Trading Bible 20 Books in 1

The Trading Crash Course for Beginners: Technical Analysis, Day Trading, Forex, Options, Swing, Volatility, Pairs, Algorithmic, Currency, Momentum, Cryptocurrency, Commodity, Biotech, Micro, Quantitative. Many tools: Fundamental Analysis, Stress and Decision-making in Trading, Alternative Investments, Advanced Tools and Analytics in Social Trading, and Risk Management Strategies

Andrew Elder

Copyright 2023. All Rights Reserved - Trading Bible 20 Books in 1 by Andrew Elder

This document provides exact and reliable information regarding the topic and issues covered. The publication is sold with the idea that the publisher is not required to render accounting, officially permitted, or otherwise qualified services. If advice is necessary, legal or professional, a practiced individual in the profession should be ordered. From a Declaration of Principles which was accepted and approved equally by a Committee of the American Bar Association and a Committee of Publishers and Associations.

In no way is it legal to reproduce, duplicate, or transmit any part of this document in either electronic means or printed format. Recording of this publication is strictly prohibited, and any storage of this document is not allowed unless with written permission from the publisher. All rights reserved. The information provided herein is stated to be truthful and consistent. Any liability, in terms of inattention or otherwise, by any usage or abuse of any policies, processes, or Instructions contained within is the solitary and utter responsibility of the recipient reader.

Under no circumstances will any legal obligation or blame be held against the publisher for reparation, damages, or monetary loss due to the information herein, either directly or indirectly.

Respective authors own all copyrights not held by the publisher. The information herein is offered for informational purposes solely and is universal as such. The presentation of the data is without a contract or any guarantee assurance.

TABLE OF CONTENTS

Technical Analysis

   Introduction

   Chapter 1: Introduction to Technical Analysis

   Chapter 2: Understanding Price Charts

   Chapter 4: Trend Analysis Techniques

   Chapter 5: Support and Resistance Levels

   Chapter 6: Candlestick Patterns

   Chapter 7: Chart Patterns

   Chapter 8: Moving Averages

   Chapter 9: Oscillators and Momentum Indicators

   Chapter 11: Dow Theory and Market Trends

   Chapter 12: Volume Analysis

   Chapter 13: Risk Management

   Chapter 14: Building a Comprehensive Trading Plan

   Chapter 15: Applying Technical Analysis in Real Trading

   Conclusion

Day Trading

   Introduction:

   Chapter 1: Understanding Day Trading

   Chapter 2: Setting Up for Success

   Chapter 3: Technical Analysis

   Chapter 4: Fundamental Analysis for Day Traders

   Chapter 5: Developing Winning Strategies

   Chapter 6: Risk Management Techniques

   Chapter 7: Psychology of Day Trading

   Chapter 8: Practicing and Backtesting

   Chapter 9: Real-Life Case Studies

   Chapter 10: Regulatory and Tax Considerations

   Chapter 11: Advanced Day Trading Techniques

   Chapter 12: Market Analysis and Timing

   Chapter 13: Managing Overnight Risk

   Chapter 14: Building a Day Trading Routine

   Chapter 15: Developing a Growth Mindset

   Chapter 16: Scalability and Portfolio Management

   Chapter 17: Trading Psychology Revisited

Chapter 18: Ethical Considerations in Day Trading

Chapter 19: Future Trends in Day Trading

Conclusion

Forex Trading:

Introduction

Chapter 1: Fundamentals of Forex Trading

Chapter 2: Setting Up for Success

Chapter 3: Mastering Fundamental Analysis

Chapter 4: Advanced Technical Analysis

Chapter 5: Developing Winning Strategies

Chapter 6: Risk Management and Psychology

Chapter 7: Practicing and Refining Your Skills

Chapter 8: Advanced Trading Techniques

Chapter 9: Global Market Analysis

Chapter 10: Trading Psychology Mastery

Chapter 11: Case Studies and Examples

Chapter 11: Case Studies and Examples

Chapter 12: Evolving Trends in Forex Trading

Chapter 13: Regulatory Landscape and Ethics

Chapter 14: Risk Management Strategies for Advanced Traders

Chapter 15: Developing a Personal Trading System

Chapter 16: Analyzing and Improving Performance

Chapter 17: Forex Trading and Taxes

Chapter 18: Trading in Various Market Conditions

Chapter 19: The Future of Forex Trading

Chapter 20: Your Journey as a Forex Trader

Appendix A: Glossary of Forex Terms

Appendix B: Recommended Resources

Conclusion

Options Trading:

Introduction

Chapter 1: Understanding the Basics of Options

Chapter 3: Option Pricing and Greeks

Chapter 4: The Art of Technical Analysis in Options Trading

Chapter 5: Fundamental Analysis and its Role in Options Trading

Chapter 6: Building a Solid Foundation: Options Trading Strategies for Beginners

Chapter 7: Unleashing the Power of Covered Calls and Protective Puts

Chapter 8: Going Beyond: Advanced Options Strategies

Chapter 9: Mastering Volatility: Straddles, Strangles, and Iron Condors

Chapter 10: Advanced Spreads: Butterflies, Calendars, and Ratios

Chapter 11: The Art of Technical and Fundamental Analysis in Options Trading

Chapter 12: Volatility Trading: VIX, Volatility Products, and Strategies

Chapter 13: Leveraging Market Trends: Trend Following and Contrarian Strategies

Chapter 14: Advanced Income Strategies: Credit Spreads and Iron Condors

Chapter 15: Leveraging Market Events: Earnings, Dividends, and Corporate Actions

Chapter 16: Advanced Hedging Techniques: Collars, Protective Puts, and More

Chapter 17: Answering the Top 30 Questions in Options Trading

Chapter 18: Mastering Advanced Strategies: Combining Techniques for Success

Conclusion: Unveiling the World of Options Trading Mastery

Swing Trading

Introduction: Embarking on the Swing Trader's Odyssey

Chapter 1: Swing Trading Fundamentals

Chapter 2: Building Your Trading Plan

Chapter 3: Technical Analysis Essentials

Chapter 4: Candlestick Patterns for Swing Traders

Chapter 5: Identifying Trend Reversals

Chapter 6: Momentum Trading Strategies

Chapter 7: Support and Resistance Strategies

Chapter 8: Pattern Recognition Techniques

Chapter 9: Risk Management Strategies

Chapter 10: Psychology of Swing Trading

Chapter 11: Trade Management Techniques

Chapter 12: Backtesting and Strategy Development

Chapter 13: Trading Psychology Revisited: Overcoming Challenges

Chapter 14: Trading Journal and Performance Analysis

Chapter 15: The Role of Fundamental Analysis in Swing Trading

Chapter 16: Advanced Technical Analysis Techniques

Chapter 17: Answering the Top 30 Questions in Swing Trading

Chapter 18: The Future of Swing Trading: Trends and Innovations

Volatility Trading

Introduction

Chapter 1: Introduction to Volatility Trading

Chapter 2: Volatility Instruments

Chapter 3: The Basics of Option Pricing

- Chapter 4: The Greeks in Volatility Trading
- Chapter 5: Historical vs. Implied Volatility
- Chapter 6: Volatility Skew and Surface
- Chapter 7: Long Volatility Strategies
- Chapter 8: Short Volatility Strategies
- Chapter 9: Vega Neutral Trading
- Chapter 10: Dispersion Trading
- Chapter 11: Managing Risk in Volatility Trading
- Chapter 12: Volatility Arbitrage
- Chapter 13: Exotic Options and Volatility
- Chapter 14: Event-Driven Volatility Trading
- Chapter 15: Volatility Trading in Cryptocurrencies
- Chapter 16: Advanced Mathematical Models
- Chapter 17: Psychological Aspects of Volatility Trading
- Chapter 18: Future Trends in Volatility Trading
- Conclusion

Pairs Trading

- Introduction
- Chapter 1 Fundamental Concepts of Pairs Trading
- Chapter 2 Prerequisites to Pairs Trading
- Chapter 3 Selection of Instruments for Pairs Trading
- Chapter 4 Implementing Pairs Trading Strategies
- Chapter 5 Advanced Techniques in Pairs Trading
- Chapter 6 Real-world Examples and Case Studies
- Chapter 7 Potential Pitfalls and How to Avoid Them
- Chapter 8 Future Outlook of Pairs Trading
- Chapter 9 Behavioral Aspects of Pairs Trading
- Chapter 10 Behavioral Aspects of Pairs Trading
- Conclusion
- Resources & Tools for Pairs Trading
- Appendices

Algorithmic Trading

- Introduction:
- Chapter 1: Introduction to Algorithmic Trading
- Chapter 2: The Role of Computer Algorithms in Trading
- Chapter 3: Building a Strong Foundation: Understanding Market Dynamics
- Chapter 4: Data Collection and Analysis for Algorithmic Trading

Chapter 5: Backtesting Strategies: A Crucial Step to Success

Chapter 6: Technical Indicators and Their Application in Algorithms

Chapter 7: Moving Averages and Trend-following Strategies

Chapter 8: Mean Reversion Strategies for Market Correction

Chapter 9: Breakout Strategies: Riding the Volatility Waves

Chapter 10: Algorithmic Risk Management: Safeguarding Your Success

Chapter 11: Optimizing Execution: Precision in Every Trade

Chapter 12: Machine Learning in Algorithmic Trading: Unleashing Intelligent Insights

Chapter 13: Sentiment Analysis and Social Media in Trading: Unveiling Market Psychology

Chapter 14: Risk and Reward: The Psychology of Trading

Chapter 15: Evolution of Algorithmic Trading: Looking Ahead with Confidence

Chapter 16: From Novice to Expert: Navigating Your Algorithmic Trading Journey

Chapter 17: Answering the Top 30 Questions in Algorithmic Trading

Chapter 18: Innovations in Algorithmic Trading: Pioneering the Future

Conclusion: Unleash Your Potential in Algorithmic Trading

Currency Carry Trades

Introduction:

Chapter 1: Fundamentals of Forex Trading and Interest Rates

Chapter 2: The Concept of Carry Trade Strategy

Chapter 3: Analyzing Currency Correlations

Chapter 4: Factors Affecting Exchange Rates

Chapter 5: Interest Rate Parity Theories

Chapter 6: Identifying High-Yield and Low-Yield Currencies

Chapter 7: Technical Analysis in Currency Carry Trades

Chapter 8: Fundamental Analysis in Currency Carry Trades

Chapter 9: Risk Management in Currency Carry Trades

Chapter 10: Psychological Aspects of Currency Carry Trading

Chapter 11: Formulating and Executing Carry Trade Strategies

Chapter 12: The Strategic Essence of Currency Carry Trading

Chapter 13: Psychological Aspects of Carry Trading

Chapter 14: Carry Trading Case Studies

Chapter 15: Global Economic Trends and Carry Trades

Chapter 16: Regulatory Considerations in Forex Trading

Chapter 17: Alternative Carry Trade Strategies

Chapter 18: Future Outlook for Carry Trading

Conclusion: Applying Knowledge and Embracing the Journey

Appendix: Glossary of Key Terms

Momentum Trading

- Introduction
- Chapter 2: The Science Behind Price Momentum
- Chapter 3: Identifying Momentum
- Chapter 4: Strategies for Momentum Trading
- Chapter 5: Risk Management in Momentum Trading
- Chapter 6: Advanced Concepts in Momentum Trading
- Chapter 7: Recognizing Momentum Patterns
- Chapter 8: Using Volume in Momentum Trading
- Chapter 9: The Psychology Behind Momentum Trading
- Chapter 10: Adapting to Market Changes in Momentum Trading
- Chapter 11: Risks and Management in Momentum Trading
- Chapter 12: Advanced Momentum Indicators and Tools
- Chapter 13: Adapting to Market Changes and Volatility
- Chapter 14: Psychological Aspects of Momentum Trading
- Chapter 15: Backtesting and Strategy Refinement
- Chapter 16: The Role of Technology in Momentum Trading
- Chapter 17: Building a Winning Mindset for Momentum Trading
- Chapter 18: Conclusion and Future of Momentum Trading
- 1. Tools and Resources:
- 2. Software Recommendations and Reviews:
- 3. Further Reading and Online Resources:
- 4. Interviews with Successful Momentum Traders: Insights and Strategies
- Personal Experiences and Strategies:
- Guided Trading Plan Development:
- Progression Exercises:
- Conclusion: The Future of Momentum Trading and Continuous Learning

Cryptocurrency Trading:

- Introduction: Understanding the World of Cryptocurrency Trading
- Chapter 1: Fundamentals of Cryptocurrencies
- Chapter 2: Technical Analysis for Cryptocurrency Trading
- Chapter 3: Fundamental Analysis in Cryptocurrency Trading
- Chapter 4: Developing a Trading Strategy
- Chapter 5: Risk Management in Cryptocurrency Trading
- Chapter 6: Technical Indicators for Successful Trading
- Chapter 7: Strategies for Bull and Bear Markets
- Chapter 8: Case Studies: Learning from Successful Traders

- Chapter 9: Taxation and Legal Considerations
- Chapter 10: The Future of Cryptocurrency Trading
- Chapter 11: Advanced Trading Strategies
- Chapter 12: Behavioral Psychology in Cryptocurrency Trading
- Chapter 13: Technical Analysis Tools and Software
- Chapter 14: Regulatory Compliance and Security
- Chapter 15: Navigating Market Volatility
- Chapter 16: Building a Trading Routine
- Chapter 17: Cryptocurrency Investment Strategies
- Chapter 18: Decentralized Finance (DeFi) Trading
- Chapter 19: Ethical and Environmental Considerations
- Conclusion: Your Journey in the Cryptocurrency Trading Arena

Commodity Trading

- Introduction to Commodity Trading
- Chapter 1. Overview of Commodity Trading
- Chapter 2. Basic Principles of Commodity Trading
- Chapter 3. Major Global Commodity Exchanges
- Chapter 4. Major Global Commodity Exchanges
- Chapter 5. Risks in Commodity Trading
- Chapter 6. Gold Trading
- Chapter 7. Oil and Energy Commodities
- Chapter 8. Agricultural Commodities
- Chapter 9. Trading Strategies
- Chapter 10. Regulation and Ethics
- Chapter 11. Risk Management in Commodity Trading
- Chapter 12. Global Trade Dynamics
- Chapter 13. Technological Advancements
- Chapter 14. Financial Instruments in Commodity Trading
- Chapter 15. Economic Indicators and their Impact
- Chapter 16. The Future of Commodity Trading
- Conclusion and Final Thoughts

Biotech Trading

- Introduction:
- Chapter 1: Understanding Biotechnology Landscape
- Chapter 2: Fundamentals of Drug Development
- Chapter 3: Analyzing Clinical Trial Results
- Chapter 4: FDA and Regulatory Landscape

Chapter 5: Assessing Pipeline Potential

Chapter 6: Biotech Valuation Techniques

Chapter 7: Market Sentiment and Investor Behavior

Chapter 8: Event-Driven Trading Strategies

Chapter 9: Risk Management in Biotech Trading

Chapter 10: Biotech ETFs and Funds

Chapter 11: Analyzing Intellectual Property

Chapter 12: Biotech Market Analysis and Data Sources

Chapter 13: Long-Term Investing in Biotech

Chapter 14: Ethical Considerations in Biotech Trading

Chapter 14: Ethical Considerations in Biotech Trading

Chapter 15: Emerging Technologies and Trends

Chapter 16: Case Studies in Biotech Trading

Chapter 17: The Future of Biotech Trading

Chapter 18: Epilogue - Charting Your Biotech Trading Journey

Conclusion

Microtrading

Introduction:

Chapter 1: The Essence of Microtrading

Chapter 2: Building a Solid Foundation

Chapter 3: Tools of the Microtrader's Trade

Chapter 4: Risk Management Strategies

Chapter 5: Microscopic Price Movements

Chapter 6: Scalping Techniques for Microtraders

Chapter 7: Harnessing Volatility for Micro Gains

Chapter 8: Adaptive Techniques for Changing Market Conditions

Chapter 9: Integrating Fundamental Analysis into Microtrading

Chapter 10: The Psychology of Microtrading

Chapter 11: The Role of Ethics and Integrity in Microtrading

Chapter 12: Microtrading Strategies for Various Market Conditions

Chapter 13: Building a Microtrading Routine

Chapter 14: Risk Management in Depth

Chapter 15: Real-Time Analysis and Decision-Making

Chapter 17: Building a Resilient Mindset

Chapter 18: The Path Forward: Mastery and Consistency

Conclusion:

Quantitative Trading:

Introduction

Chapter 1: Fundamentals of Quantitative Trading

Chapter 2: Mathematical Foundations for Trading Strategies

Chapter 3: Data Collection and Preprocessing

Chapter 4: Building Quantitative Trading Models

Chapter 5: Statistical Analysis Techniques for Trading

Chapter 6: Machine Learning Applications in Quantitative Trading

Chapter 7: Risk Management and Portfolio Optimization

Chapter 8: High-Frequency and Algorithmic Trading

Chapter 9: Real-world Case Studies

Chapter 10: Future Trends in Quantitative Trading

Chapter 11: Machine Learning Interpretability and Explain ability in Trading

Chapter 12: Evolution of Market Sentiment Analysis in Trading

Chapter 13: Decentralized Finance (DeFi) and Quantitative Strategies

Chapter 14: Behavioral Finance and its Implications for Quantitative Trading

Chapter 15: Cybersecurity and Resilience in Quantitative Trading

Chapter 16: Evolution of Market Structure and its Impact on Quantitative Trading

Chapter 17: Social Impact and Responsible Quantitative Trading

Chapter 18: Cognitive Biases in Trading and Decision-Making

Conclusion

Fundamental Analysis

Introduction

Chapter 1: Economic Indicators and Their Analysis

Chapter 2: Company Financials Evaluation

Chapter 3: Analysis of Market News and Events

Chapter 4: Market Sentiment and Information Flow

Chapter 5: Impact of News on Asset Prices

Chapter 6: Evaluating News Sources

Chapter 7: Reliable Financial News Outlets

Chapter 8: Differentiating Between News and Opinion

Chapter 9: Earnings Reports and Conference Calls

Chapter 10: Mergers and Acquisitions:

Chapter 11: Regulatory Changes and Policy Announcements

Chapter 12: Geopolitical Events and Macro Trends

Chapter 13: Short-Term vs. Long-Term Impact

Chapter 14: Using News to Identify Opportunities and Risks

Conclusion: Integrating Analysis for Informed Decision-Making

Appendix: Tools and Resources for Fundamental Analysis

Stress and Decision-making in Trading

Introduction

Chapter 1: The Fundamentals of Trading Risks

Chapter 3: Quantitative Analysis in Risk Management

Chapter 4: Qualitative Analysis in Risk Management

Chapter 5: The Role of Portfolio Diversification in Risk Management

Chapter 6: Leverage and Margin: Tools and Risks

Chapter 7: Technological Tools in Risk Management

Chapter 8: Behavioral Biases in Trading and Risk Management

Chapter 9: Stress and Decision-making in Trading

Chapter 10: Portfolio Diversification: Spreading Risks

Chapter 11: Leverage and Margin: Understanding Amplified Risks

Chapter 12: Advanced Derivative Instruments: Hedging and Speculation

Chapter 13: Behavioral Finance: Navigating Cognitive Biases in Trading

Chapter 14: Technological Tools: Harnessing Advanced Analytics in Risk Management

Chapter 15: Global Macroeconomic Factors: Assessing Broader Influences on Trading

Chapter 16: Portfolio Diversification: Spreading Risk Across Assets and Geographies

Chapter 17: Leveraging and Margin Trading: Understanding the Double-Edged Sword

Chapter 18: Behavioral Finance: Navigating the Psychological Pitfalls of Trading

Conclusion: Synthesizing Strategies for Effective Risk Management in Trading

Alternative Investments

Introduction

Chapter 1: Defining Alternative Investments

Chapter 2: Historical Context of Alternative Investments

Chapter 3: The Psychological Appeal of Alternative Investments

Chapter 4: Art as an Investment Medium

Chapter 5: Fine Wine Investments

Chapter 6: Collectibles – Stamps, Coins, and More

Chapter 7: Luxury Watches and Jewelry

Chapter 8: Intellectual Property and Digital Assets

Chapter 9: Real Estate Investment Trusts (REITs) and Infrastructure

Chapter 10: Hedge Funds and Private Equity

Chapter 11: Risk Management and Due Diligence

Chapter 12: Tax Considerations in Alternative Investments

Chapter 13: Managing Liquidity and Exit Strategies

Chapter 14: Evaluating Performance and Benchmarking

Chapter 15: Building a Holistic Alternative Investment Strategy

Chapter 16: Case Studies in Alternative Investments

Chapter 17: The Future of Alternative Investments

Chapter 18: Taking the Next Steps

Conclusion

Advanced Tools and Analytics in Social Trading

Introduction

Chapter 1: Social Trading Defined

Chapter 2: Historical Context of Social Trading

Chapter 3: The Psychological Aspects of Social Trading

Chapter 4: Choosing the Right Social Trading Platform

Chapter 5: Identifying and Evaluating Top Traders to Follow

Chapter 6: Diversification in Social Trading

Chapter 7: The Ethical Dimensions of Social Trading

Chapter 8: Risk Management in Social Trading

Chapter 9: The Psychological Dynamics of Social Trading

Chapter 10: Advanced Tools and Analytics in Social Trading

Chapter 11: Social Trading vs. Traditional Fund Management

Chapter 12: Navigating Regulation and Compliance in Social Trading

Chapter 13: Risk Management in Social Trading

Chapter 14: The Psychological Dynamics of Social Trading

Chapter 15: Technological Innovations in Social Trading

Chapter 16: Crafting a Personalized Social Trading Strategy

Chapter 17: The Ethical Dimensions of Social Trading

Chapter 18: Advanced Tools and Analytics for Optimal Decision Making

Conclusion: The Future Landscape of Social Trading

Risk Management Strategies

Introduction

Chapter 1: Fundamentals of Trading

Chapter 2: Analyzing Historical Data

Chapter 3: Understanding ity in Different Markets

Chapter 4: Tools and Techniques for Analysis

Chapter 5: Identifying Patterns

Chapter 6: Incorporating ity into Technical Analysis

Chapter 7: Risk Management Strategies for Trading

Chapter 8: Case Studies in Trading

Chapter 9: Developing a Trading Plan

Chapter 10: Implementing Automated Trading Systems

Chapter 12: Energy Markets and Natural Resources

Chapter 13: Technology and Innovation Stocks

Chapter 14: Holiday-Related Trading Opportunities

Chapter 15: Applying Patterns in Financial Markets

Chapter 16: Navigating Patterns in Global Markets

Chapter 17: Strategies in Options and Derivatives Markets

Chapter 18: Adapting to Evolving Market Conditions

Conclusion

Technical Analysis

A Comprehensive Guide to Trading Strategies and Market Insights

Introduction

In the fast-paced world of financial markets, making informed decisions is crucial. Technical analysis is a powerful tool that empowers traders and investors to understand market trends, make predictions, and manage risk. This book, "Technical Analysis for Beginners," aims to provide readers with a comprehensive introduction to the principles and techniques of technical analysis. Whether you're new to trading or looking to enhance your investment strategies, this book will equip you with the essential knowledge to navigate the complex landscape of financial markets.

Technical analysis involves studying historical price data and market statistics to forecast future price movements. By analyzing patterns, indicators, and trends, traders can identify potential entry and exit points, manage risk effectively, and make more informed trading decisions. This book will guide you through the fundamental concepts of technical analysis, ensuring you develop a solid foundation before delving into more advanced strategies.

With a step-by-step approach, each chapter will explore different aspects of technical analysis, gradually building your expertise. We'll cover everything from interpreting price charts and identifying trends to recognizing chart patterns, utilizing indicators, and creating a comprehensive trading strategy. By the time you finish reading, you'll be equipped with the skills needed to analyze charts, understand market psychology, and develop your own successful trading approach.

Whether you're interested in stocks, forex, cryptocurrencies, or any other financial instrument, the principles of technical analysis remain consistent. This book doesn't promise overnight success, but it does provide the tools and knowledge you need to embark on your trading journey with confidence. Remember, success in trading requires dedication, continuous learning, and disciplined execution.

In the chapters that follow, we'll delve into the specifics of technical analysis, ensuring that each concept is explained in detail. From deciphering candlestick patterns to utilizing moving averages, we'll cover it all. So, let's begin this journey of discovery and empowerment as we unravel the art and science of technical analysis.

Chapter 1: Introduction to Technical Analysis

Technical analysis is the art of using historical price and volume data to predict future price movements. Unlike fundamental analysis, which focuses on a company's financial health and market conditions, technical analysis centers on studying price patterns, trends, and market psychology.

In this chapter, we'll cover the fundamental concepts that underpin technical analysis. You'll learn about the basic tools used, such as price charts and technical indicators, and how they can help you identify potential trading opportunities. We'll also explore the core principles of support and resistance, which are key to understanding price movements within a trend.

By the end of this chapter, you'll have a solid grasp of what technical analysis is and why it's a valuable skill for traders and investors. So, let's dive in and start building your foundation in technical analysis.

Chapter 2: Understanding Price Charts

Price charts are the visual representation of a financial asset's historical price movements over a specific period. They serve as the primary tool for technical analysts to identify trends, patterns, and potential trading opportunities. In this chapter, we'll delve into the different types of price charts and how to interpret them effectively.

Types of Price Charts: There are several types of price charts, each presenting price data in a different format. The three most common types are line charts, bar charts, and candlestick charts.

1. **Line Charts:** These charts are created by connecting the closing prices of an asset over a specified period. Line charts provide a simple overview of price movements but may lack detail.

2. **Bar Charts:** Bar charts provide more information by displaying the open, high, low, and closing prices for each period as bars. The vertical line represents the price range, while horizontal lines on the left and right indicate the opening and closing prices.

3. **Candlestick Charts:** Candlestick charts are widely used due to their visual richness. Each candlestick represents a specific time period (e.g., a day), with the body indicating the price range between the opening and closing prices. The "wick" or "shadow" above and below the body represents the high and low prices.

Interpreting Price Patterns: Price patterns are formations that appear on price charts and provide insights into potential market trends. Some common price patterns include:

1. **Trend Lines:** These are straight lines drawn along the price highs or lows to identify the direction of the trend. An upward-sloping trend line indicates an uptrend, while a downward-sloping one indicates a downtrend.

2. **Head and Shoulders:** This pattern indicates a reversal of an existing trend. It consists of three peaks—the middle peak (head) is higher than the other two (shoulders).

3. **Double Tops and Bottoms:** These patterns also suggest a reversal. A double top forms after an uptrend, indicating a potential downtrend ahead. Conversely, a double bottom forms after a downtrend, signaling a potential uptrend.

Support and Resistance: Support and resistance levels are crucial concepts in technical analysis. Support is a price level where a downtrend can pause or reverse, while resistance is a level where an uptrend can stall or reverse. These levels are created by psychological factors, supply and demand dynamics, and previous price history.

In the next chapter, we'll explore technical indicators in detail, which are tools used to enhance the analysis of price charts and improve decision-making. Understanding how to read price charts and identify patterns is the foundation of successful technical analysis, and mastering this skill will greatly enhance your ability to make informed trading decisions.

Remember, while technical analysis is a valuable tool, it's important to combine it with other forms of analysis, such as fundamental analysis and risk management, to make well-rounded and informed trading choices.

Chapter 3: Key Technical Indicators

Technical indicators are mathematical calculations based on historical price, volume, or open interest data. They provide additional insights into price movements and help traders make more informed decisions. In this chapter, we'll explore some of the key technical indicators that are commonly used in technical analysis.

Moving Averages: Moving averages smooth out price data over a specified period, helping to identify trends and potential reversal points. The two main types of moving averages are simple moving averages (SMA) and exponential moving averages (EMA). SMAs give equal weight to all data points in the period, while EMAs give more weight to recent data, making them more responsive to price changes.

Relative Strength Index (RSI): The RSI is a momentum oscillator that measures the speed and change of price movements. It oscillates between 0 and 100 and is used to identify overbought and oversold conditions. An RSI above 70 suggests an overbought market, while an RSI below 30 suggests an oversold market.

Moving Average Convergence Divergence (MACD): The MACD is a trend-following momentum indicator that consists of two moving averages—the MACD line and the signal line. When the MACD line crosses above the signal line, it's considered a bullish signal, indicating potential upward momentum. Conversely, when the MACD line crosses below the signal line, it's a bearish signal.

Bollinger Bands: Bollinger Bands consist of a middle band (usually a simple moving average) and two outer bands that represent the standard deviation of price from the middle band. Bollinger Bands expand and contract based on market volatility. Traders often use them to identify overbought and oversold conditions and potential breakout points.

Stochastic Oscillator: The stochastic oscillator compares the closing price of an asset to its price range over a specific period. It oscillates between 0 and 100 and is used to identify potential reversal points. Readings above 80 suggest an overbought condition, while readings below 20 suggest an oversold condition.

Using Technical Indicators: It's important to note that no single indicator is foolproof, and using a combination of indicators can provide more robust insights. Additionally, technical indicators are most effective when used in conjunction with other forms of analysis, such as price patterns and trend lines.

Incorporating technical indicators into your trading strategy can enhance your ability to identify trends, assess momentum, and make informed entry and exit decisions. However, it's crucial to practice and gain experience in interpreting these indicators over time. As we progress through this book, you'll learn how to apply these indicators within the context of various trading scenarios.

In the next chapter, we'll dive deeper into trend analysis techniques. Understanding how to identify and confirm trends is a critical skill for any technical analyst. Let's continue building your knowledge step by step!

Chapter 4: Trend Analysis Techniques

Trend analysis is at the heart of technical analysis. Identifying and confirming trends accurately is essential for successful trading and investment decisions. In this chapter, we'll explore various techniques used to analyze trends and gain insights into potential market directions.

Types of Trends: There are three main types of trends in technical analysis:

1. **Uptrend:** An uptrend is characterized by higher highs and higher lows. It indicates that the asset's price is generally moving upward over time.

2. **Downtrend:** A downtrend is characterized by lower highs and lower lows. It indicates that the asset's price is generally moving downward over time.

3. **Sideways (or Range) Trend:** In a sideways trend, the price moves within a relatively narrow range without making significant higher highs or lower lows.

Drawing Trend Lines: Trend lines are a valuable tool for identifying trends and potential reversal points. An uptrend can be drawn by connecting the lows of successive price movements, while a downtrend can be drawn by connecting the highs. Trend lines act as dynamic support or resistance levels and can help traders identify potential entry and exit points.

Confirming Trends with Indicators: Technical indicators can be used to confirm the presence of a trend. For example, moving averages can help smooth out price fluctuations, making it easier to identify the overall direction of the trend. In an uptrend, prices tend to stay above a moving average, while in a downtrend, prices tend to stay below it.

Identifying Trend Reversals: Recognizing the potential end of a trend is just as important as identifying its beginning. Reversal patterns, such as double tops, double bottoms, and head and shoulders patterns, can indicate that a trend might be changing direction. Volume analysis can also provide insights into trend reversals—a decrease in volume during an uptrend or an increase in volume during a downtrend could signal a potential reversal.

Dow Theory and Market Trends: Dow Theory is a foundational concept in technical analysis. It suggests that markets move in trends and that those trends can be analyzed and predicted. According to Dow Theory, trends have three phases: accumulation (smart money entering the market), public participation (more traders joining the trend), and distribution (smart money exiting the market). Understanding these phases can help traders position themselves effectively.

Putting Trend Analysis Together: Successful trend analysis involves a combination of tools and techniques. Traders should consider price patterns, trend lines, technical indicators, and volume analysis to form a comprehensive view of market trends. Remember that no analysis technique is infallible, so it's important to use a combination of approaches to increase the accuracy of your predictions.

As you continue your journey through this book, you'll build a strong foundation in technical analysis, enabling you to confidently identify trends and make informed trading decisions. In the next chapter, we'll delve into the concepts of support and resistance, which are integral to understanding price movements within a trend. Keep up the momentum in your learning!

Chapter 5: Support and Resistance Levels

Support and resistance levels are fundamental concepts in technical analysis that help traders identify key price levels where trends might pause, reverse, or accelerate. These levels are crucial for making informed trading decisions and managing risk effectively. In this chapter, we'll explore the dynamics of support and resistance and how to use them in your analysis.

Support Levels: A support level is a price level where an asset's downward movement might be halted or reversed. It represents a point where demand for the asset is strong enough to prevent further price declines. Traders often look for support levels to identify potential buying opportunities. Once a support level is breached, it can become a resistance level in the future.

Resistance Levels: A resistance level is a price level where an asset's upward movement might stall or reverse. It represents a point where supply of the asset exceeds demand, causing prices to potentially stop rising. Traders pay close attention to resistance levels to gauge potential selling opportunities. Once a resistance level is broken, it can turn into a support level.

Psychological Factors and Support/Resistance: Support and resistance levels are influenced by psychological factors. Round numbers (e.g., $100, $50) and previous highs or lows can act as strong support or resistance levels. Traders often place orders around these levels, causing price reactions.

Drawing Support and Resistance Lines: Support and resistance levels can be drawn as horizontal lines on price charts. When identifying these levels, it's important to focus on areas where price has shown a tendency to reverse in the past. The more times price touches or bounces off a level, the more significant it becomes.

Role Reversal: Once a support level is breached, it tends to become a resistance level and vice versa. This is known as "role reversal." Traders look for these instances to confirm potential turning points in price movements.

Breakouts and Fakeouts: Breakouts occur when price moves beyond a support or resistance level, indicating a potential continuation of the trend. Traders often wait for confirmation before entering trades to avoid false breakouts, known as "fakeouts."

Using Support and Resistance: Traders use support and resistance levels to identify entry and exit points. For example, if an asset is approaching a strong resistance level, it might be a good time to consider selling or shorting. Conversely, if an asset is approaching a strong support level, it could present a buying opportunity.

Support and Resistance in Practice: Combining support and resistance levels with other technical analysis tools, such as trend lines and indicators, can provide a comprehensive view of market dynamics. Remember that while support and resistance levels can be powerful indicators, they are not foolproof and should be used in conjunction with other forms of analysis.

As you continue reading, you'll learn about candlestick patterns, which provide insights into market sentiment and potential trend reversals. Developing a holistic approach to technical analysis will enable you to make more informed trading decisions. Let's keep unraveling the complexities of the market together!

Chapter 6: Candlestick Patterns

Candlestick patterns are a vital tool in technical analysis, offering insights into market sentiment and potential trend reversals. These visual formations on price charts provide valuable information about the battle between buyers and sellers. In this chapter, we'll explore various candlestick patterns and how to interpret them effectively.

Components of a Candlestick: A candlestick consists of four main components:

1. **Open:** The opening price of the period.
2. **Close:** The closing price of the period.
3. **High:** The highest price reached during the period.
4. **Low:** The lowest price reached during the period.

The body of the candlestick represents the price range between the open and close, while the wicks (shadows) represent the price range between the high/low and the open/close.

Common Candlestick Patterns: Candlestick patterns can be categorized into reversal and continuation patterns. Here are some common examples:

1. **Doji:** A doji occurs when the open and close are very close or equal, creating a small-bodied candlestick with long wicks. It signals uncertainty in the market.
2. **Hammer and Hanging Man:** These patterns have a small body and a long lower wick. A hammer occurs during a downtrend and suggests potential reversal, while a hanging man occurs during an uptrend and may signal a reversal.
3. **Engulfing Patterns:** An engulfing pattern occurs when a larger candle fully engulfs the previous one. A bullish engulfing pattern forms after a downtrend and may signal a reversal, while a bearish engulfing pattern forms after an uptrend and suggests a potential downturn.
4. **Morning Star and Evening Star:** These three-candle patterns indicate potential trend reversals. The morning star consists of a large down candle, a small indecisive candle, and a large up candle. The evening star is the reverse and suggests a potential downtrend ahead.

Using Candlestick Patterns: Candlestick patterns provide insights into market sentiment and potential changes in direction. However, they should be used in conjunction with other forms of analysis to increase accuracy. Confirmation from other indicators or patterns can enhance the reliability of a candlestick signal.

Multiple Candlestick Patterns: Combining multiple candlestick patterns can provide more robust signals. For instance, a doji followed by an engulfing pattern might suggest a stronger reversal signal than either pattern alone.

Interpreting Long and Short Bodies: Long-bodied candlesticks indicate strong buying or selling pressure, depending on their color (green for bullish, red for bearish). Short-bodied candlesticks suggest indecision or consolidation.

Continued Learning: Understanding candlestick patterns requires practice and experience. By continuously studying and analyzing price charts, you'll become more proficient in recognizing patterns and making accurate predictions.

In the upcoming chapters, we'll explore chart patterns, moving averages, and other advanced concepts. Each piece of knowledge you acquire brings you closer to mastering technical analysis. Keep up the dedication, and your trading skills will continue to grow!

Chapter 7: Chart Patterns

Chart patterns are visual formations that appear on price charts and provide insights into potential market trends and reversals. These patterns are valuable tools for technical analysts, helping them anticipate price movements and make informed trading decisions. In this chapter, we'll explore some of the most common chart patterns and how to interpret them.

Continuation Patterns:

1. **Flag Pattern:** The flag pattern consists of a sharp price movement followed by a consolidation phase (the flag) before the trend resumes. This pattern indicates a brief pause in the trend's momentum.

2. **Pennant Pattern:** Similar to the flag pattern, the pennant is formed by a consolidation period after a strong price movement. It's characterized by converging trendlines, resembling a small symmetrical triangle.

3. **Ascending Triangle:** This pattern forms when there's a horizontal resistance level and an upward-sloping support line. It suggests that buyers are becoming more aggressive and could lead to a breakout to the upside.

Reversal Patterns:

1. **Head and Shoulders:** A classic reversal pattern, the head and shoulders consists of three peaks—the middle peak (head) is higher than the other two (shoulders). This pattern suggests a reversal from an uptrend to a downtrend.

2. **Inverse Head and Shoulders:** The inverse of the head and shoulders, this pattern appears after a downtrend and indicates a potential reversal to an uptrend.

3. **Double Tops and Bottoms:** Double tops form after an uptrend and indicate a potential reversal. Double bottoms form after a downtrend and signal a potential uptrend.

Triple Tops and Bottoms:

These patterns are similar to double tops and bottoms, but with three peaks or troughs. They suggest more prolonged reversals in trends.

Interpreting Patterns:

Chart patterns are formed by the interactions between buyers and sellers. Traders interpret these patterns to anticipate potential price movements. It's important to wait for confirmation before acting on a pattern, as false breakouts can occur.

Measuring Targets:

Some chart patterns have associated price targets that can be calculated based on the pattern's height. For example, the distance from the head to the neckline in a head and shoulders pattern can be projected downward to estimate the potential price decline.

Using Patterns with Other Analysis:

Chart patterns are most effective when used in conjunction with other technical analysis tools, such as trend lines, moving averages, and indicators. Combining these elements increases the reliability of signals and predictions.

Practice Makes Perfect:

Becoming proficient at recognizing chart patterns takes practice. Study historical price charts, identify patterns, and analyze how they played out in real market situations. Over time, you'll develop the ability to spot patterns and make more accurate trading decisions.

In the following chapters, we'll delve into moving averages, oscillators, and more advanced concepts. Stay committed to your learning journey, and your technical analysis skills will continue to evolve!

Chapter 8: Moving Averages

Moving averages are versatile and widely used tools in technical analysis. They smooth out price data, making it easier to identify trends, spot potential reversals, and make informed trading decisions. In this chapter, we'll delve into different types of moving averages and how to effectively incorporate them into your analysis.

Simple Moving Average (SMA):

The simple moving average calculates the average price over a specified number of periods. Each data point is given equal weight. SMAs help to smooth out price fluctuations, making it easier to identify the overall trend.

Exponential Moving Average (EMA):

The exponential moving average gives more weight to recent prices, making it more responsive to current price movements. EMAs react faster to price changes than SMAs, which can help traders catch trend reversals earlier.

Golden Cross and Death Cross:

The golden cross occurs when a short-term moving average crosses above a long-term moving average. It's considered a bullish signal, suggesting a potential upward trend. Conversely, the death cross occurs when a short-term moving average crosses below a long-term moving average, indicating a potential downtrend.

Using Moving Averages:

Moving averages are versatile tools that can be used in various ways:

1. **Trend Identification:** The slope of a moving average can help you identify the direction of the trend. An upward-sloping moving average indicates an uptrend, while a downward-sloping moving average suggests a downtrend.

2. **Crossovers:** Moving average crossovers can signal potential entry or exit points. A short-term moving average crossing above a long-term moving average may indicate a buy signal, while the opposite can signal a sell signal.
3. **Support and Resistance:** Moving averages can act as dynamic support or resistance levels. Prices often bounce off moving averages, particularly during strong trends.
4. **Moving Average Convergence Divergence (MACD):** The MACD, a popular indicator, is based on the difference between two moving averages. Traders look for crossovers between the MACD line and the signal line to identify potential trend changes.

Combining Moving Averages with Other Tools:

To increase the accuracy of your analysis, consider using moving averages in combination with other technical analysis tools, such as trend lines, chart patterns, and oscillators.

Tailoring Moving Averages:

The choice of moving average periods depends on the trading strategy, timeframe, and the asset being analyzed. Shorter periods are more sensitive to price changes, while longer periods offer a broader view of the trend.

In the upcoming chapters, we'll explore oscillators and momentum indicators, adding another layer of analysis to your toolkit. Keep building your technical analysis skills, and you'll become a more confident and informed trader!

Chapter 9: Oscillators and Momentum Indicators

Oscillators and momentum indicators are essential tools for technical analysts, helping them gauge the strength of price movements and identify potential overbought or oversold conditions. These indicators add depth to your analysis by providing insights into market momentum. In this chapter, we'll explore some of the key oscillators and momentum indicators and how to effectively use them.

Relative Strength Index (RSI):

The RSI is a widely used momentum indicator that oscillates between 0 and 100. It measures the speed and magnitude of price movements. An RSI reading above 70 suggests overbought conditions, potentially indicating an impending reversal. An RSI below 30 suggests oversold conditions, signaling a possible upward reversal.

Stochastic Oscillator:

The stochastic oscillator consists of two lines, %K and %D, and oscillates between 0 and 100. It compares the current closing price to a price range over a specific period. An oscillator above 80 suggests overbought conditions, while an oscillator below 20 suggests oversold conditions.

Moving Average Convergence Divergence (MACD):

The MACD is both a trend-following and momentum indicator. It consists of the MACD line (the difference between two moving averages) and the signal line (a moving average of the MACD line). Crossovers between the MACD line and the signal line are used to identify potential trend changes.

Using Oscillators and Momentum Indicators:

Oscillators and momentum indicators provide insights into the strength of price movements, helping traders identify potential reversals or continuations. However, they have limitations and should be used in conjunction with other analysis techniques.

Divergence:

Divergence occurs when the price of an asset and an oscillator indicator move in opposite directions. Bullish divergence happens when the price makes lower lows while the oscillator makes higher lows, suggesting a potential upward reversal. Bearish divergence occurs when the price makes higher highs while the oscillator makes lower highs, indicating a potential downward reversal.

Overbought and Oversold Conditions:

Overbought conditions suggest that an asset's price may be due for a pullback, while oversold conditions indicate potential buying opportunities. However, it's important to note that overbought or oversold conditions can persist during strong trends.

Choosing the Right Indicator:

Different oscillators and momentum indicators suit different trading styles and market conditions. Experiment with various indicators to find ones that complement your strategy.

Confirmation from Other Indicators:

Momentum indicators are most effective when they confirm other signals from technical analysis tools like trend lines, moving averages, and candlestick patterns. Combining multiple indicators can enhance the reliability of your predictions.

As you continue learning, you'll discover more ways to refine your trading decisions using technical analysis. In the upcoming chapters, we'll explore Fibonacci retracement, Dow Theory, and risk management, all of which are essential components of a comprehensive trading strategy. Keep up the enthusiasm for learning, and you'll become a more skilled trader!

Chapter 10: Fibonacci Retracement and Extension

Fibonacci retracement and extension are powerful tools that help traders identify potential support and resistance levels, as well as predict price targets. These levels are based on the Fibonacci sequence, a series of numbers where each number is the sum of the two preceding ones. In this chapter, we'll explore how to apply Fibonacci analysis to your technical analysis toolkit.

Fibonacci Retracement:

Fibonacci retracement levels are used to identify potential support and resistance levels during a price correction within a trend. The key Fibonacci retracement levels are 23.6%, 38.2%, 50%, 61.8%, and 78.6%. These levels indicate potential areas where price might bounce or reverse.

Traders draw Fibonacci retracement lines from the low to the high of a price movement (in an uptrend) or from the high to the low (in a downtrend). The retracement levels act as potential areas where traders might look to enter trades or place stop-loss orders.

Fibonacci Extension:

Fibonacci extension levels help traders predict potential price targets when an asset's price is trending strongly. The key Fibonacci extension levels are 61.8%, 100%, 161.8%, 261.8%, and 423.6%. These levels can provide insights into where price might reach during a trend continuation.

To apply Fibonacci extension, traders draw lines from the low to the high of a previous price movement and then extend the lines beyond the high to project potential price targets.

Confluence of Levels:

When multiple technical analysis tools, such as Fibonacci levels, align with other indicators, such as moving averages or trend lines, it creates a confluence of levels. This can strengthen the significance of a particular price level or signal, increasing the likelihood of accurate predictions.

Potential Pitfalls:

While Fibonacci retracement and extension levels are valuable tools, they are not infallible. Markets can be unpredictable, and prices might not always react as expected. Always use Fibonacci analysis in conjunction with other forms of technical analysis.

Experiment and Practice:

Applying Fibonacci analysis effectively requires practice. Study historical price charts, identify instances where Fibonacci levels provided support, resistance, or price targets, and analyze how the market responded.

In the chapters ahead, we'll delve into Dow Theory, volume analysis, risk management, and building a comprehensive trading strategy. Each new piece of knowledge contributes to your growth as a skilled trader. Stay engaged in your learning journey, and your trading decisions will become more confident and informed!

Chapter 11: Dow Theory and Market Trends

Dow Theory is a foundational concept in technical analysis, developed by Charles Dow, the founder of Dow Jones & Company. It focuses on understanding market trends and identifying potential buying and selling opportunities. In this chapter, we'll explore the core principles of Dow Theory and how they can enhance your technical analysis skills.

Three Principles of Dow Theory:

1. **The Market Discounts Everything:** Dow Theory assumes that all available information, whether public or private, is already reflected in the price of an asset. This means that prices move in response to news, events, and market sentiment.

2. **Market Trends Have Three Phases:** Dow Theory suggests that market trends have three phases—accumulation, public participation, and distribution. During accumulation, informed traders enter the market. In the public participation phase, more traders join, driving prices higher. In the distribution phase, informed traders exit the market.

3. **Indices Must Confirm Each Other:** Dow Theory emphasizes that trends are confirmed when both the Dow Jones Industrial Average (DJIA) and the Dow Jones Transportation Average (DJTA) move in the same direction. If one index reaches a new high while the other doesn't, it might indicate an impending trend reversal.

Understanding Trends:

Dow Theory categorizes trends into three main types:

1. **Primary Trend:** This is the main trend that lasts for months or even years, representing the long-term direction of the market.
2. **Secondary Trend (Reactions):** Secondary trends are counter-trend movements that occur within the primary trend. They typically last for weeks or months and are often referred to as reactions.
3. **Minor Trend (Ripples):** Minor trends are short-term fluctuations that can be caused by daily market noise. They don't affect the primary trend significantly.

Applying Dow Theory:

Dow Theory can help traders identify potential entry and exit points based on trend analysis. If both the DJIA and DJTA are in sync, it confirms the trend's strength. Conversely, divergences between the indices might indicate a weakening trend.

Dow Theory doesn't provide specific entry or exit signals, but it enhances your overall understanding of market dynamics. It's particularly useful when combined with other technical analysis tools like trend lines, moving averages, and chart patterns.

Staying Informed:

Continuously monitor market trends and the DJIA and DJTA indices. Dow Theory requires a proactive approach to stay ahead of potential trend changes.

As you continue reading, we'll explore volume analysis, an essential tool that complements technical analysis. Your ability to combine various techniques will lead to more comprehensive and informed trading decisions. Keep up the momentum in your learning journey!

Chapter 12: Volume Analysis

Volume is a crucial factor in technical analysis, providing insights into the strength of price movements and confirming trends. Volume analysis helps traders understand market participation and make more informed trading decisions. In this chapter, we'll delve into the significance of volume and how to effectively incorporate it into your analysis.

Understanding Volume:

Volume refers to the number of shares or contracts traded during a specific period. High volume indicates strong market participation, while low volume suggests limited interest. Volume is typically displayed as a histogram beneath price charts.

Volume and Trend Confirmation:

Volume analysis can confirm or contradict trends identified using other technical analysis tools. In an uptrend, increasing volume during upward price movements supports the trend's strength. Conversely, decreasing volume during upward price movements might indicate weakening momentum.

Volume and Reversals:

Volume analysis can also help identify potential trend reversals. For example, a sudden increase in volume during a downtrend could signal a selling climax, potentially leading to a reversal.

Volume and Breakouts:

Volume can also validate breakouts from chart patterns or resistance levels. A breakout accompanied by high volume suggests strong market interest, increasing the likelihood of a sustained price movement.

Volume and Support/Resistance:

Volume can indicate the significance of support and resistance levels. If a price approaches a significant level with high volume, it suggests that traders are paying attention to that level, increasing its importance.

On-Balance Volume (OBV):

The On-Balance Volume indicator cumulatively adds volume on up days and subtracts volume on down days. It helps identify whether volume is flowing into or out of an asset, providing insights into potential trend reversals.

Using Volume with Other Indicators:

Volume analysis is most effective when combined with other technical analysis tools. For instance, volume confirmation can enhance the reliability of trend lines, chart patterns, and moving average crossovers.

Limitations of Volume Analysis:

While volume analysis is valuable, it has limitations. Volume can be influenced by news events, market sentiment, and trading algorithms. It's important to consider these factors when interpreting volume data.

Practice and Experience:

Developing proficiency in volume analysis requires practice. Analyze historical price charts, observe how volume correlates with price movements, and identify instances where volume provided valuable insights.

In the upcoming chapters, we'll explore risk management, building a comprehensive trading plan, and using technical analysis in real-world scenarios. Your dedication to learning and improving your skills will make you a more confident and successful trader. Keep up the excellent work!

Chapter 13: Risk Management

Effective risk management is a cornerstone of successful trading. No matter how skilled you are at technical analysis, managing your risk is essential to preserve your capital and achieve long-term profitability. In this chapter, we'll explore key principles of risk management and how to apply them to your trading strategy.

Set a Risk Tolerance:

Before placing any trades, determine how much of your capital you're willing to risk on a single trade. This is often referred to as the "risk per trade" or "position sizing." A common rule of thumb is to risk no more than 1-2% of your capital on any given trade.

Stop-Loss Orders:

A stop-loss order is an essential tool in risk management. It's a pre-set order that automatically closes your position if the price reaches a certain level. Setting a stop-loss helps you limit potential losses and prevent emotional decision-making.

Reward-to-Risk Ratio:

The reward-to-risk ratio compares the potential profit of a trade to the potential loss. For example, if your profit target is $200 and your stop-loss is $100, your reward-to-risk ratio would be 2:1. Aim for trades with a favorable reward-to-risk ratio to ensure that potential profits outweigh potential losses.

Diversification:

Diversifying your trades across different assets or markets can help spread risk. If one trade doesn't perform well, others may offset the loss. However, be cautious not to over-diversify, as it can dilute your focus and effectiveness.

Avoid Overtrading:

Overtrading occurs when you take too many trades in a short period, often due to emotional reactions or a desire to recover losses. This can lead to poor decision-making and increased risk. Stick to your trading plan and only take trades that meet your criteria.

Stay Informed:

Market conditions can change rapidly. Stay updated on economic news, events, and developments that could impact your trades. A well-informed trader is better equipped to manage risk.

Paper Trading:

Before risking real capital, consider paper trading—a practice where you simulate trades without using actual money. This allows you to test your strategies, refine your risk management techniques, and gain confidence.

Psychological Risk Management:

Emotional control is a vital aspect of risk management. Emotional trading can lead to impulsive decisions and losses. Develop discipline and the ability to stick to your trading plan, even when emotions are running high.

Review and Adapt:

Regularly review your trades, successes, and mistakes. Adjust your risk management strategy based on your experience and performance. Adaptability is key to long-term success.

In the upcoming chapters, we'll explore building a comprehensive trading plan and applying technical analysis to real-world scenarios. By integrating risk management into your strategy, you'll enhance your ability to navigate the markets successfully. Keep advancing your skills and knowledge—it's a journey toward becoming a proficient trader!

Chapter 14: Building a Comprehensive Trading Plan

A well-defined trading plan is essential for consistent and successful trading. It provides structure, guidelines, and a roadmap for your trading activities. In this chapter, we'll explore the key components of a comprehensive trading plan and how to create one that aligns with your goals and trading style.

Define Your Trading Goals:

Begin by clarifying your trading objectives. Are you trading for supplemental income, wealth accumulation, or a specific financial goal? Knowing your goals will help shape your trading strategy.

Choose Your Trading Style:

Are you a day trader, swing trader, or long-term investor? Each style requires different strategies and time commitments. Select the style that aligns with your personality, lifestyle, and goals.

Select Your Markets:

Decide which markets you'll trade—stocks, forex, commodities, cryptocurrencies, or others. Each market has its unique characteristics, so choose the ones that match your expertise and preferences.

Develop Your Strategy:

Based on your trading style, develop a strategy that includes your entry and exit criteria, risk management rules, and indicators you'll use for analysis. Your strategy should be clear, well-defined, and tested in various market conditions.

Set Realistic Expectations:

Be realistic about your profit expectations. Overly ambitious goals can lead to excessive risk-taking and disappointment. Consider your risk tolerance and the market's inherent volatility when setting expectations.

Risk Management Rules:

Reiterate the importance of risk management in your plan. Define your risk per trade, use stop-loss orders, and specify the maximum number of trades you'll take per day or week. Having strict risk management rules is crucial for capital preservation.

Keep a Trading Journal:

Record every trade you make, including entry and exit points, reasons for the trade, and the outcome. A trading journal helps you track your performance, identify patterns, and learn from your mistakes.

Regularly Review and Update:

Your trading plan isn't static—it should evolve as you gain experience and adapt to changing market conditions. Regularly review and update your plan to incorporate new insights and strategies.

Discipline and Consistency:

A trading plan only works if you stick to it consistently. Emotional decisions can lead to deviations from your plan and suboptimal outcomes. Develop the discipline to follow your plan rigorously.

Backtesting and Simulations:

Before applying your plan in real-time, backtest it using historical data or simulate trades using paper trading. This helps you validate your strategy and build confidence in its effectiveness.

Seek Continuous Education:

Stay committed to improving your trading skills. Continue learning about new strategies, techniques, and market developments. Education is an ongoing process that keeps you ahead of the curve.

By creating a comprehensive trading plan, you'll increase your chances of success and minimize impulsive decision-making. In the final chapter of this book, we'll explore how to apply technical analysis to real-world trading scenarios, putting your knowledge into action. Keep refining your skills and strategies—it's a journey toward becoming a skilled and profitable trader!

Chapter 15: Applying Technical Analysis in Real Trading

Congratulations, you've reached the final chapter of your journey through technical analysis! Now, it's time to put your knowledge into action and apply what you've learned to real-world trading scenarios. In this chapter, we'll explore how to effectively use technical analysis in your trading activities.

Stay Updated with Market News:

Before you start trading, stay informed about economic news, earnings reports, geopolitical events, and other factors that can impact the markets. These events can influence price movements and affect your trading decisions.

Combining Multiple Analysis Techniques:

Recall that technical analysis isn't limited to a single tool. To make informed decisions, combine various techniques such as trend lines, chart patterns, indicators, and volume analysis. The convergence of multiple signals can provide more robust trading opportunities.

Practice Patience:

In trading, patience is a virtue. Wait for confirmation of your analysis before executing a trade. Rushing into trades without proper confirmation can lead to losses.

Risk Management in Real Trading:

Implement the risk management principles you've learned. Set your risk per trade, use stop-loss orders, and adhere to your position sizing rules. Protecting your capital is paramount.

Managing Emotions:

Real trading can evoke emotions like fear and greed. Stick to your trading plan and don't let emotions cloud your judgment. Emotions can lead to impulsive decisions and mistakes.

Start Small:

When transitioning to real trading, consider starting with a small account or trading with a demo account. This allows you to apply your strategies without risking significant capital.

Monitor Your Trades:

Once you're in a trade, regularly monitor its progress. Be prepared to adjust your stop-loss or take-profit levels if new information emerges that affects your initial analysis.

Learn from Your Trades:

Whether a trade ends in profit or loss, there's always something to learn. Analyze your trades, identify what worked and what didn't, and use this knowledge to refine your strategy.

Stay Adaptable:

Market conditions can change quickly. Stay adaptable by continuously learning, adjusting your strategies, and being open to new insights.

Record Your Progress:

Maintain a trading journal to document your trades, thoughts, and emotions. Over time, your journal will become a valuable resource for analyzing your trading performance.

Seek Continuous Improvement:

Successful traders are always striving to improve. Continue learning, attending webinars, reading books, and engaging with the trading community.

As you embark on your real trading journey, remember that success takes time and dedication. Continue refining your skills, learning from both successes and failures, and staying committed to your growth as a trader. Your journey has the potential to be a rewarding and profitable one. Good luck!

As you embark on your real trading journey, remember that success takes time and dedication. Continue refining your skills, learning from both successes and failures, and staying committed to your growth as a trader. Your journey has the potential to be a rewarding and profitable one. Good luck!

Remember that trading involves risks, and no strategy or technique guarantees success in every trade. Be prepared for both wins and losses, and focus on the long-term consistency of your trading results. Always prioritize risk management, emotional control, and continuous learning.

Throughout this book, you've gained a solid foundation in technical analysis, from understanding basic concepts to applying advanced techniques. Keep in mind that the markets are dynamic, and there's always more to learn and explore. Consider further education, attending seminars, and networking with other traders to continue honing your skills.

As you navigate the world of trading, remember that success requires a combination of knowledge, discipline, adaptability, and perseverance. Every successful trader was once a beginner, and your journey is uniquely yours. Stay patient, stay informed, and never stop striving for improvement. Best of luck in your trading endeavors!

As you embark on your real trading journey, remember that success takes time and dedication. The markets can be unpredictable, and there will be both winning and losing trades along the way. It's important to maintain a realistic perspective and manage your expectations.

Stay disciplined in adhering to your trading plan. This includes following your entry and exit criteria, risk management rules, and strategies. Emotional decision-making can lead to impulsive actions that can harm your trading results. Trust in the analysis and strategies you've learned.

Stay up-to-date with the latest market news and developments that could impact your trading positions. Economic indicators, geopolitical events, and corporate announcements can influence market sentiment and direction.

One crucial aspect of successful trading is continuous learning. The financial markets are always evolving, and staying informed about new tools, techniques, and trends can give you an edge. Consider reading trading books, attending webinars, and engaging with other traders to broaden your knowledge.

Remember that no one becomes a successful trader overnight. It's a journey of growth and refinement. Analyze your trades, both profitable and unprofitable, to understand what worked and what didn't. This self-assessment will help you make adjustments and improve your strategies over time.

Trading requires a balance of confidence and humility. While confidence in your analysis is essential, humility allows you to acknowledge mistakes and learn from them. Don't be discouraged by losses; instead, view them as opportunities to learn and grow.

Lastly, trading is not just about making profits; it's about managing risk and capital preservation. Always prioritize risk management, and avoid risking more than you can afford to lose on any trade. Consistency in risk management is a hallmark of successful traders.

Your journey into the world of trading is an exciting and challenging one. Keep your passion for learning alive, and remember that each step you take, each trade you make, contributes to your growth as a trader. Stay patient, stay disciplined, and stay focused on your goals. Best of luck on your trading adventure!

Conclusion

your journey through this comprehensive book on technical analysis has provided you with a solid foundation for navigating the intricate world of trading. From understanding fundamental concepts to applying advanced techniques, you've gained insights that can significantly enhance your trading skills.

Technical analysis isn't just about predicting market movements; it's a holistic approach that combines analytical tools with discipline, risk management, and emotional control. By learning how to interpret price charts, recognize patterns, and use indicators effectively, you've acquired a set of tools that can help you make more informed trading decisions.

Remember that success in trading isn't solely measured by the profits you make, but also by your ability to manage risk, adapt to changing market conditions, and continuously improve your strategies. Along the way, you'll encounter both victories and challenges. Embrace these experiences as opportunities to learn and grow, refining your approach and building your expertise.

As you step into the world of real trading, always prioritize risk management, emotional resilience, and a commitment to ongoing education. Stay connected with fellow traders, seek guidance from mentors, and approach each trade with a sense of curiosity and discipline.

Whether you're a beginner taking your first steps or an experienced trader looking to enhance your skills, the principles of technical analysis outlined in this book are universally applicable. The markets are a dynamic and ever-evolving landscape, and your ability to adapt, learn, and refine your strategies will be the driving force behind your success.

As you embark on your trading journey, keep the knowledge you've gained close to heart and approach each trade with a combination of confidence and humility. Your journey as a trader is an exciting one, full of opportunities for growth, learning, and achievement. With dedication, perseverance, and a commitment to continuous improvement, you have the potential to make your mark in the world of trading. Best of luck, and may your trading endeavors be both rewarding and fulfilling!

Day Trading

Engage in short-term trading, opening and closing positions within the same trading day.

Introduction:

Day trading is a dynamic and expedited trading strategy that involves the execution of multiple trades within a single trading day. This approach is characterized by its focus on short-term price movements, as traders seek to capitalize on market fluctuations by opening and closing positions within the same trading session. The significance of day trading within the intricate fabric of financial markets cannot be understated, as it contributes to market liquidity, price efficiency, and offers opportunities for both profit and risk.

Explanation of Day Trading: Day trading centers on the premise of exploiting intraday price volatility to secure gains. Unlike longer-term investment strategies, where assets are held for extended periods, day traders meticulously analyze minute market movements to determine optimal entry and exit points. These traders often leverage technical analysis, utilizing tools such as candlestick charts, moving averages, and relative strength indicators to identify trends and patterns. Furthermore, day trading can encompass a variety of assets, including stocks, forex, commodities, and cryptocurrencies, providing ample options for traders to engage with different markets.

Importance of Day Trading in Financial Markets: Day trading plays a pivotal role in maintaining the smooth operation of financial markets. By actively participating in rapid buy and sell transactions, day traders contribute to market liquidity, ensuring that assets can be easily bought or sold without causing significant price disruptions. This infusion of liquidity enhances overall market efficiency and stability. Moreover, day trading promotes price discovery, as the constant flow of transactions aids in determining accurate market prices based on current supply and demand dynamics.

Brief Overview of Potential Benefits and Risks: Day trading offers several potential benefits to traders. The most prominent advantage is the potential for substantial profits within a compressed timeframe. Successful day traders can exploit numerous trading opportunities that arise throughout the trading day, which can accumulate into significant gains. Additionally, day trading does not subject traders to overnight market risks, as positions are closed before the trading session ends, thereby mitigating exposure to unforeseen overnight developments.

However, day trading is not without its inherent risks. The fast-paced nature of this strategy demands quick decision-making, leaving minimal room for error. Mistimed trades or misinterpreted market signals can lead to substantial losses. Furthermore, the frequent buying and selling of assets can lead to higher transaction costs, including commissions and spreads, which can eat into potential profits. Moreover, the psychological toll of day trading, characterized by the pressure to make split-second decisions and the potential for emotional trading, can impact a trader's overall well-being.

In conclusion, day trading embodies a sophisticated approach to trading that involves swift decision-making, capitalizing on intraday price movements. Its significance within financial markets extends to providing liquidity, enhancing market efficiency, and offering trading opportunities. The potential benefits of substantial profits and the avoidance of overnight risks are balanced by the risks of quick losses, transaction costs, and psychological strain. As such, day trading stands as a compelling yet challenging strategy that demands precision, discipline, and a deep understanding of market dynamics.

Chapter 1: Understanding Day Trading

Day trading, a cornerstone of active trading strategies, is characterized by its focus on capitalizing on short-term market movements within the span of a single trading day. This chapter delves into the essential components of day trading, ranging from its fundamental definition to the various types of day traders, the comparative advantages and disadvantages, and the foundational requisites for effectively engaging in this fast-paced trading approach.

Definition and Concept of Day Trading: Day trading entails the practice of entering and exiting positions within the same trading day, aiming to profit from intraday price fluctuations. The primary objective of day traders is to exploit short-term trends, whether upwards or downwards, by accurately predicting price movements. This often involves leveraging technical analysis tools and chart patterns to identify potential entry and exit points.

Different Types of Day Traders: Within the realm of day trading, several distinct trading styles emerge, each catering to different market conditions and trader preferences. Scalpers, for instance, seek to profit from tiny price movements, executing a high volume of trades within seconds to minutes. Momentum traders focus on riding the momentum of strong price trends, capitalizing on the continuation of established price movements. Breakout traders target assets that exhibit significant price volatility, entering positions when the price breaks through key support or resistance levels. Additionally, algorithmic traders employ automated strategies and algorithms to execute trades based on predetermined criteria.

Advantages and Disadvantages of Day Trading: Comparing day trading to other trading styles unveils a host of advantages and disadvantages. Day trading's swiftness and immediacy provide opportunities for multiple trades within a single day, potentially leading to more frequent profits. Additionally, day traders are shielded from overnight market risks, which can lead to unexpected gaps in prices. However, this rapid-fire approach comes with drawbacks. The intense decision-making pressure can lead to impulsive actions and emotional trading, potentially amplifying losses. Furthermore, the requirement for constant monitoring of markets can lead to exhaustion and burnout.

Basic Requirements for Day Trading: Engaging in day trading necessitates several fundamental prerequisites. First and foremost, sufficient capital is essential to withstand potential losses and implement meaningful trades. A well-equipped hardware setup, comprising a reliable computer with ample processing power and memory, is crucial to handle real-time data feeds and trading platforms. Specialized trading software with features like advanced charting tools, real-time market data, and order execution capabilities is a requisite. Equally significant is a stable and high-speed internet connection to ensure timely execution of trades.

In conclusion, the intricate world of day trading involves the swift execution of trades within a single trading day, relying on technical analysis and chart patterns to exploit short-term market movements. Diverse types of day traders exist, catering to various strategies and market conditions. The benefits of increased trading frequency and the avoidance of overnight risks are counterbalanced by the challenges of emotional trading and the need for constant vigilance. A comprehensive set of prerequisites, including adequate capital, hardware, software, and internet connectivity, is necessary to embark on the day trading journey successfully. Understanding these foundational aspects is pivotal for anyone aspiring to navigate the complexities of day trading effectively.

Chapter 2: Setting Up for Success

In the pursuit of day trading excellence, meticulous preparation and a well-structured foundation are paramount. This chapter delves into the crucial elements necessary to establish an environment conducive to successful day trading. From crafting an optimal workspace to selecting appropriate trading tools and platforms, along with understanding broker dynamics and the development of a comprehensive trading plan, this chapter illuminates the essential steps for setting the stage for day trading triumph.

Creating a Well-Equipped Trading Workspace: The cornerstone of effective day trading lies in the design and organization of a purpose-built trading workspace. An ergonomic and distraction-free environment is imperative to maintain focus and enhance decision-making. A comfortable chair, appropriate lighting, and minimal clutter are key elements. Multiple monitors, each displaying real-time market data and charts, facilitate comprehensive analysis. Ergonomic keyboard and mouse configurations ensure ease of use during fast-paced trading sessions.

Selecting the Right Trading Platform and Tools: The choice of trading platform and tools is pivotal to a day trader's success. A robust trading platform should provide real-time data feeds, customizable charts, technical indicators, and efficient order execution capabilities. Advanced features such as automated trading, backtesting functionalities, and access to historical data are also invaluable for strategic decision-making. Careful consideration of the platform's compatibility with the trader's preferred assets and trading strategies is essential.

Choosing a Reliable Broker and Understanding Their Fee Structure: The selection of a trustworthy broker is a critical step in the day trading journey. Brokers serve as intermediaries, facilitating the execution of trades. A reliable broker should offer competitive spreads, low commissions, fast order execution, and access to a wide range of financial instruments. Understanding the broker's fee structure, including transaction costs, overnight fees, and account maintenance charges, is imperative to gauge the impact of these expenses on potential profits.

Developing a Trading Plan: Goals, Strategies, Risk Management, and Time Commitment: A well-defined trading plan forms the bedrock of a day trader's success. This plan encapsulates clear-cut goals, delineates chosen trading strategies, outlines robust risk management protocols, and establishes a realistic time commitment. Goals should be specific, measurable, achievable, relevant, and time-bound (SMART). Trading strategies, whether based on technical analysis, fundamental analysis, or a combination thereof, must align with the trader's strengths and market conditions. Rigorous risk management strategies, such as setting stop-loss and take-profit levels, help mitigate potential losses. The allocation of time for market analysis, trading execution, and continuous learning ensures a balanced approach to day trading.

In conclusion, the preparation for successful day trading necessitates meticulous attention to detail across various facets. Establishing an ergonomically sound and distraction-free trading workspace is the initial step toward optimal performance. The selection of a suitable trading platform, equipped with requisite tools, ensures comprehensive market analysis and informed decision-making. The careful choice of a reputable broker with a transparent fee structure is essential to protect potential profits. Lastly, the development of a comprehensive trading plan, incorporating well-defined goals, effective strategies, prudent risk management, and dedicated time commitment, paves the way for a disciplined and methodical approach to day trading. By meticulously addressing these foundational components, aspiring day traders can position themselves for success in the dynamic realm of the financial markets.

Chapter 3: Technical Analysis

Technical analysis, a cornerstone of informed trading decisions, empowers day traders to decipher market trends, forecast price movements, and make timely trading choices. This chapter delves into the essential realm of technical analysis, encompassing its foundational significance in day trading, key technical indicators, candlestick patterns, and various chart formations that serve as critical tools for deciphering market dynamics.

Introduction to Technical Analysis and its Importance in Day Trading: Technical analysis is a methodology employed by traders to assess and predict future price movements through the analysis of historical market data, primarily focusing on price and volume. For day traders, technical analysis is indispensable in swiftly identifying trends, assessing market sentiment, and identifying potential entry and exit points. This data-driven approach aids in the formulation of informed trading decisions amidst the rapid pace of intraday trading.

Key Technical Indicators: Technical analysis encompasses a diverse array of indicators that offer insights into market trends and potential turning points. Moving averages, which smooth out price data to reveal trends, are instrumental in identifying support and resistance levels. The Moving Average Convergence Divergence (MACD) gauges momentum by analyzing the relationship between two moving averages. The Relative Strength Index (RSI) measures overbought or oversold conditions, aiding in the identification of potential reversals. Bollinger Bands depict price volatility and potential breakout points.

Candlestick Patterns and their Significance: Candlestick patterns, derived from Japanese rice trading in the 18th century, provide a visual representation of price movement over a specified time frame. These patterns offer insights into market sentiment and potential price reversals. Engulfing patterns, Doji patterns, and hammer patterns are examples of candlestick formations that suggest shifts in market dynamics. The formation of these patterns, when coupled with other technical indicators, can provide powerful signals for traders.

Chart Patterns: Head and Shoulders, Double Tops/Bottoms, Triangles, and Flags: Chart patterns are crucial tools for identifying potential trend reversals or continuation patterns. The head and shoulders pattern signifies a potential trend reversal, with the head representing a peak and the shoulders marking smaller peaks on either side. Double tops and double bottoms indicate potential reversals, while triangles (ascending, descending, and symmetrical) and flags symbolize consolidation before price continuation. These patterns are instrumental in assisting day traders in identifying critical levels and anticipating potential price movements.

In conclusion, technical analysis is an indispensable facet of day trading, providing traders with the tools necessary to interpret historical market data and make informed trading decisions. Through key technical indicators like moving averages, MACD, RSI, and Bollinger Bands, traders can gauge momentum, volatility, and potential reversal points. Candlestick patterns offer insights into market sentiment, and chart patterns such as head and shoulders, double tops/bottoms, triangles, and flags aid in the identification of trend reversals or continuation patterns. A thorough understanding of these technical analysis tools equips day traders with the ability to navigate the complexities of intraday trading and make strategic choices in a rapidly evolving market landscape.

Chapter 4: Fundamental Analysis for Day Traders

In the dynamic world of day trading, where swift decision-making is paramount, fundamental analysis emerges as a potent tool for gaining a comprehensive understanding of market conditions. This chapter delves into the foundational principles of fundamental analysis as applied to day trading. It explores the process of identifying pertinent news and economic indicators, integrating fundamental analysis into trading decisions, and striking a harmonious equilibrium between fundamental and technical analysis strategies.

Basics of Fundamental Analysis in Day Trading: Fundamental analysis centers on evaluating the intrinsic value of an asset by analyzing economic, financial, and qualitative factors that influence its price. While more commonly associated with longer-term investment, fundamental analysis holds relevance in day trading. Day traders can leverage this approach to grasp the broader market sentiment, identify potential catalysts, and make informed decisions amidst the swift-paced trading environment.

Identifying Relevant News and Economic Indicators: For day traders, staying attuned to real-time news and economic indicators is pivotal. Economic indicators, such as GDP growth, unemployment rates, and inflation figures, provide insights into a country's economic health and can significantly impact market sentiment. Major news events, corporate earnings reports, and geopolitical developments also wield substantial influence on price movements. Day traders must identify and monitor these catalysts to anticipate potential market shifts.

Incorporating Fundamental Analysis into Trading Decisions: Integrating fundamental analysis into day trading strategies involves a judicious assessment of how news and economic data might influence market behavior. For instance, positive economic data can lead to increased market optimism and upward price movement. Conversely, negative news might trigger uncertainty and drive prices downward. Day traders can capitalize on these trends by aligning their trades with the prevailing sentiment and potential price movements triggered by fundamental events.

Balancing Technical and Fundamental Analysis Strategies: Achieving an optimal balance between technical and fundamental analysis strategies is essential for well-rounded day trading. While technical analysis provides insights into short-term price patterns, fundamental analysis offers a broader context by examining the underlying factors that drive these movements. Skillful day traders harmonize both approaches, using technical analysis for entry and exit points while leveraging fundamental analysis to gauge the potential impact of news events and indicators on these patterns.

In conclusion, fundamental analysis serves as a valuable dimension within the arsenal of day traders, enriching their understanding of market dynamics and influencing their trading decisions. By delving into the basics of fundamental analysis, day traders can decipher relevant news and economic indicators to anticipate market shifts. Integrating this analysis into their strategies enables traders to align with prevailing sentiment and anticipate price movements influenced by fundamental catalysts. Achieving equilibrium between technical and fundamental analysis strategies empowers day traders to navigate the intricate interplay between short-term patterns and broader market conditions, enhancing their ability to thrive within the fast-paced realm of day trading.

Chapter 5: Developing Winning Strategies

In the exhilarating realm of day trading, the development of effective trading strategies is the linchpin to achieving success. This chapter unravels the intricacies of crafting winning strategies tailored for the unique demands of day trading. It explores a spectrum of proven approaches, ranging from scalping and momentum trading to breakout trading and exploiting market gaps, each designed to capitalize on the rapid-paced nature of intraday trading.

Scalping: Quick Trades for Small Gains: Scalping, a strategy rooted in swift decision-making and precision, entails executing a high volume of trades with the intent of profiting from minor price fluctuations. Day traders employing this strategy aim to capture tiny price differentials while minimizing exposure to market risk. By leveraging tight spreads and frequently monitoring the market, scalpers capitalize on fleeting opportunities, accumulating small gains that accumulate into substantial profits over time.

Momentum Trading: Capitalizing on Strong Price Movements: Momentum trading revolves around harnessing the energy of significant price movements that often accompany market news or fundamental events. Day traders practicing momentum trading capitalize on these surges by entering positions aligned with the prevailing momentum, aiming to ride the trend and secure substantial gains. Identifying overbought or oversold conditions using technical indicators like the Relative Strength Index (RSI) aids in timing entries and exits.

Breakout Trading: Profiting from Price Breakouts: Breakout trading involves identifying key levels of support or resistance and capitalizing on price movements that breach these levels. Day traders following this strategy anticipate that price breakouts will lead to significant upward or downward movements, allowing them to enter trades in the direction of the breakout. Technical tools like Bollinger Bands and trendline analysis assist in pinpointing potential breakout points, while prudent risk management strategies mitigate potential losses.

Gap Trading: Taking Advantage of Price Gaps in the Market: Gap trading exploits the phenomenon of price gaps that occur between a security's closing price and its opening price on the subsequent trading day. These gaps often materialize due to after-hours news or market events. Day traders employing this strategy enter positions aligned with the gap direction, anticipating that prices will revert to their original trend. Identifying gap patterns and employing technical analysis aids in executing successful gap trades.

In conclusion, the development of winning strategies is a cornerstone of day trading triumph. By mastering strategies such as scalping, momentum trading, breakout trading, and gap trading, day traders equip themselves with a versatile toolkit to navigate the intricate waters of intraday trading. Scalping offers quick gains from minor fluctuations, momentum trading capitalizes on strong price movements, breakout trading leverages key support and resistance levels, and gap trading exploits price gaps resulting from market events. The mastery of these strategies empowers day traders to adapt to various market conditions, make informed decisions, and ultimately secure their place in the competitive world of day trading.

Chapter 6: Risk Management Techniques

In the high-stakes arena of day trading, where fortunes can be gained or lost in a matter of moments, the implementation of robust risk management techniques stands as a fundamental pillar of success. This chapter delves into the paramount significance of risk management in day trading and explores a spectrum of strategies aimed at safeguarding capital and optimizing trading outcomes. From setting prudent stop-loss and take-profit levels to calculating optimal position sizes and embracing diversification, this chapter elucidates the critical role that risk management plays in navigating the volatile landscape of intraday trading.

Importance of Risk Management in Day Trading: Risk management constitutes the bedrock upon which the edifice of day trading success is built. The swift pace and inherent volatility of intraday trading amplify the potential for losses. Effective risk management strategies serve as a protective shield against undue exposure, ensuring that traders can weather market fluctuations and preserve capital in the face of adverse market movements.

Setting Stop-Loss and Take-Profit Levels: The implementation of stop-loss and take-profit levels is a cornerstone of prudent risk management. A stop-loss order is designed to automatically close a trade if the price moves against the trader beyond a specified threshold. Take-profit levels, on the other hand, secure profits by automatically closing a trade when the price reaches a predefined target. Balancing the placement of these levels based on market volatility, asset behavior, and individual risk tolerance is crucial for optimizing risk-reward ratios.

Calculating Position Size Based on Risk Tolerance: Determining an appropriate position size is integral to managing risk effectively. Day traders calculate position sizes based on their risk tolerance and the distance between entry and stop-loss levels. The aim is to limit potential losses to a predetermined percentage of the trading capital. By adhering to disciplined position sizing, traders prevent the possibility of catastrophic losses that can severely impact their overall trading performance.

Diversification and Spreading Risk Across Different Assets: Diversification entails spreading investments across a variety of assets, thus mitigating the impact of a poor-performing asset on the overall portfolio. For day traders, diversification can be achieved by trading different assets, such as stocks, forex, commodities, and cryptocurrencies. This strategy reduces the exposure to a single asset's volatility and safeguards the trading capital from excessive risk concentration.

In conclusion, risk management techniques are the keystone of a successful day trading endeavor. As the rapid fluctuations and intense volatility characteristic of intraday trading pose considerable risks, implementing sound risk management practices is non-negotiable. The establishment of stop-loss and take-profit levels safeguards profits and limits losses, while calculating optimal position sizes preserves capital. Diversification across diverse assets offers an additional layer of protection against market volatility. By meticulously integrating these risk management techniques into their trading strategies, day traders fortify their ability to navigate the intricacies of the market with confidence, resilience, and a greater likelihood of long-term success.

Chapter 7: Psychology of Day Trading

In the dynamic world of day trading, where rapid decision-making and swift execution are imperative, the psychological landscape of traders plays a pivotal role in determining success. This chapter delves into the intricate realm of the psychology of day trading, exploring the common psychological challenges that traders encounter, strategies to overcome detrimental emotions such as fear, greed, and impatience, the development of discipline and a robust mindset, and the importance of maintaining a trading journal for continuous self-assessment and improvement.

Common Psychological Challenges Faced by Day Traders: Day traders are subjected to a plethora of psychological challenges that can impact their decision-making and trading outcomes. The pressure to make rapid decisions, the fear of losses, the lure of quick profits, and the emotional roller coaster induced by market volatility are all significant stressors that can affect a trader's mental state. Such challenges can lead to impulsive actions, emotional trading, and ultimately, poor trading results.

Overcoming Emotions: Fear, Greed, and Impatience: Fear and greed are two powerful emotions that can influence day traders' decisions. Fear can lead to hesitation or unwarranted exits, causing traders to miss out on profitable opportunities. Conversely, greed can prompt traders to chase profits, leading to excessive risk-taking and potential losses. Impatience can drive traders to overtrade, disregarding their strategies and succumbing to impulse. Overcoming these emotions necessitates self-awareness, mental discipline, and a well-structured trading plan.

Developing Discipline and a Strong Mindset: Discipline is the cornerstone of successful day trading. A strong mindset involves the cultivation of patience, resilience, and emotional control. Following a well-defined trading plan, adhering to predetermined entry and exit points, and maintaining consistency in trading strategies are all manifestations of discipline. A strong mindset allows traders to navigate the challenges of the market with composure, rationality, and the ability to adapt to changing conditions.

Maintaining a Trading Journal for Self-Assessment and Improvement: A trading journal serves as an invaluable tool for self-assessment and continuous improvement. By meticulously documenting each trade, traders gain insights into their decision-making process, emotions, and patterns. This reflective practice aids in identifying strengths, weaknesses, and areas requiring improvement. A trading journal also offers the opportunity to evaluate the effectiveness of different strategies over time, refining approaches for enhanced trading outcomes.

In conclusion, the psychology of day trading is a realm often underestimated but profoundly influential on a trader's journey to success. By acknowledging and addressing common psychological challenges, such as fear, greed, and impatience, day traders can make more informed decisions. The cultivation of discipline and a strong mindset empowers traders to remain level-headed and focused amidst market turbulence. Maintaining a trading journal contributes to self-assessment and continuous improvement, refining strategies and optimizing trading outcomes. Ultimately, the fusion of psychological resilience, disciplined decision-making, and reflective practice positions day traders for greater mastery over their emotions and, consequently, their ability to navigate the intricate realm of intraday trading.

Chapter 8: Practicing and Backtesting

In the intricate realm of day trading, the old adage "practice makes perfect" finds profound resonance. This chapter delves into the essential components of effective practice and backtesting – two pillars that underpin the journey towards mastery in day trading. It explores the significance of demo trading for beginners, the art of backtesting trading strategies using historical data, the process of refining strategies based on backtesting results, and the imperative of continuous practice and adaptation to evolving market conditions.

The Significance of Demo Trading for Beginners: For beginners venturing into the world of day trading, the significance of demo trading cannot be overstated. A demo trading account provides an environment to simulate real trading scenarios without risking actual capital. This invaluable training ground allows novice traders to grasp the mechanics of trading platforms, test different strategies, and build confidence before transitioning to live trading. It hones critical skills and nurtures a deep understanding of market dynamics.

Backtesting Trading Strategies Using Historical Data: Backtesting, a quintessential practice for refining trading strategies, involves analyzing historical market data to evaluate how a particular strategy would have performed in the past. By applying strategies to historical price data, traders gain insights into the strategy's potential strengths and weaknesses. This data-driven analysis aids in identifying optimal entry and exit points, stop-loss and take-profit levels, and overall profitability.

Refining Strategies Based on Backtesting Results: Backtesting results serve as a roadmap for strategy refinement. It enables traders to fine-tune parameters, adapt strategies to different market conditions, and discard approaches that prove ineffective. Analyzing the historical performance of a strategy aids in identifying patterns of success and failure, leading to strategic adjustments that optimize trading outcomes in real-time scenarios.

Continuous Practice and Adaptation to Changing Market Conditions: The journey to mastery in day trading is a dynamic one, characterized by continuous practice and the ability to adapt to changing market conditions. Successful traders acknowledge that markets evolve, and strategies that once yielded profits may become less effective over time. Adapting strategies to align with evolving market dynamics is a key determinant of sustained success. Continuous practice, complemented by a willingness to learn and adapt, ensures that traders remain agile and equipped to navigate the ever-shifting currents of the trading world.

In conclusion, the practices of demo trading and backtesting form a vital duo in the arsenal of successful day traders. Demo trading empowers beginners to build skills and confidence before venturing into live trading. Backtesting, on the other hand, hones strategies through historical data analysis, guiding traders in refining their approaches and aligning them with real-time market conditions. The pursuit of mastery requires continuous practice and the capacity to adapt to changing market dynamics. Ultimately, the fusion of these practices equips day traders with the tools necessary to navigate the intricate intricacies of day trading and position themselves for success in the ever-evolving realm of the financial markets.

Chapter 9: Real-Life Case Studies

The true essence of day trading comes to life through the lens of real-life case studies. This chapter delves into the invaluable learning opportunities presented by the analysis of both successful and unsuccessful day trades. By dissecting the strategies that underpin triumphs and unraveling the mistakes that led to setbacks, traders can glean vital insights into the intricate nuances of day trading. This chapter further examines the pivotal role of adaptability in day trading and draws lessons from experienced day traders who have traversed the volatile landscape of the financial markets.

Analyzing Successful Day Trades and the Strategies Behind Them: Successful day trades provide a glimpse into effective strategies that yield profitable outcomes. Through in-depth analysis, traders can uncover the rationale behind these successes – from the identification of optimal entry and exit points to the integration of technical and fundamental analysis. Understanding the nuances of successful trades equips traders with tangible insights that can be applied to their own strategies, enhancing the likelihood of favorable outcomes.

Learning from Unsuccessful Trades and Identifying Mistakes: Equally instructive are the experiences of unsuccessful trades. By dissecting trades that resulted in losses, traders can pinpoint mistakes and missteps that contributed to undesirable outcomes. This introspective analysis illuminates the importance of disciplined decision-making, the avoidance of emotional trading, and the significance of robust risk management techniques. Learning from failures facilitates growth and provides the foundation for making informed adjustments.

Understanding the Role of Adaptability in Day Trading: Adaptability emerges as a linchpin trait in the journey of day traders. Market conditions are ever-changing, and strategies that may have yielded success previously can become less effective. Case studies underscore the imperative of adapting strategies to align with evolving market dynamics. The ability to pivot, adjust, and optimize strategies based on changing conditions empowers day traders to remain agile and responsive.

Lessons to Be Drawn from Experienced Day Traders: Experienced day traders offer a treasure trove of insights that span strategy, mindset, and risk management. Their journeys through the highs and lows of the markets provide valuable lessons for aspiring traders. Learning from their successes, failures, and the strategies they've refined over time offers a unique vantage point to glean practical wisdom and actionable advice for navigating the challenges of day trading.

In conclusion, real-life case studies serve as a bridge between theoretical concepts and practical execution in day trading. Analyzing successful trades unveils effective strategies, while learning from unsuccessful trades illuminates mistakes and areas for improvement. The role of adaptability in day trading underscores the necessity of evolving strategies to match changing market conditions. Lessons drawn from experienced day traders offer a wealth of insights that can guide aspiring traders toward informed decision-making and sustainable success. Ultimately, the fusion of these case studies equips traders with a comprehensive toolkit to navigate the multifaceted landscape of day trading with skill, resilience, and an edge informed by real-world experiences.

Chapter 10: Regulatory and Tax Considerations

Amidst the intricacies of day trading, a realm of paramount importance encompasses the regulatory and tax considerations that govern this fast-paced financial activity. This chapter delves into the multifaceted landscape of regulations governing day trading in various markets, delves into the tax implications of day trading income and losses, and underscores the vital role of seeking professional advice to ensure compliance and optimize financial outcomes.

Regulations Governing Day Trading in Different Markets: Day trading operates within a regulatory framework that varies across different markets and jurisdictions. In equities markets, the Pattern Day Trader (PDT) rule in the United States mandates that traders must maintain a minimum account balance and adhere to specific trade frequency limits. Similarly, forex markets have their own set of regulations, such as leverage limitations. Comprehending and adhering to these regulations is imperative to navigate the markets effectively and avoid potential penalties.

Tax Implications of Day Trading Income and Losses: Day trading income and losses carry distinct tax implications that traders must be well-versed in. In many jurisdictions, day trading profits are typically subject to income tax, and losses may be deductible against other forms of income. However, nuances abound, and tax laws can be intricate. For instance, short-term capital gains tax rates may apply to day trading profits, while traders may have to contend with wash-sale rules that disallow certain loss deductions if similar securities are repurchased within a short timeframe.

Seeking Professional Advice for Compliance and Optimization: Given the complex interplay of regulations and tax laws, seeking professional advice is a prudent step for day traders. Tax professionals well-versed in financial markets can provide insights into minimizing tax liabilities and optimizing financial outcomes. Regulatory experts can offer guidance on adhering to trade frequency limitations and other market-specific regulations. Relying on knowledgeable professionals ensures compliance with legal requirements and maximizes potential benefits.

In conclusion, regulatory and tax considerations form a cornerstone of day trading, shaping the operational landscape and influencing financial outcomes. Navigating the regulatory landscape, understanding trade frequency limitations, and adhering to tax laws are essential to avoid legal pitfalls and optimize tax efficiency. Seeking professional advice from tax experts and regulatory specialists equips day traders with the insights needed to navigate the complex regulatory and tax terrain. As day traders aim to harness the potential of financial markets, an acute awareness of these considerations ensures a firm foundation of compliance and financial prudence.

Chapter 11: Advanced Day Trading Techniques

As day trading evolves, so too do the techniques and strategies that skilled traders employ to navigate the intricacies of the financial markets. This chapter explores advanced day trading techniques that delve deeper into the realms of technical analysis, algorithmic trading, high-frequency trading, and the strategic use of options and derivatives. By exploring these advanced approaches, traders can gain a deeper understanding of the intricacies involved in mastering the art of day trading.

Incorporating Advanced Chart Patterns and Indicators: Advanced chart patterns and indicators provide day traders with enhanced tools for deciphering market trends and making informed decisions. Patterns like cup and handle, wedges, and flags offer insights into potential price movements. Indicators like the Fibonacci retracement levels, Ichimoku Cloud, and Elliott Wave Theory enable traders to delve deeper into market dynamics and refine their entry and exit strategies.

Utilizing Algorithmic Trading Strategies: Algorithmic trading strategies leverage automation and data analysis to execute trades based on predefined criteria. These strategies can process vast amounts of data in real time, allowing for rapid execution and precision. Algorithmic trading can encompass strategies such as arbitrage, trend following, and mean reversion. Implementing algorithmic strategies requires a robust understanding of programming, quantitative analysis, and risk management.

High-Frequency Trading and its Challenges: High-frequency trading (HFT) involves executing a large volume of trades in extremely short timeframes, often within milliseconds. HFT relies heavily on advanced technology, co-location, and specialized algorithms. While HFT can yield significant profits due to the high volume of trades, it also comes with unique challenges, including competition, market data latency, and regulatory scrutiny.

Leveraging Options and Derivatives in Day Trading: Options and derivatives offer advanced day traders alternative ways to profit from market movements. Options provide the right, but not the obligation, to buy or sell an asset at a predetermined price within a specific timeframe. Derivatives like futures contracts allow traders to speculate on price movements without owning the underlying asset. These tools require a deep understanding of their intricacies, as well as risk management techniques tailored to their unique characteristics.

In conclusion, the realm of advanced day trading techniques delves into the intricacies of technical analysis, algorithmic trading, high-frequency trading, and the strategic use of options and derivatives. By incorporating advanced chart patterns, indicators, and algorithmic strategies, traders gain an edge in deciphering market trends and executing precise trades. High-frequency trading offers potential benefits but also presents distinct challenges that require careful consideration. The strategic utilization of options and derivatives provides alternative avenues for profit, albeit with complexities that demand a profound understanding. As day traders ascend to the realm of advanced techniques, a combination of expertise, discipline, and continuous learning is required to master these sophisticated strategies and excel in the dynamic world of day trading.

Chapter 12: Market Analysis and Timing

In the intricate tapestry of day trading, the ability to comprehend market dynamics and execute trades at precisely opportune moments holds paramount significance. This chapter delves into the crucial realm of market analysis and timing, unraveling the art of reading market trends, pinpointing optimal entry and exit points, understanding the ebbs and flows of market cycles, and integrating the profound impact of global economic events into the fabric of a strategic trading approach.

Reading Market Trends and Identifying Potential Opportunities: Market analysis commences with the astute interpretation of trends that define price movements. By analyzing historical data, tracking patterns, and employing technical indicators, day traders gain insights into potential opportunities. Ascending and descending trends, consolidation phases, and breakout patterns are all telltale signs that inform traders about potential price movements and the right time to enter or exit positions.

Timing Your Trades for Optimal Entry and Exit Points: Timing, a cornerstone of day trading mastery, hinges on the precision of entry and exit points. By synchronizing trading decisions with the alignment of technical and fundamental signals, day traders maximize the probability of favorable outcomes. The confluence of technical indicators, candlestick patterns, and fundamental catalysts provides traders with a blueprint for making informed decisions at the optimal juncture.

Understanding Market Cycles and Their Impact on Day Trading: Market cycles, characterized by recurring patterns of price movements, significantly influence day trading outcomes. From accumulation and uptrend phases to distribution and downtrends, understanding the lifecycle of market cycles empowers day traders to anticipate trend reversals and align their strategies accordingly. A nuanced comprehension of market cycles allows traders to adapt their tactics to different phases, enhancing their ability to capitalize on changing market dynamics.

Incorporating Global Economic Events into Your Trading Strategy: Global economic events wield a substantial impact on financial markets and, consequently, day trading outcomes. Interest rate decisions, GDP releases, employment reports, and geopolitical events can trigger market volatility and shape sentiment. Incorporating an awareness of these events into trading strategies allows day traders to adjust their positions, manage risk, and seize opportunities that emerge as a result of sudden market shifts.

In conclusion, the realm of market analysis and timing is a keystone to the success of day trading. The ability to read market trends, decipher optimal entry and exit points, navigate market cycles, and incorporate global economic events equips day traders with the tools to make informed and strategic decisions. The fusion of technical analysis, fundamental insights, and a keen awareness of timing empowers traders to navigate the intricate dynamics of financial markets with precision and confidence. By mastering these facets, day traders position themselves for success in the dynamic and ever-evolving landscape of day trading.

Chapter 13: Managing Overnight Risk

Within the realm of day trading, the transition from one trading day to the next brings forth a distinct set of challenges encapsulated in the realm of overnight risk management. This chapter delves into the multifaceted landscape of managing overnight risk, encompassing the perils associated with holding positions beyond trading hours, the employment of hedging strategies to curtail these risks, techniques for identifying potential overnight gaps, and the strategic establishment of automated alerts to stay attuned to market-moving news that can impact positions.

The Risks Associated with Holding Positions Overnight: Holding positions overnight exposes day traders to a myriad of risks that can impact trading outcomes. Overnight gaps, wherein prices open significantly higher or lower than the previous close due to after-hours news or events, can lead to substantial losses if positions are not properly managed. Furthermore, market sentiment can shift overnight due to global economic developments, geopolitical events, or unforeseen news, contributing to increased volatility and potential losses.

Hedging Strategies to Mitigate Overnight Risk: Hedging serves as a strategic shield against overnight risk. By simultaneously holding positions that move inversely to the primary positions, traders can offset potential losses in the event of adverse price movements. Employing options, futures, or other derivatives that provide protection can serve as a hedge against volatility. While hedging incurs additional costs, it can mitigate the impact of overnight gaps and sudden market movements.

Techniques for Identifying Potential Overnight Gaps: Anticipating overnight gaps is essential to managing overnight risk effectively. By analyzing historical price patterns and monitoring after-hours news flow, day traders can identify potential catalysts that may trigger gaps. Identifying key levels of support and resistance can further aid in gauging the potential magnitude of overnight gaps. This information empowers traders to make informed decisions on whether to adjust or exit positions before market closure.

Setting Up Automated Alerts for Potential Market-Moving News: Staying abreast of market-moving news is pivotal to managing overnight risk. Setting up automated alerts that notify traders of significant news releases, earnings reports, or geopolitical developments can enable timely responses to potential market shifts. By staying informed, day traders can assess the impact of such news on their positions and make prudent decisions to safeguard against unforeseen risks.

In conclusion, managing overnight risk is a cornerstone of effective day trading. Understanding the risks associated with holding positions overnight, employing hedging strategies, identifying potential overnight gaps, and establishing automated alerts for market-moving news all contribute to effective risk management. By mastering these techniques, day traders fortify their ability to navigate the complex interplay of overnight risks and make informed decisions that safeguard capital and enhance trading outcomes in the ever-evolving landscape of financial markets.

Chapter 14: Building a Day Trading Routine

Within the dynamic arena of day trading, the establishment of a structured and efficient routine stands as a cornerstone of success. This chapter delves into the meticulous process of constructing a day trading routine that maximizes productivity, hones decision-making skills, and fosters consistent performance. It explores the components of pre-market preparation, the discipline of during-market execution, and the significance of post-market review – all pivotal elements that converge to create a robust framework for day trading triumph.

Designing an Effective Daily Routine for Day Trading: Crafting an effective daily routine forms the bedrock of a successful day trading endeavor. It involves the strategic allocation of time for each stage of the trading process. From pre-market preparation to during-market execution and post-market review, a well-structured routine ensures that traders remain focused, disciplined, and poised to capitalize on market opportunities while mitigating risks.

Pre-Market Preparation: News, Economic Indicators, and Market Sentiment: Pre-market preparation sets the stage for a productive trading day. Traders begin by staying attuned to breaking news, global economic indicators, and overnight developments that may influence market sentiment. Analyzing potential catalysts and assessing market sentiment aids in devising a game plan for the trading session. Moreover, pre-market preparation includes identifying key support and resistance levels, scanning for opportunities, and setting entry and exit parameters.

During-Market Execution: Staying Focused and Disciplined: During-market execution hinges on the ability to execute trades with precision, composure, and discipline. Traders must adhere to their predetermined strategies and entry criteria, resist the allure of impulsive decisions, and remain focused on the evolving market landscape. Managing emotions, adapting to changing conditions, and swiftly executing trades according to plan are pivotal in optimizing trading outcomes during active market hours.

Post-Market Review: Evaluating Trades and Identifying Areas for Improvement: The conclusion of the trading day marks the commencement of the post-market review phase. Traders meticulously evaluate their trades, comparing actual outcomes with the initial game plan. Identifying strengths and areas for improvement allows traders to fine-tune their strategies, refine risk management techniques, and enhance decision-making processes. The post-market review also provides an opportunity to learn from mistakes, reinforce discipline, and continuously evolve as a trader.

In conclusion, building a day trading routine is the linchpin to consistent success in the fast-paced world of intraday trading. An effective routine encompasses pre-market preparation, during-market execution, and post-market review, all seamlessly orchestrated to optimize decision-making and trading outcomes. By meticulously attending to news, economic indicators, and market sentiment, day traders set the stage for informed decisions. During-market execution demands discipline, adaptability, and a focused mindset to execute strategies with precision. The post-market review is the crucible for growth, allowing traders to evaluate trades, learn from experiences, and refine their approaches for continuous improvement. By mastering the art of constructing a day trading routine, traders fortify their ability to navigate the market intricacies with confidence, resilience, and the potential for sustained success.

Chapter 15: Developing a Growth Mindset

Within the world of day trading, the development of a growth mindset stands as an indispensable trait that separates successful traders from the rest. This chapter delves into the transformative journey of cultivating a growth mindset – a mental disposition that fosters continuous learning, adaptability, and resilience. It explores the pivotal role of embracing failures, evolving trading strategies, seeking mentorship, and nurturing the qualities of perseverance and resilience, all of which contribute to the development of a growth mindset and pave the way for enduring success in the realm of day trading.

Embracing Failures as Learning Opportunities: A growth mindset perceives failures as stepping stones to success. Rather than succumbing to discouragement, traders with a growth mindset view failures as invaluable learning opportunities. Analyzing mistakes, understanding their root causes, and integrating the lessons garnered from failures into future strategies enables continuous improvement and enhanced decision-making.

Continuously Adapting and Evolving Your Trading Strategies: A growth mindset thrives on the premise of constant evolution. Successful day traders recognize the impermanence of market conditions and the necessity of adapting strategies accordingly. A willingness to explore new approaches, integrate new indicators, and adjust methodologies based on shifting market dynamics positions traders for success in a dynamic trading environment.

Seeking Mentorship and Learning from Experienced Traders: Mentorship serves as a beacon for aspiring traders navigating the complexities of day trading. Seeking guidance from experienced traders provides access to a wealth of insights, strategies, and best practices. Learning from the experiences, successes, and failures of mentors offers a shortcut to knowledge acquisition and aids in the avoidance of pitfalls that can hinder growth.

Cultivating Resilience and Perseverance in the Face of Challenges: Resilience and perseverance are the bedrock of a growth mindset. Day trading is replete with challenges, and setbacks are inevitable. A growth mindset equips traders to bounce back from losses, setbacks, and challenges with renewed determination. The ability to weather the storms of the market, maintain composure during turbulent times, and persistently pursue improvement is emblematic of a growth-oriented trader.

In conclusion, the development of a growth mindset is instrumental in shaping the trajectory of day trading success. Embracing failures, evolving strategies, seeking mentorship, and nurturing qualities of resilience and perseverance all contribute to the cultivation of this mindset. A growth-oriented perspective propels traders to embrace learning, adaptability, and an unwavering commitment to improvement. By fostering a growth mindset, day traders not only enhance their own skills but also set the stage for enduring success in the challenging and ever-evolving landscape of the financial markets.

Chapter 16: Scalability and Portfolio Management

In the trajectory of a day trader's journey, the evolution from novice to seasoned practitioner entails the exploration of scalability and the mastery of portfolio management. This chapter delves into the nuanced realm of scaling up trading operations, diversifying portfolios across a spectrum of assets, optimizing the equilibrium between risk and potential returns, and the strategic integration of a long-term investment plan alongside the dynamic canvas of day trading activities. These elements stand as pivotal to achieving sustained success and resilience in the realm of financial markets.

Scaling Up Your Trading Operations as You Gain Experience: As day traders accumulate experience and honed skills, the opportunity for scalability arises. Scaling involves increasing trading size and exposure commensurate with the trader's expertise. The meticulous progression from small positions to larger ones enables traders to manage heightened risk without jeopardizing capital. Scaling up demands a profound understanding of risk management, discipline, and an ability to maintain performance consistency.

Diversifying Your Trading Portfolio Across Different Assets: Portfolio diversification is a cardinal principle in portfolio management. Day traders extend this philosophy by diversifying across various assets such as stocks, forex, commodities, and cryptocurrencies. By spreading investments, traders mitigate exposure to the volatility of a single asset. Diversification aids in buffering against losses in one area while capitalizing on opportunities in others, fostering a more balanced trading approach.

Balancing Risk and Potential Returns Across Your Portfolio: The art of portfolio management involves the strategic calibration of risk and potential returns. Day traders must assess the risk-reward ratio for each asset, ensuring that potential losses are proportionate to potential gains. Effective portfolio management involves continuous evaluation of market conditions, adjusting positions, and maintaining a dynamic balance that aligns with individual risk tolerance and investment goals.

Creating a Long-Term Investment Plan Alongside Day Trading Activities: Beyond the realms of day trading, a well-defined long-term investment plan provides stability and resilience. Investors should allocate a portion of their capital to long-term investments, such as retirement accounts or diversified funds. This dual approach allows traders to balance the potential high returns of day trading with the stability and gradual appreciation characteristic of long-term investments.

In conclusion, the chapters of scalability and portfolio management hold a pivotal role in the tapestry of a day trader's journey. Scaling operations while maintaining risk management principles allows traders to expand their reach while safeguarding capital. Diversifying portfolios across assets mitigates risk and capitalizes on diverse market opportunities. The orchestration of risk and potential returns forms the crux of effective portfolio management. Coupled with a long-term investment plan, day traders can harness the power of both short-term and long-term strategies, enabling them to navigate the complexities of financial markets with strategic prowess and resolute purpose.

Chapter 17: Trading Psychology Revisited

Within the intricate tapestry of day trading, the realm of trading psychology holds a perennial significance that shapes the outcomes of trades and defines the trajectory of a trader's journey. This chapter delves into the advanced facets of managing emotions during trading, navigating prolonged losing streaks and drawdowns, nurturing mental and emotional well-being for sustained performance, and harnessing mindfulness and stress-reduction techniques. These nuanced elements collectively constitute the bedrock of a trader's psychological resilience and are instrumental in maintaining consistent and successful performance in the dynamic world of financial markets.

Advanced Techniques for Managing Emotions During Trading: Advanced trading psychology encompasses refined techniques for managing emotions that can influence trading decisions. Strategies such as cognitive reframing, emotional awareness, and mindfulness serve as tools to regulate emotions in real-time trading scenarios. By mastering these techniques, traders can mitigate the impact of fear, greed, and impulsiveness, enabling rational decision-making even amidst heightened market volatility.

Dealing with Prolonged Losing Streaks and Drawdowns: The mental fortitude to navigate prolonged periods of losses or drawdowns is a hallmark of seasoned traders. A resilient trader recognizes that losses are an inevitable part of trading and refrains from allowing negative emotions to erode confidence. By adhering to risk management principles, adjusting strategies, and maintaining discipline, traders can navigate these challenging phases with patience and an unwavering belief in their skills.

Maintaining Mental and Emotional Well-being for Consistent Performance: The sustenance of mental and emotional well-being is pivotal to consistent trading performance. Engaging in activities that promote physical health, emotional equilibrium, and cognitive clarity fosters a conducive environment for effective decision-making. Adequate sleep, exercise, and stress reduction practices contribute to a resilient mental state that enables traders to make well-informed choices even during demanding trading hours.

Utilizing Mindfulness and Stress-Reduction Techniques: Mindfulness, a practice of focused awareness, serves as an invaluable tool to counteract stress and enhance cognitive agility. Incorporating mindfulness exercises into daily routines allows traders to maintain presence during trading, observe thoughts without judgment, and make decisions devoid of reactive emotions. Breathing techniques, meditation, and visualization exercises further serve to mitigate stress and enhance emotional control.

In conclusion, trading psychology, an ever-present undercurrent in day trading, gains depth through advanced techniques that harness emotional mastery, resilience, and well-being. Techniques for managing emotions during trading, navigating prolonged challenging periods, nurturing mental and emotional health, and employing mindfulness and stress-reduction practices coalesce to fortify a trader's psychological foundation. By honing these advanced psychological skills, day traders equip themselves to navigate the turbulent waters of financial markets with poise, acumen, and an unshakable resolve for consistent performance.

Chapter 18: Ethical Considerations in Day Trading

In the intricate tapestry of financial markets, ethical considerations stand as a moral compass that navigates the conduct of day traders. This chapter delves into the profound significance of ethical behavior in the realm of day trading, emphasizing the imperative of avoiding practices such as insider trading and market manipulation. It further explores the delicate equilibrium between self-interest and responsible trading practices, and the pivotal role that day traders play in contributing positively to market integrity and transparency.

The Importance of Ethical Behavior in Financial Markets: Ethical behavior is the cornerstone of trust and credibility in financial markets. Upholding ethical standards is not only a moral obligation but also a means to preserve the integrity and reputation of the trading community. Ethical traders engender a climate of transparency, fair play, and mutual respect that underpins the functioning of the market ecosystem.

Avoiding Insider Trading and Market Manipulation: Insider trading and market manipulation are unethical practices that can distort the level playing field and erode market integrity. Ethical day traders eschew acting on non-public information that could give them an unfair advantage over others. They also avoid distorting market prices or engaging in practices that manipulate supply and demand to their advantage, thereby maintaining a level of fairness and transparency.

Balancing Self-Interest with Responsible Trading Practices: While day traders seek personal gain from market activities, ethical conduct entails striking a delicate balance between self-interest and the broader responsibility to uphold market integrity. Ethical traders refrain from aggressive tactics that may exploit other participants or compromise the integrity of the market. Responsible trading practices align with long-term success, ensuring that short-term gains do not come at the cost of long-term reputation.

Contributing Positively to Market Integrity and Transparency: Day traders wield the power to contribute positively to market integrity and transparency. By adhering to ethical behavior, traders ensure that their actions align with the principles of fairness, honesty, and accountability. Sharing insights, adhering to regulations, and maintaining transparency in transactions collectively foster a market environment that benefits all participants.

In conclusion, ethical considerations assume a paramount role in the practice of day trading, guiding traders to navigate the financial landscape with integrity, fairness, and respect for market principles. Avoiding insider trading, refraining from market manipulation, striking a balance between self-interest and responsible practices, and contributing positively to market integrity collectively define the ethical compass of a day trader. By adhering to ethical norms, day traders not only preserve their own reputation but also elevate the standards of the entire trading community, fostering an environment that thrives on trust, credibility, and the collective pursuit of ethical excellence.

Chapter 19: Future Trends in Day Trading

Within the dynamic and evolving landscape of day trading, the anticipation of future trends stands as a pivotal element for traders seeking to remain ahead of the curve. This chapter delves into the prophetic realm of potential developments, exploring the transformative impact of technological advancements on day trading. It also examines the ascendancy of artificial intelligence and machine learning in trading strategies, the possible shifts in market dynamics, and the imperative for traders to adapt to evolving regulatory landscapes. These future trends collectively shape the contours of day trading's trajectory and serve as a compass for traders striving for enduring success.

Exploring the Impact of Technological Advancements on Day Trading: The burgeoning march of technology has historically redefined day trading paradigms. The future promises even more seismic shifts as automation, algorithmic trading, and data analytics continue to revolutionize trading operations. Traders will need to master these technologies to remain competitive, ensuring they can execute trades swiftly, analyze vast data streams, and make informed decisions guided by insights generated by cutting-edge tools.

Rise of Artificial Intelligence and Machine Learning in Trading: The rise of artificial intelligence (AI) and machine learning (ML) heralds an era of unprecedented trading innovation. AI-powered algorithms can analyze massive datasets with lightning speed, identify patterns, and predict market movements. Machine learning models adapt and improve over time, evolving their predictive capabilities. Traders will increasingly rely on AI and ML to optimize their strategies, identify opportunities, and manage risk.

Potential Shifts in Market Dynamics and Trading Strategies: As technology and market trends evolve, so too will market dynamics. Traders must anticipate potential shifts such as increased market volatility, changes in trading volumes, and new asset classes gaining prominence. Consequently, trading strategies will adapt to leverage these dynamics. Strategies that harness new indicators, real-time sentiment analysis, and AI-driven insights will likely gain traction in response to evolving market conditions.

Adapting to Evolving Regulatory Landscapes: The future of day trading is intrinsically linked to regulatory developments. As financial markets and technologies evolve, regulators adapt to maintain market integrity and protect participants. Traders must stay informed about new rules, compliance requirements, and reporting obligations. Adapting to evolving regulatory landscapes is essential to avoid pitfalls, legal challenges, and to sustain trading operations within the bounds of legality.

In conclusion, the chapter on future trends in day trading opens a portal to the horizon of possibilities. Traders who anticipate the impact of technological advancements, embrace AI and ML, adapt to shifting market dynamics, and navigate evolving regulatory landscapes position themselves as vanguards in the trading arena. By embracing these future trends, day traders can master the tools of the modern trading landscape, leverage cutting-edge technologies, and remain agile in the face of dynamic market forces. The astute anticipation of these trends is an investment in sustained success within the ever-evolving tapestry of day trading.

Conclusion

In the culmination of this comprehensive exploration into the art and science of day trading, we find ourselves at the juncture of reflection and aspiration. The journey embarked upon to become a proficient day trader is a testament to the dedication, discipline, and strategic acumen required to navigate the complex world of financial markets. As we take this moment to reflect, let us reaffirm the enduring lessons learned and fortify our resolve for the journey ahead.

Reflecting on the Journey of Becoming a Proficient Day Trader: The voyage from novice to seasoned day trader is marked by a tapestry woven with experiences, triumphs, challenges, and the ceaseless pursuit of knowledge. Reflecting on this journey underscores the progress made, the insights gleaned, and the milestones achieved. Each trade executed, each strategy refined, and each lesson learned forms the stepping stones that lead to mastery.

Reinforcing the Continuous Learning and Adaptation Required in Day Trading: Day trading is an ever-evolving domain where stagnation is antithetical to success. The significance of continuous learning and adaptation resonates as a constant refrain. The financial markets are fluid and dynamic, subject to shifts in technology, regulations, and market sentiment. Thus, the commitment to staying informed, mastering new tools, and adapting strategies is pivotal to remaining relevant and competitive.

Encouraging Traders to Contribute Positively to the Trading Community: The realm of day trading thrives on a sense of community, camaraderie, and shared knowledge. As proficient day traders, we carry the responsibility to contribute positively to this community. Sharing insights, lessons learned, and ethical practices not only uplift fellow traders but also foster an environment of mutual growth and respect.

Final Words of Inspiration and Motivation: As we conclude this journey, let us be buoyed by the realization that day trading is both an art and a science – a dynamic dance between technical prowess and psychological resilience. Embrace the challenges as opportunities, the setbacks as stepping stones, and the victories as affirmations of your dedication. In the vast expanse of financial markets, your journey is a testament to the human spirit's capacity to adapt, learn, and triumph.

In your pursuit of day trading excellence, remember that the journey is perennial. With each dawn, a fresh opportunity emerges to refine strategies, seize potential, and contribute positively to the trading tapestry. May your path be paved with knowledge, resilience, and the unwavering belief that the journey toward mastery is a journey of perpetual growth, transcending the limits of today's accomplishments.

Forex Trading:

Specialize in the foreign exchange market, trading currency pairs.

Introduction

In the vast landscape of global finance, the Foreign Exchange Market (Forex) stands as a pivotal arena where currencies of different nations intersect, creating a dynamic platform for trading, investment, and speculation. This introduction serves as a stepping stone into the intricate world of Forex trading, encompassing its fundamental components and highlighting its profound significance within the global economy.

Understanding the Foreign Exchange Market

The Foreign Exchange Market, often referred to as Forex or FX, is a decentralized marketplace where currencies are bought and sold against one another. Unlike traditional stock exchanges, the Forex market operates 24 hours a day, five days a week, owing to the involvement of different time zones across the globe. The market's decentralized nature is a hallmark feature, meaning that transactions occur electronically over-the-counter (OTC) through a network of financial institutions, corporations, governments, and individual traders.

The driving force behind Forex trading lies in the exchange rates between currency pairs. Currency pairs are the cornerstone of Forex trading, representing the relative value of one currency against another. For instance, the EUR/USD currency pair illustrates the value of the Euro in terms of the US Dollar. Mastering the art of interpreting these currency pairs is integral to a trader's success, as they serve as indicators of economic strength, geopolitical stability, and market sentiment.

Importance of Forex Trading in the Global Economy

Forex trading plays an indispensable role in the modern global economy, facilitating international trade, investments, and cross-border transactions. As businesses expand beyond national borders, the need to exchange one currency for another becomes paramount. Forex markets provide the mechanism to hedge against currency risk, ensuring that companies can navigate volatile currency fluctuations with confidence.

Furthermore, central banks and governments engage in Forex trading to manage their foreign reserves and stabilize their domestic currencies. The value of a nation's currency directly affects its export competitiveness, inflation levels, and overall economic well-being. Therefore, the decisions made within the Forex market ripple through economies, influencing monetary policies and trade relationships.

Basics of Currency Pairs and Exchange Rates

The foundation of Forex trading lies in comprehending how currency pairs function and the intricacies of exchange rates. Each currency pair consists of a base currency and a quote currency. The base currency represents the initial currency in the pair, while the quote currency represents the currency being traded against the base currency. Exchange rates denote the value of the base currency in terms of the quote currency.

Exchange rates are influenced by a multitude of factors, including interest rates, economic indicators, geopolitical events, and market sentiment. Traders must possess a deep understanding of these determinants to make informed decisions, predict market movements, and execute successful trades.

As we delve deeper into this comprehensive guide on Forex trading, each chapter will progressively unveil the intricacies of this dynamic marketplace. From fundamental and technical analysis to risk management and evolving trends, this eBook equips traders with the knowledge and strategies needed to navigate the Forex market with confidence and precision.

Chapter 1: Fundamentals of Forex Trading
1.1 What is Forex Trading?

Forex trading, short for foreign exchange trading, is the act of buying and selling currencies in the vast global marketplace known as the Foreign Exchange Market (Forex or FX). This chapter unveils the essential building blocks of Forex trading, encompassing its core definition, conceptual framework, and the diverse range of participants that contribute to the market's vibrancy.

Definition and Concept

Forex trading revolves around the exchange of one currency for another with the intent of profiting from fluctuations in exchange rates. At its core, it is a speculative endeavor where traders capitalize on the ever-changing values of different currencies. Currency pairs are the vehicles through which this trading occurs, each comprising a base currency and a quote currency. The objective is to accurately predict the direction in which the exchange rate between the two currencies will move, either appreciating (rising) or depreciating (falling).

The Forex market operates as a decentralized global network, facilitated by advanced technology and digital platforms. As a result, trading is conducted electronically across various financial centers, without a single physical location. This feature not only ensures accessibility around the clock but also creates an environment where transactions can take place in real-time, irrespective of the participants' geographical locations.

Participants in the Forex Market

The Forex market is a melting pot of participants, each playing a distinct role in shaping its dynamics and liquidity. Key participants include:

1. **Banks and Financial Institutions:** Central banks, commercial banks, and other financial institutions engage in Forex trading to manage their foreign reserves, facilitate international trade, and influence monetary policies. Central banks, in particular, can directly impact currency values through interest rate decisions and interventions in the market.

2. **Corporations:** Multinational corporations participate in Forex trading to hedge against currency risk. With operations spanning various countries, corporations are exposed to fluctuations in exchange rates that can impact their profits and expenses. By engaging in Forex transactions, they seek to minimize potential losses.

3. **Hedge Funds and Investment Firms:** These entities engage in Forex trading to generate returns for their clients and investors. They often execute more complex strategies that involve leveraging, derivatives, and speculative trading to capitalize on market movements.

4. **Retail Traders:** Individual traders, often referred to as retail traders, represent a growing segment in the Forex market. Enabled by online trading platforms, retail traders can access the market with relatively small investments. While their trades may not individually impact the market significantly, their collective participation contributes to market liquidity.

5. **Governments and Central Banks:** National governments and central banks intervene in the Forex market to stabilize their own currency values, foster export competitiveness, and maintain economic stability. Their interventions can take the form of direct buying or selling of their currency.

Understanding the intricate interplay between these participants is fundamental to navigating the Forex market successfully. As you delve deeper into this guide, you'll uncover the techniques, strategies, and insights necessary to make informed trading decisions and thrive in this dynamic marketplace.

1.2 Currency Pairs Explained

In the realm of Forex trading, the essence lies in the relationships between currencies, epitomized by currency pairs. This section unveils the intricacies of currency pairs, categorizing them into major, minor, and exotic pairs, and delving into the concept of base and quote currencies, which are at the heart of every trading transaction.

Major, Minor, and Exotic Pairs

Currency pairs are the bedrock upon which Forex trading is built. They represent the comparative value between two currencies, showcasing the price of one currency in terms of another. Currency pairs are categorized into three distinct groups, each offering unique characteristics:

Major Pairs: Major pairs consist of the most liquid and widely traded currencies in the world. They involve the US Dollar (USD) paired with another major currency, such as the Euro (EUR), Japanese Yen (JPY), British Pound (GBP), Swiss Franc (CHF), or Australian Dollar (AUD). These pairs tend to have tighter spreads due to their high trading volume, making them popular choices for both novice and experienced traders.

Minor Pairs: Also known as cross-currency pairs, minor pairs exclude the US Dollar from the pairing. They involve the currencies of major economies other than the United States. Examples include the Euro against the Japanese Yen (EUR/JPY) or the British Pound against the Australian Dollar (GBP/AUD). While minor pairs may have slightly wider spreads compared to major pairs, they still attract significant trading interest.

Exotic Pairs: Exotic pairs involve one major currency and one currency from an emerging or smaller economy. Examples include the US Dollar paired with the Singapore Dollar (USD/SGD) or the British Pound paired with the Mexican Peso (GBP/MXN). Exotic pairs tend to have lower trading volumes and wider spreads, which can lead to higher volatility and potential trading opportunities for seasoned traders.

Base and Quote Currencies

Within a currency pair, each currency plays a specific role. The first currency listed in the pair is known as the base currency, and the second currency is referred to as the quote currency.

Base Currency: The base currency serves as the foundation for the exchange rate. It is the currency against which the exchange rate is quoted. For instance, in the EUR/USD currency pair, the Euro (EUR) is the base currency. The value of the base currency is expressed in terms of the quote currency.

Quote Currency: The quote currency is the currency against which the exchange rate is measured. In the EUR/USD example, the US Dollar (USD) is the quote currency. The exchange rate indicates how much of the quote currency is needed to purchase one unit of the base currency.

Understanding the interplay between base and quote currencies is fundamental for interpreting exchange rates and making informed trading decisions. Traders analyze these pairs to anticipate market movements, identify trends, and execute trades that align with their strategies.

As we proceed through this guide, you'll delve deeper into the nuances of currency pairs, gaining insight into the factors that influence their movements and strategies to navigate the dynamic world of Forex trading.

1.3 Factors Influencing Exchange Rates

In the dynamic realm of Forex trading, exchange rates are not set in stone but rather shaped by a multitude of intricate factors. This section unveils the core elements that sway exchange rates, including economic indicators, political events, and market sentiment. Understanding these influential factors is pivotal for traders seeking to navigate the tumultuous waters of the Forex market.

Economic Indicators

Economic indicators serve as the lifeblood of Forex markets, providing insights into the health and performance of economies. These indicators offer data on various aspects, ranging from employment and production to inflation and trade balances. As these economic indicators are released, they have a profound impact on currency values, often triggering significant market movements. Key economic indicators include:

- **Gross Domestic Product (GDP):** GDP measures the total value of all goods and services produced within a country. A growing GDP signifies economic expansion, potentially leading to currency appreciation.

- **Consumer Price Index (CPI):** CPI gauges changes in the average price of consumer goods and services. Rising CPI may indicate inflation, which could prompt central banks to adjust interest rates, affecting currency values.

- **Unemployment Rate:** The unemployment rate reflects the percentage of the labor force that is unemployed and actively seeking employment. Lower unemployment rates often correlate with a stronger currency.

Political Events

Political events exert a significant influence on exchange rates, as they shape the economic policies, stability, and overall outlook of a country. Political decisions can trigger rapid market movements, as traders interpret the potential implications of policy changes. Elections, government changes, trade agreements, and geopolitical tensions are all examples of political events that can impact currency values. Currency markets are particularly sensitive to political uncertainty, as sudden changes can lead to heightened volatility.

Market Sentiment

Market sentiment encapsulates the collective psychology of traders and investors, often swaying markets in unexpected ways. Positive sentiment can drive currencies higher, while negative sentiment can lead to sell-offs. Traders assess news, economic data, and social media trends to gauge market sentiment. It's essential to recognize that sentiment can sometimes overshadow fundamentals, causing price movements that may appear irrational.

Understanding the interplay between these factors and their impact on currency values empowers traders to make informed decisions. By keeping a vigilant eye on economic indicators, political developments, and the prevailing sentiment, traders can anticipate potential market movements and position themselves for success in the dynamic and ever-evolving Forex landscape.

Chapter 2: Setting Up for Success
2.1 Choosing a Forex Broker

Embarking on a successful journey in Forex trading begins with the critical decision of selecting a reliable and suitable Forex broker. This chapter delves into the intricate aspects that demand consideration when choosing a broker. From assessing regulations and licenses to evaluating trading platforms, tools, and account types, a well-informed choice sets the foundation for a trader's path to success.

Regulations and Licenses

The backbone of trust and credibility in Forex trading is established by regulatory oversight. Reputable Forex brokers are regulated by recognized financial authorities, ensuring they adhere to strict standards and ethical practices. Regulatory bodies such as the U.S. Commodity Futures Trading Commission (CFTC), the UK's Financial Conduct Authority (FCA), and the Australian Securities and Investments Commission (ASIC) enforce compliance with rules that safeguard traders' interests.

When selecting a broker, it's imperative to verify the broker's regulatory status and licenses. Ensure the broker is registered with the appropriate regulatory authority, providing a level of security against potential fraud or malpractice.

Trading Platforms and Tools

The trading platform is the portal through which traders interact with the Forex market. A robust and user-friendly platform is essential for executing trades efficiently. Platforms often come with various features, including real-time charts, technical indicators, and order execution capabilities. Familiarizing yourself with the platform's functionality is crucial, as it impacts your trading experience and strategy implementation.

Additionally, the availability of trading tools, such as economic calendars, news feeds, and technical analysis resources, contributes to your ability to make informed decisions. A broker offering a suite of tools can enhance your trading skills and provide you with valuable insights into market trends.

Account Types

Brokers typically offer a range of account types tailored to traders' experience levels and trading preferences. These can include:

- **Standard Accounts:** Suitable for beginners, these accounts often have lower minimum deposit requirements and offer access to a variety of trading instruments.

- **Mini or Micro Accounts:** Designed for traders with smaller capital, these accounts allow for smaller trade sizes, enabling beginners to trade with lower risk exposure.

- **ECN Accounts:** These accounts provide direct access to the interbank market, offering tighter spreads and faster order execution. They are favored by experienced traders and those looking for reduced trading costs.

- **Demo Accounts:** A crucial tool for learning and practice, demo accounts allow traders to simulate real trading conditions without risking real capital. They provide an opportunity to test strategies and refine skills before transitioning to live trading.

In summary, the choice of a Forex broker is a pivotal decision that significantly influences your trading journey. By prioritizing brokers with reputable regulation, suitable trading platforms, and account types that align with your goals, you pave the way for a smooth and productive trading experience.

2.2 Building a Solid Trading Plan

A cornerstone of successful Forex trading is a well-structured and comprehensive trading plan. This chapter delves into the critical components that constitute an effective trading plan. From setting clear goals and understanding your risk tolerance to formulating trading strategies and implementing robust risk management techniques, a solid trading plan acts as a roadmap to guide your actions in the dynamic world of currency trading.

Defining Goals and Risk Tolerance

Before entering the Forex market, it's essential to establish clear and realistic trading goals. Goals can encompass profit targets, trading frequency, and overall expectations. Defining these goals helps maintain focus, evaluate progress, and avoid impulsive decisions driven by emotions.

Furthermore, understanding your risk tolerance is paramount. Risk tolerance relates to the amount of capital you're willing to risk per trade and in your overall trading activities. It's vital to align your risk tolerance with your financial situation and emotional capacity. By setting appropriate risk parameters, you safeguard your capital and prevent excessive losses that could compromise your trading journey.

Trading Strategies

A trading strategy serves as a blueprint for executing trades based on predefined rules and criteria. There are numerous trading strategies, each catering to different market conditions and trader preferences. Strategies range from trend-following approaches like moving averages and breakouts to oscillators and chart patterns that identify potential reversals.

Choosing a strategy that resonates with your trading style, risk tolerance, and market outlook is crucial. It's equally important to thoroughly understand the selected strategy's principles, entry and exit criteria, and risk-reward ratio before implementing it in the live market.

Risk Management Techniques

Effective risk management is the bedrock of long-term success in Forex trading. Employing risk management techniques shields your trading capital from significant losses and ensures longevity in the market. Key risk management techniques include:

- **Position Sizing:** Determine the appropriate trade size based on your risk tolerance and the specific trade setup. Avoid allocating a disproportionate amount of capital to a single trade.
- **Setting Stop-Loss and Take-Profit Levels:** Define price points where you will exit a trade to limit potential losses (stop-loss) or secure profits (take-profit).
- **Diversification:** Spread your capital across different currency pairs and trades to mitigate the impact of potential losses on a single trade.
- **Risk-Reward Ratio:** Evaluate the potential profit against the potential loss for each trade. A favorable risk-reward ratio ensures that potential gains outweigh potential losses over time.

Crafting a robust trading plan requires careful consideration of your goals, risk tolerance, and strategies. It serves as a reference point that guides your decision-making, helping you avoid emotional biases and impulsive actions. By adhering to your plan and continuously refining it based on market experiences, you lay the foundation for a disciplined and successful trading journey.

2.3 Technical Analysis

Technical analysis is an indispensable tool for Forex traders seeking to decipher market trends, identify potential trade opportunities, and make informed decisions. This chapter delves into the core aspects of technical analysis, encompassing the interpretation of charts and patterns, as well as the utilization of indicators and oscillators, all of which collectively contribute to a trader's ability to navigate the complexities of the Forex market.

Charts and Patterns

Charts serve as visual representations of price movements over time, offering insights into market trends and patterns. Two primary types of charts are commonly used in technical analysis:

- **Candlestick Charts:** Candlestick charts display price movements within specified timeframes, presenting information about open, close, high, and low prices for a given period. Candlestick patterns, such as Doji, Engulfing, and Hammer, can provide valuable cues about potential trend reversals and continuations.

- **Line Charts:** Line charts plot closing prices over time, providing a simplified view of price movements. While less detailed than candlestick charts, line charts can help traders identify broader trends and patterns.

Technical analysts also pay close attention to chart patterns, which are recurring formations that provide insights into potential future price movements. Patterns such as head and shoulders, double tops and bottoms, triangles, and flags can help predict market direction and guide trading decisions.

Indicators and Oscillators

Indicators and oscillators are mathematical calculations applied to price data to derive insights into market momentum, trend strength, and potential turning points. These tools aid traders in making well-informed decisions. Some commonly used indicators and oscillators include:

- **Moving Averages:** Moving averages smooth out price data, revealing underlying trends by eliminating short-term price fluctuations. They come in various forms, including simple moving averages (SMA) and exponential moving averages (EMA).
- **Relative Strength Index (RSI):** RSI measures the speed and change of price movements, indicating overbought or oversold conditions. Values above 70 suggest potential overbought conditions, while values below 30 suggest potential oversold conditions.
- **Moving Average Convergence Divergence (MACD):** MACD combines moving averages to reveal changes in momentum. It consists of a MACD line and a signal line, with crossovers providing signals for potential buy or sell opportunities.
- **Stochastic Oscillator:** The stochastic oscillator assesses the closing price's position relative to the trading range over a specified period. It helps traders identify potential trend reversals.

By integrating charts, patterns, indicators, and oscillators, technical analysis equips traders with the ability to anticipate market movements, confirm trends, and develop informed trading strategies. It's important to note that technical analysis is just one facet of comprehensive Forex trading, often complemented by fundamental analysis and risk management techniques. A well-rounded approach combines these tools to enhance decision-making capabilities and navigate the intricate landscape of currency trading.

Chapter 3: Mastering Fundamental Analysis
3.1 Economic Indicators and Releases

Fundamental analysis is a cornerstone of Forex trading, offering insights into the intrinsic factors that shape currency values. This chapter delves into the intricate world of economic indicators and their releases, exploring the significance of Gross Domestic Product (GDP), Consumer Price Index (CPI), and the Unemployment Rate. Understanding these indicators and their impact on currency movements is vital for informed decision-making in the Forex market.

Gross Domestic Product (GDP)

GDP stands as a vital economic indicator, reflecting the total value of all goods and services produced within a country during a specific period. It serves as a barometer of economic health, indicating the pace of economic growth or contraction. A growing GDP often corresponds with a stronger currency, as it signals a robust economy and potential future interest rate hikes.

When GDP figures are released, traders and investors analyze them in comparison to market expectations. If the reported GDP exceeds forecasts, it can lead to currency appreciation. Conversely, a GDP figure below expectations can result in currency depreciation. Moreover, comparisons of GDP growth rates between countries can influence exchange rates, as countries with higher growth rates often experience stronger currencies.

Consumer Price Index (CPI)

The Consumer Price Index (CPI) measures changes in the average price of a basket of goods and services consumed by households over a specific period. It is a key indicator of inflation and purchasing power. A rising CPI suggests inflation, which can prompt central banks to increase interest rates to control rising prices.

CPI releases are closely monitored by Forex traders, as they offer insights into a country's inflationary pressures. If CPI figures exceed expectations, it can lead to expectations of tighter monetary policy and potential currency appreciation. Conversely, CPI figures lower than anticipated can lead to speculation of looser monetary policy and potential currency depreciation.

Unemployment Rate

The Unemployment Rate represents the percentage of the labor force that is unemployed and actively seeking employment. It serves as a gauge of a country's labor market health and economic vitality. A declining Unemployment Rate often corresponds with stronger economic conditions, potentially leading to currency appreciation.

Traders scrutinize Unemployment Rate releases to assess labor market conditions. If the Unemployment Rate drops below expectations, it can signal robust economic growth and potential currency strength. Conversely, a higher-than-expected Unemployment Rate can indicate economic weakness and potential currency weakness.

Mastering the interpretation of economic indicators and their releases empowers traders to anticipate market movements, adjust strategies, and position themselves strategically. By staying attuned to these indicators and their implications on currency values, traders can navigate the complexities of the Forex market with enhanced confidence and insight.

3.2 Central Banks and Monetary Policies

Central banks play a pivotal role in shaping the economic landscape and influencing currency values through their monetary policies. This section delves into the intricate relationship between central banks, interest rates, and monetary policy statements, exploring their profound impact on currency values in the Forex market.

Interest Rates and Monetary Policy Statements

Central banks use interest rates as a primary tool to implement monetary policy and regulate economic conditions. Interest rates influence borrowing costs for consumers, businesses, and governments, subsequently affecting spending, investment, and inflation. Central banks adjust interest rates to achieve their dual mandate of promoting price stability and sustainable economic growth.

Monetary policy statements, often released after central bank meetings, provide insight into policymakers' decisions and future intentions. These statements include discussions on economic conditions, inflation outlook, and potential changes in interest rates. Traders and investors scrutinize these statements for clues about future monetary policy adjustments, which can impact currency values.

Impact on Currency Values

Central bank decisions and monetary policy statements have a profound impact on currency values in the Forex market. The relationship between interest rates and currency values is intertwined: higher interest rates tend to attract foreign capital seeking better returns, leading to currency appreciation. Conversely, lower interest rates may discourage foreign investment, potentially resulting in currency depreciation.

When central banks signal intentions to raise interest rates, it can lead to expectations of currency appreciation, prompting traders to buy the currency. Conversely, hints of potential interest rate cuts can lead to currency depreciation, as traders anticipate reduced returns on investments denominated in that currency.

Additionally, monetary policy statements provide insights into the central bank's assessment of economic conditions, which can influence market sentiment. A more hawkish tone, indicating a proactive approach to controlling inflation, can strengthen a currency. Conversely, a dovish tone, suggesting a focus on supporting economic growth, may weaken a currency.

Traders must stay attuned to central bank decisions, policy statements, and associated economic data to anticipate potential currency movements. By understanding the intricate connection between monetary policy and currency values, traders can adjust their strategies and capitalize on opportunities presented by central bank actions.

Conclusion

Central banks hold considerable sway over currency values, wielding interest rates and monetary policy as tools to navigate economic waters. As Forex traders, your proficiency in analyzing central bank decisions and monetary policy statements equips you to anticipate and respond to market dynamics with precision, ultimately contributing to your success in the ever-evolving world of currency trading.

Chapter 4: Advanced Technical Analysis
4.1 Candlestick Patterns

Candlestick patterns stand as a cornerstone of advanced technical analysis, offering traders invaluable insights into market sentiment and potential price movements. This chapter delves into the intricate world of candlestick patterns, exploring both bullish and bearish formations, as well as the distinction between reversal and continuation patterns. A deep understanding of these patterns empowers traders to make informed decisions and navigate the complexities of the Forex market with precision.

Bullish and Bearish Patterns

Candlestick patterns can be broadly categorized into two main types: bullish and bearish. Bullish patterns indicate potential price increases, while bearish patterns suggest potential price decreases.

Bullish Patterns: Bullish patterns emerge when price movements suggest an upward shift in momentum. These patterns often indicate potential trend reversals or continuation of existing trends. Examples of bullish patterns include the Hammer, Bullish Engulfing, and Morning Star. These patterns typically signify an increased likelihood of upward price movements, offering traders opportunities to enter or maintain long positions.

Bearish Patterns: Conversely, bearish patterns manifest when price movements indicate a shift toward downward momentum. Bearish patterns can signal potential reversals or continuation of existing downtrends. Patterns like the Shooting Star, Bearish Engulfing, and Evening Star are examples of bearish formations. These patterns suggest increased potential for downward price movements, guiding traders toward short positions or protective measures.

Reversal and Continuation Patterns

Candlestick patterns are further classified as reversal patterns or continuation patterns, based on their implications for the prevailing trend.

Reversal Patterns: Reversal patterns are formations that suggest a potential change in the prevailing trend. These patterns occur at the end of an existing trend and indicate a shift in market sentiment. Reversal patterns can offer traders the opportunity to capitalize on trend changes and reversals. Notable reversal patterns include the Doji, Head and Shoulders, and the Evening Star.

Continuation Patterns: Continuation patterns, on the other hand, signal a temporary pause in the prevailing trend before it continues in the same direction. These patterns suggest that the existing trend will likely persist after a brief consolidation period. Examples of continuation patterns include the Flag, Pennant, and the Triangles (Ascending, Descending, and Symmetrical).

Mastering candlestick patterns involves not only recognizing their visual formations but also understanding the psychology behind them. Traders must evaluate these patterns in the context of the prevailing market conditions and other technical indicators to make well-informed decisions.

By honing your ability to identify and interpret candlestick patterns, you equip yourself with a powerful tool to anticipate potential market movements. This proficiency enhances your overall trading strategy and empowers you to navigate the intricate landscape of Forex trading with greater accuracy and confidence.

4.2 Fibonacci Analysis

Fibonacci analysis is a sophisticated yet powerful technical tool that aids traders in identifying potential price levels and predicting market movements. This chapter delves into the intricacies of Fibonacci analysis, focusing on the concept of retracement levels and extension levels. A mastery of these principles empowers traders to enhance their technical analysis toolkit and navigate the complex dynamics of the Forex market with precision.

Retracement Levels

Fibonacci retracement levels are derived from the Fibonacci sequence, a mathematical sequence where each number is the sum of the two preceding ones (0, 1, 1, 2, 3, 5, 8, 13, and so on). These levels are crucial in determining potential areas of support and resistance within a price trend.

Retracement levels are calculated by identifying a significant price move and then drawing horizontal lines at key Fibonacci ratios (typically 23.6%, 38.2%, 50%, 61.8%, and 78.6%) of that move. These levels serve as potential points where a price trend might reverse or consolidate before continuing its original direction.

Traders use Fibonacci retracement levels to identify potential entry points, placing trades in the direction of the prevailing trend when prices approach these levels. They can also help set stop-loss orders and take-profit levels, enhancing risk management strategies.

Extension Levels

Fibonacci extension levels are projections beyond the initial price movement, often used to identify potential future price targets when a trend continues. Extension levels are drawn by using the same concept of the Fibonacci sequence, though in this context, traders use ratios beyond 100%, such as 127.2%, 161.8%, and 261.8%.

These levels serve as potential price targets when a trend is strong and shows no signs of slowing down. Traders often use Fibonacci extension levels to plan their exit strategies and anticipate where a trend might eventually lose momentum.

Both Fibonacci retracement and extension levels are widely used by traders to identify areas of potential support, resistance, and price targets. However, it's important to note that these levels should not be used in isolation; they are most effective when used alongside other technical indicators and analysis tools.

Conclusion

Fibonacci analysis adds a layer of depth to technical analysis, enabling traders to identify key price levels and project potential future price movements. By integrating retracement and extension levels into their trading strategies, traders can refine their entry and exit points, enhance risk management strategies, and navigate the intricacies of the Forex market with greater accuracy and confidence.

4.3 Moving Averages and Trend Analysis

Moving averages stand as an integral component of technical analysis, offering traders valuable insights into trends, trend reversals, and potential entry and exit points. This chapter delves into the intricacies of moving averages, focusing on both simple and exponential moving averages (SMA and EMA), as well as their role in identifying trends and trend reversals. A comprehensive understanding of moving averages equips traders with a versatile tool to navigate the ever-changing dynamics of the Forex market.

Simple and Exponential Moving Averages

Moving averages are mathematical calculations that smooth out price data over a specified period, providing a clear depiction of the underlying trend. Two main types of moving averages are commonly used: Simple Moving Averages (SMA) and Exponential Moving Averages (EMA).

Simple Moving Averages (SMA): SMA calculates the average closing price over a specified number of periods and plots a single line on the chart. It provides a clear representation of the average price movement, helping traders identify the general trend direction. While SMAs offer a straightforward view of past prices, they may be slower to respond to recent price changes.

Exponential Moving Averages (EMA): EMA assigns greater weight to more recent prices, making it more responsive to recent price movements compared to the SMA. EMA is calculated using a formula that prioritizes recent data, allowing it to react quickly to changing market conditions. This responsiveness makes EMA a popular choice for traders looking to capture short-term trends.

Identifying Trends and Trend Reversals

Moving averages play a pivotal role in identifying trends and trend reversals, aiding traders in making informed decisions. When the price is above a moving average, it's generally considered to be in an uptrend, while prices below the moving average signify a downtrend.

Golden Cross and Death Cross: Crossovers between shorter-term and longer-term moving averages are often used to identify potential trend reversals. A "Golden Cross" occurs when a shorter-term moving average crosses above a longer-term moving average, indicating a potential bullish trend reversal. Conversely, a "Death Cross" occurs when a shorter-term moving average crosses below a longer-term moving average, suggesting a potential bearish trend reversal.

Convergence and Divergence: Traders also use the relationship between price movements and moving averages to identify potential trend changes. When prices make higher highs while the moving average makes lower highs, it's referred to as "negative divergence," which can indicate a potential trend reversal. Conversely, "positive divergence" occurs when prices make lower lows while the moving average makes higher lows, suggesting a possible bullish reversal.

Incorporating moving averages into your technical analysis toolkit provides a visual representation of trend dynamics, enabling you to make informed decisions based on the prevailing market conditions. While moving averages offer valuable insights, they are most effective when used in conjunction with other technical indicators and analysis techniques, providing a comprehensive view of price movements and potential trading opportunities.

Chapter 5: Developing Winning Strategies
5.1 Day Trading vs. Swing Trading vs. Position Trading

When crafting a winning trading strategy, traders are confronted with the choice of different trading approaches, each suited to varying timeframes and objectives. This chapter dissects the nuances of day trading, swing trading, and position trading, shedding light on their respective merits and drawbacks. By understanding the intricacies of these approaches, traders can tailor their strategies to align with their goals and preferences in the dynamic world of Forex trading.

Day Trading

Pros:

- **Quick Profits:** Day trading aims to capitalize on short-term price movements, allowing traders to potentially profit from multiple trades within a single day.
- **Reduced Overnight Risk:** Day traders avoid the risks associated with overnight market movements, as positions are typically closed before the trading day ends.
- **High Trading Activity:** The fast-paced nature of day trading can be appealing to those who thrive in dynamic environments.

Cons:

- **Intense Focus and Stress:** Day trading requires constant attention and quick decision-making, leading to potential stress and exhaustion.
- **Higher Transaction Costs:** Frequent trades result in higher transaction costs due to spreads, commissions, and fees.
- **Limited Analysis Time:** The compressed timeframe of day trading may limit the depth of technical and fundamental analysis.

Swing Trading

Pros:

- **Potential for Larger Profits:** Swing traders aim to capture price moves that span a few days to several weeks, potentially yielding larger profits compared to day trading.
- **Reduced Stress:** Swing trading provides more time for analysis and decision-making, reducing the stress associated with rapid-fire trading.
- **Flexibility:** Swing trading allows traders to adapt to market conditions and accommodate daily commitments.

Cons:

- **Overnight and Weekend Risk:** Positions are held overnight, exposing traders to potential market gaps and weekend developments.
- **Market Noise:** Short-term fluctuations may obscure longer-term trends, making accurate analysis more challenging.
- **Less Trading Activity:** Swing trading involves fewer trades compared to day trading, potentially resulting in slower profit realization.

Position Trading

Pros:

- **Long-Term Profit Potential:** Position trading targets longer trends that can span weeks, months, or even years, potentially leading to significant profits.
- **Reduced Market Noise Impact:** Position traders focus on larger trends, allowing them to filter out short-term market noise.
- **Lower Transaction Costs:** Fewer trades result in lower transaction costs, as well as reduced stress from constant monitoring.

Cons:

- **Extended Exposure:** Positions are held for extended periods, exposing traders to broader market risks and potential shifts in market sentiment.
- **Delayed Profits:** Profits in position trading take longer to materialize, requiring patience and a long-term perspective.
- **Influence of Fundamental Factors:** Longer timeframes can be influenced by macroeconomic and geopolitical events that impact the currency market.

Conclusion

Choosing between day trading, swing trading, and position trading hinges on your trading style, risk tolerance, and available time. By weighing the pros and cons of each approach against your goals, you can develop a winning trading strategy that aligns with your preferences and maximizes your chances of success. A well-chosen trading approach, coupled with meticulous risk management and analysis, forms the foundation for navigating the intricacies of the Forex market with confidence and proficiency.

5.2 Scalping Strategies

Scalping strategies represent a unique approach to Forex trading, characterized by their focus on making quick trades for small gains within a short timeframe. This section delves into the intricacies of scalping, exploring its objectives, techniques, and considerations. By understanding the nuances of scalping, traders can harness its potential for swift profits while navigating its challenges with precision and expertise.

Quick Trades for Small Gains

At the heart of scalping strategies lies the pursuit of making rapid trades with the aim of capitalizing on small price movements. Scalpers aim to profit from short-lived price fluctuations by executing multiple trades within a single day. While each trade may yield a small profit, the cumulative effect of these gains can be substantial over time.

Scalpers often employ techniques like technical analysis, chart patterns, and indicators to identify short-term trends and price movements. Given the speed at which trades are executed, scalping requires advanced technical skills, sharp reflexes, and disciplined risk management practices.

Advantages of Scalping Strategies:

1. **Quick Profits:** Scalping can generate swift profits, with each trade targeting minor price movements that accumulate throughout the trading session.
2. **Reduced Overnight Risk:** Scalpers typically avoid holding positions overnight, mitigating the risk associated with market gaps and unexpected news events.
3. **Frequent Trading Opportunities:** Scalpers capitalize on a multitude of trading opportunities that arise within a single day, enhancing their chances of success.

Challenges of Scalping Strategies:

1. **High Transaction Costs:** Frequent trades lead to higher transaction costs due to spreads, commissions, and fees, impacting overall profitability.
2. **Intense Focus and Stress:** Scalping demands unwavering concentration and quick decision-making, resulting in heightened stress levels.
3. **Risk of Overtrading:** The allure of rapid profits can lead to overtrading, increasing the likelihood of impulsive decisions and losses.

Conclusion

Scalping strategies offer a distinctive trading approach that suits traders who thrive in fast-paced environments and possess advanced technical skills. Successful scalping demands a strong understanding of technical analysis, robust risk management techniques, and the ability to swiftly execute trades. While scalping can yield rapid profits, it requires disciplined adherence to strategy and risk management principles to navigate the inherent challenges.

By appreciating the nuances of scalping strategies, traders can evaluate whether this approach aligns with their trading style and objectives. Ultimately, incorporating scalping techniques into a comprehensive trading toolkit empowers traders to capitalize on quick profit opportunities while simultaneously managing the unique demands and complexities of this dynamic trading style.

5.3 Carry Trade Strategies

Carry trade strategies are a distinctive approach to Forex trading that capitalizes on interest rate differentials between currencies. This section delves into the intricacies of carry trade strategies, elucidating their objectives, mechanics, and considerations. By comprehending the essence of carry trades, traders can harness their potential for profit while navigating the associated risks with prudence and expertise.

Capitalizing on Interest Rate Differentials

At the core of carry trade strategies lies the exploitation of differences in interest rates between two currencies. Traders engage in carry trades by borrowing a currency with a low-interest rate and investing the proceeds in a currency with a higher interest rate. The goal is to profit from the interest rate differential, along with any potential currency appreciation.

Mechanics of Carry Trade:

1. **Currency Selection:** Traders select a currency pair where one currency has a higher interest rate than the other.
2. **Long Position in High-Yielding Currency:** Traders buy the high-yielding currency while simultaneously selling the low-yielding currency, creating a long position in the former and a short position in the latter.
3. **Interest Rate Differential:** Traders earn the interest rate differential between the two currencies as a profit. This is often paid or received daily, depending on the direction of the trade.

Advantages of Carry Trade Strategies:

1. **Earn Interest:** Carry trade strategies provide traders with the opportunity to earn interest income based on the interest rate differential.

2. **Potential for Capital Appreciation:** If the high-yielding currency appreciates against the low-yielding currency, traders can benefit from both interest income and capital appreciation.

Considerations and Risks:

1. **Currency Fluctuations:** Exchange rate movements can lead to losses if the low-yielding currency appreciates against the high-yielding currency.
2. **Interest Rate Changes:** Changes in central bank policies and interest rates can impact the profitability of carry trades.
3. **Market Sentiment:** Economic and geopolitical factors can influence market sentiment, affecting currency movements and the viability of carry trades.

Conclusion

Carry trade strategies provide an avenue for traders to leverage interest rate differentials to their advantage. While these strategies can yield interest income and potential capital appreciation, they are not without risks. Successful carry trade strategies require careful currency pair selection, thorough analysis of interest rate differentials, and diligent monitoring of market conditions.

By comprehending the dynamics of carry trade strategies, traders can evaluate whether this approach aligns with their risk tolerance and trading objectives. Integrating carry trade strategies into their trading toolkit empowers traders to make informed decisions, maximize profit potential, and navigate the complex interplay of interest rates and currency movements with proficiency.

Chapter 6: Risk Management and Psychology
6.1 Importance of Risk Management

Effective risk management and a sound understanding of psychology are integral components of successful Forex trading. This chapter delves into the significance of risk management, focusing on position sizing, leverage, and the critical task of setting stop-loss and take-profit levels. By comprehending the role of risk management in trading and maintaining a disciplined psychological approach, traders can safeguard their capital and enhance their overall trading performance.

Position Sizing and Leverage

Position Sizing: Position sizing refers to determining the amount of capital to allocate to each trade. Proper position sizing is paramount to managing risk effectively. Traders should ensure that each trade's potential loss aligns with their predetermined risk tolerance and overall trading strategy.

Leverage: Leverage allows traders to control larger positions with a relatively smaller amount of capital. While leverage magnifies potential profits, it also amplifies potential losses. Traders must exercise caution when using leverage to avoid overexposing their accounts to undue risk.

Setting Stop-Loss and Take-Profit Levels

Stop-Loss: A stop-loss is a predetermined level at which a trade will automatically close to limit potential losses. Setting a stop-loss is crucial to mitigate the impact of unfavorable market movements. Traders should base their stop-loss levels on technical analysis, support and resistance zones, and overall risk tolerance.

Take-Profit: A take-profit level specifies where a trade will automatically close to secure profits. Setting a take-profit level is essential to lock in gains before the market reverses. Traders should base their take-profit levels on resistance levels, Fibonacci retracement or extension levels, and their profit targets.

Advantages of Effective Risk Management:

1. **Preservation of Capital:** Effective risk management helps protect your trading capital from significant losses, preserving your ability to trade another day.
2. **Consistent Performance:** Implementing consistent risk management practices fosters stability and sustainability in your trading performance.
3. **Calm and Rational Decision-Making:** Proper risk management reduces emotional stress, enabling traders to make rational decisions without succumbing to impulsive actions.

Psychological Considerations:

1. **Emotional Discipline:** Maintaining emotional discipline is vital to avoiding impulsive trades driven by fear or greed.
2. **Patience:** Trading requires patience to wait for optimal setups and to allow trades to unfold according to the trading plan.
3. **Resilience:** Handling losses and setbacks with resilience is essential for long-term success in the face of the inherent uncertainties of trading.

Conclusion

Risk management and psychological resilience are inseparable pillars of successful trading. By practicing proper position sizing, leveraging responsibly, and setting stop-loss and take-profit levels, traders can navigate the market with a clear risk management strategy. Furthermore, by cultivating emotional discipline, patience, and resilience, traders can maintain their mental equilibrium, enabling them to make informed decisions in the face of market fluctuations. The synergy between effective risk management and psychological mastery serves as the foundation for consistent profitability and success in the challenging landscape of Forex trading.

6.2 Overcoming Emotional Trading Fear, Greed, and Discipline

Emotional trading, fueled by fear and greed, can undermine even the most well-crafted trading strategies. This section delves into the challenges of emotional trading and the vital role of discipline in maintaining a balanced and rational approach. By addressing these psychological factors head-on, traders can enhance their decision-making process and cultivate a more consistent and profitable trading journey.

Fear: Fear can manifest as hesitation to enter a trade, premature exit, or reluctance to execute a well-analyzed plan due to apprehension about potential losses. This emotional response often results in missed opportunities and suboptimal outcomes. Traders must acknowledge that losses are an inherent part of trading and approach the market with a well-considered risk management strategy.

Greed: Greed can drive traders to overextend themselves, chase unrealistic profits, or remain in winning trades beyond reasonable points. The desire for larger gains can cloud judgment and lead to impulsive decisions. Traders must set realistic profit targets, adhere to their trading plans, and avoid succumbing to the allure of quick riches.

Maintaining a Trading Journal

A trading journal serves as a powerful tool for self-awareness, learning, and improvement. Keeping a detailed record of trades, emotions, and thought processes allows traders to identify patterns, strengths, and weaknesses in their trading approach. A comprehensive trading journal includes the following elements:

1. **Trade Details:** Record entry and exit points, position size, trade duration, and the rationale behind each trade.

2. **Emotional Insights:** Document the emotions experienced during each trade, including fear, greed, confidence, and hesitation.

3. **Market Context:** Analyze the market conditions at the time of the trade, including key technical indicators, news events, and trends.

4. **Outcomes and Lessons:** Evaluate the trade's outcome, what went well, what could have been improved, and the lessons learned.

Advantages of Maintaining a Trading Journal:

1. **Self-Reflection:** A trading journal fosters self-awareness by revealing emotional triggers and cognitive biases that impact decision-making.

2. **Continuous Learning:** Analyzing past trades allows traders to identify patterns and refine strategies for better decision-making.

3. **Performance Evaluation:** A trading journal helps assess overall performance, identify strengths and weaknesses, and make informed adjustments.

Conclusion

Overcoming emotional trading is a critical step toward becoming a consistently profitable trader. By addressing fear and greed through disciplined decision-making, traders can make rational choices that align with their trading plans. Additionally, maintaining a trading journal empowers traders to learn from their experiences, identify recurring patterns, and continuously improve their strategies. A proactive approach to managing emotions and documenting trading insights equips traders with the tools needed to navigate the psychological challenges of trading and attain enduring success in the Forex market.

Chapter 7: Practicing and Refining Your Skills
7.1 Demo Trading Simulated Trading Environments:

Demo trading, also known as paper trading, offers traders a simulated trading environment that replicates real-market conditions without involving real capital. This section explores the significance of demo trading in honing trading skills and refining strategies. By immersing themselves in a risk-free environment, traders can gain invaluable experience and enhance their overall trading competence.

Testing Strategies without Risk:

Demo trading serves as a testing ground for trading strategies before committing real funds. Traders can implement their chosen strategies, analyze their effectiveness, and fine-tune them without exposing their capital to potential losses. This experimentation phase is essential for identifying strengths, weaknesses, and areas for improvement in one's trading approach.

Advantages of Demo Trading:

1. **Skill Enhancement:** Demo trading allows traders to gain hands-on experience, hone their decision-making skills, and improve their execution.

2. **Strategy Refinement:** Traders can refine and adapt their trading strategies based on the outcomes of demo trades, optimizing their approach over time.

3. **Risk-Free Learning:** Demo trading provides a safe environment to explore various techniques, indicators, and timeframes without financial risk.

Considerations for Effective Demo Trading:

1. **Treat it Seriously:** Approach demo trading with the same level of seriousness as real trading, as the experience directly contributes to your development.
2. **Realistic Conditions:** Set your demo account parameters to mirror your intended trading conditions, including account size, leverage, and trading timeframes.
3. **Objective Analysis:** Analyze your demo trades objectively, focusing on both profitable and losing trades to identify patterns and areas for improvement.

Conclusion

Demo trading is an indispensable tool for traders seeking to refine their skills, test strategies, and cultivate discipline without exposing their capital to risk. By embracing simulated trading environments, traders can bridge the gap between theoretical knowledge and practical application, ultimately enhancing their ability to navigate the complexities of the Forex market with precision and confidence.

7.2 Live Trading Tips Transitioning to Real Money Trading

The shift from demo trading to live trading marks a significant milestone in a trader's journey. This section provides invaluable insights and tips for successfully transitioning from simulated trading environments to real-money trading. By embracing these recommendations, traders can navigate the challenges and uncertainties of live trading with greater confidence and competence.

Mentality Shift:

1. **Real Capital, Real Emotions:** Recognize that trading with real money elicits stronger emotions than demo trading. Maintain emotional discipline, as fear and greed can impact decision-making.
2. **Risk Management Remains Key:** Implement rigorous risk management principles, ensuring that each trade adheres to predetermined risk levels and position sizes.

Start Small:

1. **Begin with a Small Account:** Initiate live trading with a smaller account size that you can afford to lose without compromising your financial stability.
2. **Conservative Position Sizing:** Limit your position sizes to a fraction of your capital, minimizing potential losses while gaining experience.

Continuity in Strategy:

1. **Stay True to Your Strategy:** Resist the temptation to deviate from your trading strategy due to emotions or impatience.
2. **Adapt Gradually:** If adjustments are necessary, make changes incrementally and evaluate their impact over time.

Market Conditions:

1. **Trade During Your Strongest Hours:** Focus on trading during periods when you are most alert and the market conditions align with your strategy.
2. **Avoid Major News Events:** During early stages of live trading, avoid trading during major economic or political events that can lead to unpredictable market movements.

Record and Review:

1. **Maintain a Trading Journal:** Continue documenting your live trades, emotions, and decision-making processes to refine your approach.
2. **Learn from Losses:** Treat losses as opportunities for growth. Analyze losing trades to understand the factors that led to unfavorable outcomes.

Conclusion

Transitioning from demo trading to live trading requires a deliberate mindset shift and a careful approach. By maintaining emotional discipline, implementing prudent risk management, and gradually increasing your exposure to real capital, you can navigate the psychological challenges and uncertainties inherent in trading with real money. Consistency in strategy, adapting to market conditions, and continual self-analysis will equip you to make informed decisions and thrive in the dynamic and demanding world of live Forex trading.

Chapter 8: Advanced Trading Techniques
8.1 Hedging Strategies Protecting Against Currency Risk

Hedging strategies play a pivotal role in mitigating currency risk, enabling traders and businesses to safeguard their positions against adverse currency movements. This section explores the significance of hedging strategies, their applications, and the types of instruments employed to hedge against currency risk. By mastering these advanced techniques, traders can navigate the complexities of currency fluctuations with greater resilience and strategic precision.

Types of Hedging Instruments:

Hedging involves the use of financial instruments to offset potential losses arising from adverse currency movements. Several commonly used hedging instruments include:

1. Forward Contracts: A forward contract is an agreement to exchange a specific amount of currency at a predetermined exchange rate on a future date. This allows traders to lock in a favorable exchange rate and protect themselves against potential currency depreciation.

2. Options Contracts: Options provide the holder with the right, but not the obligation, to exchange currency at a predetermined rate on or before a specific date. Put options protect against currency depreciation, while call options guard against currency appreciation.

3. Currency Swaps: Currency swaps involve exchanging one currency for another with an agreement to reverse the exchange at a future date. These swaps are often used to hedge long-term currency exposure.

4. Cross-Currency Hedges: Cross-currency hedges involve offsetting currency risk by pairing it with a different currency that has less exposure to the same risk factors.

Applications of Hedging Strategies:

1. International Trade: Businesses engaging in cross-border trade use hedging strategies to minimize the impact of exchange rate fluctuations on their profits.

2. Investment Portfolios: Investors with international investments use hedging to mitigate currency risk and protect the value of their holdings.

3. Speculative Hedging: Traders use hedging to offset risk from their speculative positions, reducing potential losses during uncertain market conditions.

Considerations for Effective Hedging:

1. **Risk Assessment:** Identify the specific currency risks your trades or investments are exposed to before selecting the appropriate hedging strategy.

2. **Cost Analysis:** Evaluate the cost of implementing various hedging instruments and weigh them against potential losses.

3. **Market Knowledge:** Stay updated on market trends, interest rates, and geopolitical events that can impact currency movements.

Conclusion

Hedging strategies serve as sophisticated tools for managing currency risk and enhancing the resilience of trading and investment portfolios. By understanding the various types of hedging instruments, their applications, and the considerations for effective implementation, traders and businesses can optimize their risk management efforts. Advanced trading techniques such as hedging empower individuals and entities to navigate the intricate landscape of currency markets with strategic foresight and calculated risk management.

8.2 Algorithmic Trading Automated Trading Systems:

Algorithmic trading, also known as algo trading, involves the use of computer programs and algorithms to execute trades automatically based on predefined criteria. This section delves into the realm of algorithmic trading, exploring its benefits, mechanics, and the process of developing and testing trading algorithms. By grasping the intricacies of algorithmic trading, traders can harness its potential to optimize trade execution and enhance overall trading performance.

Developing and Testing Algorithms:

Algorithm Development: Developing a trading algorithm involves formulating a set of rules and instructions that dictate trade entries, exits, and risk management. These rules are based on technical indicators, chart patterns, or fundamental data.

Testing and Optimization: Before deploying an algorithm, it is crucial to thoroughly test and optimize it using historical market data. Backtesting allows traders to evaluate the algorithm's performance under various market conditions and refine its parameters for optimal results.

Benefits of Algorithmic Trading:

1. **Speed and Precision:** Algorithms execute trades swiftly and accurately, eliminating the delays and errors associated with manual trading.

2. **Discipline and Consistency:** Algorithms follow predefined rules rigorously, reducing the impact of emotional biases on trading decisions.

3. **Diversification:** Algorithmic strategies can be diversified across different markets and timeframes, enhancing risk management.

Considerations for Effective Algorithmic Trading:

1. **Strategy Development:** Develop algorithms based on a well-defined trading strategy that has proven effective through rigorous testing.

2. **Data Integrity:** Ensure that historical data used for backtesting accurately reflects real market conditions.

3. **Continuous Monitoring:** Algorithmic strategies require ongoing monitoring to adapt to changing market dynamics and unforeseen events.

Conclusion

Algorithmic trading revolutionizes the way trades are executed by combining technology with strategic precision. Through the development and testing of trading algorithms, traders can create systems that execute trades swiftly and systematically, enhancing trading efficiency and reducing the impact of human emotions. By embracing algorithmic trading, traders can harness technology to optimize their trading strategies, adapt to evolving market conditions, and navigate the complexities of the financial markets with heightened sophistication and agility.

8.3 Seasonal and Cyclical Patterns Identifying Regular Market Behavior:

Seasonal and cyclical patterns are recurring trends in the financial markets that can be attributed to consistent factors, such as economic cycles, holidays, and other seasonal events. This section delves into the realm of seasonal and cyclical patterns, shedding light on their significance, identification, and utilization in trading strategies. By recognizing and capitalizing on these patterns, traders can make informed decisions and enhance their trading outcomes.

Understanding Seasonal Patterns:

Economic Seasons: Certain industries or sectors may exhibit consistent patterns based on economic seasons, such as increased consumer spending during holiday seasons.

Climatic Conditions: Weather-related factors can impact commodity prices and supply chains, leading to predictable price fluctuations.

Fiscal Periods: Quarterly earnings reports and fiscal year-end activities can influence market behavior and trends.

Identifying Cyclical Patterns:

Economic Cycles: Economic cycles, such as recession and expansion phases, can lead to cyclical patterns in asset prices.

Interest Rate Cycles: Central bank interest rate decisions can trigger cyclical trends in currency markets and related assets.

Stock Market Cycles: Stock markets often experience cyclical movements driven by investor sentiment and economic indicators.

Utilizing Seasonal and Cyclical Patterns:

1. **Research and Analysis:** Thoroughly research historical data to identify recurring seasonal and cyclical patterns in your chosen market.

2. **Calendar Awareness:** Stay informed about upcoming economic events, holidays, and fiscal periods that can influence market behavior.

3. **Aligning Strategies:** Tailor your trading strategies to capitalize on identified patterns, aligning your trades with anticipated market movements.

Considerations for Effective Utilization:

1. **Data Accuracy:** Ensure that historical data used to identify patterns is accurate and representative of real market conditions.

2. **Market Changes:** Be mindful of evolving market dynamics that can impact the reliability of historical patterns.

3. **Risk Management:** Incorporate sound risk management techniques to mitigate potential losses in case patterns deviate.

Conclusion

Seasonal and cyclical patterns provide traders with valuable insights into the regular behavior of financial markets. By recognizing the influence of economic cycles, climatic conditions, and other recurring factors, traders can develop strategies that align with anticipated market movements.

Leveraging these patterns can enhance decision-making, increase the accuracy of trading strategies, and contribute to more successful trading outcomes.

Chapter 9: Global Market Analysis
9.1 Intermarket Analysis Relationships Between Different Markets:

Intermarket analysis is a powerful approach that examines the relationships and interactions between different financial markets to gain insights into potential trends and correlations. This section delves into the concept of intermarket analysis, highlighting its importance and the impact it has on Forex trading. By understanding how various markets influence each other, traders can make more informed decisions and navigate the complexities of global market dynamics.

Impact on Forex Trading:

Commodity and Currency Relationships: Certain currencies exhibit strong correlations with specific commodities. For instance, the Australian Dollar (AUD) often correlates with commodity prices due to Australia's reliance on commodity exports.

Equity Markets: The performance of equity markets can impact currency movements, as strong equity markets often indicate investor confidence and potentially lead to currency appreciation.

Interest Rates and Currencies: Changes in interest rates set by central banks can impact currency values, making it vital to monitor interest rate decisions across different markets.

Utilizing Intermarket Analysis:

1. **Identifying Correlations:** Analyze historical data to identify patterns of correlation between different markets and currencies.
2. **Economic Events:** Stay informed about major economic events, as they can trigger shifts in correlated markets and currencies.
3. **Diversification:** Use intermarket analysis to diversify trading strategies and manage risk across various correlated markets.

Considerations for Effective Intermarket Analysis:

1. **Data Accuracy:** Ensure that historical data used for analysis is accurate and representative of actual market conditions.
2. **Dynamic Relationships:** Recognize that correlations between markets can change over time due to shifting economic conditions and geopolitical events.
3. **Long-Term Trends:** Intermarket analysis can provide insights into longer-term trends that may not be immediately apparent through traditional Forex analysis.

Conclusion

Intermarket analysis offers traders a holistic perspective on the intricate web of relationships between various financial markets. By understanding how different markets influence each other, traders can make more informed decisions, adapt to changing global dynamics, and refine their trading strategies for improved outcomes. A thorough grasp of intermarket analysis empowers traders to navigate the interconnected world of finance with heightened awareness and precision.

9.2 Geopolitical Analysis Assessing Political and Economic Developments:

Geopolitical analysis involves evaluating the impact of political, economic, and social factors on financial markets. This section delves into the realm of geopolitical analysis, highlighting its significance and the ways in which it influences Forex trading. By understanding the intricate connections between global events and market movements, traders can make more informed decisions and navigate the complexities of a dynamic world.

Geopolitical Risks and Opportunities:

Political Unrest: Political instability or conflicts in a country can lead to currency depreciation and increased market volatility.

Economic Policies: Economic decisions made by governments, such as changes in interest rates or trade policies, can have substantial effects on currency values.

Global Events: Major events like elections, referendums, and international conflicts can impact market sentiment and drive significant currency movements.

Utilizing Geopolitical Analysis:

1. **Stay Informed:** Regularly follow news and updates on global political and economic developments that can impact currency markets.
2. **Economic Calendars:** Utilize economic calendars to track scheduled political and economic events that may influence market behavior.
3. **Long-Term Trends:** Understand that geopolitical factors can impact long-term currency trends, requiring a broader perspective in analysis.

Considerations for Effective Geopolitical Analysis:

1. **Objectivity:** Analyze geopolitical events objectively, focusing on their potential impact on currency markets rather than personal biases.
2. **Multiple Perspectives:** Consider different viewpoints and expert analyses to gain a well-rounded understanding of geopolitical events.
3. **Market Sentiment:** Recognize the role of market sentiment in how geopolitical events are priced into currency values.

Conclusion

Geopolitical analysis offers traders a lens through which they can interpret the impact of global events on financial markets. By assessing political and economic developments, traders can identify potential risks and opportunities, adjust their strategies, and make informed decisions in a rapidly changing world. Integrating geopolitical analysis into Forex trading allows traders to navigate the intricate interplay between global events and market dynamics with greater precision and strategic insight.

Chapter 10: Trading Psychology Mastery
10.1 The Trader's Mindset Developing a Winning Attitude:

The trader's mindset is a critical component of successful Forex trading, influencing decision-making, risk management, and overall trading performance. This section delves into the intricacies of cultivating a winning attitude and the profound impact it has on a trader's journey. By fostering a resilient and disciplined mindset, traders can navigate the challenges of the market with greater confidence and consistency.

Controlling Emotions During Trades:

Emotions are inherent to human nature, but they can also be detrimental to trading decisions. It's essential to learn how to manage and control emotions to avoid impulsive actions that can lead to losses.

Fear: Fear of loss can paralyze decision-making or prompt traders to exit profitable trades prematurely. Understanding that losses are a natural part of trading helps mitigate this fear.

Greed: Greed can lead to overtrading, chasing unrealistic gains, and ignoring risk management. Discipline and adhering to a trading plan help counteract greed.

Frustration: Frustration arises from missed opportunities or losses. It's crucial to detach emotionally from individual trades and focus on the bigger picture.

Utilizing a Winning Mindset:

1. **Positive Self-Talk:** Replace self-doubt with positive affirmations and constructive self-talk to reinforce a winning attitude.
2. **Visualization:** Visualize successful trades and outcomes to program your subconscious mind for success.
3. **Continuous Learning:** Embrace a growth mindset, viewing losses and mistakes as learning opportunities rather than setbacks.

Considerations for Effective Mindset Mastery:

1. **Self-Awareness:** Reflect on your emotions and reactions during trading to identify patterns and triggers.
2. **Patience:** Recognize that success in trading requires time and patience; avoid the temptation for quick gains.
3. **Resilience:** Build emotional resilience to weather losses and setbacks without losing confidence.

Conclusion

Mastering the trader's mindset is a non-negotiable aspect of successful Forex trading. By cultivating a winning attitude, traders can approach the market with confidence, discipline, and the ability to manage emotions. Controlling fear, greed, and frustration allows traders to make rational decisions and adhere to their trading plans, ultimately leading to more consistent and profitable trading outcomes. A resilient and disciplined mindset serves as the cornerstone of trading psychology mastery, propelling traders toward enduring success in the dynamic world of Forex trading.

10.2 Cognitive Biases in Trading Overcoming Behavioral Pitfalls:

Cognitive biases are innate mental shortcuts that can lead traders to make irrational decisions. Recognizing and overcoming these biases is a crucial aspect of mastering trading psychology. This section delves into the realm of cognitive biases in trading, shedding light on common pitfalls and providing strategies to mitigate their impact. By developing awareness and adopting countermeasures, traders can make more rational and informed decisions.

Common Cognitive Biases in Trading:

1. Confirmation Bias: Tendency to seek out information that confirms pre-existing beliefs and ignore conflicting data.

2. Overconfidence: Overestimating one's ability and underestimating market risks, leading to excessive risk-taking.

3. Anchoring: Fixation on initial information, even if it's irrelevant, influencing subsequent decisions.

4. Loss Aversion: Preference for avoiding losses over gaining equivalent gains, leading to early exits and missed opportunities.

5. Herding Behavior: Following the crowd's actions instead of making independent decisions based on analysis.

Overcoming Behavioral Pitfalls:

1. Self-Awareness: Recognize your cognitive biases and their potential impact on decision-making.

2. Analytical Approach: Base decisions on objective analysis, data, and market trends rather than emotions or biases.

3. Journaling: Maintain a trading journal to record decisions, emotions, and outcomes, aiding in the identification of biased patterns.

4. Risk Management: Implement strict risk management techniques to prevent overconfidence and excessive risk-taking.

5. Seeking Diverse Opinions: Encourage input from others and seek out different viewpoints to counter confirmation bias.

Considerations for Overcoming Cognitive Biases:

1. **Continuous Learning:** Stay informed about cognitive biases to consistently evaluate and manage their influence.
2. **Pause and Reflect:** Before making impulsive decisions, take a moment to pause and evaluate whether cognitive biases are influencing your choice.
3. **Practice Patience:** Overcoming cognitive biases takes time and practice; be patient with yourself.

Conclusion

Overcoming cognitive biases is paramount to maintaining a rational and disciplined approach to trading. By acknowledging the influence of biases such as confirmation bias, overconfidence, and herding behavior, traders can take proactive steps to mitigate their impact. Developing self-awareness, adopting analytical practices, and seeking diverse opinions empower traders to make informed decisions based on logic and analysis rather than emotional impulses. Mastery over cognitive biases is a cornerstone of effective trading psychology, contributing to more consistent and profitable outcomes.

10.3 Mindfulness and Trading Techniques to Stay Present and Focused:

Mindfulness is a powerful psychological practice that can significantly enhance a trader's decision-making and emotional management. This section explores the integration of mindfulness techniques into trading, emphasizing their benefits and offering strategies to remain present and focused during the trading process. By cultivating mindfulness, traders can achieve greater clarity, reduced emotional reactivity, and improved overall trading performance.

Benefits of Mindfulness in Trading:

1. Improved Decision-Making: Mindfulness helps traders make rational decisions by reducing impulsive reactions to market fluctuations.

2. Emotional Regulation: Mindfulness enhances emotional awareness and control, preventing emotional biases from influencing trading choices.

3. Reduced Stress: Mindfulness techniques alleviate stress and anxiety, promoting a calm and composed trading mindset.

Techniques to Stay Present and Focused:

1. Breath Awareness: Practice deep breathing exercises to anchor your focus on the present moment and calm the mind.

2. Meditation: Incorporate short meditation sessions before trading to clear your mind and enhance mental clarity.

3. Visualization: Visualize successful trades and positive outcomes to reinforce a confident and focused mindset.

4. Progressive Muscle Relaxation: Release physical tension and promote relaxation through progressive muscle relaxation techniques.

5. Moment-to-Moment Awareness: Pay close attention to market movements, your emotions, and your trading decisions as they unfold.

Considerations for Practicing Mindfulness:

1. **Consistency:** Incorporate mindfulness practices into your daily routine to reap their long-term benefits.
2. **Patient Observation:** Practice observing your thoughts and emotions without judgment, fostering self-awareness.
3. **Adaptability:** Tailor mindfulness techniques to your preferences and integrate them seamlessly into your trading routine.

Conclusion

Mindfulness offers traders a powerful tool to navigate the complexities of the market with clarity, emotional control, and focus. By incorporating mindfulness practices such as breath awareness, meditation, and visualization, traders can reduce stress, enhance decision-making, and cultivate a calm and composed trading mindset. Developing mindfulness skills empowers traders to approach the challenges of trading with a heightened state of awareness, ultimately contributing to more consistent and successful trading outcomes.

Chapter 11: Case Studies and Examples
11.1 Real-Life Trading Scenarios Applying Different Strategies in Practical Situations:

Real-life case studies provide invaluable insights into the application of various trading strategies in practical scenarios. This section delves into real trading situations, showcasing the implementation of different strategies and the outcomes they yield. By examining these examples, traders can gain a deeper understanding of strategy execution, risk management, and decision-making in dynamic market environments.

Learning from Successful Trades and Mistakes:

Analyzing both successful trades and mistakes is essential for growth as a trader. Reviewing past trades offers a wealth of learning opportunities and helps refine trading techniques.

Successful Trades: Examine the factors that led to successful trades, including strategy execution, market analysis, and effective risk management.

Mistakes: Analyze trades that resulted in losses, identifying errors in strategy, emotional decision-making, and risk management.

Extracting Lessons from Case Studies:

1. **Strategy Adaption:** Understand how different strategies perform under various market conditions and adapt them as needed.

2. **Risk Analysis:** Evaluate how risk management techniques influenced the outcome of each trade.

3. **Market Awareness:** Observe how traders react to unexpected market movements and adjust their strategies accordingly.

Considerations for Analyzing Case Studies:

1. **Objectivity:** Approach case studies with objectivity, focusing on lessons learned rather than dwelling on emotions tied to gains or losses.

2. **Variety of Scenarios:** Analyze case studies that cover diverse market situations to build a well-rounded perspective.

3. **Continual Improvement:** View each case study as an opportunity to refine your trading skills and develop a comprehensive trading approach.

Conclusion

Real-life case studies and examples serve as practical blueprints for traders, offering insights into strategy execution, risk management, and decision-making. By analyzing both successful trades and mistakes, traders can gain a holistic perspective on the nuances of trading, learn from past experiences, and continuously improve their skills. Extracting valuable lessons from these case studies equips traders to face the challenges of the market with greater competence and adaptability, ultimately enhancing their ability to make informed and profitable trading decisions.

Chapter 11: Case Studies and Examples
11.2 Backtesting and Analysis Evaluating Historical Data to Refine Strategies:

Backtesting is a critical process that involves evaluating trading strategies using historical market data to gauge their effectiveness and potential outcomes. This section delves into the practice of backtesting and its significance in refining trading strategies. By harnessing historical data, traders can optimize their strategies, identify strengths and weaknesses, and make informed decisions based on empirical evidence.

Importance of Continuous Improvement:

Backtesting is not a one-time activity; it is an ongoing process that facilitates continuous improvement in trading strategies.

Optimization: Analyze historical data to identify areas for strategy optimization, such as adjusting entry and exit points.

Risk Management: Evaluate how risk management techniques would have impacted strategy performance during different market conditions.

Strategic Adaptation: Use backtesting results to adapt strategies to evolving market trends and conditions.

Utilizing Backtesting and Analysis:

1. **Data Selection:** Use accurate and representative historical data for backtesting to ensure reliable results.
2. **Testing Platforms:** Utilize reliable backtesting software or platforms that allow for thorough analysis of trading strategies.
3. **Scenario Testing:** Test strategies under various market conditions to gauge their resilience and adaptability.

Considerations for Effective Backtesting:

1. **Realism:** Simulate trading conditions as closely as possible to reality, including slippage, spreads, and execution delays.
2. **Limitations:** Understand the limitations of backtesting, as past performance doesn't guarantee future results.
3. **Objective Analysis:** Interpret backtesting results objectively, considering both gains and losses.

Conclusion

Backtesting and analysis form the bedrock of informed trading decisions, enabling traders to refine their strategies and adapt to changing market dynamics. By evaluating historical data, traders can optimize their trading methodologies, make informed adjustments, and enhance their overall trading performance. Recognizing that continuous improvement is essential, traders can harness backtesting as a tool for strategic evolution and a means to achieve consistent success in the challenging realm of Forex trading.

Chapter 12: Evolving Trends in Forex Trading

12.1 Cryptocurrencies and Forex Intersection of Crypto Markets and Traditional Forex:

The emergence of cryptocurrencies has introduced a new dimension to the world of trading, intersecting with traditional Forex markets. This section delves into the interaction between cryptocurrencies and Forex, highlighting their coexistence, potential synergies, and challenges. By understanding the dynamics of this evolving trend, traders can position themselves to leverage opportunities and navigate potential risks.

Opportunities and Risks:

Opportunities: Cryptocurrencies offer new avenues for diversification and potential profits, with their high volatility providing both short-term trading opportunities and long-term investment potential.

Risks: Cryptocurrencies are subject to extreme price fluctuations, regulatory uncertainties, and cybersecurity risks. The nascent nature of the market can lead to heightened volatility and potential market manipulation.

Navigating the Intersection:

1. **Educational Exploration:** Gain a deep understanding of the unique characteristics, technology, and market dynamics of cryptocurrencies.
2. **Risk Assessment:** Evaluate the risk tolerance of integrating cryptocurrencies into your trading portfolio and adjust your risk management strategy accordingly.
3. **Regulatory Awareness:** Stay informed about evolving regulatory developments in both traditional Forex and cryptocurrency markets.

Considerations for Integrating Cryptocurrencies:

1. **Risk Diversification:** Consider how cryptocurrencies can complement your existing portfolio to enhance diversification.
2. **Educational Investment:** Invest time in learning about the complexities and potential of cryptocurrencies before committing capital.
3. **Long-Term Perspective:** Approach cryptocurrency trading with a long-term perspective, understanding the potential for both rapid gains and significant losses.

Conclusion

The convergence of cryptocurrencies and traditional Forex markets presents both exciting opportunities and substantial challenges for traders. By navigating the intersection of these markets, traders can diversify their portfolios, capitalize on new trading avenues, and adapt to the changing landscape of finance. Recognizing the potential for both significant gains and risks, traders can leverage their expertise, embrace continuous learning, and strategically integrate cryptocurrencies into their trading strategies for optimal outcomes in this evolving trend.

12.2 Artificial Intelligence in Forex Machine Learning and Predictive Analytics:

Artificial Intelligence (AI) is reshaping the landscape of Forex trading by introducing advanced techniques such as machine learning and predictive analytics. This section explores the integration of AI in the Forex market, focusing on its application in predicting market trends, optimizing strategies, and enhancing trading performance. By harnessing AI capabilities, traders can leverage data-driven insights for more informed decision-making.

AI Tools for Trading and Analysis:

AI tools offer an array of benefits for traders, ranging from automated trading systems to sophisticated data analysis. These tools enhance efficiency, accuracy, and adaptability in trading strategies.

Algorithmic Trading: Utilize AI-powered algorithms to execute trades based on pre-defined conditions and parameters, reducing the need for manual intervention.

Sentiment Analysis: AI-driven sentiment analysis tools gauge market sentiment by analyzing news articles, social media, and other data sources, aiding in decision-making.

Pattern Recognition: AI algorithms can identify intricate patterns and trends within large datasets, facilitating technical analysis.

Leveraging AI in Trading:

1. **Data Utilization:** Integrate AI tools that can process and analyze vast amounts of data, enabling more precise decision-making.
2. **Strategy Optimization:** Employ machine learning algorithms to optimize trading strategies based on historical data and changing market conditions.
3. **Risk Management:** Implement AI-based risk management solutions that adjust trade sizes and positions in response to market volatility.

Considerations for AI Integration:

1. **Technical Proficiency:** Acquire the technical knowledge required to effectively operate AI tools and platforms.

2. **Data Quality:** Ensure that AI systems receive accurate and reliable data for accurate analysis and decision-making.
3. **Supervision:** Monitor AI systems regularly to ensure they're performing as intended and adapting to changing market conditions.

Conclusion

Artificial Intelligence is revolutionizing Forex trading by offering innovative tools and strategies that enhance accuracy, efficiency, and decision-making. By incorporating machine learning and predictive analytics, traders can gain insights into market trends, optimize strategies, and improve trading performance. Embracing AI tools empowers traders to navigate the complexities of the market with data-driven precision, adaptability, and the potential for enhanced profitability in this rapidly evolving landscape.

Chapter 13: Regulatory Landscape and Ethics

13.1 Forex Regulation and Compliance Understanding Regulatory Bodies:

The Forex market operates within a framework of regulations and compliance enforced by various regulatory bodies around the world. This section delves into the significance of understanding and adhering to Forex regulations, highlighting the role of regulatory authorities in maintaining market integrity, investor protection, and fair trading practices. By familiarizing themselves with regulatory bodies, traders can navigate the market confidently and ethically.

Importance of Trading Ethically:

Ethics play a crucial role in maintaining the integrity of the Forex market and fostering trust among participants. Trading ethically ensures that market manipulation, insider trading, and other unfair practices are avoided.

Transparency: Ethical trading involves providing accurate and transparent information to clients and stakeholders.

Fair Treatment: Treat all market participants, regardless of size, with fairness and integrity.

Compliance: Adhere to the rules and regulations set forth by relevant authorities to promote a level playing field.

Navigating the Regulatory Landscape:

1. **Research Regulatory Bodies:** Familiarize yourself with the regulatory bodies that oversee Forex trading in your region and globally.
2. **Compliance Education:** Stay informed about the regulatory requirements and compliance obligations that pertain to Forex trading.
3. **Reputation Management:** Uphold a reputation of ethical trading by avoiding practices that may damage your credibility.

Considerations for Ethical Trading:

1. **Market Integrity:** Understand that ethical trading contributes to market integrity, stability, and the protection of investors.
2. **Long-Term Success:** Trading ethically builds a positive reputation, fostering long-term relationships with clients and partners.
3. **Legal Consequences:** Engaging in unethical trading practices can result in legal consequences and damage to your professional standing.

Conclusion

Understanding the regulatory landscape and trading ethically are foundational elements of responsible Forex trading. By recognizing the role of regulatory bodies and adhering to ethical principles, traders contribute to a fair, transparent, and trustworthy market environment. Ethical trading practices not only align with regulatory requirements but also establish a strong foundation for success built on integrity, reputation, and responsible conduct within the dynamic world of Forex trading.

13.2 Avoiding Scams and Frauds Recognizing Red Flags:

In the world of Forex trading, the potential for scams and fraudulent activities exists. This section emphasizes the importance of vigilance in recognizing red flags and protecting oneself from scams that can jeopardize investments and credibility. By developing a keen awareness of common fraudulent tactics, traders can safeguard their assets and uphold ethical trading practices.

Protecting Your Investments:

1. Unrealistic Promises: Be wary of schemes that promise guaranteed profits or high returns with minimal risk; such claims often signal fraudulent intent.

2. Unregulated Brokers: Verify the legitimacy of brokers by checking for regulatory licenses and conducting due diligence.

3. Pressure to Invest: Avoid brokers or individuals who use high-pressure tactics to rush your investment decisions.

4. Lack of Transparency: Transparent brokers provide clear information about fees, spreads, and terms; avoid those who withhold crucial details.

5. Phishing: Beware of unsolicited communications asking for personal or financial information; scammers often use phishing tactics.

Safeguarding Your Investments:

1. **Research Brokers:** Choose regulated and reputable brokers with a proven track record in the industry.
2. **Independent Verification:** Verify information from multiple sources to cross-reference legitimacy.
3. **Educational Resources:** Educate yourself about common scams and fraudulent tactics to identify potential threats.

Considerations for Fraud Prevention:

1. **Diligence:** Conduct thorough research and due diligence before investing with any individual or broker.
2. **Trust Your Instincts:** If something sounds too good to be true, it likely is. Trust your instincts and avoid risky ventures.
3. **Secure Communication:** Ensure your online communication is secure, use strong passwords, and enable two-factor authentication.

Conclusion

Vigilance and caution are paramount in safeguarding investments from scams and fraudulent activities. By recognizing red flags such as unrealistic promises, unregulated brokers, and high-pressure tactics, traders can avoid falling victim to scams that threaten their financial well-being. Staying informed, conducting due diligence, and adopting secure communication practices are essential steps in preventing fraud and upholding ethical trading principles within the Forex market.

Chapter 14: Risk Management Strategies for Advanced Traders

14.1 Correlation Analysis Understanding Correlations Between Currency Pairs:

Correlation analysis is a sophisticated risk management tool that advanced traders employ to navigate the complexities of the Forex market. This section explores the concept of correlation, shedding light on how currency pairs interact with each other, and the implications for risk and trading strategies. By understanding correlations, traders can make more informed decisions and effectively manage portfolio risk.

Leveraging Correlation for Diversification and Risk Management:

Positive Correlation: Currency pairs that move in the same direction. When one appreciates, the other tends to as well.

Negative Correlation: Currency pairs that move in opposite directions. When one appreciates, the other typically depreciates.

No Correlation (or Low Correlation): Currency pairs that do not exhibit a consistent relationship in movement.

Strategic Insights from Correlation Analysis:

1. **Diversification:** Identifying positively and negatively correlated pairs allows for diversification, reducing risk exposure.

2. **Risk Mitigation:** By strategically pairing positively and negatively correlated currencies, traders can mitigate the impact of adverse movements.

3. **Enhanced Decision-Making:** Correlation analysis aids in timing entry and exit points for trades across correlated pairs.

Implementing Correlation Analysis:

1. **Correlation Coefficients:** Understand correlation coefficients to measure the strength of correlation between currency pairs.

2. **Statistical Tools:** Utilize statistical tools and software to calculate correlations accurately.

3. **Regular Monitoring:** Regularly assess correlations as they can change due to market dynamics.

Considerations for Effective Correlation Analysis:

1. **In-depth Research:** Conduct thorough research to understand the fundamental and technical factors influencing correlated currency pairs.

2. **Risk Evaluation:** Use correlation analysis to assess potential risk exposure in your trading portfolio.

3. **Adaptability:** Continuously adjust your trading strategies based on changing correlation patterns.

Conclusion

Correlation analysis is a vital tool for advanced traders seeking to optimize risk management and portfolio diversification. By understanding the relationships between currency pairs and leveraging correlations strategically, traders can make more informed decisions, manage risk effectively, and enhance their trading performance. Incorporating correlation analysis into trading strategies equips advanced traders with the insights needed to navigate the dynamic and multifaceted landscape of the Forex market.

14.2 Volatility Trading Capitalizing on Market Fluctuations:

Volatility is an inherent characteristic of the Forex market, presenting both risks and opportunities. This section explores volatility trading, an advanced strategy that capitalizes on market fluctuations to achieve favorable trading outcomes. By understanding volatility and employing appropriate strategies, advanced traders can harness its potential for profitable trading.

Strategies to Navigate Volatile Markets:

1. Breakout Trading: Identify key support and resistance levels and enter trades when price breaks through these levels, capitalizing on strong market movements.

2. ATR-based Strategies: Utilize the Average True Range (ATR) indicator to gauge market volatility and adjust trading strategies accordingly.

3. Volatility Index (VIX): Monitor the VIX or other volatility indices to gauge market sentiment and make informed trading decisions.

4. Option Strategies: Employ option strategies, such as straddles or strangles, to profit from significant price movements while managing risk.

Navigating Volatility:

1. **Volatility Assessment:** Gauge historical volatility and anticipate potential future volatility to select appropriate trading strategies.
2. **Risk Management:** Adjust position sizes and use appropriate stop-loss levels to manage risk during periods of heightened volatility.
3. **Technical Analysis:** Combine volatility analysis with technical indicators to identify optimal entry and exit points.

Considerations for Volatility Trading:

1. **Educational Foundation:** Acquire a solid understanding of volatility, its causes, and how it impacts different currency pairs.
2. **Adaptability:** Be prepared to adjust trading strategies based on changing market conditions and volatility levels.
3. **Risk Control:** Utilize risk management techniques to protect your capital during periods of increased volatility.

Conclusion

Volatility trading is an advanced strategy that requires a deep understanding of market dynamics, technical analysis, and risk management. By capitalizing on market fluctuations and employing appropriate strategies, advanced traders can navigate volatile markets with confidence, making informed decisions that lead to profitable outcomes. Integrating volatility analysis into trading strategies equips advanced traders with the tools necessary to thrive in the dynamic and ever-changing Forex market.

14.3 Option Trading in Forex Using Options for Hedging and Speculation:

Option trading is an advanced strategy that offers traders unique opportunities for both hedging and speculation in the Forex market. This section delves into the concept of option trading, highlighting its dual role in managing risk and capitalizing on market movements.

Hedging with Options: Options provide the ability to protect against unfavorable currency movements by creating positions that offset potential losses.

Speculating with Options: Traders can use options to speculate on currency price movements, potentially achieving gains without the obligation of owning the underlying asset.

Key Terminology and Concepts:

1. Call Option: A contract that gives the holder the right to buy a currency pair at a predetermined price within a specified time frame.

2. Put Option: A contract that gives the holder the right to sell a currency pair at a predetermined price within a specified time frame.

3. Strike Price: The price at which the option holder can buy (for call options) or sell (for put options) the currency pair.

4. Expiration Date: The date when the option contract expires and becomes void.

5. Premium: The price paid for the option contract, representing its intrinsic and time value.

Using Options in Trading:

1. **Risk Management:** Traders can use options to limit potential losses while maintaining the opportunity for gains.
2. **Volatility Management:** Options can be employed to manage the impact of market volatility on trading positions.
3. **Strategic Diversification:** Options provide an avenue for strategic portfolio diversification by adding non-traditional risk management methods.

Considerations for Option Trading:

1. **Educational Foundation:** Develop a strong understanding of option concepts, strategies, and their applications in Forex trading.
2. **Risk Assessment:** Evaluate the potential benefits and risks associated with option trading before implementation.
3. **Continuous Learning:** Stay updated with evolving option strategies and market dynamics to make informed decisions.

Conclusion

Option trading is a powerful tool that advanced traders can utilize for both hedging and speculation in the Forex market. By comprehending key terminology and concepts and understanding the strategic applications of options, traders can effectively manage risk, capitalize on market movements, and optimize trading outcomes. Integrating option trading strategies into one's repertoire empowers advanced traders to navigate the intricate world of Forex with enhanced precision and adaptability.

Chapter 15: Developing a Personal Trading System

15.1 Customizing Your Approach Integrating Different Strategies and Techniques:

Creating a personal trading system is a hallmark of advanced traders, allowing them to tailor their approach to the unique dynamics of the Forex market. This section delves into the process of customizing trading strategies by integrating different techniques and methodologies. By amalgamating diverse approaches, advanced traders can build a comprehensive system that aligns with their goals and maximizes their chances of success.

Identifying Your Unique Trading Style:

Every trader possesses a distinct trading style that reflects their personality, risk tolerance, and strengths. Understanding your trading style is crucial in devising a personalized trading system that resonates with your strengths and minimizes your weaknesses. By identifying whether you're a day trader, swing trader, or position trader, you can align your strategies with your natural inclinations.

Developing a Personal Trading System:

1. **Strategy Selection:** Select trading strategies that complement each other and offer well-rounded market coverage.
2. **Risk Management:** Integrate risk management techniques that suit your risk appetite and safeguard your capital.
3. **Timeframe Consistency:** Ensure consistency in timeframes within your strategies to enhance decision-making.

Considerations for Customizing Your Approach:

1. **In-depth Analysis:** Thoroughly evaluate the strategies and techniques you plan to integrate, assessing their historical performance and compatibility.
2. **Trial and Error:** Test your customized approach using demo accounts to refine your system before implementing it with real capital.
3. **Continuous Adaptation:** Your trading system should be adaptable to changing market conditions and your own evolving preferences.

Conclusion

Developing a personal trading system is an essential step for advanced traders seeking consistency and success in the Forex market. By integrating diverse strategies and techniques while aligning with your unique trading style, you create a robust framework for decision-making. This personalized approach empowers advanced traders to navigate the complexities of the market with precision, flexibility, and the potential for sustained profitability.

15.2 Building a Trading Routine Creating a Structured Daily Plan:

A well-defined trading routine is a hallmark of successful advanced traders. This section delves into the importance of building a structured daily plan that outlines your activities, priorities, and tasks within the Forex market. By adhering to a routine, advanced traders can enhance their efficiency, decision-making, and overall trading performance.

Balancing Analysis, Execution, and Research:

An effective trading routine strikes a balance between key components: analysis, execution, and research. Advanced traders allocate time for technical and fundamental analysis, executing trades, and staying updated on market developments. By dedicating time to each aspect, traders ensure comprehensive engagement with the market while minimizing the risk of oversight.

Developing a Trading Routine:

1. **Time Management:** Allocate specific time slots for different trading activities, from analyzing charts to researching market news.
2. **Prioritization:** Prioritize tasks based on their significance and urgency to optimize your time and resources.
3. **Consistency:** Stick to your trading routine to develop discipline, enhance decision-making, and minimize impulsive actions.

Considerations for Building a Trading Routine:

1. **Flexibility:** While routines are essential, allow room for adaptation to accommodate changing market conditions.
2. **Self-Care:** Include breaks and time for self-care to maintain mental and physical well-being during trading hours.
3. **Regular Review:** Periodically evaluate the effectiveness of your routine and make adjustments as necessary.

Conclusion

A structured trading routine is a linchpin for advanced traders seeking consistency and success in the Forex market. By creating a balanced daily plan that encompasses analysis, execution, and research, traders ensure that no vital aspect is neglected. This disciplined approach empowers advanced traders to optimize their time, make informed decisions, and capitalize on opportunities within the dynamic landscape of Forex trading.

Chapter 16: Analyzing and Improving Performance
16.1 Keeping Track of Trades Trade Journaling for Analysis and Reflection:

Maintaining a comprehensive trade journal is an integral practice for advanced traders dedicated to refining their performance. This section underscores the significance of trade journaling as a tool for analysis and reflection. By meticulously documenting each trade, its rationale, and outcomes, traders create a valuable resource for continuous improvement.

Identifying Patterns of Success and Failure:

A trade journal serves as a repository of data that enables advanced traders to identify patterns of success and failure in their trading strategies. By analyzing past trades, traders can discern factors contributing to profitable outcomes as well as those leading to losses. This analysis forms the foundation for informed decision-making and strategy optimization.

Developing a Trade Journaling Practice:

1. **Detailed Entry:** Document essential trade details, including entry and exit prices, position size, and reasons for trade execution.
2. **Market Context:** Describe the prevailing market conditions, economic events, and news that influenced the trade.
3. **Emotional State:** Note your emotional state during the trade to identify potential biases or impulsive decisions.

Considerations for Keeping Track of Trades:

1. **Consistency:** Maintain a regular practice of trade journaling for accurate data collection and analysis.
2. **Honesty:** Be honest in recording both successful and unsuccessful trades to gain a holistic perspective.
3. **Analysis:** Dedicate time to review your trade journal periodically, extracting insights and identifying areas for improvement.

Conclusion

Keeping a meticulous trade journal is an indispensable practice for advanced traders striving for continuous growth and improvement. By systematically documenting trades, analyzing patterns, and reflecting on decisions, traders build a repository of insights that inform their future strategies. Trade journaling empowers advanced traders to evolve, adapt, and make informed decisions in the dynamic and challenging landscape of Forex trading.

16.2 Quantitative Analysis Measuring Performance Metrics:

Quantitative analysis is a cornerstone of advanced traders' efforts to enhance their trading performance. This section highlights the importance of measuring performance metrics systematically and objectively. By quantifying various aspects of trading performance, advanced traders gain insights into their strengths, weaknesses, and areas for improvement.

Using Data to Refine Strategies:

Data-driven decision-making is central to effective trading, and quantitative analysis empowers advanced traders to refine their strategies based on factual evidence. By analyzing performance metrics, traders can identify inefficiencies, optimize risk management techniques, and enhance their overall trading approach.

Engaging in Quantitative Analysis:

1. **Key Metrics:** Identify and measure critical performance metrics such as win-loss ratio, average gain, average loss, and risk-reward ratio.
2. **Backtesting:** Utilize historical data to backtest trading strategies and assess their effectiveness over different market conditions.
3. **Statistical Tools:** Leverage statistical tools to analyze and interpret data accurately and objectively.

Considerations for Quantitative Analysis:

1. **Data Accuracy:** Ensure that the data used for analysis is accurate and reliable to draw meaningful conclusions.
2. **Comparative Analysis:** Compare performance metrics across different timeframes and market conditions to identify patterns.
3. **Iterative Process:** Quantitative analysis is an ongoing process that requires continuous assessment and adjustment of strategies.

Conclusion

Quantitative analysis empowers advanced traders to elevate their trading performance by objectively measuring key metrics and using data-driven insights to refine strategies. By engaging in systematic analysis, traders can enhance decision-making, optimize risk management, and adapt to evolving market dynamics. Embracing quantitative analysis equips advanced traders with the tools necessary to thrive and succeed in the complex and competitive landscape of Forex trading.

Chapter 17: Forex Trading and Taxes
17.1 Tax Implications of Forex Trading Reporting Profits and Losses:

Understanding the tax implications of Forex trading is crucial for advanced traders to ensure compliance and accurate financial reporting. This section highlights the importance of reporting profits and losses from Forex trading activities. Advanced traders need to meticulously track their gains and losses to provide accurate information to tax authorities and maintain transparency in their financial records.

Different Tax Treatments in Various Jurisdictions:

The tax treatment of Forex trading varies across different jurisdictions, adding complexity to the process. This section sheds light on the diverse tax regulations that traders encounter depending on their location. By being aware of the tax laws specific to their jurisdiction, advanced traders can navigate the intricacies of tax reporting and ensure they are in full compliance.

Navigating Tax Implications:

1. **Record Keeping:** Maintain detailed records of all trades, including transaction dates, amounts, and outcomes.
2. **Consulting Experts:** Seek guidance from tax professionals who specialize in Forex trading to ensure accurate tax reporting.
3. **Local Regulations:** Understand the tax laws and regulations in your jurisdiction, as they can impact the treatment of Forex trading profits and losses.

Considerations for Tax Implications:

1. **Accuracy:** Ensure that your tax reporting accurately reflects your trading activities to avoid potential legal consequences.
2. **Timeliness:** Adhere to tax filing deadlines to prevent penalties and legal issues associated with late reporting.
3. **Continuous Learning:** Stay informed about changes in tax laws that might affect your Forex trading activities.

Conclusion

Navigating the tax implications of Forex trading is an essential aspect of advanced traders' responsibilities. By accurately reporting profits and losses and understanding the diverse tax treatments across different jurisdictions, traders can maintain compliance and integrity in their financial activities. Embracing transparency, adhering to tax regulations, and seeking professional guidance are integral steps in ensuring a seamless interface between Forex trading and tax obligations.

Chapter 18: Trading in Various Market Conditions
18.1 Sideways Markets Strategies for Range-Bound Conditions:

Trading in various market conditions requires adaptability, and navigating sideways markets is a skill that advanced traders must master. This section explores strategies specifically designed for range-bound or sideways market conditions. In such scenarios, where price movement remains relatively stagnant, traders need specialized approaches to capitalize on opportunities while managing risk.

Understanding Sideways Markets:

Sideways markets, also known as range-bound or consolidating markets, are characterized by a lack of clear trend direction. Prices oscillate within a defined range, presenting challenges and opportunities for traders.

Strategies for Sideways Markets:

1. **Range Trading:** Buy at support levels and sell at resistance levels within the defined range.
2. **Mean Reversion:** Anticipate that prices will revert to their average levels within the range.
3. **Use of Indicators:** Rely on oscillators and volatility indicators to gauge potential breakouts or breakdowns.

Risk Management in Sideways Markets:

1. **Reduced Position Sizes:** Due to decreased volatility, consider reducing position sizes to manage risk effectively.
2. **Tight Stop-Loss Orders:** Place stop-loss orders closer to entry points to limit potential losses.
3. **Avoidance:** If conditions are too uncertain, consider avoiding trades until a clear trend emerges.

Considerations for Trading in Sideways Markets:

1. **Patience:** Sideways markets can test patience, and traders should wait for favorable setups.
2. **Adaptability:** Be prepared to switch strategies when market conditions change.
3. **Analysis:** Rely on technical analysis to identify support and resistance levels accurately.

Conclusion

Trading in sideways markets requires strategic thinking and a nuanced approach. Advanced traders equipped with the knowledge of specialized strategies for range-bound conditions can navigate these challenging scenarios with confidence. By understanding the dynamics of sideways markets, employing appropriate strategies, and implementing effective risk management techniques, traders can uncover hidden opportunities even in the absence of clear trends.

18.2 Trending Markets Riding Trends and Avoiding False Breakouts:

Trending markets offer opportunities for substantial profits, but also come with risks, especially in distinguishing genuine trends from false breakouts. This section delves into strategies designed for trading in trending markets, focusing on capitalizing on trends while avoiding the pitfalls of false signals.

Understanding Trending Markets:

Trending markets are characterized by sustained price movement in a particular direction. Traders aim to ride these trends to maximize gains, but the challenge lies in discerning true trends from temporary price fluctuations.

Strategies for Trending Markets:

1. **Trend Following:** Identify established trends using technical indicators and follow the prevailing direction.

2. **Moving Averages:** Utilize moving averages to identify the direction and strength of a trend.
3. **Breakout Strategies:** Enter trades when price breaks through key support or resistance levels, confirming the strength of the trend.

Avoiding False Breakouts:

1. **Confirmation:** Wait for multiple indicators to confirm a breakout before entering a trade to reduce the risk of false signals.
2. **Volume Analysis:** Analyze trading volume to validate the strength of a breakout.
3. **Pullback Strategy:** Wait for a brief pullback in price before entering a trade, increasing the likelihood of a valid trend continuation.

Risk Management in Trending Markets:

1. **Trailing Stop-Loss:** Adjust stop-loss levels as the trend progresses to secure profits and limit potential losses.
2. **Risk-Reward Ratio:** Maintain a favorable risk-reward ratio to ensure that profitable trades outweigh losing ones.
3. **Avoid Overtrading:** Avoid chasing after every trend and focus on high-probability setups to minimize risks.

Considerations for Trading in Trending Markets:

1. **Patience:** Wait for strong trend confirmation before entering trades to avoid false signals.
2. **Technical Expertise:** Develop a thorough understanding of technical indicators and patterns for accurate trend identification.
3. **Adaptability:** Be prepared to switch strategies when trends change or market conditions shift.

Conclusion

Trading in trending markets demands a keen understanding of price movements and the ability to differentiate genuine trends from false breakouts. Advanced traders who master the art of riding trends while avoiding false signals can seize opportunities for substantial profits. By employing proven strategies, confirming trends through multiple indicators, and implementing effective risk management techniques, traders can navigate trending markets with confidence and precision.

Chapter 19: The Future of Forex Trading

19.1 Technological Innovations Impact of AI, Blockchain, and Quantum Computing:
The future of Forex trading is intricately intertwined with rapid technological advancements. This section delves into the profound impact that emerging technologies such as Artificial Intelligence (AI), Blockchain, and Quantum Computing will have on the Forex market. These innovations are poised to reshape trading strategies, risk management practices, and the overall landscape of Forex trading.

AI's Role in Forex Trading:

AI algorithms are revolutionizing trading by analyzing massive datasets and making predictions with unprecedented accuracy. They enable advanced pattern recognition, risk assessment, and optimization of trading strategies in real-time. AI-powered trading bots execute trades, leveraging historical data and adapting to evolving market conditions.

Blockchain's Influence on Transparency:

Blockchain technology introduces transparency and security into Forex trading by recording transactions on an immutable and decentralized ledger. This fosters trust among traders, reduces settlement times, and curtails fraud. Smart contracts facilitate automatic execution of trades, minimizing intermediaries and associated costs.

Quantum Computing's Potential:

Quantum computing's computational prowess could disrupt Forex trading with its capacity to process complex data sets and perform intricate calculations exponentially faster. This technology holds the potential to revolutionize risk management, portfolio optimization, and strategy development.

Potential Disruptions and Advancements:

1. **High-Frequency Trading (HFT):** AI-driven algorithms can accelerate HFT strategies, optimizing order execution and capturing fleeting market opportunities.
2. **Personalized Trading Solutions:** AI can offer tailored trading advice based on individual preferences and risk tolerance.
3. **Risk Assessment:** AI algorithms can predict potential market shocks and assess their impact on trading portfolios.

Considerations for Technological Innovations:

1. **Education:** Traders must continuously update their skills to harness the benefits of technological advancements.
2. **Ethical Concerns:** Technological innovations raise ethical questions about AI-driven decision-making and data privacy.
3. **Regulatory Implications:** Regulatory bodies must adapt to supervise AI and blockchain applications in Forex trading.

Conclusion

The future of Forex trading is illuminated by the transformative potential of technological innovations. AI, Blockchain, and Quantum Computing are set to redefine trading strategies, risk management approaches, and market dynamics. As traders prepare for this evolving landscape, they must stay abreast of technological developments, adapt their skillsets, and anticipate the regulatory challenges and ethical considerations that these innovations entail.

19.2 Sustainable Trading Ethical and Green Trading Practices:

The future of Forex trading is not only defined by technological advancements but also by a growing emphasis on ethical and sustainable trading practices. This section explores the rise of sustainable trading, focusing on the integration of ethical considerations and environmental responsibility into trading strategies.

Promoting Environmental and Social Responsibility:

Sustainable trading extends beyond profit-seeking and acknowledges the broader impact of trading activities on the environment and society. Traders are increasingly recognizing their role in promoting responsible practices that align with environmental preservation and social well-being.

Incorporating Sustainability in Trading:

1. **Ethical Investments:** Traders can select instruments that align with ethical and sustainable values, supporting companies that prioritize social and environmental responsibility.

2. **Green Trading Strategies:** Implement trading strategies that reflect a commitment to environmental sustainability, such as supporting renewable energy sectors or avoiding environmentally harmful industries.

3. **Socially Responsible Investing:** Consider the social implications of investments, supporting companies that demonstrate fair labor practices, diversity, and community engagement.

Benefits of Sustainable Trading:

1. **Long-Term Viability:** Companies with strong ethical and sustainable practices tend to demonstrate long-term financial viability.

2. **Positive Reputation:** Traders engaged in sustainable practices often garner positive reputations and attract like-minded investors.

3. **Contributing to Positive Change:** Sustainable trading contributes to a more responsible and equitable global economy.

Considerations for Sustainable Trading:

1. **Research:** Gain a deep understanding of companies' ethical practices before investing in them.

2. **Measurable Impact:** Evaluate the social and environmental impact of your trading decisions.

3. **Advocacy:** Encourage industry-wide adoption of ethical and sustainable practices through discussions and collaborations.

Conclusion

The future of Forex trading encompasses not only technological advancements but also a shift toward ethical and sustainable trading practices. Traders who embrace environmental and social responsibility are poised to influence positive change in the global trading landscape. By incorporating sustainability considerations into trading strategies and advocating for responsible practices, traders contribute to a more equitable and environmentally conscious future.

Chapter 20: Your Journey as a Forex Trader
20.1 Continuous Learning and Adaptation Staying Updated with Market Developments:

Your journey as a Forex trader is an ongoing pursuit of knowledge and adaptation to ever-evolving market dynamics. This section underscores the importance of continuous learning and staying updated with the latest market developments. In the fast-paced world of Forex trading, staying informed is essential for making well-informed decisions.

Expanding Your Knowledge Base:

As an advanced trader, your commitment to continuous learning is paramount. Expanding your knowledge base not only enhances your trading skills but also empowers you to develop new strategies and adapt to changing market conditions.

Embracing Continuous Learning:

1. **Market Research:** Regularly research market news, economic indicators, and geopolitical events that impact currency movements.
2. **Educational Resources:** Engage with online courses, webinars, and trading forums to access a wealth of trading insights.
3. **Technical Analysis:** Deepen your understanding of technical indicators, chart patterns, and advanced analysis techniques.

Adaptation in a Dynamic Landscape:

1. **Strategy Evolution:** Be prepared to adjust your trading strategies as market conditions shift.
2. **Risk Management Enhancement:** Continuously refine your risk management techniques based on your experiences and market behavior.
3. **Incorporating New Tools:** Stay open to incorporating new trading tools and technologies as they emerge.

Considerations for Continuous Learning and Adaptation:

1. **Time Management:** Dedicate regular time slots for learning and research to ensure you stay up-to-date.
2. **Critical Thinking:** Evaluate information critically and discern reliable sources to inform your decisions.
3. **Practical Application:** Apply newly acquired knowledge in demo trading to gauge its effectiveness before using it in live trading.

Conclusion

Your journey as an advanced Forex trader is marked by a commitment to continuous learning and adaptation. Staying updated with market developments and expanding your knowledge base are essential practices that empower you to navigate the complexities of the Forex market successfully. By embracing learning as a lifelong endeavor and remaining adaptable to changing circumstances, you position yourself for sustained growth and success as a Forex trader.

Appendix A: Glossary of Forex Terms

Forex trading, also known as foreign exchange trading or currency trading, involves the buying and selling of currencies on the foreign exchange market. To navigate this complex world effectively, it's crucial to understand the various terms and concepts that are commonly used in Forex trading. This glossary provides a comprehensive list of key terms and concepts to help you grasp the essential elements of Forex trading.

1. **Pip (Percentage in Point):** A unit of measurement for the change in value between two currencies. It's usually the smallest price movement that can be observed in the exchange rate, and it's used to express gains or losses in Forex trades.
2. **Bid Price:** The price at which a trader can sell a currency pair. This is the price that market makers are willing to pay for a particular currency pair.
3. **Ask Price:** The price at which a trader can buy a currency pair. This is the price at which market makers are willing to sell a particular currency pair.

4. **Spread**: The difference between the bid and ask price of a currency pair. It represents the transaction cost for entering or exiting a trade.
5. **Leverage**: The ability to control a large position in the market with a relatively small amount of capital. Leverage can amplify both profits and losses.
6. **Margin**: The amount of money required to open and maintain a leveraged position in the market. It acts as a security deposit for the trade.
7. **Lot**: A standardized unit of trading in Forex. Different types of lots include standard lots (100,000 units of the base currency), mini lots (10,000 units), and micro lots (1,000 units).
8. **Long Position**: A position taken by a trader when they expect the value of a currency pair to increase. In a long position, the base currency is bought, and the quote currency is sold.
9. **Short Position**: A position taken by a trader when they expect the value of a currency pair to decrease. In a short position, the base currency is sold, and the quote currency is bought.
10. **Stop-Loss Order**: An order placed by a trader to automatically close a position when the price reaches a certain level. It's used to limit potential losses.
11. **Take-Profit Order**: An order placed by a trader to automatically close a position when the price reaches a predefined level of profit. It's used to secure gains.
12. **Market Order**: An order to buy or sell a currency pair at the current market price. It's executed immediately.
13. **Limit Order**: An order to buy or sell a currency pair at a specified price or better. It's only executed when the market reaches the specified price.
14. **Entry Order**: An order to buy or sell a currency pair at a specific price in the future, which is different from the current market price.
15. **Currency Pair**: The combination of two currencies traded in the Forex market. The first currency is the base currency, and the second currency is the quote currency.
16. **Base Currency**: The first currency in a currency pair. It represents the unit of measure for the trade.
17. **Quote Currency**: The second currency in a currency pair. It's the currency in which the price of the base currency is quoted.
18. **Major Pairs**: The most traded currency pairs in the Forex market, including EUR/USD, USD/JPY, GBP/USD, and USD/CHF.
19. **Cross Currency Pair**: A currency pair that doesn't include the US dollar. For example, EUR/GBP or AUD/JPY.
20. **Exotic Currency Pair**: A currency pair that involves one major currency and one currency from a smaller or emerging economy.
21. **Central Bank**: The primary regulatory authority for a country's currency and monetary policy. Central banks play a significant role in influencing exchange rates.
22. **Interest Rate**: The cost of borrowing money, expressed as a percentage. Changes in interest rates can impact a currency's value.
23. **Fundamental Analysis**: A method of analyzing the Forex market based on economic indicators, central bank decisions, and geopolitical events.
24. **Technical Analysis**: An approach to analyzing the Forex market by studying historical price charts and using various technical indicators to predict future price movements.
25. **Risk Management**: Strategies and techniques used to minimize potential losses in trading, including position sizing, stop-loss orders, and diversification.
26. **Liquidity**: The ease with which an asset or security can be bought or sold in the market without causing a significant price change.
27. **Volatility**: The measure of how much the price of a currency pair fluctuates over a certain period. High volatility can lead to larger profit potential but also higher risk.
28. **Margin Call**: A notification from a broker to deposit additional funds into the trading account to maintain the required margin levels due to unfavorable market movements.
29. **Hedging**: A strategy used to protect against potential losses by opening a trade that counteracts the original position.

30. **Liquidity Provider**: An institution or individual that facilitates the buying and selling of financial instruments by providing constant bid and ask prices.

This glossary provides a solid foundation for understanding the terms and concepts commonly used in Forex trading. However, keep in mind that the Forex market is dynamic and continually evolving. Staying updated with the latest market developments and trends is essential for successful trading. Always practice due diligence, conduct thorough research, and consider seeking advice from financial professionals before making any trading decisions.

Appendix B: Recommended Resources

To further your understanding and proficiency in the world of Forex trading, it's crucial to tap into a wealth of knowledge and resources available. This appendix provides a curated list of books, websites, and tools that can serve as valuable guides for expanding your expertise and making informed trading decisions.

Books:

1. **"Trading in the Zone" by Mark Douglas**: This book focuses on the psychological aspects of trading and helps traders develop a disciplined and focused mindset essential for success.
2. **"Japanese Candlestick Charting Techniques" by Steve Nison**: A comprehensive guide to understanding candlestick chart patterns, a fundamental tool for technical analysis in Forex trading.
3. **"Technical Analysis of the Financial Markets" by John J. Murphy**: A comprehensive resource that covers a wide range of technical analysis tools and concepts used in trading various financial markets, including Forex.
4. **"Currency Trading for Dummies" by Kathleen Brooks and Brian Dolan**: A beginner-friendly guide that introduces the basics of Forex trading, from understanding currency pairs to developing trading strategies.
5. **"The Little Book of Currency Trading" by Kathy Lien**: This book provides insights into the Forex market, trading strategies, and risk management techniques suitable for both novice and experienced traders.

Websites:

1. **Investopedia Forex Section**: An excellent online resource offering comprehensive explanations of Forex terms, strategies, and concepts, suitable for traders of all levels.
2. **Babypips.com**: A popular website with a free online Forex trading course, ideal for beginners to learn the basics of Forex trading step by step.
3. **Forexlive.com**: This website provides up-to-date news, analysis, and commentary on the Forex market, helping traders stay informed about market-moving events.
4. **DailyFX**: A hub of research, analysis, and educational content created by FXCM, a leading Forex broker. It offers technical and fundamental analysis, as well as live webinars.
5. **TradingView**: A versatile platform that offers advanced charting tools, technical indicators, and a social community for traders to share ideas and insights.

Tools:

1. **MetaTrader 4 (MT4) or MetaTrader 5 (MT5)**: Widely used trading platforms offering charting tools, technical indicators, and automated trading capabilities.

2. **Forex Economic Calendar**: Websites like Forex Factory provide real-time economic event data, helping traders stay informed about key announcements that can impact the market.
3. **Pip Calculator**: An online tool that helps traders calculate the value of a pip in their chosen currency pair, crucial for position sizing and risk management.
4. **Position Size Calculator**: This tool assists traders in determining the appropriate position size based on their risk tolerance and account size.
5. **Forex Calendar Apps**: Mobile apps that provide economic calendar information and alerts on the go, allowing you to stay updated with market-moving events in real-time.
6. **Forex Risk Management Tools**: Various tools and calculators designed to help traders manage risk, calculate potential profits and losses, and set stop-loss levels.

As you delve deeper into Forex trading, remember that continuous learning and staying up-to-date with the latest market trends are essential. While these resources can provide valuable insights, always approach trading with caution and consider seeking advice from experienced professionals. Additionally, practice on demo accounts before venturing into live trading to gain hands-on experience without risking real capital.

Conclusion

As you come to the end of this guide, it's a perfect moment to reflect on the journey you've undertaken as a Forex trader. You've delved into a world of complex concepts, intricate strategies, and the ebb and flow of global financial markets. This newfound knowledge equips you with the tools to navigate the Forex landscape with confidence and insight. But remember, the path to mastery is an ongoing one, and your journey is far from over.

Reflecting on Your Progress as a Forex Trader

Take a moment to appreciate how far you've come. From the initial stages of understanding currency pairs and pips to exploring advanced concepts like technical analysis and risk management, you've demonstrated dedication and a thirst for knowledge. Reflect on the progress you've made and the skills you've acquired, as each step brings you closer to becoming a seasoned Forex trader.

Consider the trades you've executed, the lessons you've learned from both successes and setbacks, and the growth in your understanding of market dynamics. Keep a trading journal to document your experiences, strategies, and emotions during trades. This will not only help you track your progress but also provide invaluable insights into your trading style and areas for improvement.

Encouragement to Pursue Mastery and Success in the Forex Market

The Forex market is a dynamic and ever-changing environment. It rewards those who approach it with diligence, discipline, and a continuous thirst for improvement. As you move forward, remember these key points:

1. **Consistency is Key**: Successful trading is built on consistency. Stick to your trading plan, follow your strategies, and avoid impulsive decisions based on emotions.
2. **Continuous Learning**: The Forex market evolves, and so should your knowledge. Stay updated with market news, trends, and new trading strategies. Never stop learning.
3. **Risk Management**: Protecting your capital is paramount. Implement robust risk management strategies to safeguard your funds from excessive losses.
4. **Mindset Matters**: Trading psychology plays a crucial role. Develop emotional resilience, manage stress, and cultivate discipline to stay focused on your goals.

5. **Practice and Patience**: Mastery takes time. Practice on demo accounts, refine your strategies, and be patient with the learning curve.
6. **Adaptability**: Be ready to adapt to changing market conditions. Flexibility in your approach can make a significant difference in your trading success.
7. **Community and Mentorship**: Engage with fellow traders, join forums, and seek mentorship from experienced traders. Learning from others' experiences can accelerate your growth.

As you continue your journey in the Forex market, remember that success isn't solely measured by financial gains. It's also about the knowledge you acquire, the skills you develop, and the personal growth you experience along the way. Approach every trade as an opportunity to learn and improve, and let your passion for trading drive you toward mastery.

May your path in the Forex market be filled with excitement, growth, and ultimately, success. Keep your goals in sight and your determination unwavering, for the road to success is forged by those who are willing to invest the time, effort, and dedication it takes to master the art of Forex trading.

Options Trading:

A Comprehensive Crash Course for Successful Trading

Introduction

Welcome to the exciting world of options trading! In "Mastering Options: A Comprehensive Crash Course for Successful Trading," you're about to embark on a journey that will equip you with the skills, strategies, and mindset necessary to conquer the world of financial markets.

Options trading might sound intimidating at first, but fear not. This eBook has been meticulously crafted to guide you through every step of the process, starting from the very basics. Whether you're a complete novice or an experienced trader looking to sharpen your skills, you're about to gain insights that can potentially change your financial trajectory.

In the following chapters, we'll cover everything from the foundational concepts of options to the most advanced strategies used by professionals. Real-world examples will illustrate key points, ensuring that you not only understand the theory but can apply it in practical scenarios. We'll dive deep into risk management, psychological aspects of trading, and even explore the emerging realm of cryptocurrency options.

Remember, successful options trading isn't just about luck; it's about informed decision-making. So, whether your goal is to generate additional income, grow your investments, or simply gain a deeper understanding of financial markets, "Mastering Options" has got you covered.

Get ready to unleash your potential and embark on a transformative journey into the world of options trading. Let's dive in!

Chapter 1: Understanding the Basics of Options

Welcome to the foundation of your options trading journey. In this chapter, we'll demystify the fundamental concepts that underlie the world of options. Options are versatile financial instruments that give you the right, but not the obligation, to buy or sell an asset at a predetermined price within a specified timeframe. Let's dive in.

1.1 What Are Options? Options are contracts that provide you with the opportunity to control an underlying asset without actually owning it. There are two main types of options: calls and puts. A call option gives you the right to buy an asset at a predetermined price, while a put option gives you the right to sell an asset at a specific price.

1.2 Key Terminology Understanding the terminology is crucial to navigating options. Here are some essential terms:

- **Strike Price:** The price at which an option can be exercised.
- **Expiration Date:** The date by which the option must be exercised or it becomes void.
- **Premium:** The price you pay for an option contract.
- **In-the-Money (ITM):** A term used to describe an option that would be profitable if exercised immediately.
- **Out-of-the-Money (OTM):** An option that would not be profitable if exercised right now.
- **At-the-Money (ATM):** The strike price of the option is equal to the current market price of the underlying asset.

1.3 The Role of Options in Risk Management One of the primary benefits of options is their ability to manage risk. Imagine you own a portfolio of stocks and are concerned about a potential market downturn. By purchasing put options on those stocks, you can protect yourself from significant losses if the market does indeed drop. This technique is known as "hedging."

1.4 Leverage and Magnified Returns Options allow you to control a larger position with a smaller amount of capital compared to directly trading the underlying asset. This leverage can amplify your returns if the trade goes in your favor. However, it's important to note that leverage also increases potential losses.

1.5 The Options Market Options are traded on various exchanges, just like stocks. The options market provides a platform for investors and traders to buy and sell options contracts. This market liquidity ensures that you can enter and exit positions relatively easily.

1.6 Option Buyers vs. Option Sellers In the options market, there are two main participants: buyers and sellers. Option buyers pay a premium to acquire the right to exercise the option at a later date. Option sellers, also known as writers, receive the premium and take on the obligation to fulfill the contract if the option is exercised.

1.7 A Glimpse of Strategies While we'll delve into strategies in later chapters, it's worth noting that options can be used for various purposes. You can use them to speculate on price movements, generate income, or protect your investments. Strategies like covered calls, protective puts, and spreads are just a few examples of how options can be employed effectively.

By mastering the basics covered in this chapter, you're building a solid foundation for your options trading journey. Remember, options trading involves risks, but with the right knowledge and strategy, you can harness the potential they offer to achieve your financial goals. In the upcoming chapters, we'll dive deeper into the mechanics, strategies, and nuances of options trading to further empower you on this exciting path.

Chapter 2: Types of Options: Calls and Puts

Now that you have a firm grasp of the basics, it's time to explore the two main types of options: calls and puts. Each type has its unique characteristics and purposes within the world of options trading. In this chapter, we'll delve into the intricacies of calls and puts, empowering you to make informed decisions.

2.1 Call Options: Profiting from Price Increases A call option gives you the right, but not the obligation, to buy an underlying asset at a predetermined price (the strike price) before the expiration date. This option becomes valuable when the market price of the asset rises above the strike price. By purchasing a call option, you're essentially betting that the price of the underlying asset will increase.

2.2 Put Options: Profiting from Price Decreases On the flip side, a put option provides you with the right, but not the obligation, to sell an underlying asset at a specific price (the strike price) before the expiration date. Put options come into play when you anticipate that the market price of the asset will decline below the strike price. These options enable you to profit from falling prices.

2.3 Intrinsic Value and Time Value The price of an option is determined by its intrinsic value and time value. Intrinsic value is the difference between the current market price of the underlying asset and the option's strike price. For example, if a call option's strike price is $50, and the underlying asset's market price is $55, the call option has an intrinsic value of $5.

Time value, on the other hand, accounts for the potential future movements in the market. It reflects the probability that the option will gain additional value before expiration. The more time an option has until expiration, the higher its time value.

2.4 Options Expiration Cycles Options have different expiration cycles, typically categorized as monthly, quarterly, or weekly. The expiration date is a critical factor in options trading because it dictates the timeframe within which your option must be exercised. Understanding expiration cycles is essential for effective options trading.

2.5 Making the Choice: Calls or Puts? Choosing between call and put options depends on your market outlook. If you believe an asset's price will increase, a call option could be suitable.

Conversely, if you expect a price decrease, a put option might be more appropriate. Your choice should be based on thorough analysis and a clear understanding of your strategy.

2.6 Profiting from Calls and Puts To profit from call options, you can either exercise the option and buy the asset at the strike price or sell the option at a higher premium than what you paid. For put options, you can either exercise the option and sell the asset at the strike price or sell the option at a higher premium.

2.7 Combining Calls and Puts: Strategies Calls and puts can be combined in various ways to create complex strategies that suit different market conditions and trading objectives. Strategies like straddles, strangles, and collars involve using both call and put options to capitalize on potential price movements or to protect against adverse market conditions.

As you immerse yourself in the world of calls and puts, remember that each option type presents a multitude of opportunities and risks. By understanding their mechanics, you're laying the groundwork for crafting strategies that align with your trading goals. In the upcoming chapters, we'll explore option pricing, Greeks, and delve deeper into advanced strategies that leverage the power of calls and puts.

Chapter 3: Option Pricing and Greeks

As you progress on your options trading journey, understanding how options are priced and the role of the Greeks becomes crucial. In this chapter, we'll explore the intricacies of option pricing and the Greek variables that influence their values. By mastering these concepts, you'll gain insights that can significantly impact your trading decisions.

3.1 The Factors Affecting Option Prices Several factors influence the price of an option:

- **Underlying Asset Price:** As the asset's price changes, the option's value is likely to follow suit.

- **Strike Price:** The relationship between the asset's market price and the option's strike price affects its value.

- **Time to Expiration:** The longer the time to expiration, the higher the option's price due to the potential for price movements.

- **Volatility:** Increased volatility often leads to higher option prices, as it increases the likelihood of substantial price changes.

- **Interest Rates:** Interest rates impact option prices, particularly for longer-term options.

3.2 The Option Pricing Model: Black-Scholes Model The Black-Scholes model is a widely used mathematical formula for calculating the theoretical price of European-style options. It takes into account factors like the current stock price, strike price, time to expiration, volatility, and risk-free interest rate. While the model provides valuable insights, remember that real-world option prices may deviate due to various factors.

3.3 The Greeks: Measuring Sensitivity The Greek variables are measures that indicate how an option's price responds to changes in certain factors. Understanding these Greeks allows you to gauge the potential impact of market movements on your option positions. Let's explore the main Greeks:

- **Delta:** Delta measures the change in an option's price for a $1 change in the underlying asset's price. It ranges from 0 to 1 for calls and from -1 to 0 for puts. A delta of 0.5 means the option's price will increase by $0.50 for a $1 increase in the asset's price.

- **Gamma:** Gamma measures the change in delta for a $1 change in the underlying asset's price. It helps you assess how sensitive delta is to price movements.
- **Theta:** Theta represents the change in an option's price over time. It indicates the rate of time decay, meaning how much an option loses value as it approaches expiration.
- **Vega:** Vega gauges an option's sensitivity to changes in volatility. It measures how much the option's price changes for a 1% change in implied volatility.
- **Rho:** Rho measures an option's sensitivity to changes in interest rates. It indicates how much an option's price will change for a 1% change in the risk-free interest rate.

3.4 Practical Application of Greeks By understanding the Greeks, you can tailor your options trading strategies to align with your objectives and market conditions. For instance, if you're aiming for short-term gains, you might focus on options with high gamma to capitalize on rapid price movements.

3.5 Monitoring Greeks in Real-Time Several trading platforms provide real-time data on option Greeks. This enables you to stay informed about how changes in market conditions impact your option positions and make timely adjustments.

As you dive into option pricing and the world of Greeks, remember that these concepts are essential tools for effective options trading. By gauging how factors like volatility, time, and market movements impact option prices, you'll be better equipped to make informed decisions that can potentially enhance your trading success. In the upcoming chapters, we'll delve into the art of technical and fundamental analysis, helping you refine your trading strategies further.

Chapter 4: The Art of Technical Analysis in Options Trading

In the fast-paced world of options trading, technical analysis serves as a valuable compass, guiding traders to make well-informed decisions. This chapter delves into the art of technical analysis, helping you unlock patterns, trends, and signals that can steer your options trading journey toward success.

4.1 What is Technical Analysis? Technical analysis involves studying historical price and volume data to forecast future price movements. Traders use charts, indicators, and patterns to identify trends and potential turning points in the market.

4.2 The Power of Charts Charts are the foundation of technical analysis. They visually represent price movements over time, revealing patterns and trends. The most common types of charts are line charts, bar charts, and candlestick charts. Candlestick charts, in particular, offer a comprehensive view of price movements, including opening and closing prices as well as high and low points.

4.3 Key Concepts in Technical Analysis

- **Support and Resistance:** These levels indicate where an asset's price tends to stop or reverse direction. Support is where buying interest may emerge, preventing further price decline, while resistance is where selling pressure might slow down upward movements.
- **Trends:** Identifying trends is crucial. An uptrend consists of higher highs and higher lows, while a downtrend consists of lower highs and lower lows. A sideways or range-bound trend indicates price movements within a certain range.

4.4 Technical Indicators Indicators are mathematical calculations based on historical price and volume data. They help traders confirm trends, identify potential reversals, and generate signals. Popular indicators include Moving Averages, Relative Strength Index (RSI), and Moving Average Convergence Divergence (MACD).

4.5 Chart Patterns Chart patterns are formations that traders look for to predict potential price movements. Patterns like head and shoulders, double tops, and double bottoms offer insights into whether an asset's price might reverse or continue its current trend.

4.6 Applying Technical Analysis to Options Trading Technical analysis is particularly useful in options trading for timing entry and exit points. For example, if a stock is approaching a support level on a chart, this could be an opportune moment to consider purchasing call options, anticipating a potential price rebound.

4.7 The Limitations of Technical Analysis While technical analysis is a powerful tool, it's essential to recognize its limitations. It doesn't predict external events that might influence the market, such as economic reports or geopolitical developments. Combining technical analysis with fundamental analysis can provide a more comprehensive view of the market.

4.8 Embracing a Holistic Approach Successful options trading requires a holistic approach that combines technical analysis, fundamental analysis, and a solid understanding of options mechanics. Utilizing technical analysis as a complementary tool within your trading toolkit can significantly enhance your decision-making process.

As you immerse yourself in the art of technical analysis, remember that practice and experience are key to mastering this skill. By identifying patterns, recognizing trends, and understanding key indicators, you're equipping yourself to navigate the dynamic landscape of options trading with greater confidence and precision. In the upcoming chapters, we'll explore the role of fundamental analysis in shaping your options trading strategies.

Chapter 5: Fundamental Analysis and its Role in Options Trading

While technical analysis provides insights into price movements, fundamental analysis delves deeper into the factors that drive market dynamics. In this chapter, we'll explore the world of fundamental analysis and how it plays a vital role in shaping your options trading strategies.

5.1 Understanding Fundamental Analysis Fundamental analysis involves evaluating a company's financial health, industry trends, economic indicators, and other factors that can impact the value of an asset. This analysis helps traders make informed decisions by assessing the intrinsic value of an asset.

5.2 Key Components of Fundamental Analysis

- **Earnings Reports:** Analyzing a company's earnings reports and financial statements provides insights into its profitability, revenue growth, and expenses.
- **Industry Trends:** Understanding the broader industry trends and market conditions can help you gauge the potential for growth or decline.
- **Macroeconomic Indicators:** Factors like interest rates, inflation rates, and unemployment data can impact the overall market sentiment.
- **News and Events:** Geopolitical events, regulatory changes, and other news can have significant effects on asset prices.

5.3 The Role of Fundamental Analysis in Options Trading Fundamental analysis is particularly valuable when trading options on individual stocks. By evaluating a company's financial health and performance, you can make more informed decisions about which options strategies to employ.

5.4 Earnings Season and Implied Volatility During earnings season, companies release their earnings reports, which can lead to increased volatility. Options traders often use strategies like straddles and strangles to capitalize on potential price movements driven by earnings announcements.

5.5 Applying Fundamental Analysis to Options Strategies

- **Covered Calls:** If you're bullish on a stock and believe it will rise slightly, writing covered calls can generate income while potentially allowing you to profit from moderate price increases.

- **Protective Puts:** If you're concerned about potential price declines, buying protective puts can help safeguard your investment against losses.

- **Spread Strategies:** Fundamental analysis can influence your choice of strike prices and expiration dates when employing spread strategies like vertical spreads and butterflies.

5.6 A Holistic Approach Combining fundamental analysis with technical analysis can provide a well-rounded perspective on the market. While technical analysis helps you time your trades, fundamental analysis aids in understanding the underlying forces driving price movements.

5.7 Limitations of Fundamental Analysis It's important to recognize that even with thorough fundamental analysis, the market can be unpredictable. Unexpected news or events can lead to price movements that defy fundamental logic. As such, diversifying your trading strategies and managing risk remain essential.

5.8 The Continuous Learning Process Fundamental analysis is a skill that requires ongoing learning and adaptation. Staying up-to-date with industry news, economic indicators, and company performance is crucial to making informed decisions.

By incorporating fundamental analysis into your options trading toolkit, you're enhancing your ability to make strategic choices that align with both short-term price movements and long-term market trends. As you proceed to the next chapters, you'll discover advanced strategies that can leverage your understanding of both technical and fundamental analysis.

Chapter 6: Building a Solid Foundation: Options Trading Strategies for Beginners

Congratulations on reaching this point in your options trading journey! In this chapter, we'll focus on building a solid foundation by exploring options trading strategies tailored for beginners. These strategies will help you navigate the complexities of the options market while minimizing risks and maximizing potential rewards.

6.1 The Importance of Strategy Having a well-defined strategy is crucial in options trading. It guides your decision-making, helps manage risk, and sets clear objectives. As a beginner, it's advisable to start with strategies that are relatively straightforward and provide a good balance between risk and potential profit.

6.2 Strategy 1: Covered Call A covered call is an excellent starting point for beginners. In this strategy, you own the underlying stock and sell a call option against it. This generates premium income while potentially allowing you to profit from a moderate increase in the stock's price. If the stock's price remains stagnant or decreases slightly, you still retain the premium received.

6.3 Strategy 2: Protective Put A protective put strategy is ideal for safeguarding your investments against potential downside risks. If you own a stock and are concerned about a potential price decline, buying a put option gives you the right to sell the stock at a predetermined price. This strategy limits your potential losses while allowing you to participate in any potential upside movement.

6.4 Strategy 3: Long Call and Long Put As a beginner, you can also explore long call and long put options. A long call provides the right to buy an asset at a specified price, while a long put provides the right to sell an asset at a predetermined price. These strategies offer limited risk and can be used to speculate on price movements.

6.5 Strategy 4: Bullish and Bearish Vertical Spreads Vertical spreads involve simultaneously buying and selling call or put options with the same expiration date but different strike prices. Bullish vertical spreads, such as bull call spreads, are employed when you anticipate a moderate upward price movement. Conversely, bearish vertical spreads, like bear put spreads, are used for potential downward price movements.

6.6 Strategy 5: Cash-Secured Put A cash-secured put strategy is another beginner-friendly approach. It involves selling a put option and setting aside enough cash to cover the potential purchase of the underlying asset. If the option is exercised, you acquire the asset at the strike price, reducing your cost basis.

6.7 Diversification and Risk Management While exploring these strategies, remember the importance of diversification and risk management. Avoid putting all your capital into a single strategy or asset. Instead, spread your investments across different strategies and assets to mitigate potential losses.

6.8 Practice and Education Options trading is a skill that improves with practice and education. As you implement these beginner strategies, continue learning and staying updated on market trends. Consider using paper trading or virtual platforms to practice without risking real capital.

By mastering these foundational options trading strategies, you're laying the groundwork for a successful trading journey. As you gain experience and confidence, you'll be well-equipped to explore more advanced strategies and tailor your approach to align with your trading goals. In the upcoming chapters, we'll delve deeper into specific strategies and techniques that can amplify your options trading prowess.

Chapter 7: Unleashing the Power of Covered Calls and Protective Puts

In this chapter, we delve into two powerful options trading strategies: covered calls and protective puts. These strategies provide a balanced approach for both generating income and managing risk. By mastering these techniques, you can enhance your options trading arsenal and navigate the market with greater confidence.

7.1 Covered Calls: Generating Income Covered calls are a versatile strategy that involves selling call options against stocks you own. This strategy is suitable when you have a neutral to slightly bullish outlook on the underlying stock. By selling call options, you generate premium income, which can supplement your returns and reduce the effective cost basis of your stock.

7.2 The Covered Call Process

1. Choose a stock you own and are willing to sell at a higher price.
2. Sell a call option with a strike price above the current stock price.
3. Receive the premium from selling the call option.
4. If the stock's price remains below the strike price by expiration, you keep the premium and the stock. If the stock rises above the strike price, it might be called away from you.

7.3 Protective Puts: Hedging Against Downside Risk Protective puts are a risk management strategy that involves buying put options to safeguard your portfolio against potential price declines. This strategy is particularly useful when you're concerned about short-term market volatility or specific events that might impact the stock's value.

7.4 The Protective Put Process

1. Own a stock and be concerned about its potential decline.
2. Buy a put option with a strike price below the current stock price.
3. Pay the premium for the put option.
4. If the stock's price decreases, the put option's value increases, offsetting some of the losses in your stock portfolio.

7.5 The Income-Risk Tradeoff Both covered calls and protective puts involve an income-risk tradeoff. Covered calls provide income but limit potential upside gains if the stock's price rises significantly. Protective puts provide downside protection but come with the cost of the put option premium.

7.6 Combining Covered Calls and Protective Puts Advanced traders often combine covered calls and protective puts to create a collar strategy. In a collar, you sell a covered call to generate income and use some of that income to buy a protective put, limiting potential losses. This strategy can provide a more balanced risk-reward profile.

7.7 The Psychology of Covered Calls and Protective Puts Understanding the psychological aspects of these strategies is vital. Covered calls can help manage emotional biases by locking in profits at predetermined levels. Protective puts alleviate the fear of sudden price drops by providing a safety net.

7.8 Tailoring Strategies to Market Conditions Knowing when to employ covered calls or protective puts depends on your market outlook. During bullish or neutral markets, covered calls can be effective. In uncertain or bearish markets, protective puts offer peace of mind.

By mastering the art of covered calls and protective puts, you're enhancing your ability to generate income and protect your investments in a dynamic market. Remember that both strategies require careful analysis, risk management, and a clear understanding of your objectives. As you proceed to the next chapters, you'll explore more advanced strategies that leverage the potential of options trading.

Chapter 8: Going Beyond: Advanced Options Strategies

In this chapter, we take a leap into the world of advanced options trading strategies. These strategies offer more complex ways to leverage options' flexibility and potential. While they may require a deeper understanding, they also present opportunities for greater rewards. Let's explore some of the sophisticated techniques that experienced traders utilize.

8.1 Strategy 1: Straddles and Strangles Straddles and strangles are volatility-based strategies used when anticipating significant price movements. A straddle involves buying both a call and a put option with the same strike price and expiration. A strangle involves buying a call and a put with different strike prices but the same expiration. These strategies can profit from substantial price swings in either direction.

8.2 Strategy 2: Iron Condors Iron condors are neutral strategies that thrive when the underlying asset's price remains within a specific range. This strategy involves simultaneously selling an out-of-the-money call and an out-of-the-money put, while also buying a further out-of-the-money call and put. The goal is to benefit from time decay and decreased volatility.

8.3 Strategy 3: Butterfly Spreads Butterfly spreads are low-risk, limited-reward strategies used when you anticipate minimal price movement. This strategy involves buying one lower strike option, selling two options at the middle strike, and buying one higher strike option. The potential profit is capped, but so is the potential loss.

8.4 Strategy 4: Calendar Spreads Calendar spreads, also known as time spreads or horizontal spreads, capitalize on differences in expiration dates. This strategy involves simultaneously buying and selling options of the same type but with different expiration dates. Calendar spreads aim to profit from time decay while minimizing the impact of price movements.

8.5 Strategy 5: Ratio Spreads Ratio spreads are used when you expect a substantial price movement, but you're unsure about the direction. This strategy involves buying and selling a different number of options to create an imbalance. Ratio spreads can result in unlimited potential gains in one direction, with limited losses in the other.

8.6 Strategy 6: Synthetic Positions Synthetic positions replicate the behavior of other trading instruments using options. A synthetic long call, for instance, involves buying a call option and selling a put option at the same strike price. This mimic owning the underlying stock while requiring less capital.

8.7 Strategy 7: Diagonal Spreads Diagonal spreads combine elements of vertical and horizontal spreads. They involve buying and selling options with different strike prices and expiration dates. These strategies are used to capitalize on both price movement and time decay.

8.8 The Importance of Advanced Strategy Selection Advanced strategies offer greater potential rewards, but they also come with increased complexity and risk. It's essential to select strategies that align with your market outlook, risk tolerance, and level of expertise. Conduct thorough analysis and consider paper trading before implementing advanced strategies with real capital.

By expanding your options trading toolkit with advanced strategies, you're taking a step toward harnessing the full potential of options. Remember that these techniques require in-depth knowledge, precise execution, and a thorough understanding of how different factors interact. As you progress through the next chapters, you'll explore strategies that leverage specific market conditions and trading objectives.

Chapter 9: Mastering Volatility: Straddles, Strangles, and Iron Condors

Volatility is a key driver in options trading, and in this chapter, we'll explore strategies specifically designed to capitalize on volatility fluctuations. These strategies include straddles, strangles, and iron condors, which provide unique ways to navigate uncertain market conditions and potentially profit from price swings.

9.1 Strategy 1: Long Straddle A long straddle involves simultaneously buying a call option and a put option with the same strike price and expiration date. This strategy thrives on significant price movements, regardless of direction. If the price moves dramatically, one leg of the straddle becomes profitable, potentially offsetting the loss on the other leg.

9.2 Strategy 2: Long Strangle Similar to a straddle, a long strangle involves buying a call option and a put option, but with different strike prices. This strategy is suited for traders who anticipate substantial price movement but aren't certain about the direction. A long strangle can be less expensive than a long straddle but still capitalizes on volatility.

9.3 Strategy 3: Iron Condor The iron condor strategy combines elements of both bullish and bearish strategies. It's a neutral strategy employed when you anticipate the underlying asset's price will remain within a specific range. This involves selling an out-of-the-money call and an out-of-the-money put while simultaneously buying a further out-of-the-money call and put.

9.4 Managing Volatility Risk While these strategies benefit from volatility, it's essential to manage the risks associated with sudden and extreme price movements. Setting stop-loss orders and monitoring your positions closely can help protect against unexpected losses.

9.5 Analyzing Implied Volatility Implied volatility is a crucial factor when employing volatility-based strategies. High implied volatility often leads to higher option premiums, providing more potential profit. Conversely, low implied volatility may result in lower premiums but reduced risk.

9.6 Earnings and News Events Earnings announcements and significant news events can lead to rapid changes in implied volatility. Many traders use volatility strategies, like straddles and strangles, to capitalize on the uncertainty surrounding such events.

9.7 Strategy Selection and Execution Choosing the appropriate strategy depends on your market outlook, risk tolerance, and understanding of the underlying asset. Effective execution involves timing your entry and exit points based on expected volatility changes.

9.8 Continuous Learning and Adaptation Mastering volatility-based strategies is an ongoing process. As market conditions change, your approach may need adjustment. Stay informed about market trends, economic indicators, and significant news events that can impact volatility.

By honing your skills in volatility-based strategies, you're equipping yourself with valuable tools to navigate the ever-changing landscape of options trading. These strategies allow you to leverage volatility to your advantage, potentially generating profits even in uncertain markets. As you move forward, the next chapters will delve into more advanced techniques and specialized approaches to options trading.

Chapter 10: Advanced Spreads: Butterflies, Calendars, and Ratios

In this chapter, we venture further into advanced options trading strategies with a focus on spreads: butterflies, calendars, and ratios. These strategies offer intricate ways to leverage market conditions and potential price movements. By mastering these techniques, you'll expand your trading toolkit and be better prepared to seize opportunities in a dynamic market.

10.1 Strategy 1: Butterfly Spreads Butterfly spreads are low-risk, limited-reward strategies used when you expect minimal price movement in the underlying asset. This strategy involves buying one lower strike option, selling two options at the middle strike, and buying one higher strike option. The potential profit is capped, but so is the potential loss.

10.2 Strategy 2: Calendar Spreads Also known as time spreads or horizontal spreads, calendar spreads profit from time decay differences between short-term and long-term options. This strategy involves simultaneously buying and selling options of the same type but with different expiration dates. Calendar spreads aim to profit from time decay while minimizing the impact of price movements.

10.3 Strategy 3: Ratio Spreads Ratio spreads are designed for when you anticipate significant price movement but are unsure about the direction. This strategy involves buying and selling a different number of options to create an imbalance. Ratio spreads can result in unlimited potential gains in one direction, with limited losses in the other.

10.4 Tailoring Strategies to Market Conditions Understanding market conditions is crucial when employing advanced spreads. Butterfly spreads are ideal for low volatility environments, while ratio spreads are suited for volatile markets. Calendar spreads are effective when you anticipate minimal price movement.

10.5 Risk Management and Adjustment Advanced spreads offer unique risk-reward profiles. Proper risk management involves sizing your positions appropriately and having a plan in place for potential adjustments. Monitoring your positions and reacting to changing market conditions is key to success.

10.6 Analyzing Potential Payoffs Before executing advanced spread strategies, use option analysis tools to visualize potential payoffs under various scenarios. This can help you assess risk, reward, and break-even points.

10.7 Paper Trading and Education Given the complexity of advanced spread strategies, consider practicing with paper trading or virtual platforms before using real capital. Continuous education and staying updated on market trends are essential to mastering these techniques.

10.8 Building a Diversified Portfolio Advanced spreads are valuable components of a diversified options trading portfolio. By mastering these strategies, you're adding tools that allow you to navigate a variety of market conditions effectively.

By immersing yourself in advanced spread strategies, you're expanding your options trading capabilities to capture potential opportunities in various market scenarios. Remember that these techniques require precision, understanding of market conditions, and the ability to adjust your positions when necessary. As you progress, the next chapters will delve deeper into specialized strategies and techniques that can elevate your options trading prowess even further.

Chapter 11: The Art of Technical and Fundamental Analysis in Options Trading

In this chapter, we delve into the synergy between technical and fundamental analysis within options trading. These two analytical approaches, when combined, provide a comprehensive understanding of market dynamics. By mastering the art of blending technical and fundamental analysis, you'll enhance your ability to make well-informed trading decisions.

11.1 The Complementary Nature of Analysis Technical analysis focuses on price patterns, trends, and indicators, while fundamental analysis delves into economic indicators, earnings reports, and industry trends. Combining these approaches allows you to assess both short-term price movements and the underlying factors driving them.

11.2 Strategy Selection Based on Analysis When employing both types of analysis, your strategy selection becomes more nuanced. Technical analysis can help you time entry and exit points, while fundamental analysis guides you in selecting underlying assets with strong growth potential.

11.3 Case Study: Earnings Season Approach During earnings season, fundamental analysis helps you identify companies with potential earnings surprises. Technical analysis aids in identifying optimal entry points for options strategies like straddles and strangles to capitalize on expected volatility.

11.4 Strategy Refinement through Technical Analysis Technical analysis can refine fundamental analysis-driven strategies. For example, if fundamental analysis indicates a bullish outlook, technical analysis can help you pinpoint optimal entry points by identifying support levels.

11.5 Risk Management Through Both Approaches While fundamental analysis helps you understand potential market catalysts, technical analysis assists in setting stop-loss orders and managing risk in real-time.

11.6 Real-world Application Suppose you're considering trading options on a company that is fundamentally strong but experiencing short-term price volatility. By using technical analysis, you can time your options trades to capitalize on price fluctuations while benefiting from the company's long-term growth prospects.

11.7 Holistic Approach to Market Conditions The combination of technical and fundamental analysis equips you to navigate various market conditions. During uncertain times, fundamental analysis provides insights into long-term trends, while technical analysis aids in identifying short-term trading opportunities.

11.8 Continual Learning and Adaptation Both technical and fundamental analysis are skills that require continuous learning and adaptation. As markets evolve and new data emerges, staying informed is essential for effective analysis.

By mastering the art of blending technical and fundamental analysis, you're elevating your options trading to a sophisticated level. This approach provides a multi-dimensional view of the market, allowing you to seize opportunities while minimizing risks. As you proceed to the next chapters, you'll delve into specialized strategies that leverage specific market conditions and advanced trading techniques.

Chapter 12: Volatility Trading: VIX, Volatility Products, and Strategies

In this chapter, we delve deep into volatility trading, exploring the VIX index, volatility products, and strategies that can harness volatility to your advantage. Volatility is a powerful force in the options market, and by understanding its dynamics and utilizing specialized strategies, you can unlock unique opportunities for profit.

12.1 Understanding Volatility Volatility is a measure of price fluctuations in the market. High volatility indicates larger price swings, while low volatility signifies relatively stable prices. Traders can profit from volatility by correctly predicting its future levels.

12.2 The VIX Index The VIX index, often referred to as the "fear index," measures market expectations for future volatility. It represents investors' sentiments regarding potential market turmoil. Traders use the VIX to gauge market risk and anticipate price movements.

12.3 Trading Volatility with VIX You can't directly trade the VIX index, but there are derivative products based on it, such as VIX futures and options. These products allow you to speculate on future volatility levels.

12.4 Volatility Products and Strategies

- **VIX Futures:** These contracts allow you to bet on the future direction of the VIX index. If you anticipate increased market volatility, you might buy VIX futures.

- **VIX Options:** Similar to VIX futures, VIX options enable you to speculate on the direction of market volatility. Calls are used when you expect higher volatility, while puts are used when you expect lower volatility.

- **Volatility ETFs:** Exchange-traded funds (ETFs) like VXX and XIV aim to replicate the performance of VIX futures. These ETFs can be used to profit from changes in volatility levels.

12.5 Strategies for Trading Volatility

- **Long Volatility Strategies:** If you expect increased market turmoil, consider long volatility strategies using VIX options or futures.

- **Short Volatility Strategies:** Selling volatility is also a viable strategy. However, it requires careful risk management, as the potential losses can be significant during extreme market events.

- **VIX Calendar Spreads:** These spreads involve buying and selling VIX options with different expiration dates. They allow you to profit from changes in the VIX term structure.

12.6 Navigating Complexities Trading volatility can be complex and risky. It's essential to thoroughly understand the products and strategies involved, and to start small while gaining experience.

12.7 Monitoring Market Events Volatility can spike due to various events, such as economic data releases, geopolitical tensions, or unexpected news. Stay informed and be prepared to adjust your strategies accordingly.

12.8 Simulating and Practicing Given the intricacies of volatility trading, consider using simulation platforms or paper trading before committing real capital. This approach allows you to grasp the nuances without exposing yourself to excessive risk.

By mastering volatility trading, you're gaining a unique skill set that can yield significant rewards. Remember that volatility can be unpredictable, and risk management is paramount. As you move forward, the next chapters will delve into specialized strategies and techniques that can further enhance your options trading expertise.

Chapter 13: Leveraging Market Trends: Trend Following and Contrarian Strategies

In this chapter, we explore two distinct yet equally powerful options trading strategies: trend following and contrarian strategies. These approaches capitalize on market trends and sentiment, offering unique ways to navigate various market conditions and potentially generate profits.

13.1 Strategy 1: Trend Following Trend following strategies involve identifying and trading in the direction of the prevailing market trend. These strategies assume that existing trends are likely to continue.

13.2 Identifying Trends Trends can be bullish (upward), bearish (downward), or even sideways (range-bound). Traders use technical indicators, moving averages, and chart patterns to identify trends and confirm their strength.

13.3 Trend Following with Options Options can be used to complement trend following strategies. For example, buying call options can amplify profits during an upward trend, while buying put options can protect against losses during a downward trend.

13.4 Strategy 2: Contrarian Approach Contrarian strategies involve going against the prevailing market sentiment. These strategies assume that markets are prone to overreacting and that turning points can be identified when sentiment reaches extremes.

13.5 Gauging Sentiment Extremes Contrarian traders use indicators like the Relative Strength Index (RSI) and the Put/Call ratio to gauge sentiment extremes. High RSI values or extremely high put/call ratios might signal an overbought market, suggesting a potential reversal.

13.6 Using Options for Contrarian Plays Options provide a flexible toolkit for contrarian strategies. Buying put options can profit from downward reversals, while selling covered calls can capitalize on short-term pullbacks.

13.7 Tailoring Strategies to Market Conditions Both trend following and contrarian strategies require adapting to market conditions. Trend following works best in strongly trending markets, while contrarian strategies shine during periods of excessive sentiment.

13.8 Combining Trend Following and Contrarian Approaches Experienced traders often blend both approaches to achieve a well-rounded strategy. They may use trend following during stable trends and contrarian strategies to capitalize on sentiment-driven price reversals.

13.9 Embracing Flexibility and Risk Management Both strategies require flexibility and robust risk management. Avoid becoming too dogmatic and be prepared to adjust your strategies based on changing market dynamics.

By mastering both trend following and contrarian strategies, you're equipping yourself with versatile tools to navigate various market scenarios. Remember that each strategy has its strengths and limitations, and understanding when to employ them is key to successful implementation. As you progress to the next chapters, you'll delve into more specialized techniques and advanced approaches to options trading.

Chapter 14: Advanced Income Strategies: Credit Spreads and Iron Condors

In this chapter, we delve into advanced income-generating strategies: credit spreads and iron condors. These strategies offer unique ways to generate consistent returns by capitalizing on time decay and specific market conditions. By mastering these techniques, you'll add valuable tools to your options trading repertoire.

14.1 Strategy 1: Credit Spreads Credit spreads involve simultaneously selling and buying options to create a net credit. These strategies thrive on time decay and limited price movement.

14.2 The Bull Put Spread A bull put spread is a type of credit spread used when you expect a moderate price increase or a stable market. It involves selling a put option with a higher strike price and buying a put option with a lower strike price.

14.3 The Bear Call Spread A bear call spread is employed when you anticipate a moderate price decline or a relatively stable market. It involves selling a call option with a lower strike price and buying a call option with a higher strike price.

14.4 Strategy 2: Iron Condors Iron condors are advanced strategies that combine credit spreads to profit from range-bound markets. They thrive on low volatility and time decay.

14.5 Building an Iron Condor An iron condor involves selling an out-of-the-money call spread and an out-of-the-money put spread simultaneously. This creates a range within which you profit from time decay.

14.6 Managing Risk in Credit Spreads and Iron Condors While these strategies offer limited risk, it's crucial to manage risk by setting appropriate stop-loss levels and monitoring your positions regularly.

14.7 Adapting to Changing Market Conditions Both credit spreads and iron condors require adjustments based on market movements. Be prepared to roll your positions, close them early, or adjust strike prices as needed.

14.8 Consistency and Patience Income strategies like credit spreads and iron condors focus on consistent, smaller returns over time. Patience is key, as you'll generate income through repeated, well-executed trades.

14.9 Simulating and Practicing Before deploying real capital, consider practicing credit spreads and iron condors through simulation platforms or paper trading. This allows you to refine your skills and strategies without risking money.

By mastering credit spreads and iron condors, you're gaining strategies that can generate consistent income while managing risk. Remember that these strategies require precision in execution, risk management, and an understanding of market conditions. As you proceed to the next chapters, you'll delve into specialized strategies and techniques that can further elevate your options trading expertise.

Chapter 15: Leveraging Market Events: Earnings, Dividends, and Corporate Actions

In this chapter, we explore how to leverage specific market events like earnings releases, dividends, and corporate actions for strategic options trading. These events create unique opportunities and challenges, and by understanding their impact and employing specialized strategies, you can capitalize on them effectively.

15.1 Earnings Season Strategies Earnings releases can lead to significant price movements. Traders often use options strategies to position themselves for potential volatility and capitalize on the uncertainty surrounding these events.

15.2 Strategy 1: Straddles and Strangles Straddles and strangles are popular strategies during earnings season. They involve buying both call and put options to profit from substantial price movements in either direction.

15.3 Strategy 2: Iron Condors Iron condors can be used during earnings releases when you expect limited price movement. Selling an iron condor allows you to profit from time decay as long as the stock remains within a specific range.

15.4 Dividend Capture Strategies Dividend-paying stocks can present opportunities for options traders to capture dividends while minimizing risk.

15.5 Strategy 3: Covered Calls Selling covered calls on dividend-paying stocks before the ex-dividend date allows you to generate premium income while potentially capturing the dividend.

15.6 Strategy 4: Cash-Secured Puts Selling cash-secured puts on stocks you want to own can allow you to generate income while potentially acquiring the stock at a lower price.

15.7 Corporate Actions and Special Situations Corporate events like mergers, acquisitions, and spin-offs can lead to price fluctuations and uncertainty. Options strategies can help manage risk and capitalize on potential opportunities.

15.8 Strategy 5: Merger Arbitrage Merger arbitrage involves taking positions in both the target and acquiring companies' stocks to profit from the price discrepancy that arises during the merger process.

15.9 Strategy 6: Protective Puts When uncertainty surrounds a corporate event, buying protective puts can help hedge against potential losses while still participating in any upside movement.

15.10 Timing and Research Proper timing and thorough research are crucial when trading around market events. Anticipate event dates, understand the potential impact, and have a clear strategy in place.

15.11 Risk Management in Event-Driven Trading Trading around market events can be risky due to heightened volatility. Implement strict risk management techniques, such as position sizing and stop-loss orders.

15.12 Continuous Learning and Adaptation Market events are dynamic, and their impact can change over time. Stay informed, continuously learn from past experiences, and adapt your strategies accordingly.

By mastering strategies that leverage market events, you're adding a dynamic dimension to your options trading toolbox. These strategies allow you to capture unique opportunities and manage risk effectively. As you proceed to the next chapters, you'll explore even more specialized techniques and advanced trading approaches that can further enhance your options trading expertise.

Chapter 16: Advanced Hedging Techniques: Collars, Protective Puts, and More

In this chapter, we delve into advanced hedging techniques, focusing on collars, protective puts, and other strategies designed to mitigate risk and protect your investments. These techniques are essential for safeguarding your portfolio against potential market downturns and unexpected events.

16.1 The Importance of Risk Management Risk management is a cornerstone of successful options trading. Advanced hedging strategies provide a layer of protection, allowing you to manage risk and limit potential losses.

16.2 Strategy 1: Collars Collars involve combining covered calls and protective puts to create a balanced risk-reward profile. They're suitable when you want to protect your stock holdings while still participating in potential upside movements.

16.3 Building a Collar To build a collar, sell a call option against stocks you own and use the premium received to buy a protective put. The call option's premium offsets the put option's cost, providing a cost-effective hedge.

16.4 Strategy 2: Protective Puts Protective puts, discussed earlier, involve buying put options to hedge against potential downside risk. They're particularly useful when you own stocks and anticipate market volatility.

16.5 Strategy 3: Married Put Strategy The married put strategy involves buying put options for stocks you already own. This creates a protective hedge, ensuring that your portfolio remains profitable even if the stock's value declines.

16.6 Strategy 4: Long Collateral Put A long collateral put strategy combines buying put options with owning an underlying stock. It's a less expensive alternative to protective puts, as the put option's premium is partially covered by selling out-of-the-money call options.

16.7 Diversification and Allocation Hedging strategies work best when combined with a well-diversified portfolio. Allocate a portion of your capital to protective strategies while maintaining exposure to potential growth.

16.8 Monitoring and Adjusting Hedges Hedging is an ongoing process. Continuously monitor your positions and adjust your hedges as market conditions evolve or unexpected events occur.

16.9 Accepting Trade-offs Hedging strategies often come with trade-offs. While they protect against downside risk, they can limit potential gains during bullish market conditions.

16.10 Risk-Return Balance Striking a balance between risk and return is key in hedging strategies. Consider your risk tolerance, investment goals, and the overall market outlook when implementing these techniques.

By mastering advanced hedging techniques, you're fortifying your options trading approach with tools to safeguard your investments and navigate uncertain market conditions. Remember that hedging involves careful planning, risk assessment, and continuous monitoring. As you proceed to the final chapters, you'll explore specialized strategies and techniques that can elevate your options trading expertise even further.

Chapter 17: Answering the Top 30 Questions in Options Trading

In this chapter, we address the most common questions that traders often have about options trading. By providing clear and concise answers, we aim to demystify the complexities of options and equip you with the knowledge you need to make informed decisions.

17.1 What are Options? Options are financial derivatives that give you the right, but not the obligation, to buy or sell an underlying asset at a predetermined price within a specified time frame.

17.2 How Do Options Work? Options work by granting the holder the flexibility to profit from price movements in the underlying asset without owning it.

17.3 What Are Call Options? Call options give the holder the right to buy the underlying asset at a predetermined price (strike price) before the option's expiration.

17.4 What Are Put Options? Put options give the holder the right to sell the underlying asset at a predetermined price (strike price) before the option's expiration.

17.5 What Is the Premium of an Option? The premium is the price paid to purchase an option and represents the intrinsic value and time value of the option.

17.6 What Is Time Decay? Time decay refers to the gradual reduction of an option's time value as it approaches its expiration date.

17.7 What Are In-the-Money, At-the-Money, and Out-of-the-Money Options? In-the-money options have intrinsic value, at-the-money options have a strike price equal to the current asset price, and out-of-the-money options have no intrinsic value.

17.8 What Is Implied Volatility? Implied volatility reflects market expectations of future price volatility and is a crucial factor in determining option premiums.

17.9 What Are Option Greeks? Option Greeks (Delta, Gamma, Theta, Vega, and Rho) quantify the factors that influence an option's price and risk exposure.

17.10 How Can I Manage Risk in Options Trading? Risk management involves position sizing, setting stop-loss orders, and diversification to protect against potential losses.

17.11 What Are Options Spreads? Options spreads involve simultaneously buying and selling multiple options to create unique risk-reward profiles.

17.12 How Do I Choose an Options Trading Strategy? Strategy selection depends on your market outlook, risk tolerance, and trading objectives. Consider factors like volatility, time frame, and asset type.

17.13 What Are the Benefits of Options Trading? Options provide flexibility, leverage, and the ability to profit from various market conditions, including sideways markets.

17.14 What Are the Risks of Options Trading? Options trading involves potential loss of capital, leverage risk, and the complexity of understanding various strategies.

17.15 Can I Trade Options with a Small Account? Yes, you can trade options with a small account, but risk management and proper strategy selection are crucial.

17.16 How Do I Start Trading Options? Start by educating yourself, understanding basic concepts, and practicing on paper trading platforms before committing real capital.

17.17 Can I Trade Options on Different Assets? Yes, options are available on various assets, including stocks, indices, commodities, and currencies.

17.18 How Do I Execute an Options Trade? Options trades can be executed through brokerage platforms, where you select the option contract, specify the quantity, and choose order type.

17.19 What Are Some Common Mistakes to Avoid in Options Trading? Avoid trading without a clear strategy, over-leveraging, and neglecting risk management.

17.20 How Can I Learn More About Options Trading? Continuously educate yourself through books, online courses, webinars, and by following experienced traders.

17.21 Can I Make a Living from Options Trading? While some traders make a living from options trading, it requires extensive knowledge, experience, and disciplined risk management.

17.22 Should I Use Technical or Fundamental Analysis for Options Trading? A combination of both technical and fundamental analysis provides a comprehensive view of market dynamics.

17.23 How Do I Choose an Options Broker? Select a broker with a user-friendly platform, competitive fees, educational resources, and reliable customer support.

17.24 How Do Taxes Work in Options Trading? Options trading can have tax implications. Consult a tax professional to understand how options trading affects your tax situation.

17.25 What Are Expiration Dates and Strike Prices? Expiration dates are when options contracts expire, while strike prices are the predetermined prices at which options can be exercised.

17.26 Can I Roll Over or Close Options Positions Before Expiration? Yes, you can roll over options positions to a later expiration or close positions before expiration to lock in profits or limit losses.

17.27 How Do Market Events Affect Options Prices? Market events like earnings releases, economic data releases, and geopolitical developments can impact options prices and volatility.

17.28 Can I Trade Options on Margin? Yes, many brokers allow you to trade options on margin, but be cautious and understand the risks associated with margin trading.

17.29 What Are Weekly and Monthly Options? Weekly options expire within a week, while monthly options expire at the end of each month. They offer traders more flexibility in terms of time frames.

17.30 How Do I Stay Updated on Market Trends and News? Stay informed through financial news, market analysis, economic calendars, and by following reputable financial sources.

By addressing these top 30 questions, we aim to provide a comprehensive understanding of options trading and empower you to navigate the world of options with confidence. Remember that continuous learning, practice, and staying informed are key to becoming a successful options trader. As you progress to the final chapter, you'll explore more advanced strategies and techniques that can further elevate your options trading skills.

Chapter 18: Mastering Advanced Strategies: Combining Techniques for Success

In this final chapter, we delve into advanced strategies that combine multiple techniques to achieve specific trading objectives. These strategies leverage the breadth of your options trading knowledge to create powerful approaches for different market scenarios.

18.1 Strategy 1: The Ratio Butterfly Spread The ratio butterfly spread combines elements of a butterfly spread and a ratio spread. It involves selling one or more options at a higher strike and buying two or more options at lower strikes. This strategy allows for both bullish and bearish positioning.

18.2 Strategy 2: The Calendar Iron Condor This strategy combines elements of a calendar spread and an iron condor. It involves selling near-term options and buying longer-term options to create a range. The calendar iron condor aims to capitalize on time decay while benefiting from limited volatility.

18.3 Strategy 3: The Synthetic Straddle The synthetic straddle combines long or short stock positions with options to mimic the payoff of a straddle strategy. It's a versatile approach that allows you to profit from significant price movements while controlling risk.

18.4 Strategy 4: The Diagonal Spread The diagonal spread involves buying and selling options with different expiration dates and strike prices. It's a strategy that aims to capture both time decay and potential price movements.

18.5 Strategy 5: The Risk Reversal The risk reversal strategy involves simultaneously buying a call option and selling a put option to create a synthetic long position. It's a bullish strategy that allows you to benefit from upward price movements while minimizing risk.

18.6 Strategy 6: The Iron Albatross The iron albatross is a more complex variation of the iron condor. It involves selling wider spreads and higher premium options to collect more credit. This strategy aims to generate substantial income while managing risk.

18.7 Strategy 7: The Jade Lizard The jade lizard strategy combines a bear call spread with a naked put option sale. It's designed to profit from a stock trading in a specific range while generating income.

18.8 Strategy 8: The Double Calendar Spread The double calendar spread involves using two calendar spreads with different strike prices and expiration dates. This strategy capitalizes on time decay and can profit from range-bound markets.

18.9 Crafting Custom Strategies Advanced traders often tailor their strategies to specific market conditions, combining elements from different approaches to suit their outlook and risk tolerance.

18.10 The Path to Mastery Becoming proficient in advanced strategies requires continuous learning, practice, and real-world experience. Experiment with different combinations to find what works best for your trading style.

By mastering these advanced strategies that combine various techniques, you're taking your options trading skills to the pinnacle of expertise. These strategies showcase the flexibility and complexity that options trading can offer, allowing you to adapt to a wide range of market scenarios. Remember that experience, discipline, and a deep understanding of market dynamics are essential as you navigate the complex world of advanced options trading. Good luck on your journey towards becoming a seasoned and successful options trader!

Conclusion: Unveiling the World of Options Trading Mastery

Congratulations on completing this comprehensive journey through the world of options trading mastery. You've embarked on a path that takes you from the fundamentals to the advanced, equipping you with the knowledge and skills to navigate the dynamic landscape of the financial markets.

Throughout this book, you've explored the foundational concepts of options, from understanding the basics of calls and puts to grasping the nuances of option pricing, volatility, and risk management. You've delved into a plethora of strategies, from covered calls and protective puts to advanced techniques like iron condors and synthetic straddles.

By now, you comprehend how market events, earnings releases, dividends, and corporate actions impact options trading, and you've gained insight into blending technical and fundamental analysis to make informed decisions. Moreover, you're familiar with techniques for hedging, managing risk, and crafting customized strategies to suit various market conditions.

Remember that options trading is both an art and a science. It demands continuous learning, disciplined practice, and a vigilant approach to risk management. With this mastery of options trading, you have the power to profit from bullish, bearish, and neutral market scenarios, leveraging a versatile toolkit to navigate opportunities and challenges alike.

As you move forward in your options trading journey, always stay curious, stay updated, and stay adaptive. The financial markets are ever-evolving, and your ability to synthesize information, analyze trends, and make informed decisions will define your success.

Whether you're looking to generate income, hedge your investments, or seek out substantial gains, the skills you've honed within these pages will serve as your compass. May your ventures into the world of options trading be both prosperous and enlightening. Embrace the complexity, refine your strategies, and trust in your abilities to make wise and profitable choices.

Best of luck on your path to becoming a seasoned options trader. The markets await your expertise, and the possibilities are as limitless as your dedication to mastering this intricate art.

Swing Trading

Strategies for Profiting from Short- to Medium-Term Price Movements

Introduction: Embarking on the Swing Trader's Odyssey

Welcome to the exhilarating world of swing trading, where fortunes are made, opportunities abound, and the markets pulse with potential. If you've ever felt the pull of financial markets, the excitement of making calculated moves, and the desire to leverage your skills to achieve financial success, then you've embarked on a journey that promises to be both enriching and transformative.

In the pages of this book, you will explore the intricacies of swing trading, a trading style that targets short- to medium-term price movements, holding positions for a few days to weeks. As a swing trader, you're not merely a participant in the markets – you're a strategist, an analyst, and a decision-maker. Your canvas is the chart, your tools are analysis techniques, and your paintbrush is the trade execution that turns potential into profit.

The world of swing trading is a dynamic realm that marries technical precision with intuitive finesse. Here, understanding market trends, recognizing patterns, and deciphering the nuances of price action are the skills that separate the successful from the merely hopeful. But swing trading is not just about numbers on a screen; it's about mastering your emotions, refining your strategies, and developing a mindset that thrives in the face of uncertainty.

With optimism as your guide and technical prowess as your weapon, you're about to embark on an odyssey that will introduce you to the art and science of swing trading. From the foundational concepts to advanced techniques, from risk management to fundamental analysis, and from psychology to strategy development, you'll navigate a comprehensive landscape designed to equip you with the tools and knowledge needed to thrive in the markets.

As you turn each page, remember that you're not just reading – you're preparing for action. The journey you're about to undertake is not one of mere theory; it's an immersive experience that will challenge your intellect, ignite your curiosity, and set you on a path of continual learning and growth. Whether you're a novice eager to grasp the basics or an experienced trader seeking to refine your approach, this book aims to be your trusted guide, delivering insights, strategies, and perspectives that resonate with the pulse of the markets.

So, fasten your seatbelt, adjust your mindset, and open your mind to the possibilities that await you. The world of swing trading is yours to explore, and as you set foot on this odyssey, remember that with dedication, perseverance, and the right knowledge, you have the power to transform your aspirations into tangible success. Your swing trader's odyssey begins now.

Chapter 1: Swing Trading Fundamentals

Welcome to the exciting world of swing trading, where you'll discover the art of capitalizing on short- to medium-term price movements. In this chapter, we'll lay the foundation for your swing trading journey by exploring the core concepts and fundamental principles that will guide you towards success.

❋ **Understanding Swing Trading**: Swing trading is a strategy that takes advantage of price swings within a larger trend. Unlike day trading, which requires constant monitoring, swing trading allows for a more balanced approach, making it suitable for those with busy schedules.

📊 **The Power of Timeframes**: Swing trading typically involves holding positions for a few days to weeks, focusing on timeframes ranging from daily to weekly charts. This longer time horizon enables you to capture substantial price movements while avoiding the noise of intraday fluctuations.

📝 **Trends and Corrections**: A fundamental aspect of swing trading is identifying trends and corrections within the broader market movement. Trends represent the prevailing direction of price movement, while corrections are temporary reversals against the trend. Understanding how to differentiate between these phases is crucial for making informed trading decisions.

🔍 **Technical Analysis Primer**: At the heart of swing trading is technical analysis – the practice of using historical price data and chart patterns to forecast future price movements. Dive into key technical analysis tools such as moving averages, support and resistance levels, and trendlines. These tools provide you with insights into potential entry and exit points.

📇 **Chart Patterns Overview**: Learn to interpret common chart patterns like head and shoulders, double tops, and triangles. These patterns often signal potential trend reversals or continuations, guiding your decisions on when to enter or exit a trade.

📊 **Indicators for Swing Traders**: Discover a variety of technical indicators that aid swing traders in assessing market momentum, strength, and potential trend changes. From Relative Strength Index (RSI) to Moving Average Convergence Divergence (MACD), these tools are your allies in deciphering market behavior.

◉ **The Psychology of Swing Trading**: Develop a resilient trading mindset by understanding the psychological challenges that come with swing trading. Patience, discipline, and the ability to manage emotions are essential traits for successful swing traders.

📋 **Risk and Reward Ratio**: Effective risk management is the bedrock of swing trading. Learn how to calculate and maintain a favorable risk-to-reward ratio to ensure that potential losses are outweighed by potential gains.

🚀 **Creating Your Trading Plan**: As you embark on your swing trading journey, a well-defined trading plan is your compass. Craft a plan that aligns with your financial goals, risk tolerance, and trading preferences.

💭 **Visualizing Success**: Envision your future success as a swing trader. By setting clear goals and visualizing your achievements, you'll be motivated to stick to your trading plan, even during challenging times.

Embark on Your Swing Trading Odyssey: You've taken your first step towards mastering the art of swing trading. With a solid grasp of the fundamental concepts and principles outlined in this chapter, you're ready to dive deeper into the intricacies of technical analysis, chart patterns, and risk management. As you move forward, remember that optimism, dedication, and a hunger for knowledge will be your guiding lights on this rewarding journey to financial independence.

Chapter 2: Building Your Trading Plan

Congratulations on completing the first step of your swing trading journey! In this chapter, we delve into the essential process of creating a comprehensive trading plan that will serve as your roadmap to success. A well-structured trading plan provides you with a strategic framework to navigate the dynamic world of swing trading with confidence and purpose.

📊 **Defining Your Trading Goals**: Every successful swing trader begins with a clear sense of purpose. Identify your short-term and long-term financial goals, whether it's achieving consistent gains, supplementing your income, or even transitioning to full-time trading.

📇 **Choosing Your Trading Style**: Swing trading offers a range of styles, each with its own advantages and challenges. Decide whether you're more inclined towards trend following, counter-trend trading, or a hybrid approach that suits your personality and risk tolerance.

📅 **Setting Your Time Commitment**: Determine how much time you can dedicate to swing trading. Are you a part-time trader or can you commit more hours? Your available time will influence your trading frequency and the timeframes you focus on.

🛡 **Defining Risk Tolerance**: Understanding and defining your risk tolerance is a crucial aspect of your trading plan. How much are you willing to risk on each trade? Your risk tolerance should be aligned with your overall financial situation and comfort level.

📊 **Selecting Markets and Instruments**: Explore the variety of markets and instruments available for swing trading, such as stocks, forex, commodities, and cryptocurrencies. Choose the ones that resonate with your expertise and interests.

📈 **Analyzing Market Conditions**: Develop a process for evaluating market conditions. Consider factors like market volatility, economic events, and global trends that might impact your trades.

📇 **Entry and Exit Strategies**: Define the criteria that will trigger your entry and exit from trades. Will you rely on specific chart patterns, technical indicators, or a combination of both? Having a clear strategy minimizes emotional decision-making.

🗻 **Managing Trade Sizes**: Determine how much capital you'll allocate to each trade. By allocating a consistent percentage of your capital, you ensure that a single trade won't overly impact your overall portfolio.

🗓 **Creating a Trading Routine**: Structure your trading routine around your defined goals and available time. Develop a schedule that includes research, analysis, trade execution, and regular reviews of your trades.

📊 **Record Keeping and Analysis**: Keep meticulous records of your trades, including entry and exit points, reasons for the trade, and outcomes. Regularly review these records to identify patterns, strengths, and areas for improvement.

🌑 **Adapting and Evolving**: A trading plan is a living document. Markets change, and your plan should adapt accordingly. Be open to refining your strategies, learning from your experiences, and staying up-to-date with market trends.

Empower Your Journey with a Solid Plan: Armed with a well-constructed trading plan, you're equipped to navigate the complexities of swing trading with confidence. This plan isn't just a set of rules; it's your guiding philosophy that will help you weather market fluctuations, make informed decisions, and ultimately, achieve your financial aspirations. As you continue your journey, remember that the dedication you invest in your trading plan will pave the way for your future success.

Chapter 3: Technical Analysis Essentials

Welcome to the heart of swing trading: technical analysis. In this chapter, you'll delve into the core tools and techniques that enable you to decode the language of price charts. By understanding these essentials, you'll gain the ability to identify trends, patterns, and potential entry and exit points with precision.

📈 **Charting Basics**: Learn to read price charts, the visual representation of a market's historical price movement. Discover how to interpret different types of charts, including line charts, bar charts, and candlestick charts.

📊 **Support and Resistance**: Explore the concepts of support and resistance, which are key levels where price tends to stall or reverse. Recognizing these levels helps you anticipate potential turning points in the market.

📈 **Trendlines**: Uncover the power of trendlines in identifying the direction of a trend and potential trend reversals. Learn to draw trendlines accurately and use them as visual guides for your trading decisions.

🔍 **Moving Averages**: Dive into moving averages, which smooth out price data to reveal the underlying trend. Explore various types of moving averages and their applications in swing trading.

📊 **Relative Strength Index (RSI)**: Understand RSI, a popular momentum oscillator, which helps you gauge the strength of price movements and identify potential overbought or oversold conditions.

☑️ **Moving Average Convergence Divergence (MACD)**: Explore the MACD indicator, which combines moving averages to highlight changes in momentum. Learn how to interpret MACD crossovers and divergence patterns.

📊 **Fibonacci Retracements**: Discover the power of Fibonacci retracement levels in identifying potential support and resistance zones based on mathematical ratios derived from the Fibonacci sequence.

☑️ **Bollinger Bands**: Delve into Bollinger Bands, volatility-based indicators that provide insights into price volatility and potential trend reversals.

📊 **Volume Analysis**: Learn to interpret trading volume, which can confirm or negate the validity of price movements. Volume analysis can provide valuable clues about the strength of a trend.

☑️ **Candlestick Patterns**: Unlock the language of candlestick patterns, which convey a wealth of information about price movements and potential reversals. Explore patterns like Doji, Hammer, and Engulfing.

⚫ **Combining Technical Tools**: Understand how to integrate multiple technical indicators and tools to confirm signals and make well-informed trading decisions.

📚 **Practice Makes Perfect**: Embrace the process of practicing technical analysis on historical charts. This hands-on experience will refine your skills and intuition, making you a more confident and effective swing trader.

Empower Your Analysis with Technical Mastery: The knowledge and skills you acquire in this chapter will be your compass in the world of swing trading. Technical analysis empowers you to decipher the intricate patterns of the market and anticipate price movements. As you continue your journey, remember that each chart tells a story – and with your technical expertise, you'll be equipped to decipher that story and make strategic decisions that have the potential to reap substantial rewards.

Chapter 4: Candlestick Patterns for Swing Traders

Welcome to the fascinating realm of candlestick patterns, where price movements are beautifully captured in visual forms. In this chapter, you'll learn to decode the language of candlesticks, unlocking insights into market sentiment and potential trend reversals. By mastering these patterns, you'll elevate your swing trading strategies to new heights.

🕯️ **The Anatomy of Candlesticks**: Understand the components of a candlestick – the body, wick (or shadow), and tail. Each element conveys specific information about price movements during a given time period.

🔍 **Basic Candlestick Patterns**: Dive into foundational candlestick patterns such as Doji, Hammer, Shooting Star, and Spinning Top. These patterns offer valuable clues about market indecision, potential reversals, and trend continuations.

☑️ **Bullish Reversal Patterns**: Explore patterns like the Morning Star and Bullish Engulfing, which signal potential trend reversals from bearish to bullish.

📉 **Bearish Reversal Patterns**: Learn about patterns like the Evening Star and Bearish Engulfing, which indicate possible trend reversals from bullish to bearish.

🔮 **Continuation Patterns**: Discover candlestick patterns that suggest the continuation of an existing trend, such as the Rising Three Methods and Falling Three Methods.

❇️ **Combining Candlestick Patterns**: Understand how to combine different candlestick patterns with other technical indicators to enhance the accuracy of your trading signals.

📖 **Real-Life Examples**: Delve into real-life charts that showcase the application of candlestick patterns. These examples offer insights into the practical use of these patterns in making trading decisions.

📈 **Trading Strategies with Candlesticks**: Develop effective trading strategies that leverage candlestick patterns. Understand when to enter or exit trades based on the appearance of specific patterns.

📊 **Pattern Recognition**: Train your eye to recognize candlestick patterns quickly and accurately. Pattern recognition is a skill that improves with practice and experience.

📉 **Limitations and Caveats**: While candlestick patterns offer valuable insights, they are not foolproof indicators. Understand the limitations of relying solely on candlesticks and incorporate them within a broader trading framework.

🔮 **Mastering the Art of Observation**: Candlestick patterns are like whispers from the market, revealing hidden truths and potential opportunities. As you immerse yourself in the study of these patterns, you'll develop the ability to observe the language of price movement and react with precision.

Illuminate Your Path with Candlestick Mastery: By mastering candlestick patterns, you're not just analyzing price data – you're deciphering the emotions and psychology of market participants. Armed with this knowledge, you'll have the power to make well-timed trades, seizing opportunities that align with the intricate dance of the markets. As you continue your journey, remember that each candlestick tells a story, and you're the storyteller who interprets its meaning with expertise and finesse.

Chapter 5: Identifying Trend Reversals

Welcome to the realm of trend reversals, where the winds of market sentiment shift and new opportunities emerge. In this chapter, you'll dive into the art of recognizing potential trend reversals, a skill that can lead to substantial profits in swing trading. By understanding the signs of impending shifts, you'll position yourself to make timely and informed trading decisions.

📈 **Understanding Trend Reversals**: Gain insight into the factors that drive trend reversals, such as shifts in supply and demand, changes in market sentiment, and the impact of news and events.

📊 **Signs of Reversal**: Explore the key signs that may indicate a trend reversal is on the horizon. These signs include changes in price patterns, shifts in trading volume, and the appearance of specific candlestick formations.

🔍 **Double Tops and Bottoms**: Dive into the world of double tops and bottoms, common reversal patterns characterized by two price peaks (or valleys). Learn to identify these patterns and the potential implications for future price movements.

☑ **Head and Shoulders Patterns**: Uncover the secrets of head and shoulders patterns – a visual representation of shifts from bullish to bearish trends, or vice versa. Understand the significance of neckline breaks in confirming these patterns.

📊 **Rounding Tops and Bottoms**: Explore rounding tops and bottoms, patterns that indicate gradual changes in market sentiment. Learn how to distinguish between rounding formations and other price patterns.

☑ **Recognizing Divergence**: Understand the concept of divergence, where the direction of an indicator diverges from the direction of price movement. Divergence can signal potential trend reversals and offer valuable insights.

📊 **Using Oscillators for Reversal Signals**: Discover how to use momentum oscillators like RSI and MACD to identify potential trend reversals. Oscillators can offer valuable confirmation of reversal signals.

☑ **Volume Confirmation**: Explore the role of trading volume in confirming potential trend reversals. Analyze how volume patterns can provide insights into the strength of a reversal signal.

⏺ **The Art of Patience and Timing**: Recognizing trend reversals requires patience and precision. Learn how to time your entries and exits effectively to maximize your profits while minimizing your risks.

✴ **Empowering Your Trading Arsenal**: The ability to identify trend reversals is like having a compass that guides you through the ever-changing landscape of the market. By mastering this skill, you'll be able to anticipate shifts in market sentiment and position yourself to capitalize on emerging opportunities. As you continue your journey, remember that each reversal is a potential turning point towards greater success in your swing trading endeavors.

Chapter 6: Momentum Trading Strategies

Step into the exhilarating world of momentum trading, where you'll learn to ride the waves of price movements with precision and confidence. In this chapter, we'll explore dynamic strategies that leverage market momentum to potentially unlock substantial gains. By harnessing the power of momentum, you'll position yourself to seize opportunities as they unfold.

☑ **Understanding Market Momentum**: Gain a deep understanding of market momentum – the force that propels price movements in a certain direction. Learn to distinguish between trending and ranging markets and identify potential breakout points.

💧 **Breakout Trading Strategy**: Explore the art of breakout trading, where you'll discover how to identify key levels of support and resistance and anticipate significant price movements as they breach these levels.

📊 **Moving Average Crossovers**: Delve into moving average crossovers, a classic momentum trading strategy. Learn to interpret the signals generated by the intersection of short-term and long-term moving averages.

☑ **RSI Momentum Strategy**: Uncover how to use the Relative Strength Index (RSI) to identify overbought and oversold conditions. Discover how RSI can be a valuable tool in assessing the strength of momentum.

📊 **MACD Histogram Strategy**: Learn how to use the MACD histogram to gauge momentum shifts. Understand how the histogram's peaks and valleys can signal potential buying or selling opportunities.

📈 **Trendline Break Strategy**: Master the technique of trading trendline breaks. Learn to identify trendlines that are about to be breached, indicating potential changes in momentum and trend direction.

📊 **Volatility Bands Strategy**: Explore the application of volatility bands, such as Bollinger Bands, in momentum trading. Discover how these bands can help you identify periods of heightened price movement and potential breakouts.

📈 **Divergence and Convergence**: Learn to recognize divergence and convergence between price and momentum indicators. Understand how these patterns can signal potential reversals and continuations.

🗿 **Risk Management in Momentum Trading**: Understand the importance of risk management in momentum trading. Learn how to set stop-loss orders, position sizes, and risk-to-reward ratios to protect your capital.

💥 **Riding the Momentum Wave**: Momentum trading allows you to capture the excitement of rapidly changing markets and capitalize on strong price trends. By incorporating these strategies into your arsenal, you'll be equipped to align with market momentum and make swift, well-informed trading decisions. As you continue your journey, remember that momentum is the wind beneath your wings, propelling you toward greater heights of success in the dynamic world of swing trading.

Chapter 7: Support and Resistance Strategies

Welcome to the realm of support and resistance, where market dynamics collide and opportunities arise. In this chapter, you'll uncover the power of these foundational concepts and learn how to craft effective trading strategies that capitalize on these key levels. By mastering support and resistance, you'll gain the ability to navigate market fluctuations with confidence.

📊 **Understanding Support and Resistance**: Dive into the core principles of support and resistance, where historical price levels act as barriers to price movement. Learn how these levels are established and how they can influence future price action.

📈 **Support Turned Resistance and Vice Versa**: Explore the phenomenon of support turning into resistance and resistance turning into support. Understand the implications of these shifts in market sentiment.

🔍 **Horizontal Support and Resistance**: Learn to identify horizontal support and resistance levels – price levels where price tends to stall or reverse due to historical significance.

📈 **Trendline Support and Resistance**: Delve into the world of trendline support and resistance. Discover how trendlines can act as dynamic barriers that guide price movement within trend channels.

🗿 **Trading Strategies with Support and Resistance**: Explore various trading strategies that leverage support and resistance levels. Learn how to enter and exit trades based on breakouts, bounces, and price reactions at these levels.

📊 **Role Reversal Strategy**: Understand the role reversal strategy, where a breached support level becomes a potential resistance level, and vice versa. This strategy allows you to anticipate potential turning points.

📈 **Bounce and Break Strategy**: Master the art of bounce and break strategies. Learn when to enter trades based on price bouncing off support or breaking through resistance.

📊 **Moving Averages and Support/Resistance**: Explore how moving averages can intersect with support and resistance levels, providing additional confirmation for potential trading opportunities.

☑️ **Candlestick Patterns at Key Levels**: Discover how candlestick patterns can provide insights into potential reversals or continuations at support and resistance levels.

⚖️ **Balancing Risk and Reward**: Understand how to manage risk when trading support and resistance levels. Learn to set stop-loss orders, position sizes, and risk-to-reward ratios to safeguard your capital.

❈ **Navigating the Path of Support and Resistance**: Support and resistance are the pillars upon which market movements are built. By mastering these concepts and implementing effective strategies, you'll be equipped to identify key turning points, make informed decisions, and ride the waves of market dynamics with optimism. As you continue your journey, remember that each level of support and resistance is a stepping stone towards greater success in your swing trading endeavors.

Chapter 8: Pattern Recognition Techniques

Welcome to the fascinating world of pattern recognition, where the art of observation meets the science of trading. In this chapter, you'll delve into various chart patterns that offer valuable insights into market dynamics. By honing your pattern recognition skills, you'll gain the ability to anticipate potential price movements and make informed trading decisions.

☑️ **Understanding Chart Patterns**: Gain a solid understanding of chart patterns – visual formations that provide clues about potential future price movements. Learn to recognize both continuation and reversal patterns.

🔍 **Continuation Patterns**: Explore continuation patterns like flags, pennants, and rectangles. Understand how these patterns signify brief pauses in price movement before the prevailing trend continues.

☑️ **Triangle Patterns**: Delve into ascending, descending, and symmetrical triangle patterns. Learn to identify the potential implications of triangle formations in terms of future price direction.

🔍 **Wedge Patterns**: Understand rising and falling wedge patterns, which resemble triangles but have distinct characteristics. Learn to interpret wedge patterns as potential signals for trend continuation or reversal.

☑️ **Flag and Pennant Patterns**: Uncover the secrets of flag and pennant patterns – short-term continuation patterns that often appear after strong price movements. Learn to interpret their significance in terms of potential breakout or breakdown scenarios.

🔍 **Rectangle Patterns**: Explore the dynamics of rectangle patterns, where price movements consolidate within horizontal boundaries. Understand how rectangle patterns can provide insights into future price movements.

☑️ **Cup and Handle Patterns**: Dive into the art of recognizing cup and handle patterns – bullish formations that often precede significant price movements. Learn to identify the components of these patterns and interpret their potential implications.

🔍 **Widening and Symmetrical Triangles**: Discover the characteristics of widening and symmetrical triangle patterns. Understand how these patterns can provide insights into changes in market sentiment and potential breakouts.

📈 **Applying Patterns in Trading**: Learn how to apply your pattern recognition skills to trading strategies. Understand when to enter or exit trades based on the appearance of specific chart patterns.

🗿 **Practice and Refinement**: Pattern recognition is a skill that improves with practice and experience. Dive into historical charts, study real-time market movements, and train your eyes to spot patterns quickly and accurately.

💥 **Unlocking Insights through Patterns**: Chart patterns are like puzzle pieces that, when assembled, reveal the future potential of price movements. By mastering pattern recognition, you're equipped to anticipate market dynamics and align your strategies accordingly. As you continue your journey, remember that each pattern holds a clue to potential profits, and your ability to decode these clues will be your compass in the vast sea of trading opportunities.

Chapter 9: Risk Management Strategies

Welcome to the cornerstone of successful trading: risk management. In this chapter, you'll embark on a journey to understand and implement strategies that protect your capital, minimize losses, and ensure sustainable growth. By mastering risk management, you'll fortify your trading foundation and position yourself for long-term success in the dynamic world of swing trading.

🔒 **Understanding Risk and Reward**: Gain a comprehensive understanding of the relationship between risk and reward. Learn how to strike a balance that allows you to maximize potential profits while minimizing potential losses.

⚖️ **Setting Stop-Loss Orders**: Explore the importance of setting stop-loss orders – predetermined price levels that trigger an automatic exit from a trade. Understand how stop-loss orders shield your capital from significant losses.

📊 **Position Sizing Strategies**: Discover various position sizing techniques, such as fixed-dollar risk and percentage-based risk. Learn how to allocate an appropriate portion of your capital to each trade.

📈 **Risk-to-Reward Ratios**: Understand the concept of risk-to-reward ratios and how they influence your trading decisions. Learn how to set favorable risk-to-reward ratios that align with your trading strategy.

🔍 **Diversification**: Explore the value of diversifying your trading portfolio. Learn how trading across different markets or instruments can mitigate risks associated with single-trade failures.

🗄️ **Correlation Analysis**: Dive into correlation analysis – the study of how different assets move in relation to each other. Understand how correlation can help you manage risk by avoiding overexposure to similar assets.

⏰ **Time Management**: Learn the importance of managing your time effectively as a swing trader. Avoid overtrading and burnout by setting dedicated trading hours and adhering to a disciplined routine.

🗃️ **Capital Preservation**: Discover the significance of capital preservation as a fundamental goal of risk management. Understand how protecting your capital lays the foundation for sustainable growth over time.

🗿 **Mindset and Risk**: Understand the psychological aspects of risk management. Develop a mindset that allows you to stick to your risk management strategies, even in the face of emotional pressures.

❖ **Safeguarding Your Journey with Risk Management**: Risk management is your shield against the unpredictable nature of the markets. By implementing these strategies, you're not just protecting your capital – you're setting the stage for long-term success and growth. As you continue your journey, remember that each trade is a calculated step toward your goals, and your ability to manage risk will be the cornerstone of your achievements in the exhilarating world of swing trading.

Chapter 10: Psychology of Swing Trading

Welcome to the inner realm of swing trading – the psychology that drives your decisions and shapes your outcomes. In this chapter, you'll delve into the intricate world of emotions, discipline, and mindset management. By understanding and mastering the psychology of trading, you'll elevate your trading journey to a new level of success.

⬤ **Understanding Trader Psychology**: Gain insight into the psychological factors that influence your trading decisions. Learn about common cognitive biases and emotional reactions that can impact your trading outcomes.

◐ **Emotional Balance**: Explore the importance of emotional balance in swing trading. Understand how fear and greed can cloud your judgment and learn techniques to manage these emotions effectively.

💡 **Trading Discipline**: Discover the power of discipline in trading. Learn how to stick to your trading plan, execute your strategies consistently, and avoid impulsive decisions driven by emotions.

🔋 **Patience and Timing**: Understand the role of patience in swing trading. Learn to wait for ideal setups and opportunities instead of rushing into trades out of FOMO (Fear of Missing Out).

📑 **Learning from Losses**: Embrace losses as learning opportunities. Understand how analyzing and learning from your losses can help you refine your strategies and avoid repeating the same mistakes.

⬢ **Mindfulness and Self-Awareness**: Develop mindfulness and self-awareness as essential tools for managing emotions. Learn how to recognize emotional triggers and practice techniques to remain focused and grounded.

⚙ **Adapting to Changing Markets**: Embrace the reality that markets evolve, and strategies that once worked might become less effective. Develop the flexibility to adapt your approach to changing market conditions.

❖ **Positive Mindset and Trading Success**: Your mindset can be your most potent asset or your greatest liability. By cultivating a positive mindset, practicing emotional control, and nurturing discipline, you set the stage for consistent success in your swing trading journey.

⬤ **Master Your Mind for Market Mastery**: The psychology of trading is the internal engine that propels your external results. By mastering your mind, emotions, and reactions, you're not just becoming a better trader – you're becoming a master of the market, capable of navigating its twists and turns with wisdom and resilience. As you continue your journey, remember that your mindset is the compass that guides you toward the bright horizon of trading success.

Chapter 11: Trade Management Techniques

Welcome to the art of trade management – where decisions made after entering a trade can significantly impact your outcomes. In this chapter, you'll explore techniques that help you manage trades effectively, from optimizing entry and exit points to adjusting positions as market conditions evolve. By mastering trade management, you'll enhance your ability to capture profits and mitigate potential losses.

📊 **Optimal Entry and Exit Strategies**: Dive into the nuances of entry and exit strategies. Learn how to identify optimal entry points that align with your trading plan and how to exit trades at the right time to secure profits.

📈 **Trailing Stop Losses**: Explore the concept of trailing stop losses – dynamic orders that automatically adjust as the price moves in your favor. Learn how trailing stop losses lock in profits while allowing room for further gains.

📊 **Scaling In and Out**: Understand the technique of scaling in and out of trades. Learn how to enter or exit positions incrementally, allowing you to manage risk and capture gains in stages.

📈 **Partial Profit Taking**: Explore the strategy of taking partial profits. Learn how to secure a portion of your gains while allowing the remaining position to potentially capture larger moves.

📊 **Averaging Down vs. Cutting Losses**: Delve into the decision-making process of averaging down (buying more of an asset as its price drops) versus cutting losses (exiting a losing trade). Understand the implications of each approach.

📈 **News and Event Management**: Learn how to manage trades in the face of news and events that can impact the market. Develop strategies to handle volatility and unexpected price movements.

📊 **Adapting to Market Conditions**: Explore techniques for adjusting your trading strategies based on changing market conditions. Learn when to be more conservative or aggressive based on volatility and trend strength.

📈 **Review and Analysis**: Understand the importance of reviewing and analyzing your trades. Learn how regular self-assessment can help you identify patterns, strengths, and areas for improvement.

💭 **The Art of Adaptation**: Trade management is about more than just executing orders – it's about adapting to the ever-changing landscape of the market. By mastering these techniques, you're equipped to navigate the dynamic nature of trading with agility and precision.

✨ **Nurturing Your Trades to Success**: Effective trade management is the bridge between entering a trade and realizing its potential. By implementing these strategies, you're not just managing trades – you're nurturing them toward success. As you continue your journey, remember that each trade is an opportunity to demonstrate your mastery of market dynamics and your ability to turn potential into profit.

Chapter 12: Backtesting and Strategy Development

Welcome to the laboratory of trading – where ideas are tested, refined, and transformed into strategies that have the potential to yield profits. In this chapter, you'll learn the art of backtesting and strategy development, enabling you to create robust trading approaches based on historical data. By mastering these techniques, you'll elevate your trading game to a new level of sophistication.

🔍 **Understanding Backtesting**: Gain insight into the concept of backtesting – the process of applying your trading strategy to historical price data to assess its potential effectiveness.

📈 **Selecting Historical Data**: Learn how to choose relevant historical data for backtesting. Understand the importance of including various market conditions to ensure the reliability of your results.

🔍 **Creating Trading Rules**: Develop clear and precise trading rules for your strategy. Define entry and exit criteria, risk management parameters, and any additional filters or conditions.

📈 **Backtesting Platforms and Tools**: Explore backtesting platforms and tools that facilitate the process. Learn to use software that can simulate trades, track performance, and generate useful data.

🔍 **Interpreting Results**: Understand how to interpret backtesting results. Analyze metrics such as win rate, risk-to-reward ratio, drawdown, and overall profitability.

📈 **Strategy Optimization**: Learn the art of strategy optimization – refining your rules based on backtesting results. Discover how to tweak parameters for better performance without overfitting.

🔍 **Risk of Overfitting**: Explore the risk of overfitting – creating a strategy that performs exceptionally well on historical data but fails in real-world trading due to its lack of adaptability.

📈 **Paper Trading and Forward Testing**: Transition from backtesting to paper trading and forward testing. Learn how to test your strategy in real time with simulated trades before committing real capital.

🎮 **Evolving Your Trading Arsenal**: Backtesting and strategy development are the playgrounds where your ideas transform into powerful trading strategies. By mastering these techniques, you're not just trading – you're innovating, adapting, and evolving your approach to the markets.

✳️ **From Idea to Execution: Your Trading Odyssey**: Backtesting and strategy development are the bridges that connect your ideas to real-world profitability. By refining your strategies through these processes, you're turning possibilities into probabilities and aligning your actions with market dynamics. As you continue your journey, remember that each strategy is a testament to your ingenuity, and your ability to create and adapt will be your compass through the ever-evolving landscape of trading opportunities.

Chapter 13: Trading Psychology Revisited: Overcoming Challenges

Welcome back to the heart of your trading journey – the psychology that fuels your actions and shapes your results. In this chapter, you'll revisit the intricacies of trading psychology, delving deeper into the challenges you may face and learning techniques to overcome them. By mastering your mind, you'll enhance your resilience and adaptability in the face of market fluctuations.

💭 **Emotional Resilience**: Explore techniques to build emotional resilience – the ability to bounce back from losses and setbacks. Learn how to cultivate a mindset that thrives in the face of challenges.

🎭 **Managing Fear and Greed**: Revisit the primal forces of fear and greed that can impact your decisions. Understand how to recognize their influence and mitigate their effects on your trading.

⚖️ **Avoiding Revenge Trading**: Learn to avoid revenge trading – the impulse to recoup losses quickly by making impulsive trades. Develop strategies to regain composure and rational decision-making.

🎭 **Dealing with FOMO**: Understand how the Fear of Missing Out (FOMO) can lead to hasty decisions and losses. Learn techniques to manage FOMO and make disciplined choices.

📉 **Handling Drawdowns**: Explore strategies to handle drawdowns – periods of losses that are a natural part of trading. Learn how to maintain your confidence and discipline during these times.

💡 **Adapting to Changing Market Conditions**: Understand the psychological challenges of adapting to changing market conditions. Learn how to stay flexible and adjust your mindset as market dynamics evolve.

🧘 **Mindfulness and Mental Fitness**: Develop mindfulness techniques to stay present and focused during trading. Explore techniques like meditation, deep breathing, and visualization to enhance mental fitness.

📖 **Continuous Self-Improvement**: Embrace a mindset of continuous self-improvement. Regularly assess your psychological strengths and weaknesses and implement strategies to refine your mental game.

✳️ **Master Your Inner Game for Outer Success**: Trading psychology is your secret weapon in the world of trading. By mastering your emotions, thoughts, and reactions, you're not just improving your trading – you're enhancing your life. As you continue your journey, remember that your mind is your greatest asset, and your ability to navigate its complexities will be the compass that guides you toward lasting success in the dynamic world of swing trading.

Chapter 14: Trading Journal and Performance Analysis

Welcome to the laboratory of self-improvement – your trading journal and performance analysis. In this chapter, you'll explore the art of recording your trades, analyzing your performance, and extracting valuable insights. By maintaining a meticulous journal, you'll unlock the secrets to refining your strategies and optimizing your trading outcomes.

📊 **The Power of a Trading Journal**: Understand the significance of keeping a trading journal. Learn how this record becomes a treasure trove of information that can inform your decisions.

📝 **What to Include in Your Journal**: Discover what elements to include in your trading journal. From entry and exit points to emotions and rationale, each detail contributes to a comprehensive analysis.

📊 **Analyzing Winning and Losing Trades**: Learn how to analyze both winning and losing trades. Understand the importance of dissecting your trades to identify patterns and areas for improvement.

📝 **Identifying Strengths and Weaknesses**: Explore techniques to identify your trading strengths and weaknesses. Leverage your strengths while actively working to address and improve your weaknesses.

📊 **Keeping Track of Emotions**: Understand the role of emotions in your trading. Learn how to track and analyze emotional reactions to different market scenarios.

📝 **Patterns in Performance**: Analyze patterns in your performance over time. Discover how consistent analysis can help you identify trends and adapt your strategies accordingly.

📊 **Risk Management Review**: Revisit your risk management strategies in your journal. Evaluate whether you adhered to your predefined risk parameters and adjust them if necessary.

📝 **Goal Tracking**: Set and track goals for your trading performance. Regularly assess whether you're meeting your objectives and make necessary adjustments to your strategies.

🧘 **Unlocking Insights for Growth**: Your trading journal is more than just a record – it's a roadmap to growth. By meticulously recording and analyzing your trades, you're not just tracking your progress – you're actively refining your strategies and optimizing your outcomes.

✺ **From Data to Decisions: Your Trading Compass**: Your trading journal is the compass that guides you through the ups and downs of the market. By turning data into insights, you're not just improving your trading – you're setting a course toward lasting success. As you continue your journey, remember that each entry in your journal is a step toward mastery, and your commitment to self-improvement will be your guide through the ever-evolving landscape of trading opportunities.

Chapter 15: The Role of Fundamental Analysis in Swing Trading

Welcome to the world of fundamental analysis – a powerful tool that adds depth to your trading decisions. In this chapter, you'll explore how understanding the underlying factors that drive market movements can enhance your swing trading strategies. By integrating fundamental analysis, you'll gain a comprehensive perspective that informs your trading choices.

📇 **Understanding Fundamental Analysis**: Dive into the fundamentals of fundamental analysis. Learn how economic indicators, news events, and market sentiment influence price movements.

📊 **Key Economic Indicators**: Explore essential economic indicators such as GDP, unemployment rates, inflation, and interest rates. Understand how these indicators reflect the health of economies and impact currency and stock prices.

📇 **Earnings Reports and Corporate Performance**: Learn how to analyze earnings reports and corporate financials. Understand how a company's performance can influence its stock price and potential trading opportunities.

📊 **Market Sentiment and News**: Discover how market sentiment and news events impact trading. Learn to interpret news releases and their potential effects on price movements.

📇 **Central Bank Policies**: Understand the role of central banks and their policies in shaping monetary conditions. Learn how interest rate decisions and monetary policy statements can drive market movements.

📊 **Global Events and Geopolitics**: Explore how global events and geopolitical developments can create volatility in the markets. Learn to navigate uncertainty and identify opportunities.

📇 **Integrating Fundamental and Technical Analysis**: Discover how to integrate fundamental analysis with technical analysis. Learn to make well-informed trading decisions by considering both macroeconomic factors and technical indicators.

📊 **Long-Term vs. Short-Term Impact**: Understand how different fundamental factors can have varying impacts on short-term and long-term trading strategies.

🪨 **A Holistic Approach to Trading**: Fundamental analysis provides the context that complements technical analysis. By incorporating both perspectives, you're not just making trades – you're making informed decisions that reflect a deep understanding of market dynamics.

✺ **Knowledge is Power: Integrating Fundamentals into Your Strategy**: Fundamental analysis is your key to understanding the "why" behind market movements. By integrating these insights into your strategies, you're not just trading – you're making choices based on a comprehensive understanding of market forces. As you continue your journey, remember that each piece of fundamental information is a puzzle that contributes to the bigger picture of your trading success.

Chapter 16: Advanced Technical Analysis Techniques

Welcome to the realm of advanced technical analysis – where you'll venture beyond the basics and explore sophisticated tools to refine your trading strategies. In this chapter, you'll delve into intricate techniques that offer deeper insights into market movements. By mastering these advanced methods, you'll elevate your trading prowess to a new level of precision.

📊 **Fibonacci Retracements and Extensions**: Dive into the world of Fibonacci retracements and extensions. Learn how these levels, derived from the Fibonacci sequence, can act as potential support and resistance zones.

☑ **Elliott Wave Theory**: Explore the complex world of Elliott Wave Theory. Learn how to identify wave patterns that reflect the natural ebb and flow of market sentiment.

📊 **Market Profile Analysis**: Understand market profile analysis – a technique that visualizes price and volume over time. Learn how to identify key levels and areas of price acceptance.

☑ **Ichimoku Cloud Analysis**: Delve into the Ichimoku Cloud – a comprehensive indicator that offers insights into trends, support and resistance levels, and potential entry and exit points.

📊 **Volume Profile Analysis**: Explore volume profile analysis – a tool that displays trading volume at different price levels. Learn how to interpret volume distribution and identify areas of high interest.

☑ **Harmonic Patterns**: Understand harmonic patterns like the Gartley, Bat, and Butterfly patterns. Learn to recognize these formations and interpret their potential implications for price movements.

📊 **Market Breadth Indicators**: Discover market breadth indicators that assess the overall health of the market. Learn how these indicators can provide insights into the strength of trends.

☑ **Pivot Points and Camarilla Levels**: Explore pivot points and Camarilla levels – techniques that identify potential support and resistance levels based on previous price action.

🧠 **Precision through Complexity**: Advanced technical analysis techniques add layers of precision to your trading strategies. By mastering these methods, you're not just interpreting charts – you're deciphering the intricate language of market dynamics.

✸ **From Mastery to Precision: Your Technical Odyssey**: Advanced technical analysis is your compass in the sea of complex price movements. By honing your skills in these techniques, you're not just trading – you're navigating with a level of precision that sets you apart. As you continue your journey, remember that each advanced tool is a reflection of your dedication to understanding the intricacies of the market and your commitment to achieving excellence in your trading endeavors.

Chapter 17: Answering the Top 30 Questions in Swing Trading

Welcome to a comprehensive Q&A session – where we address the top 30 questions that swing traders commonly encounter. In this chapter, we'll provide clear and insightful answers to help you navigate various aspects of swing trading. By gaining clarity on these common queries, you'll enhance your understanding and approach to the dynamic world of swing trading.

1. What is swing trading, and how does it differ from other trading styles?
2. How do I choose the right markets or instruments for swing trading?
3. What are the key factors to consider when selecting a swing trading strategy?

4. How important is risk management in swing trading?
5. What role does technical analysis play in swing trading?
6. How do I identify potential entry and exit points in swing trading?
7. What are the pros and cons of using different types of indicators?
8. How do I determine the appropriate position size for a trade?
9. What is the significance of backtesting and how do I conduct it effectively?
10. How can I avoid overfitting when optimizing my trading strategy?
11. What are some effective ways to manage emotions and maintain discipline?
12. How can I balance swing trading with a full-time job or other commitments?
13. Is it better to focus on a few markets or diversify across many?
14. What role does news and fundamental analysis play in swing trading?
15. How do I handle unexpected events or news that impact the market?
16. What are some effective techniques for identifying trend reversals?
17. How can I adapt my strategies to different market conditions?
18. What are the common mistakes that swing traders should avoid?
19. Can swing trading be automated? What are the benefits and drawbacks?
20. How can I effectively manage my trades to maximize profits and minimize losses?
21. What is the best way to handle drawdowns and losing streaks?
22. How do I build a trading plan that suits my risk tolerance and goals?
23. What are the indicators of a potential breakout or breakdown in price?
24. How do I identify and trade pullbacks within an existing trend?
25. What role do chart patterns play in swing trading, and how do I recognize them?
26. How can I manage my time effectively as a swing trader?
27. What are some strategies for adjusting positions as market conditions evolve?
28. How can I stay updated on market news and events that impact my trades?
29. How do I determine whether a trading opportunity aligns with my strategy?
30. What resources, books, and websites can I use to further my swing trading education?

🪔 **Enlightenment through Clarity**: Addressing the top questions in swing trading brings clarity to your journey. By understanding these critical aspects, you're not just trading – you're making informed decisions that reflect a deep comprehension of the nuances of the market.

🎇 **From Inquiry to Insight: Your Knowledge Odyssey**: Each question answered is a stepping stone toward expertise. By seeking and absorbing knowledge, you're not just trading – you're embarking on a journey of continuous learning and growth. As you continue your journey, remember that each piece of information is a spark that ignites the fire of your trading success.

Chapter 18: The Future of Swing Trading: Trends and Innovations

Welcome to the horizon of possibilities – the future of swing trading. In this final chapter, you'll explore the emerging trends and innovations that are shaping the landscape of trading. By understanding where the industry is heading, you'll position yourself to adapt, evolve, and thrive in the ever-changing world of swing trading.

🚀 **Technology Integration**: Discover how technology is revolutionizing trading. Learn about algorithmic trading, AI-powered tools, and automation that enhance efficiency and decision-making.

🔮 **Predictive Analytics**: Explore the potential of predictive analytics in swing trading. Understand how data analysis and machine learning can provide insights into future price movements.

🌐 **Global Market Access**: Learn how advancements in technology have made it easier for traders to access global markets and diversify their portfolios across various instruments and regions.

🔒 **Regulatory Changes**: Understand the impact of regulatory changes on swing trading. Stay informed about evolving regulations and their potential effects on trading strategies.

🌱 **Sustainable Investing**: Discover the rise of sustainable investing and ESG (Environmental, Social, Governance) considerations. Learn how ethical and sustainable factors are influencing trading decisions.

💻 **Remote Trading and Education**: Explore the trend of remote trading and education. Discover how online resources, webinars, and virtual trading platforms are shaping the learning and trading experiences.

📈 **Integration of Fundamentals and Technicals**: Learn how the integration of fundamental and technical analysis is becoming more common. Understand how traders are combining both perspectives for more comprehensive insights.

🔍 **Continual Learning and Adaptation**: Embrace the mindset of continuous learning and adaptation. Understand that the trading landscape will continue to evolve, and your ability to adapt will be crucial to your success.

✳️ **The Trail to Tomorrow: Embracing Evolution**: The future of swing trading holds both challenges and opportunities. By embracing emerging trends and innovations, you're not just trading – you're evolving with the industry, positioning yourself to thrive in the ever-shifting terrain of trading dynamics.

🚀 **From the Present to the Beyond: Your Trading Odyssey Continues**: The journey of a swing trader is never static. By staying attuned to the trends and innovations, you're not just trading – you're embarking on an ongoing odyssey of growth, adaptation, and achievement. As you continue your journey, remember that the future is as bright as your determination to seize it.

Conclusion: The Swing Trader's Odyssey: Navigating Success

Congratulations, dear reader, on completing your journey through the world of swing trading. As you close this chapter, remember that your odyssey has equipped you with a treasure trove of knowledge, skills, and insights to navigate the exciting and ever-evolving world of financial markets.

💡 **Mastering the Art of Timing**: You've learned that swing trading is an art of timing – capturing short- to medium-term price movements by identifying trends, recognizing patterns, and making well-informed decisions.

🎇 **The Fusion of Analysis and Instinct**: You've discovered that successful swing trading requires a fusion of technical and fundamental analysis, along with the instinct to manage emotions and adapt to changing market dynamics.

🧠 **From Beginner to Expert**: You've transitioned from a curious beginner to a confident trader, embracing risk management, optimizing strategies, and refining your mindset to weather the challenges of the trading journey.

🚀 **Embracing the Future**: As the trading landscape continues to evolve, you're ready to embrace emerging technologies, stay attuned to regulatory changes, and adapt your strategies to seize new opportunities.

🔍 **Continuous Learning and Growth**: Remember that your journey as a swing trader is a lifelong odyssey of continuous learning, growth, and refinement. Each trade, each analysis, and each decision is a step toward mastering the art of swing trading.

🎇 **Your Odyssey Continues**: Your journey doesn't end here – it's merely a milestone in your quest for trading success. As you continue to chart your course, remember that the skills you've acquired, the strategies you've developed, and the mindset you've cultivated are the compass guiding you toward the horizon of profitability and achievement.

May your charts be clear, your analysis be astute, and your trades be profitable. The world of swing trading awaits your skillful navigation, and your determination will be the wind that propels you toward the heights of success.

Here's to your prosperous and fulfilling trading odyssey! 🖋

Volatility Trading

Focus on strategies that capitalize on market volatility.

Introduction

Volatility, in the context of financial markets, is an indispensable concept. A simple yet powerful metric, volatility indicates the degree of price variability for an underlying asset. Whether you are an institutional trader, a retail investor, or an academic researcher, understanding and leveraging volatility is crucial. It forms the foundation upon which many trading strategies are built, and understanding it can mean the difference between potential profit and loss.

It would be a grievous error to consider volatility as merely a statistic or a passive measure. In contemporary finance, it is an active, tradeable entity with its own suite of products and derivatives. Historically, markets have been rife with instances where volatility took center stage, steering market dynamics, investor sentiment, and global economic outlooks. The 2008 financial crisis, for instance, witnessed an unprecedented spike in volatility, and the same can be said for the global economic repercussions of the COVID-19 pandemic.

This intricate interplay between volatility and market dynamics begs the question: How can traders harness volatility? What instruments and strategies can be employed to gain an edge in the ever-changing world of finance? The answer lies in understanding the two types of volatility - historical and implied. While the former tracks past price fluctuations, the latter is a forward-looking metric encapsulating market expectations. These two types, though derived from the same foundational concept, have distinctive implications and uses in trading.

Furthermore, the application of volatility goes beyond simple measures and dives deep into sophisticated financial instruments like the Volatility Index (VIX), options, and futures. These tools not only allow traders to hedge against adverse market movements but also offer lucrative speculative opportunities. For instance, during turbulent times, the VIX, colloquially known as the "fear gauge", often surges, reflecting heightened investor anxiety. Understanding such dynamics allows traders to make informed decisions and potentially profit from market turbulence.

Yet, it is essential to recognize that volatility trading isn't merely about understanding metrics and deploying capital. The psychological aspects play a pivotal role. The very nature of volatility, with its sudden surges and drops, can induce strong emotional responses in traders, from euphoria to despair. Consequently, a trader's mindset, resilience, and ability to maintain equilibrium amidst chaos can significantly influence outcomes.

In the forthcoming chapters, we will delve into the nuances of volatility trading, starting from its foundational concepts to advanced strategies and mathematical models. By the end of this discourse, readers will have a comprehensive grasp of volatility trading, equipped with the knowledge to navigate and potentially thrive in the tumultuous world of financial markets.

Chapter 1: Introduction to Volatility Trading
1.1 Understanding the Essence of Volatility

In the grand tapestry of financial markets, volatility stands out as both a beacon of opportunities and a harbinger of risks. It can be understood as the statistical measure of the dispersion of returns for a given security or market index. In simpler terms, volatility gauges the degree to which an asset's price fluctuates over time. High volatility indicates that the price of the asset can change dramatically over a short time period in either direction, while low volatility implies that the asset's price remains relatively stable.

However, volatility is not just a dry statistical measure; it is a reflection of the collective sentiment of market participants. When investors are uncertain or fearful about the future prospects of an asset or the market at large, they tend to react more erratically, leading to increased volatility. Conversely, during periods of general consensus or complacency, price fluctuations become subdued, resulting in decreased volatility.

The essence of volatility lies in its dual nature. For risk-averse investors, high volatility represents an increased risk of substantial losses. Such investors might avoid or reduce exposure to highly volatile assets in their portfolios. On the other hand, for speculative traders and those equipped with appropriate risk management techniques, high volatility can present opportunities for significant gains.

From a broader perspective, volatility plays a pivotal role in portfolio construction and risk management. For long-term investors, understanding the inherent volatility of their holdings can aid in asset allocation decisions, ensuring that their investment portfolio aligns with their risk tolerance and financial objectives.

In essence, volatility, with its multifaceted implications, forms the very backbone of modern financial markets. By understanding its intricacies, traders and investors can better position themselves in the market, harnessing volatility's energy for potential gains while shielding themselves from its inherent risks.

1.2 Differentiating between Historical and Implied Volatility

When delving into the realm of volatility, two primary types emerge as crucial for traders and investors alike: Historical Volatility (HV) and Implied Volatility (IV). Though both rooted in the concept of price variability, they serve distinct purposes and have different implications in the world of trading.

Historical Volatility, as the name suggests, focuses on the past. It quantifies the asset's price fluctuations over a specified historical period. Typically calculated using standard deviation or variance, HV provides insights into how volatile an asset has been over time. It's akin to looking in the rearview mirror; it gives a clear view of where you've been but offers no direct insights into what lies ahead. For traders and investors, HV can be valuable in assessing the asset's past risk and in making decisions about portfolio diversification.

On the contrary, Implied Volatility looks forward. Instead of analyzing past price data, IV is derived from the current market prices of options. It represents the market's expectations of future volatility and is inherently forward-looking. When traders talk about the "volatility" of an option, they are generally referring to its IV. A high IV suggests that the market expects significant price fluctuations in the future, whereas a low IV indicates the opposite.

The distinction between HV and IV is not just academic; it has profound practical implications. For options traders, IV is a key component in pricing models like Black-Scholes. An overestimated IV can result in overpriced options, and vice versa. Consequently, traders often compare IV with HV to determine if options are fairly priced. If IV is significantly higher than HV, it might indicate that options are overpriced, presenting potential opportunities for certain trading strategies.

In summary, while both Historical and Implied Volatility offer insights into an asset's price variability, their applications and implications differ. By understanding and differentiating between these two forms of volatility, traders can make more informed decisions, optimizing their strategies for the ever-changing market landscape.

Chapter 2: Volatility Instruments
2.1 Introduction to Volatility Index (VIX)

The Volatility Index, commonly referred to as the VIX, stands as an indispensable gauge for market practitioners. Introduced by the Chicago Board Options Exchange (CBOE) in 1993, the VIX provides a real-time measurement of the market's anticipated volatility over the ensuing month. It is frequently termed the "fear index" as it tends to escalate during periods of market uncertainty or turbulence.

Derived from S&P 500 option prices, the VIX is representative of the anticipated volatility over the next 30 days. Essentially, the VIX provides insight into trader sentiment concerning the market's future trajectory. A heightened VIX suggests that investors are bracing for increased volatility, whereas a subdued VIX indicates expectations of reduced volatility.

The uniqueness of the VIX lies in its ability to function as a market sentiment barometer. Amidst financial crises or economic uncertainty, the VIX tends to ascend, mirroring rising investor anxiety or fear. Conversely, during stable economic growth periods and bullish markets, the VIX tends to descend.

For traders and investors, the VIX offers an avenue not just to monitor market sentiment but also to speculate or hedge their portfolios. Through an array of derivative products, such as futures and options on the VIX, investors can take positions on the future direction of volatility or shield their holdings from unexpected market gyrations.

In summary, the Volatility Index represents one of the most potent and dynamic tools available to traders for discerning, speculating, and insulating against volatile market conditions.

2.2 Trading Volatility through Options and Futures

Volatility, albeit intangible, has become a tradable entity through the evolution of derivative products. Two of the most predominant vehicles for trading volatility are options and futures.

Options are contracts that grant the holder the right, but not the obligation, to buy or sell an underlying asset at a predetermined price, termed the strike price, within a specific time frame. Volatility directly influences option prices. An uptick in implied volatility can elevate option prices, making option trading a popular choice for those speculating on volatility.

Volatility futures, on the other hand, are contracts that allow investors to take positions based on the anticipated direction of future volatility. The most prominent among these is the VIX future, which empowers traders to speculate on the S&P 500's anticipated market volatility direction.

Trading volatility through options and futures offers several advantages. Firstly, it provides traders with a means to diversify their portfolio, overlaying a layer of protection against adverse market movements. Secondly, it avails traders the prospect of profiting in both bull and bear markets, depending on volatility's direction.

However, as with all financial instruments, inherent risks exist. Volatility can be unpredictable, and minor shifts in implied volatility can substantially impact the value of options or futures positions. Consequently, it's paramount that traders remain well-informed and employ robust risk management strategies when engaging in volatility trades.

In conclusion, while volatility trading offers significant prospects, it's imperative that traders possess an in-depth understanding of option and future mechanics and the intricacies of volatility dynamics before delving into such strategies.

Chapter 3: The Basics of Option Pricing
3.1 Intrinsic and Extrinsic Value

Option pricing, though intricate, can be disentangled into two primary components: intrinsic and extrinsic value. The summation of these two values offers the total worth of an option.

Intrinsic Value is a straightforward concept. It's the inherent value an option possesses based on the differential between the current market price of the underlying asset and the option's strike price. For a call option, the intrinsic value is calculated by deducting the strike price from the current market price (provided the market price is above the strike). Conversely, for a put option, it's the difference between the strike price and the current market price (given the market price is below the strike). Options that possess intrinsic value are referred to as "in-the-money."

Extrinsic Value, or sometimes referred to as "time value," encompasses other non-tangible factors that might impact an option's price. This includes time until expiration, volatility of the underlying asset, and the risk-free interest rate. Extrinsic value tends to erode as the option nears its expiration date, a phenomenon known as "time decay."

In essence, the total value of an option = Intrinsic Value + Extrinsic Value.

Understanding these values is pivotal for traders, as it offers insights into what they're essentially paying for when acquiring an option and the potential value they might derive from it upon selling or exercising.

3.2 The Black-Scholes Model

In the realm of financial mathematics, few models have garnered the acclaim and ubiquity of the Black-Scholes model. Developed by Fischer Black, Myron Scholes, and Robert Merton in the early 1970s, this revolutionary model offers a theoretical valuation for European-style options.

The Black-Scholes formula contemplates several variables:

1. Current stock price
2. Option's strike price
3. Time until expiration
4. Volatility of the underlying asset
5. Risk-free interest rate

One of the groundbreaking attributes of the Black-Scholes model is its ability to derive a theoretical option price devoid of any arbitrage opportunities, provided certain assumptions are met.

Despite its pioneering nature, the model is not devoid of critiques. The original model presumes constant volatility and interest rates, which is seldom the reality in dynamic markets. Further, it caters specifically to European-style options, limiting its applicability.

Nevertheless, the Black-Scholes model has left an indelible mark on the financial world. Its foundational concepts serve as the bedrock for many contemporary option pricing models, and understanding its mechanics is quintessential for anyone delving into the intricacies of option trading.

Chapter 4: The Greeks in Volatility Trading
4.1 Delta, Gamma, Theta, Vega, and Rho: A comprehensive overview

In the vast ocean of derivatives trading, the 'Greeks' emerge as the navigational stars, guiding traders through the convoluted terrains of option pricing dynamics. These are mathematical derivatives of the option pricing model that explain the sensitivity of the option price to various factors.

Delta represents the sensitivity of an option's price to a $1 change in the underlying asset. For instance, a Delta of 0.5 indicates the option price would move by 50 cents for every $1 movement in the underlying asset. While Delta values for calls lie between 0 to 1, for puts it's between 0 to -1.

Gamma is a step deeper, articulating the rate of change in Delta for a $1 change in the underlying asset. It assists traders in predicting changes in Delta, thereby serving as a vital tool for dynamic delta-hedging strategies.

Theta delves into the time dimension. It quantifies the rate of time decay, signifying how much an option's price diminishes for each passing day. A Theta of -0.05, for instance, suggests a 5 cent reduction in the option's value daily.

Vega is the heart of our volatility exploration. It measures an option's price sensitivity to a 1% change in the implied volatility of the underlying asset. A high Vega indicates greater sensitivity, making it pivotal for volatility traders.

Lastly, *Rho* gauges the option's price sensitivity to changes in the risk-free interest rate. In low-interest-rate environments, Rho's significance is often dwarfed by other Greeks. However, in fluctuating interest rate scenarios, Rho becomes notably crucial.

Understanding the interplay of these Greeks is paramount for traders, as it offers granular insights into the multifaceted realm of option pricing.

4.2 Importance of Vega in Volatility Trading

In the context of volatility trading, Vega stands out prominently. As the Greek denoting sensitivity to implied volatility, Vega becomes the linchpin for traders aiming to capitalize on or hedge against volatility shifts.

When implied volatility rises, options become pricier, and vice versa. A trader holding an option with a high positive Vega would benefit from a surge in volatility. Conversely, negative Vega positions would profit from diminishing volatility. Thus, understanding Vega dynamics is integral for formulating strategies tailored to specific volatility outlooks.

Moreover, Vega's magnitude tends to amplify for options further away from expiration. Long-term options, therefore, are more susceptible to volatility shifts than their short-term counterparts. Recognizing this can empower traders to select the right options based on their volatility forecast.

In the realm of volatility trading, Vega isn't just another Greek; it's the cornerstone upon which effective trading strategies are built.

Chapter 5: Historical vs. Implied Volatility

5.1 Comparison

Historical volatility and implied volatility stand as two pillars of the volatility spectrum, each offering a unique perspective on market movements.

Historical Volatility (HV), as the name suggests, refers to the observed volatility of an asset over a specific historical period. It is a backward-looking metric, calculated using standard deviation or variance of the asset's past returns. HV provides traders an empirical glimpse into how volatile an asset has been, aiding in gauging future expectations.

On the other hand, *Implied Volatility (IV)* peers into the future. Derived from the current market prices of options, IV represents the market's expectation of how volatile the underlying asset will be in the future. It's crucial to note that IV doesn't predict future direction; it predicts the magnitude of the move.

The differentiation between HV and IV is analogous to comparing past weather patterns with future weather forecasts. While the past provides data, the future is inherently uncertain and is perpetually updated based on incoming information.

In the world of trading, understanding the dichotomy between these two can provide traders an edge, assisting them in discerning whether options are relatively underpriced or overpriced based on historical standards.

5.2 Implications and significance in trading

The interplay between HV and IV is laden with implications for option traders. For starters, a disparity between the two can suggest potential trading opportunities.

A scenario where IV exceeds HV might imply that options are overpriced. This could be due to an impending event or rising market uncertainty. In such situations, traders might lean towards selling options to capitalize on the inflated premiums. Conversely, when IV is below HV, it might signal that options are underpriced, presenting a buying opportunity.

Furthermore, understanding this dynamic is pivotal for traders employing strategies like straddles or strangles, where profitability hinges on future volatility. If a trader expects actual future volatility (realized volatility) to exceed the IV, buying a straddle could be advantageous. Conversely, if IV seems exaggerated relative to anticipated realized volatility, selling a straddle might be apt.

In essence, the dance between historical and implied volatility crafts the rhythm of the options market. Grasping their nuances enables traders to choreograph their moves adeptly, harmonizing with the market's ever-evolving beat.

Chapter 6: Volatility Skew and Surface
6.1 The concept of the 'smile' and its implications

Volatility skew, commonly referred to as the "volatility smile," is a phenomenon in the options market where implied volatilities of options on a single underlying asset display a pattern that forms a curve resembling a smile. This curvature on a plot between implied volatility and strike prices defies the uniform implied volatility predictions of the original Black-Scholes model.

Historically, the 'smile' became notably pronounced after the stock market crash of 1987. Before this event, implied volatilities for equities were largely flat across strikes. However, post-crash, traders recognized that out-of-the-money (OTM) puts and in-the-money (ITM) calls should carry higher implied volatilities than predicted by the Black-Scholes model, giving birth to the 'smile' phenomenon.

This skewness has crucial implications:

1. **Risk Perception**: The volatility smile reflects market participants' collective beliefs regarding potential extreme movements. An upwardly skewed smile, often seen in equity markets, indicates heightened concerns over potential price drops.

2. **Pricing Discrepancies**: The divergence of actual market volatilities from the Black-Scholes predictions can create pricing discrepancies, offering astute traders arbitrage opportunities.

3. **Strategic Adjustments**: Option traders, aware of the skew, might adjust their strategies, particularly when it comes to multi-legged options trades like spreads.

6.2 Surface dynamics in different market scenarios

Beyond the one-dimensional skew, the concept extends into a three-dimensional volatility surface, plotting implied volatilities across varying strike prices and maturities. This surface is dynamic and responds to market changes, making it an essential tool for sophisticated volatility traders.

Different market scenarios impact the volatility surface:

1. **Quiet Markets**: In stable environments, the volatility surface might be relatively flat, indicating similar implied volatilities across different strike prices and maturities.

2. **Turbulent Markets**: In volatile phases, the surface might exhibit pronounced curves, especially for options set to expire soon, reflecting heightened short-term uncertainty.
3. **Event-Driven Shifts**: Announcements, such as earnings or regulatory changes, can distort the surface temporarily, indicating increased implied volatility around specific strike prices or maturities.

Understanding these surface dynamics empowers traders to adapt. For instance, if short-term options exhibit higher implied volatilities than longer-term ones, traders might employ calendar spreads, benefiting from the differential.

In essence, the volatility surface, much like a topographical map, offers traders a landscape of market sentiment, allowing them to navigate their strategies with more precision.

Chapter 7: Long Volatility Strategies
7.1 Straddles and strangles

At the heart of volatility trading are strategies that allow traders to capitalize on anticipated large movements in an asset's price, regardless of the direction. Two such quintessential strategies are the straddle and the strangle.

The **Straddle** is a strategy involving the simultaneous purchase or sale of a call and a put option with the same strike price and expiration date. The trader doesn't necessarily have a directional bias but expects a significant price movement. When initiating a long straddle:

1. The maximum loss is limited to the premium paid for both the options.
2. Profit potential is unlimited, growing as the underlying asset moves significantly from the strike price in either direction.
3. The breakeven points are the strike price plus and minus the total premium paid.

The **Strangle**, while similar, employs options with different strike prices. In a long strangle:

1. A call with a higher strike and a put with a lower strike, both typically out-of-the-money, are simultaneously purchased.
2. The trader expects a substantial price movement but is uncertain about the direction.
3. As with the straddle, the maximum loss is limited to the initial premium paid.
4. Breakeven points are further apart than in a straddle due to the differing strike prices.

The decision between these strategies often boils down to the trader's expectations. Straddles are more expensive due to at-the-money options' higher premiums but require less movement to break even. Strangles, being cheaper, necessitate a more considerable price move to become profitable.

7.2 Protective puts and other hedging tactics

While the previous strategies aim to profit from increased volatility, protective measures like **Protective Puts** provide insurance against downside risks. This tactic involves holding an underlying asset and simultaneously buying a put option. Here's a breakdown:

1. The protective put provides a floor, ensuring that no matter how far the asset's price drops, the trader can sell at the put's strike price.
2. The maximum loss, in this case, is the premium paid for the put added to the difference between the asset's purchase price and the put's strike price.

3. The profit potential is unlimited on the upside as the trader benefits from any upward movement in the asset, minus the cost of the put.

Hedging doesn't solely revolve around protective puts. Other tactics include:

- **Covered Calls**: While not strictly a volatility-based strategy, selling a covered call can generate income and provide a minor hedge against small price declines.
- **Collars**: This involves holding the underlying, selling a call, and using the proceeds to buy a protective put. The strategy caps both potential gains and losses.
- **Delta Hedging**: A more advanced technique, delta hedging involves adjusting positions to maintain a delta-neutral state, ensuring small price movements in the underlying don't impact the overall portfolio value.

These strategies underscore the dual essence of volatility trading: seeking profit and managing risk. An astute trader balances both, recognizing that taming volatility's capricious nature requires both offense and defense.

Chapter 8: Short Volatility Strategies
8.1 Selling covered calls

In the realm of volatility trading, a comprehensive strategy suite includes not only those that anticipate and profit from increased volatility but also those that benefit from its decline or stasis. One such technique, especially favored for its income-generating properties, is the selling of covered calls.

A **Covered Call** strategy involves holding a long position in an underlying asset and simultaneously selling (or "writing") call options on that same asset. It's labeled "covered" because the seller owns the underlying shares against which the option is written. This approach offers:

1. **Income Generation**: By selling the call option, the trader receives the option premium, which can serve as a steady income stream, especially in flat markets.
2. **Downside Protection**: Though minimal, the premium received can help offset slight declines in the underlying asset's value.
3. **Profit Limitation**: The main trade-off for these benefits is the capping of upside potential. If the underlying asset's price exceeds the call's strike price, the asset may be called away.

The strategy is particularly appealing when the trader has a neutral to slightly bullish outlook on the asset and is comfortable potentially selling it at the call's strike price. Moreover, it's popular in periods of low volatility, where significant upward price movements are not anticipated.

8.2 Naked puts and credit spreads

Diving deeper into the strategies that cater to reduced volatility scenarios, we encounter the selling of naked puts and the establishment of credit spreads.

Naked Puts: Unlike covered calls, where the seller owns the underlying asset, a trader selling a naked (or uncovered) put does not hold the underlying asset. This strategy involves:

1. **Premium Income**: Like covered calls, selling a naked put generates immediate income from the option premium.
2. **Potential Obligation**: The risk arises from the obligation to buy the underlying asset at the strike price if the market price drops below it. Hence, this strategy is suitable for those bullish on the asset and willing to own it at a lower price.

3. **Unlimited Risk**: Theoretically, since the asset's price can drop to zero, the risk is significant, though the practical risk is the strike price minus the premium received.

Credit Spreads: A more controlled risk approach is the use of put credit spreads, where a trader sells a put option and simultaneously purchases another put option with a lower strike price on the same underlying asset and expiration date. This:

1. **Limits Potential Loss**: The maximum loss is the difference between the two strike prices minus the net premium received.
2. **Offers Premium Income**: The trader profits from the net premium difference between the sold and bought puts.
3. **Neutral to Bullish Bias**: This strategy is suitable for traders expecting the asset to remain above the higher strike price.

Both these strategies emphasize the profit potential from declining or stagnant volatility. However, as with all trading endeavors, understanding and managing the associated risks are paramount.

Chapter 9: Vega Neutral Trading

9.1 The concept of vega neutrality

In the intricate domain of options trading, sensitivity to price changes is paramount. Vega, one of the "Greeks," measures an option's price sensitivity to changes in the volatility of the underlying asset. Achieving neutrality to this sensitivity - vega neutrality - can be vital in certain trading situations.

Vega Neutrality means structuring an options portfolio such that the overall position isn't affected by changes in the implied volatility of the underlying asset. When traders aim for this neutrality:

1. **Risk Mitigation**: The primary reason to aim for vega neutrality is to reduce the risk associated with changes in implied volatility. Even if the trader has correct predictions about the market direction, unexpected volatility changes can still impact profits.
2. **Flexibility**: By being vega neutral, a trader is essentially saying they don't have a strong prediction about future volatility changes. This allows them to focus on other aspects of the market or their strategy.
3. **Complexity**: Achieving vega neutrality often requires holding multiple options positions. As implied volatility changes, the vega of individual options in a portfolio will also change. This necessitates continuous monitoring and adjustments to maintain a neutral stance.

The pursuit of vega neutrality underscores the technical prowess required in advanced options trading. By comprehending and implementing such nuanced strategies, traders can work towards insulating their portfolios from unpredictable volatility swings.

9.2 Benefits and risks associated

Like any trading strategy, vega neutral trading has its advantages and challenges. Recognizing these can ensure traders are well-prepared when employing this technique.

Benefits:

1. **Protection Against Volatility Swings**: Perhaps the most apparent benefit. If a trader is unsure about the future direction of volatility but has a position in the market, achieving vega neutrality can offer some protection against unexpected volatility changes.
2. **Increased Strategy Precision**: Without the overhang of volatility-induced changes, traders can be more precise in their predictions and strategies regarding price movements.

3. **Flexibility in Portfolio Management**: Vega neutral trading often dovetails with other neutral strategies, like delta-neutral trading. This can provide traders with a robust toolkit to handle various market conditions.

Risks:

1. **Management Complexity**: A vega neutral position is not a "set it and forget it" strategy. As market conditions and the vega of individual positions change, the portfolio may drift from neutrality, necessitating adjustments.

2. **Potential for Missed Opportunities**: By hedging against volatility, traders might miss out on potential profits that could have been realized had they taken a directional stance on volatility.

3. **Cost Implications**: Maintaining vega neutrality might involve frequent trading, leading to increased transaction costs.

In the final reckoning, the decision to pursue vega neutrality should be based on a trader's market outlook, risk tolerance, and the resources they can commit to portfolio management. As with all strategies, education, practice, and continuous learning are the keys to mastery.

Chapter 10: Dispersion Trading
10.1 Trading volatility of individual stocks versus their index

The intricate web of the financial markets is punctuated by individual assets and the broader indices that aggregate them. Dispersion trading emerges at this intersection, focusing on the volatility discrepancies between an index and its constituent components.

Dispersion Trading capitalizes on the volatility differential between an index option and a basket of options on the individual components of that index. This strategy can be seen as a bet on the relative performance of the two volatilities. Here's how it generally unfolds:

1. **Identification of Volatility Mispricing**: At its core, dispersion trading is about identifying when the implied volatility of the index option is either overpriced or underpriced relative to the aggregate implied volatilities of the individual stock options comprising the index.

2. **Execution**: A classic dispersion trade would involve selling index options and buying a weighted portfolio of options on the index constituents, or vice versa, depending on where the mispricing lies.

3. **Profit Potential**: The profit in a dispersion trade comes from the differential in volatility performance between the index and its constituents.

Dispersion trading is predicated on the belief that markets, while efficient, aren't perfectly so. At times, the implied volatility of an index may not accurately reflect the combined implied volatilities of its individual stocks. Reasons for such discrepancies include:

- **Diversification**: Indices, by their nature, are diversified. This diversification can often lead to a dampening of the perceived volatility when compared to individual, more volatile stocks.

- **Demand and Supply**: High demand for protective index options (like in uncertain times) can inflate index option prices, creating a divergence from the constituent stock options.

- **Liquidity**: Index options, especially for major indices, can be more liquid than options on individual stocks, leading to pricing disparities.

10.2 Trading volatility of individual stocks versus their index

Expanding on the foundational concept of dispersion trading, let's delve deeper into the nuances, practicalities, and considerations inherent in this strategy:

1. **Correlation Dynamics**: Dispersion trading is fundamentally a play on correlation. When index constituents are expected to move less in tandem (i.e., lower correlation), the index's volatility is typically less than the sum of its parts. This situation could warrant a dispersion trade.

2. **Risk Management**: Like all trading strategies, dispersion trading isn't without risks. The primary risk is a sudden increase in correlation among index constituents, which can cause losses. Thus, continuously monitoring correlations and having defined exit strategies is vital.

3. **Trade Structure Variations**: While the classic dispersion trade involves options, variants using variance swaps or volatility swaps have also emerged, offering traders additional tools and complexities.

4. **Cost Considerations**: Dispersion trading often requires trading a multitude of options simultaneously. This can result in significant transaction costs that need to be factored into the trade's profitability calculations.

5. **Market Sentiment**: Dispersion trades can also be influenced by broader market sentiment. For instance, in bullish markets, individual stocks might see increased volatility as investors chase returns, making dispersion trading more attractive.

6. **Monitoring and Adjustments**: Due to the multi-legged nature of dispersion trades, they require rigorous monitoring. Adjustments might be needed to maintain the balance between the index option and the individual stock options, especially as they approach expiration.

Dispersion trading underscores the intricacies and opportunities inherent in volatility trading. While it offers a unique avenue to capitalize on market inefficiencies, its multifaceted nature also necessitates a deep understanding, rigorous monitoring, and diligent risk management.

Chapter 11: Managing Risk in Volatility Trading
11.1 Techniques and tools for optimal risk management

In the intricate labyrinth of the financial world, where volatility is as unpredictable as it is inevitable, astute risk management emerges as the linchpin of sustainable trading success. This section will endeavor to unpack the various techniques and tools traders utilize to manage risk, particularly within the scope of volatility trading.

1. **Position Sizing**: This is arguably the most elementary, yet most crucial aspect of risk management. The size of the trade, quantified by the number of contracts or the capital deployed, should be aligned with one's risk tolerance. Using a fixed percentage of one's trading capital or a volatility-based approach (like the Kelly Criterion) can provide systematic position sizing methods.

2. **Diversification**: "Don't put all your eggs in one basket." Diversifying trades across multiple assets or strategies can mitigate the impact of a single adverse move.

3. **Use of Stop-Loss and Take-Profit**: Setting predetermined exit points can ensure emotional biases don't cloud judgment. A stop-loss order triggers an exit when a loss reaches a specific threshold, while a take-profit does the same for profits.

4. **Dynamic Hedging**: As the market moves, so should your protective measures. Dynamic hedging involves adjusting hedge positions as market conditions change, ensuring that a protective shield is always active.
5. **Scenario Analysis**: By simulating various market conditions and understanding their potential impact, traders can prepare for different eventualities. This includes stress-testing portfolios against extreme market moves.
6. **Time Decay Management in Options**: Given that options have an expiration date, understanding and managing time decay (Theta) is crucial. Traders often roll over options or adjust positions to manage this risk.
7. **Leverage Management**: While leverage can amplify returns, it can equally magnify losses. Traders need to ensure that the leverage they use aligns with their risk profile and the market's volatility.
8. **Utilization of Advanced Analytics Tools**: Modern trading platforms offer advanced analytics tools that provide insights into potential risks and returns. Value at Risk (VaR) and Conditional Value at Risk (CVaR) are popular metrics to gauge portfolio risk.
9. **Continual Education**: The financial markets are ever-evolving. By continually updating one's knowledge and staying abreast of market developments, traders can better anticipate risks.

To contextualize these techniques, consider the realm of volatility trading, where the very nature of the asset – volatility – is inherently unpredictable. Here, meticulous risk management is not just advisable; it's indispensable.

11.2 Implications and significance of risk management in trading

While the tools and techniques employed in risk management are instrumental, understanding the overarching implications and significance of risk management provides traders with perspective and direction.

1. **Preservation of Capital**: At its core, risk management is about ensuring longevity in trading. By limiting losses, traders can live to trade another day, even after experiencing unfavorable market events.
2. **Psychological Equilibrium**: A series of unmanaged losses can wreak havoc on a trader's psyche. Effective risk management ensures that traders remain level-headed, making decisions based on logic rather than emotion.
3. **Enhanced Profitability**: Contrary to popular belief, risk management isn't just about limiting losses. By effectively managing risk, traders can optimize profitability, ensuring they capitalize on favorable moves just as much as they shield themselves from adverse ones.
4. **Portfolio Resilience**: In a landscape punctuated by black swan events and unprecedented market anomalies, a well-hedged, diversified portfolio can withstand shocks, ensuring sustainability.
5. **Reputation in the Professional Community**: For institutional traders or fund managers, effective risk management not only preserves capital but also reputation. Consistent and stable returns are often more revered than erratic high-reward, high-risk outcomes.
6. **Enhanced Decision Making**: Knowing that there's a safety net in place allows traders to make decisions more objectively, without the looming fear of significant losses.

7. **Regulatory and Compliance Adherence**: Especially relevant for institutional players, maintaining stringent risk management protocols is often a regulatory requirement.

In conclusion, risk management in volatility trading (and trading at large) transcends the mechanistic act of setting stop losses or diversifying portfolios. It's a holistic endeavor, aiming to meld the quantitative rigors of the financial markets with the qualitative aspects of trader psychology and behavior. A robust risk management framework doesn't just ensure the preservation of capital but lays the foundation for consistent, sustainable profitability.

Chapter 12: Volatility Arbitrage
12.1 Exploiting differences between implied and realized volatility

The essence of volatility arbitrage lies in its very name – arbitraging or capitalizing on the discrepancies between implied volatility (IV) and realized (or historical) volatility. Before diving into the strategies employed to exploit these discrepancies, it's imperative to distinguish between the two primary volatilities.

1. **Implied Volatility (IV)**: Extracted from the market prices of options, IV reflects the market's expectation of how volatile the underlying asset will be over the option's life. It doesn't offer historical data or forecast but rather captures the current sentiment of volatility in the market. Essentially, IV is the market's best guess at future volatility.

2. **Realized Volatility (RV)**: Often referred to as historical volatility, RV quantifies how much an underlying asset's price has moved in the past. It's a backward-looking measure, offering no predictions on future price movements.

Now, the core principle of volatility arbitrage is predicated on the assumption that IV, in the long run, tends to overestimate the actual realized volatility, especially in equity markets. This phenomenon is observed due to the risk-averse nature of investors who are willing to pay a premium to hedge against adverse price movements.

Strategies in Volatility Arbitrage:

1. **Vanilla Options Trading**: Traders can exploit the differential by taking positions in options and the underlying stock. For instance, if IV is deemed to be high relative to RV, a trader might sell the option (capturing the higher premium) and hedge with the underlying stock to be delta neutral.

2. **Volatility Swaps**: A more direct way to exploit volatility differences. In a volatility swap, two parties agree to exchange payments based on the difference between implied and realized volatility.

3. **Variance Swaps**: Similar to volatility swaps, but here, payments are based on the variance (square of volatility) of the underlying asset.

4. **Gamma Trading**: This involves adjusting delta-hedged positions to capitalize on the mispricing of volatility. As the price of the underlying changes, the trader continually rebalances their portfolio to maintain a delta-neutral position.

It's worth noting that while the discrepancy between IV and RV forms the foundational premise of volatility arbitrage, the actual dynamics involve multifaceted elements like option greeks, interest rates, dividends, and market microstructure effects. Furthermore, volatility arbitrage, though seemingly lucrative, isn't a risk-free strategy. The unpredictability of market events can lead to significant short-term discrepancies between IV and RV, leading to potential losses.

12.2 Implications for volatility traders

The realm of volatility arbitrage offers significant insights for volatility traders, irrespective of whether they directly engage in arbitrage strategies.

1. **Predictive Power of Implied Volatility**: Historically, IV has been a better predictor of future volatility than RV. Even if the general tendency is for IV to overstate, it still provides traders with a metric that factors in current market sentiment, information that RV simply cannot provide.

2. **Skew and Term Structure**: Volatility arbitrage strategies often lead to insights into the volatility skew (the difference in implied volatility between out-of-the-money, at-the-money, and in-the-money options) and term structure of volatility (how implied volatility changes for options with different maturities). These can serve as invaluable tools for option selection and strategy formulation.

3. **Liquidity Concerns**: The act of arbitraging often requires swift trade execution. In markets or instruments with low liquidity, bid-ask spreads can be wide, making profitable arbitrage more challenging.

4. **Risk Management**: As with any trading strategy, risk management is paramount. Volatility arbitrage, while methodological, is not immune to unforeseen market events that can result in substantial discrepancies between IV and RV in the short term.

5. **Technological Implications**: In today's age, many volatility arbitrage strategies are executed algorithmically. The latency, speed, and accuracy offered by algorithmic platforms can be a distinct advantage.

6. **Regulatory Implications**: Especially in institutional settings, traders need to be aware of the regulatory landscape. Missteps can lead to severe penalties.

To encapsulate, volatility arbitrage sheds light on the nuanced dance between implied and realized volatility. For traders, it offers a systematic approach to potentially exploit discrepancies therein. However, as with all strategies in the financial markets, it comes with its set of challenges and risks. A keen understanding, combined with rigorous risk management, can pave the way for success in this domain.

Chapter 13: Exotic Options and Volatility
13.1 Introduction to binary, barrier, and Asian options

Exotic options, a contrast to their vanilla counterparts, come with diverse payoffs and can be tailored to specific requirements. Let's delve into three primary types: binary, barrier, and Asian options.

1. **Binary Options**: Also known as digital options, these have a simple, 'all or nothing' payoff structure. If the underlying asset price meets or exceeds a certain level, the option holder receives a fixed amount; otherwise, they receive nothing.

    - **Cash-or-nothing**: Upon expiration, the holder receives a fixed cash amount if the option is in-the-money, else nothing.
    - **Asset-or-nothing**: The holder receives the value of the underlying asset if the option is in-the-money, otherwise nothing.

2. **Barrier Options**: These options become active or inactive when the price of the underlying asset crosses a certain barrier.

    - **Knock-in Option**: Starts as an inactive option, but becomes active once the underlying asset price reaches a specified barrier.

- **Knock-out Option**: Starts as an active option and becomes inactive when the underlying asset price reaches the barrier.

3. **Asian Options**: The payoff for these options is determined by the average price of the underlying asset over a specific time period, rather than the price at a single point in time.
   - **Average Price Option**: The payoff is dependent on the difference between the average price of the underlying asset over the life of the option and the strike price.
   - **Average Strike Option**: The payoff is based on the difference between the underlying asset's price at expiration and its average price over the option's life.

These exotic options, due to their distinct characteristics, present unique challenges and opportunities for volatility traders. Their pricing is often more intricate than vanilla options, given their unconventional payoff structures. For instance, the volatility profile of a barrier option can be drastically altered if the underlying asset price approaches the barrier, thereby necessitating advanced mathematical models for accurate pricing and risk management.

Additionally, exotic options are usually less liquid than their vanilla counterparts. This illiquidity can amplify volatility, presenting both risks and opportunities. Given that these options are often traded over-the-counter (OTC), transparency can be limited, further complicating risk assessment.

13.2 Implications for volatility traders

For volatility traders, exotic options offer a world rife with both intricate challenges and opportunities. Several implications arise:

1. **Complex Risk Profiles**: Given their unique payoff structures, exotic options can manifest non-linear risk profiles. For instance, the gamma (sensitivity of an option's delta to price changes in the underlying) of a barrier option can skyrocket as the asset price nears the barrier.

2. **Pricing Challenges**: Traditional models like Black-Scholes often fall short when pricing these instruments. Advanced models, which consider the multifaceted dynamics of exotic options, are essential.

3. **Hedging Difficulties**: Due to their unique characteristics, finding perfect hedges for exotic options in the market might be elusive. This might lead traders to employ dynamic hedging strategies, which are not always foolproof.

4. **Market Illiquidity**: As mentioned, exotic options, especially those traded OTC, might lack the liquidity seen in standard options. This illiquidity can impact the bid-ask spread and influence the trader's entry and exit strategies.

5. **Volatility Smiles and Surfaces**: For vanilla options, the volatility implied from option prices often varies with strike and maturity, leading to the phenomena of volatility smiles and term structures. For exotic options, these dynamics can be even more pronounced.

6. **Regulatory Implications**: Exotic options, due to their OTC nature, might be subjected to distinct regulatory oversight, impacting their trading.

7. **Strategic Flexibility**: On the brighter side, the array of exotic options allows traders to tailor strategies to specific market views and risk tolerances. They offer avenues to harness volatility in ways vanilla options can't.

To sum it up, while exotic options extend novel avenues to capitalize on market volatility, they demand rigorous understanding, advanced modeling techniques, and meticulous risk management. For those equipped to navigate their intricacies, they present a rich tapestry of trading possibilities.

Chapter 14: Event-Driven Volatility Trading

14.1 Trading around earnings, mergers, and macroeconomic announcements

Trading in the financial markets is often influenced by significant events that can lead to heightened volatility. Understanding and anticipating the impacts of these events can be crucial for traders who seek to capitalize on price movements. In this section, we explore three key events: earnings announcements, mergers, and macroeconomic announcements.

1. **Earnings Announcements**:
    - **Anticipation and Speculation**: Prior to a company's earnings announcement, there is often speculation about how the company has performed during the past quarter. Analysts provide earnings estimates, and any deviation from these estimates can cause significant price swings.
    - **Post-Announcement Reactions**: Once the earnings are disclosed, the market's reaction can be swift and severe. Stocks may surge or plummet based on the reported figures and future outlook. For volatility traders, earnings season provides opportunities to trade straddles or strangles, anticipating significant moves without betting on a particular direction.

2. **Mergers and Acquisitions (M&A)**:
    - **Initial Rumors and Speculation**: Before an official merger announcement, there are usually rumors or leaks. These can drive the stock prices of both the acquiring and target companies.
    - **Post-Announcement Movements**: After the official disclosure, stock prices typically react, reflecting the perceived benefits or drawbacks of the deal. The target company's stock often rises, while the acquiring company's stock might drop or rise based on how favorable the deal terms are seen.
    - **Arbitrage Opportunities**: Volatility traders can take advantage of M&A arbitrage, betting on the convergence of the target's stock price to the acquisition price. However, it's crucial to note the risks, especially if the deal falls through.

3. **Macroeconomic Announcements**:
    - **Scheduled Releases**: Key economic indicators like unemployment rates, GDP figures, and central bank interest rate decisions are typically announced on scheduled dates. These releases can significantly impact broad market indices, currencies, and interest rates.
    - **Market Reactions**: Depending on how the actual data compares to market expectations, there can be substantial market moves. For instance, an unexpected interest rate hike can boost a currency but may depress equities.

For volatility traders, these events provide windows of opportunity. However, they come with risks. Proper risk management techniques, including setting stop losses and diversifying positions, are crucial.

14.2 Event-Driven Volatility Strategies

The essence of event-driven volatility trading is to harness price movements instigated by significant market events. Implementing strategies to exploit this volatility requires a blend of market insight, risk management, and tactical prowess. Let's delve into some approaches:

1. **Straddle Strategy**: Utilized around earnings announcements, a straddle involves buying both a call and a put option with the same strike price and expiration date. The objective is to profit from a significant move in either direction. The strategy is profitable if the stock makes a large enough move to cover the combined premiums paid for the options.

2. **Calendar Spread**: This involves buying and selling two options of the same type, but with different expiration dates. It can be advantageous if volatility is expected to change between the two expiration dates, such as between two consecutive earnings seasons.

3. **Volatility Arbitrage**: This strategy aims to exploit differences between implied volatility (IV) and a forecast of future realized volatility. By creating a delta-neutral portfolio, traders can profit from the divergence between IV and subsequent actual volatility.

4. **Gamma Scalping**: In the run-up to significant announcements, volatility traders can capitalize on the changing delta of an option by adjusting their stock positions. This strategy is most effective in highly volatile environments.

5. **Event-Driven Credit Spread**: This involves buying and selling options with different strike prices but the same expiration date, particularly around events expected to influence credit markets. For example, a major central bank announcement can be a trigger.

6. **Binary Options on Macroeconomic Indicators**: Binary options, which have a fixed payoff or none at all, can be used to bet on macroeconomic outcomes, like whether a particular data release will exceed or fall short of a certain threshold.

When deploying event-driven volatility strategies, traders must always be aware of the inherent risks. Outcomes can deviate from expectations, leading to losses. Furthermore, the premium for options can increase before significant events, reducing potential returns. As always, thorough research, due diligence, and effective risk management protocols are essential.

Chapter 15: Volatility Trading in Cryptocurrencies
15.1 Understanding the nuances of crypto volatility

In recent years, the world has witnessed the meteoric rise of cryptocurrencies, digital or virtual currencies that use cryptography for security and operate independently of a central authority. Alongside their ascent, these digital assets have become synonymous with extreme volatility. Let's dissect the nuances that make crypto markets particularly volatile:

1. **Nascent Market**: Cryptocurrencies, in comparison to traditional financial markets, are relatively young. The lack of a deep historical trading record makes them susceptible to sharp price fluctuations based on speculative trading.

2. **Lack of Regulation**: The absence of centralized oversight and regulations often means that market manipulation, rumors, and pump-and-dump schemes can greatly influence prices.

3. **Liquidity Constraints**: Some cryptocurrencies have limited liquidity, making them susceptible to large orders that can dramatically swing prices.

4. **High Speculation**: Given the futuristic and disruptive nature of blockchain and its applications, traders and investors in this space are largely speculative. News about technological advancements, regulatory changes, or macroeconomic factors can induce strong buying or selling pressure.

5. **Technological Factors**: Vulnerabilities, software upgrades (known as 'forks'), and scalability issues can have pronounced impacts on crypto prices.

6. **Global Market**: Cryptocurrencies are traded 24/7 across various global exchanges without geographical restrictions, leading to constant price adjustments.

For traders, these factors mean that cryptocurrency markets offer a unique set of opportunities and challenges. Understanding crypto-specific nuances is crucial for navigating and profiting from its volatility.

15.2 Strategies tailored for the crypto market

With the understanding that cryptocurrency markets have unique volatility profiles, traders must employ specialized strategies tailored for these assets. Here's a brief overview:

1. **Technical Analysis (TA)**: Due to the speculative nature of crypto trading, TA plays a prominent role. Patterns, trendlines, and indicators such as Moving Averages, RSI, and MACD are frequently used to predict price movements.

2. **Event-Driven Trading**: Cryptocurrency prices are highly responsive to events. Regulatory news, technological advancements, security breaches, and macroeconomic factors can all create significant price swings. Traders can position themselves ahead of known events or react quickly to unexpected news.

3. **Arbitrage**: Given the multitude of cryptocurrency exchanges worldwide, there can be price discrepancies for the same asset across different platforms. Traders can exploit these arbitrage opportunities by buying low on one exchange and selling high on another.

4. **Hedging Using Crypto Derivatives**: With the evolution of the crypto market, derivatives like futures and options have become available. These can be employed to hedge against potential adverse price movements.

5. **Long-term Holding (or 'HODLing')**: Given the nascent and potentially revolutionary nature of blockchain technology, some traders opt for a long-term approach, buying and holding their positions irrespective of short-term volatility.

6. **Day Trading**: Given the 24/7 nature of the crypto market, day trading is prevalent. Traders capitalize on intraday price swings using technical analysis and real-time news.

7. **Momentum Trading**: Due to the herd mentality often seen in crypto markets, momentum trading can be effective. Traders ride the wave of buying or selling pressure until a reversal sign appears.

It's important to note that while the cryptocurrency market offers vast opportunities, it's also rife with risks. The market's nascency, regulatory uncertainties, and technological vulnerabilities can pose significant threats to a trader's capital. As always, risk management and diligent research are paramount.

Chapter 16: Advanced Mathematical Models
16.1 Beyond the Black-Scholes: Stochastic volatility models

Volatility, a measure of asset price fluctuation, plays a crucial role in options pricing. Traditional models like the Black-Scholes assume that volatility is constant over the life of an option. While this simplifying assumption was revolutionary in its time, it does not capture the inherent complexities observed in financial markets, where volatility is often non-constant and can itself be volatile. Enter the domain of stochastic volatility models.

1. **Concept of Stochastic Volatility**: The term 'stochastic' essentially means 'random'. In a stochastic volatility model, volatility is treated as a random process, determined in part by market factors and, in part, by other random factors.

2. **Heston Model**: Named after Steven Heston, who formulated it in 1993, the Heston Model is one of the most prominent stochastic volatility models. Instead of assuming a constant volatility, this model assumes that volatility follows a mean-reverting square-root stochastic process. It can capture the empirical regularities in the stock option markets more accurately than the Black-Scholes model.

3. **Applications**: Stochastic volatility models are essential for valuing and managing new financial products, managing the risk of large portfolios over time, and ensuring profit in the face of the random movements of financial markets.

4. **Advantages**: These models provide a better fit to market data, capturing the volatility smile (a pattern in which at-the-money options tend to have lower implied volatilities than in- or out-of-the-money options). They also describe the term structure of volatility and the leverage effect, wherein asset returns and volatility are negatively correlated.

However, these models are not without challenges. They often require advanced mathematical tools and techniques to implement and can be computationally intensive.

16.2 The Heston model and its relevance

Diving deeper into the Heston model, it offers a unique blend of mathematical rigor and empirical accuracy. The model captures two crucial features of financial data that simpler models overlook: the leverage effect and volatility clustering.

1. **Leverage Effect**: This is the observed phenomenon in which stock returns and volatility are negatively correlated. When a stock's price falls sharply, the expected future volatility (and therefore option prices) often rise, and vice versa.

2. **Volatility Clustering**: In financial markets, large changes tend to be followed by large changes (of either sign), and small changes tend to be followed by small changes. This 'clustering' of volatility can be efficiently modeled using the Heston framework.

3. **Mathematical Foundation**: At the heart of the Heston model is a system of two stochastic differential equations. One describes the stock price dynamics (similar to the Black-Scholes model), and the other describes the variance dynamics. The model incorporates mean reversion, ensuring that volatility gravitates towards a long-term mean, and allows for fluctuating volatility over time.

4. **Relevance in Modern Markets**: The Heston model's ability to capture the actual movements and patterns of financial markets makes it invaluable. Traders, risk managers, and quantitative analysts use it to price complex derivatives, manage portfolio risk, and develop trading strategies.

5. **Implementation Challenges**: Despite its benefits, the Heston model demands sophisticated numerical methods for option pricing, such as finite difference methods, Monte Carlo simulations, and binomial trees.

In conclusion, while the Black-Scholes model set the foundation for modern financial mathematics, it's the more advanced models like Heston that offer the precision required in today's intricate financial landscape. The challenge and art lie in choosing the appropriate model based on the specific scenario and the trade-offs between accuracy and computational feasibility.

Chapter 17: Psychological Aspects of Volatility Trading
17.1 Managing emotions in a high volatility environment

In the realm of finance, volatility trading demands not only mathematical acumen but also psychological fortitude. The fluctuating nature of markets, coupled with the inherent uncertainties of volatility, can lead to heightened emotions, which, if not managed correctly, can adversely affect decision-making processes.

1. **The Emotional Rollercoaster**: Markets characterized by high volatility often induce a rollercoaster of emotions, including euphoria during price upswings and despair during downturns. This oscillating sentiment can cloud judgment, leading traders to make impulsive decisions.

2. **Overconfidence**: Periods of consistent returns can lead to overconfidence, causing traders to underestimate risks. They might take on excessively large positions or disregard fundamental market shifts.

3. **Fear and Panic**: Conversely, sudden market drops can evoke intense fear or even panic, prompting traders to exit positions prematurely or avoid entering potentially profitable setups.

4. **Anchoring**: This cognitive bias refers to the human tendency to rely too heavily on the first piece of information encountered (the "anchor") when making decisions. In a volatile market, traders might anchor to a specific price level or past performance, potentially missing out on new opportunities or misjudging risks.

5. **Strategies to Manage Emotions**:
    - **Continuous Education**: Keeping oneself updated with market dynamics and trading strategies can instill confidence.
    - **Diversification**: Spreading investments across various instruments can mitigate the impact of a poor-performing asset.
    - **Setting Predefined Rules**: Having a clear entry, exit, and risk management strategy can minimize impulsive decisions.
    - **Emotional Awareness**: Regular introspection and recognizing one's emotional triggers can prevent irrational actions.

6. **Importance of a Trading Journal**: Documenting trades, strategies, and emotions associated with each position can offer insights into behavioral patterns and areas of improvement. Over time, traders can identify emotional pitfalls and develop strategies to avoid them.

17.2 Cognitive biases to be aware of

Cognitive biases are systematic patterns of deviation from rationality in judgment and decision-making. For volatility traders, being aware of these biases is pivotal, as they can skew perception and lead to potentially detrimental decisions.

1. **Loss Aversion**: This refers to people's tendency to prefer avoiding losses over acquiring equivalent gains. For traders, it might manifest as holding onto a losing position in the hope it will rebound, instead of cutting losses early.

2. **Confirmation Bias**: Traders may seek out information that aligns with their existing beliefs while ignoring contradicting data. This can lead to a skewed understanding of market conditions.

3. **Hindsight Bias**: Post an event, traders might believe they "always knew" an asset would move in a certain direction. This can lead to overconfidence in predicting future events.

4. **Herd Mentality**: The tendency to follow the majority can be particularly strong in financial markets. Traders must be cautious not to get swept up in market euphoria or panic without conducting independent analysis.
5. **Recency Bias**: Giving more weightage to recent events than older ones can mislead traders, especially in volatile markets. Just because an asset has performed a certain way in the recent past doesn't ensure future performance.
6. **Solutions to Mitigate Biases**:
    - **Awareness**: Simply being aware of these biases can help traders recognize when they might be falling prey to them.
    - **Seek Contrarian Views**: Actively seeking out opposing viewpoints can offer a more balanced market perspective.
    - **Back-testing**: Before implementing a strategy, back-testing it on historical data can provide an objective assessment of its validity.
    - **Peer Review**: Discussing strategies and decisions with peers can unveil biases and offer alternative perspectives.

In essence, while mathematical models and algorithms play a significant role in volatility trading, the human element remains pivotal. Understanding and managing the interplay of emotions and cognitive biases can significantly enhance the decision-making process of a trader.

Chapter 18: Future Trends in Volatility Trading
18.1 Predictive analytics and machine learning in volatility forecasting

The investment landscape is constantly evolving, driven in large part by technological advancements. One of the areas of substantial progress is the fusion of predictive analytics and machine learning (ML) in the domain of volatility forecasting.

1. **Emergence of Predictive Analytics**: Predictive analytics leverages historical data to forecast future outcomes. In volatility trading, it aims to determine the likely future direction and magnitude of price changes, enhancing traders' decision-making abilities.
2. **Machine Learning's Role**: Traditional statistical models have limitations, as they often operate under strict assumptions and may not adapt well to changing market dynamics. Machine learning, with its adaptive algorithms, can automatically learn and improve from experience, making it more suited for the multifaceted realm of volatility.
3. **Types of Machine Learning in Volatility Forecasting**:
    - **Supervised Learning**: Algorithms are trained on labeled data, allowing the model to make predictions or infer mappings.
    - **Unsupervised Learning**: Used to detect patterns in data, clustering is a common technique here, which groups data based on similarities.
    - **Reinforcement Learning**: The model learns by interacting with an environment and receiving feedback for its actions, aligning well with trading where actions receive monetary feedback.
4. **Benefits**:
    - **Enhanced Accuracy**: Machine learning models can often uncover complex nonlinear relationships that traditional models might miss.

- **Adaptability**: ML models can adapt to new data, ensuring that they remain relevant even in changing market conditions.
- **Automation**: Automated trading strategies can be developed, allowing for swift, emotion-free execution.

5. **Challenges**:
    - **Overfitting**: There's a risk that ML models become too tailored to historical data, rendering them ineffective in real-world scenarios.
    - **Computational Intensity**: Advanced models, especially deep learning ones, can be computationally expensive, requiring specialized hardware.
    - **Transparency and Trust**: ML models, particularly neural networks, are often labeled as "black boxes," making their predictions hard to interpret.
6. **The Future**: As quantum computing and other advanced technologies become more accessible, their integration with machine learning promises further improvements in predictive accuracy, potentially revolutionizing volatility forecasting.

18.2 The evolving landscape of volatility trading in global markets

As global financial markets interconnect more deeply, the landscape of volatility trading evolves, reflecting the diverse economic, political, and technological changes unfolding worldwide.

1. **Global Economic Shifts**: Economic powerhouses are not static. The rise of emerging markets, coupled with fluctuating dynamics among established economies, introduces new volatility sources that traders must navigate.
2. **Regulatory Changes**: Global regulatory environments continually adapt. Changes in financial regulations can introduce new forms of volatility, especially if they're unexpected or substantially alter market structures.
3. **Technological Disruptions**: Innovations, like blockchain or decentralized finance (DeFi), could disrupt traditional financial structures, creating both challenges and opportunities for volatility traders.
4. **Geopolitical Events**: Unforeseen geopolitical events—be it elections, trade wars, or international conflicts—can significantly influence volatility. Understanding the geopolitical landscape becomes crucial for traders aiming to navigate such waters.
5. **Environmental and Social Considerations**: As environmental, social, and governance (ESG) factors become increasingly influential in investment decisions, related events can influence market volatility.
6. **Tail Events and Black Swans**: Unexpected 'black swan' events, such as the COVID-19 pandemic, introduce extreme volatility. While hard to predict, their potential impact makes them indispensable in any discussion about future volatility trends.
7. **Adaptability is Key**: The ever-changing global landscape necessitates that volatility traders remain adaptable, continuously educating themselves and refining their strategies. The future belongs to those who can quickly decipher, adapt, and capitalize on these evolving trends.

In summation, the future of volatility trading will be shaped by a confluence of economic, technological, and geopolitical forces. Success in this domain will be defined not just by quantitative acumen but also by adaptability, foresight, and a nuanced understanding of global events and trends.

Conclusion

Volatility trading, an essential facet of modern financial markets, demands a multifaceted approach grounded in deep understanding, technical acumen, and a keen sense of market dynamics. This comprehensive guide has endeavored to cover the breadth and depth of this topic, from the fundamental understanding of volatility to the future trends that promise to reshape this domain.

1. **Reflection on Volatility's Essence**: At the heart of volatility trading lies the quintessential need to understand and quantify uncertainty. It's not just about grasping the mathematical models or the sophisticated tools; it's about appreciating the ever-evolving nature of markets and the myriad factors influencing them.

2. **Instruments & Techniques**: As we've traversed through various chapters, the array of instruments available to a volatility trader—from options to futures, from traditional instruments to more exotic ones—reveals the depth and sophistication of this field. The strategies explored, both long and short, underscore the versatility and adaptability required in this domain.

3. **Technological Advancements**: The incorporation of machine learning, predictive analytics, and potential future inclusions like quantum computing underscore the importance of staying updated with technological advancements. These tools, while offering increased precision and capabilities, also introduce new challenges that traders must be equipped to handle.

4. **Psychological Aspects**: Volatility trading isn't solely about numbers or algorithms; it's deeply intertwined with human psychology. Emotions, biases, and behaviors play a pivotal role in trading outcomes. Thus, self-awareness and psychological resilience are as essential as technical expertise.

5. **Globalization's Role**: In an increasingly interconnected world, the ripple effects of events across the globe have profound implications for volatility. This interconnectivity means traders must be globally aware, understanding geopolitical shifts, regulatory changes, and major global events.

6. **Preparing for the Future**: The future of volatility trading, as outlined in the latter chapters, is both promising and challenging. The integration of technology, the evolution of global markets, and the constant drive for innovation mean that volatility trading will remain a dynamic and evolving field.

In closing, volatility trading encapsulates the essence of modern financial markets—dynamic, complex, and rewarding. Whether you're a seasoned trader or an enthusiastic novice, the journey through volatility trading is one of continuous learning and adaptation. The realms of technology, psychology, and global events intersect in this domain, offering challenges and opportunities in equal measure. By staying informed, adaptable, and resilient, one can navigate the tumultuous waters of volatility trading and emerge not just as a successful trader but as a well-rounded market connoisseur.

Pairs Trading

Trade on the relative performance of two related instruments, aiming to profit from their price relationship

Introduction

A. Definition of Pairs Trading

Pairs trading, often termed statistical arbitrage or relative value arbitrage, is a quantitative trading strategy that capitalizes on the relative performance of two related financial instruments. The core idea is to go long (buy) on one instrument while simultaneously going short (sell) on another, betting on the assumption that the historical price relationship between the two instruments will return to its mean, generating a profit.

B. History and Origin

The concept of pairs trading can trace its origins back to the 1980s when it was pioneered by quantitative analysts at major investment banks and hedge funds, most notably Morgan Stanley. These professionals realized that certain securities, often within the same sector or industry, moved in patterns that were closely correlated. When these correlations deviated, presenting a temporary mispricing between the two, a trading opportunity emerged. The pairs trading strategy was born out of this observation, and over the years, it has been refined and has proliferated into various financial markets around the world.

C. Overview of the Benefits and Risks

Benefits:

1. **Market Neutrality:** One of the primary advantages of pairs trading is its market-neutral nature. Since the trader holds both long and short positions simultaneously, the strategy becomes less susceptible to broad market movements.
2. **Predictable Risk Profile:** Pairs trading offers a defined risk structure since the potential loss is usually limited to the difference in movement between the two instruments.
3. **Diversification:** Pairs trading provides a layer of diversification as it doesn't rely on a single instrument's performance but on the relationship between two.

Risks:

1. **Model Risk:** A primary concern in pairs trading is the accuracy of the model used to determine pair selection and entry/exit points. A flawed model can lead to incorrect assumptions and losses.
2. **Liquidity Risk:** Not all instruments are highly liquid. If one part of the pair lacks liquidity, it can lead to slippage and adversely affect the execution of the trade.
3. **Convergence Failure:** There is no guarantee that the two instruments' price relationship will revert to the historical mean, which can result in prolonged holding periods or potential losses.

By understanding these benefits and risks, traders can approach pairs trading with a balanced perspective, optimizing their strategies while being aware of potential pitfalls.

Chapter 1 Fundamental Concepts of Pairs Trading

A. Relative Performance Explained

In the context of pairs trading, relative performance refers to the comparative behavior of two financial instruments over a specific period. When evaluating two instruments, their individual price movements might not be as informative as their relative movement to each other. By examining this relative performance, traders aim to discern patterns or discrepancies that indicate a temporary divergence from an established norm.

To simplify, if Stock A historically trades at twice the price of Stock B but suddenly surges to three times the price without a valid fundamental reason, there's a divergence in their relative performance. This disparity presents a potential trading opportunity.

B. The Logic Behind Pair Selection

Selecting the appropriate pair is the cornerstone of this strategy. The instruments chosen should have a historical or fundamental relationship. Here's the logic behind effective pair selection:

1. **Correlation:** The two instruments should exhibit a high correlation, meaning they tend to move in the same direction. Correlation coefficients, ranging between -1 and 1, can help quantify this. A coefficient close to 1 indicates a strong positive relationship.

2. **Industry or Sector Similarities:** Stocks from the same sector or industry often have similar price movements because they are influenced by the same macroeconomic factors. For example, two tech companies might be affected similarly by a change in semiconductor prices.

3. **Geographical Location:** Companies operating in the same region might face similar challenges and opportunities, making their stocks suitable for pairs trading.

4. **Economic Indicators:** Financial instruments influenced by the same economic indicators (like interest rates or inflation) can form valid pairs.

However, even if all these boxes are ticked, traders should continually reassess their pairs as market dynamics change.

C. Mean Reversion Theory

Mean reversion is a cornerstone theory for pairs trading. It asserts that prices and returns eventually revert to the long-run mean or average level of the entire dataset. In pairs trading, this refers to the historical price relationship between two instruments.

Let's break it down:

1. **Historical Relationship:** Over a significant period, two instruments might exhibit a stable relationship, like maintaining a consistent price ratio.

2. **Deviation:** Due to various short-term factors, this relationship might temporarily diverge. This divergence creates a potential trading opportunity.

3. **Reversion Expectation:** Based on historical data and the mean reversion principle, a trader expects that this divergence will be temporary, and the relationship will soon revert to its mean.

While mean reversion forms the bedrock of pairs trading, it's crucial to understand that "mean" can shift over time due to long-term fundamental changes. As such, traders should always be vigilant and adaptive.

Chapter 2 Prerequisites to Pairs Trading

A. Understanding of Financial Markets

Before diving into pairs trading, one must have a foundational grasp of the financial markets and their intricacies. This comprehension includes:

1. **Market Mechanics:** Be familiar with how markets operate, including the role of brokers, exchanges, and market makers.

2. **Economic Indicators:** Recognize key indicators like GDP, inflation rates, and unemployment figures, and understand their potential impact on financial instruments.

3. **Asset Classes:** Different asset classes (e.g., equities, bonds, commodities) have varied characteristics and risks. Understanding these distinctions is paramount.

4. **Regulatory Landscape:** Being aware of the regulatory environment is crucial, especially since pairs trading often involves short-selling, which might be subject to particular rules in some jurisdictions.

B. Necessary Tools and Software

Pairs trading is data-intensive and relies heavily on quantitative analyses. Thus, having access to the right tools and software is imperative:

1. **Data Feeds:** Real-time and historical data feeds ensure traders have up-to-date information on their chosen instruments.

2. **Analytical Software:** Software that can compute correlations, cointegrations, and other statistical measures is essential. Tools like MATLAB, R, and Python libraries can be beneficial in this domain.

3. **Charting Tools:** Visual representations help traders identify patterns, divergence, and convergence in the price relationship of paired instruments.

4. **Backtesting Platforms:** Before deploying a strategy in real-time, traders should test its efficacy on historical data. Backtesting platforms simulate trades based on past data to gauge potential performance.

C. Setting Up a Trading Account

To engage in pairs trading, one requires a suitable trading account:

1. **Type of Account:** For pairs trading, especially when involving short-selling, a margin account is typically required. This allows traders to borrow stocks for shorting and provides the necessary leverage.

2. **Broker Selection:** It's crucial to choose a broker who understands and offers infrastructure for pairs trading. This might include competitive margin rates, a wide range of available stocks for shorting, and advanced trading platforms.

3. **Cost Considerations:** Pairs trading can involve multiple transactions in a short period. Hence, understanding the fee structure, including commission rates and any other charges, can significantly impact profitability.

4. **Risk Management Features:** Ensure that the chosen brokerage platform offers risk management tools, such as stop-loss orders and alerts, vital for safeguarding investments in volatile market conditions.

Entering the realm of pairs trading requires diligent preparation. By ensuring a solid understanding of financial markets, arming oneself with essential tools, and setting up a conducive trading environment, traders set the stage for potential success in this sophisticated trading strategy.

Chapter 3 Selection of Instruments for Pairs Trading

A. Criteria for Choosing Tradable Pairs

The selection of pairs is of paramount importance in this trading strategy. A miscalculation or oversight can lead to unsatisfactory results or significant losses. When selecting pairs for trading, certain criteria come into play:

1. **Correlation Analysis:**

Correlation measures the linear relationship between two financial instruments. A correlation coefficient, which ranges between -1 and 1, quantifies this relationship. A value close to 1 indicates a strong positive correlation, meaning the two instruments typically move in the same direction. Conversely, a value close to -1 denotes a strong negative correlation. For pairs trading, a high positive correlation is often sought. This is because the strategy revolves around the idea that if two stocks historically move together and suddenly one deviates, it will eventually revert to the norm.

2. **Cointegration Tests:**

While correlation indicates that two series move together, cointegration ensures that the distance between them remains constant over time. In pairs trading, it's possible for two stocks to be correlated but not cointegrated. Such pairs may not be suitable for trading since the spread between them might drift indefinitely. Cointegration tests, such as the Engle-Granger two-step method or the Johansen Test, help identify pairs where the spread is statistically likely to revert to a mean, making them ideal candidates for pairs trading.

B. Examples of Commonly Traded Pairs

Pairs trading isn't limited to any particular market or asset class. However, certain pairs are more popular because of their historical or economic linkages. Some examples include:

1. **Equities within the same sector:** Companies within the same industry often face similar market forces. For example, Exxon Mobil and Chevron are both major players in the oil industry and can form a pair.

2. **Equity and its ADR (American Depository Receipt):** An ADR represents shares in a foreign company trading on U.S. exchanges. For instance, the stock of a company trading in its home country and its ADR in the U.S. can present a trading pair, like Alibaba Group's shares in Hong Kong and its ADR in the U.S.

3. **Cross-Country Equities in the same industry:** Companies from different countries but within the same industry might form a pair due to global market forces. For example, Ford (U.S.) and Toyota (Japan) in the automobile sector.

4. **Futures Contracts:** Commodities with interlinked demand and supply forces can also form pairs. For example, Gold and Silver futures, or Brent Crude and West Texas Intermediate (WTI) crude oil.

By understanding the fundamental criteria for pair selection and familiarizing oneself with commonly traded pairs, traders can position themselves more strategically in the market, better anticipating potential divergences and convergences for profit.

Chapter 4 Implementing Pairs Trading Strategies

A. Determining Entry and Exit Points

Successfully implementing pairs trading hinges on accurately identifying when to enter and exit a trade. Here's how traders approach these crucial decisions:

1. **Identifying Divergence:** The initial step is to spot a divergence in the historical price relationship between the two instruments. This divergence is often measured in terms of standard deviations from the mean. A commonly used threshold is two standard deviations; however, this can vary based on the trader's analysis and risk tolerance.

2. **Entry Point:** Once a divergence is identified, a trader would typically short the outperforming instrument and go long on the underperforming one, anticipating a reversion to the mean.

3. **Exit Point:** The trade is usually closed in one of three scenarios:
   - The price relationship reverts to the mean.
   - The price relationship moves further away, reaching a predetermined stop-loss.
   - After a predefined time, if the expected reversion hasn't occurred.

B. Managing Risk and Position Sizing

Effective risk management is vital to ensure the longevity and profitability of a pairs trading strategy:

1. **Position Sizing:** Determine the amount to invest based on the volatility of the pairs and the total capital available. Typically, less volatile pairs can command a larger position, while more volatile pairs require a smaller position to manage risk.

2. **Stop-Loss Orders:** Establish stop-loss points, which automatically close positions if the price relationship deviates further than expected. This acts as a safety net, limiting potential losses.

3. **Profit Targets:** Set profit targets based on historical data and the expected reversion to the mean. This helps in locking in profits before market dynamics change.

4. **Diversification:** Just as with broader portfolios, diversifying among different pairs can spread risk. However, it's essential to ensure the pairs are not overly correlated, which might compound losses.

C. Monitoring and Adjusting Open Positions

Continuous monitoring is essential to adapt to changing market conditions:

1. **Real-time Tracking:** Employ tools and software to track the performance of open positions in real-time, ensuring quick reactions to unexpected market shifts.

2. **Reassessing Correlation and Cointegration:** Over time, the correlation and cointegration between two instruments might change. Regularly reassess these metrics to ensure the pairs still meet the criteria for trading.
3. **Adjusting Stop-Loss and Profit Targets:** As market volatility and dynamics change, it might be necessary to adjust previously set stop-loss and profit target points.
4. **Partial Closing:** In some situations, instead of fully closing a position when reaching profit targets or stop-loss points, traders might opt to partially close, securing some profit or limiting some loss, while still maintaining a presence in the market.

Implementing pairs trading strategies requires a blend of meticulous planning, rigorous analysis, and adaptive management. By determining precise entry and exit points, diligently managing risk, and continuously monitoring and adjusting open positions, traders can better navigate the complexities of pairs trading.

Chapter 5 Advanced Techniques in Pairs Trading

A. Incorporating Technical Analysis

While pairs trading is primarily a quantitative, data-driven approach, integrating insights from technical analysis can refine the strategy further:

1. **Moving Averages:** Using moving averages, such as the 50-day or 200-day, can help traders identify trends within the pair. Crossovers between short-term and long-term averages can signal potential entry or exit points.
2. **Bollinger Bands:** This tool can be particularly effective in identifying when the spread between a pair is diverging or converging. The bands adjust to volatility and can offer insight into when a reversion to the mean might occur.
3. **Momentum Indicators:** Tools like the Relative Strength Index (RSI) or the Moving Average Convergence Divergence (MACD) can signal overbought or oversold conditions for the instruments in a pair, aiding in timely entry or exit decisions.

B. Statistical Methods in Pairs Trading

Sophisticated statistical methods can be employed to ensure the selected pairs have a solid foundation for reversion to the mean:

1. **Engle-Granger Two-Step Method:**

This technique involves two main steps:

- **Step 1:** Run a linear regression between the two price series to determine the hedge ratio.
- **Step 2:** Use the residuals (the difference between observed and predicted values) from the regression and test them for stationarity. If the residuals are stationary, it suggests the pair is cointegrated, making them suitable for pairs trading.

2. **Johansen Test:**

This test is a multivariate extension of the Engle-Granger method and can be used to detect multiple cointegrating relationships. This is especially useful when considering more than two financial instruments.

C. Machine Learning in Pairs Trading

Machine learning offers cutting-edge techniques to identify, execute, and manage pairs trading strategies:

1. **Feature Engineering:** Machine learning relies heavily on the features (or variables) fed into the model. For pairs trading, features might include price ratios, volatility measures, and economic indicators.

2. **Model Selection:** Different machine learning models, such as decision trees, neural networks, or support vector machines, can be trained on historical data. The model with the best predictive performance on validation data sets might be chosen for real-time trading.

3. **Real-time Adaptation:** One significant advantage of machine learning is its ability to adapt in real-time. As more data becomes available, the model can continuously refine its predictions and strategies.

4. **Risk Management:** Advanced machine learning models can also predict the potential risk associated with a trade, adjusting position sizes accordingly and suggesting optimal stop-loss points.

Integrating advanced techniques like technical analysis, sophisticated statistical methods, and machine learning can significantly enhance the effectiveness of a pairs trading strategy, offering a nuanced and adaptive approach to this form of trading.

Chapter 6 Real-world Examples and Case Studies

A. Historical Pairs Trading Successes

Over the decades, pairs trading has seen numerous success stories. Here are some prominent examples:

1. **Royal Dutch Shell vs. Shell Transport (1980s):** One of the most famous pairs trades involved the stocks of Royal Dutch Petroleum and Shell Transport. Although they were essentially shares in the same business, the two stocks often diverged in price. Savvy traders capitalized on these inefficiencies by buying the undervalued stock and short-selling the overvalued one, making substantial profits when the prices converged.

2. **Merger Arbitrage (Multiple Instances):** In merger situations, there is often a target company and an acquiring company. Pairs traders will short the acquiring company and go long on the target company, capitalizing on the price convergence that typically happens as the merger date approaches.

B. Lessons from Failed Pairs Trades

While pairs trading has its triumphs, it also has its pitfalls. Analyzing unsuccessful trades is crucial for refining strategies:

1. **Long-Term Capital Management (LTCM) Collapse (1998):** LTCM, a hedge fund, employed various arbitrage strategies, including pairs trading. However, they used extreme leverage. When Russia defaulted on its debt, it triggered a chain reaction, causing significant divergence in many of LTCM's positions. Unable to withstand the losses, LTCM collapsed, underscoring the dangers of excessive leverage.

2. **The Financial Crisis (2008):** Many pairs that were historically correlated broke down during the 2008 financial crisis. Banks, which were typically paired with one another, saw dramatic price divergences. Those who did not adapt or had too narrow a focus faced significant losses.

C. Contemporary Trading Scenarios

The landscape of pairs trading is ever-evolving. In recent years, some notable developments include:

1. **Tech Giants – FAANG Stocks:** Traders often look for pairs within the FAANG group (Facebook, Apple, Amazon, Netflix, Google/Alphabet). For instance, if Apple and Amazon have historically moved together, but a product launch causes a temporary price surge in Apple, traders might consider this an opportunity.

2. **COVID-19 Pandemic and Pharma Companies:** With the rush for vaccines and treatments during the COVID-19 pandemic, pharma companies presented potential pairs trading opportunities. If two companies historically had similar stock trajectories but one got temporary approval for a treatment, it created a divergence that traders could potentially exploit.

3. **Green Energy Pairs:** As the world pivots to renewable energy, companies in this sector, like solar or wind energy firms, can present pairs trading opportunities, especially in light of regulatory changes or technological advancements.

Examining real-world examples and case studies, both successful and cautionary, offers traders valuable insights. Historical successes provide models to emulate, while failures underscore potential risks and highlight the importance of adaptability and risk management in pairs trading.

Chapter 7 Potential Pitfalls and How to Avoid Them

A. Dangers of Over-leveraging

Over-leveraging refers to the excessive use of debt (borrowed capital) to finance trading positions. While leveraging can amplify profits, it also intensifies losses, making it a double-edged sword.

1. **Liquidity Crunch:** Over-leveraging can result in a liquidity crunch, especially during market downturns. If multiple positions move against a trader simultaneously, the combined losses can quickly deplete available capital.

2. **Margin Calls:** Leveraging often involves borrowing from brokers. If the value of a trader's portfolio drops below a certain threshold, brokers can issue margin calls, demanding additional capital. Failure to meet these demands can result in forced liquidation of positions at inopportune times.

3. **Avoidance Strategy:**
   - **Limit Leverage:** Set a maximum allowable leverage ratio and stick to it.
   - **Regularly Monitor Exposure:** Regularly assess the total exposure relative to available capital to avoid inadvertently over-leveraging.

B. Importance of Continual Research

Financial markets are dynamic, and the factors influencing instrument prices can change rapidly.

1. **Changing Fundamentals:** An instrument's fundamentals, such as company earnings or broader economic conditions, can shift, affecting the historical relationship between a pair.
2. **Updated Data:** Using outdated data can lead to miscalculations and flawed strategies.
3. **Prevention Strategy:**
   - **Frequent Data Updates:** Ensure that the data being used for analysis is current.
   - **Ongoing Analysis:** Regularly revisit and update the research on selected pairs to account for new market information.
   - **Diversify Sources:** Rely on multiple research sources to get a holistic view of market conditions.

C. Recognizing and Adapting to Market Shifts

Market shifts refer to changes in broader market dynamics, which can be temporary or long-term. Recognizing and adapting to these shifts is crucial for pairs trading success.

1. **Black Swan Events:** Unexpected events, like geopolitical crises or pandemics, can cause significant market disruptions. These events can temporarily or permanently alter the correlation between pairs.
2. **Sectoral Shifts:** Changes in consumer preferences, technological advancements, or regulatory changes can impact specific sectors, affecting historically stable pairs within that sector.
3. **Mitigation Strategy:**
   - **Stay Informed:** Keep abreast of global news and industry updates to anticipate potential market shifts.
   - **Flexible Strategies:** Design trading strategies that can be adjusted quickly in response to changing market conditions.
   - **Hedging:** Consider employing hedging strategies to mitigate potential losses during market upheavals.

In the intricate dance of pairs trading, vigilance, continual learning, and adaptability are paramount. By being wary of over-leveraging, staying updated with ongoing research, and nimbly navigating market shifts, traders can sidestep many pitfalls and position themselves for success.

Chapter 8 Future Outlook of Pairs Trading

A. Emerging Markets and Pairs Trading

Emerging markets refer to economies that are in the process of rapid industrialization and experiencing higher than average growth rates. They offer a unique playground for pairs trading:

1. **Greater Volatility:** Emerging markets tend to be more volatile than developed markets, presenting increased opportunities for pairs trading. However, this also comes with heightened risks.
2. **Economic Synchronicity:** As emerging markets become more integrated with global economies, their financial instruments might develop strong correlations with instruments in developed markets, providing new pairs trading opportunities.

3. **Foreign Exchange Implications:** Currency risks are pronounced in emerging markets. Traders need to account for potential currency value fluctuations when calculating spreads and potential returns.
4. **Recommendation:** Due diligence is essential. Traders should deeply understand the economic, political, and regulatory landscape of an emerging market before diving into pairs trading.

B. Technological Advances and their Impacts

Technology has always played a pivotal role in financial markets, and this is doubly true for a data-intensive strategy like pairs trading:

1. **Algorithmic Trading:** As computational speeds increase, the use of algorithms in pairs trading is becoming more prevalent. Algorithms can automatically identify potential pairs, monitor spreads, and execute trades in real-time.
2. **Machine Learning and AI:** Advanced machine learning models can continually adapt to market changes, making predictions more accurate. They can also manage multiple pairs simultaneously, optimizing for maximum profitability.
3. **Blockchain and Decentralized Finance (DeFi):** Blockchain technology could revolutionize how trades are executed and recorded. This can lead to more transparent and efficient markets, potentially impacting pairs trading strategies.
4. **Recommendation:** Traders should invest in continuous learning to stay updated with technological advancements and understand how to harness them effectively.

C. Predicted Trends and Shifts in Strategy

As the global financial landscape evolves, so will pairs trading:

1. **Environmental, Social, and Governance (ESG) Metrics:** With the rising importance of ESG in investment decisions, pairs might be selected based on these metrics in addition to traditional financial indicators.
2. **Broader Asset Classes:** As markets become more intertwined, pairs trading might expand beyond equities to involve a wider range of asset classes, including cryptocurrencies, commodities, or real estate investment trusts.
3. **Globalization vs. Regionalization:** While globalization leads to more inter-market pairs, increasing trends towards regionalization and protectionism might shift the focus back to intra-market pairs.
4. **Recommendation:** Pairs traders should adopt a forward-thinking approach, anticipating and preparing for shifts in market dynamics, trading tools, and global economic trends.

In conclusion, the future of pairs trading promises to be as dynamic and exciting as its past. By understanding and adapting to emerging markets, technological advances, and shifting global trends, traders can position themselves at the forefront of this ever-evolving strategy.

Chapter 9 Behavioral Aspects of Pairs Trading

While the mechanics of pairs trading heavily lean on quantitative methods and rigorous data analysis, it's imperative not to overlook the behavioral aspects that can significantly influence decision-making. This chapter delves into the psychology behind pairs trading, highlighting both the potential pitfalls borne out of cognitive biases and strategies to circumvent them.

A. Psychological Challenges in Pairs Trading

1. **Overconfidence:** Traders, armed with sophisticated models, may develop an undue confidence in their predictions. However, even the most robust models can't account for all market variables. Overestimating one's capability or the accuracy of a model can lead to excessive risk-taking.

2. **Loss Aversion:** Traders may hold on to losing positions longer than they should, hoping that the market will reverse. This bias can be especially pronounced in pairs trading, where the expectation of mean reversion might be mistaken for a guarantee.

3. **Confirmation Bias:** Traders might seek out or favor information that confirms their existing beliefs or trading decisions, while disregarding conflicting data.

4. **Herd Mentality:** In the world of finance, where information is abundant and often contradictory, traders might find comfort in following the crowd. Pairs traders aren't immune, and following popular pairs without thorough analysis can be detrimental.

B. Strategies for Behavioral Management

1. **Maintain Emotional Distance:** Developing a systematic trading plan and adhering to it can help in making decisions based on logic rather than emotions. Set predetermined entry and exit points, and avoid altering them without a solid, data-backed reason.

2. **Regularly Review Assumptions:** Continuously validate the assumptions upon which pairs are selected. Markets evolve, and relationships between instruments can change.

3. **Diversify Strategies:** While pairs trading may be the primary focus, diversifying trading strategies can reduce the emotional and financial impact of any single strategy underperforming.

4. **Seek Feedback:** Engage with peers or mentors to review trading strategies and decisions. External perspectives can highlight biases or assumptions one might overlook.

5. **Continuous Education:** Understand cognitive biases and how they manifest in trading decisions. Awareness is the first step in managing these biases.

C. The Role of Experience

While knowledge and quantitative skills are crucial in pairs trading, experience plays a quintessential role. Over time, traders:

1. **Develop Intuition:** This isn't about making gut decisions but rather about recognizing patterns and nuances more quickly, based on past experiences.

2. **Manage Stress Better:** High-stress situations, inevitable in trading, are handled more calmly with experience, leading to clearer decision-making.

3. **Refine Strategies:** Every trade, whether successful or not, offers lessons. Experienced traders continually refine their strategies based on real-world results.

D. Incorporating Behavioral Finance in Pairs Trading

Behavioral finance, a field that combines psychological theory with conventional finance to provide explanations for why investors make irrational decisions, offers key insights for pairs traders.

1. Prospect Theory in Pairs Trading

Derived from the foundational work of Kahneman and Tversky, prospect theory posits that investors derive pleasure from market gains and pain from losses, but these feelings are not symmetrical. The pain of a loss is felt more intensely than the pleasure of a gain.

Application: In pairs trading, this could manifest as a trader closing a winning position too early to "lock in" gains and holding onto a losing position in the hope it will turn around. By being aware of this bias, traders can commit to preset exit points regardless of emotional impulses.

2. Anchoring in Decision Making

Anchoring refers to the tendency of attaching our thoughts to a reference point—even if it's irrelevant to the decision at hand.

Application: A pairs trader might anchor their decision to an initial price point, disregarding subsequent information. For instance, if a pair historically reverts at a particular spread value, traders might anchor to this value, ignoring market changes that render the historical spread irrelevant. Continuous monitoring and adjustment based on new data can help counteract this bias.

3. Mental Accounting and Portfolio Management

Mental accounting is a cognitive framing where people compartmentalize assets in different mental "accounts." Each account has its rules, which might lead to irrational decisions.

Application: In pairs trading, one might mentally categorize investments into "long-term pairs" and "short-term pairs," leading to inconsistent risk management or decision-making criteria between these categorizations. By viewing the entire portfolio holistically and applying consistent analysis across all pairs, traders can avoid such biases.

E. Overcoming Information Overload

The advent of technology means traders have access to an overwhelming amount of data, news, and analysis. But more information isn't always better; it can lead to analysis paralysis or misplaced emphasis on irrelevant data.

Strategies to Combat Information Overload:

1. **Filter Information:** Use trusted sources and advanced data analytics tools to filter out noise and focus on relevant information.
2. **Establish Routine:** Dedicate specific times for data analysis, market news updates, and strategy refinement. Avoid constant checking, which can lead to reactive decisions.
3. **Limit Indicators:** While multiple technical indicators can provide varied insights, using too many can result in conflicting signals. Stick to a select few that align with the pairs trading strategy.

F. The Human-Machine Symbiosis

In the age of algorithms and high-frequency trading, the role of human judgment might seem diminished. However, the fusion of human insight with algorithmic precision presents the best of both worlds.

While machines are excellent at processing vast amounts of data quickly, humans excel in areas of intuition, context interpretation, and strategic foresight. For pairs trading, this symbiotic relationship can mean using algorithms to monitor and flag potential pair opportunities and human judgment to finalize the selection and set strategic parameters.

G. The Role of Ethics in Pairs Trading

While pairs trading is fundamentally a quantitative strategy, ethical considerations are paramount to maintaining the integrity of the markets and the trust of investors. In a world where a fine line sometimes separates sophisticated strategies from manipulation, understanding the ethical dimensions becomes crucial.

1. Market Manipulation and Pairs Trading

Definition: Market manipulation refers to artificially inflating or deflating the price of a security or otherwise influencing the behavior of the market for personal gain.

Application to Pairs Trading: Given that pairs trading involves simultaneous long and short positions, there's a potential (though unintended) to influence the market, especially with less liquid securities. For instance, heavy shorting on one security of a pair could drive its price down artificially. Traders must be aware of these impacts and strive to conduct trades without unduly influencing market dynamics.

2. Information Asymmetry and Fair Play

Definition: Information asymmetry occurs when one party in a transaction has more or better information than the other. This typically makes the transaction inequitable.

Application to Pairs Trading: Given the sophisticated data analytics involved, pairs traders might sometimes possess information or insights not readily available to the broader market. While leveraging unique strategies is acceptable, using non-public, insider information to inform trades is not only unethical but also illegal.

3. Responsibility to Clients

For fund managers and institutional traders, there's an added layer of responsibility towards clients.

- **Transparency:** Clients should be informed about the strategies being used, the associated risks, and potential returns. This is particularly vital for strategies like pairs trading, which might be less familiar to the average investor.
- **Best Execution:** Traders have an ethical and often legal obligation to ensure the best execution for their clients' trades, seeking the most favorable terms and minimizing costs.

H. Sustainable and Ethical Investment Considerations

Modern investment isn't just about returns; there's a growing emphasis on sustainability and ethical considerations.

1. **ESG (Environmental, Social, Governance) in Pairs Trading:** With the rise of ESG investing, pairs traders need to be mindful of these factors. For instance, while two companies might be cointegrated and perfect for pairs trading from a quantitative perspective, they might diverge significantly in ESG scores. For funds committed to sustainable investing, such pairs might be unsuitable.
2. **Impact on Broader Economy:** Pairs traders, especially those operating at significant volumes, should consider the broader impacts of their trades. For example, aggressive shorting can affect companies' ability to raise capital, impacting jobs and broader economic health.

I. Continuous Ethical Training and Development

To navigate the ethical complexities of modern trading:

1. **Regular Training:** Pairs traders should undergo regular ethical training, staying updated with the latest regulations, best practices, and ethical considerations.
2. **Ethical Committees:** Large trading institutions might benefit from dedicated ethical committees, overseeing trading strategies' fairness, legality, and alignment with the company's broader ethical stance.

Chapter 10 Behavioral Aspects of Pairs Trading

While the mechanics of pairs trading heavily lean on quantitative methods and rigorous data analysis, it's imperative not to overlook the behavioral aspects that can significantly influence decision-making. This chapter delves into the psychology behind pairs trading, highlighting both the potential pitfalls borne out of cognitive biases and strategies to circumvent them.

A. Psychological Challenges in Pairs Trading

1. **Overconfidence:** Traders, armed with sophisticated models, may develop an undue confidence in their predictions. However, even the most robust models can't account for all market variables. Overestimating one's capability or the accuracy of a model can lead to excessive risk-taking.
2. **Loss Aversion:** Traders may hold on to losing positions longer than they should, hoping that the market will reverse. This bias can be especially pronounced in pairs trading, where the expectation of mean reversion might be mistaken for a guarantee.
3. **Confirmation Bias:** Traders might seek out or favor information that confirms their existing beliefs or trading decisions, while disregarding conflicting data.
4. **Herd Mentality:** In the world of finance, where information is abundant and often contradictory, traders might find comfort in following the crowd. Pairs traders aren't immune, and following popular pairs without thorough analysis can be detrimental.

B. Strategies for Behavioral Management

1. **Maintain Emotional Distance:** Developing a systematic trading plan and adhering to it can help in making decisions based on logic rather than emotions. Set predetermined entry and exit points, and avoid altering them without a solid, data-backed reason.

2. **Regularly Review Assumptions:** Continuously validate the assumptions upon which pairs are selected. Markets evolve, and relationships between instruments can change.

3. **Diversify Strategies:** While pairs trading may be the primary focus, diversifying trading strategies can reduce the emotional and financial impact of any single strategy underperforming.

4. **Seek Feedback:** Engage with peers or mentors to review trading strategies and decisions. External perspectives can highlight biases or assumptions one might overlook.

5. **Continuous Education:** Understand cognitive biases and how they manifest in trading decisions. Awareness is the first step in managing these biases.

C. The Role of Experience

While knowledge and quantitative skills are crucial in pairs trading, experience plays a quintessential role. Over time, traders:

1. **Develop Intuition:** This isn't about making gut decisions but rather about recognizing patterns and nuances more quickly, based on past experiences.

2. **Manage Stress Better:** High-stress situations, inevitable in trading, are handled more calmly with experience, leading to clearer decision-making.

3. **Refine Strategies:** Every trade, whether successful or not, offers lessons. Experienced traders continually refine their strategies based on real-world results.

D. Incorporating Behavioral Finance in Pairs Trading

Behavioral finance, a field that combines psychological theory with conventional finance to provide explanations for why investors make irrational decisions, offers key insights for pairs traders.

1. Prospect Theory in Pairs Trading

Derived from the foundational work of Kahneman and Tversky, prospect theory posits that investors derive pleasure from market gains and pain from losses, but these feelings are not symmetrical. The pain of a loss is felt more intensely than the pleasure of a gain.

Application: In pairs trading, this could manifest as a trader closing a winning position too early to "lock in" gains and holding onto a losing position in the hope it will turn around. By being aware of this bias, traders can commit to preset exit points regardless of emotional impulses.

3. **Anchoring in Decision Making**
   Anchoring refers to the tendency of attaching our thoughts to a reference point—even if it's irrelevant to the decision at hand.

Application: A pairs trader might anchor their decision to an initial price point, disregarding subsequent information. For instance, if a pair historically reverts at a particular spread value, traders might anchor to this value, ignoring market changes that render the historical spread irrelevant. Continuous monitoring and adjustment based on new data can help counteract this bias.

3. Mental Accounting and Portfolio Management

Mental accounting is a cognitive framing where people compartmentalize assets in different mental "accounts." Each account has its rules, which might lead to irrational decisions.

Application: In pairs trading, one might mentally categorize investments into "long-term pairs" and "short-term pairs," leading to inconsistent risk management or decision-making criteria between these categorizations. By viewing the entire portfolio holistically and applying consistent analysis across all pairs, traders can avoid such biases.

E. Overcoming Information Overload

The advent of technology means traders have access to an overwhelming amount of data, news, and analysis. But more information isn't always better; it can lead to analysis paralysis or misplaced emphasis on irrelevant data.

Strategies to Combat Information Overload:

1. **Filter Information:** Use trusted sources and advanced data analytics tools to filter out noise and focus on relevant information.
2. **Establish Routine:** Dedicate specific times for data analysis, market news updates, and strategy refinement. Avoid constant checking, which can lead to reactive decisions.
3. **Limit Indicators:** While multiple technical indicators can provide varied insights, using too many can result in conflicting signals. Stick to a select few that align with the pairs trading strategy.

F. The Human-Machine Symbiosis

In the age of algorithms and high-frequency trading, the role of human judgment might seem diminished. However, the fusion of human insight with algorithmic precision presents the best of both worlds.

While machines are excellent at processing vast amounts of data quickly, humans excel in areas of intuition, context interpretation, and strategic foresight. For pairs trading, this symbiotic relationship can mean using algorithms to monitor and flag potential pair opportunities and human judgment to finalize the selection and set strategic parameters.

Conclusion

A. Summarizing Key Points

Pairs trading, as a market-neutral strategy, has stood the test of time due to its potential for consistent returns irrespective of broader market movements. Throughout this eBook, we delved into:

1. **Foundations of Pairs Trading:** Originating from the quant desks of major investment banks, this strategy hinges on the relative performance of two correlated instruments.

2. **Mechanics and Prerequisites:** Successful pairs trading requires an understanding of financial markets, the right tools and software, and a well-set trading account.
3. **Instrument Selection and Strategy Implementation:** Pairs must be carefully chosen based on criteria like correlation and cointegration, after which determining entry/exit points, managing risks, and monitoring positions becomes paramount.
4. **Advanced Techniques:** Modern pairs trading incorporates technical analysis, statistical methods, and even machine learning to refine strategies.
5. **Real-world Examples and Pitfalls:** History offers both successful examples to emulate and cautionary tales that highlight potential pitfalls.
6. **Future Outlook:** The landscape of pairs trading is continually evolving, influenced by emerging markets, technological advancements, and global economic shifts.

B. Recommended Further Reading

For those keen on deepening their understanding of pairs trading, the following resources are invaluable:

1. **"Pairs Trading: Quantitative Methods and Analysis" by Ganapathy Vidyamurthy:** A comprehensive guide that delves into the quantitative aspects of pairs trading.
2. **"Quantitative Trading: How to Build Your Own Algorithmic Trading Business" by Ernie Chan:** While not exclusively about pairs trading, this book offers insights into algorithmic strategies, many of which apply to pairs trading.
3. **"Trading Pairs: Capturing Profits and Hedging Risk with Statistical Arbitrage Strategies" by Mark Whistler:** A practitioner's guide that explains the logic and strategies behind pairs trading.

C. Staying Updated in the World of Pairs Trading

The dynamic nature of financial markets necessitates continuous learning for pairs traders:

1. **Financial News Outlets:** Regularly follow reputable financial news sources such as Bloomberg, Reuters, and the Financial Times to stay informed about global economic developments.
2. **Academic Journals:** Periodicals like The Journal of Finance or The Journal of Financial Economics often publish research on new trading strategies and market analyses.
3. **Online Forums and Blogs:** Communities like Quantopian or Elite Trader offer a platform for traders to discuss strategies, tools, and recent market developments.
4. **Continuous Training:** Consider enrolling in courses or seminars focused on advanced trading strategies, quantitative methods, or financial market developments.

Resources & Tools for Pairs Trading

Pairs trading, an intricate quantitative strategy, demands a robust arsenal of resources and tools. These instruments are pivotal in facilitating accurate analysis, timely decision-making, and efficient execution. Here's a comprehensive look at essential resources and tools beneficial for pairs trading:

1. Data Providers

Accurate and up-to-date data forms the foundation of pairs trading. Here are some leading data providers:

- **Bloomberg Terminal:** A comprehensive software platform providing real-time and historical data, news, and analytics.
- **Reuters Eikon:** Another industry-standard platform offering data, news, analytics, and trading capabilities.
- **Quandl:** A platform specializing in alternative data, Quandl offers a vast repository of datasets useful for pairs traders.

2. Statistical Software & Libraries

Analyzing data to uncover potential pairs and to test trading strategies requires robust statistical tools:

- **R and RStudio:** Open-source software environment and IDE for statistical computing and graphics. Useful packages for pairs trading include "quantmod" and "tseries."
- **Python:** A versatile programming language with libraries like "pandas" for data manipulation, "statsmodels" for statistical methods, and "scikit-learn" for machine learning.
- **MATLAB:** A high-performance language tailored for technical computing, particularly matrix operations which are prevalent in pairs trading analytics.

3. Algorithmic & Automated Trading Platforms

Automating trading strategies is essential for reacting swiftly to market changes:

- **MetaTrader 4/5:** Popular platforms for forex trading but can also be tailored for pairs trading with custom scripts.
- **TradeStation:** Offers advanced analysis capabilities and can automate complex trading strategies.
- **Interactive Brokers (TWS platform):** Offers API access to facilitate algorithmic trading.

4. Backtesting Tools

Before implementing a strategy, it's imperative to test its viability:

- **Backtrader:** An open-source Python framework that facilitates strategy development and backtesting.
- **QuantConnect:** Provides a platform for algorithm development in multiple languages and offers extensive backtesting capabilities.
- **Quantopian:** While it has shifted its focus from a crowdsourced hedge fund, its platform still offers rich resources for strategy development and backtesting.

5. Educational Resources

Continuous learning is the cornerstone of success in pairs trading:

- **Coursera & Udemy:** Online platforms offering numerous courses on quantitative finance, algorithmic trading, and related fields.
- **CQF (Certificate in Quantitative Finance):** A comprehensive program that delves deep into quantitative analysis, financial mathematics, and programming.

6. Community & Forums

Engaging with peers can provide new insights, strategies, and feedback:

- **Elite Trader:** An active community discussing various trading strategies including pairs trading.
- **QuantNet:** Focused more on the quantitative side, it's an excellent resource for discussions on mathematical models and algorithmic strategies.

Appendices

The following appendices aim to complement the primary content of the eBook on pairs trading. They delve into supplemental materials, examples, calculations, and references to give readers a comprehensive understanding of the subject.

Appendix A: Glossary of Terms

A detailed list of technical terms and jargon commonly associated with pairs trading and quantitative finance. This glossary will help readers familiarize themselves with the specific terminology used.

Example:

- **Cointegration:** A statistical property where two or more time series move together over time, even if they might be non-stationary when considered individually.

Appendix B: Mathematical Derivations

A deep dive into the mathematical concepts and formulas that underline pairs trading strategies. This section will break down equations, explain variables, and walk readers through calculations step-by-step.

Example:

- **Engle-Granger Two-Step Method:** A detailed explanation of the method, complete with formulae, illustrative examples, and potential applications in pairs trading.

Appendix C: Sample Code Snippets

For those inclined towards algorithmic trading, this section will offer sample code snippets in popular languages such as Python and R. These samples can serve as a starting point for building and testing one's strategies.

Example:

- **Python Code for Correlation Analysis:** A simple script to calculate and visualize the correlation between two financial instruments using the pandas and matplotlib libraries.

Appendix D: List of Notable Research Papers and Publications

A curated list of seminal research papers, articles, and publications relevant to pairs trading. This list will guide readers looking for in-depth academic insights into the strategy.

Example:

- *"Pairs Trading: Performance of a Relative Value Arbitrage Rule"* by Evan Gatev, William N. Goetzmann, and K. Geert Rouwenhorst.

Appendix E: Comparative Analysis of Tools

A comparative table highlighting the features, benefits, and costs associated with different trading platforms, data providers, and backtesting tools. This will help readers make informed decisions based on their specific needs.

Example:

- **Comparison Between Bloomberg Terminal and Reuters Eikon:** A side-by-side analysis of their features, data coverage, integration capabilities, and pricing.

Appendix F: Frequently Asked Questions (FAQs)

A compilation of common questions and answers about pairs trading. This section addresses typical concerns, misconceptions, and clarifications that readers might seek after going through the main content.

Example:

- **Q:** Is pairs trading restricted only to stocks? **A:** No, pairs trading can be applied to any set of financial instruments that demonstrate a stable, long-term relationship, including commodities, currencies, and bonds.

Algorithmic Trading

Mastering Automated Strategies for Financial Success

Introduction:

Welcome to the exciting realm of algorithmic trading, where cutting-edge technology meets the financial markets to create unprecedented opportunities. In "Algorithmic Trading Unleashed," we embark on a journey to explore the captivating world of automated trading strategies driven by computer algorithms. Whether you're a seasoned investor seeking new approaches or a novice eager to learn, this book is your ultimate companion in deciphering the complexities of algorithmic trading.

The financial landscape has evolved rapidly, and manual trading is no longer the sole player in the game. Algorithmic trading, driven by powerful algorithms and data analysis, has revolutionized how we engage with the markets. From traditional stocks and commodities to the world of cryptocurrencies, algorithms have become the driving force behind smarter, more efficient, and more profitable trading strategies.

Throughout this book, you'll learn the art and science of creating algorithms that can navigate market dynamics with precision. We'll start by laying a solid foundation, covering the basics of algorithmic trading, the role of computer algorithms, and the essential understanding of market dynamics. As we progress, you'll delve into the depths of data collection, analysis, and backtesting – the crucial stages that precede the deployment of any successful trading strategy.

Chapters on technical indicators, trend-following, mean reversion, and breakout strategies will equip you with a diverse set of tools to deploy in various market scenarios. Machine learning's integration into algorithmic trading opens up a whole new dimension of possibilities, while risk management techniques ensure you're prepared for the unpredictable.

Join us in exploring real-world case studies, learning from successful algorithms, and uncovering the ethical and legal considerations that shape algorithmic trading. And to address your burning questions, we've dedicated an entire chapter to answering the top 30 queries about this fascinating field.

Get ready to unleash the potential of algorithmic trading and embark on a journey that could redefine your financial future. "Algorithmic Trading Unleashed" isn't just a book; it's your guide to conquering the world of automated trading strategies and securing your place in the ever-evolving world of finance.

Chapter 1: Introduction to Algorithmic Trading

In the realm of financial markets, where split-second decisions can mean the difference between success and failure, algorithmic trading emerges as a game-changing strategy. This chapter serves as your compass, guiding you through the foundational concepts and principles that underpin algorithmic trading's transformative power.

Understanding Algorithmic Trading: A New Era of Trading Excellence

Algorithmic trading, often referred to as algo trading or automated trading, is a method of executing trades using pre-programmed computer algorithms. These algorithms follow a set of rules and criteria, enabling them to analyze market data, identify trading opportunities, and execute trades at lightning speed. The era of manual trading, marked by human biases and limitations, has paved the way for algorithmic trading to step into the spotlight.

Advantages of Algorithmic Trading

Algorithmic trading offers a plethora of advantages over traditional manual trading methods:

1. **Speed**: Algorithms execute trades in milliseconds, leveraging speed to seize fleeting opportunities that human traders might miss.

2. **Precision**: Algorithms operate based on predefined rules, eliminating emotional and impulsive decisions.
3. **Efficiency**: Automated trading systems can manage and execute a large number of trades simultaneously.
4. **Backtesting**: Algorithms can be tested on historical data, allowing traders to refine strategies before deploying them.
5. **Diversification**: Algorithms can implement multiple strategies across various assets, reducing risk.
6. **Reduced Costs**: Manual trading often incurs higher costs, while algorithms cut down on transaction fees.

Components of Algorithmic Trading

Algorithmic trading involves several key components:

1. **Data**: Algorithms rely on a steady stream of accurate and relevant market data to make informed decisions.
2. **Strategy**: The trading strategy defines the rules and conditions that guide algorithmic decisions.
3. **Execution System**: The mechanism that translates algorithmic decisions into actual trades within the market.
4. **Risk Management**: Strategies include risk parameters to prevent excessive losses.
5. **Infrastructure**: Fast and reliable internet connectivity and server infrastructure are crucial for timely execution.

Market Evolution and Algorithmic Trading

The financial markets have undergone a significant transformation with the rise of algorithmic trading:

1. **Increased Liquidity**: Algorithms contribute to market liquidity by executing a high volume of trades.
2. **Market Fragmentation**: Multiple trading venues and electronic exchanges have grown due to algorithmic trading's demand.
3. **Volatility and Regulation**: The speed and volume of algorithmic trading have raised concerns, leading to regulatory responses.
4. **High-Frequency Trading (HFT)**: HFT is a subset of algorithmic trading characterized by ultra-fast trades executed in fractions of a second.

Ethical Considerations

As algorithms gain prominence, ethical concerns arise:

1. **Market Manipulation**: Algorithms can be exploited to manipulate markets, prompting regulatory scrutiny.
2. **Flash Crashes**: Rapid algorithmic trading can inadvertently trigger severe market fluctuations, known as flash crashes.

3. **Transparency**: The complexity of algorithms raises questions about transparency and accountability.

The journey into algorithmic trading is both exciting and intricate. As you delve deeper, you'll uncover the mechanics behind algorithmic strategies, the role of data analysis, and the nuances of backtesting. Brace yourself for a transformational experience, as the chapters ahead guide you from novice to expert in the art of algorithmic trading.

Chapter 2: The Role of Computer Algorithms in Trading

In the digital age, where data flows ceaselessly and technology shapes every aspect of our lives, it's only natural that the world of trading has undergone a profound transformation. Chapter 2 takes you on a journey through the pivotal role of computer algorithms in modern trading practices, unveiling the mechanics behind their success and exploring their impact on the financial landscape.

The Algorithmic Advantage

Computer algorithms, fueled by vast computational power, have become the driving force behind the evolution of trading. These sophisticated mathematical models process data at lightning speed, enabling traders to make informed decisions with unprecedented accuracy. The algorithmic advantage extends across various domains, including speed, precision, and efficiency, reshaping the way markets function.

Types of Trading Algorithms

Trading algorithms come in various flavors, each designed to tackle specific market conditions and objectives:

1. **Trend-Following Algorithms**: These algorithms track market trends and aim to capitalize on price movements in the same direction.
2. **Mean Reversion Algorithms**: These strategies focus on assets whose prices deviate from their historical averages, anticipating a return to normalcy.
3. **Arbitrage Algorithms**: Arbitrageurs exploit price discrepancies between different markets, making risk-free profits.
4. **Market Making Algorithms**: Market makers provide liquidity by continuously quoting bid and ask prices, earning from the spread.
5. **Statistical Arbitrage Algorithms**: These models identify statistical relationships between assets and trade based on statistical deviations.

Algorithm Components and Process

The anatomy of an algorithm involves several components:

1. **Signal Generation**: Algorithms generate trading signals based on various indicators, patterns, or market conditions.
2. **Risk Management**: Risk parameters are integrated to ensure trades align with acceptable levels of risk.
3. **Order Execution**: Algorithms convert trading signals into actual orders, executing them in the market.
4. **Feedback Loop**: Algorithms continuously adapt based on market feedback, refining strategies over time.

Quantitative vs. Qualitative Analysis

Algorithmic trading introduces a paradigm shift from qualitative to quantitative analysis. Traditional traders relied on subjective interpretations of news and charts, while algorithms process vast amounts of data objectively. This transition has amplified the importance of data collection, accuracy, and interpretation.

Impact on Market Structure

Algorithmic trading has left an indelible mark on market structure:

1. **Market Liquidity**: Algorithms contribute substantial liquidity, enhancing market efficiency.
2. **Trading Venues**: The proliferation of algorithmic trading has driven the growth of electronic exchanges.
3. **Microstructure Changes**: High-frequency trading (HFT) and algorithmic trading have altered the microstructure of markets.

Challenges and Considerations

The rise of algorithmic trading has brought forth a series of challenges and considerations:

1. **Technological Infrastructure**: Reliable infrastructure is imperative for seamless execution.
2. **Risk Management**: Algorithms must be equipped with robust risk management protocols to avoid catastrophic losses.
3. **Regulatory Scrutiny**: Regulators closely monitor algorithmic trading to prevent market manipulation and maintain fairness.

In a world where milliseconds make a difference and data reigns supreme, understanding the role of computer algorithms in trading is paramount. As you progress through this book, you'll unlock the secrets of designing, implementing, and optimizing these algorithms, transforming your approach to trading and positioning yourself at the forefront of the financial frontier. Get ready to dive into the intricate world of algorithmic trading strategies that stand to redefine your financial success.

Chapter 3: Building a Strong Foundation: Understanding Market Dynamics

Welcome to the heart of trading mastery: understanding the intricate dance of market dynamics. Chapter 3 delves deep into the factors that influence price movements, the psychology driving market participants, and the fundamental principles that underpin successful algorithmic trading.

The Market Ecosystem

Markets are living ecosystems influenced by a multitude of factors:

1. **Supply and Demand**: The foundation of market pricing, influenced by economic indicators, news, and events.
2. **Market Participants**: Individuals, institutions, and algorithms collectively shape market sentiment.
3. **Psychology**: Human emotions, such as fear and greed, drive short-term price fluctuations.

Market Efficiency

Market efficiency refers to how quickly prices adjust to new information. Understanding efficiency levels helps traders identify opportunities:

1. **Weak-Form Efficiency**: Prices instantly reflect all past trading information.
2. **Semi-Strong Form Efficiency**: Prices reflect all publicly available information.
3. **Strong-Form Efficiency**: Prices incorporate all public and private information.

Market Trends and Patterns

Recognizing market trends and patterns is essential for traders:

1. **Uptrends and Downtrends**: Markets often exhibit upward or downward price movement over time.
2. **Sideways Trends (Consolidation)**: Prices move within a range, signaling indecision.
3. **Reversal Patterns**: Indicators suggest a trend change, like head and shoulders or double tops/bottoms.
4. **Continuation Patterns**: Suggest the resumption of an existing trend, such as flags or pennants.

Market Indicators

Indicators provide insights into market conditions and can be used as components of algorithmic strategies:

1. **Moving Averages**: Smoothed price lines that reveal trend direction.
2. **Relative Strength Index (RSI)**: Measures the speed and change of price movements.
3. **Moving Average Convergence Divergence (MACD)**: Combines moving averages to indicate trend momentum.

Sentiment Analysis

Market sentiment captures the emotional state of traders and investors:

1. **Bullish Sentiment**: Optimism about rising prices.
2. **Bearish Sentiment**: Pessimism about falling prices.

News and Events Impact

News and events have a profound influence on markets:

1. **Economic Indicators**: Reports on economic performance impact market expectations.
2. **Corporate Announcements**: Earnings reports, mergers, and acquisitions affect stock prices.
3. **Geopolitical Events**: Political instability, wars, and diplomatic developments influence market sentiment.

Market Regimes

Market regimes define different market conditions:

1. **Trending Regime**: Clear directional movement.
2. **Range-Bound Regime**: Price stays within a defined range.
3. **Volatility Regime**: Rapid price fluctuations.

Behavioral Finance and Market Anomalies

Behavioral finance studies how human biases impact financial decisions:

1. **Loss Aversion**: People feel the pain of losses more than the joy of gains.
2. **Overconfidence Bias**: Individuals overestimate their ability to predict outcomes.

Understanding market dynamics equips you with the tools to navigate the ever-changing landscape of financial markets. As you progress through this book, you'll uncover how to harness this understanding to craft robust and effective algorithmic trading strategies. Prepare to embark on a journey of discovery that will elevate your trading game and set you on a path toward sustainable success.

Chapter 4: Data Collection and Analysis for Algorithmic Trading

In the era of algorithmic trading, data is the lifeblood that fuels success. Chapter 4 immerses you in the world of data collection, analysis, and the vital role it plays in developing effective trading strategies. From raw data to actionable insights, this chapter unravels the mysteries behind data-driven trading.

The Data Revolution

The digital age has birthed an unprecedented data revolution, inundating traders with vast streams of information:

1. **Market Data**: Real-time prices, trade volumes, and order book data.
2. **Fundamental Data**: Company financials, economic indicators, and news.
3. **Alternative Data**: Satellite images, social media sentiment, and more.

The Process of Data Analysis

Data analysis is a multi-step process that transforms raw information into actionable insights:

1. **Data Collection**: Aggregating data from various sources, ensuring accuracy and timeliness.
2. **Data Cleaning**: Identifying and rectifying errors, inconsistencies, and missing values.
3. **Data Exploration**: Exploring relationships, patterns, and trends within the data.
4. **Feature Engineering**: Creating new features that enhance predictive power.
5. **Model Building**: Constructing predictive models using machine learning algorithms.
6. **Backtesting**: Testing strategies on historical data to evaluate performance.

Technical vs. Fundamental Analysis

Traders employ two primary methods of analysis:

1. **Technical Analysis**: Utilizes price charts, patterns, and indicators to predict future price movements.
2. **Fundamental Analysis**: Assesses economic, financial, and qualitative factors that impact asset value.

Quantitative Data Analysis

Quantitative analysis involves crunching numbers to identify trends and patterns:

1. **Correlation Analysis**: Identifies relationships between different assets.

2. **Volatility Analysis**: Measures the extent of price fluctuations.
3. **Statistical Tests**: Validates trading hypotheses using statistical techniques.

Big Data and Machine Learning

The advent of big data and machine learning has revolutionized trading:

1. **Predictive Analytics**: Machine learning algorithms predict future price movements.
2. **Pattern Recognition**: Algorithms identify complex patterns humans might miss.
3. **Algorithmic Pattern Trading**: Trades executed based on machine-identified patterns.

Overfitting and Bias

Two pitfalls in data analysis are overfitting and bias:

1. **Overfitting**: Creating models too tailored to historical data, which might not perform well in the future.
2. **Bias**: Letting personal beliefs or external factors influence data interpretation.

Data-Driven Strategy Development

Successful algorithmic trading hinges on a data-driven approach:

1. **Strategy Hypothesis**: Formulating a hypothesis based on data analysis.
2. **Backtesting**: Simulating the strategy on historical data to assess viability.
3. **Optimization**: Tweaking parameters for optimal performance.

In a landscape saturated with data, your ability to extract valuable insights and translate them into profitable trades becomes a powerful asset. As you journey through this chapter, you'll learn to wield the tools of data collection, analysis, and interpretation, paving the way for crafting robust and successful algorithmic trading strategies that thrive on the foundations of precision and knowledge.

Chapter 5: Backtesting Strategies: A Crucial Step to Success

In the world of algorithmic trading, success isn't just about formulating strategies; it's about rigorously testing them. Chapter 5 delves into the critical process of backtesting, where strategies are put through the ultimate trial on historical data. Prepare to uncover the secrets of evaluating strategy performance and refining your trading approach for optimal results.

What is Backtesting?

Backtesting is the process of applying a trading strategy to historical market data to evaluate its performance. This simulation allows traders to gauge how the strategy would have performed in the past before risking real capital.

The Importance of Backtesting

Backtesting offers invaluable benefits:

1. **Performance Evaluation**: Assess how well a strategy would have performed historically.
2. **Risk Analysis**: Understand potential drawdowns and losses the strategy might incur.
3. **Parameter Tuning**: Optimize strategy parameters for improved performance.
4. **Confidence Building**: Gain confidence in the viability of your trading approach.

The Backtesting Workflow

Effective backtesting follows a structured workflow:

1. **Data Preparation**: Ensure historical data is clean, accurate, and complete.
2. **Strategy Implementation**: Code the strategy's rules and conditions for execution.
3. **Simulation**: Apply the strategy to historical data, tracking trades and performance.
4. **Performance Metrics**: Measure key metrics like profit, loss, win rate, and drawdown.
5. **Analysis and Interpretation**: Analyze results to understand strategy strengths and weaknesses.
6. **Optimization**: Adjust parameters to enhance performance, then retest.

Common Backtesting Pitfalls

Avoid falling into these common backtesting traps:

1. **Data Snooping Bias**: Overfitting the strategy to historical data.
2. **Survivorship Bias**: Neglecting delisted or obsolete assets in historical data.
3. **Transaction Costs and Slippage**: Not accounting for real-world trading costs.

Performance Metrics

Assess strategy performance with these metrics:

1. **Profit and Loss**: Overall earnings or losses.
2. **Win Rate**: Percentage of winning trades.
3. **Risk-Reward Ratio**: Comparison of potential profit to potential loss.
4. **Drawdown**: Maximum decline in capital from a peak.
5. **Sharpe Ratio**: Measures risk-adjusted return.

Reality Check and Forward Testing

While backtesting is insightful, it's essential to move beyond historical data and perform forward testing:

1. **Reality Check**: Evaluate how well the strategy adapts to unseen market conditions.
2. **Paper Trading**: Test the strategy in a simulated environment with real-time data.
3. **Live Testing**: Deploy the strategy with a small amount of real capital.

Iterative Process of Refinement

Backtesting is not a one-and-done activity; it's an iterative process:

1. **Analyze Results**: Interpret backtesting outcomes to identify strategy weaknesses.
2. **Adjust Parameters**: Fine-tune strategy parameters based on analysis.
3. **Re-test and Validate**: Re-run backtests to validate improvements.

Backtesting serves as a litmus test for your trading strategies. This chapter empowers you to make informed decisions based on historical data, enabling you to refine your approach and align it with market realities. As you continue your journey through algorithmic trading mastery, remember that the rigor of backtesting is a crucial step toward achieving sustainable success in the dynamic world of finance.

Chapter 6: Technical Indicators and Their Application in Algorithms

In the realm of algorithmic trading, technical indicators stand as powerful tools to interpret market data and guide trading decisions. Chapter 6 unravels the intricate world of technical indicators, delving into their diverse types, functionalities, and the art of integrating them into algorithmic strategies to optimize trading performance.

Understanding Technical Indicators

Technical indicators are mathematical calculations based on historical price, volume, or open interest data. They offer insights into market trends, momentum, volatility, and more:

1. **Trend Indicators**: Reveal the direction of price movement, e.g., Moving Averages.
2. **Momentum Indicators**: Measure the speed and strength of price movement, e.g., RSI, MACD.
3. **Volatility Indicators**: Gauge the level of market volatility, e.g., Bollinger Bands, Average True Range.

Types of Technical Indicators

Technical indicators are classified into different categories:

1. **Leading Indicators**: Signal potential trend changes before they occur.
2. **Lagging Indicators**: Confirm trend changes that have already happened.
3. **Oscillators**: Fluctuate within a range, indicating overbought or oversold conditions.
4. **Trend-following Indicators**: Identify and confirm trends.

Moving Averages: A Fundamental Indicator

Moving Averages (MA) are foundational indicators used to smooth out price data and identify trends:

1. **Simple Moving Average (SMA)**: Calculates the average price over a specified period.
2. **Exponential Moving Average (EMA)**: Gives more weight to recent prices, reacting faster to market changes.

Relative Strength Index (RSI)

RSI is a popular momentum oscillator that measures the speed and change of price movements:

1. **Overbought and Oversold Levels**: RSI values above 70 indicate overbought conditions, while values below 30 indicate oversold conditions.

Moving Average Convergence Divergence (MACD)

MACD combines moving averages to identify trend momentum:

1. **MACD Line**: The difference between the short-term and long-term moving averages.
2. **Signal Line**: The moving average of the MACD line, smoothing out its fluctuations.

Fibonacci Retracements

Fibonacci retracements are ratios used to predict potential levels of price retracement in a trend:

1. **Golden Ratio**: Key retracement levels are 38.2%, 50%, and 61.8%.

Applying Indicators in Algorithms

Integrating technical indicators into algorithmic strategies requires careful consideration:

1. **Signal Generation**: Determine conditions that trigger trades based on indicator values.
2. **Filtering and Confirmation**: Use multiple indicators to filter out false signals and confirm trends.

Optimizing Indicator Parameters

Fine-tuning indicator parameters is crucial for effective strategy performance:

1. **Sensitivity**: Adjust indicator settings to match the asset's volatility and trading style.
2. **Optimization**: Use backtesting to find optimal parameter values.

Technical indicators are like compasses guiding traders through the maze of market data. This chapter equips you with the knowledge to wield these tools effectively, deciphering trends, identifying opportunities, and optimizing your algorithmic strategies. As you delve deeper into the art of algorithmic trading, harness the power of technical indicators to sharpen your decision-making prowess and elevate your trading game to new heights.

Chapter 7: Moving Averages and Trend-following Strategies

In the dynamic world of algorithmic trading, understanding market trends is paramount. Chapter 7 shines a spotlight on one of the most essential tools for trend analysis: Moving Averages (MA). Prepare to unravel the intricacies of MAs and how they lay the foundation for powerful trend-following strategies that can propel your trading success to new heights.

The Power of Moving Averages

Moving Averages (MAs) are bedrock tools for traders seeking to uncover underlying trends amidst market noise. MAs offer a smoothed representation of price data, aiding in trend identification, entry points, and risk management.

Simple Moving Average (SMA)

SMA calculates the average of prices over a specific time period:

1. **SMA Calculation**: Add up closing prices over the chosen period and divide by the number of periods.

SMA's Role in Trend Identification

SMA serves as a trend filter:

1. **Golden Cross**: When a short-term SMA crosses above a long-term SMA, it indicates a potential uptrend.
2. **Death Cross**: When a short-term SMA crosses below a long-term SMA, it indicates a potential downtrend.

Exponential Moving Average (EMA)

EMA gives more weight to recent price data, making it more responsive to recent market changes:

1. **EMA Calculation**: Considers both recent and historical prices, weighting recent prices more heavily.

Utilizing MAs in Strategies

MAs play a pivotal role in crafting trend-following strategies:

1. **Crossover Strategies**: Buy when short-term MA crosses above long-term MA; sell on the opposite crossover.
2. **Trend Confirmation**: Use MAs to confirm trends identified by other indicators.

Golden and Death Cross Strategies

The Golden Cross and Death Cross strategies capitalize on MA crossovers:

1. **Golden Cross Strategy**: Buy when the short-term MA crosses above the long-term MA.
2. **Death Cross Strategy**: Sell when the short-term MA crosses below the long-term MA.

Risk Management with MAs

MAs aren't just about entry signals; they help manage risk:

1. **Trailing Stops**: Adjust stops based on the distance from the moving average.
2. **Reversion to the Mean**: MAs can indicate when a price deviates significantly from the trend, suggesting a potential reversal.

Choosing the Right Timeframes

Selecting appropriate MA timeframes is crucial:

1. **Short-term MAs**: Provide more responsive signals but may be more prone to noise.
2. **Long-term MAs**: Offer smoother signals but respond slower to trend changes.

MAs in Different Markets

MAs can be applied across various assets:

1. **Stocks**: Used for position trading and trend identification.
2. **Forex**: Valuable for capturing longer-term currency trends.
3. **Cryptocurrencies**: Applied to identify trends in volatile markets.

Harness the power of Moving Averages to decipher trends, refine entry and exit points, and optimize your trend-following strategies. As you journey through this chapter, you'll gain insights into how these foundational tools can guide your algorithmic trading decisions, transforming your approach and leading you toward greater trading success in the ever-changing world of finance.

Chapter 8: Mean Reversion Strategies for Market Correction

In the intricate landscape of algorithmic trading, understanding market dynamics is key to unlocking profit opportunities. Chapter 8 delves into the fascinating realm of mean reversion strategies, offering you a comprehensive guide on identifying overextended markets and capitalizing on potential price corrections for successful algorithmic trading.

Mean Reversion: A Contrarian Approach

Mean reversion strategies are built on the concept that prices tend to revert to their historical average over time. This contrarian approach allows traders to capitalize on market extremes.

Understanding Mean Reversion

Mean reversion strategies revolve around two primary concepts:

1. **Overbought**: When prices rise significantly above their average, signaling potential overextension.
2. **Oversold**: When prices fall substantially below their average, suggesting potential undervaluation.

Applying Bollinger Bands

Bollinger Bands are a popular tool for mean reversion strategies:

1. **Bollinger Bands Construction**: Consist of a central moving average and upper and lower bands based on standard deviations.
2. **Overbought and Oversold Conditions**: Prices nearing the upper band indicate overbought conditions; prices nearing the lower band indicate oversold conditions.

Pair Trading

Pair trading is a mean reversion strategy involving two correlated assets:

1. **Cointegration**: Ensures the assets move together over the long term.
2. **Relative Deviation**: When the spread between asset prices diverges, a mean reversion trade can be initiated.

RSI and Stochastic Oscillator

The RSI and Stochastic Oscillator are valuable indicators for mean reversion:

1. **RSI**: Identifies overbought and oversold conditions.
2. **Stochastic Oscillator**: Measures the relative position of a closing price within a price range.

Combining Indicators for Confirmation

Mean reversion strategies can be enhanced with additional indicators:

1. **Confirmation Indicators**: Validate potential reversal signals from other indicators.
2. **Moving Averages**: Use MAs to identify the trend before deploying mean reversion strategies.

Risk Management in Mean Reversion

Risk management is crucial in mean reversion strategies:

1. **Stop Loss and Take Profit**: Set levels to manage risk and secure profits.
2. **Diversification**: Spread risk across multiple mean reversion strategies and assets.

Market Conditions and Drawbacks

Mean reversion strategies excel in specific market conditions:

1. **Sideways Markets**: When prices move within a range.
2. **Low Volatility**: Stable markets are conducive to mean reversion.

However, there are limitations:

1. **Trend Continuations**: Mean reversion strategies might fail in strongly trending markets.
2. **Uncertain Environments**: Political events, news, or economic shifts can disrupt mean reversion.

By understanding the dynamics of mean reversion, you're equipped to identify potential turning points in the market and capitalize on price corrections. This chapter immerses you in the art of contrarian trading, empowering you to harness the power of mean reversion strategies and navigate market fluctuations with confidence as you continue your journey in algorithmic trading mastery.

Chapter 9: Breakout Strategies: Riding the Volatility Waves

In the fast-paced world of algorithmic trading, adapting to market volatility is crucial. Chapter 9 introduces you to breakout strategies – a dynamic approach that capitalizes on sudden price movements. Get ready to explore how to identify potential breakouts, ride volatility waves, and harness the power of this strategy to enhance your trading success.

Unveiling Breakout Strategies

Breakout strategies focus on moments when prices escape from their established trading ranges:

1. **Volatility Expansion**: Breakouts occur when volatility increases.
2. **Trend Acceleration**: Breakouts signal the emergence of new trends.

Identifying Breakout Patterns

Various patterns indicate potential breakouts:

1. **Rectangle and Flag Patterns**: Consistent price range followed by a sudden price movement.
2. **Triangle Patterns**: Converging trendlines that lead to a breakout.
3. **Head and Shoulders Patterns**: Reversal pattern followed by a breakout.

Implementing Breakout Strategies

Breakout strategies require precise execution:

1. **Entry Triggers**: Enter the market when prices breach a significant level.
2. **Confirmation Indicators**: Validate breakouts with other indicators.

Donchian Channels

Donchian Channels are a popular tool for breakout strategies:

1. **Construction**: Consist of an upper and lower channel line representing high and low price extremes over a specific period.
2. **Entry Points**: Buy when prices breach the upper channel; sell when prices fall below the lower channel.

ATR (Average True Range) Breakouts

ATR measures volatility and can guide breakout strategies:

1. **ATR Calculation**: Measures the range between high and low prices over a specific period.

2. **Entry Points**: Buy when prices move above a certain ATR value; sell when prices move below it.

False Breakouts and Risk Management

False breakouts are a challenge in breakout strategies:

1. **Whipsaws**: Occur when prices briefly breach a level and reverse.
2. **Confirmation Indicators**: Use volume and other indicators to confirm breakouts.

Risk Management

Risk management is crucial in breakout strategies:

1. **Stop Loss**: Set below the breakout level to limit losses in case of false breakouts.
2. **Position Sizing**: Allocate a portion of capital to each breakout trade.

Market Conditions and Limitations

Breakout strategies excel in volatile markets:

1. **News Announcements**: Breakouts often follow significant news releases.
2. **Volatility Cycles**: Market volatility tends to go through cycles.

However, there are limitations:

1. **Choppy Markets**: Breakouts might lead to false signals in choppy conditions.
2. **Market Manipulation**: Breakout points might be targeted by manipulative traders.

Breakout strategies offer a dynamic approach to algorithmic trading, allowing you to capitalize on sudden market movements and adapt to changing conditions. As you delve into this chapter, you'll gain insights into the intricacies of breakout patterns, tools, and techniques, positioning yourself to ride volatility waves and enhance your trading success in the dynamic world of algorithmic trading.

Chapter 10: Algorithmic Risk Management: Safeguarding Your Success

In the exhilarating realm of algorithmic trading, success is intertwined with prudent risk management. Chapter 10 is your compass to navigate the intricate landscape of risk, providing you with a comprehensive guide on how to safeguard your trading endeavors. From capital preservation to position sizing, prepare to embrace a strategic approach that secures your trading success.

The Role of Risk Management

In the dynamic world of algorithmic trading, risk management is not just a strategy – it's a lifeline. It's the shield that protects your capital from unforeseen market turbulence and safeguards your hard-earned profits. Effective risk management is the bedrock upon which successful trading endeavors are built.

Capital Preservation: The First Line of Defense

Preserving your capital is paramount:

1. **Risk per Trade**: Determine the maximum percentage of your capital you're willing to risk on each trade.
2. **Risk of Ruin**: Calculate the probability of depleting your capital beyond recovery.

Position Sizing: The Art of Allocation

Position sizing is a delicate balance:

1. **Optimal Position Size**: Allocate a portion of your capital based on risk per trade.
2. **Trade Frequency**: Adjust position size based on the frequency of your trades.

Setting Stop Losses: Protecting Your Profits

Stop losses are your safety net:

1. **Volatility-based Stops**: Set stops based on market volatility.
2. **Technical Stops**: Place stops below support levels to limit losses.

Diversification: Spreading Risk

Diversifying your portfolio mitigates risk:

1. **Asset Classes**: Spread investments across different types of assets.
2. **Strategy Diversification**: Deploy multiple algorithmic strategies to reduce reliance on a single approach.

Backtesting Risk Management

Backtest your risk management strategy:

1. **Simulation**: Apply your risk management rules to historical trades to assess their effectiveness.
2. **Adjustments**: Fine-tune risk management parameters based on backtesting outcomes.

Market Conditions and Adaptability

Adapt your risk management to market conditions:

1. **Volatility Shifts**: Adjust risk parameters in volatile and stable markets.
2. **News and Events**: Increase risk mitigation during high-impact news releases.

Emotional Discipline: The Ultimate Risk Manager

Maintain emotional discipline:

1. **Stick to the Plan**: Follow your risk management strategy even when emotions run high.
2. **Avoid Revenge Trading**: Resist the urge to recover losses with impulsive trades.

Continuous Review and Improvement

Risk management is an evolving process:

1. **Regular Assessment**: Continuously evaluate your risk management strategy's effectiveness.
2. **Adaptation**: Adjust risk parameters based on changing market conditions and personal growth.

Embrace risk management as your steadfast ally in the journey of algorithmic trading. This chapter empowers you with the knowledge to proactively shield your trading capital, optimize position sizing, and navigate the complexities of market volatility. As you implement these strategies, you'll fortify your trading success and embark on a path of confident and resilient trading excellence.

Chapter 11: Optimizing Execution: Precision in Every Trade

In the fast-paced world of algorithmic trading, execution speed and accuracy are paramount. Chapter 11 illuminates the path to optimizing trade execution, ensuring your strategies translate seamlessly into profitable actions. Get ready to explore the intricacies of order types, routing, and execution strategies that will elevate your trading endeavors to new heights of precision.

The Essence of Execution Optimization

In the realm of algorithmic trading, execution optimization isn't a luxury – it's a necessity. The difference between success and missed opportunities often lies in how swiftly and precisely your trades are executed. This chapter unveils the strategies and tools that empower you to seize the moment with precision.

Understanding Order Types

Selecting the right order type is crucial:

1. **Market Orders**: Execute at the current market price, ensuring immediate execution.
2. **Limit Orders**: Execute at a specific price or better, offering control over execution price.
3. **Stop Orders**: Trigger a market order when a specified price is reached.

Routing Strategies: Choosing the Right Path

Routing determines where your orders are sent for execution:

1. **Smart Order Routing (SOR)**: Directs orders to the best available market venue for execution.
2. **Dark Pools**: Private trading venues that offer anonymity and reduced market impact.

Slippage and Market Impact

Slippage can impact execution quality:

1. **Price Impact**: Movement in the market caused by your order.
2. **Liquidity Impact**: Effect of your order on the asset's liquidity.

Algorithmic Execution Strategies

Algorithmic execution strategies enhance precision:

1. **VWAP (Volume Weighted Average Price)**: Executes orders to match the average traded price.
2. **TWAP (Time Weighted Average Price)**: Distributes orders evenly over a specified time period.
3. **Implementation Shortfall**: Balances urgency and execution price.

Direct Market Access (DMA)

DMA offers direct access to market venues:

1. **Benefits**: Faster execution, control over order routing, and reduced information leakage.
2. **Challenges**: Increased market impact and risk management complexity.

High-Frequency Trading (HFT)

HFT leverages speed for rapid execution:

1. **Speed Advantage**: Leveraging technology to execute orders in milliseconds.
2. **Market Making**: Providing liquidity by continuously quoting bid and ask prices.

Backtesting Execution Strategies

Backtest your execution strategies:

1. **Simulated Environment**: Test execution strategies on historical data.
2. **Fine-tuning**: Adjust execution parameters for optimal results.

Real-time Monitoring and Adaptation

Monitor execution in real-time:

1. **Slippage Tracking**: Compare executed price to desired price.
2. **Adaptation**: Adjust execution strategies based on changing market conditions.

Optimizing trade execution is the cornerstone of successful algorithmic trading. This chapter empowers you to make informed decisions on order types, routing strategies, and execution methods. As you implement these strategies, you'll execute trades with the precision of a master, ensuring that your trading endeavors thrive on speed, accuracy, and confidence, all within the exhilarating realm of algorithmic trading.

Chapter 12: Machine Learning in Algorithmic Trading: Unleashing Intelligent Insights

In the era of data-driven decision-making, machine learning stands as a beacon of intelligence in algorithmic trading. Chapter 12 delves into the realm of machine learning, unveiling its transformative potential to uncover patterns, predict market movements, and optimize trading strategies. Get ready to embark on a journey of intelligent insights that can elevate your trading success to unprecedented heights.

The Intersection of Machine Learning and Trading

Machine learning's ascendancy has revolutionized algorithmic trading:

1. **Data Analysis Power**: Machine learning extracts insights from vast datasets.
2. **Predictive Modeling**: Algorithms forecast market movements with remarkable accuracy.

Machine Learning Algorithms

Explore the spectrum of machine learning algorithms:

1. **Supervised Learning**: Algorithms learn from labeled historical data to make predictions.
2. **Unsupervised Learning**: Algorithms uncover hidden patterns in unlabeled data.
3. **Reinforcement Learning**: Algorithms learn through trial and error interactions with an environment.

Predictive Modeling with Regression

Regression models predict future prices based on historical data:

1. **Linear Regression**: Fits a linear relationship between variables.
2. **Polynomial Regression**: Models complex relationships between variables.

Pattern Recognition with Neural Networks

Neural networks mimic human brain functions:

1. **Deep Learning**: Neural networks with multiple hidden layers for intricate pattern recognition.
2. **Convolutional Neural Networks (CNNs)**: Specialized for image and sequence data.

Clustering and Classification

Unsupervised learning aids in classification and clustering:

1. **K-Means Clustering**: Groups data points into clusters based on similarities.
2. **Support Vector Machines (SVM)**: Classifies data into distinct categories.

Ensemble Methods for Robustness

Ensemble methods enhance model accuracy:

1. **Random Forests**: Combine multiple decision trees for improved predictive power.
2. **Gradient Boosting**: Iteratively builds strong models by focusing on misclassified data.

Backtesting Machine Learning Models

Backtest machine learning models like traditional strategies:

1. **Train-Test Split**: Divide data for training and testing.
2. **Validation**: Assess model performance on unseen data.

Challenges and Future Possibilities

Machine learning isn't devoid of challenges:

1. **Overfitting**: Models performing well on training data but poorly on new data.
2. **Interpretability**: Complex models can be difficult to interpret.

Ethical Considerations

Navigate ethical concerns in algorithmic trading:

1. **Bias**: Ensure models aren't influenced by discriminatory factors.
2. **Market Impact**: Large-scale automated trading can influence markets.

Machine learning holds the promise of intelligent trading insights. This chapter empowers you to harness its potential, uncover patterns hidden in data, and predict market movements with unprecedented precision. As you venture into the world of machine learning, you'll revolutionize your trading strategies, unveiling the possibilities of intelligent algorithms in the dynamic landscape of algorithmic trading.

Chapter 13: Sentiment Analysis and Social Media in Trading: Unveiling Market Psychology

In the digital age, understanding market sentiment is a gateway to unparalleled insights in algorithmic trading. Chapter 13 delves into the fascinating world of sentiment analysis and the impact of social media on trading decisions. Prepare to decode market psychology, harness sentiment data, and infuse your strategies with a profound understanding of market emotions for remarkable trading success.

Unleashing Sentiment Analysis

Market sentiment is a force that drives market movements:

1. **Human Emotions**: Sentiments like fear, greed, and optimism influence trading decisions.
2. **Impact on Prices**: Positive or negative sentiment can lead to price shifts.

Sentiment Analysis Tools and Techniques

Sentiment analysis extracts insights from text data:

1. **Natural Language Processing (NLP)**: Analyzes and interprets human language.
2. **Sentiment Lexicons**: Databases that assign sentiment scores to words.

Social Media's Role

Social media is a treasure trove of sentiment data:

1. **Twitter**: A hub for real-time sentiment updates.
2. **Forums and Blogs**: Platforms where traders express opinions.

News Sentiment Analysis

News sentiment impacts trading decisions:

1. **Event Detection**: Identify news events that influence sentiment.
2. **Market Reaction**: Measure how sentiment affects price movements.

Incorporating Sentiment in Strategies

Integrate sentiment analysis into your trading strategies:

1. **Sentiment-based Signals**: Trade based on positive or negative sentiment signals.
2. **Confirmation Indicator**: Use sentiment to validate other trading signals.

Sentiment Analysis Challenges

Sentiment analysis isn't without challenges:

1. **Contextual Understanding**: Language nuances impact sentiment interpretation.
2. **False Signals**: Sentiment can be influenced by noise or manipulation.

Combining Sentiment and Technical Analysis

Fuse sentiment with technical analysis:

1. **Trend Reversals**: Sentiment can signal potential trend changes.
2. **Volatility Indications**: Extreme sentiment might foreshadow market volatility.

Real-time Data and Rapid Adaptation

Sentiment analysis demands real-time adaptation:

1. **News Releases**: Sentiment changes can coincide with news events.
2. **Social Media Impact**: Sentiment can swiftly shift due to social media posts.

Ethical Considerations

Ethics matter in sentiment analysis:

1. **Misinformation**: Rely on credible sources to avoid acting on false information.
2. **Impact on Markets**: Large-scale automated sentiment-based trading can affect markets.

Sentiment analysis unveils the human element in trading. This chapter empowers you to tap into market psychology, interpret sentiment data, and fuse it with your trading strategies. As you embark on this journey, you'll harness the power of emotions in trading decisions, aligning yourself with the heartbeat of the market and transforming your approach in the captivating world of algorithmic trading.

Chapter 14: Risk and Reward: The Psychology of Trading

In the captivating world of algorithmic trading, understanding the psychology of trading is your key to enduring success. Chapter 14 delves into the intricate realm of trader psychology, unraveling the emotions that can impact your decisions and providing strategies to cultivate a resilient and disciplined mindset. Get ready to master the art of staying calm amidst market fluctuations and achieving optimal risk and reward in every trade.

The Mindset of a Successful Trader

In the tumultuous landscape of trading, a strong psychological foundation is essential:

1. **Emotional Resilience**: Maintain composure during losses and gains.
2. **Disciplined Decision-Making**: Avoid impulsive decisions driven by emotions.

Emotions and Their Impact

Emotions can cloud rational decision-making:

1. **Fear and Greed**: Drive decisions based on avoiding loss or maximizing gain.
2. **Overconfidence**: Can lead to excessive risk-taking.

Loss Aversion and Risk Management

Loss aversion can impact risk management:

1. **Avoiding Losses**: Traders might hold losing positions hoping for a reversal.
2. **Risk Management**: Set predefined stop losses to mitigate losses.

Developing Emotional Discipline

Cultivating emotional discipline is a journey:

1. **Mindfulness**: Stay present and aware of your emotions while trading.
2. **Trading Journal**: Document trades and emotions to identify patterns.

Overcoming Cognitive Biases

Cognitive biases can lead to suboptimal decisions:

1. **Confirmation Bias**: Seeking information that confirms preconceived notions.
2. **Anchoring**: Holding onto a specific value as a reference point.

Positive Self-talk and Visualization

Positive self-talk reinforces a resilient mindset:

1. **Affirmations**: Use positive statements to counter negative thoughts.

2. **Visualization**: Imagine successful trades to boost confidence.

Maintaining Consistency

Consistency is key to successful trading:

1. **Trading Plan**: Develop a well-defined trading plan and stick to it.
2. **Routine**: Create a structured trading routine for consistency.

Psychology and Algorithmic Trading

Algorithmic trading isn't immune to psychology:

1. **Monitoring Bots**: Avoid compulsively checking trading algorithms in live markets.
2. **Tweaking Obsession**: Resist the urge to constantly adjust algorithms.

Holistic Well-being

Maintain overall well-being for better trading psychology:

1. **Physical Health**: Exercise and proper nutrition boost cognitive function.
2. **Rest and Recovery**: Adequate sleep supports emotional resilience.

Trading psychology is the bedrock of trading success. This chapter empowers you to master your emotions, build discipline, and make decisions based on sound logic rather than impulses. As you delve into the realm of trader psychology, you'll elevate your algorithmic trading journey to a realm of calm confidence and resilience, ensuring that your trading endeavors thrive amidst market fluctuations and uncertainties.

Chapter 15: Evolution of Algorithmic Trading: Looking Ahead with Confidence

In the ever-evolving landscape of finance and technology, the future of algorithmic trading is brimming with exciting possibilities. Chapter 15 takes you on a journey to explore the future trends, innovations, and challenges that lie ahead. With an optimistic outlook, you'll gain insights into how to stay ahead of the curve, adapt to changing dynamics, and continue your algorithmic trading journey with confidence.

The Promise of Technological Advancements

Technological advancements are shaping the future of algorithmic trading:

1. **Artificial Intelligence**: AI-powered algorithms will refine decision-making.
2. **Quantum Computing**: Speed up complex calculations for faster strategies.

Machine Learning and Big Data Fusion

Machine learning's integration with big data will revolutionize trading:

1. **Enhanced Insights**: Machine learning extracts deeper insights from massive datasets.
2. **Predictive Power**: Accurate predictions based on historical and real-time data.

Automated Portfolio Management

Algorithmic trading extends to portfolio management:

1. **Diversification**: Algorithms will optimize portfolios across asset classes.
2. **Risk Management**: Algorithms will dynamically adjust portfolios to market conditions.

Ethical and Regulatory Considerations

Ethical and regulatory aspects will gain prominence:

1. **Algorithm Transparency**: Ensure algorithms' behavior is understandable and explainable.
2. **Regulatory Compliance**: Adapt to evolving trading regulations.

Decentralized Finance (DeFi) Integration

DeFi will reshape trading paradigms:

1. **Smart Contracts**: Automated trade execution based on predefined conditions.
2. **Tokenization**: Real-world assets will be represented as tradable tokens.

Quantitative ESG Strategies

Environmental, Social, and Governance (ESG) factors will influence trading:

1. **Sustainability Integration**: Algorithms will consider ESG criteria in trading decisions.
2. **Impact Investing**: Trading strategies will align with socially responsible goals.

Cryptocurrencies and Digital Assets

Cryptocurrencies will continue to disrupt traditional finance:

1. **Algorithmic Stablecoins**: Stable cryptocurrencies driven by algorithms.
2. **Automated Trading on Decentralized Exchanges**: Algorithmic trading on blockchain platforms.

Continuous Learning and Adaptation

Staying relevant requires continuous learning:

1. **Stay Curious**: Embrace emerging technologies and trends.
2. **Community Engagement**: Participate in trading communities for knowledge exchange.

Adapting to Market Dynamics

Market dynamics will remain dynamic:

1. **Volatility and Calm**: Be prepared for both turbulent and stable periods.
2. **Data Privacy**: Manage personal and sensitive data in compliance with regulations.

The future of algorithmic trading is an exciting frontier. This chapter empowers you to embrace innovation, adapt to changing technologies, and navigate the challenges of an evolving financial landscape. As you embark on this journey into the future, you'll cultivate an agile mindset, harness the power of emerging tools, and continue your algorithmic trading endeavors with optimism, resilience, and a keen eye on the endless possibilities that lie ahead.

Chapter 16: From Novice to Expert: Navigating Your Algorithmic Trading Journey

The path from novice to expert in algorithmic trading is a rewarding expedition filled with growth and discovery. Chapter 16 serves as your compass, guiding you through the stages of this transformative journey. With unwavering optimism, you'll uncover the strategies to navigate challenges, refine your skills, and emerge as a seasoned algorithmic trader with a profound understanding of the financial markets.

The Novice Phase: Building Foundations

In the initial phase, lay strong foundations:

1. **Education**: Immerse yourself in learning the basics of algorithmic trading.
2. **Paper Trading**: Practice trading without real money to understand strategies.

The Learning Phase: Expanding Horizons

In this phase, expand your knowledge:

1. **Market Analysis**: Dive into technical and fundamental analysis.
2. **Coding Skills**: Acquire programming proficiency to develop trading algorithms.

The Experimentation Phase: Testing Strategies

Experiment with different strategies:

1. **Backtesting**: Test strategies on historical data to gauge their potential.
2. **Forward Testing**: Implement strategies in real-time, observing their performance.

The Refinement Phase: Improving Strategies

Refine strategies based on insights:

1. **Data Analysis**: Analyze trading results to identify strengths and weaknesses.
2. **Optimization**: Fine-tune strategies for better risk-reward ratios.

The Mindset Phase: Cultivating Discipline

Cultivate a disciplined mindset:

1. **Risk Management**: Prioritize capital preservation and risk control.
2. **Emotional Discipline**: Master emotions to make rational decisions.

The Mastery Phase: Achieving Consistency

Attain trading mastery:

1. **Consistent Results**: Trade with a strategy that consistently generates profits.
2. **Adaptability**: Adjust strategies to evolving market conditions.

The Mentorship Phase: Guiding Others

Share your knowledge with others:

1. **Trading Communities**: Contribute to trading forums and communities.
2. **Mentoring**: Guide aspiring traders on their journey.

The Expert Phase: Embracing Challenges

Become an algorithmic trading expert:

1. **Innovation**: Develop novel strategies and adapt to emerging technologies.
2. **Market Evolution**: Navigate challenges and opportunities with expertise.

Continuous Learning and Growth

Growth is perpetual:

1. **Stay Current**: Keep abreast of market trends and technological advancements.
2. **Humility**: Acknowledge that learning is an ongoing process.

Your algorithmic trading journey is a path of perpetual growth. This chapter empowers you to embrace each stage with optimism, from novice to expert. As you navigate the complexities, refine your skills, and cultivate a resilient mindset, you'll emerge as a seasoned algorithmic trader, ready to conquer challenges, seize opportunities, and embark on a journey of constant evolution within the dynamic realm of algorithmic trading.

Chapter 17: Answering the Top 30 Questions in Algorithmic Trading

In the quest for algorithmic trading mastery, questions abound. Chapter 17 serves as your comprehensive guide, addressing the top 30 questions that traders often seek answers to. With an optimistic outlook, you'll gain clarity on crucial aspects, debunk common misconceptions, and pave the way for confident decision-making in the exhilarating world of algorithmic trading.

Question 1: What is Algorithmic Trading?

Algorithmic trading involves executing trades using pre-programmed rules:

1. **Automation**: Algorithms execute trades based on predefined conditions.
2. **Speed and Accuracy**: Algos process orders swiftly and precisely.

Question 2: Can I Start Algorithmic Trading with Limited Knowledge?

A foundation in trading and programming is essential:

1. **Learning Curve**: Invest time in understanding markets and coding.
2. **Continuous Learning**: Evolve your knowledge as markets and tech advance.

Question 3: What Programming Languages are Suitable for Algorithmic Trading?

Languages like Python and R are popular:

1. **Python**: Known for simplicity and extensive libraries.
2. **R**: Offers statistical capabilities for data analysis.

Question 4: How Do I Backtest Trading Strategies?

Backtesting involves testing strategies on historical data:

1. **Data Quality**: Accurate data is vital for reliable backtesting.
2. **Robustness**: Test strategies across different market conditions.

Question 5: What Are Some Common Backtesting Pitfalls?

Avoid common pitfalls:

1. **Overfitting**: Strategies may perform well on past data but fail in real markets.
2. **Survivorship Bias**: Ignoring strategies that failed in the past.

Question 6: How Can I Manage the Emotional Aspect of Trading?

Emotions impact trading decisions:

1. **Emotional Discipline**: Cultivate mindfulness and emotional control.

2. **Trading Journal**: Document emotions and learn from them.

Question 7: Are There Successful Algorithmic Trading Strategies?

Numerous successful strategies exist:

1. **Diversification**: A diverse portfolio of strategies is key.
2. **Adaptation**: Strategies must evolve to match changing markets.

Question 8: Can Algorithmic Trading Beat Human Traders?

Algorithms can outperform human traders:

1. **Speed and Accuracy**: Algorithms process data faster and execute with precision.
2. **Removal of Emotion**: Algorithms don't succumb to emotional biases.

Question 9: How Can I Deal with Market Volatility?

Volatility is part of trading:

1. **Adaptation**: Adjust strategies to thrive in volatile conditions.
2. **Risk Management**: Prioritize capital preservation.

Question 10: What's the Role of Fundamental Analysis in Algorithmic Trading?

Fundamental analysis informs long-term strategies:

1. **Economic Indicators**: Data like GDP and employment influence strategies.
2. **News Sentiment**: Fundamental data can impact market sentiment.

From the basics to complexities, this chapter answers your burning questions. Armed with accurate information, you'll navigate the algorithmic trading landscape with clarity and confidence. Each question you explore leads you closer to the realm of successful algorithmic trading, empowering you to make informed decisions and thrive in the dynamic world of finance and technology.

Chapter 18: Innovations in Algorithmic Trading: Pioneering the Future

Innovation is the heartbeat of algorithmic trading, propelling it into new dimensions of success. Chapter 18 immerses you in the world of cutting-edge advancements, exploring innovations that are shaping the future of trading. With unwavering optimism, you'll gain insights into AI-driven strategies, quantum computing, blockchain integration, and more, positioning yourself at the forefront of trading excellence.

Innovation in Quantitative Analysis

Quantitative analysis evolves with new tools:

1. **AI and Machine Learning**: Enhance data analysis for better insights.
2. **High-Frequency Trading (HFT)**: Leveraging microsecond-level trading.

Quantum Computing and Trading

Quantum computing revolutionizes speed and complexity:

1. **Faster Algorithms**: Quantum computers solve complex problems faster.
2. **Portfolio Optimization**: Efficiently analyze countless scenarios.

Blockchain and Decentralization

Blockchain transforms trading:

1. **Decentralized Exchanges**: Pave the way for automated, secure trading.
2. **Smart Contracts**: Automate trade execution with trustless contracts.

Algorithmic Trading for Retail Traders

Algorithmic trading reaches retail traders:

1. **User-friendly Platforms**: Accessible interfaces for non-experts.
2. **Strategy Marketplaces**: Buy and sell algorithms.

Neural Networks and Sentiment Analysis

Neural networks fuel sentiment analysis:

1. **Advanced Insights**: Uncover nuanced market sentiments.
2. **Adaptive Strategies**: Algorithms adapt to changing sentiment.

Hybrid Strategies for Optimal Performance

Hybrid strategies combine different approaches:

1. **Trend Following and Mean Reversion**: Balance profit potential and risk.
2. **Adaptation to Market Conditions**: Switch strategies based on market trends.

Biometric Authentication for Security

Biometric authentication ensures security:

1. **Fingerprint and Facial Recognition**: Secure access to trading platforms.
2. **Two-factor Authentication**: Enhance account protection.

Regtech and Algorithmic Trading

Regtech streamlines compliance:

1. **Automation**: Algorithms ensure trading adheres to regulations.
2. **Reporting**: Generate necessary compliance reports.

Continuous Learning and Adaptation

Embrace innovation with open arms:

1. **Learning Attitude**: Stay curious about emerging technologies.
2. **Agility**: Adapt to changes in the trading landscape.

The future of algorithmic trading is brimming with possibilities. This chapter empowers you to embrace innovation, from AI to blockchain, and explore groundbreaking advancements. As you step into the realm of cutting-edge strategies and technologies, you'll position yourself as a trailblazer in the world of algorithmic trading, ready to seize opportunities, overcome challenges, and pioneer the future of trading with optimism and a spirit of continuous evolution.

Conclusion: Unleash Your Potential in Algorithmic Trading

Congratulations, dear reader, on completing your journey through the realm of algorithmic trading. As you stand at the threshold of this exhilarating world, armed with knowledge and insights, the possibilities are boundless. This conclusion encapsulates the essence of your journey, reinforcing the optimism that fuels your path towards algorithmic trading success.

Reflecting on Your Journey

Your journey began with a spark of curiosity, a desire to delve into the world where finance and technology converge. Throughout the chapters, you've traversed the intricacies of algorithmic trading, from foundational concepts to advanced strategies. You've explored the realms of data analysis, coding, risk management, and psychology, weaving together a tapestry of skills that culminate in trading excellence.

Embracing Growth and Adaptation

Algorithmic trading is not static; it's a voyage of growth and adaptation. As markets evolve and technologies advance, your knowledge will also flourish. The optimism that has driven you through this journey will be your compass as you embrace emerging trends, technologies, and strategies. Your willingness to learn, adapt, and innovate will propel you to new heights of trading success.

Crafting Your Trading Identity

Algorithmic trading is more than a pursuit; it's an identity you're crafting. Armed with the technical prowess and the psychological resilience you've acquired; you're poised to navigate the dynamic waves of the market with confidence. Your decisions will be rooted in data, guided by strategies, and executed with precision, marking you as a seasoned algorithmic trader.

Connecting with the Trading Community

Remember that you're not alone on this journey. The algorithmic trading community is a wellspring of knowledge, camaraderie, and support. Engage with fellow traders, share insights, and contribute to the collective growth. Collaboration fosters innovation, and as you contribute, you'll discover new dimensions of trading excellence.

The Road Ahead

As you embark on your algorithmic trading adventure, stand tall with optimism. The road ahead is illuminated with possibilities waiting to be explored. The tools, strategies, and insights you've gained are your companions on this exciting voyage. Continue to learn, adapt, and refine your approach, and with each trade, you'll inch closer to realizing your trading goals.

In the vast arena of algorithmic trading, you're not merely a participant; you're an architect of your trading destiny. Armed with optimism, technical acumen, and a relentless pursuit of excellence, you're ready to conquer the markets, shape your financial future, and embark on a journey that's as rewarding as it is exhilarating. Your journey in algorithmic trading has just begun – embrace it with confidence and stride towards a future of trading success.

Currency Carry Trades

Focus on exploiting the interest rate differential between two currencies

Introduction:

Currency Carry Trades: Exploiting Interest Rate Differentials for Profit

In the complex realm of global financial markets, the concept of currency carry trades has emerged as a strategic avenue for capitalizing on the nuances of interest rate differentials between various currencies. This book delves into the intricate interplay of forex trading, economics, and financial strategy, providing an in-depth exploration of how traders and investors can harness these differentials to their advantage. Understanding the dynamics of currency carry trades is imperative for anyone seeking to navigate the highly competitive world of foreign exchange.

The Significance of Interest Rate Differentials:

At the heart of the currency carry trade strategy lies the fundamental notion of interest rate differentials. In essence, these differentials reflect the variance between the interest rates of two distinct currencies. This variance is not merely a numerical difference; it is a catalyst that drives currency valuations, influences market sentiment, and shapes trading decisions. To illustrate this, consider the following scenario:

Suppose the Central Bank of Country A maintains a relatively high interest rate compared to the Central Bank of Country B. As a result, the currency of Country A tends to offer a higher return to investors who choose to hold it. This higher yield presents a lucrative opportunity for traders looking to profit from the interest rate differential. By borrowing the lower-yielding currency of Country B, traders can invest in the higher-yielding currency of Country A, effectively capitalizing on the interest rate spread. This process, known as the carry trade, exposes the trader to potential profits stemming not only from exchange rate fluctuations but also from the interest rate differential.

Navigating the Forex Landscape:

Before embarking on a journey into the intricacies of currency carry trades, it is essential to establish a solid understanding of the forex landscape. The foreign exchange market, often referred to as forex or FX, is the global marketplace where currencies are bought and sold. It is the largest and most liquid financial market, with an average daily trading volume exceeding $6 trillion USD as of the latest available data. This vast market encompasses a diverse range of participants, including central banks, financial institutions, corporations, and individual traders.

Within this dynamic market, the movement of currency pairs—such as the EUR/USD, USD/JPY, and GBP/USD—forms the foundation of forex trading. Each currency pair represents the exchange rate between two major currencies and serves as a primary instrument for traders to speculate on currency movements. The interplay between these pairs creates a complex web of relationships, influenced by economic indicators, geopolitical events, and shifts in market sentiment.

Purpose and Structure of the Book:

As the foreign exchange market evolves and adapts to changing economic landscapes, currency carry trades remain a steadfast strategy employed by traders to seek alpha. The primary purpose of this book is to provide a comprehensive guide to mastering the art of currency carry trading. Whether you are a novice trader seeking to understand the fundamental principles or an experienced investor looking to refine your strategies, this book aims to equip you with the knowledge and tools necessary for successful carry trading.

The chapters that follow delve into various aspects of currency carry trades, each addressing a unique facet of the strategy. From understanding the fundamentals of forex trading and the concept of carry trades to exploring risk management, technical and fundamental analysis, and even psychological aspects, this book endeavors to offer a holistic approach to mastering the intricate world of carry trading.

By combining theoretical insights with practical applications and real-world examples, this book seeks to bridge the gap between academic knowledge and effective execution. Through a meticulous examination of interest rate parity theories, case studies, alternative carry trade strategies, and the future outlook of the strategy, readers will gain a comprehensive understanding of how to exploit interest rate differentials effectively and responsibly.

In the following chapters, we will embark on a journey through the terrain of currency carry trades. We will delve into the nuances of interest rate differentials, examine the methods of identifying high-yield and low-yield currencies, explore the role of technical and fundamental analysis in shaping trading decisions, and dissect the intricate interplay between risk management and profit potential. Furthermore, we will explore the psychological aspects that can influence trading decisions and study real-life case scenarios to derive valuable insights.

It is our hope that by the end of this comprehensive guide, you will not only possess the knowledge required to navigate the world of currency carry trades but also the wisdom to do so responsibly and ethically. As you progress through the subsequent chapters, we encourage you to approach the material with an open mind and a thirst for knowledge. The world of forex trading is ever-evolving, and the strategies outlined in this book are designed to equip you with the skills necessary to adapt and succeed in this dynamic environment.

As we embark on this journey together, let us explore the depths of currency carry trades and uncover the strategies that have the potential to transform the way you perceive and engage with the global financial markets.

Chapter 1: Fundamentals of Forex Trading and Interest Rates

In the realm of financial markets, the foreign exchange (forex) market stands as a multifaceted arena where currencies from around the world are traded. Understanding the fundamentals of forex trading is a crucial stepping stone toward comprehending the intricacies of currency carry trades. This chapter is dedicated to providing an in-depth exploration of these fundamentals, offering readers a comprehensive foundation upon which to build their knowledge.

Understanding Forex Trading:

Forex trading revolves around the exchange of one currency for another. Currency pairs, such as EUR/USD or GBP/JPY, represent the relative value of two currencies. The value of a currency pair is denoted by the exchange rate, which indicates how much of one currency is required to purchase a unit of the other currency. The forex market operates 24 hours a day, five days a week, due to its global nature and the presence of various trading sessions in different time zones.

The forex market's liquidity and accessibility make it an attractive platform for traders and investors alike. Unlike traditional stock markets, the forex market lacks a central exchange. Instead, it operates as an over-the-counter (OTC) market, facilitated by a network of financial institutions, brokers, and electronic trading platforms. This decentralization enhances market efficiency and allows for seamless execution of trades.

Interest Rates and Currency Valuation:

Interest rates play a pivotal role in currency valuation, forming the bedrock upon which the concept of currency carry trades is built. Central banks, as custodians of monetary policy, dictate interest rates to achieve specific economic objectives. A higher interest rate generally attracts foreign capital seeking greater returns, leading to an increased demand for the currency. Consequently, the currency appreciates in value against other currencies.

Conversely, a lower interest rate tends to discourage foreign investment, potentially resulting in a depreciation of the currency's value. Traders and investors scrutinize these interest rate differentials as they directly impact currency pairs and drive market sentiment. This dynamic relationship lays the groundwork for the carry trade strategy, where disparities in interest rates between currencies create opportunities for profit.

Role of Economic Indicators:

Economic indicators wield significant influence over forex markets. These indicators provide insights into a country's economic health, thereby affecting its currency's perceived value. Key economic indicators include gross domestic product (GDP), inflation rates, unemployment figures, and trade balances. Positive economic data often bolsters a currency's value, while negative data can lead to depreciation.

The release of economic indicators prompts market participants to make swift trading decisions, leading to heightened volatility during such events. Traders who engage in carry trades must be vigilant in tracking economic calendars to anticipate these releases. Analyzing economic data enables traders to forecast potential currency movements and make informed decisions that align with their trading strategies.

Market Sentiment and Risk Aversion:

In the forex market, investor sentiment is a driving force behind price movements. Positive sentiment can lead to a higher demand for a currency, causing its value to appreciate. Conversely, negative sentiment can trigger currency depreciation. This sentiment is influenced by a multitude of factors, including geopolitical events, global economic conditions, and shifts in central bank policies.

Traders engaged in currency carry trades must be attuned to shifts in market sentiment. Sudden changes can result in rapid currency movements that may impact trading positions. A thorough understanding of geopolitical events, market news, and global economic trends is essential for mitigating risk and making informed trading decisions.

Conclusion of Chapter 1:

As we conclude this comprehensive exploration of the fundamentals of forex trading and their connection to currency carry trades, it becomes evident that a strong grasp of these concepts lays the groundwork for successful trading endeavors. The foreign exchange market's dynamics are intricately tied to interest rates, economic indicators, market sentiment, and geopolitical events. These interconnected factors shape the landscape in which currency carry trades unfold.

In the chapters that follow, we will delve deeper into the mechanics of the carry trade strategy. Armed with the foundational knowledge provided in this chapter, readers are well-equipped to embark on a journey through the various facets of this strategy. From analyzing currency correlations and interest rate parity theories to identifying high-yield and low-yield currencies, we will navigate the intricate world of carry trades with precision and insight.

Join us as we continue to unravel the intricacies of currency carry trades and equip ourselves with the tools needed to capitalize on interest rate differentials in the pursuit of profitable trading endeavors.

Chapter 2: The Concept of Carry Trade Strategy

Understanding the Carry Trade Strategy:

At the core of currency carry trading lies the concept of capitalizing on interest rate differentials between two currencies. The carry trade strategy involves borrowing a currency with a low-interest rate and investing in a currency with a higher interest rate. This disparity in interest rates creates a yield differential, or "carry," which can result in profit for the trader.

Consider a hypothetical scenario: The Bank of Country A maintains an interest rate of 5%, while the Bank of Country B has an interest rate of 1%. A trader borrows the currency of Country B and converts it into the currency of Country A to invest at the higher interest rate. Over time, the trader earns the interest rate differential as profit, known as the "carry."

Advantages of Carry Trading:

Carry trading offers several advantages that appeal to traders seeking consistent returns in the forex market. One primary advantage is the potential for positive returns regardless of market direction. Unlike other trading strategies that rely on market appreciation, carry trades generate profits from the interest rate spread, which can lead to income even when exchange rates remain relatively stable.

Additionally, carry trades can provide diversification benefits to an investment portfolio. Since carry trading is less dependent on market direction, it can serve as a hedge against other investments that might be influenced by market volatility. This diversification potential makes carry trading an attractive strategy for both individual traders and institutional investors.

Risks and Considerations:

While carry trading presents enticing profit potential, it is not without risks. Market volatility can lead to sudden and unexpected currency movements that impact the profit potential of carry trades. For example, a change in market sentiment due to geopolitical events or economic data releases can cause rapid currency fluctuations that affect the carry trade's outcome.

Leverage, a double-edged sword, can amplify both gains and losses in carry trading. The use of leverage increases the trader's exposure to market movements, heightening the importance of effective risk management. Traders must be prepared for the possibility of significant losses if market conditions turn unfavorable.

Factors Influencing Carry Trade Profitability:

Several factors influence the profitability of carry trades beyond interest rate differentials. Currency appreciation or depreciation can offset or enhance the interest rate spread. Traders must consider not only the interest rate differential but also the potential for exchange rate movements that might impact their overall profitability.

Economic indicators, central bank decisions, geopolitical events, and shifts in market sentiment can all influence exchange rates and consequently affect the profitability of carry trades. Traders must stay informed about these factors to make timely decisions and manage their positions effectively.

Conclusion of Chapter 2:

As we conclude this exploration of the concept of the carry trade strategy, it becomes evident that this approach is built upon a nuanced interplay between interest rate differentials, market movements, and risk management. The carry trade strategy offers distinct advantages, including the potential for consistent returns and portfolio diversification.

However, traders must navigate potential risks, including market volatility and leverage, to ensure a balanced and well-informed trading approach. As we proceed to subsequent chapters, we will delve further into the intricacies of carry trading, exploring the identification of high-yield and low-yield currencies, the analysis of currency correlations, and the application of interest rate parity theories. Equipped with the insights gained in this chapter, readers are well-prepared to embark on a journey of comprehensive carry trade knowledge and practical application.

Join us as we continue our exploration of the world of currency carry trades, unveiling strategies and insights that can empower traders to effectively harness interest rate differentials and navigate the complexities of the forex market.

Chapter 3: Analyzing Currency Correlations

Understanding Currency Correlations:

In the world of currency trading, understanding the relationships between currency pairs is paramount. Currency correlations measure the degree to which two currency pairs move in relation to each other. These correlations can be positive, negative, or neutral, indicating how closely or inversely the two currencies tend to move.

Positive correlations imply that two currency pairs move in the same direction. For instance, if the EUR/USD and GBP/USD pairs both appreciate, this reflects a positive correlation between the euro and the British pound. Conversely, negative correlations suggest that two currency pairs move in opposite directions. Understanding these correlations is vital for managing risk and constructing a diversified portfolio of carry trades.

Importance of Diversification:

Diversification is a fundamental principle in investment, and it holds particular significance in the context of carry trading. By diversifying across different currency pairs, traders can reduce their exposure to the risk associated with a single currency pair's movement. The goal is to create a portfolio of carry trades that are less likely to move in unison, thereby mitigating the potential impact of adverse market events on the overall portfolio.

Diversification, however, requires a comprehensive understanding of currency correlations. Traders must identify currency pairs that have a lower correlation to ensure that their portfolio remains well-balanced and resilient to market fluctuations.

Measuring Currency Correlations:

Currency correlations can be measured numerically, with values ranging from -1 to +1. A correlation coefficient of +1 indicates a perfect positive correlation, while a coefficient of -1 indicates a perfect negative correlation. A coefficient close to 0 suggests a weak or no correlation between currency pairs.

Correlation coefficients can be calculated using historical price data and statistical methods. Traders can utilize various tools and software to obtain correlation coefficients and identify pairs that exhibit strong correlations or those that tend to move independently.

Applying Currency Correlations to Carry Trades:

When constructing a portfolio of carry trades, understanding currency correlations helps traders avoid overexposure to a single currency or region. By selecting currency pairs with lower correlations, traders can diversify their risk and reduce the impact of unfavorable market movements on their overall portfolio.

For instance, if a trader is already engaged in a carry trade involving the USD/JPY pair, which carries a high correlation to the AUD/USD pair, opening an additional carry trade with the AUD/USD pair might result in an overexposure to the Japanese yen. To manage this risk, the trader might consider selecting a currency pair with a low correlation to the yen.

Conclusion of Chapter 3:

As we conclude this chapter dedicated to the analysis of currency correlations, it becomes clear that comprehending these relationships is a pivotal aspect of successful currency carry trading. By grasping the intricacies of positive, negative, and neutral correlations, traders can construct portfolios that are diversified and less susceptible to adverse market conditions.

The ability to measure and apply currency correlations empowers traders to make informed decisions when selecting currency pairs for carry trades. As we progress to the subsequent chapters, we will delve further into the theories of interest rate parity, explore the identification of high-yield and low-yield currencies, and examine the methods of risk management in the context of currency carry trades.

Armed with the insights gained in this chapter, readers are prepared to navigate the complexities of currency correlations and integrate them effectively into their carry trading strategies. Join us as we continue our journey through the realm of currency carry trades, uncovering strategies that optimize the exploitation of interest rate differentials while managing the intricacies of correlated currency pairs.

Chapter 4: Factors Affecting Exchange Rates

Understanding Exchange Rate Determinants:

In the intricate tapestry of the foreign exchange market, exchange rates are influenced by a myriad of factors. These determinants collectively shape the value of currencies in relation to each other. Understanding these factors is essential for currency carry traders, as they provide insights into potential future movements that can impact the profitability of carry trades.

Economic Indicators and Data Releases:

Economic indicators serve as vital gauges of a country's economic health and play a pivotal role in shaping exchange rates. Key indicators, such as gross domestic product (GDP), inflation rates, unemployment figures, and trade balances, provide a snapshot of a country's economic performance. Positive economic data can lead to currency appreciation, while negative data can result in depreciation.

Traders closely monitor economic calendars to anticipate the release of these indicators. The actual data compared to market expectations can influence market sentiment and lead to swift currency movements. Carry traders must remain vigilant during data releases, as the resulting volatility can impact open positions.

Central Bank Policies and Monetary Decisions:

Central banks hold considerable influence over exchange rates through their monetary policy decisions. Interest rate decisions, quantitative easing programs, and forward guidance can impact a currency's attractiveness to investors. A central bank raising interest rates, for example, often leads to increased demand for the currency due to higher yields.

Traders engaged in carry trades must closely follow central bank announcements and statements to gauge potential shifts in monetary policy. These decisions can trigger market movements and influence the profitability of carry trades.

Geopolitical Events and Market Sentiment:

Geopolitical events, such as elections, trade negotiations, and geopolitical tensions, can create sudden shifts in market sentiment. Market participants react to these events by adjusting their trading positions, leading to increased volatility in exchange rates. Positive developments can lead to currency appreciation, while negative events can cause depreciation.

Understanding the potential impact of geopolitical events on market sentiment is vital for carry traders. A sudden change in sentiment can trigger currency movements that impact the profitability of carry trades. Traders must stay informed about global events and consider their implications when formulating trading strategies.

Conclusion of Chapter 4:

As we conclude this chapter focused on the factors affecting exchange rates, it becomes evident that the foreign exchange market's intricate dynamics are influenced by a complex interplay of economic indicators, central bank policies, and geopolitical events. The ability to anticipate and interpret these determinants is instrumental for currency carry traders seeking to maximize profits while managing risks.

By delving into economic data releases, central bank decisions, and the impact of geopolitical events, traders can enhance their ability to forecast potential currency movements. As we progress to the subsequent chapters, we will explore interest rate parity theories, methods for identifying high-yield and low-yield currencies, and the techniques of technical and fundamental analysis in the context of currency carry trades.

Equipped with the insights gained in this chapter, readers are prepared to navigate the multifaceted landscape of exchange rate determinants and integrate this knowledge into their carry trading strategies. Join us as we continue our exploration of the world of currency carry trades, unveiling strategies that optimize the exploitation of interest rate differentials while navigating the complexities of exchange rate dynamics.

Chapter 5: Interest Rate Parity Theories

Uncovered Interest Rate Parity (UIP) Theory:

The concept of interest rate parity forms a cornerstone of currency carry trading strategies. Uncovered Interest Rate Parity (UIP) is a theoretical framework that posits that the difference in interest rates between two countries should be reflected in the exchange rate movement between their currencies. In essence, UIP suggests that a currency with a higher interest rate will depreciate relative to a currency with a lower interest rate, to compensate for the potential difference in returns.

For carry traders, understanding UIP theory helps anticipate potential exchange rate movements based on interest rate differentials. If a trader is considering a carry trade involving a high-yield currency, UIP theory suggests that this currency might experience depreciation due to the higher interest rate, potentially impacting the overall profitability of the trade.

Covered Interest Rate Parity (CIP) Theory:

Covered Interest Rate Parity (CIP) theory builds upon the concept of UIP by incorporating the role of forward exchange rates. CIP theory asserts that when accounting for the interest rate differential and forward exchange rates, there should be no arbitrage opportunity in the forex market. In other words, it suggests that the returns from investing in domestic currency and converting it to foreign currency through the forward market should be equivalent to the returns from investing directly in the foreign currency.

Traders engaged in carry trades often consider CIP theory when deciding between holding the currency directly or entering a forward contract. If the forward contract provides a yield equivalent to that of investing directly in the high-yield currency, there might be little incentive to engage in a carry trade. However, real-world market conditions and transaction costs can influence the practical application of CIP theory.

Application of Parity Theories in Carry Trade Strategies:

While the UIP and CIP theories provide theoretical frameworks for understanding interest rate differentials and exchange rate movements, real-world currency markets can deviate from these models. Various factors, such as market sentiment, geopolitical events, and central bank interventions, can influence currency movements beyond the scope of these theories.

For carry traders, the key is to use parity theories as tools for analysis rather than as strict predictors of future movements. By incorporating the insights gained from these theories into their overall trading strategy, traders can make informed decisions about their carry trade positions. Understanding the underlying principles of parity theories enables traders to navigate the complexities of interest rate differentials and exchange rate dynamics.

Conclusion of Chapter 5:

As we conclude this chapter dedicated to interest rate parity theories, it becomes clear that these theoretical frameworks provide valuable insights into the interplay between interest rates and exchange rates. Uncovered Interest Rate Parity (UIP) and Covered Interest Rate Parity (CIP) theories offer perspectives on how interest rate differentials influence currency movements and the potential implications for carry trading strategies.

While parity theories serve as valuable analytical tools, carry traders must be aware of the limitations and deviations that can occur in real-world markets. As we progress to the subsequent chapters, we will delve into the identification of high-yield and low-yield currencies, explore the techniques of technical and fundamental analysis, and discuss risk management strategies in the context of currency carry trades.

Equipped with the insights gained in this chapter, readers are prepared to integrate the principles of interest rate parity theories into their carry trading strategies. Join us as we continue our exploration of the world of currency carry trades, unveiling strategies that optimize the exploitation of interest rate differentials while acknowledging the complexities of real-world market dynamics.

Chapter 6: Identifying High-Yield and Low-Yield Currencies
Evaluating Interest Rate Differentials:

In the realm of currency carry trading, the ability to identify high-yield and low-yield currencies is paramount. Interest rate differentials form the foundation of carry trades, making the assessment of these differentials a crucial step in strategy development. Traders must evaluate the interest rates set by central banks of various countries and compare them to ascertain which currencies offer the potential for favorable returns.

High-yield currencies are those associated with central banks offering relatively high interest rates. These currencies tend to attract investors seeking greater returns on their investments. Low-yield currencies, on the other hand, correspond to central banks with lower interest rates and are often borrowed to fund carry trades.

Carry Trade Selection Criteria:

When selecting currency pairs for carry trades, traders should consider a range of factors beyond interest rate differentials. Economic indicators, central bank policies, geopolitical events, and market sentiment all influence the profitability of carry trades. A comprehensive analysis that includes both fundamental and technical aspects can provide a well-rounded understanding of potential trade opportunities.

Additionally, traders must consider the level of volatility associated with a currency pair. While high-yield currencies may offer attractive returns, they can also be more volatile, leading to increased risk. Low-yield currencies might offer lower returns but can also exhibit more stable price movements. Traders must balance the potential for profit with their risk tolerance when selecting currency pairs.

Monitoring Economic Data and Events:

To identify high-yield and low-yield currencies effectively, traders must stay informed about economic data releases and events that can impact central bank decisions. Positive economic data, such as strong GDP growth or low unemployment figures, can influence central banks to consider raising interest rates. Conversely, negative economic data can lead to interest rate cuts.

Traders should also track central bank statements and press conferences, as these provide insights into policymakers' views on economic conditions and potential future actions. Geopolitical events, such as elections and trade negotiations, can create sudden shifts in market sentiment that impact currency valuations. A holistic approach to monitoring events and data ensures that traders are well-prepared to identify opportunities and potential risks.

Conclusion of Chapter 6:

As we conclude this chapter dedicated to identifying high-yield and low-yield currencies, it becomes clear that the process involves a nuanced evaluation of interest rate differentials, economic indicators, central bank policies, and market sentiment. A multidimensional analysis is essential for selecting currency pairs that align with a trader's risk tolerance, trading strategy, and profit objectives.

The ability to identify currencies with attractive interest rate differentials and growth potential empowers traders to make informed decisions when constructing their carry trade portfolios. As we progress to the subsequent chapters, we will delve into the techniques of technical and fundamental analysis, explore risk management strategies, and address the psychological aspects of trading in the context of currency carry trades.

Equipped with the insights gained in this chapter, readers are prepared to navigate the complexities of currency selection and integration into their carry trading strategies. Join us as we continue our exploration of the world of currency carry trades, unveiling strategies that optimize the exploitation of interest rate differentials while considering the intricacies of market dynamics and risk management.

Chapter 7: Technical Analysis in Currency Carry Trades

Understanding Technical Analysis:

Technical analysis is a valuable tool in the arsenal of currency carry traders. It involves analyzing historical price data and chart patterns to forecast future price movements. Technical analysis operates on the premise that historical price patterns tend to repeat themselves, providing insights into potential market trends and turning points.

Key Components of Technical Analysis:

Several key components form the foundation of technical analysis in currency carry trading:

1. **Price Charts:** Price charts display the historical price movement of a currency pair over time. Different chart types, such as line charts, bar charts, and candlestick charts, offer various perspectives on price behavior.

2. **Support and Resistance Levels:** Support levels represent price points where a currency pair tends to find buying interest and reverse upward. Resistance levels are price points where selling interest surfaces, potentially leading to price declines.

3. **Trend Analysis:** Identifying trends is a fundamental aspect of technical analysis. Trends can be upward (bullish), downward (bearish), or sideways (neutral). Traders often use trendlines and moving averages to identify and confirm trends.

4. **Technical Indicators:** Technical indicators are mathematical calculations applied to price data. Examples include moving averages, relative strength index (RSI), and stochastic oscillators. These indicators provide insights into potential market reversals or continuation patterns.

Application of Technical Analysis in Carry Trades:

For currency carry traders, technical analysis aids in timing entry and exit points for trades. By identifying support and resistance levels, traders can set stop-loss and take-profit orders to manage risk and capture potential profits. Technical indicators help confirm potential trends, assess market momentum, and identify potential overbought or oversold conditions.

Carry traders often combine technical analysis with fundamental analysis to make well-informed trading decisions. For instance, if a high-yield currency pair is showing signs of an upward trend based on technical analysis, a trader might analyze economic indicators and central bank policies to validate the trade's potential.

Limitations and Considerations:

While technical analysis offers valuable insights, it is not infallible. Market sentiment, unexpected news events, and geopolitical developments can disrupt established price patterns. Traders must also be aware of the possibility of false signals and avoid relying solely on technical analysis without considering fundamental factors.

Additionally, carry traders should be mindful of the timeframe they are analyzing. Different timeframes can yield varying technical signals, and it's important to align the chosen timeframe with the trader's trading style and objectives.

Conclusion of Chapter 7:

As we conclude this chapter dedicated to technical analysis in currency carry trades, it becomes evident that technical analysis is a powerful tool for identifying trends, potential reversals, and entry and exit points in the forex market. The ability to integrate technical analysis into carry trading strategies empowers traders to make more informed decisions based on historical price data and chart patterns.

By combining technical analysis with fundamental analysis and risk management strategies, traders can develop a comprehensive approach to currency carry trading. As we progress to the subsequent chapters, we will delve into risk management techniques, explore the psychological aspects of trading, and discuss the process of formulating and executing carry trade strategies.

Equipped with the insights gained in this chapter, readers are prepared to navigate the world of technical analysis and apply it effectively to their currency carry trading endeavors. Join us as we continue our exploration of the world of currency carry trades, unveiling strategies that optimize the exploitation of interest rate differentials while harnessing the power of technical insights.

Chapter 8: Fundamental Analysis in Currency Carry Trades
Understanding Fundamental Analysis:

Fundamental analysis is a cornerstone of successful currency carry trading. This approach involves studying economic, geopolitical, and market data to understand the factors influencing currency values. Traders engaged in carry trades must possess a strong grasp of fundamental analysis to make informed trading decisions.

Key Components of Fundamental Analysis:

Several key components form the foundation of fundamental analysis in currency carry trading:

1. **Economic Indicators:** Economic indicators, such as GDP growth, inflation rates, and unemployment figures, provide insights into a country's economic health. Positive economic data can lead to currency appreciation, while negative data can result in depreciation.
2. **Central Bank Policies:** Central banks play a pivotal role in shaping currency values through their monetary policy decisions. Interest rate changes, quantitative easing programs, and forward guidance can impact a currency's attractiveness to investors.
3. **Geopolitical Events:** Geopolitical events, such as elections, trade negotiations, and conflicts, can create sudden shifts in market sentiment. These events can impact currency values as traders adjust their positions in response to changing conditions.
4. **Market Sentiment:** Market sentiment reflects the collective perception of traders and investors about the market's future direction. Positive sentiment can lead to currency appreciation, while negative sentiment can cause depreciation.

Application of Fundamental Analysis in Carry Trades:

For currency carry traders, fundamental analysis provides insights into potential market trends and turning points. By analyzing economic indicators, central bank policies, and geopolitical events, traders can anticipate potential currency movements and adjust their trading strategies accordingly.

For example, if a trader is considering a carry trade involving a currency pair with a high-yield currency, they might analyze the economic indicators of both countries to assess the potential for interest rate changes. Positive economic data and indications of potential interest rate hikes can bolster the attractiveness of the high-yield currency.

Limitations and Considerations:

Fundamental analysis has its limitations, including the potential for unexpected events that can disrupt established trends. Additionally, interpreting fundamental data can be complex, and different traders might interpret the same data differently. Traders must also be aware of the impact of market sentiment, as sentiment can sometimes override fundamental factors in the short term.

Moreover, fundamental analysis often requires a longer time horizon than technical analysis. Economic indicators and central bank policies take time to influence currency values, and traders must be patient in waiting for their analysis to play out in the market.

Conclusion of Chapter 8:

As we conclude this chapter dedicated to fundamental analysis in currency carry trades, it becomes evident that this approach is a vital tool for understanding the forces that influence currency values. By integrating fundamental analysis into carry trading strategies, traders can make more informed decisions based on economic data, central bank policies, and geopolitical events.

By combining fundamental analysis with technical analysis, risk management strategies, and an understanding of market sentiment, traders can develop a comprehensive approach to currency carry trading. As we progress to the subsequent chapters, we will explore risk management techniques, address the psychological aspects of trading, and discuss the process of formulating and executing carry trade strategies.

Equipped with the insights gained in this chapter, readers are prepared to navigate the world of fundamental analysis and apply it effectively to their currency carry trading endeavors. Join us as we continue our exploration of the world of currency carry trades, unveiling strategies that optimize the exploitation of interest rate differentials while harnessing the power of fundamental insights.

Chapter 9: Risk Management in Currency Carry Trades

Understanding Risk Management:

In the world of currency carry trading, effective risk management is a non-negotiable aspect of success. The forex market's volatile nature demands careful consideration of potential risks and the implementation of strategies to mitigate them. Risk management involves setting parameters that define the amount of capital to risk on a trade and mechanisms to protect against excessive losses.

Key Components of Risk Management:

Several key components form the foundation of risk management in currency carry trading:

1. **Position Sizing:** Position sizing involves determining the appropriate amount of capital to allocate to a trade. This ensures that losses on individual trades do not disproportionately impact the trader's overall capital. Traders often use a percentage of their account balance as a guide for position sizing.

2. **Stop-Loss Orders:** Stop-loss orders automatically close a trade if the market moves against the trader's position beyond a predefined point. This helps prevent significant losses and ensures that individual trades do not excessively impact the trader's overall capital.

3. **Take-Profit Orders:** Take-profit orders automatically close a trade when the market reaches a predetermined profit level. This ensures that traders capture profits before the market potentially reverses, protecting their gains.

4. **Diversification:** Diversification involves spreading risk across multiple currency pairs and assets. By diversifying their portfolio of carry trades, traders reduce their exposure to the risk associated with a single trade or currency pair.

Applying Risk Management in Carry Trades:

For currency carry traders, risk management is paramount due to the potential for rapid and unexpected currency movements. By setting appropriate stop-loss and take-profit levels and adhering to position sizing guidelines, traders can manage their risk exposure effectively.

Additionally, diversification plays a crucial role in risk management. Traders must avoid overconcentration in a single currency pair or region, as adverse market movements can impact their entire portfolio. Diversification helps mitigate the impact of individual trade losses on the overall capital.

Limitations and Considerations:

While risk management strategies are essential, no approach can completely eliminate the inherent risks of trading. Currency markets can experience extreme volatility due to unforeseen events, leading to rapid and significant price movements. Traders must be prepared for the possibility of unexpected outcomes and take measures to protect their capital.

Moreover, risk management should be a continuous process that evolves with changing market conditions and individual trading performance. Traders should regularly assess and adjust their risk management strategies to ensure they remain aligned with their trading objectives and risk tolerance.

Conclusion of Chapter 9:

As we conclude this chapter dedicated to risk management in currency carry trades, it becomes clear that effective risk management is a foundational element of successful trading. The ability to integrate risk management strategies, such as position sizing, stop-loss and take-profit orders, and diversification, empowers traders to protect their capital and navigate the challenges of the forex market.

By combining risk management with technical and fundamental analysis, traders can develop a comprehensive approach to currency carry trading. As we progress to the subsequent chapters, we will address the psychological aspects of trading, discuss the process of formulating and executing carry trade strategies, and provide a holistic view of currency carry trading as a strategic endeavor.

Equipped with the insights gained in this chapter, readers are prepared to implement effective risk management strategies and navigate the dynamic world of currency carry trading with a focus on capital preservation. Join us as we continue our exploration of the world of currency carry trades, unveiling strategies that optimize the exploitation of interest rate differentials while safeguarding against potential losses

Chapter 10: Psychological Aspects of Currency Carry Trading
Understanding the Role of Psychology:

In the realm of currency carry trading, the psychological aspects of trading play a pivotal role in determining success. The forex market's fast-paced nature, potential for quick gains or losses, and emotional ups and downs can challenge even the most seasoned traders. Developing a strong psychological mindset is essential for maintaining discipline, making rational decisions, and managing emotions.

Key Psychological Factors:

Several key psychological factors influence currency carry traders:

1. **Emotional Discipline:** Emotional discipline involves controlling emotions such as fear, greed, and anxiety that can cloud judgment and lead to impulsive trading decisions. Traders must cultivate emotional resilience and adhere to their trading plans, even in the face of market volatility.

2. **Patience:** Patience is a virtue in trading. Traders must be patient in waiting for favorable trading opportunities to align with their strategies. Impatient decisions can lead to entering trades that do not align with the trader's analysis.

3. **Confidence:** Confidence in one's trading strategy and analysis is crucial. Doubt and overthinking can lead to hesitation and missed opportunities. Traders should trust their skills and decisions while remaining open to learning and improvement.

4. **Risk Management Mindset:** Embracing risk management as a central tenet of trading is vital. Traders should prioritize capital preservation and understand that losses are an inherent part of trading. A risk management mindset helps traders make rational decisions and avoid emotional overreactions to losses.

Managing Psychological Challenges:

Managing psychological challenges requires self-awareness and continuous effort. Traders can implement several strategies to maintain a healthy psychological mindset:

1. **Develop a Trading Plan:** A well-defined trading plan outlines entry and exit strategies, risk management guidelines, and trading objectives. Following a plan helps traders stay focused and disciplined, reducing the influence of emotions.

2. **Practice Mindfulness:** Mindfulness techniques, such as deep breathing and meditation, can help traders stay calm and focused during stressful trading moments. These practices promote emotional control and prevent impulsive decisions.

3. **Review and Learn:** Regularly reviewing trades, both successful and unsuccessful, helps traders learn from their experiences. Analyzing mistakes and successes fosters continuous improvement and builds confidence in decision-making.

4. **Set Realistic Expectations:** Realistic expectations about trading outcomes are crucial. Traders should understand that trading is not a guaranteed path to quick riches and that losses are a natural part of the process.

Conclusion of Chapter 10:

As we conclude this chapter focused on the psychological aspects of currency carry trading, it becomes evident that the trader's mindset is a critical factor in achieving success. The ability to cultivate emotional discipline, patience, confidence, and a risk management mindset empowers traders to make informed decisions and navigate the challenges of the forex market.

By addressing psychological challenges through self-awareness and the implementation of psychological strategies, traders can enhance their trading performance and overall well-being. As we progress to the final chapters, we will discuss the process of formulating and executing carry trade strategies and provide a comprehensive overview of currency carry trading as a strategic endeavor.

Equipped with the insights gained in this chapter, readers are prepared to address the psychological aspects of trading and foster a mindset conducive to success in currency carry trading. Join us as we continue our exploration of the world of currency carry trades, unveiling strategies that optimize the exploitation of interest rate differentials while embracing the challenges of the human psyche.

Chapter 11: Formulating and Executing Carry Trade Strategies

Crafting a Carry Trade Strategy:

Crafting a successful carry trade strategy involves synthesizing various elements discussed in previous chapters. Traders must consider interest rate differentials, economic indicators, central bank policies, technical and fundamental analysis, risk management, and psychological factors to create a cohesive and effective strategy.

Steps in Formulating a Carry Trade Strategy:

1. **Currency Pair Selection:** Identify high-yield and low-yield currency pairs based on interest rate differentials and a comprehensive analysis of economic and market factors.

2. **Analysis:** Combine technical and fundamental analysis to validate potential trading opportunities. Look for alignment between technical signals and fundamental drivers.

3. **Risk Management:** Determine appropriate position sizes, set stop-loss and take-profit levels, and diversify the portfolio to manage risk exposure.

4. **Psychological Preparation:** Cultivate a disciplined and patient mindset, embracing emotional resilience and confidence in your strategy.

Executing the Strategy:

Executing a carry trade strategy involves putting the formulated plan into action with precision and discipline:

1. **Entry:** Enter the trade when all criteria align, and technical and fundamental analysis indicate a high probability of success. Ensure that the trade conforms to your risk management guidelines.

2. **Monitoring:** Continuously monitor the trade's progress and remain vigilant for potential changes in market conditions or unforeseen events that might necessitate adjustments.
3. **Exit:** Exit the trade when the conditions defined in your strategy are met. This includes reaching predetermined profit targets or stop-loss levels.

Adapting to Market Dynamics:

Market dynamics can change rapidly, requiring traders to adapt their strategies as needed. Economic indicators, central bank policies, geopolitical events, and unexpected news can influence currency movements. Traders should be prepared to adjust their strategies based on evolving market conditions.

Conclusion of Chapter 11:

As we conclude this chapter focused on formulating and executing carry trade strategies, it becomes evident that success in currency carry trading relies on a comprehensive approach that integrates various elements. The ability to synthesize interest rate differentials, economic indicators, technical and fundamental analysis, risk management, and psychological preparedness empowers traders to execute strategies with precision.

By mastering the process of formulating and executing carry trade strategies, traders can navigate the forex market's complexities and achieve consistent results over time. As we approach the final chapter, we will provide a comprehensive overview of currency carry trading as a strategic endeavor and offer insights for readers embarking on their own carry trading journeys.

Equipped with the insights gained in this chapter, readers are prepared to develop and implement their carry trade strategies with confidence and precision. Join us as we conclude our exploration of the world of currency carry trades, unveiling the strategic essence of exploiting interest rate differentials while embracing the dynamic nature of the forex market.

Chapter 12: The Strategic Essence of Currency Carry Trading
A Holistic Perspective on Currency Carry Trading:

As we conclude our journey through the world of currency carry trading, it's essential to reflect on the strategic essence that underpins this trading approach. Currency carry trading is more than a series of individual trades; it's a strategic endeavor that requires a deep understanding of market dynamics, a disciplined mindset, and a comprehensive approach to analysis and risk management.

Embracing the Dual Nature:

Currency carry trading embodies a dual nature that combines the exploitation of interest rate differentials with the complexities of global market dynamics. Traders must navigate the intricate interplay of economic indicators, central bank policies, geopolitical events, and market sentiment while capitalizing on the potential returns offered by interest rate disparities.

The Role of Analysis:

Technical and fundamental analysis serve as guiding lights for currency carry traders. Technical analysis offers insights into historical price patterns and potential trends, while fundamental analysis provides a window into the macroeconomic factors that influence currency values. By integrating these analyses, traders can make informed decisions that align with their strategies.

Risk Management as the Bedrock:

Effective risk management serves as the bedrock of currency carry trading. Position sizing, stop-loss and take-profit orders, and diversification are not mere afterthoughts; they are critical components that protect traders from excessive losses and ensure capital preservation. A strong risk management strategy provides the necessary framework for executing trades with confidence.

The Psychological Frontier:

The psychological aspects of trading cannot be overlooked. A trader's emotional discipline, patience, confidence, and risk management mindset determine their ability to execute their strategy with consistency. Managing emotions, adhering to trading plans, and maintaining a resilient mindset are key to overcoming the psychological challenges that arise in the fast-paced world of forex trading.

A Strategic Journey:

Currency carry trading is a journey that requires continuous learning and adaptation. Traders must stay attuned to evolving market conditions, adjust their strategies as needed, and continually refine their skills. Success is not measured by individual trades but by a consistent and disciplined approach that yields sustainable results over time.

Conclusion of Chapter 12:

As we conclude this final chapter on the strategic essence of currency carry trading, it becomes clear that this approach is a comprehensive and multifaceted endeavor. The strategic essence of currency carry trading lies in the ability to integrate interest rate differentials, technical and fundamental analysis, risk management, and psychological preparedness into a cohesive and effective trading strategy.

By embracing this strategic essence, traders can navigate the challenges and opportunities presented by the forex market and embark on a journey of consistent growth and success. Equipped with the insights gained throughout this book, readers are prepared to embark on their own currency carry trading journeys, armed with the knowledge, tools, and mindset necessary to thrive in this dynamic and rewarding field.

Chapter 13: Psychological Aspects of Carry Trading

In the world of carry trading, the psychological aspects are as crucial as the technical and analytical components. This chapter delves into the intricate realm of emotions, mindset, and discipline that shape the success of a carry trader. Understanding and managing these psychological factors are key to maintaining a balanced and strategic approach to trading.

Emotions and Their Impact:

Emotions are an integral part of human nature, but they can also be a double-edged sword in trading. Fear, greed, excitement, and frustration are just a few emotions that can significantly influence trading decisions. Traders often find themselves making impulsive choices driven by emotions, which can lead to losses and hinder consistent performance.

Developing a Disciplined Trading Mindset:

One of the cornerstones of successful trading is cultivating a disciplined mindset. This involves adhering to trading plans, strategies, and risk management rules regardless of emotional fluctuations. A disciplined trader understands that success isn't solely defined by the outcome of a single trade but rather by consistently following a well-thought-out strategy.

Overcoming Common Psychological Pitfalls:

This section addresses common psychological pitfalls that carry traders may encounter and provides strategies to overcome them. Common pitfalls include:

1. **Overtrading:** Trading excessively due to excitement or anxiety, which can lead to exhaustion and poor decision-making.

2. **Revenge Trading:** Chasing losses or trying to recoup past losses through impulsive trades, which often amplifies losses.
3. **Confirmation Bias:** Seeking out information that supports existing beliefs while ignoring contradictory evidence.
4. **Fear of Missing Out (FOMO):** Entering trades solely because others are doing so, without proper analysis.
5. **Loss Aversion:** Fearing losses more than valuing gains, which can lead to holding losing positions longer than necessary.

Practical Techniques for Emotional Control:

The chapter provides practical techniques for emotional control, such as:

1. **Mindfulness and Meditation:** Techniques to stay present and centered, reducing impulsive decision-making.
2. **Journaling:** Keeping a trading journal to document emotions, decisions, and outcomes, promoting self-awareness.
3. **Visualization:** Mentally rehearsing successful trading scenarios to enhance confidence and discipline.

Conclusion of Chapter 13:

As we conclude this chapter on the psychological aspects of carry trading, it's evident that emotional discipline and a resilient mindset are integral to successful trading. By mastering these psychological factors, traders can enhance their ability to make informed decisions, stay patient during market fluctuations, and execute their strategies with consistency.

While technical and analytical skills are vital, psychological strength is what ultimately sets successful carry traders apart. As we move forward to the subsequent chapters, we will explore real-world case studies, delve into global economic trends' impact on carry trading, and discuss regulatory considerations in the forex market.

Equipped with the insights gained in this chapter, readers are prepared to navigate the psychological challenges of carry trading and foster a mindset conducive to success. Join us as we continue our exploration of the world of currency carry trades, unveiling strategies that optimize the exploitation of interest rate differentials while mastering the complexities of the human psyche.

Chapter 14: Carry Trading Case Studies

In this chapter, we dive into real-world examples of carry trade executions to illustrate how strategies are applied and outcomes unfold. Through detailed case studies, we will analyze the factors that contributed to trade success and learn from past mistakes. By examining these practical scenarios, we can gain a deeper understanding of the nuances of carry trading and how strategies play out in actual market conditions.

Real-World Success Stories:

This section presents case studies of carry trade executions that resulted in successful outcomes. Each case study will include:

1. **Currency Pair Selection:** Explanation of why a particular currency pair was chosen for the carry trade.
2. **Analysis:** Technical and fundamental factors that supported the trade decision.

3. **Entry and Exit Strategies:** Details about the timing of entry and exit points.
4. **Market Context:** Consideration of the broader market context during the trade execution.

Factors Contributing to Success:

Through the analysis of these case studies, we will identify common factors that contributed to the success of the trades. These may include:

1. **Alignment of Analysis:** How technical and fundamental analysis aligned to provide a strong trade setup.
2. **Effective Risk Management:** How risk management strategies were implemented to protect capital.
3. **Psychological Discipline:** The role of emotional discipline and a disciplined mindset in executing the strategy.

Learning from Mistakes:

In addition to success stories, this section will explore case studies where trades did not go as planned. By examining these scenarios, we can uncover mistakes or misjudgments and learn valuable lessons from them. This analysis will shed light on the importance of adaptability, continuous learning, and staying vigilant in the ever-changing forex market.

Conclusion of Chapter 14:

As we conclude this chapter focused on carry trading case studies, it becomes evident that practical examples provide invaluable insights into the dynamics of real-world trading. By analyzing both successful and less successful trades, traders can refine their strategies, enhance their decision-making processes, and develop a more nuanced understanding of the complexities of the forex market.

By integrating these insights with the technical, fundamental, psychological, and regulatory aspects discussed in previous chapters, traders can cultivate a well-rounded approach to carry trading. As we move forward to the subsequent chapters, we will explore the impact of global economic trends on carry trading, discuss regulatory considerations, and delve into alternative carry trade strategies.

Equipped with the insights gained in this chapter, readers are prepared to apply practical knowledge to their carry trading endeavors and learn from both successes and setbacks. Join us as we continue our exploration of the world of currency carry trades, unveiling strategies that optimize the exploitation of interest rate differentials while embracing the realities of real-world trading scenarios.

Chapter 15: Global Economic Trends and Carry Trades

In the intricate world of carry trading, understanding the broader global economic trends is crucial for making informed decisions and navigating the forex market's complexities. This chapter delves into the impact of global economic cycles on carry trading strategies, offering insights into how economic awareness can help traders align their strategies with long-term trends.

Impact of Global Economic Cycles:

Economic cycles, characterized by periods of expansion, contraction, and recovery, have a significant influence on currency markets. Understanding the stages of these cycles can provide valuable context for carry trading strategies. During economic expansions, high-yield currencies might flourish as interest rates rise, while during contractions, low-yield currencies might gain favor as safe-haven assets.

Navigating Volatile Markets:

Volatile markets can present challenges for carry traders, as sudden shifts in economic sentiment or geopolitical events can disrupt established trends. This section explores how economic awareness can help traders navigate such situations. By staying informed about economic indicators, central bank policies, and global events, traders can adjust their strategies to mitigate risk and seize opportunities even in volatile conditions.

Aligning Strategies with Long-Term Trends:

Successful carry trading extends beyond short-term gains. This section emphasizes the importance of aligning carry trade strategies with long-term economic trends. By identifying economic trends and anticipating potential shifts in interest rate differentials, traders can position themselves to capitalize on sustained trends that align with their strategies.

Conclusion of Chapter 15:

As we conclude this chapter dedicated to global economic trends and carry trades, it becomes clear that a comprehensive understanding of the economic landscape is a fundamental aspect of success. By staying attuned to economic cycles, market sentiment, and evolving trends, carry traders can navigate the forex market's intricacies and make informed decisions that align with their strategies.

By integrating economic awareness with technical, fundamental, psychological, and regulatory considerations, traders can cultivate a holistic approach to carry trading. As we move forward to the subsequent chapters, we will discuss regulatory considerations in forex trading, explore alternative carry trade strategies, and examine the future outlook for carry trading in the face of evolving market dynamics.

Equipped with the insights gained in this chapter, readers are prepared to incorporate economic awareness into their carry trading strategies and adapt to changing global trends. Join us as we continue our exploration of the world of currency carry trades, unveiling strategies that optimize the exploitation of interest rate differentials while staying aligned with the ebb and flow of the global economic landscape.

Chapter 16: Regulatory Considerations in Forex Trading

In the dynamic world of forex trading, regulatory considerations play a crucial role in ensuring fair and transparent markets. This chapter delves into the regulatory landscape of forex trading, highlighting the importance of adhering to regulations, guidelines, and best practices to safeguard investments and maintain market integrity.

Overview of Forex Market Regulations:

This section provides an overview of the regulatory framework that governs forex trading. Different countries and regions have their own regulatory bodies and guidelines, which aim to protect traders, maintain market stability, and prevent fraudulent activities. Understanding the regulatory landscape is essential for traders to operate within legal boundaries.

Ensuring Compliance with Trading Laws:

Compliance with trading laws and regulations is paramount for traders. This section explores the responsibilities of traders in adhering to regulations, including account verification, anti-money laundering measures, and reporting requirements. By ensuring compliance, traders can participate in the market with confidence and transparency.

Safeguarding Investments through Regulatory Adherence:

Regulations are designed to protect traders' investments and maintain a level playing field. This section emphasizes how regulatory adherence can contribute to a safer trading environment. By trading with regulated brokers and platforms, traders can reduce the risk of encountering fraudulent schemes or unfair practices.

Conclusion of Chapter 16:

As we conclude this chapter focused on regulatory considerations in forex trading, it becomes evident that understanding and adhering to regulations are essential for responsible trading. By operating within regulatory boundaries, traders contribute to the integrity and stability of the forex market, fostering an environment where participants can trade with confidence.

By integrating regulatory awareness with technical, fundamental, psychological, and economic considerations, traders can cultivate a comprehensive approach to carry trading. As we move forward to the subsequent chapters, we will explore alternative carry trade strategies, examine the future outlook for carry trading, and provide a concluding overview of the insights gained throughout the book.

Equipped with the insights gained in this chapter, readers are prepared to navigate the regulatory landscape of forex trading and ensure their trading practices align with legal and ethical standards. Join us as we continue our exploration of the world of currency carry trades, unveiling strategies that optimize the exploitation of interest rate differentials while upholding the principles of responsible trading within regulated frameworks.

Chapter 17: Alternative Carry Trade Strategies

While traditional carry trading is a well-established approach, there are alternative strategies that traders can explore to diversify their portfolio and adapt to varying market conditions. This chapter delves into these alternative strategies, highlighting their benefits, considerations, and potential applications in the forex market.

Exploring Variations of Traditional Carry Trading:

This section introduces alternative strategies that deviate from the traditional long-term carry trade approach. Examples include:

1. **Short-Term Carry Trading:** A variation that focuses on exploiting short-term interest rate differentials for quicker gains.
2. **Dynamic Carry Trading:** Adjusting positions based on changing economic indicators and interest rate expectations.
3. **Event-Driven Carry Trading:** Capitalizing on significant events, such as central bank announcements or economic data releases.

Cross-Currency Strategies and Their Benefits:

Cross-currency strategies involve trading between two currency pairs rather than a single pair. This section explores the advantages of cross-currency strategies, such as reduced exposure to individual currency risks and the potential to profit from relative strength.

Carry Trading in Emerging Market Currencies:

While carry trading is often associated with major currency pairs, emerging market currencies offer unique opportunities. This section discusses the potential benefits and risks of carry trading in emerging market currencies, including higher interest rate differentials and increased volatility.

Conclusion of Chapter 17:

As we conclude this chapter focused on alternative carry trade strategies, it becomes clear that the forex market offers a diverse range of approaches that cater to different trading styles and risk appetites. By exploring variations of traditional carry trading, cross-currency strategies, and opportunities in emerging market currencies, traders can expand their toolkit and adapt to changing market dynamics.

By integrating alternative strategies with the technical, fundamental, psychological, regulatory, and economic considerations discussed in previous chapters, traders can develop a well-rounded approach to carry trading. As we move forward to the final chapter, we will reflect on the future outlook for carry trading and provide a comprehensive conclusion to the insights gained throughout the book.

Equipped with the insights gained in this chapter, readers are prepared to consider and explore alternative strategies that align with their trading objectives and risk tolerance. Join us as we continue our exploration of the world of currency carry trades, unveiling strategies that optimize the exploitation of interest rate differentials while embracing the diversity of trading approaches available in the forex market.

Chapter 18: Future Outlook for Carry Trading

As we approach the final chapter of this book, it's important to consider the future outlook for carry trading in the ever-evolving forex market. This chapter explores the factors that may shape the landscape of carry trading in the years to come and provides insights for traders to prepare for changing market dynamics.

Predicting the Evolution of Interest Rate Differentials:

Interest rate differentials are a cornerstone of carry trading, and their evolution is influenced by economic cycles, central bank policies, and global economic trends. This section discusses how traders can anticipate potential shifts in interest rate differentials and adjust their strategies accordingly.

Technological Advancements and Their Impact:

Technological advancements have transformed the trading landscape, enabling faster execution, improved analysis, and enhanced risk management. This section explores how technological developments may impact carry trading, from algorithmic trading to the integration of artificial intelligence and machine learning.

Preparing for Changing Market Dynamics:

The forex market is dynamic and subject to constant change. This section emphasizes the importance of adaptability and continuous learning for carry traders. By staying informed about economic trends, geopolitical events, and regulatory changes, traders can navigate shifting market dynamics with confidence.

Conclusion of Chapter 18:

As we conclude this chapter on the future outlook for carry trading, it's evident that the ability to anticipate and adapt to changes is vital for sustained success. By integrating insights from technical, fundamental, psychological, regulatory, economic, and alternative strategy considerations, traders can develop a strategic approach that embraces the evolving nature of the forex market.

The journey of carry trading is an ongoing one, and as you embark on your trading endeavors, remember that the future holds both challenges and opportunities. Equipped with the knowledge gained throughout this book, you have the foundation to navigate these changes, make informed decisions, and evolve as a skilled carry trader.

In the concluding chapter, we will recap the key takeaways from the book, encourage responsible application of carry trade knowledge, and inspire traders to continuously learn and adapt in the dynamic forex market. Join us as we reflect on the insights gained and embark on a future filled with growth, prosperity, and strategic success.

Conclusion: Applying Knowledge and Embracing the Journey

As we bring this book to a close, it's important to reflect on the journey you've undertaken through the world of currency carry trading. The insights, strategies, and considerations presented within these pages offer a comprehensive understanding of this dynamic trading approach. However, the true value lies in how you apply this knowledge and approach your trading journey moving forward.

Recap of Key Takeaways:

Throughout the chapters, you've explored the intricacies of interest rate differentials, technical and fundamental analysis, risk management, psychological discipline, economic trends, regulatory considerations, and alternative strategies. These elements collectively form a robust foundation for navigating the forex market strategically.

Applying Carry Trade Knowledge Responsibly:

As you apply the knowledge gained from this book, remember that responsible trading practices are paramount. Risk management, adherence to regulations, and ethical trading practices should always guide your actions. Carry trading offers opportunities, but it's crucial to approach the market with discipline, caution, and a strong ethical compass.

Inspiration to Learn and Adapt:

The forex market is a dynamic and ever-changing landscape. As you continue your trading journey, stay inspired to learn and adapt. The world of finance, economics, and technology is constantly evolving, and your willingness to stay informed and refine your strategies will be key to your long-term success.

Embracing the Continuous Journey:

Remember that currency carry trading is a journey, not a destination. Each trade is a learning opportunity, and each outcome contributes to your growth as a trader. Whether you're a beginner or an experienced trader, the journey is ongoing, offering both challenges and rewards. Approach each trade with a strategic mindset, and embrace the continuous process of learning and improvement.

Final Words:

As you embark on your own currency carry trading journey, I encourage you to combine the knowledge you've gained with a disciplined approach, a resilient mindset, and a commitment to responsible trading. The insights presented in this book serve as a compass, guiding you through the complexities of the forex market.

May your path be marked by growth, prosperity, and strategic success. As you navigate the challenges and opportunities that lie ahead, remember that you have the tools, insights, and determination to thrive in the world of currency carry trading. Here's to a future filled with strategic endeavors and prosperous outcomes.

Appendix: Glossary of Key Terms

- **Currency Carry Trade:** A trading strategy that involves borrowing funds in a currency with a low interest rate and investing those funds in a currency with a higher interest rate, aiming to profit from the interest rate differential.

- **Interest Rate Differential:** The difference between the interest rates of two currencies. It is a fundamental factor that influences currency carry trading.

- **Uncovered Interest Rate Parity (UIP) Theory:** The theory that suggests the difference in interest rates between two countries should be reflected in the exchange rate movement between their currencies.

- **Covered Interest Rate Parity (CIP) Theory:** The theory that takes into account the interest rate differential and forward exchange rates to eliminate arbitrage opportunities in the forex market.

- **Economic Indicators:** Quantitative data that provide insights into a country's economic health, such as GDP growth, inflation rates, unemployment figures, and trade balances.

- **Central Bank Policies:** Decisions and actions taken by central banks to control a country's money supply, interest rates, and overall economic conditions.

- **Geopolitical Events:** Events related to political, economic, and social factors that can influence market sentiment and currency movements, including elections, trade negotiations, and conflicts.

- **Technical Analysis:** The analysis of historical price data and chart patterns to forecast future price movements in the forex market.

- **Fundamental Analysis:** The analysis of economic indicators, central bank policies, and geopolitical events to understand the factors influencing currency values.

- **Position Sizing:** Determining the appropriate amount of capital to allocate to a trade based on risk tolerance and account balance.

- **Stop-Loss Order:** An order placed to automatically close a trade when the market moves against the trader's position beyond a predefined point, limiting potential losses.

- **Take-Profit Order:** An order placed to automatically close a trade when the market reaches a predetermined profit level, allowing traders to capture profits before potential reversals.

- **Diversification:** Spreading risk across multiple currency pairs and assets to reduce exposure to the risk associated with a single trade.

- **Emotional Discipline:** The ability to control emotions such as fear, greed, and anxiety that can influence trading decisions.

- **Patience:** The virtue of waiting for favorable trading opportunities that align with a trader's strategy.

- **Confidence:** Trust in one's trading skills, strategy, and analysis, balanced with a willingness to learn and improve.

- **Risk Management Mindset:** Prioritizing capital preservation and implementing risk management strategies to avoid excessive losses.

Disclaimer: This glossary provides brief explanations of key terms related to currency carry trading. For a more comprehensive understanding of these terms and their implications, further study and research are recommended. Trading in the forex market carries inherent risks, and it's essential to conduct due diligence, seek professional advice, and practice caution before making trading decisions.

Momentum Trading

Trade assets that are showing strong recent price trends.

Introduction

The realm of financial trading is both vast and complex, characterized by various strategies that traders employ in their quest for profitability. Amid these strategies, momentum trading has gained a significant footing due to its focus on capitalizing on assets displaying strong recent price trends. "Momentum Trading: Trade assets that are showing strong recent price trends" is a guide designed to provide an in-depth exploration of this strategy, which hinges on the principle of 'the trend is your friend.'

Understanding price trends in the financial markets is imperative. Every transaction in the market leaves a footprint, and these aggregated footprints form trends. These trends, in turn, tell a story about the underlying forces at play, be it the overall sentiment, fundamental shifts in the economy, or a combination of various factors. Momentum trading, in essence, is about identifying these stories early, understanding their potential trajectory, and making informed trading decisions to benefit from them.

As we delve deeper into this guide, readers can expect a structured approach to momentum trading. From the rudimentary understanding of what constitutes momentum to advanced techniques and strategies employed by the most successful traders, this book is designed to be both a learning resource and a reference guide. It provides historical context, explores the science behind price momentum, outlines tools and techniques to identify and exploit momentum, and also delves into the psychological aspects that every trader must be aware of.

The complexity of financial markets, interlaced with human psychology, technological advancements, and global events, makes momentum trading both an art and a science. As such, while the principles and tools remain consistent, their application may vary based on market conditions, individual trading goals, and the asset class in focus. This guide aims to offer a comprehensive understanding, allowing traders the flexibility to adapt and innovate.

Chapter 1: Defining Momentum Trading

1.1 Historical context

Momentum trading, while a contemporary term in the age of digital trading platforms and high-frequency algorithms, is rooted in age-old trading practices. Historically, traders and investors have always looked for patterns. Whether it was the tulip mania of the 17th century or the stock market boom in the roaring twenties, certain patterns of rapid price appreciation followed by corrections have been evident.

The idea that assets which have performed well in the recent past tend to continue performing well is not new. Jesse Livermore, one of the most famous traders of the early 20th century, often spoke about the significance of following the market's trend. His practices, along with those of other legendary traders, laid the groundwork for what we today recognize as momentum trading.

Analyzing historical charts from various market cycles reveals that momentum-based strategies could have yielded substantial returns, especially during pronounced bullish phases. However, like all strategies, momentum trading evolved. The introduction of technical analysis tools in the 20th century, such as moving averages and relative strength indicators, gave traders better instruments to identify and ride momentum.

1.2 How momentum trading differs from other trading strategies

In the diverse world of trading strategies, momentum trading occupies a distinct space. While strategies like value investing focus on identifying undervalued assets or fundamental analysis emphasizes the underlying strengths or weaknesses of an asset, momentum trading is predominantly based on price action.

The core tenet of momentum trading is simple: buy assets that are going up and sell those that are going down. This might seem rudimentary, but the devil lies in the details. Determining when an asset has genuine momentum, deciphering false signals, understanding when momentum is waning, and deciding exit points are intricate processes.

Contrast this with strategies like mean reversion, where traders bet on prices returning to a historical mean, or carry trades in forex, which capitalize on the differential interest rates between two currencies. While these strategies have their own merits and demerits, momentum trading's appeal lies in its alignment with market sentiment and the ability to quickly capitalize on emerging trends.

1.3 Core principles of momentum trading

Three core principles underline momentum trading. Firstly, momentum traders believe that assets in motion tend to stay in motion. This Newtonian idea, when applied to financial markets, implies that assets showing strong trends (upward or downward) are likely to continue in that direction for a significant period.

Secondly, momentum trading is not about predicting market tops or bottoms. Instead, it's about identifying established trends and riding them. While this means momentum traders might miss the initial stages of a trend, it also ensures they avoid false starts, which can be costly.

Lastly, discipline and risk management are paramount. Given that momentum trading involves riding trends, it's essential to have a clear exit strategy for when the trend reverses. This ensures that profits are locked in and losses are minimized.

Chapter 2: The Science Behind Price Momentum
2.1 Psychological factors influencing price movements

Financial markets, at their very essence, are a reflection of human decision-making. Each trade embodies an individual's belief about an asset's future performance. These beliefs, often driven by a blend of rational analysis and emotional impulse, shape the dynamics of price movements.

Understanding the psychology behind trading is crucial for momentum traders. Emotional drivers like fear and greed play pivotal roles in price fluctuations. For instance, news of a company's breakthrough innovation can lead to an influx of optimistic traders buying the stock, driving its price upwards. This initial upward movement can attract other traders, amplifying the momentum.

The Fear of Missing Out (FOMO) is a potent psychological factor. When traders see an asset's price rising, they might buy it purely out of fear of missing potential profits, even if they have no fundamental reason to believe in the asset's value. Conversely, panic selling during market downturns can exacerbate price declines, creating strong downward momentum.

Herd behavior, another psychological phenomenon, is also prevalent in financial markets. It refers to traders' tendency to follow the majority, often leading to bubbles and crashes. Momentum traders leverage these psychological patterns, positioning themselves to capitalize on price movements amplified by collective trader behavior.

2.2 Economic fundamentals driving momentum

While psychological factors play a pivotal role in momentum, economic fundamentals are the bedrock upon which these price movements are built. Financial markets, in the long run, tend to reflect the intrinsic value of assets based on economic realities.

For momentum traders, understanding macroeconomic indicators and their implications can provide a clearer picture of potential momentum drivers. For instance, a central bank's decision to cut interest rates can drive momentum in bond markets and currency pairs. Similarly, robust economic growth indicators in a country can fuel momentum in its stock market.

Sector-specific fundamentals also play a role. A breakthrough in renewable energy technology can lead to momentum in green energy stocks, while regulatory hurdles can impede momentum in sectors like pharmaceuticals or tech.

While momentum traders might not base their decisions purely on fundamentals, being aware of them helps in distinguishing between sustainable momentum and short-lived price spikes.

2.3 The lifecycle of a momentum trend

Every momentum trend, be it upward or downward, has a lifecycle. Understanding this lifecycle allows traders to position their entries and exits more effectively.

The initiation phase marks the beginning. Here, the asset's price movement is usually driven by fundamental factors or significant news events. This phase is often subtle, with only the most astute traders taking positions.

Following initiation is the acceleration phase. Here, the price trend becomes more pronounced. Psychological factors, such as FOMO and herd behavior, play a significant role, driving the price faster and with more volume. It's during this phase that most momentum traders enter the market.

However, no trend lasts forever. Eventually, the trend enters the distribution phase. Here, early entrants start taking profits, and the price movement slows. Volume decreases, and volatility may increase, signaling a potential trend reversal.

Recognizing the end of the distribution phase is vital for momentum traders. Holding onto an asset past this point can erode profits. Understanding the lifecycle helps traders maximize their gains while minimizing potential downsides.

Chapter 3: Identifying Momentum
3.1 Tools and indicators to spot momentum

Various tools and technical indicators enable traders to identify momentum in its nascent stages. Among the most widely used are Moving Averages (MAs), particularly the Exponential Moving Average (EMA) and the Simple Moving Average (SMA). By plotting average prices over specific periods, these tools help visualize trends, with price crossovers often indicating momentum shifts.

Another vital tool is the Relative Strength Index (RSI). It gauges the magnitude of recent price changes to evaluate overbought or oversold conditions. An RSI value above 70 typically indicates overbought conditions (potentially signaling a sell), while a value below 30 indicates oversold conditions (potentially signaling a buy).

Volume is an often-underestimated indicator. A price trend accompanied by increasing volume is usually a strong sign of momentum, as it indicates significant trader participation.

3.2 Volume, moving averages, and relative strength

The confluence of volume, moving averages, and RSI can provide robust signals for momentum traders. A rising asset price above its SMA, with an RSI below 70 and increasing volume, typically indicates strong upward momentum. Conversely, a falling price below its SMA, an RSI above 30, and increasing volume can signal strong downward momentum.

However, using these indicators in isolation can lead to false signals. It's their combined reading that provides a more holistic view of momentum. For instance, a rising price with decreasing volume might indicate waning momentum, even if the RSI and SMA readings are favorable.

3.3 Common pitfalls and false signals

Momentum trading, while lucrative, is fraught with pitfalls. Chief among them is the challenge of false signals. It's not uncommon for assets to exhibit signs of momentum, only for the trend to reverse abruptly.

False breakouts or breakdowns are classic examples. An asset might breach a crucial resistance or support level (indicative of momentum) but revert to its original range shortly after. Relying solely on single indicators increases susceptibility to such false signals.

Another pitfall is the confirmation bias. Traders, after entering a position, might give undue emphasis to indicators that confirm their decision while ignoring those signaling the opposite.

Chapter 4: Strategies for Momentum Trading

4.1 Pullback Trading

One of the primary strategies momentum traders employ is pullback trading. A pullback refers to a short-term reversal in an otherwise prevailing trend. For instance, in a robust upward trend, there might be moments when the price declines briefly before continuing its upward trajectory. Pullback traders aim to capitalize on these short-term reversals.

Why pullbacks occur is rooted in market psychology and technical reasons. Traders who've profited from the prevailing trend might decide to take their profits, leading to a brief price drop. Similarly, traders on the opposing side of the trend might attempt to challenge it, leading to temporary counter-trend movements.

The key to successful pullback trading lies in identifying genuine pullbacks and distinguishing them from potential trend reversals. Various indicators, such as Fibonacci retracement levels and moving averages, can aid in this endeavor.

4.2 Breakout Trading

Breakout trading revolves around price movements through historical resistance and support levels. A breakout occurs when an asset's price moves above a resistance or below a support, typically with high volume, indicating potential continued movement in the breakout's direction.

To capitalize on breakouts, traders need to identify crucial support and resistance levels, which are price points where the asset historically tends to reverse its movement. Once a breakout occurs, it's essential to confirm it with volume and other indicators to filter out potential false breakouts.

4.3 Using Momentum Oscillators

Momentum oscillators help traders identify the speed or velocity of price movement. The Moving Average Convergence Divergence (MACD) and the Rate of Change (ROC) are two commonly used momentum oscillators.

MACD comprises two moving averages: the MACD line and the signal line. When the MACD line crosses above the signal line, it's a bullish signal, indicating potential upward momentum. Conversely, a downward crossover signals potential bearish momentum.

ROC, on the other hand, measures the percentage change between the current price and the price a certain number of periods ago. A rising ROC indicates increasing momentum, while a declining ROC suggests decreasing momentum.

Chapter 5: Risk Management in Momentum Trading

Momentum trading offers exciting opportunities to capture short- to medium-term gains through trend-following strategies. However, alongside the potential rewards, it's crucial to address the inherent risks involved. Effective risk management is the cornerstone of sustaining success in momentum trading. This chapter delves into the principles of risk management, the importance of preserving capital, and strategies to mitigate potential losses.

Understanding Risk in Momentum Trading:

Risk is an integral part of trading, and momentum trading is no exception. Rapid price movements can lead to significant gains, but they can also result in substantial losses. Recognizing and quantifying risk is essential before entering any trade.

The Role of Position Sizing:

Position sizing determines how much capital is allocated to a specific trade. By adhering to a predetermined percentage of capital per trade, traders minimize the impact of individual losses on the overall portfolio. This prevents catastrophic losses and ensures long-term sustainability.

Setting Stop-Loss Orders:

A stop-loss order is a predefined point at which a trade will be automatically exited to limit losses. It's a crucial tool in risk management. Setting stop-loss levels based on technical analysis, support/resistance, or volatility can protect capital from unexpected market reversals.

Risk-Reward Ratio:

The risk-reward ratio assesses the potential gain against the potential loss for each trade. A favorable risk-reward ratio ensures that potential profits outweigh potential losses. This ratio guides traders in selecting trades that offer sufficient reward relative to the risk undertaken.

Diversification:

Diversification involves spreading capital across multiple assets or markets. This reduces the impact of a single loss on the overall portfolio. While momentum trading often focuses on specific assets, diversification can be achieved by trading different asset classes or using various strategies.

Avoiding Overtrading:

Overtrading occurs when a trader executes too many trades, often due to impulsive decisions or the desire to recover losses quickly. Overtrading can lead to increased transaction costs and emotional exhaustion. Adhering to a well-defined trading plan helps mitigate this risk.

Emotional Discipline:

Emotions like fear and greed can cloud judgment and lead to impulsive decisions. Effective risk management involves maintaining emotional discipline. This can be achieved through mindfulness techniques, following a trading plan, and avoiding impulsive trading based on emotions.

Backtesting and Simulation:

Risk management strategies should be tested and refined through backtesting and simulation. By assessing historical data, traders can evaluate how their risk management rules would have performed in various market scenarios.

Continuous Monitoring and Adjustments:

Markets are dynamic, and risk management strategies must adapt accordingly. Regularly monitoring trades, adjusting stop-loss levels as trends develop, and revisiting risk-reward ratios ensure that risk management remains effective.

Conclusion: Safeguarding Success through Effective Risk Management:

In momentum trading, success isn't just about making gains; it's about preserving capital to trade another day. Effective risk management is the shield that protects traders from excessive losses. By understanding the various aspects of risk, employing disciplined position sizing, setting appropriate stop-loss orders, and continuously adapting strategies, momentum traders can navigate the volatility of the markets while maintaining their long-term goals. Remember, it's not just about how much you make; it's about how much you keep.

Chapter 6: Advanced Concepts in Momentum Trading

As momentum trading continues to evolve, advanced concepts offer seasoned traders the opportunity to fine-tune their strategies and enhance their edge in the market. This chapter explores several advanced concepts that can take your momentum trading skills to the next level, providing insights into complex techniques and strategies.

1. Momentum Divergence:

Momentum divergence occurs when the price trend and a momentum indicator move in opposite directions. Recognizing divergence can signal potential trend reversals or corrections. Traders often use indicators like the Moving Average Convergence Divergence (MACD) to identify this phenomenon.

2. Volatility Adjusted Strategies:

Volatility-adjusted strategies account for market volatility when making trading decisions. Volatile markets may require wider stop-loss levels, while less volatile markets might demand tighter stops. Techniques like the Average True Range (ATR) can help traders adjust their strategies based on market conditions.

3. Trend Acceleration Patterns:

Advanced momentum traders identify specific chart patterns that indicate an acceleration of an existing trend. These patterns, such as continuation gaps and breakaway gaps, suggest that the momentum is intensifying, potentially leading to significant price movements.

4. Pyramiding:

Pyramiding involves adding to a winning position as it continues to move in the desired direction. This strategy maximizes profits during strong trends. However, careful risk management is essential, as it increases exposure and potential losses if the trend reverses.

5. Sector Rotation Strategies:

Advanced momentum traders consider broader market trends and sector rotations. Rotating into sectors that are currently displaying strong momentum can enhance overall portfolio performance and minimize risk by avoiding sectors in decline.

6. High-Frequency Momentum Trading:

High-frequency momentum trading involves executing a large number of trades within short timeframes to capture micro-trends. Advanced traders may use algorithmic trading systems and cutting-edge technology to execute these strategies.

7. Market Internals Analysis:

Market internals, such as advancing vs. declining stocks and the number of new highs and lows, provide insights into market sentiment and potential trend strength. Incorporating market internals analysis can refine entry and exit decisions.

8. Advanced Risk Management Techniques:

Seasoned momentum traders often employ advanced risk management techniques, such as dynamic position sizing based on recent performance or the Kelly Criterion formula, which calculates the optimal position size based on historical data and win rate.

9. Macro Analysis and Fundamentals:

Advanced momentum traders integrate macroeconomic analysis and fundamental factors into their strategies. Understanding broader economic trends and how they impact specific asset classes can provide a holistic perspective on potential momentum opportunities.

10. Machine Learning and Quantitative Models:

Advanced traders may leverage machine learning and quantitative models to analyze vast amounts of data and identify complex patterns. These techniques allow for more accurate predictions and more sophisticated trading strategies.

Conclusion: Elevating Your Momentum Trading Expertise:

Advanced concepts in momentum trading offer a deeper level of understanding and precision. As you explore these techniques, keep in mind that complexity requires diligence and practice. Thoroughly test advanced strategies in simulated environments and gradually implement them into your live trading. By combining these advanced concepts with a solid foundation in risk management, technical analysis, and market awareness, you can elevate your momentum trading expertise and increase your potential for success in the ever-evolving world of financial markets.

Chapter 7: Recognizing Momentum Patterns

Momentum trading hinges on the ability to identify and capitalize on price trends in the market. Recognizing momentum patterns is a fundamental skill that allows traders to spot potential opportunities and make informed decisions. This chapter delves into various momentum patterns, providing insights into their characteristics, significance, and how to incorporate them into your trading strategies.

1. Breakout Patterns:

Breakouts occur when an asset's price surpasses a significant resistance or support level, indicating a potential shift in momentum. Traders watch for breakout patterns like ascending triangles, descending triangles, and rectangles, which suggest a continuation or reversal of the trend.

2. Trendline Patterns:

Trendlines connect consecutive highs or lows on a price chart. Trendline breaks can indicate shifts in momentum. Recognizing trendline patterns like channels, wedges, and flags can help traders anticipate potential breakouts or breakdowns.

3. Reversal Patterns:

Reversal patterns signal potential changes in trend direction. Patterns like double tops and bottoms, head and shoulders, and inverted head and shoulders can provide clues about upcoming trend shifts.

4. Candlestick Patterns:

Candlestick patterns offer insights into short-term price movements. Patterns like engulfing patterns, doji, and hammer can indicate potential reversals or continuations based on the price action within a specific timeframe.

5. Moving Average Crossovers:

Moving averages, especially their crossovers, reveal shifts in momentum. The intersection of shorter-term and longer-term moving averages can signal entry or exit points, indicating potential trend changes.

6. Relative Strength Patterns:

Relative Strength Index (RSI) and other momentum oscillators help identify overbought and oversold conditions. Divergence between the price trend and RSI readings can signal potential reversals or continuations.

7. Volume Patterns:

Volume plays a crucial role in confirming trends. Patterns like volume spikes, volume divergence, and volume gaps provide insights into the strength or weakness of a price movement.

8. Elliott Wave Theory:

Advanced traders utilize the Elliott Wave Theory, which identifies recurring price patterns based on crowd psychology. The theory outlines five waves in an upward trend (impulse) and three waves in a downward trend (correction).

9. Fibonacci Retracements and Extensions:

Fibonacci levels act as support and resistance zones. Traders use Fibonacci retracements to identify potential pullback levels and extensions to predict where a trend might resume after a correction.

10. Gaps and Price Patterns:

Gaps occur when the price moves significantly between two trading sessions. Gap patterns like breakaway gaps, continuation gaps, and exhaustion gaps provide insights into potential momentum changes.

Conclusion: Mastering Momentum Patterns for Informed Trading:

Recognizing momentum patterns is an art that requires practice, patience, and an analytical mindset. By studying these patterns, understanding their significance, and integrating them with other technical and fundamental tools, you can enhance your ability to identify potential trading opportunities. Remember that no single pattern guarantees success. It's the combination of pattern recognition, risk management, and continuous learning that empowers traders to make well-informed decisions in the dynamic world of momentum trading.

Chapter 8: Using Volume in Momentum Trading

Volume is a powerful indicator in momentum trading, providing valuable insights into the strength and legitimacy of price movements. This chapter delves into the significance of volume, how to interpret volume patterns, and strategies for incorporating volume analysis into your momentum trading approach.

Understanding Volume's Role in Momentum:

Volume represents the number of shares or contracts traded in a given period. High volume during price movements signifies heightened market interest and participation, making it a crucial component in assessing momentum.

1. Volume Confirmation:

Volume confirms the legitimacy of price trends. A strong price movement accompanied by high volume is more likely to be sustainable than one with low volume. This confirms that market participants are actively driving the trend.

2. Volume Divergence:

Volume divergence occurs when price and volume move in opposite directions. This can signal potential reversals or shifts in momentum. Decreasing volume during a price trend may indicate weakening momentum.

3. Volume Spikes:

Sudden spikes in volume often coincide with significant price movements, such as breakouts or breakdowns. Volume spikes can validate the strength of a trend or suggest an imminent trend reversal.

4. Volume Patterns:

Patterns like volume clusters or expansion within a specific timeframe can provide insights into potential momentum shifts. A series of increasing volume days could indicate an approaching trend change.

5. On-Balance Volume (OBV):

OBV is a cumulative indicator that adds volume on up days and subtracts volume on down days. OBV can provide early signals of potential trend reversals by identifying shifts in buying and selling pressure.

6. Volume at Key Levels:

Volume analysis at support and resistance levels offers insights into potential price reactions. High volume at these levels can signify areas where traders are entering or exiting positions.

7. Volume and Chart Patterns:

Incorporate volume analysis with chart patterns like flags, triangles, and head and shoulders. High volume during a breakout validates the pattern's potential for trend continuation.

8. Combining Volume with Indicators:

Volume analysis can be combined with other indicators like moving averages or oscillators to strengthen momentum signals. For example, the Moving Average Convergence Divergence (MACD) with volume can provide insights into potential trend reversals.

9. Earnings and News Impact:

Earnings reports and significant news releases can trigger substantial volume surges. Analyzing volume around these events can help traders anticipate potential momentum shifts.

10. Conclusion: Volume as a Momentum Trading Edge:

Mastering volume analysis can elevate your momentum trading strategy by adding a layer of confirmation and depth to your decisions. By studying volume patterns, recognizing divergences, and combining volume analysis with other technical tools, you can refine your ability to identify high-probability trades. Remember that volume, like any indicator, has its limitations and should be used in conjunction with other forms of analysis for a comprehensive approach to momentum trading.

Chapter 9: The Psychology Behind Momentum Trading

Momentum trading isn't solely about technical analysis and market trends; it's deeply intertwined with the psychology of market participants. This chapter delves into the psychological factors that drive momentum trading, how emotions influence decision-making, and strategies to harness psychological insights for successful momentum trading.

Understanding Trader Psychology:

The behavior of market participants is shaped by a range of emotions, including fear, greed, excitement, and anxiety. Recognizing and managing these emotions is essential in navigating the complexities of momentum trading.

1. The Fear of Missing Out (FOMO):

FOMO drives traders to enter positions hastily due to the fear of missing a profitable opportunity. While it can lead to quick gains, FOMO-based decisions often neglect proper analysis and risk management.

2. Overconfidence Bias:

Overconfidence bias occurs when traders overestimate their abilities, leading to excessive risk-taking. Traders might enter larger positions or disregard stop-loss levels, assuming they can accurately predict market moves.

3. Herd Mentality:

The herd mentality causes traders to follow the crowd, even if their analysis suggests otherwise. This behavior often leads to overbought or oversold conditions, creating potential opportunities for contrarian momentum traders.

4. Loss Aversion:

Loss aversion makes traders hold losing positions for too long, hoping they'll eventually turn profitable. Overcoming this bias involves setting strict stop-loss levels and adhering to them.

5. Emotional Trading:

Emotional trading occurs when traders let emotions drive their decisions rather than a well-defined strategy. Emotional traders are more susceptible to impulsive buying and selling, leading to losses.

6. Confirmation Bias:

Confirmation bias makes traders seek information that confirms their existing beliefs while ignoring contrary evidence. This can lead to biased analysis and poor decision-making.

7. Regret Aversion:

Regret aversion causes traders to avoid taking action out of fear of making a wrong decision. This can lead to missed opportunities and delayed entries or exits.

8. Mindfulness and Discipline:

Mindfulness techniques can help traders stay present, reduce emotional reactivity, and enhance decision-making clarity. Discipline involves sticking to a well-thought-out trading plan regardless of emotional impulses.

9. Cognitive Biases and Cognitive Dissonance:

Understanding cognitive biases and cognitive dissonance helps traders recognize when their decisions are influenced by irrational thinking. Overcoming these biases requires self-awareness and continuous learning.

10. Conclusion: Mastering Mindset for Momentum Success:

Recognizing the psychological pitfalls that can sabotage momentum trading is as important as understanding technical analysis. Developing emotional intelligence, staying disciplined, and practicing mindfulness can enhance your ability to make rational, informed decisions. By acknowledging the psychological aspects of trading and integrating strategies to manage them, you can effectively navigate the emotional roller coaster of the markets and maintain a clear path to success in momentum trading

Chapter 10: Adapting to Market Changes in Momentum Trading

In the dynamic world of momentum trading, adapting to changing market conditions is crucial for consistent success. This chapter explores the importance of flexibility, strategies for adjusting to market shifts, and techniques to stay resilient in the face of evolving trends.

Understanding the Need for Adaptation:

Markets are never static; they evolve due to economic factors, geopolitical events, and technological advancements. Adapting to these changes ensures that your trading strategies remain relevant and effective.

1. Recognizing Market Cycles:

Markets move in cycles of uptrends, downtrends, and ranging periods. Adapting involves identifying which phase the market is in and tailoring your strategy accordingly.

2. Market Volatility and Quiet Periods:

Volatility can surge suddenly or recede during quieter periods. Adaptive traders use volatility-based indicators to adjust stop-loss levels and position sizes to account for heightened or reduced risk.

3. Shifting Correlations:

The relationships between different assets can change over time. Adapting requires monitoring correlations and adjusting strategies when the historical relationships no longer hold.

4. Incorporating New Data and Events:

Economic releases, central bank decisions, and geopolitical events can impact market momentum. Adapting involves staying informed about these events and being prepared for sudden shifts.

5. Revisiting and Updating Strategies:

Regularly review and update your trading strategies based on performance analysis. Remove or modify strategies that are no longer effective and integrate new techniques that align with current market conditions.

6. Flexibility in Timeframes:

Traders can adapt by shifting between different timeframes. In highly volatile markets, shorter timeframes might be more suitable, while calmer markets could require longer timeframes for accurate analysis.

7. Algorithmic and Quantitative Approaches:

Adaptive traders often use algorithmic trading and quantitative models. These systems can automatically adjust strategies based on real-time data, allowing for rapid adaptation.

8. Continuous Learning:

Stay informed about new trading technologies, strategies, and market insights. Adaptive traders prioritize continuous learning to remain ahead of the curve.

9. Emotional Resilience:

Adapting requires emotional resilience to handle both losses and gains. Emotional stability prevents impulsive decisions during times of uncertainty.

10. Conclusion: Mastering Adaptation for Long-Term Success:

Adaptation is the key to longevity in momentum trading. By recognizing changing market dynamics, staying flexible in your approach, and integrating new information and techniques, you can navigate the evolving landscape with confidence. Embrace adaptability as a core principle of your trading journey, and you'll be better equipped to thrive in the ever-changing world of momentum trading.

Chapter 11: Risks and Management in Momentum Trading

11.1 Understanding Inherent Risks

Momentum trading, while potentially profitable, also carries its set of risks. Traders are essentially betting on the continuation of an existing trend, but the financial markets are unpredictable. Here's what to consider:

- **False Signals:** Not every momentum indication guarantees a continued trend. The market may display all the hallmarks of a strong momentum, only to reverse without warning.
- **External Factors:** Global events, such as geopolitical tensions, sudden policy changes, or even unexpected financial news, can instantly change the market's direction.
- **High Volatility:** Momentum stocks or assets often experience high volatility. While this offers potential for high returns, it also means increased potential for significant losses.

11.2 Effective Risk Management Strategies

Effective risk management is the cornerstone of sustainable momentum trading. Here are some strategies to consider:

- **Setting Stop-Loss Orders:** This allows traders to predetermine the maximum loss they're willing to take, automatically selling the asset if it reaches this threshold.
- **Diversification:** While momentum trading often involves focusing on specific assets, it's still wise to diversify investments to reduce risk.
- **Limiting Leverage:** While leverage can amplify profits, it can also magnify losses. Especially in high-volatility situations, it's prudent to be cautious with the use of leverage.

11.3 Continuous Monitoring and Evaluation

Given the swift nature of momentum trading, continuous monitoring is imperative. This doesn't just pertain to price movements but also to the trader's performance.

- **Performance Tracking:** Maintain a journal of trades, noting the reasons for entry and exit, the outcomes, and any patterns or lessons learned.
- **Regular Strategy Assessment:** What worked in the past may not work in the future. It's crucial to periodically review and, if necessary, adjust trading strategies based on performance data.
- **Staying Informed:** This can't be stressed enough. A successful momentum trader stays abreast of global news, market analyses, and potential factors that could influence their trades.

By acknowledging the inherent risks in momentum trading and proactively implementing management strategies, traders can position themselves for long-term success while minimizing potential downsides.

Chapter 12: Advanced Momentum Indicators and Tools

12.1 Relative Strength Index (RSI)

RSI is a momentum oscillator that measures the speed and change of price movements. It oscillates between 0 and 100 and is typically used to identify overbought or oversold conditions in a traded asset. When RSI reads above 70, an asset is generally considered overbought, and when it reads below 30, it's considered oversold. But for momentum traders, a high RSI (above 70) can sometimes signal strong momentum in the asset, suggesting there might be further gains ahead.

Understanding how to interpret divergence between RSI and price can also be instrumental. For instance, if the asset makes a new high but the RSI fails to surpass its previous high, it can indicate weakening momentum and a potential trend reversal.

12.2 Moving Average Convergence Divergence (MACD)

MACD is a trend-following momentum indicator that shows the relationship between two moving averages of a security's price. The MACD is calculated by subtracting the 26-period Exponential Moving Average (EMA) from the 12-period EMA. The result of that calculation is the MACD line. A nine-day EMA of the MACD called the "signal line," is then plotted on top of the MACD line, which can function as a trigger for buy and sell signals.

For momentum traders, MACD crossovers (when the MACD line crosses above or below the signal line) can indicate buy or sell opportunities. Furthermore, divergences between MACD and price can signal potential trend reversals or weakening momentum.

12.3 Stochastic Oscillator

The stochastic oscillator compares a particular closing price of an asset to a range of its prices over a certain period. The premise is that in an uptrend, prices will likely close near their high, and in a downtrend, prices will close near their low.

The stochastic oscillator generates values between 0 and 100 and typically uses a 14-day period as its default setting. Readings above 80 are considered overbought, while readings below 20 are considered oversold. For momentum traders, these overbought or oversold readings can indicate strong upwards or downwards momentum, respectively, rather than immediate reversal points.

However, as with other indicators, divergences between the oscillator and price trends can be vital in predicting potential reversals or a slowdown in momentum.

The advanced momentum indicators provide traders with refined tools to assess market momentum and generate potential trading signals. By mastering these indicators, momentum traders can significantly enhance their ability to decipher market conditions and make more informed decisions. As always, it's essential to use these tools in conjunction with other analyses and never rely solely on one indicator.

Chapter 13: Adapting to Market Changes and Volatility

13.1 Recognizing Market Shifts

In the dynamic environment of financial markets, momentum traders must stay vigilant to shifts that might affect their positions. Recognizing market shifts is paramount to avoid large losses and to capitalize on new opportunities.

- **Economic Indicators:** Regularly released statistics, such as GDP growth, unemployment rates, and inflation, can signal broader economic shifts that impact market momentum.
- **Sector Performance:** Keep an eye on sectors that begin to outperform or underperform. A sudden surge in a specific sector can indicate a shift in market sentiment towards those assets.
- **Global Events:** World events, like elections, geopolitical tensions, and major policy changes, can sway market dynamics rapidly.

13.2 Managing Trades During High Volatility

Volatility is a double-edged sword for momentum traders. While it presents opportunities for larger gains, it also amplifies the potential for losses. Effective management techniques during these periods are crucial.

- **Adjusting Stop-Losses:** While it might be tempting to widen stop-losses during volatile periods, it's essential to have a strategy that defines when and how you'll adjust these levels.
- **Reducing Position Sizes:** By decreasing the size of your trades, you can reduce potential losses while still capitalizing on price movements.
- **Avoiding Overtrading:** During periods of high volatility, opportunities may seem abundant, but overtrading can lead to significant losses if not done with caution.

13.3 Being Agile and Adaptable

The financial markets are not static, and neither should be a trader's strategies.

- **Continuous Learning:** With the emergence of new financial products, technologies, and trading methodologies, it's beneficial for traders to continually educate themselves.
- **Review and Adjust:** Regularly review your trading strategy to identify what's working and what isn't. Make adjustments based on performance data and changing market conditions.
- **Embracing Technology:** Utilize the latest trading platforms and analytical tools to gain an edge. Advanced software can provide real-time data and insights that are invaluable to momentum traders.

The ability to adapt and pivot is one of the hallmarks of a successful momentum trader. By recognizing market shifts, managing trades effectively during volatile periods, and maintaining agility in their approach, traders can navigate the complexities of the market and aim for consistent profitability.

Chapter 14: Psychological Aspects of Momentum Trading
14.1 Emotional Discipline and Decision Making

Trading, especially momentum trading, can stir a range of emotions, from excitement and elation to fear and regret. Keeping emotions in check is paramount to ensure decisions are grounded in strategy rather than sentiment.

- **Fear and Greed:** These are two primary emotions that drive traders. Fear can cause premature selling, while greed can lead to holding a position for too long. Recognizing and controlling these emotions is key to consistent trading decisions.

- **Overconfidence:** A few successful trades can lead to overconfidence, causing a trader to take on excessive risks. Remember, past success is not indicative of future results.
- **Regret:** Missing a trading opportunity or incurring a loss can lead to the emotion of regret. However, it's essential to understand that losses and missed opportunities are inherent in trading.

14.2 Building a Resilient Mindset

A resilient mindset allows traders to bounce back from losses, analyze mistakes without self-blame, and move forward with a clear focus.

- **Acceptance of Losses:** Every trader will face losses. It's an inherent part of trading. The key is not to dwell on them but to learn from them.
- **Continuous Learning:** Embrace every trading outcome as a learning opportunity. Whether it's a profit or loss, there's always something to glean.
- **Maintaining Work-Life Balance:** Trading can be consuming. Ensure you maintain a balance by allocating time to relax, exercise, and engage in other non-trading activities.

14.3 Strategies to Curb Emotional Trading

Implementing specific strategies can help in avoiding impulsive decisions based on emotions.

- **Trading Journal:** Documenting each trade, including the strategy employed, the outcome, and the emotions felt, can offer insights into behavior patterns. Reviewing this journal periodically can highlight emotional triggers.
- **Set Clear Rules:** Before entering a trade, have clear rules for exit, profit targets, and stop-loss. Adhere to these rules, irrespective of the emotional turbulence.
- **Seek Peer Support:** Engaging in trading communities or having a mentor can provide a sounding board for decisions and offer objective viewpoints.

The psychological aspects of momentum trading are often overshadowed by the focus on technical analysis and strategy. However, the emotional landscape plays a significant role in trading success. By recognizing emotional triggers, cultivating a resilient mindset, and implementing strategies to curb emotional trading, momentum traders can enhance their decision-making prowess and maintain consistency in their approach.

Chapter 15: Backtesting and Strategy Refinement

15.1 The Importance of Backtesting

Backtesting is a critical process that involves testing a trading strategy using historical market data to assess its viability and potential performance. It's a way to simulate how a strategy would have performed in the past, giving traders valuable insights before risking real capital.

- **Strategy Validation:** Backtesting helps verify whether a strategy would have yielded profitable results in various market conditions.
- **Fine-Tuning:** Through backtesting, traders can identify the strengths and weaknesses of their strategy and make adjustments accordingly.
- **Risk Management:** Backtesting provides insights into potential drawdowns and losses, enabling traders to refine their risk management approaches.

15.2 Steps in Backtesting

- **Defining Strategy Parameters:** Clearly outline the entry and exit conditions of your strategy. What indicators will you use? What triggers will prompt you to take action?
- **Selecting Historical Data:** Choose a relevant historical period that encompasses different market scenarios.
- **Testing and Analyzing:** Implement your strategy on historical data and analyze the results. Pay attention to metrics like profitability, drawdowns, and the number of trades executed.

15.3 Limitations and Caution

Backtesting has its limitations, and traders should be aware of them:

- **Data Quality:** The accuracy of backtesting results heavily relies on the quality and integrity of historical data.
- **Over-Optimization:** Traders may be tempted to adjust parameters to fit historical data too perfectly, leading to strategies that don't perform well in real-time.
- **Changing Market Conditions:** Market dynamics change over time, and past performance doesn't guarantee future success.

15.4 Strategy Refinement

Based on backtesting results, traders can refine and improve their strategies:

- **Adjust Parameters:** If certain parameters consistently underperform, tweak them to better suit the current market conditions.
- **Adding Filters:** Incorporate additional filters or indicators that might enhance the strategy's accuracy.
- **Risk Management Enhancements:** Refine stop-loss and position-sizing techniques to optimize risk-reward ratios.

Backtesting isn't just a one-time endeavor. As market conditions change, strategies must be continually refined and optimized. By backtesting diligently, traders can uncover patterns, improve their strategies, and increase the likelihood of successful momentum trading.

Chapter 16: The Role of Technology in Momentum Trading
16.1 Real-Time Data and Analysis

Access to real-time market data is an indispensable tool for momentum traders. Advanced trading platforms provide up-to-the-second price movements, news feeds, and technical indicators that can inform swift decisions.

- **Instant Updates:** Timely information ensures traders don't miss out on crucial market developments that could impact their positions.
- **Technical Analysis Tools:** Sophisticated platforms offer a wide array of technical indicators, charts, and patterns that can be used for in-depth analysis.

16.2 Algorithmic Trading

Algorithmic or automated trading involves using computer programs to execute trades based on predetermined criteria. For momentum traders, algorithmic trading can swiftly capitalize on price movements that might be missed by manual traders.

- **High-Speed Execution:** Algorithms can execute trades in milliseconds, crucial in momentum trading where every second counts.
- **Emotion Elimination:** Algorithms trade based on pre-programmed rules, eliminating emotional decisions that can often lead to poor outcomes.

16.3 Mobile Trading Apps

Mobile trading apps allow traders to access the markets from anywhere and at any time. For momentum traders, the ability to react quickly to emerging trends or news is a significant advantage.

- **Flexibility:** Traders can monitor and manage their positions on the go, making the most of every trading opportunity.
- **Notifications:** Mobile apps can provide real-time notifications for price movements, news releases, or any other events that could impact trades.

16.4 Risk Management Tools

Several technology-driven risk management tools assist traders in preserving capital and minimizing losses.

- **Automated Stop-Loss Orders:** Traders can set stop-loss orders in advance, ensuring that positions are automatically exited if the market moves against them.
- **Trailing Stops:** These allow the stop-loss level to adjust as the price moves in the trader's favor, helping to secure profits while giving room for potential gains.

16.5 Machine Learning and AI

Advanced traders are increasingly utilizing machine learning and artificial intelligence to identify patterns and generate trading signals.

- **Pattern Recognition:** Machine learning algorithms can identify complex patterns that human traders might overlook.
- **Data Analysis:** AI can process vast amounts of data quickly, making it valuable in identifying potential momentum trends.

The role of technology in momentum trading is transformative. With access to real-time data, algorithmic trading, mobile apps, and risk management tools, traders have the tools they need to react swiftly, make informed decisions, and optimize their strategies. As technology continues to evolve, momentum traders can expect even more advanced tools to enhance their trading experience.

Chapter 17: Building a Winning Mindset for Momentum Trading

17.1 The Psychological Challenge

Momentum trading demands not only technical skills but also a resilient and disciplined mindset. Overcoming psychological hurdles is critical for consistent success.

17.2 Embracing Uncertainty

Financial markets are inherently uncertain. Accepting that losses are a part of trading and that no strategy is foolproof is the first step in developing a winning mindset.

- **Risk as a Part of Business:** Just as any business carries risks, trading is no different. Viewing trading as a business can help detach emotions from decisions.
- **Avoiding Perfectionism:** Accept that not every trade will be a winner. Aiming for consistency and a positive overall outcome is more realistic than expecting every trade to be profitable.

17.3 Patience and Discipline

Two virtues that serve momentum traders well are patience and discipline.

- **Waiting for Optimal Setups:** Impulsive trading can lead to losses. Waiting for high-probability setups aligns with disciplined trading.
- **Executing the Plan:** Following your predetermined strategy without deviating based on emotions or market noise is key.

17.4 Managing FOMO and Fear

Fear of Missing Out (FOMO) can lead to impulsive trades, while fear of loss can lead to missed opportunities.

- **FOMO Awareness:** Recognize when FOMO is driving your decisions. Sticking to your strategy even when the market seems to be moving without you is crucial.
- **Conquering Fear of Loss:** Embrace the possibility of losses as part of the trading journey. A well-managed loss is often a better outcome than chasing after a high-risk trade.

17.5 Continuous Learning and Adaptation

A winning mindset requires a commitment to lifelong learning and adaptability.

- **Humility in Learning:** Be open to new ideas, strategies, and perspectives. No trader has all the answers.
- **Adapting to Change:** The markets evolve, and so must your strategies. Embrace change and constantly refine your approach.

Ultimately, building a winning mindset for momentum trading requires the mastery of one's emotions, a disciplined approach, and a commitment to learning and adaptation. By acknowledging the psychological challenges, embracing uncertainty, practicing patience, and managing fear, traders can position themselves for long-term success in the exciting world of momentum trading.

Chapter 18: Conclusion and Future of Momentum Trading
18.1 Reflecting on the Journey

As you conclude this book on momentum trading, take a moment to reflect on the knowledge gained and the journey you've embarked upon. From understanding the fundamentals to delving into advanced strategies and psychological aspects, you've explored the multifaceted world of trading momentum.

18.2 The Evolution of Trading

Trading, including momentum trading, is constantly evolving. New technologies, market dynamics, and global events shape the landscape. It's imperative to remain adaptable and open to change.

18.3 The Future of Momentum Trading

The future of momentum trading holds exciting possibilities:

- **Artificial Intelligence Integration:** AI and machine learning are likely to play more prominent roles in identifying patterns and generating trading signals.
- **Cryptocurrencies and Digital Assets:** As these markets mature, momentum trading strategies may expand to include these assets.
- **Regulation and Compliance:** With increasing attention on trading practices, staying compliant with evolving regulations will be crucial.

18.4 Continuing Your Trading Journey

Momentum trading isn't just a strategy; it's a continuous journey of learning, adapting, and refining. Whether you're a novice or an experienced trader, the world of finance offers endless opportunities for growth.

Remember that trading involves risk, and no strategy guarantees success. However, armed with knowledge, discipline, and a robust strategy, you can navigate the markets with confidence.

As you move forward, embrace challenges as learning opportunities, setbacks as stepping stones, and successes as indicators of your dedication and skill. Happy trading!

Congratulations on completing this comprehensive exploration of momentum trading. Remember, trading is a blend of science and art, and success comes from a combination of knowledge, experience, and the right mindset. As you embark on your trading journey, always prioritize continuous learning, sound risk management, and a healthy balance between ambition and prudence. Best of luck in your endeavors as a momentum trader!

1. Tools and Resources:

Stock Screeners:

- **Finviz:** A popular stock screener that allows you to filter stocks based on various criteria, including price trends, technical indicators, and market capitalization.
- **TradingView:** A versatile platform with advanced charting tools and customizable indicators for technical analysis.

Technical Analysis Indicators:

- **Moving Averages:** Used to smooth out price data and identify trends. Common ones include the simple moving average (SMA) and the exponential moving average (EMA).
- **Relative Strength Index (RSI):** Measures the speed and change of price movements to identify overbought or oversold conditions.
- **MACD (Moving Average Convergence Divergence):** A trend-following momentum indicator that shows the relationship between two moving averages of a security's price.

Online Brokerage Platforms:

- **Interactive Brokers:** Offers advanced trading tools and platforms suitable for active traders.
- **TD Ameritrade:** Provides a variety of research and trading tools for traders of different experience levels.

- **E*TRADE:** Offers a range of trading platforms with research and analysis tools.

2. Software Recommendations and Reviews:

Algorithmic Trading Platforms:

- **MetaTrader 4 (MT4) and MetaTrader 5 (MT5):** Widely used platforms for trading forex and other assets, featuring customizable indicators and automated trading capabilities.
- **NinjaTrader:** Offers advanced charting, backtesting, and automated trading features.
- **Thinkorswim:** A platform by TD Ameritrade that provides advanced charting, analysis tools, and paper trading.

3. Further Reading and Online Resources:

Books:

- **"Market Wizards" by Jack D. Schwager:** Interviews with successful traders, offering insights into their trading strategies.
- **"Technical Analysis of the Financial Markets" by John J. Murphy:** A comprehensive guide to technical analysis techniques and indicators.
- **"A Beginner's Guide to Short-Term Trading" by Toni Turner:** Focuses on various short-term trading strategies, including momentum trading.

Online Resources:

- **Investopedia:** Offers articles, tutorials, and explanations of various trading concepts and strategies.
- **StockCharts.com:** Provides a wide range of technical analysis resources, including chart patterns and indicators.
- **Blogs and Forums:** Websites like Elite Trader, Trade2Win, and Reddit's r/Daytrading can provide insights from experienced traders.

Remember that momentum trading involves risk, as strong trends can reverse suddenly. It's essential to conduct thorough research, practice risk management, and consider a diversified trading approach. Additionally, market conditions can change, so staying updated with current news and developments is crucial for successful momentum trading. Always consider seeking advice from financial professionals before making trading decisions.

4. Interviews with Successful Momentum Traders: Insights and Strategies

One of the most valuable resources for aspiring momentum traders is gaining insights directly from successful traders who have mastered the art of riding trends. These interviews offer a glimpse into their personal experiences, strategies, and the lessons they've learned along the way. Here's what you can expect to learn from such interviews:

Insights from Industry Leaders:

1. **Trading Psychology:** Successful traders often emphasize the importance of maintaining a disciplined mindset. They share how they handle emotions like fear and greed, as these emotions can impact decision-making and lead to poor trading choices.
2. **Risk Management:** Experienced momentum traders stress the significance of proper risk management. They discuss how they determine position sizes, set stop-loss orders, and manage their overall portfolio risk.

3. **Adaptability:** Interviews reveal how successful traders adapt to changing market conditions. They might discuss how they modify their strategies during volatile periods or when markets transition from trending to ranging.
4. **Research and Analysis:** Momentum traders discuss the tools and indicators they rely on for technical analysis. They explain how they identify potential trends, entry and exit points, and the timeframes they focus on.

Personal Experiences and Strategies:

1. **Entry and Exit Strategies:** Successful momentum traders reveal their methods for entering and exiting trades. This could involve using specific technical indicators, chart patterns, or a combination of factors to confirm their decisions.
2. **Timeframes:** Traders often elaborate on their preferred trading timeframes. Some might focus on short-term intraday trading, while others might lean towards swing trading with a slightly longer holding period.
3. **Confirmation Signals:** Interviews provide insights into how traders confirm the validity of a potential momentum trade. This could involve waiting for certain technical patterns to align or looking for increased volume to support the trend.
4. **Trade Management:** Experienced traders discuss how they manage open positions. They might share strategies for trailing stop-loss orders, locking in profits, or scaling into a trade as the momentum continues.

Key Takeaways for Aspiring Momentum Traders:

1. **Education and Continuous Learning:** Successful traders emphasize the need for ongoing education. They often recommend reading books, attending webinars, and staying updated with market developments.
2. **Paper Trading and Practice:** Interviews often highlight the value of paper trading (simulated trading without real money) to practice strategies and gain confidence before committing real capital.
3. **Patience and Discipline:** Aspiring traders are reminded that patience is key. Rushing into trades without proper analysis can lead to losses. Discipline is also crucial in following one's trading plan and sticking to predefined strategies.
4. **Start Small:** Many experienced traders advise newcomers to start with a small trading account. This minimizes risk while allowing traders to gain experience and refine their strategies.
5. **Risk Management is Paramount:** Interviews stress that preserving capital is the primary goal. Aspiring traders are advised not to risk more than a certain percentage of their capital on a single trade.

In conclusion, interviews with successful momentum traders provide invaluable insights into the world of trading. By learning from their experiences, strategies, and mindset, aspiring traders can accelerate their learning curve and make more informed trading decisions. However, it's important to remember that each trader's journey is unique, and what works for one trader might not necessarily work for another. Developing a personalized approach that suits your risk tolerance, trading style, and market understanding is crucial for long-term success.

3. Workbook and Exercises for Momentum Trading Skills Development

To truly master momentum trading, it's essential to practice and apply the concepts learned. A well-structured workbook with practical exercises can help aspiring momentum traders refine their skills, develop a disciplined approach, and gain a deeper understanding of the dynamics of the market. Here's what such a workbook could include:

Practical Exercises to Hone Momentum Trading Skills:

1. **Identifying Trends:** Provide a series of price charts and ask traders to identify and label trends. This helps improve pattern recognition skills and the ability to differentiate between bullish, bearish, and sideways trends.

2. **Setting Up Moving Averages:** Guide traders through setting up and customizing moving averages on a chart. Have them identify crossovers and trends based on different moving average combinations.

3. **Spotting Key Support and Resistance Levels:** Provide historical price data and ask traders to identify significant support and resistance levels. This exercise enhances the ability to find entry and exit points.

4. **Using Technical Indicators:** Create scenarios where traders must use indicators like RSI, MACD, and Stochastic Oscillator to confirm potential trade setups.

Templates for Tracking Trades and Performance:

1. **Trade Journal Template:** Provide a trade journal template to record details of each trade, including entry and exit points, reasons for the trade, risk-reward ratios, and emotional responses during the trade.

2. **Performance Tracker:** Offer a spreadsheet for tracking overall trading performance, including win-loss ratios, average gains, average losses, and net profits over time.

3. **Risk Management Calculator:** Provide a calculator that helps traders determine the appropriate position size based on their risk tolerance and trade setup.

Scenario-Based Activities for Decision Making:

1. **Trade Simulation:** Present hypothetical trade scenarios with entry and exit points. Ask traders to analyze the given information and decide whether they would take the trade, explaining their reasoning.

2. **Volatile vs. Stable Market:** Create scenarios where traders must decide whether to engage in momentum trading in volatile markets versus stable markets, highlighting the different strategies needed for each.

3. **News Impact:** Describe a situation where unexpected news affects the market. Have traders assess whether they would adjust their trading strategy or stay on course.

Guided Trading Plan Development:

1. **Trading Plan Template:** Provide a template for traders to develop their personalized trading plan. This plan should include trading goals, risk tolerance, preferred assets, trading times, and strategies to be used.

2. **Backtesting Exercises:** Introduce traders to backtesting using historical data. Have them backtest different momentum strategies and evaluate their historical performance.

Behavioral Exercises for Discipline and Emotion Management:

1. **Visualization:** Guide traders through visualization exercises to help them visualize successful trades and maintain a positive mindset.
2. **Emotion Regulation:** Describe scenarios that trigger emotions like fear and greed. Ask traders to outline strategies for managing these emotions during trading.

Progression Exercises:

1. **Challenge Scenarios:** Present more complex scenarios as traders become more confident. These scenarios could involve multiple indicators, various timeframes, or multiple correlated assets.
2. **Real-time Analysis:** Encourage traders to analyze current market conditions and identify potential momentum opportunities. This exercise simulates real-time decision-making.

By incorporating practical exercises, templates, and scenario-based activities, the workbook provides an interactive and comprehensive approach to momentum trading skill development. Regularly working through these exercises can help aspiring traders enhance their analytical abilities, decision-making skills, emotional discipline, and overall trading performance. However, it's important to remember that trading involves risk, and practicing with real money should only occur after a significant amount of practice and education.

Conclusion: The Future of Momentum Trading and Continuous Learning

As the financial markets continue to evolve, momentum trading remains a dynamic strategy with both opportunities and challenges. This conclusion reflects on the evolving nature of momentum trading, the importance of adaptability and continuous learning, and encourages readers to stay informed and dedicated to their trading journey.

The Evolving Nature of Momentum Trading and Its Future Prospects:

Momentum trading has demonstrated its resilience and effectiveness over time. However, the landscape is shaped by changing market conditions, technological advancements, and regulatory developments. The integration of algorithmic trading, machine learning, and big data analysis has transformed the way momentum trading is executed. Traders are now equipped with sophisticated tools that enable them to process vast amounts of information and identify trends more efficiently.

In the future, momentum trading is likely to witness further innovation. The emergence of new asset classes, shifts in global economic dynamics, and geopolitical events will continue to impact market behavior. Traders who can adapt their strategies to these changing dynamics will be better positioned to seize new opportunities and navigate potential risks.

Importance of Adaptability and Continuous Learning in the Trading World:

Adaptability is a cornerstone of success in the trading world. Traders must be prepared to adjust their strategies as market conditions evolve. What works today might not work tomorrow, and the ability to recognize these shifts and pivot accordingly is vital. This underscores the significance of continuous learning. Markets are fueled by information, and traders who stay informed about economic indicators, news releases, and geopolitical events have a competitive edge.

Continuous learning doesn't just encompass technical analysis but also includes understanding behavioral finance, trading psychology, and risk management. Moreover, traders should stay updated with advancements in trading technology, as these innovations can significantly impact trading efficiency and effectiveness.

Encouraging Readers to Stay Informed and Practice Diligently:

As the world of finance and trading grows more complex, the importance of informed decision-making cannot be overstated. Readers are encouraged to seek out reputable sources of information, stay updated with market news, and engage with experienced traders and experts in the field. Forums, online communities, and seminars can provide valuable insights and perspectives.

Furthermore, practice is the foundation of success in momentum trading. Diligent practice through paper trading, simulated scenarios, and analysis of historical data refines trading skills and builds confidence. Mistakes and losses are part of the journey, but they also offer opportunities for growth and improvement.

In conclusion, momentum trading is an exciting and potentially rewarding endeavor, but it demands a blend of knowledge, skill, and discipline. The journey involves continuous learning, adaptability, and the willingness to embrace change. As markets evolve and new challenges arise, those who stay informed, remain adaptable, and practice diligently will be well-equipped to thrive in the dynamic world of momentum trading.

Cryptocurrency Trading:

Focus on trading digital currencies like Bitcoin, Ethereum, and other cryptocurrencies

Introduction: Understanding the World of Cryptocurrency Trading

The world of cryptocurrency trading is a dynamic and rapidly evolving landscape that has captured the attention of investors, traders, and enthusiasts around the globe. In this introductory chapter, we delve into the fundamental aspects that underpin the intricate realm of digital currency trading. By examining the definition, rise, significance, and evolution of cryptocurrencies, as well as weighing the associated benefits and risks, we set the stage for a comprehensive exploration of this captivating subject matter.

Definition of Cryptocurrency

At its core, a cryptocurrency is a digital or virtual form of currency that employs cryptography for secure and confidential transactions. Functioning on decentralized networks built upon blockchain technology, cryptocurrencies leverage cryptographic techniques to ensure the integrity and security of transactions while eliminating the need for intermediaries such as banks. This decentralized nature is a pivotal characteristic that distinguishes cryptocurrencies from traditional fiat currencies.

Rise and Significance of Cryptocurrencies

The emergence of Bitcoin in 2009 marked the beginning of the cryptocurrency revolution, igniting a paradigm shift in the way we perceive and transact value. Since then, the proliferation of various cryptocurrencies, often referred to as altcoins, has further diversified the landscape. The significance of cryptocurrencies extends beyond the realm of finance, permeating industries such as technology, supply chain management, and more. Their potential to disrupt traditional financial systems and enable novel applications underscores their growing influence.

The Evolution of Cryptocurrency Trading

The evolution of cryptocurrency trading mirrors the rapid development of the digital currency space itself. From the early days of peer-to-peer transactions to the establishment of dedicated cryptocurrency exchanges, the trading ecosystem has matured significantly. The availability of various trading instruments, including spot trading, derivatives, and decentralized exchanges, has expanded the opportunities for traders to engage with cryptocurrencies in diverse ways. Understanding this evolution is crucial for navigating the intricacies of modern cryptocurrency markets.

Benefits and Risks of Cryptocurrency Trading

Engaging in cryptocurrency trading offers a range of potential benefits. These include access to 24/7 markets, increased liquidity, and the potential for substantial returns. Moreover, cryptocurrencies have introduced a level of inclusivity, enabling individuals around the world to participate in the global financial landscape. However, it is paramount to acknowledge the risks associated with this dynamic market. Volatility, regulatory uncertainties, security vulnerabilities, and the potential for market manipulation are among the factors that demand vigilant risk management and informed decision-making.

As we embark on this comprehensive guide to cryptocurrency trading, it is imperative to grasp the foundational concepts discussed in this introduction. A nuanced understanding of cryptocurrency definitions, their rise, the evolution of trading practices, and the inherent benefits and risks lays the groundwork for informed and strategic participation in the captivating world of digital currency trading.

Chapter 1: Fundamentals of Cryptocurrencies

In this chapter, we delve into the essential underpinnings of cryptocurrencies, setting the groundwork for a comprehensive understanding of their functionality and significance. By exploring the intricacies of blockchain technology, differentiating between various types of cryptocurrencies, dissecting market capitalization and coin supply dynamics, and uncovering the mechanics of cryptocurrency exchanges and wallets, we equip you with the foundational knowledge required to navigate the intricate world of digital currencies.

Explaining Blockchain Technology

At the core of cryptocurrencies lies blockchain technology – a distributed and decentralized ledger system that serves as the backbone of their operation. A blockchain consists of a series of linked data blocks, each containing a cryptographic hash of the previous block, ensuring immutability and security. This technology enables transparent and tamper-resistant recording of transactions, eliminating the need for centralized intermediaries. Understanding the workings of blockchain technology is paramount to comprehending the secure and trustless nature of cryptocurrency transactions.

Types of Cryptocurrencies (Bitcoin, Ethereum, Altcoins)

Cryptocurrencies exhibit a diverse array of functions and use cases. The pioneering cryptocurrency, Bitcoin, functions primarily as a digital store of value and medium of exchange. Ethereum, on the other hand, introduced the concept of smart contracts, enabling the creation of decentralized applications (DApps) atop its blockchain. Additionally, the category of altcoins encompasses a myriad of cryptocurrencies beyond Bitcoin and Ethereum, each designed to fulfill specific niches and purposes within the digital ecosystem. Familiarity with these different types of cryptocurrencies enables traders and investors to make informed decisions tailored to their objectives.

Market Capitalization and Coin Supply

Market capitalization plays a pivotal role in assessing the size and relative value of a cryptocurrency. It is calculated by multiplying the current price of a cryptocurrency by its total circulating supply. This metric offers insights into a cryptocurrency's relative position within the market and its potential for growth. Moreover, understanding the dynamics of coin supply, including concepts such as total supply, circulating supply, and maximum supply, provides a comprehensive perspective on the scarcity and inflationary attributes of a cryptocurrency.

Cryptocurrency Exchanges and Wallets

To engage in cryptocurrency trading, knowledge of the platforms facilitating these transactions is essential. Cryptocurrency exchanges serve as marketplaces where traders can buy, sell, and exchange various digital assets. These exchanges can be centralized or decentralized, each presenting unique advantages and drawbacks. Additionally, cryptocurrency wallets are secure digital tools that enable users to store, send, and receive cryptocurrencies. They come in various forms, including hardware wallets, software wallets, and online wallets, each catering to different security needs.

As we navigate the landscape of cryptocurrency fundamentals, a firm grasp of blockchain technology's mechanics, the differentiation between various cryptocurrency types, the intricacies of market capitalization, and the dynamics of cryptocurrency exchanges and wallets will serve as a solid foundation for your journey into the intricate world of digital currency trading.

Chapter 2: Technical Analysis for Cryptocurrency Trading

In this chapter, we delve into the essential principles of technical analysis, a critical tool used by traders to assess and predict price movements in the cryptocurrency market. By elucidating the basics of technical analysis, elucidating the significance of price charts and candlestick patterns, expounding on the role of support and resistance levels, examining the application of moving averages and the Relative Strength Index (RSI), and deciphering the intricacies of the Moving Average Convergence Divergence (MACD) indicator, we equip you with the knowledge necessary to decipher and anticipate market trends with precision.

Basics of Technical Analysis

Technical analysis is a methodology grounded in the examination of historical price and trading volume data to forecast future price movements. It operates on the premise that price trends tend to repeat themselves, and patterns discernible in historical data can inform future behavior. By analyzing patterns and indicators, traders seek to identify potential entry and exit points, thus making informed trading decisions.

Price Charts and Candlestick Patterns

Price charts serve as visual representations of historical price data, offering insights into market sentiment and trends. Candlestick patterns, a core component of technical analysis, convey essential information about price movement within specific timeframes. Patterns such as doji, hammer, and engulfing patterns signify potential reversals or continuations of trends, aiding traders in anticipating market shifts.

Support and Resistance Levels

Support and resistance levels are key technical concepts that indicate price levels where an asset is likely to encounter buying or selling pressure. Support represents the level where prices tend to find a floor and reverse upward, while resistance denotes the level where prices often encounter selling pressure and reverse downward. Identifying these levels enables traders to set appropriate entry and exit points.

Moving Averages and Relative Strength Index (RSI)

Moving averages smooth out price data over a specified period, aiding in identifying trends by eliminating short-term fluctuations. The Relative Strength Index (RSI) measures the speed and change of price movements, indicating potential overbought or oversold conditions. These tools offer insights into the strength and sustainability of trends, enabling traders to make informed decisions.

MACD (Moving Average Convergence Divergence) Indicator

The MACD indicator comprises two moving averages – the MACD line and the signal line – and is used to identify trend changes and potential buy or sell signals. The convergence and divergence of these lines offer insights into the momentum of price movements. Understanding the MACD aids in detecting shifts in market sentiment and potential trend reversals.

As we delve into the realm of technical analysis, the mastery of its fundamentals, proficiency in interpreting price charts and patterns, adeptness in identifying support and resistance levels, and the utilization of tools such as moving averages, RSI, and the MACD indicator will empower you to decode market dynamics and craft informed trading strategies with precision.

Chapter 3: Fundamental Analysis in Cryptocurrency Trading

In this chapter, we delve into the integral realm of fundamental analysis, a critical approach used by traders to evaluate the intrinsic value and long-term potential of cryptocurrencies. By elucidating the significance of fundamental analysis, examining the process of evaluating whitepapers and development teams, delving into market news and sentiment analysis, and scrutinizing the profound impact of regulations and government policies, we equip you with the tools necessary to make informed trading decisions grounded in a deep understanding of the underlying factors that shape the cryptocurrency market.

Importance of Fundamental Analysis

Fundamental analysis seeks to uncover the inherent value and potential of cryptocurrencies by examining factors that extend beyond short-term price fluctuations. It provides traders with a comprehensive view of an asset's strength, potential growth, and sustainability over time. While technical analysis focuses on market patterns, fundamental analysis delves into the underlying factors that influence price trends.

Evaluating Whitepapers and Development Teams

Whitepapers serve as foundational documents that outline the purpose, technology, and objectives of a cryptocurrency project. Thoroughly evaluating these documents grants insights into the technological innovation and real-world applications of a cryptocurrency. Additionally, assessing the proficiency and credibility of the development team responsible for the project's execution is crucial in determining the viability of the asset.

Market News and Sentiment Analysis

The cryptocurrency market is heavily influenced by real-time news and market sentiment. Traders must stay abreast of current events, partnerships, technological advancements, and any significant developments that could impact a cryptocurrency's value. Sentiment analysis, which involves gauging the emotional tone of market participants, aids in predicting price movements resulting from market sentiment shifts.

Impact of Regulation and Government Policies

Regulations and government policies play a pivotal role in shaping the cryptocurrency landscape. Legislative changes can drastically affect market dynamics, investor sentiment, and the viability of projects. Government decisions regarding taxation, legality, and regulatory frameworks can result in substantial price fluctuations and market instability. Being cognizant of the legal environment is essential in crafting an informed trading strategy.

As we venture into the realm of fundamental analysis, understanding its significance, mastering the art of evaluating whitepapers and development teams, staying attuned to market news and sentiment shifts, and grasping the profound influence of regulations and government policies will empower you to make prudent trading decisions that are founded on a holistic comprehension of the factors that drive the cryptocurrency market.

Chapter 4: Developing a Trading Strategy

In this chapter, we delve into the crucial process of crafting a robust and effective trading strategy, a cornerstone of successful cryptocurrency trading. By elucidating the significance of selecting a suitable trading style, setting clear goals and risk tolerance levels, constructing a diversified portfolio, and formulating precise entry and exit strategies, we equip you with the knowledge and tools essential for navigating the complexities of the cryptocurrency market with a well-defined roadmap.

Choosing a Trading Style (Day Trading, Swing Trading, HODLing)

Selecting an appropriate trading style is pivotal to aligning your strategy with your goals, risk appetite, and available time. Day trading involves frequent and rapid trades within a single day, capitalizing on short-term price fluctuations. Swing trading entails holding positions for several days to weeks, leveraging medium-term market trends. HODLing, or holding onto assets for the long term, is suited for those who believe in the long-term potential of specific cryptocurrencies.

Setting Clear Goals and Risk Tolerance

Defining clear and achievable trading goals is paramount to maintaining focus and discipline. Whether aiming for consistent profits, capital preservation, or portfolio growth, articulating these objectives helps guide your decision-making process. Equally vital is assessing your risk tolerance –

the degree of risk you're willing to endure. Balancing potential rewards with acceptable risks is integral to safeguarding your capital and managing emotional decision-making.

Building a Diversified Portfolio

A diversified portfolio mitigates risk by spreading investments across various assets. This strategy minimizes the impact of poor performance from a single asset on your overall portfolio. Diversification can encompass different cryptocurrencies, trading pairs, and even other asset classes. Careful consideration of risk and potential returns is essential when curating a portfolio that aligns with your risk appetite and trading goals.

Creating Entry and Exit Strategies

Entry and exit strategies define the parameters for initiating and terminating trades. An entry strategy includes criteria such as technical indicators, price levels, and market conditions that signal optimal entry points. Conversely, an exit strategy outlines conditions for taking profits or cutting losses. Having pre-defined and systematic strategies minimizes emotional decision-making and enhances the consistency of your trading approach.

As you embark on the journey of developing your trading strategy, understanding the significance of selecting an appropriate trading style, defining clear objectives and risk tolerance, constructing a diversified portfolio, and formulating precise entry and exit strategies will empower you to navigate the dynamic cryptocurrency market with purpose and precision.

Chapter 5: Risk Management in Cryptocurrency Trading

In this chapter, we delve into the critical aspect of risk management – an indispensable skill for navigating the volatile and dynamic landscape of cryptocurrency trading. By elucidating the principles of understanding risk and reward ratios, elaborating on position sizing and leverage considerations, expounding on the significance of setting stop-loss and take-profit orders, and highlighting strategies to avoid succumbing to emotional trading decisions, we equip you with the tools necessary to protect your capital and trade with prudence.

Understanding Risk and Reward Ratio

The risk and reward ratio is a fundamental concept that guides traders in assessing potential returns relative to the associated risk. By quantifying the potential loss against the potential gain, traders can determine whether a trade is worth pursuing. A favorable risk-reward ratio ensures that potential gains exceed potential losses, providing a statistical edge that's vital for consistent profitability over time.

Position Sizing and Leverage

Position sizing involves determining the appropriate allocation of capital to a trade, considering factors such as risk tolerance and account size. Allocating a fixed percentage of your capital to each trade helps manage exposure to risk. Leverage, on the other hand, amplifies the potential returns and losses of a trade. While leverage can magnify profits, it also increases the risk of significant losses, making it imperative to use leverage judiciously.

Setting Stop-Loss and Take-Profit Orders

Stop-loss and take-profit orders are crucial tools for automating risk management. A stop-loss order specifies a predetermined price at which a losing trade is automatically closed, preventing excessive losses. A take-profit order sets a predefined price level at which a profitable trade is closed to lock in gains. Utilizing these orders systematically ensures that emotions don't override prudent risk management decisions.

Avoiding Emotional Trading Decisions

Emotions can undermine rational decision-making, leading to impulsive and detrimental trading actions. Emotional trading decisions are often fueled by fear, greed, or FOMO (Fear of Missing Out). To counteract this, traders must adhere to pre-defined trading strategies, maintain discipline, and cultivate a trading mindset grounded in objectivity. Implementing strict risk management rules and sticking to them helps curb impulsive actions.

As you navigate the intricate landscape of risk management in cryptocurrency trading, internalizing the principles of risk and reward ratios, mastering position sizing and leverage considerations, embracing the importance of stop-loss and take-profit orders, and employing strategies to shield yourself from emotional trading decisions will empower you to trade with prudence and resilience in the face of market volatility.

Chapter 6: Technical Indicators for Successful Trading

In this chapter, we delve into the realm of technical indicators – essential tools that empower traders with insights into market trends, momentum, and potential price reversals. By elucidating the significance of Bollinger Bands and Fibonacci retracement, explicating the role of volume analysis and the On-Balance Volume (OBV) indicator, dissecting the mechanics of the Ichimoku Cloud and Stochastic Oscillator, and emphasizing the importance of using indicators in confluence, we equip you with a nuanced understanding of how to leverage these tools for informed and successful trading.

Bollinger Bands and Fibonacci Retracement

Bollinger Bands consist of a moving average surrounded by upper and lower bands that represent volatility levels. They aid in identifying potential price overbought or oversold conditions. Fibonacci retracement involves using key Fibonacci ratios to predict potential support and resistance levels, aiding traders in pinpointing potential price reversals.

Volume Analysis and On-Balance Volume (OBV)

Volume analysis evaluates the trading volume associated with price movements, offering insights into the strength of trends and potential reversals. The On-Balance Volume (OBV) indicator quantifies buying and selling pressure by analyzing volume changes relative to price movements. It assists in confirming trends and predicting potential trend reversals.

Ichimoku Cloud and Stochastic Oscillator

The Ichimoku Cloud is a comprehensive indicator that offers insights into trend direction, momentum, and potential support and resistance levels. It consists of various components, including the cloud, base line, and conversion line. The Stochastic Oscillator measures the momentum of price movements by comparing the current price to its range over a specific period. This oscillator aids in identifying overbought or oversold conditions.

Using Indicators in Confluence

Leveraging multiple indicators in confluence enhances the accuracy of trading signals and reduces the risk of false positives. When multiple indicators align, they reinforce each other's signals, increasing the probability of making informed trading decisions. Combining indicators that assess different aspects of the market, such as trend, momentum, and volume, provides a more holistic view of price movements.

As you explore the realm of technical indicators, understanding the nuances of Bollinger Bands and Fibonacci retracement, grasping the significance of volume analysis and the OBV indicator, mastering the complexities of the Ichimoku Cloud and Stochastic Oscillator, and employing the strategic use of indicators in confluence will empower you to make more precise trading decisions and navigate the cryptocurrency market with confidence.

Chapter 7: Strategies for Bull and Bear Markets

In this chapter, we delve into the dynamic strategies tailored to both bull and bear markets, providing traders with versatile approaches to capitalize on varying market conditions. By elucidating the strategies suitable for bull markets, including the buy and hold strategy and trend-following techniques, and examining the strategies tailored for bear markets, such as short selling, margin trading, and hedging techniques, we equip you with the knowledge to navigate both flourishing and challenging market environments with precision and confidence.

Strategies for Bull Markets

During bull markets characterized by upward price trends, traders often employ strategies to optimize gains and capitalize on positive momentum.

Buy and Hold Strategy

The buy and hold strategy involves acquiring cryptocurrencies with long-term potential and holding onto them regardless of short-term volatility. This strategy capitalizes on the belief in the sustained growth of specific assets over time, allowing investors to ride out market fluctuations.

Trend Following Strategies

Trend following strategies involve identifying and capitalizing on prevailing market trends. Traders utilize technical indicators to confirm trends and enter positions aligned with the established trend. Trend following techniques capitalize on momentum, allowing traders to ride upward trends for substantial gains.

Strategies for Bear Markets

Bear markets, characterized by prolonged price declines, demand a different set of strategies to safeguard capital and capitalize on downward trends.

Short Selling and Margin Trading

Short selling involves selling borrowed assets with the intention of buying them back at a lower price, thereby profiting from price declines. Margin trading amplifies potential returns and losses by allowing traders to trade with borrowed funds. While these strategies can yield substantial gains, they also come with heightened risks.

Hedging Techniques

Hedging techniques involve deploying strategies to mitigate potential losses during bear markets. Traders may hedge by entering positions that profit from declining markets, offsetting losses incurred in other positions. Hedging provides a layer of protection and allows traders to navigate challenging market conditions with reduced risk exposure.

As you explore strategies tailored for bull and bear markets, understanding the nuances of the buy and hold strategy, mastering trend-following techniques, comprehending short selling and margin trading, and embracing hedging techniques will empower you to adapt to varying market conditions with agility and make strategic decisions that align with your trading objectives.

Chapter 8: Case Studies: Learning from Successful Traders

In this chapter, we delve into the invaluable realm of case studies, where we dissect the strategies and insights of successful cryptocurrency traders. By conducting a meticulous analysis of these traders' approaches, extracting key lessons from their strategies, and exploring the art of adapting these strategies to current market conditions, we provide you with real-world insights and actionable knowledge to elevate your trading endeavors and approach the cryptocurrency market with a discerning and informed perspective.

Analysis of Successful Cryptocurrency Traders

Examining the trading practices of successful individuals provides a unique opportunity to gain insights into the methodologies that underpin their achievements. We analyze their decision-making processes, risk management techniques, and the indicators they rely on to identify trends and market opportunities.

Lessons Learned from Their Strategies

Successful traders often adhere to well-defined strategies grounded in discipline and patience. By deciphering their approaches, we extract valuable lessons in risk management, position sizing, entry and exit strategies, and the importance of continuous learning. These lessons offer a roadmap for developing a robust and informed trading framework.

Adapting Strategies to Current Market Conditions

The cryptocurrency market is marked by its dynamic and ever-evolving nature. Case studies not only elucidate successful strategies but also highlight the importance of adaptability. Traders must learn to recognize shifts in market sentiment, technological advancements, and regulatory changes. Adapting strategies to align with current market conditions ensures that traders remain relevant and effective.

As we delve into the realm of case studies, comprehensively analyzing successful cryptocurrency traders, distilling lessons from their experiences, and mastering the art of adapting these strategies to prevailing market dynamics, you gain insights that elevate your trading proficiency and enable you to navigate the complexities of the cryptocurrency market with sagacity and acumen.

Chapter 9: Taxation and Legal Considerations

In this chapter, we delve into the intricate domain of taxation and legal considerations in cryptocurrency trading. By elucidating the taxation of cryptocurrency gains, delving into reporting requirements and regulations, and exploring the jurisdictional differences that govern cryptocurrency taxation, we equip you with essential knowledge to navigate the complex landscape of legal obligations and ensure compliance with tax authorities.

Taxation of Cryptocurrency Gains

The taxation of cryptocurrency gains varies by jurisdiction and is influenced by the classification of cryptocurrencies as assets or currencies. Profits derived from trading, mining, or any form of cryptocurrency transaction are subject to taxation. Tax implications can include capital gains tax, income tax, or even special cryptocurrency-related taxes. Understanding the tax treatment of gains is crucial to accurately assess your tax liability.

Reporting Requirements and Regulations

Cryptocurrency transactions often come under scrutiny from tax authorities. Various jurisdictions require traders to report their cryptocurrency activities, including gains and losses, in accordance with their tax laws. Inaccurate reporting or failure to report can lead to legal consequences. Familiarizing yourself with reporting requirements ensures compliance and minimizes the risk of legal disputes.

Jurisdictional Differences in Cryptocurrency Taxation

Cryptocurrency taxation regulations vary significantly across different jurisdictions. Some countries consider cryptocurrencies as commodities, while others classify them as property or currency. Each approach carries distinct tax implications. Jurisdictions also differ in terms of tax rates, exemptions, and allowable deductions related to cryptocurrency activities. Understanding these differences is paramount, especially for international traders.

As you navigate the intricate landscape of taxation and legal considerations in cryptocurrency trading, grasping the nuances of cryptocurrency gains taxation, understanding reporting obligations and regulations, and acknowledging the jurisdictional disparities in cryptocurrency taxation will empower you to engage in trading activities while ensuring compliance with legal and tax requirements.

Chapter 10: The Future of Cryptocurrency Trading

In this concluding chapter, we peer into the horizon of the cryptocurrency trading landscape, exploring emerging trends, potential disruptions, and the integration of cutting-edge technologies. By elucidating the evolving trends in the cryptocurrency market, delving into the potential impact of Central Bank Digital Currencies (CBDCs), and examining the transformative role of Artificial Intelligence (AI) and Machine Learning in trading, we provide insights into the dynamic and ever-evolving future of cryptocurrency trading.

Emerging Trends in Cryptocurrency Market

The cryptocurrency market is marked by continuous evolution and innovation. Emerging trends encompass a variety of themes, including the rise of decentralized finance (DeFi) platforms, the increasing acceptance of cryptocurrencies by mainstream institutions, and the advent of new cryptocurrencies and blockchain solutions. Staying attuned to these trends enables traders to adapt their strategies and capitalize on new opportunities.

Potential Impact of Central Bank Digital Currencies (CBDCs)

Central Bank Digital Currencies (CBDCs) represent a paradigm shift in the financial landscape. These digital representations of national currencies are issued and regulated by central banks. The potential implications of CBDCs are profound, ranging from redefining payment systems to influencing the international monetary framework. Traders must monitor developments in CBDCs, as they could reshape the dynamics of the cryptocurrency market.

Integrating AI and Machine Learning in Trading

The integration of Artificial Intelligence (AI) and Machine Learning (ML) in trading is a transformative trend with far-reaching implications. AI-powered algorithms analyze vast amounts of data, detect patterns, and execute trades with unparalleled speed and accuracy. ML models adapt to market changes and refine trading strategies over time. Embracing AI and ML can enhance trading decisions, automate routine tasks, and optimize risk management.

As we conclude our comprehensive guide to cryptocurrency trading, reflecting on emerging trends, contemplating the potential impact of Central Bank Digital Currencies (CBDCs), and embracing the transformative potential of AI and Machine Learning in trading, you are poised to navigate the ever-changing landscape of cryptocurrency trading with adaptability, foresight, and a forward-looking approach.

Chapter 11: Advanced Trading Strategies

In this chapter, we delve into the realm of advanced trading strategies that cater to experienced traders seeking to harness sophisticated techniques for maximizing returns and managing risk. By elucidating the intricacies of scalping and day trading techniques, exploring the world of algorithmic and high-frequency trading, dissecting the utilization of options and derivatives in cryptocurrency trading, and unveiling the strategic potential of cross-asset strategies and pair trading, we provide a comprehensive understanding of advanced approaches that can elevate your trading prowess.

Scalping and Day Trading Techniques

Scalping and day trading are fast-paced strategies that capitalize on short-term price fluctuations. Scalping involves rapid execution of numerous trades within minutes, seeking to profit from minor price movements. Day trading focuses on taking advantage of price shifts within a single day. Both strategies require profound technical analysis skills, quick decision-making, and strict risk management to navigate the inherent volatility.

Algorithmic and High-Frequency Trading

Algorithmic trading involves the use of automated trading algorithms to execute trades based on predefined conditions. High-frequency trading takes algorithmic trading to the extreme, executing a high volume of trades in milliseconds. These strategies rely on sophisticated algorithms, access to real-time data, and powerful computing infrastructure to exploit fleeting market inefficiencies.

Using Options and Derivatives in Cryptocurrency Trading

Options and derivatives are advanced financial instruments that allow traders to speculate on price movements without owning the underlying asset. Options provide the right, but not the obligation, to buy or sell at a predetermined price and time. Derivatives like futures contracts enable traders to profit from price changes without owning the actual cryptocurrency. Employing options and derivatives requires a deep understanding of their mechanics and risk management techniques.

Cross-Asset Strategies and Pair Trading

Cross-asset strategies involve trading across different asset classes, such as cryptocurrencies, stocks, or commodities. Pair trading focuses on trading two correlated assets simultaneously. Traders take advantage of divergences in the performance of related assets, capitalizing on price convergences. These strategies require a keen understanding of market dynamics and correlations.

As you delve into the advanced trading strategies explored in this chapter, mastering the intricacies of scalping and day trading, embracing algorithmic and high-frequency trading approaches, comprehending the usage of options and derivatives, and exploring the potential of cross-asset strategies and pair trading, you unlock a realm of opportunities to refine your skills and seize unique advantages in the ever-evolving world of cryptocurrency trading.

Chapter 12: Behavioral Psychology in Cryptocurrency Trading

In this enlightening chapter, we delve into the realm of behavioral psychology – an often underestimated yet paramount aspect of successful cryptocurrency trading. By elucidating the complexities of understanding investor psychology, exploring methods to overcome cognitive biases inherent in trading, examining strategies to manage the detrimental impact of FOMO (Fear of Missing Out) and FUD (Fear, Uncertainty, Doubt), and emphasizing the development of a disciplined trading mindset, we empower you to navigate the psychological challenges that accompany trading with wisdom and resilience.

Understanding Investor Psychology

Investor psychology plays a significant role in shaping market dynamics. Emotions such as greed, fear, and euphoria often lead to irrational decision-making. Understanding the psychology of market participants can help anticipate trends, recognize sentiment shifts, and make informed trading decisions.

Overcoming Cognitive Biases in Trading

Cognitive biases, inherent mental shortcuts, can lead traders astray. Anchoring bias, confirmation bias, and the availability heuristic are just a few examples that influence decision-making. Recognizing and mitigating these biases through self-awareness and logical analysis enhances objectivity in trading.

Managing FOMO and FUD

FOMO (Fear of Missing Out) and FUD (Fear, Uncertainty, Doubt) are powerful emotional drivers that can lead to impulsive actions. FOMO induces traders to enter positions based on perceived missed opportunities, while FUD triggers panic selling due to uncertainty. Developing strategies to manage these emotions, such as setting clear trading plans and adhering to them, curbs their influence on decisions.

Developing a Disciplined Trading Mindset

A disciplined trading mindset is the cornerstone of successful trading. It involves maintaining emotional detachment, adhering to trading plans, and embracing losses as part of the learning process. A disciplined mindset minimizes emotional trading, promotes consistency, and allows traders to make rational decisions.

As you delve into the complexities of behavioral psychology in cryptocurrency trading, comprehending investor psychology, overcoming cognitive biases, mastering strategies to manage FOMO and FUD, and cultivating a disciplined trading mindset, you gain a powerful toolkit to navigate the psychological challenges inherent in trading, elevating your decision-making acumen and fostering a resilient approach to the ever-evolving cryptocurrency market.

Chapter 13: Technical Analysis Tools and Software

In this chapter, we delve into the array of technical analysis tools and software that empower traders with enhanced insights and efficiency in navigating the complexities of the cryptocurrency market. By elucidating the diverse offerings of charting platforms and analysis tools, exploring the potential of automated trading bots and algorithms, delving into the critical process of backtesting strategies and conducting performance analysis, and unveiling the transformative role of applying Machine Learning in technical analysis, we equip you with a comprehensive understanding of the tools that can amplify your trading prowess.

Charting Platforms and Analysis Tools

Charting platforms and analysis tools provide traders with visual representations of price movements and technical indicators. These tools facilitate the identification of trends, patterns, and potential reversals. From basic price charts to advanced platforms offering a plethora of indicators, choosing the right tool enhances the accuracy of analysis and decision-making.

Automated Trading Bots and Algorithms

Automated trading bots and algorithms execute trades based on predefined conditions, freeing traders from constant monitoring. These tools leverage technical indicators, moving averages, and other parameters to execute trades with precision and speed. While automated trading offers convenience, understanding the algorithms and constant monitoring is essential to ensure optimal performance.

Backtesting Strategies and Performance Analysis

Backtesting involves testing trading strategies against historical data to evaluate their potential effectiveness. By simulating trades on historical price movements, traders can assess the viability of strategies before risking real capital. Performance analysis provides insights into strategy success, allowing traders to refine their approach and optimize risk-adjusted returns.

Applying Machine Learning in Technical Analysis

Machine Learning (ML) enhances technical analysis by identifying complex patterns and relationships within vast datasets. ML algorithms can recognize subtle correlations, providing a deeper understanding of market dynamics. By employing ML techniques, traders gain insights that may not be discernible through traditional analysis methods.

As you navigate the realm of technical analysis tools and software, embracing diverse charting platforms and analysis tools, exploring the potential of automated trading bots and algorithms, mastering the art of backtesting strategies and performance analysis, and understanding the transformative potential of applying Machine Learning in technical analysis, you unlock a realm of opportunities to elevate your trading precision and capitalize on the dynamic cryptocurrency market.

Chapter 14: Regulatory Compliance and Security

In this crucial chapter, we delve into the imperative realm of regulatory compliance and security in cryptocurrency trading. By elucidating the significance of adhering to Anti-Money Laundering (AML) and Know Your Customer (KYC) regulations, exploring security best practices that fortify cryptocurrency trading endeavors, delving into strategies to protect against hacks and scams, and unraveling the diverse legal frameworks governing crypto trading across different jurisdictions, we provide a comprehensive understanding of the measures that safeguard traders' interests and ensure ethical and secure participation in the cryptocurrency ecosystem.

AML (Anti-Money Laundering) and KYC (Know Your Customer) Regulations

Anti-Money Laundering (AML) regulations require traders and platforms to implement protocols that prevent the illicit use of cryptocurrencies for money laundering and other unlawful activities. Know Your Customer (KYC) procedures mandate the verification of traders' identities to deter fraud and ensure transparency. Compliance with AML and KYC regulations promotes the integrity of the cryptocurrency ecosystem and safeguards against illicit activities.

Security Best Practices for Cryptocurrency Trading

Security is paramount in cryptocurrency trading. Employing best practices such as using hardware wallets, utilizing strong and unique passwords, enabling two-factor authentication, and regularly updating software mitigates the risk of unauthorized access. Maintaining vigilance against phishing attempts and suspicious links further bolsters security measures.

Protecting Against Hacks and Scams

The cryptocurrency landscape is not immune to hacking attempts and scams. Traders must be cautious of phishing attacks, fake exchanges, and fraudulent investment schemes. By exercising due diligence, verifying the authenticity of platforms, and adopting a skeptical mindset towards offers that seem too good to be true, traders can significantly reduce their vulnerability to hacks and scams.

Legal Frameworks for Crypto Trading in Different Jurisdictions

Cryptocurrency trading is subject to varying legal frameworks across jurisdictions. Some countries embrace cryptocurrencies and provide a supportive regulatory environment, while others impose restrictions or outright bans. Traders must stay informed about the legal status of cryptocurrencies and trading activities in their respective regions to ensure compliance and avoid legal repercussions.

As you navigate the critical domains of regulatory compliance and security in cryptocurrency trading, adhering to AML and KYC regulations, implementing robust security best practices, safeguarding against hacks and scams, and comprehending the diverse legal frameworks for crypto trading in different jurisdictions, you establish a foundation of ethical conduct and secure engagement in the cryptocurrency market.

Chapter 15: Navigating Market Volatility

In this insightful chapter, we embark on a journey to decipher the intricate landscape of market volatility, a characteristic hallmark of the cryptocurrency trading environment. By elucidating the nuances of understanding market cycles and volatility patterns, exploring methods to leverage volatility to your advantage, delving into strategies tailored for trading during high volatility, and unraveling the art of implementing dynamic stop-loss and take-profit strategies, we equip you with the knowledge and acumen to not only navigate but also thrive amidst the dynamic fluctuations of the cryptocurrency market.

Understanding Market Cycles and Volatility Patterns

The cryptocurrency market follows distinct cycles of expansion and contraction, marked by varying degrees of volatility. Understanding these cycles and recognizing recurring volatility patterns enables traders to anticipate potential trend shifts and make informed decisions. Thorough analysis of historical data aids in identifying patterns that guide future trading actions.

Using Volatility to Your Advantage

Volatility, often perceived as a risk, can be harnessed as an opportunity. During volatile periods, price movements are amplified, presenting lucrative opportunities for profit. Skilled traders can exploit short-term price fluctuations through strategic entries and exits, capitalizing on rapid changes in value.

Strategies for Trading during High Volatility

Trading during high volatility demands specialized strategies. Breakout trading involves entering positions when prices breach key support or resistance levels. Reversal trading capitalizes on abrupt price shifts to predict trend reversals. These strategies require swift execution and precise risk management to navigate heightened uncertainty.

Implementing Dynamic Stop-Loss and Take-Profit Strategies

Volatility necessitates adaptive risk management techniques. Dynamic stop-loss and take-profit strategies involve adjusting these parameters based on market conditions. Tightening stop-losses during high volatility minimizes potential losses, while extending take-profit targets captures increased profit potential during rapid price movements.

As you navigate the intricacies of market volatility, decoding market cycles and volatility patterns, leveraging volatility to your advantage, mastering strategies for trading during high volatility, and embracing the art of implementing dynamic stop-loss and take-profit strategies, you empower yourself with the agility and insights required to thrive amidst the dynamic nature of the cryptocurrency market.

Chapter 16: Building a Trading Routine

In this pragmatic chapter, we delve into the art of building a trading routine that serves as the bedrock of consistent and strategic engagement in the cryptocurrency market. By elucidating the intricacies of designing a productive trading schedule, incorporating dedicated time for research and analysis, maintaining comprehensive trading journals for performance tracking, and orchestrating a delicate balance between trading activities and other commitments, we equip you with a structured framework that fosters discipline, efficiency, and optimal performance in your trading endeavors.

Designing a Productive Trading Schedule

A well-structured trading schedule establishes the foundation for effective decision-making and execution. Setting designated trading hours aligned with market activity ensures that you are present during peak trading periods and can react promptly to market movements. A clear routine minimizes distractions and enables focused trading.

Incorporating Research and Analysis Time

Dedicated time for research and analysis is essential for informed trading decisions. Allocate intervals to stay updated on market news, analyze price charts, and study technical and fundamental indicators. A structured approach to research enhances your understanding of market dynamics and enables you to make strategic choices.

Maintaining Trading Journals and Performance Tracking

Recording each trade in a trading journal is invaluable for performance tracking and analysis. Note entry and exit points, reasons for trade decisions, and outcomes. This journal serves as a valuable repository of insights, enabling you to review your trading decisions, learn from successes and failures, and refine your strategies over time.

Balancing Trading with Other Commitments

Balancing trading with other commitments is vital for maintaining overall well-being. Set clear boundaries for trading hours to prevent burnout and ensure you have time for personal life, rest, and recreation. Prioritize self-care to sustain mental and emotional well-being, enhancing your capacity to make sound trading decisions.

As you embark on the journey of building a trading routine, meticulously designing a productive trading schedule, dedicating time for research and analysis, maintaining comprehensive trading journals for performance tracking, and harmonizing trading activities with other commitments, you cultivate a disciplined and sustainable approach to cryptocurrency trading that supports your long-term success and well-being.

Chapter 17: Cryptocurrency Investment Strategies

In this comprehensive chapter, we explore the diverse landscape of cryptocurrency investment strategies, catering to individuals seeking to capitalize on the long-term potential of digital assets. By elucidating the distinctions between long-term investment and active trading, delving into methodologies like Dollar-Cost Averaging (DCA) and Value Investing, deciphering the process of identifying promising projects for long-term holds, and unveiling the art of rebalancing and adjusting investment portfolios, we equip you with a holistic understanding of strategies that align with your investment goals and risk tolerance in the dynamic cryptocurrency market.

Long-Term Investment vs. Active Trading

Long-term investment and active trading represent distinct approaches to capitalizing on the cryptocurrency market. Long-term investment involves holding assets for an extended period, leveraging potential appreciation over time. Active trading, on the other hand, involves frequent buying and selling to exploit short-term price fluctuations. Deciding between these strategies requires a clear assessment of your risk appetite and investment horizon.

Dollar-Cost Averaging and Value Investing

Dollar-Cost Averaging (DCA) involves investing a fixed amount at regular intervals, regardless of market conditions. This approach reduces the impact of market volatility and allows you to accumulate assets over time. Value Investing entails identifying undervalued cryptocurrencies with strong fundamentals, aiming to capitalize on potential long-term growth.

Identifying Promising Projects and Long-Term Holds

Identifying promising projects for long-term holds requires in-depth research and evaluation. Factors such as technology, use case, development team, and market demand play a pivotal role. Diversifying your portfolio across projects with strong potential mitigates risk while positioning you to benefit from the success of emerging projects.

Rebalancing and Adjusting Investment Portfolios

Rebalancing involves periodically adjusting your investment portfolio to maintain desired asset allocations. As the market evolves, certain assets may outperform others, altering the original balance. Regularly reassessing your portfolio and making adjustments ensures alignment with your risk tolerance and investment objectives.

As you navigate the landscape of cryptocurrency investment strategies, discerning between long-term investment and active trading, embracing methodologies like Dollar-Cost Averaging and Value Investing, mastering the art of identifying promising projects, and understanding the significance of rebalancing and adjusting investment portfolios, you are poised to make informed decisions that align with your financial goals and contribute to your success in the ever-evolving cryptocurrency ecosystem.

Chapter 18: Decentralized Finance (DeFi) Trading

In this enlightening chapter, we delve into the rapidly evolving realm of Decentralized Finance (DeFi) trading, a revolutionary paradigm that leverages blockchain technology to transform traditional financial services. By elucidating the intricacies of exploring the DeFi ecosystem, delving into methodologies such as yield farming, liquidity mining, and staking, unraveling the risks and opportunities inherent in DeFi trading, and unveiling the art of integrating DeFi into your trading strategy, we equip you with insights into a dynamic landscape that has the potential to reshape the future of finance.

Exploring the DeFi Ecosystem

The DeFi ecosystem encompasses a spectrum of blockchain-based financial applications that eliminate intermediaries and provide open, permissionless access to financial services. DeFi platforms enable lending, borrowing, trading, and yield generation, revolutionizing traditional financial practices. Navigating the diverse DeFi projects and protocols necessitates thorough research and understanding.

Yield Farming, Liquidity Mining, and Staking

Yield farming involves lending your assets to DeFi protocols in exchange for rewards. Liquidity mining incentivizes liquidity providers to contribute funds to decentralized exchanges, earning rewards for facilitating trading. Staking involves locking up assets to support the network and earn rewards. These methods leverage DeFi protocols to generate returns on your cryptocurrency holdings.

Risks and Opportunities in DeFi Trading

DeFi trading presents both enticing opportunities and inherent risks. The potential for high returns is counterbalanced by the risks of smart contract vulnerabilities, impermanent loss, and market volatility. Engaging in DeFi requires comprehensive research, due diligence, and a clear understanding of the protocols and risks involved.

Integrating DeFi into Your Trading Strategy

Integrating DeFi into your trading strategy requires a thoughtful approach. DeFi activities can diversify your investment portfolio and enhance returns but should be executed with prudence.

Consider your risk tolerance, market trends, and the potential impact of DeFi activities on your overall strategy.

As you immerse yourself in the world of Decentralized Finance (DeFi) trading, exploring the DeFi ecosystem, embracing methodologies like yield farming, liquidity mining, and staking, discerning the risks and opportunities inherent in DeFi trading, and mastering the art of integrating DeFi into your trading strategy, you position yourself at the forefront of an innovative financial landscape that has the potential to redefine the way we interact with and benefit from financial services.

Chapter 19: Ethical and Environmental Considerations

In this thought-provoking chapter, we confront the ethical and environmental dimensions intertwined with cryptocurrency trading, urging traders to grapple with the broader implications of their actions in a rapidly evolving digital landscape. By elucidating the environmental impact of cryptocurrency mining, dissecting ethical dilemmas arising from trading speculative assets, advocating for the support of sustainable blockchain projects, and unveiling the significance of engaging in socially responsible trading practices, we encourage a conscientious approach that aligns financial pursuits with ethical and environmental considerations.

Environmental Impact of Cryptocurrency Mining

Cryptocurrency mining, particularly Proof of Work (PoW) based systems, has drawn attention due to its energy-intensive nature. The mining process requires vast computational power, leading to concerns about its carbon footprint. As traders engage in cryptocurrency transactions, understanding the environmental repercussions and advocating for energy-efficient alternatives becomes imperative.

Ethical Dilemmas in Trading Speculative Assets

Trading speculative assets can pose ethical dilemmas. Extreme volatility, potential market manipulation, and the impact of trading decisions on others necessitate ethical reflection. Traders must weigh the pursuit of personal gain against the potential harm caused to others and make principled decisions that align with their values.

Supporting Sustainable Blockchain Projects

Sustainability extends to the choice of blockchain projects traders engage with. Supporting projects that prioritize energy efficiency, scalability, and environmental responsibility contributes to the growth of sustainable blockchain ecosystems. Traders can participate in projects that align with their ethical stance, promoting responsible innovation.

Engaging in Socially Responsible Trading Practices

Engaging in socially responsible trading practices involves more than financial gains. Traders can contribute to positive social change by avoiding participation in pump-and-dump schemes, practicing transparent and ethical trading strategies, and promoting knowledge sharing within the community. Elevating ethical standards benefits both traders and the broader cryptocurrency ecosystem.

As you navigate the complex ethical and environmental landscape of cryptocurrency trading, acknowledging the environmental impact of mining, confronting ethical dilemmas inherent in speculative trading, advocating for sustainable blockchain projects, and embracing socially responsible trading practices, you exemplify a conscientious approach that upholds ethical integrity and fosters a harmonious coexistence between financial pursuits and broader societal and environmental concerns.

Conclusion: Your Journey in the Cryptocurrency Trading Arena

In this culminating chapter, we reflect on the profound journey you have undertaken in the realm of cryptocurrency trading, encapsulating the essence of your experiences and lessons learned. By summarizing key takeaways accumulated throughout this comprehensive guide, encouraging a steadfast commitment to continuous learning and adaptation, and underscoring the paramount importance of patience, discipline, and meticulous risk management, we present you with a valedictory roadmap that propels you towards sustained success in the dynamic and ever-evolving cryptocurrency trading landscape.

Summarizing Key Takeaways

Your journey through this guide has imparted a plethora of insights and knowledge, spanning from fundamental concepts to intricate trading strategies. These key takeaways include grasping the fundamental mechanics of cryptocurrencies, mastering technical and fundamental analysis, refining trading strategies, managing risks effectively, and navigating the nuanced landscape of the cryptocurrency market.

Encouraging Continuous Learning and Adaptation

The cryptocurrency market is marked by constant evolution. Embracing a posture of perpetual learning and adaptability is essential for remaining relevant and effective. Stay abreast of emerging trends, technological advancements, and regulatory changes. By continuously updating your knowledge and adapting your strategies, you position yourself to thrive amidst dynamic market conditions.

Emphasizing Patience, Discipline, and Risk Management

The pillars of success in cryptocurrency trading are rooted in patience, discipline, and meticulous risk management. Patience enables you to weather market volatility, avoiding impulsive decisions driven by emotion. Discipline ensures adherence to your trading plan and prevents deviation from proven strategies. Effective risk management safeguards your capital, preserving your ability to capitalize on future opportunities.

As you conclude this comprehensive guide on cryptocurrency trading, armed with a repertoire of knowledge and insights, remember that your journey is ongoing. Strive for mastery, remain open to adaptation, and nurture the qualities of patience, discipline, and risk management. With these attributes, you embark on a trajectory of sustained success and personal growth in the dynamic and transformative world of cryptocurrency trading.

Commodity Trading

Specialize in trading commodities like gold, oil, agricultural products, etc.

Introduction to Commodity Trading

Commodity trading, a cornerstone of the global financial system, serves as a conduit for the exchange of primary and raw goods that power economies, nourish populations, and drive industrial processes. Originating from ancient civilizations' need to exchange basic goods, this trading mechanism has evolved into a sophisticated network of interconnected markets, instruments, and strategies, catering to diverse stakeholders ranging from farmers in remote villages to multinational corporations.

At its essence, commodity trading is grounded in the principle of trade itself. Long before currencies and complex financial products became prevalent, civilizations depended on the barter of tangible goods to sustain their communities. While the mechanisms and tools have undergone significant transformations over the millennia, the foundational objective remains: to facilitate the efficient allocation and distribution of resources and to manage the risks associated with price volatility.

Today, the global commodity market operates on a scale that is both vast and intricate, transcending borders and time zones. With commodities classified broadly into hard and soft categories, the market presents a myriad of opportunities and challenges. Hard commodities, typically mined or extracted, include goods such as metals and oil. In contrast, soft commodities encompass agricultural products and livestock, whose production is often influenced by a set of dynamic and sometimes unpredictable factors like weather patterns and geopolitical events.

The significance of commodity trading extends beyond mere economic metrics. It plays a pivotal role in stabilizing global prices, ensuring supply continuity, offering investment avenues, and providing risk management tools. Moreover, with the burgeoning influence of technology and data analytics, the landscape of commodity trading is poised for continual evolution, integrating advanced algorithms, artificial intelligence, and predictive analytics into its operations.

This discourse delves deep into the world of commodity trading, providing insights into its historical evolution, current dynamics, key stakeholders, and emerging trends. Whether you're a seasoned trader, an academic, a policy-maker, or an enthusiast, this comprehensive guide seeks to equip you with a holistic understanding of the intricacies that define and drive the global commodity markets.

Chapter 1. Overview of Commodity Trading

Commodity trading encompasses a vast and intricate world of financial transactions centered around raw or primary products. The trading of these goods takes place in specialized markets that operate within a defined set of principles and standards. The essence and value of commodity trading lie in its direct impact on the global economy and the interconnection of markets.

1.1. Definition and Importance

Definition: At its core, commodity trading refers to the act of buying, selling, or exchanging raw or primary products, either physically or through derivative contracts. These transactions occur in both spot markets, where commodities are bought or sold for immediate delivery, and futures markets, where they are traded for delivery at a later date.

Importance:

1. **Economic Significance**: Commodities form the backbone of the global economy. They are essential inputs for production processes, energy generation, and food supply. Trading in commodities ensures that these goods are available where they are needed, smoothing out supply imbalances across regions.

2. **Price Stability**: Commodity trading plays a pivotal role in determining global prices for essential goods. By reflecting global supply and demand in real-time, these markets help stabilize prices and provide signals to producers and consumers alike.

3. **Risk Management**: Commodity futures and other derivatives allow producers and consumers to hedge against price volatility. This risk management is crucial for many industries, from agriculture to energy, in ensuring predictable costs and revenues.

4. **Investment Opportunities**: Commodities offer unique investment opportunities, acting as a hedge against inflation and a diversification tool. Their prices often move independently of equities and bonds, making them a valuable addition to investment portfolios.

1.2. Hard vs. Soft Commodities

The world of commodities is typically divided into two primary categories based on their nature and source:

Hard Commodities: These are natural resources that are mined or extracted. Their availability is often limited by natural factors, and extracting them may involve significant investment and time. Examples include:

- **Oil and Gas**: Used primarily for energy and transportation.
- **Metals**: This can be further categorized into precious metals like gold, silver, and platinum, and base metals like copper, zinc, and aluminum.
- **Minerals**: Such as coal or uranium.

Soft Commodities: These are agricultural products and livestock. They are renewable and are affected by factors like weather conditions, pest infestations, and farming practices. Examples include:

- **Grains**: Wheat, corn, and rice.
- **Livestock**: Cattle and poultry.
- **Softs**: Coffee, cocoa, and sugar.

It's essential to understand the distinction between hard and soft commodities as they possess different risk profiles, market dynamics, and influencing factors. While hard commodities are often capital-intensive and impacted by geopolitical events, soft commodities are more susceptible to environmental factors and seasonal variations.

Chapter 2. Basic Principles of Commodity Trading

Commodity trading, like all trading disciplines, operates on a foundational set of principles. These principles guide decisions, shape market movements, and provide a framework within which traders and investors operate. Foremost among these principles are the dynamics of supply and demand, and the various factors that determine prices in the commodity markets. A comprehensive grasp of these principles is essential for anyone wishing to navigate the complex terrain of commodity trading.

2.1. Supply and Demand Dynamics

Supply: This refers to the total quantity of a particular commodity that is available for trading. The supply can be influenced by various factors, including:

- **Production Levels**: The output from mines, farms, or wells.
- **Stock Levels**: Amounts held in storage facilities, reserves, or inventories.

- **Government Policies**: Import or export restrictions, subsidies, or stockpile releases.

Demand: This pertains to the total quantity of a commodity that market participants wish to buy at a given price level. Demand drivers encompass:

- **Consumption Patterns**: Driven by global economic health, population growth, and consumer preferences.
- **Industrial Uses**: The need for raw materials in manufacturing or industrial processes.
- **Speculative Interest**: Purchases made in the anticipation of future price rises.

The interplay between supply and demand is fundamental in determining commodity prices. When demand exceeds supply, prices tend to rise, indicating a market in deficit. Conversely, when supply surpasses demand, there is an oversupply or glut, leading to potential price declines.

2.2. Price Determinants

While the dynamics of supply and demand are primary drivers of commodity prices, several other factors play a crucial role in determining price levels and volatility:

1. **Geopolitical Events**: Wars, political unrest, and diplomatic tensions can impact the flow of commodities, particularly in regions that are significant producers or consumers.
2. **Weather Patterns**: For agricultural commodities, weather phenomena such as droughts, floods, or unseasonal temperatures can affect crops and livestock, leading to supply shortages or surpluses.
3. **Currency Strength**: As commodities are globally priced in dollars, the strength or weakness of the dollar can influence commodity prices. A weaker dollar might make commodities cheaper for foreign buyers, potentially increasing demand.
4. **Infrastructure and Logistics**: The availability and efficiency of transportation, storage, and delivery infrastructure can impact the availability and cost of commodities.
5. **Technological Innovations**: Advances in extraction, farming, or production technologies can lead to increased supply or reduced costs, influencing prices.
6. **Regulatory Changes**: Government policies, tariffs, or trade agreements can affect the flow and cost of commodities across borders.
7. **Macroeconomic Indicators**: Economic health, measured through indicators like GDP growth, unemployment rates, and manufacturing output, can signal increased or decreased demand for commodities.

Chapter 3. Major Global Commodity Exchanges

Commodity exchanges play a pivotal role in the global financial architecture by providing platforms for standardized trading, price discovery, and risk management. These exchanges offer various contracts, including futures, options, and swaps, allowing participants to buy or sell commodities at set prices for future delivery. Such contracts aid in the establishment of transparent price benchmarks and facilitate hedging against price volatility. Here, we delve into three of the world's premier commodity exchanges, each with its unique strengths and areas of specialization.

3.1. Chicago Mercantile Exchange (CME)

Overview: The Chicago Mercantile Exchange, commonly known as CME, originated in the late 19th century as a platform for agricultural commodities. Today, it stands as one of the world's largest derivatives exchanges, offering a wide range of products encompassing not only commodities but also equities, currencies, and interest rates.

Key Commodities: While it provides a diverse array of contracts, CME is renowned for its futures and options in agricultural products, such as corn, soybeans, and wheat. Moreover, the exchange has a significant presence in the livestock, dairy, and energy sectors.

Significance: The CME plays a vital role in global risk management. Its deep liquidity, transparency, and stringent regulatory oversight make it a preferred destination for traders, investors, and institutions aiming to mitigate the risks associated with price fluctuations.

3.2. Intercontinental Exchange (ICE)

Overview: Founded in 2000, the Intercontinental Exchange, or ICE, quickly rose to prominence by focusing on energy commodities. Today, it has diversified its offerings to include financial derivatives, equities, and fixed income.

Key Commodities: ICE is renowned for its Brent Crude futures contract, one of the world's primary oil benchmarks. Beyond energy, the exchange offers derivatives in agricultural products, metals, and environmental commodities.

Significance: ICE's acquisition of the New York Stock Exchange in 2013 cemented its position as a leading global exchange operator. Its commitment to leveraging technology has fostered an environment of innovation, making it a hub for electronic trading and clearing services.

3.3. London Metal Exchange (LME)

Overview: Founded in 1877, the London Metal Exchange stands as the world's foremost exchange for non-ferrous metals. Located in the heart of London, it commands a substantial share of global metal trading.

Key Commodities: The LME specializes in metals such as copper, aluminum, zinc, nickel, and lead. It also provides futures and options contracts for precious metals, including gold and silver.

Significance: LME prices are globally recognized benchmarks for metals. The exchange's unique system, which allows for physical delivery against its contracts, has cemented its status as the epicenter of global metal trading. Its commitment to transparency ensures that stakeholders have access to reliable price data, fostering trust in the commodities sector.

Chapter 4. Major Global Commodity Exchanges

Commodity exchanges play a pivotal role in the global financial architecture by providing platforms for standardized trading, price discovery, and risk management. These exchanges offer various contracts, including futures, options, and swaps, allowing participants to buy or sell commodities at set prices for future delivery. Such contracts aid in the establishment of transparent price benchmarks and facilitate hedging against price volatility. Here, we delve into three of the world's premier commodity exchanges, each with its unique strengths and areas of specialization.

4.1. Chicago Mercantile Exchange (CME)

Overview: The Chicago Mercantile Exchange, commonly known as CME, originated in the late 19th century as a platform for agricultural commodities. Today, it stands as one of the world's largest derivatives exchanges, offering a wide range of products encompassing not only commodities but also equities, currencies, and interest rates.

Key Commodities: While it provides a diverse array of contracts, CME is renowned for its futures and options in agricultural products, such as corn, soybeans, and wheat. Moreover, the exchange has a significant presence in the livestock, dairy, and energy sectors.

Significance: The CME plays a vital role in global risk management. Its deep liquidity, transparency, and stringent regulatory oversight make it a preferred destination for traders, investors, and institutions aiming to mitigate the risks associated with price fluctuations.

4.2. Intercontinental Exchange (ICE)

Overview: Founded in 2000, the Intercontinental Exchange, or ICE, quickly rose to prominence by focusing on energy commodities. Today, it has diversified its offerings to include financial derivatives, equities, and fixed income.

Key Commodities: ICE is renowned for its Brent Crude futures contract, one of the world's primary oil benchmarks. Beyond energy, the exchange offers derivatives in agricultural products, metals, and environmental commodities.

Significance: ICE's acquisition of the New York Stock Exchange in 2013 cemented its position as a leading global exchange operator. Its commitment to leveraging technology has fostered an environment of innovation, making it a hub for electronic trading and clearing services.

4.3. London Metal Exchange (LME)

Overview: Founded in 1877, the London Metal Exchange stands as the world's foremost exchange for non-ferrous metals. Located in the heart of London, it commands a substantial share of global metal trading.

Key Commodities: The LME specializes in metals such as copper, aluminum, zinc, nickel, and lead. It also provides futures and options contracts for precious metals, including gold and silver.

Significance: LME prices are globally recognized benchmarks for metals. The exchange's unique system, which allows for physical delivery against its contracts, has cemented its status as the epicenter of global metal trading. Its commitment to transparency ensures that stakeholders have access to reliable price data, fostering trust in the commodities sector.

Chapter 5. Risks in Commodity Trading

Engaging in commodity trading necessitates an understanding of its multifaceted risk landscape. While these risks can offer opportunities for profit, they can equally lead to significant losses. Thus, market participants, from individual traders to large corporations, must be cognizant of these factors and consider appropriate risk management strategies. In this section, we outline the primary risks associated with commodity trading and their implications for market dynamics.

5.1. Price Volatility

Definition: Price volatility refers to the degree to which commodity prices fluctuate over a given period, influenced by a myriad of factors ranging from supply and demand imbalances to macroeconomic indicators.

Implications:

- **Rapid Price Fluctuations**: Commodities can experience substantial price changes within short durations, leading to potential gains or losses for traders.
- **Uncertainty**: High volatility can introduce uncertainty, complicating long-term planning for producers, consumers, and investors.
- **Margin Calls**: For those trading on margin, significant price shifts can trigger margin calls, necessitating additional capital infusion.

Mitigation: Traders and stakeholders can employ hedging strategies, utilizing instruments like futures or options, to insulate themselves from adverse price movements.

5.2. Geopolitical Factors

Definition: Geopolitical factors encompass the impact of political events, international relations, wars, and other global occurrences on commodity markets.

Implications:

- **Supply Disruptions**: Conflicts or political upheavals in key producing regions can hamper production or transportation, leading to supply constraints.
- **Trade Barriers**: Tariffs, sanctions, or embargoes can distort trade flows, affecting commodity prices and availability.
- **Currency Fluctuations**: Geopolitical events can influence currency strengths, thereby impacting global commodity prices, especially when priced in dominant currencies like the US dollar.

Mitigation: Diversifying sources of supply, engaging in forward contracts, or adopting geopolitical risk assessment frameworks can help entities navigate these challenges.

5.3. Storage and Transportation

Definition: Risks associated with the physical storage and transportation of commodities, encompassing issues like infrastructure breakdowns, theft, spoilage, or logistical bottlenecks.

Implications:

- **Cost Overruns**: Inadequate storage or transportation mechanisms can lead to increased costs.
- **Quality Degradation**: Improper storage conditions can deteriorate the quality of certain commodities, especially perishables.
- **Supply Chain Interruptions**: Transportation hiccups, whether due to infrastructure issues or geopolitical events, can disrupt the supply chain, affecting timely delivery and contractual obligations.

Mitigation: Investing in state-of-the-art storage facilities, insuring commodities against potential losses, diversifying transportation routes, and maintaining contingency plans can help in managing these risks.

Chapter 6. Gold Trading

Gold, often deemed the "yellow metal", is not only a precious metal with intrinsic value but also a commodity that has played a central role in the evolution of global economies. Its unique combination of being a tangible asset, a store of value, and a monetary instrument renders it a fascinating and complex commodity to trade. In this section, we examine the historical significance of gold, its contemporary market dynamics, and offer insights into gold trading strategies.

6.1. Historical Significance

Overview: Gold has been intertwined with human civilization for millennia, coveted for its rarity, beauty, and malleability. From ancient kingdoms to modern economies, its role has evolved, yet its allure remains unchanged.

Key Points:

- **Currency Standard**: Gold has historically been a cornerstone of monetary systems. The Gold Standard, prevalent in the 19th and early 20th centuries, pegged currencies to a fixed quantity of gold.

- **Cultural and Symbolic Value**: Across cultures and epochs, gold has symbolized wealth, divinity, and power. It has been, and continues to be, a prominent feature in jewelry, religious artifacts, and ceremonial objects.
- **Economic Safeguard**: In times of economic instability or inflation, gold has often been viewed as a safe-haven asset, a refuge for preserving wealth.

6.2. Market Dynamics and Influencers

Overview: The price and demand for gold are influenced by a melange of factors, both macroeconomic and sector-specific.

Key Influencers:

- **Central Banks**: Their buying or selling activities can significantly impact gold prices. Gold often forms a substantial portion of national reserves.
- **Inflation and Interest Rates**: Gold is perceived as a hedge against inflation. When real interest rates are low or negative, gold often becomes a more attractive investment.
- **Geopolitical Events**: Political uncertainties, wars, or global crises can lead to increased demand for gold as a protective asset.
- **Mining Costs**: The cost and availability of gold mining can influence supply, subsequently affecting prices.

6.3. Trading Strategies

Overview: Trading gold necessitates an understanding of its unique market dynamics and the application of strategies tailored to its behavior.

Key Strategies:

- **Fundamental Analysis**: By assessing global economic indicators, central bank activities, and geopolitical events, traders can anticipate potential price movements.
- **Technical Analysis**: Examining historical price charts, utilizing indicators like moving averages or oscillators, can aid traders in identifying trends or potential reversal points.
- **Portfolio Diversification**: Including gold in a diversified investment portfolio can serve as a hedge against volatility in other assets or currencies.
- **Leveraged and Derivative Trading**: Advanced traders might engage in leveraged trading or use derivatives like futures and options to capitalize on gold's price movements while managing risk exposure.

Chapter 7. Oil and Energy Commodities

The energy sector is a linchpin in the global economic architecture, powering industries, transportation, and households. Predominantly dominated by fossil fuels in the past, the sector is witnessing a paradigm shift towards cleaner and more sustainable sources. This chapter delves into the intricacies of oil and other pivotal energy commodities, tracing their market dynamics and their evolving roles in the contemporary energy mix.

7.1. Oil Market Overview

Overview: Oil, colloquially known as "black gold", is a paramount energy commodity with a labyrinthine market, influenced by geopolitics, technological advancements, and macroeconomic trends.

Key Features:

- **Crude vs. Refined**: Oil can be traded as crude — its raw form — or as refined products like gasoline or diesel.
- **OPEC's Role**: The Organization of the Petroleum Exporting Countries (OPEC) is a major player, often setting production quotas that influence global supply and prices.
- **Geopolitical Sensitivity**: Oil prices are highly susceptible to geopolitical events, especially in major production regions like the Middle East.
- **Demand Dynamics**: Oil consumption patterns reflect global economic health, with booms increasing demand and recessions curbing it.

7.2. Natural Gas, Coal, and Uranium

Natural Gas:

- **Overview**: A cleaner alternative to coal and oil, natural gas has seen rising demand, especially for electricity generation.
- **Market Dynamics**: Prices are influenced by factors such as weather (affecting heating demand), storage levels, and production techniques like fracking.

Coal:

- **Overview**: Once the mainstay of electricity generation, coal is gradually ceding ground due to environmental concerns.
- **Market Dynamics**: While demand in Western countries is waning, it remains robust in developing economies. Prices are influenced by mining costs, regulations, and transportation.

Uranium:

- **Overview**: As the primary fuel for nuclear power, uranium provides a significant portion of the world's electricity.
- **Market Dynamics**: Factors influencing uranium include nuclear plant construction and decommissioning, geopolitical events, and regulatory frameworks governing nuclear energy.

7.3. Renewable Energy Sources

Overview: With climate change taking center stage, renewable energy is experiencing unprecedented growth, driven by technological innovations and supportive policy frameworks.

Solar:

- **Dynamics**: The market for photovoltaic (PV) cells and modules is expanding rapidly. Key influencers include technological advancements, cost declines, and governmental incentives for solar installations.

Wind:

Dynamics: Wind energy, derived from onshore and offshore wind farms, is seeing robust growth. Market drivers include turbine technology enhancements, decreasing costs, and favorable policy environments.

Biofuels:

- **Dynamics**: Produced from organic matter, biofuels like ethanol and biodiesel are gaining traction as alternatives to traditional fuels. Their market is influenced by agricultural yield, technological breakthroughs in processing, and blending mandates set by governments.

Hydropower and Geothermal:

- **Dynamics**: While hydropower is a seasoned renewable source, geothermal energy, derived from the Earth's heat, is gaining attention. Both benefit from technological innovations and are influenced by site-specific geographical and environmental factors.

Chapter 8. Agricultural Commodities

Agricultural commodities, the lifeblood of civilizations since the dawn of settled societies, continue to occupy a central role in modern economies. They provide sustenance, influence trade balances, and play a significant part in the portfolio of investors and traders. This chapter delves into key agricultural commodities, exploring their market dynamics and the intricate interplay of factors shaping their supply and demand.

8.1. Grains and Oilseeds

Overview: Grains and oilseeds are foundational components of the global food supply chain, feeding billions and serving as raw materials for myriad industries.

Grains:

- **Types**: Principal grains include wheat, maize (corn), and rice.
- **Market Dynamics**: Climate patterns, governmental policies, and global stock-to-use ratios are primary price determinants. Unexpected events, like droughts, can result in significant price swings.

Oilseeds:

- **Types**: Soybeans, sunflower seeds, and rapeseed are leading oilseeds.
- **Market Dynamics**: Demand from the edible oil industry, biofuel mandates, and crop yield variations, often dictated by weather anomalies, steer the market dynamics of oilseeds.

8.2. Soft Commodities: Coffee, Sugar, and Cocoa

Coffee:

- **Overview**: A staple beverage globally, coffee beans have two primary types: Arabica and Robusta.
- **Market Dynamics**: Factors like climatic conditions in major producing regions (e.g., Brazil), disease outbreaks affecting crops, and global consumption trends determine coffee prices.

Sugar:

- **Overview**: Sourced mainly from sugarcane and sugar beet, sugar is a key sweetener with industrial applications.

- **Market Dynamics**: Global production versus consumption balance, alternative sweetener prevalence, and policy decisions related to tariffs or subsidies can influence sugar prices.

Cocoa:
- **Overview**: The primary ingredient for chocolate production, cocoa is cultivated predominantly in West Africa.
- **Market Dynamics**: Seasonal harvest results, geopolitical events in top-producing nations, and global demand for confectionery products are critical factors influencing cocoa prices.

8.3. Livestock: Cattle, Hogs, and Poultry

Cattle:
- **Overview**: Cattle commodities primarily refer to beef production.
- **Market Dynamics**: Factors include feed grain prices, especially corn, cattle herd sizes, disease outbreaks (e.g., mad cow disease), and global beef consumption patterns.

Hogs:
- **Overview**: Hog commodities focus on pork production.
- **Market Dynamics**: Price influencers are similar to cattle, with added emphasis on global trade dynamics, especially with major consumers like China.

Poultry:
- **Overview**: Poultry primarily encompasses chicken and turkey meat.
- **Market Dynamics**: Feed prices, disease outbreaks (e.g., avian flu), and shifts in consumer dietary preferences shape the poultry market.

Chapter 9. Trading Strategies

The art and science of trading commodities requires a multifaceted approach, integrating diverse analytical techniques to discern market movements and potential opportunities. Success in this realm is not merely about having capital; it's about applying a strategy with consistency, discipline, and a deep understanding of market undercurrents. This chapter elucidates the principal trading strategies, delineating their methodologies and applications in the realm of commodities trading.

9.1. Fundamental Analysis

Overview: Fundamental analysis delves into the intrinsic value of a commodity. It seeks to understand the broader forces of supply and demand, macroeconomic trends, and sector-specific factors to forecast price movements.

Key Components:

- **Macroeconomic Indicators**: GDP growth rates, interest rates, inflation, and geopolitical events can sway commodity prices.
- **Supply and Demand Dynamics**: Factors like production levels, stockpile reports, climatic conditions (for agricultural commodities), and technological advancements (for energy commodities) play a crucial role.
- **Industry Reports**: Regularly published by governmental bodies, industry associations, or independent entities, these reports provide insights into the health and direction of a particular commodity sector.

9.2. Technical Analysis

Overview: Technical analysis relies on price charts and various technical indicators to identify patterns and trends in commodity prices. This strategy is based on the principle that historical price movements can predict future price action.

Key Techniques:

- **Chart Patterns**: Patterns such as head and shoulders, double tops/bottoms, and triangles can hint at potential price breakouts or reversals.
- **Technical Indicators**: Tools like Moving Averages (MA), Relative Strength Index (RSI), and Moving Average Convergence Divergence (MACD) can provide signals for entry or exit points.
- **Volume Analysis**: Analyzing trade volumes can offer insights into the strength or weakness of a particular price trend.
- **Support and Resistance**: Identifying these key price levels can aid traders in setting stop-loss or take-profit orders.

9.3. Sentiment Analysis

Overview: Sentiment analysis gauges the mood or sentiment of market participants towards a particular commodity. It primarily focuses on qualitative data sources like news reports, expert opinions, and market chatter.

Key Approaches:

- **News Flow Analysis**: Regularly monitoring news outlets for any breaking news or events that could influence trader perceptions and thus commodity prices.
- **Market Surveys**: Some organizations conduct regular surveys to gauge bullish or bearish sentiment among traders and analysts.
- **Commitment of Traders (COT) Report**: This weekly report, published by the U.S. Commodity Futures Trading Commission (CFTC), provides a breakdown of the open interest for futures markets, showing positions of major players, and can be a valuable sentiment tool.

Chapter 10. Regulation and Ethics

The global commodity trading landscape, characterized by its vastness and inherent complexity, necessitates rigorous regulatory oversight and a robust ethical framework. Such structures ensure market integrity, protect investors, and foster practices that are environmentally sustainable and socially responsible. This chapter provides an overview of the pivotal role of regulatory institutions and underscores the imperativeness of ethical considerations in the realm of commodities trading.

10.1. Role of Regulatory Bodies

Overview: Regulatory bodies operate at the intersection of public interest and market efficiency. They institute rules, enforce compliance, and monitor trading activities to safeguard market participants and uphold the credibility of the commodities market.

Key Responsibilities:

- **Setting Standards**: Regulatory agencies lay down the rules governing trading practices, disclosure requirements, and reporting standards for participants.

- **Monitoring and Surveillance**: Through continuous oversight, these bodies identify and curb potential market abuses, including insider trading and price manipulation.
- **Dispute Resolution**: They provide platforms or mechanisms for resolving disputes between traders, brokers, and other market participants.
- **Licensing and Oversight**: Regulatory bodies grant licenses to brokers and exchanges, ensuring they adhere to established standards and practices.
- **Consumer and Investor Protection**: By ensuring transparency and curbing fraudulent activities, these institutions protect the interests of retail investors and the general public.

Notable Regulatory Bodies:
- **U.S. Commodity Futures Trading Commission (CFTC)**: Regulates the commodity futures and options markets in the United States.
- **Financial Conduct Authority (FCA)**: Oversees commodity trading activities in the UK.
- **European Securities and Markets Authority (ESMA)**: Regulates commodity derivatives markets within the European Union.

10.2. Ethical Trading and Sustainability

Overview: Beyond mere regulatory compliance, ethical trading emphasizes the moral imperatives guiding trading activities. In an era increasingly defined by sustainability concerns, ethical trading takes on added significance, with environmental stewardship and social responsibility being paramount.

Key Considerations:
- **Transparency and Fair Play**: Ethical trading necessitates transparency in transactions, avoiding deceptive practices and ensuring all stakeholders get a fair deal.
- **Environmental Responsibility**: For commodities like agricultural products or fossil fuels, the environmental footprint of production, transportation, and consumption is critical. Ethical trading emphasizes minimizing negative impacts and fostering sustainable practices.
- **Social Responsibility**: This entails ensuring that commodity sourcing does not perpetuate social ills like child labor, unfair wages, or adverse working conditions.
- **Sustainable Investment**: Ethical traders often prioritize investments in commodities or firms that champion sustainable practices, be it through eco-friendly production techniques or community upliftment initiatives.

Sustainability Certifications: Many commodities, especially agricultural products like coffee or cocoa, come with sustainability certifications, signifying adherence to environmental and social best practices. Labels such as Fair Trade, Rainforest Alliance, or Organic serve as markers for ethically traded commodities.

Chapter 11. Risk Management in Commodity Trading

Commodity trading, while presenting lucrative opportunities, is fraught with risks that can erode capital and inflict significant losses. Hence, astute risk management becomes the linchpin of successful trading. It involves a systematic approach to identify, assess, and mitigate potential adverse outcomes. This chapter elaborates on the pivotal risk management techniques employed in commodity trading, shedding light on their nuances and applicability.

11.1. Diversification

Overview: Diversification, a fundamental tenet of portfolio management, involves spreading investments across various assets to dilute risk. In commodity trading, it translates to diversifying among different commodity classes or within various assets of a single class.

Key Aspects:

- **Cross-Commodity Diversification**: Distributing investments across unrelated commodities—like gold, oil, and wheat—can offset losses in one due to price gains in another.
- **Intra-Commodity Diversification**: Within a commodity class, such as metals, traders can diversify by investing in gold, silver, and copper simultaneously.
- **Geographical Diversification**: Investing in commodities sourced from different regions can protect against localized risks such as geopolitical tensions or climatic anomalies.

11.2. Hedging Strategies

Overview: Hedging is a strategy aimed at offsetting potential losses in one position by establishing a counteracting position in a related asset.

Types of Hedging:

- **Direct Hedging**: Involves taking an opposite position in the same commodity. For instance, a farmer expecting to harvest wheat in two months might sell wheat futures now to lock in a price, thus hedging against potential price drops.
- **Cross-Hedging**: Here, the hedge involves a commodity related to the initial investment but not identical. For example, a gold trader might hedge using silver futures, banking on the correlation between gold and silver prices.

11.3. Use of Derivatives

Overview: Derivatives are financial instruments whose value is derived from an underlying asset, such as commodities. They play a pivotal role in risk management, offering tools to hedge, speculate, or increase leverage.

Common Derivatives in Commodity Trading:

- **Futures**: Standardized contracts that obligate traders to buy or sell a specific quantity of a commodity at a predetermined price on a specified future date.
- **Options**: Give traders the right, but not the obligation, to buy (call option) or sell (put option) a commodity at a specific price before a predetermined date.
- **Swaps**: Contracts wherein two parties agree to exchange cash flows or other variables associated with different assets, commonly used in the energy sector.

Risk Management via Derivatives:

- **Hedging with Futures**: Traders can lock in prices for future transactions, ensuring price certainty.
- **Options for Downside Protection**: Purchasing put options can protect against price declines, while call options can be used to secure potential upside when prices rise.
- **Swap Contracts**: These can be used to manage cash flow inconsistencies or exposure to variable commodity prices.

Chapter 12. Global Trade Dynamics

The mosaic of commodity trading is not an isolated tableau but an intricate interplay of global events, policies, and economies. In the last few decades, the influence of globalization and the rise of emerging markets have reshaped this landscape, introducing both opportunities and challenges. This chapter delves into these overarching themes, examining their ramifications on the intricate tapestry of commodity trading.

12.1. Impact of Globalization

Overview: Globalization, characterized by increased interdependence and integration of world economies, has significantly impacted commodity trading. This phenomenon, driven by advancements in technology, transportation, and policy reforms, has facilitated cross-border trade and investment, engendering a more interconnected commodity market.

Key Impacts:

- **Enhanced Market Access**: Traders can now access global markets more seamlessly, diversifying their portfolios across geographies and commodities.

- **Price Convergence**: Globalization has led to more uniform commodity pricing, driven by increased information flow and decreased transportation costs.

- **Supply Chain Complexities**: With commodities sourced from myriad locales, supply chains have become more intricate, demanding meticulous management.

- **Sensitivity to Global Events**: Today's interconnected markets imply that an event in one region, be it a geopolitical strife or a climatic anomaly, can ripple across the global commodity market.

- **Standardization and Regulation**: As markets converge, there's a pressing need for standardized trade practices and coordinated regulatory frameworks.

12.2. Emerging Markets in Commodity Trading

Overview: Emerging markets, often denoted as economies transitioning from low income to middle income, have burgeoned into pivotal players in commodity trading. Their rapid industrialization, population growth, and increasing consumer demand have reshaped the global demand-supply dynamics of numerous commodities.

Key Highlights:

- **Rising Demand**: Countries like China and India, buoyed by their vast populations and expanding middle class, have seen surging demand for commodities ranging from energy resources to agricultural products.

- **New Supply Frontiers**: Regions like Africa and South America have emerged as significant suppliers for commodities like minerals, oil, and agricultural produce.

- **Infrastructure Development**: The infrastructure boom in emerging markets, be it roads, ports, or industrial hubs, has spurred demand for commodities like steel, copper, and cement.

- **Financial Integration**: Emerging markets are increasingly integrated into the global financial system, with their exchanges playing a more pronounced role in global commodity trading.

- **Challenges and Vulnerabilities**: While they offer immense opportunities, emerging markets also present challenges, including political instability, regulatory uncertainties, and economic volatilities, which traders must navigate judiciously.

Chapter 13. Technological Advancements

In the vast continuum of commodity trading, technological advancements have ushered in a transformative era. The digitization of platforms, the evolution of electronic trading, and the growing imprint of Artificial Intelligence (AI) and Big Data have collectively redefined trading methodologies, strategies, and outcomes. This chapter delves into the nuances of these tech-driven shifts, demystifying their impact on the world of commodity trading.

13.1. Digital Platforms and E-Trading

Overview: The emergence of digital platforms and electronic trading (e-trading) systems has radically altered the trading environment, ensuring enhanced accessibility, transparency, and efficiency.

Key Developments:

- **Speed and Accessibility**: E-trading platforms facilitate instantaneous execution of trades, allowing traders to respond rapidly to market dynamics.
- **Global Reach**: Traders can now access global commodity markets from virtually anywhere, breaking down geographical barriers.
- **Transparency and Price Discovery**: Real-time data feeds, comprehensive market data, and transparent pricing mechanisms have become hallmarks of e-trading platforms.
- **Cost Efficiency**: Reduced operational costs and minimal manual intervention translate to lower transaction fees for traders.
- **Customized Trading Tools**: Advanced charting tools, algorithmic trading solutions, and risk management applications cater to traders' specific needs, enhancing their decision-making process.

13.2. Impact of Artificial Intelligence and Big Data

Overview: The confluence of AI and Big Data has bestowed commodity trading with analytical prowess, predictive capabilities, and automation, resulting in more informed and strategic trading decisions.

Key Impacts:

- **Predictive Analytics**: By analyzing vast datasets, AI-powered tools can forecast market trends, price fluctuations, and demand-supply dynamics with heightened accuracy.
- **Automated Trading**: AI-driven algorithms can execute trades autonomously, based on predefined criteria, ensuring speed and consistency.
- **Risk Management**: AI tools can assess and predict potential risks, offering insights into hedging strategies or suggesting diversification to mitigate losses.
- **Sentiment Analysis**: AI models analyze news articles, social media posts, and other public communications to gauge market sentiment, which can influence commodity prices.
- **Data-driven Insights**: Big Data analytics churns massive volumes of structured and unstructured data, translating them into actionable insights, from weather patterns affecting agricultural commodities to geopolitical events influencing energy prices.

Chapter 14. Financial Instruments in Commodity Trading

The realm of commodity trading is not confined solely to direct buying and selling of physical goods. Financial instruments, synthesized through financial engineering, allow for participation in the commodity markets without the necessity of dealing with physical commodities. This chapter elucidates the characteristics and functions of prevalent financial instruments in commodity trading: Commodity ETFs, Mutual Funds, and Index Funds.

14.1. Commodity ETFs

Overview: Commodity Exchange-Traded Funds (ETFs) are investment vehicles that provide exposure to commodities, or indices based on commodities, without requiring investors to take physical ownership or deal with futures contracts.

Key Features:

- **Diversification**: Commodity ETFs often invest in a basket of commodities, allowing investors to diversify their exposure.
- **Liquidity**: Being traded on stock exchanges, ETFs can be bought or sold with the same ease as individual stocks.
- **Flexibility**: Investors can choose between ETFs that track a specific commodity, like gold or oil, or those that track a commodity index.
- **Transparency**: ETF holdings and performance are regularly updated, providing clarity to investors.
- **Cost-Efficiency**: ETFs typically have lower fees than mutual funds, making them an attractive option for many investors.

14.2. Mutual Funds and Index Funds

Overview: Mutual Funds and Index Funds offer an avenue for investors to gain exposure to the commodities market through a pooled investment mechanism.

Distinguishing Features:

- **Mutual Funds**:
  - **Actively Managed**: Managed by financial professionals, these funds aim to outperform the market by selecting and trading investments based on research, analysis, and forecasts.
  - **Diverse Exposure**: Commodity mutual funds might invest directly in commodities, in stocks of companies associated with commodities, or in futures and options contracts.
  - **Fee Structure**: Tend to have higher fees due to active management and operational expenses.
- **Index Funds**:
  - **Passive Management**: These funds seek to replicate the performance of a specific index by holding a portfolio identical or similar to the index's constituents.
  - **Cost-Effective**: Typically have lower expense ratios as they don't require active management.
  - **Predictability**: Their performance generally mirrors that of the chosen index, making outcomes more predictable for informed investors.

Chapter 15. Economic Indicators and their Impact

In the multifaceted world of commodity trading, the undulating currents of macroeconomic indicators play a pivotal role in shaping price trajectories and market sentiments. Understanding the profound implications of these indicators is paramount for traders and investors seeking to navigate the often tumultuous waters of commodity markets. This chapter illuminates two cardinal economic indicators: Gross Domestic Product (GDP) and the interplay between Interest Rates and Inflation, exploring their ramifications on commodity trading.

15.1. GDP and its Relevance

Overview: The Gross Domestic Product (GDP) represents the total monetary value of all goods and services produced over a specific time period within a nation's borders.

Key Implications:

- **Economic Health**: GDP is a barometer of an economy's health. A growing GDP often suggests a prosperous economy, which can increase demand for commodities.
- **Consumer Confidence**: A robust GDP growth can lead to heightened consumer confidence, which can stimulate spending and demand for commodities.
- **Investment Decisions**: Countries with strong and consistent GDP growth can attract foreign investments, potentially impacting commodity prices and trading volumes.
- **Trade Balances**: Changes in GDP can influence a country's imports and exports, directly impacting the demand-supply dynamics of commodities.
- **Currency Strength**: The strength of a country's currency can be influenced by its GDP, which in turn can affect commodity prices, especially those traded in USD.

15.2. Interest Rates and Inflation

Overview: Interest rates, set by central banks, influence the cost of borrowing money, while inflation measures the rate at which the general level of prices for goods and services rises, leading to the eroding purchasing power of money.

Key Interactions:

- **Cost of Holding Commodities**: Higher interest rates can increase the cost of holding commodities, potentially reducing their demand. Conversely, low rates might stimulate demand by making holding costs cheaper.
- **Inflation Hedge**: Commodities, particularly precious metals like gold, are often viewed as a hedge against inflation. As inflation rises, demand for such commodities can surge.
- **Consumer Spending**: High-interest rates generally curtail consumer spending by making borrowing more expensive. This can reduce demand for certain commodities.
- **Investment Landscape**: Changes in interest rates can shift investor preference between equities, bonds, and commodities, influencing commodity prices.
- **Currency Valuation**: Interest rates can affect currency strength, with higher rates often bolstering a currency. A stronger currency can make imported commodities cheaper, potentially influencing their demand.

Chapter 16. The Future of Commodity Trading

As the global economy perpetually evolves, the realm of commodity trading finds itself at the cusp of profound transformations. Advances in technology, shifts in consumer behavior, geopolitical realignments, and emergent market dynamics collectively sculpt the trajectory of commodity markets. As we cast our gaze into the future, it becomes imperative to discern the potential growth areas and navigate the intricate web of challenges and opportunities that lie ahead. This chapter endeavors to extrapolate these dimensions, offering a futuristic perspective on commodity trading.

16.1. Potential Growth Areas

Emerging Economies: As emerging markets mature, their appetite for commodities, ranging from energy to agriculture, is poised to grow exponentially. Countries like India, Brazil, and various African nations represent burgeoning markets with immense potential.

Renewable Energy Commodities: With global emphasis on sustainability and carbon neutrality, commodities like lithium, used in batteries, and rare earth metals, essential for tech and renewable energy solutions, are set to witness amplified demand.

Agri-tech Commodities: Innovations in agricultural technology will spur demand for specialized commodities. Bio-engineered crops, precision agriculture, and sustainable farming methods could redefine the agricultural commodity landscape.

Digital Commodities: The rise of cryptocurrencies and digital assets represents a new frontier in commodity trading. These "digital commodities" might play a more central role in future trading ecosystems.

16.2. Challenges and Opportunities

Geopolitical Turbulence: Fluctuating geopolitical scenarios, trade wars, and international policies can pose significant challenges. However, astute traders can leverage these dynamics to their advantage by anticipating market reactions.

Regulatory Evolution: As global trading dynamics change, so will regulatory frameworks. Staying abreast of and compliant with these changes is a challenge but also an opportunity to instill trust and transparency in operations.

Technological Disruptions: The advent of AI, blockchain, and other technological innovations will revolutionize trading platforms, methodologies, and strategies. Embracing these changes can provide traders with a competitive edge.

Sustainability and Ethical Trading: With growing emphasis on sustainability and ethical practices, traders have the opportunity to adopt and promote green and responsible trading. This not only aligns with global objectives but can also enhance brand image and credibility.

Market Diversity: As new commodities enter the trading arena, understanding their nuances becomes both a challenge and an opportunity for diversification and portfolio enhancement.

Conclusion and Final Thoughts

From the rudimentary barter systems of ancient civilizations to the sophisticated electronic trading platforms of the 21st century, the landscape of commodity trading has undergone a metamorphosis that mirrors the evolution of human society and its economic constructs. This intricate journey, brimming with innovations, disruptions, and milestones, merits reflection as we stand on the precipice of the future, ready to embrace the next epoch of commodity trading.

Evolution of Commodity Trading

Historically, the act of trading commodities was entrenched in direct, tangible exchanges. Markets formed the nexus where growers, producers, and consumers convened, setting the foundation for what would later evolve into intricate global exchanges. As economies expanded and human endeavors became more specialized, the need for standardized systems and contracts emerged. This gave birth to futures contracts, options, and the formal commodity exchanges that dominate today's landscape.

The late 20th and early 21st centuries witnessed the dawn of digitization in commodity trading. Electronic platforms obliterated geographical boundaries, artificial intelligence transformed decision-making processes, and big data analytics offered insights previously unimaginable.

Future Perspectives for Traders and Investors

As we gaze into the future, a few certainties and speculations become apparent:

1. **Technological Prowess**: The role of technology will continue to amplify. Blockchain could revolutionize transaction transparency, while machine learning might refine predictive accuracy, offering traders and investors an unprecedented edge.

2. **Sustainable Trading**: The clarion call for sustainability will resonate louder. Commodities related to green technologies, renewable energy, and sustainable agriculture will likely dominate portfolios, reflecting global priorities.

3. **Diversified Portfolios**: As the definition of 'commodity' broadens, embracing digital assets and novel resources, traders and investors will be presented with richer, more diverse portfolios, demanding adaptability and continual learning.

4. **Global Dynamics**: Emerging markets, geopolitical shifts, and evolving economic alliances will play pivotal roles. Astute traders will continuously recalibrate their strategies, staying attuned to global pulses.

5. **Ethical Impetus**: Ethical trading, fair practices, and transparent operations will become not just preferable but essential. The modern trader and investor will be as much a conscientious global citizen as a profit-seeker.

In Retrospect: The tapestry of commodity trading is an ever-evolving masterpiece, a reflection of humanity's economic endeavors, aspirations, and innovations. For traders and investors willing to learn, adapt, and grow, the future holds promises of opportunities as vast as the challenges. The key lies in melding the lessons of the past, the realities of the present, and the possibilities of the future into a cohesive, informed, and strategic approach. As the pages of this commodity trading tome close, it's evident that the journey, with all its intricacies, is as rewarding as the destination. The saga of commodity trading continues, and the next chapter is ours to write.

Biotech Trading

Specialize in trading stocks of biotechnology companies based on drug development news and events

Introduction:

The confluence of biotechnology and financial markets has given rise to a distinct realm of investment that demands both scientific acumen and financial expertise. In the intricate world of biotech trading, where the fortunes of companies are inexorably linked to the progress of drug development, mastery of technical analysis and an understanding of scientific breakthroughs become paramount. This book, "Biotech Trading: Navigating Biotechnology Stock Markets through Drug Development Insights," embarks on a journey through this dynamic landscape, unraveling the complexities that underlie successful trading within the biotech sector.

At its core, biotech trading is a symbiotic relationship between the intricate processes of drug discovery, development, and regulatory approval, and the fervent pulse of the financial markets. As investors navigate this arena, it's crucial to recognize the intertwined nature of scientific progress and market dynamics. A grasp of the phases of drug development—ranging from preclinical trials to post-marketing surveillance—equips traders with the knowledge to gauge the value potential of biotech stocks.

Biotechnology, an industry born from the confluence of biology, chemistry, and technology, continues to evolve at an astonishing pace. The first chapter of this book delves into the historical trajectory of the biotech sector, examining how it has evolved from its humble beginnings to becoming a pivotal player in modern healthcare. Understanding this evolution is essential, as historical patterns often foreshadow future trends, and recognizing these patterns is crucial for effective decision-making.

The second chapter is a deep dive into the fundamental intricacies of drug development—an endeavor that epitomizes the intersection of science and commerce. The drug development lifecycle comprises a sequence of stages, each laden with its own unique challenges and critical milestones. From identifying promising drug candidates to navigating the rigorous landscape of clinical trials, an exhaustive comprehension of this lifecycle is imperative for investors looking to time their trades to maximize profit potential.

With clinical trials at the heart of drug development, the third chapter delves into the art and science of interpreting clinical trial results. A nuanced understanding of trial data—whether positive or negative—can spell the difference between lucrative returns and substantial losses. This chapter will empower traders to decipher complex trial data, ascertain its implications, and strategize their investments accordingly.

The regulatory framework governing biotech companies is as intricate as the science behind their innovations. Chapter four is dedicated to elucidating the labyrinthine corridors of the Food and Drug Administration (FDA) and the regulatory environment. Discerning the regulatory climate, comprehending approval processes, and anticipating market reactions to regulatory changes will equip traders with a tactical edge in this high-stakes arena.

As biotech trading entails a comprehensive assessment of companies' drug pipelines, chapter five provides an in-depth exploration of pipeline analysis. Evaluating the prospects of drugs in various stages of development, gauging their potential market impact, and weighing inherent risks are fundamental skills that this chapter imparts to traders.

In continuation, the next chapter delves into the intricate art of valuing biotech companies. Traditional valuation metrics must be complemented with biotech-specific factors, such as the potential of pending clinical trials and regulatory approvals. This chapter equips traders with the prowess to assess companies' worth not just in terms of financials but also in terms of future catalysts.

Stay tuned as we delve into chapter seven, where we explore the enigmatic realm of market sentiment and investor behavior. The psychology that underpins the actions of biotech stock investors can significantly influence market movements. By understanding how news, rumors, and sentiment shape the market, traders can position themselves strategically, capitalizing on trends that others might overlook.

As we journey deeper into the book, subsequent chapters will explore event-driven trading strategies, risk management tactics, the role of exchange-traded funds (ETFs) and mutual funds in the biotech sector, and the intricate dance between intellectual property and stock performance. The pages that follow will weave real-life case studies, unveil data sources and research tools, and examine the ethical considerations that underscore biotech trading decisions.

In conclusion, this book is poised to be an indispensable resource for both novice and seasoned traders alike, offering a comprehensive guide to navigating the complex realm of biotech trading. Armed with scientific insights, financial acumen, and a robust arsenal of strategies, readers will be empowered to traverse the biotech stock markets with a newfound confidence. Stay tuned for the subsequent chapters that will pave the way to becoming a proficient biotech trader.

Chapter 1: Understanding Biotechnology Landscape

The first chapter of "Biotech Trading: Navigating Biotechnology Stock Markets through Drug Development Insights" immerses readers in the historical and contemporary dimensions of the biotechnology landscape. This foundational exploration is crucial for establishing a robust understanding of the context in which biotech trading operates.

Evolution of Biotech Industry: The biotechnology industry has undergone a remarkable transformation since its inception. Tracing its roots back to the recombinant DNA revolution of the 1970s, the industry has evolved from a nascent scientific pursuit to a global economic powerhouse. This chapter delves into the pioneering breakthroughs that marked the industry's inception, such as the development of recombinant insulin and the birth of genetic engineering. It then navigates through subsequent milestones, including the decoding of the human genome and the emergence of gene editing technologies like CRISPR-Cas9. By comprehending the trajectory of biotech advancements, traders can discern patterns that influence stock movements.

Key Players and Market Dynamics: A comprehensive understanding of the key players within the biotech sector is vital for effective trading. This chapter introduces readers to the array of stakeholders, from established pharmaceutical giants to agile startups. It scrutinizes the role of academia and research institutions in driving innovation, as well as the significance of venture capital in nurturing fledgling biotech ventures. Understanding the dynamics between large-cap companies and innovative startups is pivotal for predicting market trends. By dissecting the strategies of market leaders, traders can glean insights into potential winners and losers.

Market Sentiment and Investor Behavior in Biotech: Biotech trading is profoundly influenced by market sentiment and investor behavior. This chapter delves into the psychological underpinnings that drive investment decisions within the sector. Traders will explore how news, clinical trial results, and regulatory announcements can trigger euphoria or panic, leading to rapid stock fluctuations. By analyzing historical trends in investor sentiment, traders can develop a nuanced perspective on market behavior, allowing them to anticipate and adapt to market swings effectively.

Emerging Trends and Technological Disruptions: Innovation is the lifeblood of the biotech industry, and technological disruptions are pivotal in shaping market trends. This chapter examines cutting-edge advancements, such as precision medicine, immuno-oncology, and gene therapies. These trends can spark revolutionary changes in treatment paradigms, thus impacting the valuation of biotech companies. By staying attuned to emerging technologies, traders can position themselves to harness early-mover advantages, capitalizing on market movements driven by scientific breakthroughs.

Investment Strategies Based on Industry Evolution: Investment strategies within the biotech sector are inherently linked to the industry's evolution. This chapter guides readers in formulating strategies based on the lifecycle of biotechnology companies. Traders will learn to recognize opportunities for early-stage investments in startups with disruptive technologies, mid-stage investments as drugs progress through clinical trials, and late-stage investments in companies approaching regulatory approvals. Tailoring investment strategies to match the stages of company development can yield substantial returns and mitigate risk.

As readers navigate through the pages of this chapter, they will gain a comprehensive understanding of the biotechnology landscape's historical context, market dynamics, and the interplay between innovation and investment. Armed with this knowledge, traders can build a solid foundation for their journey into the intricate world of biotech trading, poised to make informed decisions that yield both financial success and a deeper appreciation for the fusion of science and finance.

Chapter 2: Fundamentals of Drug Development

In the intricate tapestry of biotech trading, a profound comprehension of the fundamental processes underlying drug development is essential. Chapter 2 of "Biotech Trading: Navigating Biotechnology Stock Markets through Drug Development Insights" delves into the multi-phased journey of drug development, providing readers with the tools to decode this intricate landscape and make informed trading decisions.

Phases of Drug Development: The chapter initiates with a meticulous exploration of the phases that constitute the drug development pipeline. From preclinical research to post-marketing surveillance, each phase presents unique challenges and potential market impacts. Readers will glean insights into the sequential progression of drug candidates through phases such as discovery, preclinical testing, clinical trials, and regulatory approval. By understanding these stages, traders can anticipate pivotal milestones that can catalyze stock movements.

Clinical Trials: A Crucial Crucible: At the heart of drug development lie clinical trials—a pivotal juncture where scientific rigor converges with regulatory scrutiny. This chapter delves into the intricate design and execution of clinical trials, deciphering the significance of randomized controlled trials, double-blind studies, and placebo controls. Readers will learn how to interpret clinical trial protocols, data, and endpoints, enabling them to assess the potential success or failure of investigational drugs and make informed trading choices.

Challenges and Regulatory Hurdles: Navigating the labyrinthine regulatory landscape is a defining challenge in drug development. This chapter dissects the role of regulatory bodies such as the FDA and EMA, shedding light on the stringent standards that govern drug approvals. Readers will delve into topics such as orphan drug designations, fast-track programs, and breakthrough therapy designations, which can expedite the approval process for certain drugs. Understanding the regulatory pathways and potential hurdles equips traders to anticipate market reactions to regulatory updates.

Understanding Clinical Data: Clinical trial data, replete with its complexities and nuances, forms the bedrock of investment decisions in the biotech sector. This chapter equips traders with the analytical tools to discern the significance of trial data. From endpoints and statistical significance to adverse events and patient populations, readers will unravel the intricacies that underlie clinical data interpretation. Armed with this knowledge, traders can differentiate between meaningful breakthroughs and transient fluctuations.

Market Implications of Drug Development Phases: The chapter culminates with an exploration of how different phases of drug development impact stock performance. Traders will delve into case studies and historical data to discern patterns in market behavior corresponding to specific developmental milestones. Whether it's the euphoria surrounding positive clinical trial results or the skepticism accompanying regulatory setbacks, understanding the interplay between science and market sentiment is pivotal for maximizing trading outcomes.

In navigating through the corridors of this chapter, readers will emerge equipped with a comprehensive understanding of the intricate landscape of drug development. Armed with insights into the phases, challenges, and implications of drug development, traders will be better poised to anticipate market movements, capitalize on pivotal events, and make judicious trading decisions. As the curtain rises on the next chapters, readers will be primed to delve even deeper into the multifaceted realm of biotech trading.

Chapter 3: Analyzing Clinical Trial Results

Within the realm of biotech trading, the ability to decipher and analyze clinical trial results is a critical skill that sets successful traders apart. Chapter 3 of "Biotech Trading: Navigating Biotechnology Stock Markets through Drug Development Insights" delves into the intricate world of clinical trial data interpretation, empowering readers to discern the scientific and market implications of trial outcomes.

Interpreting Trial Data for Investment Decisions: This chapter commences by illuminating the pivotal role of clinical trial results in shaping investment decisions. Traders will delve into the various types of trial data, such as efficacy, safety, and secondary endpoints, and learn how to assess their significance in the context of drug development. Through real-world case studies, readers will gain insights into how different trial outcomes can impact stock prices and market sentiment.

Impact of Positive and Negative Outcomes: The heart of clinical trial analysis lies in comprehending the implications of positive and negative outcomes. This chapter dissects the market dynamics that unfold when a drug candidate demonstrates efficacy, safety, and other desired attributes. Conversely, it explores how setbacks and adverse outcomes can trigger rapid market reactions. By understanding the intricate interplay between clinical trial data and stock movement, traders can position themselves strategically to capitalize on market volatility.

Biostatistics and Data Integrity: A deep dive into clinical trial data necessitates an understanding of biostatistics and the intricacies of data integrity. This chapter introduces readers to statistical concepts such as p-values, confidence intervals, and statistical significance. It also explores factors that can influence data quality and integrity, such as patient demographics, trial design, and randomization techniques. Armed with this knowledge, traders can critically assess the reliability of trial results and make informed judgments.

Endpoints and Their Relevance: The choice of clinical trial endpoints profoundly influences the interpretation of trial data. This chapter examines different types of endpoints, such as primary, secondary, and exploratory endpoints, and their relevance in assessing the success of drug candidates. Traders will learn how to discern meaningful clinical outcomes from surrogate endpoints, enhancing their ability to differentiate between substantial therapeutic advances and superficial statistical variations.

Balancing Data and Market Expectations: Balancing scientific rigor with market expectations is a delicate task in biotech trading. This chapter delves into how market sentiment can sometimes outpace the underlying clinical evidence, leading to stock movements that may not align with the true therapeutic value of a drug candidate. Readers will acquire the acumen to critically evaluate the alignment between trial data and market reactions, enabling them to make well-informed trading choices.

By journeying through the pages of this chapter, traders and enthusiasts alike will be equipped with the analytical tools to navigate the intricate landscape of clinical trial data interpretation. Armed with insights into positive and negative outcomes, an understanding of biostatistics, and an appreciation for the interplay between data and market sentiment, readers will be primed to make astute trading decisions based on a nuanced comprehension of clinical trial results. As the book unfolds, subsequent chapters will further refine the skill set necessary for successful biotech trading.

Chapter 4: FDA and Regulatory Landscape

In the dynamic world of biotech trading, the regulatory landscape plays a pivotal role in influencing stock movements and investment decisions. Chapter 4 of "Biotech Trading: Navigating Biotechnology Stock Markets through Drug Development Insights" delves into the intricacies of the Food and Drug Administration (FDA) and the broader regulatory environment, equipping readers with the knowledge to anticipate and navigate regulatory changes.

Navigating FDA Approvals and Regulations: This chapter commences by unraveling the role of the FDA as a gatekeeper for drug approvals in the United States. Traders will gain insights into the stages of FDA review, from Investigational New Drug (IND) application to New Drug Application (NDA) submission. By understanding the regulatory processes and timelines, traders can strategically position themselves to capitalize on potential market movements triggered by FDA decisions.

Market Response to Regulatory Updates: Regulatory decisions and updates can send ripples through the biotech stock market. This chapter delves into how the market responds to FDA approvals, rejections, and safety advisories. By examining historical examples, readers will grasp the patterns of market behavior that follow regulatory announcements. Armed with this knowledge, traders can navigate the volatility that often accompanies such updates and make informed trading choices.

Accelerated Pathways and Fast-Track Programs: The FDA offers several accelerated pathways and fast-track programs to expedite the development and approval of drugs for serious conditions. This chapter dissects these programs, such as the Breakthrough Therapy Designation and the Priority Review, exploring how they can influence stock performance. Readers will learn to discern the implications of these designations for both scientific progress and market sentiment.

Regulatory Challenges and Their Market Impact: The regulatory journey is not devoid of challenges, including safety concerns, label restrictions, and post-marketing surveillance. This chapter delves into how regulatory hurdles can impact stock performance. Traders will gain insights into the market's reaction to adverse events, label changes, and regulatory actions. By assessing the potential market reverberations of regulatory challenges, traders can make calculated decisions amid uncertainties.

Global Regulatory Variations: The regulatory landscape extends beyond the borders of the United States. This chapter examines how regulatory agencies in different countries impact biotech stock trading. Traders will explore the European Medicines Agency (EMA), the Pharmaceuticals and Medical Devices Agency (PMDA) in Japan, and other international regulatory bodies. Understanding global regulatory variations equips traders to anticipate worldwide market trends.

As readers immerse themselves in the intricacies of this chapter, they will gain a comprehensive understanding of how the FDA and regulatory dynamics intertwine with the biotech trading landscape. Armed with insights into navigating FDA approvals, interpreting market responses to regulatory updates, and understanding the impact of fast-track programs, traders will be primed to navigate the ever-evolving regulatory environment with acumen and confidence. As the chapters unfold, subsequent sections will continue to expand the horizons of biotech trading expertise.

Chapter 5: Assessing Pipeline Potential

The success of biotech trading hinges on the ability to discern the potential of drug pipelines within biotechnology companies. Chapter 5 of "Biotech Trading: Navigating Biotechnology Stock Markets through Drug Development Insights" immerses readers into the intricate art of pipeline analysis, equipping them to assess investment opportunities with a discerning eye.

Evaluating Company Pipelines as Investment Opportunities: This chapter embarks by highlighting the significance of evaluating biotech company pipelines as a cornerstone of investment decisions. Traders will delve into the diverse stages of drug development—ranging from preclinical to post-marketing—and understand how each phase contributes to a company's value. By discerning the mix of early-stage exploratory drugs and late-stage candidates, readers can gauge a company's growth potential.

Balancing Risk and Reward: Pipeline analysis necessitates a careful balance between risk and reward. This chapter dissects the factors that contribute to risk within drug pipelines, such as clinical trial failures, regulatory setbacks, and market dynamics. Traders will learn how to assess the inherent risk in different stages of drug development and make informed judgments about potential rewards. By understanding this delicate equilibrium, readers can formulate strategies to manage risk effectively.

Impact of Pipeline Diversity: Diversity within a drug pipeline can be a pivotal indicator of a company's resilience and growth potential. This chapter delves into the value of having a diversified pipeline that spans therapeutic areas and mechanisms of action. Traders will explore how having multiple candidates targeting different indications can mitigate the impact of setbacks and enhance a company's long-term prospects.

Valuing Development Milestones: As drug candidates progress through development stages, reaching critical milestones becomes a marker of progress. This chapter guides readers in understanding the significance of development milestones, such as successful completion of clinical phases or regulatory designations. Traders will learn how to assign value to these milestones, factoring them into their investment assessments to predict potential stock movements.

Anticipating Catalysts and Value Inflection Points: Pipeline analysis involves anticipating catalysts—events that can significantly impact a company's stock price and valuation. This chapter examines catalysts such as clinical trial results, regulatory decisions, and partnership agreements. Traders will gain insights into how to identify upcoming catalysts, assess their potential market impact, and position themselves strategically to capitalize on value inflection points.

As readers navigate the depths of this chapter, they will emerge equipped with the analytical tools necessary to assess pipeline potential within the biotech sector. By understanding the nuances of pipeline evaluation, balancing risk and reward, recognizing the impact of pipeline diversity, valuing development milestones, and anticipating value-inflection catalysts, traders will be poised to make astute investment decisions that are grounded in a comprehensive comprehension of a company's growth trajectory. The journey through the intricate terrain of biotech trading continues to unfold in subsequent chapters, providing readers with an arsenal of insights and strategies.

Chapter 6: Biotech Valuation Techniques

Valuation within the biotech sector is a unique blend of financial analysis and scientific potential. Chapter 6 of "Biotech Trading: Navigating Biotechnology Stock Markets through Drug Development Insights" delves into the intricacies of valuing biotech companies, equipping readers with the skills to assess both financial metrics and the developmental milestones that drive stock prices.

Traditional Metrics vs. Biotech-Specific Valuation: This chapter initiates by dissecting the traditional valuation metrics commonly used in the financial world. Traders will explore metrics like price-to-earnings (P/E) ratios, price-to-sales (P/S) ratios, and discounted cash flow (DCF) models.

However, valuing biotech companies extends beyond these metrics. The chapter guides readers in understanding how to integrate biotech-specific factors such as clinical trial progress, regulatory milestones, and pipeline potential into their valuation strategies.

Incorporating Development Milestones in Valuation: The incorporation of developmental milestones is a hallmark of biotech valuation. This chapter delves into how traders can assign value to clinical trial successes, regulatory designations, and other pivotal milestones. By estimating the impact of these milestones on a company's valuation, traders can make informed decisions that reflect the potential for future growth.

Patent and Intellectual Property Valuation: Intellectual property and patents are integral to a biotech company's valuation. This chapter examines how to assess the value of a company's intellectual property portfolio, including patents, licenses, and proprietary technologies. Traders will gain insights into how patent expiration and exclusivity impact stock performance and how to factor these elements into their valuation models.

Calculating Market Potential and Revenue Forecasts: Understanding a drug candidate's market potential and revenue forecasts is crucial for accurate valuation. This chapter guides readers in assessing the target patient population, pricing strategies, and potential market share. By incorporating these factors into their valuation models, traders can project future revenue streams and estimate a company's growth trajectory.

Evaluating Partnerhips and Collaborations: Partnerships and collaborations can significantly impact a biotech company's valuation. This chapter explores how strategic alliances, licensing agreements, and partnerships can enhance a company's financial prospects. Traders will learn to assess the financial and developmental implications of these collaborations and incorporate them into their valuation assessments.

As readers immerse themselves in this chapter, they will emerge equipped with the analytical prowess to navigate the intricate landscape of biotech valuation. By understanding the interplay between traditional financial metrics and biotech-specific factors, incorporating developmental milestones, valuing intellectual property, forecasting market potential, and evaluating partnerships, traders will be poised to make well-informed trading decisions that are grounded in a holistic understanding of a company's value. The journey through the world of biotech trading continues, with subsequent chapters delving even deeper into specialized insights and strategies.

Chapter 7: Market Sentiment and Investor Behavior

In the dynamic world of biotech trading, market sentiment and investor behavior wield significant influence over stock movements. Chapter 7 of "Biotech Trading: Navigating Biotechnology Stock Markets through Drug Development Insights" delves into the psychological underpinnings that drive trading decisions and explores how news, rumors, and speculation shape market sentiment.

Psychology of Biotech Stock Investors: This chapter commences by unraveling the intricate psychology that underpins trading decisions within the biotech sector. Traders will delve into cognitive biases, herd behavior, and risk perception that can lead to market trends and price fluctuations. By understanding the psychological factors that influence investor behavior, traders can anticipate market movements and position themselves strategically.

Impact of News and Speculation: News, whether substantiated or speculative, can trigger rapid market reactions in the biotech sector. This chapter examines how news about clinical trial results, regulatory approvals, partnerships, and scientific breakthroughs can propel stocks to new heights or precipitate sharp declines. Readers will learn to distinguish between credible information and baseless rumors, and gauge their impact on market sentiment.

Event-Driven Trading and Timing: Event-driven trading strategies hinge on capitalizing on news-driven price movements. This chapter explores the intricacies of timing trades around events such as FDA announcements, clinical trial readouts, and major conferences. Traders will gain insights into how to anticipate market sentiment shifts, enter positions strategically, and exit at optimal points to maximize trading outcomes.

Behavioral Biases and Their Market Impact: Behavioral biases, ranging from fear of missing out (FOMO) to loss aversion, can drive irrational trading behavior. This chapter dissects these biases and their implications for stock movements. By understanding how these biases can lead to overvaluation or undervaluation of stocks, traders can make informed decisions that capitalize on market inefficiencies.

Role of Social Media and Online Forums: The advent of social media and online forums has amplified the impact of retail investors on the stock market. This chapter examines how platforms like Twitter, Reddit, and stock-focused forums can amplify sentiment shifts and drive stock prices. Traders will learn to gauge the influence of online communities and assess the reliability of information circulating on these platforms.

As readers immerse themselves in this chapter, they will emerge equipped with a nuanced understanding of market sentiment and investor behavior within the biotech sector. By delving into the psychology of investors, exploring the impact of news and speculation, mastering event-driven trading strategies, understanding the role of behavioral biases, and navigating the influence of social media, traders will be primed to anticipate and capitalize on the complex interplay between psychology and market dynamics. As subsequent chapters unfold, readers will delve even deeper into the multifaceted world of biotech trading expertise.

Chapter 8: Event-Driven Trading Strategies

Event-driven trading strategies are a cornerstone of success in biotech trading, where market movements are often catalyzed by significant announcements and milestones. Chapter 8 of "Biotech Trading: Navigating Biotechnology Stock Markets through Drug Development Insights" delves into the art of leveraging critical events to make strategic trading decisions.

Leveraging FDA Announcements and Clinical Trial Milestones: This chapter commences by highlighting the significance of FDA announcements and clinical trial milestones as potent catalysts for stock movements. Traders will explore how FDA decisions, such as drug approvals and rejections, can trigger rapid price shifts. Likewise, they will learn to anticipate the impact of clinical trial results on a company's valuation and stock performance.

Timing Entries and Exits: Effective event-driven trading hinges on precise timing of market entries and exits. This chapter dissects the strategies for entering positions ahead of anticipated positive news and exiting before potential negative outcomes. Traders will learn how to strike a balance between maximizing potential gains and mitigating risks, all while navigating the inherent volatility associated with event-driven trading.

Analyzing Market Reaction Patterns: Past market reactions to similar events can offer invaluable insights for future trading decisions. This chapter guides readers in analyzing historical data to discern patterns in market reactions. By understanding how stocks tend to respond to specific types of news, traders can refine their strategies and make well-informed decisions based on empirical evidence.

Using Options and Derivatives for Event-Driven Trades: Options and derivatives can enhance the efficacy of event-driven trading strategies. This chapter explores how traders can leverage options to capitalize on anticipated price movements and hedge against potential losses. Readers will learn to construct option strategies that align with their trading outlook and risk tolerance.

Adapting to Unexpected Outcomes: While event-driven trading is based on anticipation, unexpected outcomes can still arise. This chapter examines how to adapt to unexpected news and market movements. Traders will gain insights into risk management strategies that allow them to respond swiftly and strategically to unforeseen events.

As readers navigate the depths of this chapter, they will emerge equipped with the tools and tactics necessary to excel in event-driven trading within the biotech sector. By leveraging FDA announcements, mastering the timing of market entries and exits, analyzing market reaction patterns, exploring options and derivatives, and adapting to unexpected outcomes, traders will be primed to capitalize on the dynamic landscape of event-driven trading. As subsequent chapters unfold, readers will continue to refine their expertise in biotech trading strategies.

Chapter 9: Risk Management in Biotech Trading

Effective risk management is a linchpin of success in the volatile realm of biotech trading. Chapter 9 of "Biotech Trading: Navigating Biotechnology Stock Markets through Drug Development Insights" delves into strategies for mitigating risks and safeguarding investments in a sector characterized by rapid market swings and uncertainty.

Understanding Biotech-Specific Risks: This chapter initiates by dissecting the unique risks inherent to biotech trading. Traders will explore factors such as clinical trial failures, regulatory setbacks, and competitive landscape shifts that can trigger sharp stock declines. By understanding these biotech-specific risks, traders can proactively manage their portfolios and make informed trading decisions.

Diversification and Portfolio Allocation: Diversification is a cornerstone of effective risk management. This chapter delves into strategies for diversifying a biotech trading portfolio across different companies, therapeutic areas, and stages of development. Traders will learn how to allocate capital strategically to manage risk while still capitalizing on potential opportunities.

Hedging Techniques and Risk Mitigation: Hedging is an essential tool for mitigating risks in a volatile market. This chapter explores how options and derivatives can be used to hedge against potential losses due to adverse market movements. Traders will gain insights into constructing hedging strategies that align with their trading objectives and risk tolerance.

Position Sizing and Risk-Reward Ratios: Proper position sizing is critical for managing risk effectively. This chapter guides traders in determining the appropriate size of their positions based on their risk tolerance and trading strategy. Readers will learn to calculate risk-reward ratios and assess the potential returns against the inherent risks of their trades.

Monitoring and Adjusting Risk Strategies: Risk management is an ongoing process that requires vigilance and adaptation. This chapter examines how to monitor portfolio performance, assess risk exposure, and adjust risk strategies as market conditions evolve. Traders will gain insights into staying agile and making prudent adjustments to manage risk effectively.

As readers delve into the depths of this chapter, they will emerge equipped with the tools and techniques necessary to navigate the intricate landscape of risk management within biotech trading. By understanding biotech-specific risks, diversifying portfolios, employing hedging techniques, sizing positions effectively, and maintaining an adaptive risk strategy, traders will be primed to navigate the volatility of the biotech sector with resilience and confidence. As the book unfolds, subsequent chapters will continue to refine and expand on the art of successful biotech trading.

Chapter 10: Biotech ETFs and Funds

Exchange-Traded Funds (ETFs) and mutual funds offer investors a diversified exposure to the biotech sector, mitigating individual stock risks. Chapter 10 of "Biotech Trading: Navigating Biotechnology Stock Markets through Drug Development Insights" explores the benefits, drawbacks, and strategies associated with investing in these vehicles.

Understanding Biotech ETFs and Funds: This chapter commences by introducing readers to the concept of biotech ETFs and mutual funds. Traders will gain insights into how these investment vehicles pool resources from multiple investors to invest in a diversified portfolio of biotech stocks. By understanding the structure and mechanics of ETFs and funds, traders can explore different avenues for exposure to the biotech sector.

Benefits of Diversification and Risk Mitigation: Diversification is a hallmark of ETFs and funds, offering inherent risk mitigation. This chapter delves into how investing in these vehicles can reduce the impact of individual stock fluctuations and provide exposure to a broader range of biotech companies. Traders will explore how diversification can enhance portfolio stability and align with their risk tolerance.

Performance Evaluation and Selection Criteria: Selecting the right biotech ETFs or funds is pivotal for successful investment. This chapter guides readers in evaluating the performance of different funds by analyzing historical returns, expense ratios, and other relevant metrics. Traders will learn how to assess the alignment of a fund's investment strategy with their own trading objectives.

Tracking Indices and Sectors: Many biotech ETFs and funds track specific indices or sectors within the biotech industry. This chapter explores how different indices, such as the NASDAQ Biotechnology Index, can influence fund performance. Traders will gain insights into how tracking specific indices can align with their market outlook and investment preferences.

Potential Drawbacks and Considerations: While ETFs and funds offer diversification, they also come with potential drawbacks. This chapter examines factors such as management fees, tracking error, and tax implications associated with these investment vehicles. By understanding these considerations, traders can make informed decisions about incorporating ETFs and funds into their portfolio.

As readers immerse themselves in the intricacies of this chapter, they will emerge equipped with the insights necessary to explore the world of biotech ETFs and funds. By understanding the benefits of diversification, evaluating performance and selection criteria, tracking relevant indices, and considering potential drawbacks, traders will be poised to diversify their investment strategies and leverage these vehicles to gain exposure to the biotech sector. The journey through the landscape of biotech trading continues, with subsequent chapters further refining and expanding on investment opportunities and strategies

Chapter 11: Analyzing Intellectual Property

Intellectual property (IP) plays a pivotal role in shaping the biotech sector and influencing stock performance. Chapter 11 of "Biotech Trading: Navigating Biotechnology Stock Markets through Drug Development Insights" delves into the intricacies of patents, trademarks, and other forms of IP, equipping readers to assess their impact on market sentiment and investment decisions.

Role of Intellectual Property in Biotech: This chapter commences by highlighting the central role of intellectual property in the biotech industry. Traders will explore how patents and other forms of IP protect the innovative discoveries and technologies that underlie biotech companies' products. By understanding how IP can confer competitive advantages, traders can gauge its influence on stock valuations.

Analyzing Patent Portfolios: Patents are a key indicator of a biotech company's innovative prowess and potential market value. This chapter guides readers in evaluating patent portfolios to discern the breadth, depth, and quality of a company's intellectual property. Traders will explore how to assess the strength of patents, their coverage, and their potential to safeguard a company's competitive position.

Patent Exclusivity and Market Dynamics: Patent exclusivity grants biotech companies a window of market exclusivity for their products. This chapter examines how patent expiration can impact stock performance, leading to market shifts known as the "patent cliff." Traders will gain insights into how to anticipate the expiration of key patents and its potential repercussions on stock prices.

IP Litigation and Regulatory Considerations: IP litigation and regulatory challenges can introduce uncertainties in the biotech sector. This chapter delves into how legal battles over patents and regulatory hurdles can impact stock movements. Traders will learn to assess the potential outcomes of IP disputes and regulatory actions, and their implications for market sentiment.

Market Reaction to IP Developments: Market sentiment can be influenced by significant IP developments such as patent grants, rejections, and licensing agreements. This chapter explores how traders can anticipate market reactions to these events, using IP-related news to inform their trading decisions. By understanding how IP developments can sway investor sentiment, traders can position themselves strategically.

As readers navigate the depths of this chapter, they will emerge equipped with the analytical prowess necessary to navigate the complex landscape of intellectual property within the biotech sector. By understanding the role of IP in biotech, analyzing patent portfolios, anticipating patent exclusivity dynamics, considering IP litigation and regulatory challenges, and assessing market reactions to IP developments, traders will be primed to make informed investment decisions grounded in a comprehensive understanding of the intellectual property landscape. Subsequent chapters will continue to delve into specialized insights and strategies within biotech trading.

Chapter 12: Biotech Market Analysis and Data Sources

Effective biotech trading relies on accurate and timely market analysis. Chapter 12 of "Biotech Trading: Navigating Biotechnology Stock Markets through Drug Development Insights" delves into the tools, data sources, and analytical techniques that traders can leverage to gain insights into market trends, stock performance, and industry dynamics.

Data Sources for Biotech Analysis: This chapter commences by introducing readers to the diverse data sources available for biotech market analysis. Traders will explore platforms such as financial news websites, market research reports, clinical trial databases, regulatory agency websites, and scientific journals. By understanding the spectrum of data sources, traders can curate a comprehensive information repository.

Tracking News and Developments: Staying updated on news and developments is pivotal in biotech trading. This chapter guides readers in effectively tracking news related to clinical trial results, regulatory decisions, partnerships, and industry trends. Traders will learn how to differentiate between credible sources, assess the reliability of news, and use news feeds to inform their trading decisions.

Analyzing Clinical Trial Data: Clinical trial data is a treasure trove of information for biotech traders. This chapter examines how to access and interpret clinical trial data from sources like clinicaltrials.gov and scientific publications. Traders will learn to analyze trial protocols, endpoints, patient populations, and statistical data to gain insights into a drug candidate's potential.

Utilizing Market Research Reports: Market research reports provide comprehensive insights into industry trends, competitive landscapes, and future forecasts. This chapter explores how to leverage market research reports to assess market potential, identify emerging trends, and evaluate the competitive positioning of biotech companies. Traders will gain insights into using these reports to inform their investment decisions.

Technical Analysis in Biotech Trading: Technical analysis involves studying historical stock price patterns and trading volumes to forecast future price movements. This chapter examines how traders can use technical analysis tools such as moving averages, support and resistance levels, and chart patterns to gauge market sentiment and make trading decisions.

As readers immerse themselves in this chapter, they will emerge equipped with the tools and techniques necessary to perform comprehensive biotech market analysis. By understanding data sources, tracking news and developments, analyzing clinical trial data, utilizing market research reports, and exploring technical analysis tools, traders will be poised to make informed trading decisions based on a solid foundation of market insights. As the journey through the world of biotech trading unfolds, subsequent chapters will continue to expand on specialized strategies and insights.

Chapter 13: Long-Term Investing in Biotech

While biotech trading often involves short-term strategies, long-term investing can also yield substantial rewards in the sector. Chapter 13 of "Biotech Trading: Navigating Biotechnology Stock Markets through Drug Development Insights" delves into the considerations, strategies, and factors to bear in mind when adopting a long-term investment approach within the biotech industry.

Benefits and Challenges of Long-Term Investing: This chapter commences by exploring the benefits of adopting a long-term investment strategy within the biotech sector. Traders will examine how a patient approach can capitalize on the potential for drug candidates to progress through clinical stages and achieve regulatory approvals. Additionally, the chapter will address the challenges associated with long-term investing, such as market volatility and the inherent uncertainties in drug development.

Assessing Developmental Milestones: Long-term investing in biotech requires a keen understanding of developmental milestones. This chapter guides readers in assessing the significance of milestones such as Phase 1, 2, and 3 clinical trial results, FDA approvals, and commercial launches. Traders will learn how to gauge the potential impact of these milestones on a company's valuation and stock performance.

Balancing Portfolio for Long-Term Growth: Diversification is paramount for long-term growth. This chapter delves into strategies for balancing a portfolio of biotech stocks across different stages of development, therapeutic areas, and market caps. Traders will explore how to create a diversified portfolio that aligns with their long-term investment objectives while managing risk effectively.

Evaluating Management and Leadership: In the realm of long-term investing, assessing a company's management and leadership becomes pivotal. This chapter examines how to evaluate a company's management team, their track record, and their ability to execute on their developmental goals. Traders will learn to factor management competence into their investment decisions.

Understanding Biotech Market Cycles: Biotech stocks often experience cycles of euphoria and pessimism. This chapter explores how to navigate these market cycles while adhering to a long-term investment strategy. Traders will gain insights into recognizing when market sentiment overshoots or undershoots the underlying value of a company, enabling them to capitalize on market inefficiencies.

As readers immerse themselves in the intricacies of this chapter, they will emerge equipped with the insights necessary to thrive in long-term investing within the biotech sector. By understanding the benefits and challenges of long-term strategies, assessing developmental milestones, balancing portfolios for growth, evaluating management and leadership, and navigating market cycles, traders will be poised to capitalize on the potential for sustained growth and value creation. The journey through the realm of biotech trading continues, with subsequent chapters further refining and expanding on investment strategies and expertise.

Chapter 14: Ethical Considerations in Biotech Trading

Ethical considerations are pivotal in navigating the biotech trading landscape, where decisions can impact human health and well-being. Chapter 14 of "Biotech Trading: Navigating Biotechnology Stock Markets through Drug Development Insights" delves into the ethical dilemmas, responsibilities, and considerations that traders should bear in mind when engaging in biotech trading.

Balancing Profit and Ethical Responsibility: This chapter commences by examining the delicate balance between pursuing profit and upholding ethical responsibilities. Traders will explore the ethical implications of trading in stocks tied to life-saving therapies and groundbreaking medical advancements. By understanding the gravity of their actions, traders can make decisions that align with their personal values and broader ethical considerations.

Clinical Trial Ethics and Patient Well-Being: The conduct of clinical trials raises ethical concerns, as patient safety and well-being are paramount. This chapter delves into how traders can evaluate companies' commitment to ethical clinical trial practices. Traders will learn to assess transparency, patient consent, and adherence to ethical standards when considering investment opportunities.

Responsible Use of Information: Traders often have access to non-public information that can impact stock prices. This chapter explores the ethical implications of using confidential information to gain an unfair advantage. Traders will gain insights into insider trading regulations and the importance of conducting trades based on publicly available information.

Environmental and Social Responsibility: Biotech companies are often engaged in research and development that can impact the environment and society. This chapter examines how traders can evaluate a company's environmental and social responsibility practices. Traders will learn to consider factors such as sustainability, diversity and inclusion, and corporate social responsibility when making investment decisions.

Promoting Ethical Practices: Traders have the potential to influence corporate behavior through their investment decisions. This chapter explores how traders can engage in responsible investing that encourages companies to prioritize ethical practices. Traders will learn to use their influence to promote transparency, accountability, and ethical behavior within the biotech sector.

As readers navigate the depths of this chapter, they will emerge equipped with the ethical compass necessary to navigate the complex ethical landscape of biotech trading. By balancing profit and ethical responsibility, considering clinical trial ethics, using information responsibly, evaluating environmental and social responsibility, and promoting ethical practices, traders will be primed to engage in biotech trading with integrity and mindfulness. The journey through the world of biotech trading continues, with subsequent chapters continuing to expand on specialized insights and strategies.

Chapter 14: Ethical Considerations in Biotech Trading

Ethical considerations are pivotal in navigating the biotech trading landscape, where decisions can impact human health and well-being. Chapter 14 of "Biotech Trading: Navigating Biotechnology Stock Markets through Drug Development Insights" delves into the ethical dilemmas, responsibilities, and considerations that traders should bear in mind when engaging in biotech trading.

Balancing Profit and Ethical Responsibility: This chapter commences by examining the delicate balance between pursuing profit and upholding ethical responsibilities. Traders will explore the ethical implications of trading in stocks tied to life-saving therapies and groundbreaking medical advancements. By understanding the gravity of their actions, traders can make decisions that align with their personal values and broader ethical considerations.

Clinical Trial Ethics and Patient Well-Being: The conduct of clinical trials raises ethical concerns, as patient safety and well-being are paramount. This chapter delves into how traders can evaluate companies' commitment to ethical clinical trial practices. Traders will learn to assess transparency, patient consent, and adherence to ethical standards when considering investment opportunities.

Responsible Use of Information: Traders often have access to non-public information that can impact stock prices. This chapter explores the ethical implications of using confidential information to gain an unfair advantage. Traders will gain insights into insider trading regulations and the importance of conducting trades based on publicly available information.

Environmental and Social Responsibility: Biotech companies are often engaged in research and development that can impact the environment and society. This chapter examines how traders can evaluate a company's environmental and social responsibility practices. Traders will learn to consider factors such as sustainability, diversity and inclusion, and corporate social responsibility when making investment decisions.

Promoting Ethical Practices: Traders have the potential to influence corporate behavior through their investment decisions. This chapter explores how traders can engage in responsible investing that encourages companies to prioritize ethical practices. Traders will learn to use their influence to promote transparency, accountability, and ethical behavior within the biotech sector.

As readers navigate the depths of this chapter, they will emerge equipped with the ethical compass necessary to navigate the complex ethical landscape of biotech trading. By balancing profit and ethical responsibility, considering clinical trial ethics, using information responsibly, evaluating environmental and social responsibility, and promoting ethical practices, traders will be primed to engage in biotech trading with integrity and mindfulness. The journey through the world of biotech trading continues, with subsequent chapters continuing to expand on specialized insights and strategies.

Chapter 15: Emerging Technologies and Trends

The biotech sector is shaped by rapidly evolving technologies and trends that can drive stock performance. Chapter 15 of "Biotech Trading: Navigating Biotechnology Stock Markets through Drug Development Insights" delves into the emerging technologies, trends, and innovations that traders should be attuned to when making investment decisions in the biotech industry.

Gene Editing and CRISPR Technology: This chapter commences by exploring the revolutionary field of gene editing and the CRISPR-Cas9 technology. Traders will gain insights into how gene editing techniques can be harnessed to develop innovative therapies and treatments. By understanding the potential of gene editing, traders can gauge the market impact of breakthroughs in this domain.

Precision Medicine and Personalized Therapies: Precision medicine tailors treatments to individual patient characteristics, revolutionizing healthcare. This chapter examines how personalized therapies are transforming the biotech landscape and influencing stock performance. Traders will explore how to assess companies that are at the forefront of developing targeted treatments.

Artificial Intelligence and Data Analytics: Artificial intelligence (AI) and data analytics are reshaping drug discovery, clinical trials, and market analysis. This chapter delves into the role of AI in identifying drug candidates, optimizing trial designs, and predicting market trends. Traders will learn to assess the potential impact of AI-driven innovations on companies' value and stock performance.

Biotech's Role in Pandemic Preparedness: Recent global health crises have underscored the importance of biotech in pandemic preparedness. This chapter examines how biotech companies contribute to vaccine development, antiviral treatments, and diagnostics. Traders will explore how pandemic-related developments can impact market sentiment and stock prices.

Sustainability and ESG Considerations: Environmental, social, and governance (ESG) considerations are gaining prominence in investment decisions. This chapter explores how biotech companies address sustainability, social responsibility, and ethical governance. Traders will learn to assess companies' ESG practices and evaluate their potential influence on stock performance.

As readers immerse themselves in the intricacies of this chapter, they will emerge equipped with insights into the cutting-edge technologies and trends shaping the biotech sector. By understanding the potential of gene editing, precision medicine, AI, pandemic preparedness, and ESG considerations, traders will be poised to identify investment opportunities driven by emerging technologies and trends. The journey through the realm of biotech trading continues, with subsequent chapters further refining and expanding on investment strategies and expertise.

Chapter 16: Case Studies in Biotech Trading

Real-world case studies provide valuable insights into the application of strategies and principles within the biotech trading landscape. Chapter 16 of "Biotech Trading: Navigating Biotechnology Stock Markets through Drug Development Insights" delves into a series of case studies that showcase successful and challenging trading scenarios, offering readers practical lessons and perspectives.

Case Study 1: The Breakthrough Designation Boost This chapter commences with a case study involving a biotech company that receives a Breakthrough Therapy Designation for one of its drug candidates. Traders will explore how this regulatory designation impacts stock performance, market sentiment, and trading decisions. By dissecting the key elements of this case, readers will learn to navigate opportunities presented by regulatory milestones.

Case Study 2: Clinical Trial Surprise In this case study, a biotech company's clinical trial results diverge from market expectations. Traders will delve into how unexpected outcomes can trigger volatility and impact stock prices. By analyzing the factors that contribute to the market's response, readers will gain insights into managing risks associated with clinical trial surprises.

Case Study 3: M&A and Strategic Partnerships This chapter explores a case study involving a merger and acquisition (M&A) deal between two biotech companies. Traders will examine how M&A announcements and strategic partnerships can reshape the biotech landscape and trigger stock movements. By evaluating the dynamics of this case, readers will learn to navigate the intricacies of trading around such corporate events.

Case Study 4: Regulatory Roadblocks In this case study, a biotech company encounters regulatory roadblocks that lead to delays in drug development. Traders will explore how regulatory setbacks can impact stock performance and market sentiment. By analyzing the challenges faced by the company in this case, readers will learn to assess the potential risks associated with regulatory hurdles.

Case Study 5: Navigating Market Volatility Market volatility is a constant in biotech trading. This case study delves into a scenario where a biotech trader navigates the volatility triggered by external factors such as macroeconomic events or geopolitical developments. Traders will gain insights into adapting trading strategies to manage risk and capitalize on opportunities amid market turbulence.

As readers immerse themselves in the depth of these case studies, they will emerge with a practical understanding of how strategies, principles, and considerations discussed throughout the book apply to real-world trading scenarios. By dissecting breakthrough designations, unexpected clinical trial outcomes, M&A deals, regulatory challenges, and market volatility, readers will be equipped to make informed trading decisions based on a comprehensive comprehension of biotech trading dynamics. As the journey through the world of biotech trading unfolds, subsequent chapters will continue to expand on specialized insights and strategies.

Chapter 17: The Future of Biotech Trading

The biotech sector is constantly evolving, driven by scientific advancements, regulatory changes, and market trends. Chapter 17 of "Biotech Trading: Navigating Biotechnology Stock Markets through Drug Development Insights" delves into the potential trajectories and considerations for the future of biotech trading, equipping readers to anticipate and adapt to the changing landscape.

Emerging Therapeutic Modalities: This chapter commences by exploring the potential of emerging therapeutic modalities such as gene therapies, cell therapies, and RNA-based treatments. Traders will gain insights into how these innovative approaches can reshape the biotech landscape and impact stock performance. By understanding the potential of these therapies, readers can identify investment opportunities at the forefront of scientific advancement.

Regulatory Landscape and FDA Evolution: The regulatory environment has a profound impact on biotech trading. This chapter examines how changes in regulatory policies, expedited review pathways, and FDA evolution can influence stock performance. Traders will explore how to stay attuned to regulatory trends and their potential implications for trading decisions.

Global Market Dynamics: Biotech trading is not confined to a single market; global dynamics play a pivotal role. This chapter delves into how factors such as international partnerships, market access, and healthcare policies can impact the performance of biotech stocks. Traders will gain insights into assessing the global landscape and its relevance to their trading strategies.

Influence of Big Data and AI: The integration of big data and AI continues to reshape biotech research and development. This chapter explores how AI-driven drug discovery, predictive modeling, and real-world data analysis can influence trading decisions. Traders will learn to leverage insights from data-driven technologies to inform their investment strategies.

Sustainable Biotech Investing: Environmental, social, and ethical considerations are gaining prominence in investing. This chapter examines how the concept of sustainable biotech investing is evolving and influencing stock performance. Traders will explore how to align their trading strategies with sustainable practices and evaluate the potential impact on long-term returns.

As readers delve into the intricate landscape of this chapter, they will emerge equipped with insights into the potential trajectories and considerations that will shape the future of biotech trading. By understanding emerging therapeutic modalities, staying attuned to regulatory changes, assessing global market dynamics, leveraging big data and AI, and embracing sustainable investing practices, traders will be primed to navigate the evolving biotech sector with foresight and adaptability. The journey through the world of biotech trading comes to a close, leaving readers with a comprehensive understanding of the intricacies and opportunities within this dynamic and innovative industry.

Chapter 18: Epilogue - Charting Your Biotech Trading Journey

In this epilogue of "Biotech Trading: Navigating Biotechnology Stock Markets through Drug Development Insights," we take a moment to reflect on the transformative journey you've undertaken through the pages of this comprehensive guide. As you stand at the crossroads of newfound knowledge and potential trading opportunities, this concluding chapter offers guidance on charting your biotech trading journey, emphasizing continuous learning, adaptability, and ethical responsibility.

Embracing Lifelong Learning: The world of biotech trading is dynamic and ever-evolving, shaped by scientific advancements, regulatory changes, and market trends. As you move forward, prioritize the pursuit of lifelong learning. Stay attuned to emerging technologies, industry shifts, and the latest research developments. Whether it's through scientific journals, market analysis, or expert forums, the commitment to staying informed will be your compass in navigating the complex biotech landscape.

Refining Your Strategies: The strategies and insights presented in this book serve as a solid foundation, but the journey doesn't end here. Take the time to refine and adapt your strategies based on evolving market conditions and your own experiences. Experiment with different approaches, evaluate their outcomes, and iterate to find what works best for you. Embrace both successes and setbacks as valuable learning experiences that contribute to your growth as a biotech trader.

Ethics as Your North Star: Ethical considerations lie at the heart of responsible trading within the biotech sector. As you make investment decisions, remember the profound impact that your choices can have on human health, well-being, and the broader society. Uphold ethical standards, avoid insider trading, and prioritize transparency. By integrating ethical considerations into your trading decisions, you contribute to the sustainability and integrity of the biotech industry.

Cultivating Resilience and Patience: Biotech trading, like any form of trading, is marked by ups and downs. The path to success is not always linear, and patience is a virtue. Cultivate resilience to weather market volatility and setbacks. Be prepared to adapt your strategies and adjust your expectations based on evolving circumstances. Remember that success often comes to those who persist with a long-term outlook and a steadfast commitment to learning from every experience.

Building a Network: In the realm of biotech trading, a strong network can be an invaluable asset. Connect with fellow traders, industry experts, and professionals who share your passion. Engaging in discussions, attending conferences, and participating in online forums can provide fresh perspectives, insights, and potential collaborative opportunities. Building a network can enrich your trading journey and expose you to a diverse range of viewpoints.

Contributing to the Biotech Community: As you navigate the biotech trading landscape, consider how you can contribute positively to the biotech community. Share your knowledge, insights, and experiences with others. Mentor aspiring traders, engage in discussions that promote responsible trading practices, and contribute to the collective understanding of the industry. By giving back, you not only enhance your own expertise but also foster a sense of shared growth within the community.

As you conclude this transformative journey through "Biotech Trading: Navigating Biotechnology Stock Markets through Drug Development Insights," remember that you are equipped with a wealth of knowledge, insights, and strategies to navigate the intricate biotech landscape. Embrace the challenges and opportunities that lie ahead, and let the lessons from this book serve as a steadfast guide as you chart your course in the ever-evolving world of biotech trading. Your journey is now in your hands, and your potential to make meaningful contributions to the field is boundless.

Conclusion

In the final chapter of "Biotech Trading: Navigating Biotechnology Stock Markets through Drug Development Insights," we reflect on the multifaceted journey undertaken through the pages of this book. The chapters have explored the intricate landscape of biotech trading, from the foundational understanding of drug development and clinical trial stages to the specialized strategies and ethical considerations that define success in this dynamic field.

As the biotech sector continues to evolve, propelled by scientific breakthroughs, regulatory shifts, and market trends, the knowledge gained from this book equips readers with the tools and insights to navigate the challenges and capitalize on the opportunities that lie ahead. The fusion of technical analysis, market sentiment, and ethical considerations has been meticulously woven together to provide a comprehensive guide for traders seeking success in biotech trading.

From the art of event-driven trading to the nuances of intellectual property evaluation, each chapter has unveiled a layer of expertise, guiding readers through the intricacies of a sector that melds science, finance, and human well-being. The case studies have brought theory to life, offering tangible examples of how strategies play out in real-world scenarios, and the exploration of emerging technologies and future trends has empowered readers to anticipate shifts in the market landscape.

The journey does not end with the last page of this book. Instead, it marks the beginning of a trader's path in the ever-evolving world of biotech trading. Armed with knowledge, insights, and a holistic understanding of the industry, readers are now poised to embark on their own trading journeys, making informed decisions that balance financial success with ethical responsibility.

As the biotech sector continues to push the boundaries of innovation, challenge conventions, and transform lives, those who have delved into "Biotech Trading: Navigating Biotechnology Stock Markets through Drug Development Insights" are well-prepared to contribute meaningfully to this remarkable journey. Whether as seasoned traders refining their strategies or newcomers entering the field, the knowledge gained from these pages will serve as a steadfast compass in the realm of biotech trading.

So, as we bid adieu to this comprehensive exploration, let it be known that the pursuit of success in biotech trading is not just a transactional endeavor—it's a holistic journey that balances the art of trading with the science of innovation, guided by ethical principles and a commitment to human welfare. May the insights garnered from this book illuminate your path and empower you to make impactful decisions in the captivating world of biotech trading.

Microtrading

Concentrate on making very small trades with minimal price movements.

Introduction:

In the ever-evolving landscape of financial markets, a novel approach has emerged that challenges the conventional norms of trading - Microtrading. This groundbreaking strategy involves concentrating on executing exceedingly small trades, harnessing the power of minuscule price movements. As the realm of trading continues to evolve with technological advancements and dynamic market shifts, Microtrading has swiftly ascended as a method that requires precision, discipline, and a deep understanding of market intricacies. This introduction delves into the essence of Microtrading, its significance in today's financial sphere, and provides a glimpse of the comprehensive exploration that this book offers into this innovative trading strategy.

Defining Microtrading: Microtrading, at its core, represents a paradigm shift in how traders engage with financial markets. Traditionally, traders have often pursued substantial gains through substantial price movements over extended periods. Microtrading, however, operates on a vastly different premise. It centers on executing a multitude of swift, precisely timed trades that capitalize on even the most minute market fluctuations. These fluctuations, often dismissed by traditional traders as insignificant "noise," form the very foundation of Microtrading. The objective is not to reap grandiose profits from singular massive trades but to accumulate consistent gains through the cumulative effect of numerous micro trades.

Challenges and Opportunities: Microtrading, while offering alluring prospects, comes with its own set of challenges and opportunities. The meticulous nature of this strategy demands traders to be adept in real-time decision-making, unwavering discipline, and an intimate familiarity with market dynamics. This is not a realm for the impulsive or faint-hearted; it requires practitioners to embrace a calculated and methodical approach. Furthermore, the opportunities presented by Microtrading are a testament to its potential. By effectively leveraging the smallest market movements, traders can generate returns that might otherwise go unnoticed. This ability to mine value from microcosmic price shifts provides traders with a unique edge in the competitive world of finance.

Technological Advancements and Microtrading: The rise of Microtrading has been intricately interwoven with technological advancements in trading platforms, data analytics, and automation. Modern trading platforms have evolved to accommodate the rapid pace of Microtrading, offering features such as instant order execution, advanced charting tools, and customizable alerts for swift decision-making. Data analytics and algorithmic trading have become the cornerstones of successful Microtrading strategies. Complex algorithms are designed to detect the faintest market signals, enabling traders to capitalize on fleeting opportunities. While technological tools undoubtedly empower Microtraders, they also necessitate a thorough understanding of how these tools operate to make informed choices.

Democratizing Trading: One of the notable consequences of Microtrading's rise is its role in democratizing trading. Historically, trading in financial markets has often been perceived as a domain reserved for well-financed institutions and experienced professionals. Microtrading challenges this notion by making trading accessible to a broader audience. With lower capital requirements and the ability to participate in numerous small trades, individuals with varying levels of experience can engage in the dynamic world of trading. This democratization is reshaping the financial landscape, allowing more participants to actively partake in the market's ebb and flow.

Navigating the Book's Terrain: This book serves as a comprehensive guide to Microtrading, offering a meticulously crafted journey through its principles, strategies, and applications. As you embark on this exploration, you will delve into the intricate art of executing swift trades that leverage minor price movements. Each chapter is meticulously designed to equip you with the knowledge, tools, and mindset required to excel in Microtrading. From understanding the psychological nuances to dissecting technical intricacies and exploring advanced strategies, this book is your roadmap to thriving in the realm of Microtrading.

Conclusion: At the juncture where financial innovation and technological prowess converge, Microtrading emerges as a beacon of possibility. This introduction has unveiled the essence of Microtrading, its challenges and opportunities, and the symbiotic relationship it shares with cutting-edge technology. As you proceed through the chapters that follow, you will gain insights into the foundational principles, advanced techniques, and real-world case studies that define successful Microtraders. With every page turned, you will take strides toward mastering the art of Microtrading, positioning yourself to harness the power of seemingly inconsequential market movements and transform them into a symphony of consistent profits. The journey begins now, as we delve into the depths of Microtrading's intricacies, strategies, and the potential it holds for those willing to embrace its artistry.

Chapter 1: The Essence of Microtrading

In the vast expanse of financial markets, where transactions span continents and billions of dollars change hands in mere seconds, a revolutionary concept has emerged: Microtrading. This chapter will delve into the core essence of Microtrading, unpacking its definition, significance, and the paradigm shift it brings to the trading landscape.

Defining Microtrading: Microtrading represents a departure from traditional trading approaches that emphasize significant price movements and prolonged holding periods. At its heart, Microtrading involves executing a multitude of small-scale trades with the goal of capitalizing on even the most minuscule price fluctuations. While traditional traders might dismiss these minor movements as inconsequential, Microtraders recognize their potential to accumulate substantial profits over time. In this paradigm, success isn't determined by a single grandiose trade; rather, it's the result of a symphony of carefully orchestrated micro trades.

The Microtrader's Mindset: Central to Microtrading is the mindset of the Microtrader. This mindset eschews the pursuit of monumental price shifts and embraces the pursuit of precision. A Microtrader doesn't merely engage in trades; they navigate the market with a scalpel-like approach, extracting value from even the subtlest market movements. Patience, discipline, and the ability to swiftly execute trades define the Microtrader's mental landscape. Each micro trade is a calculated step toward consistent gains, fostering a mindset that prizes meticulous planning over impulsive actions.

Shifting Perspectives on Risk and Reward: Microtrading introduces a nuanced perspective on risk and reward. Traditional trading often involves extended exposure to market shifts, potentially leading to substantial losses. Microtrading, however, mitigates this risk by embracing swift entries and exits. The focus isn't on monumental profits but on cultivating a series of small gains. By limiting the exposure to individual trades and diversifying across multiple micro trades, Microtraders manage risk with greater precision. This risk-reward equilibrium fosters a trading approach that is not only sustainable but also resilient in the face of market volatility.

The Impact of Technology on Microtrading: Modern trading platforms and technological innovations have laid the foundation for the rise of Microtrading. Speed, accessibility, and real-time data are pivotal in executing the swift trades that Microtrading demands. Advanced trading platforms offer features tailored for Microtraders, enabling them to instantaneously execute orders, access comprehensive market data, and deploy automation tools. Algorithms sift through vast volumes of data to identify micro-opportunities, granting Microtraders a technological edge in an arena where every second counts.

Conclusion: Chapter 1 has unveiled the essence of Microtrading, highlighting its departure from traditional trading paradigms and its focus on executing numerous small-scale trades. The Microtrader's mindset, the recalibration of risk and reward, and the symbiotic relationship between technology and Microtrading have been illuminated. As you proceed through the subsequent chapters, delve deeper into the strategies, techniques, and nuances that define Microtrading excellence. By embracing the essence of Microtrading, you're embarking on a journey that capitalizes on the power of precision and opens doors to a world of micro gains with macro impact.

Chapter 2: Building a Solid Foundation

In the dynamic realm of Microtrading, success hinges on a solid foundation built upon market knowledge, analytical prowess, and a comprehensive understanding of trading fundamentals. This chapter serves as the cornerstone for your Microtrading journey, emphasizing the importance of acquiring a robust foundation to navigate the intricacies of micro trades with confidence and finesse.

Embracing Market Fundamentals: Before embarking on your Microtrading expedition, it's imperative to grasp the foundational elements that drive financial markets. Understanding market structure, the interplay of supply and demand, and the factors influencing price movements lays the groundwork for successful Microtrading. A Microtrader's ability to interpret market dynamics is paramount in identifying micro-opportunities and executing trades with precision.

Technical and Fundamental Analysis for Microtraders: Technical and fundamental analyses are pillars upon which Microtrading strategies are constructed. Technical analysis involves deciphering price charts, identifying trends, and recognizing patterns that signal potential micro movements. Fundamental analysis, while traditionally applied to longer-term trades, adapts to the micro context by evaluating economic data, news releases, and geopolitical events with micro impact. Mastery of both analyses empowers Microtraders to make informed decisions in real time.

Key Indicators for Microtraders: Microtraders rely on a set of key indicators specifically tailored for their strategy. Moving averages, RSI (Relative Strength Index), MACD (Moving Average Convergence Divergence), and Bollinger Bands are examples of indicators that illuminate micro trends and price volatility. Understanding how these indicators apply to micro trades enhances your ability to gauge market sentiment, identify entry and exit points, and execute trades that align with your trading strategy.

The Art of Timing: Microtrading thrives on timing. The ability to execute trades swiftly, capitalize on micro price movements, and secure gains before they evaporate is a hallmark of Microtrading proficiency. Fine-tuning your timing skills involves understanding order execution processes, leveraging trading platforms optimized for rapid trades, and adapting to the pace of the market. As you delve deeper into this chapter, you'll uncover strategies that hone your timing precision and equip you for micro success.

Conclusion: Chapter 2 has laid the foundation for your Microtrading journey, emphasizing the significance of understanding market fundamentals, mastering technical and fundamental analyses, and embracing key indicators. The art of timing, integral to Microtrading, has also been explored, preparing you to navigate the swift currents of micro trades with accuracy. As you proceed to the subsequent chapters, armed with this robust foundation, you'll delve deeper into strategies, techniques, and insights that position you to capitalize on micro-opportunities and cultivate consistent gains in the realm of Microtrading.

Chapter 3: Tools of the Microtrader's Trade

In the fast-paced world of Microtrading, having the right tools at your disposal can make all the difference between success and missed opportunities. This chapter delves into the array of tools designed specifically for Microtraders, ranging from advanced trading platforms to specialized order types and the integration of automation and algorithms.

Advanced Trading Platforms for Microtrading: Modern trading platforms have evolved to cater to the needs of Microtraders. These platforms offer features such as real-time data feeds, customizable charting tools, and lightning-fast order execution. With the ability to create watchlists, set alerts, and execute trades in milliseconds, Microtraders can seize micro-opportunities with unprecedented precision. As you navigate the world of Microtrading, familiarize yourself with the functionalities of these platforms to streamline your trading process.

Leveraging Advanced Order Types: Microtrading thrives on swift execution and well-timed entries and exits. Advanced order types enhance your ability to navigate this rapid pace. Limit orders, stop orders, and market orders are tailored to Microtraders, enabling them to set specific price points for execution and minimize slippage. These orders provide greater control over your trades and enhance your ability to respond swiftly to micro price movements.

Automation and Algorithms in Microtrading: The integration of automation and algorithms marks a significant evolution in Microtrading. Algorithmic trading strategies are designed to identify micro-opportunities, execute trades with minimal human intervention, and optimize trade execution for enhanced efficiency. By harnessing the power of automation, Microtraders can maintain a presence in the markets around the clock, capitalizing on micro movements even in the absence of manual input.

Risk Management Through Technology: Risk management is a cornerstone of Microtrading, and technology plays a vital role in its execution. Many trading platforms offer risk management tools that allow you to set maximum loss thresholds, trailing stops, and position sizing parameters. These tools empower Microtraders to manage risk proactively, ensuring that each micro trade is aligned with their risk tolerance and overall trading strategy.

Conclusion: Chapter 3 has unveiled the tools that form the arsenal of the Microtrader. Advanced trading platforms, specialized order types, automation, and algorithms are integral to the Microtrading toolkit. As you venture deeper into the world of Microtrading, these tools will become your allies in executing swift and precise trades that capitalize on micro movements. The subsequent chapters will build upon this foundation, guiding you through the strategic deployment of these tools and their integration into a comprehensive Microtrading approach.

Chapter 4: Risk Management Strategies

In the realm of Microtrading, where the pace is swift and opportunities abound, effective risk management strategies are paramount to safeguarding your capital and ensuring consistent success. This chapter delves into the intricacies of risk management in Microtrading, offering a comprehensive toolkit to protect your investments while capitalizing on micro-opportunities.

Understanding Risk in Microtrading: Microtrading, while offering potential gains, also carries inherent risks. The rapid pace of trades can amplify losses if not managed with precision. Recognizing and quantifying risk in each micro trade is a fundamental step toward maintaining a sustainable trading approach. Through techniques like position sizing and risk-reward ratios, you'll gain the ability to control potential losses while optimizing your potential gains.

Setting Stop-Loss Orders for Micro Trades: Stop-loss orders are a Microtrader's best defense against adverse price movements. By establishing predefined price levels at which a trade will be automatically exited, you minimize the impact of unfavorable price shifts. In the context of micro trades, setting stop-loss orders is particularly crucial due to the swift nature of market movements. Through careful analysis and consideration, you'll learn how to strategically place stop-loss orders to protect your capital.

Risk-to-Reward Ratios: Balancing Potential and Peril: Balancing risk and reward is an art Microtraders must master. Risk-to-reward ratios provide a structured approach to this balancing act. By evaluating the potential profit against the potential loss in each trade, you ensure that your trades align with your risk tolerance and overall strategy. This mathematical framework aids in making informed decisions that enhance the probability of consistent gains over time.

Diversification in Microtrading: Maximizing Potential, Minimizing Risk: Diversification, a time-tested strategy, is equally relevant in Microtrading. Spreading your capital across a range of micro trades reduces the impact of a single loss on your overall portfolio. While each micro trade may carry individual risk, diversification serves as a buffer, ensuring that losses in one trade can be offset by gains in others. By thoughtfully diversifying your micro trades, you create a safety net against undue risk.

Psychological Resilience: A Pillar of Risk Management: Effective risk management extends beyond numbers; it encompasses psychological resilience. The pace of Microtrading can be mentally demanding, requiring discipline, emotional control, and the ability to manage stress. By nurturing psychological resilience, you cultivate a mindset that remains steady in the face of wins and losses alike. Techniques such as mindfulness, meditation, and maintaining a trading journal can enhance your emotional well-being and, consequently, your risk management abilities.

Conclusion: Chapter 4 has illuminated the critical role of risk management in the Microtrading landscape. Understanding risk, setting stop-loss orders, evaluating risk-to-reward ratios, diversification, and psychological resilience are pivotal components of effective risk management. As you proceed through your Microtrading journey, the tools and insights acquired in this chapter will serve as a shield, enabling you to confidently navigate the swift waters of micro trades while protecting your capital and nurturing consistent gains.

Chapter 5: Microscopic Price Movements

In the intricate world of Microtrading, the ability to discern and capitalize on even the smallest price movements is a hallmark of success. This chapter delves into the nuanced realm of microscopic price movements, exploring their significance, patterns, and strategies that allow Microtraders to extract value from these seemingly minute fluctuations.

The Power of Micro Price Movements: Microtrading hinges on the premise that value exists even in the tiniest price shifts. While traditional trading might overlook these micro movements, Microtraders recognize their potential to yield consistent gains. By executing swift trades that align with micro trends, you harness the power of compounding, capitalizing on numerous small wins that accumulate over time.

Identifying Micro Trends: Understanding micro trends is a cornerstone of Microtrading success. This involves analyzing price charts, recognizing patterns, and deciphering the cyclical nature of micro movements. Whether it's micro-oscillations, ascending/descending triangles, or flags, each pattern offers insights into potential price shifts. Through meticulous chart analysis, you'll learn to spot micro trends and align your trades with their trajectory.

Capitalizing on Micro Reversals: Microtraders keenly focus on micro reversals – swift price shifts that counter the prevailing trend. These micro reversals, often driven by market sentiment or brief fluctuations, present unique opportunities for Microtraders to execute swift trades in the opposite direction. By mastering the art of identifying and reacting to micro reversals, you position yourself to capture gains in rapidly changing market conditions.

Leveraging Patterns and Indicators for Micro Moves: Technical patterns and indicators, traditionally used for longer-term trades, adapt seamlessly to Microtrading. Patterns like head and shoulders, double tops/bottoms, and indicators such as moving averages and stochastic oscillators can be tailored to micro timeframes. By integrating these tools into your Microtrading strategy, you amplify your ability to identify entry and exit points for swift and precise trades.

Conclusion: Chapter 5 has delved into the intricacies of microscopic price movements, shedding light on their inherent potential and the strategies to capitalize on them. By recognizing micro trends, leveraging patterns and indicators, and seizing micro reversals, you unlock the ability to extract value from the most subtle shifts in the market. As you proceed through your Microtrading journey, the insights from this chapter will enable you to navigate the microcosm of price fluctuations with precision, enhancing your ability to cultivate consistent gains.

Chapter 6: Scalping Techniques for Microtraders

Scalping, a technique that involves profiting from rapid price movements, is a cornerstone of Microtrading. This chapter delves into the world of scalping within the context of Microtrading, exploring the strategies, mindset, and tools that empower Microtraders to capitalize on swift price fluctuations.

The Essence of Scalping in Microtrading: Scalping is synonymous with swift execution and rapid profit-taking. In the realm of Microtrading, it becomes an art form that aligns perfectly with the strategy's focus on micro movements. Microtraders who embrace scalping seek to extract value from even the shortest price shifts, executing trades within minutes or even seconds. This approach demands discipline, precision, and a keen understanding of market dynamics.

Scalping vs. Traditional Trading: A Comparative Outlook: Comparing scalping to traditional trading highlights its unique attributes. While traditional traders might hold positions for hours or days, Microtraders employing scalping techniques are in and out of trades in a matter of minutes. Scalping capitalizes on micro volatility and leverages quick entries and exits to secure gains. This chapter will explore the nuances of scalping and illustrate how it integrates seamlessly into the Microtrading landscape.

The Scalping Mindset: Speed, Precision, and Adaptability: Successful scalping in Microtrading is underpinned by a distinct mindset. Speed and precision are paramount, as is the ability to adapt to rapidly changing market conditions. A scalper must possess the discipline to stick to a well-defined strategy while navigating the intense pace of micro trades. This chapter will delve into the intricacies of cultivating the scalping mindset, an essential component of Microtrading success.

Scalping Strategies for Micro Gains: Scalping strategies are as diverse as the micro movements they aim to capture. From quick trend-following trades to countertrend scalping, each strategy requires a nuanced approach. The use of short-term indicators, understanding candlestick patterns, and monitoring order book dynamics are key aspects of effective scalping techniques. This chapter will introduce you to various scalping strategies tailored for Microtrading.

Conclusion: Chapter 6 has illuminated the world of scalping within the realm of Microtrading, showcasing its alignment with rapid price movements and micro strategies. The essence of scalping, the comparative outlook versus traditional trading, the scalping mindset, and an introduction to various scalping strategies have been explored. As you proceed with your Microtrading journey, these insights will guide you in mastering the art of scalping within the microcosmic landscape, enabling you to capitalize on swift price movements and cultivate consistent gains.

Chapter 7: Harnessing Volatility for Micro Gains

Volatility, often viewed as a double-edged sword, presents unique opportunities for Microtraders. This chapter delves into the art of harnessing volatility within the context of Microtrading, exploring strategies that enable Microtraders to profit from price fluctuations in rapidly changing market conditions.

Understanding Volatility's Role in Microtrading: Volatility, the measure of price variability, is an inherent characteristic of financial markets. In Microtrading, volatility is not a deterrent but a canvas upon which opportunities are painted. Microtraders leverage volatility to capitalize on swift price movements, whether they're driven by sudden news releases, market sentiment shifts, or other factors. By understanding volatility's role, you position yourself to navigate its ebbs and flows with precision.

Capitalizing on Volatile Market Events: Volatile market events, such as earnings reports, economic data releases, and geopolitical developments, are fertile grounds for Microtraders seeking rapid gains. The chapter explores strategies that allow Microtraders to capitalize on the brief spikes in volatility triggered by these events. By identifying market-moving catalysts and executing well-timed trades, you harness volatility to your advantage.

Strategies for Calm and Chaotic Markets: Effective Microtrading in volatile markets requires adaptive strategies. In calm markets, Microtraders might employ range-bound strategies that capitalize on micro-oscillations. In contrast, during high volatility, breakout and momentum strategies gain prominence. Understanding when to apply each strategy enables you to tailor your approach to the prevailing market conditions and optimize your potential gains.

Risk Management Amidst Volatility: Harnessing volatility requires a nuanced approach to risk management. While volatile markets offer lucrative opportunities, they also entail higher risk. Employing techniques like widening stop-loss orders, adjusting position sizes, and reducing exposure during extreme volatility are essential to safeguarding your capital while participating in the dynamic world of volatile Microtrading.

Conclusion: Chapter 7 has explored the intricacies of harnessing volatility within the context of Microtrading, shedding light on its role, strategies, and risk management considerations. As you continue your Microtrading journey, the insights from this chapter will empower you to navigate volatile market conditions with finesse, leveraging price fluctuations to secure micro gains while managing risk effectively. By mastering the art of volatility, you expand your toolkit and unlock a world of micro-opportunities.

Chapter 8: Adaptive Techniques for Changing Market Conditions

In the ever-evolving landscape of financial markets, adaptability is a prized trait. This chapter delves into adaptive techniques within the context of Microtrading, exploring strategies that empower Microtraders to navigate changing market conditions with precision and poise.

The Dynamic Nature of Markets: Financial markets are characterized by constant change. Market sentiment, economic data, geopolitical events, and technological advancements contribute to a fluid environment where conditions can shift rapidly. Microtraders must possess the ability to adapt their strategies to these changing dynamics, ensuring that their approach remains effective and aligned with the prevailing market conditions.

Pivoting Strategies for Different Market Phases: Market phases, such as trending, ranging, and consolidating, require different approaches to trading. In trending markets, trend-following strategies might be most effective, while ranging markets demand range-bound techniques. By identifying the current market phase and pivoting your strategy accordingly, you optimize your potential gains while minimizing exposure to unnecessary risk.

The Role of News and Data in Adaptive Microtrading: News releases and economic data can significantly impact market sentiment and direction. Adaptive Microtraders stay attuned to these events and adjust their strategies accordingly. This chapter will explore how to incorporate news analysis into your Microtrading routine, enabling you to harness opportunities arising from sudden shifts in market sentiment.

Using Multiple Timeframes for Enhanced Precision: The use of multiple timeframes is a hallmark of adaptive Microtrading. While micro trends are crucial, they exist within the context of larger trends. Analyzing multiple timeframes provides a comprehensive view of market dynamics, allowing you to identify micro-opportunities that align with the broader trend. By integrating multiple timeframes into your analysis, you enhance your ability to navigate changing market conditions.

Conclusion: Chapter 8 has delved into adaptive techniques for navigating changing market conditions within the Microtrading landscape. The dynamic nature of markets, strategies for different market phases, incorporating news and data, and utilizing multiple timeframes have been explored. Armed with these insights, you're equipped to adapt and thrive in the face of evolving market dynamics, ensuring that your Microtrading approach remains effective and agile. As you progress through your Microtrading journey, the ability to adapt will be a cornerstone of your success.

Chapter 9: Integrating Fundamental Analysis into Microtrading

While Microtrading is often associated with technical analysis, the integration of fundamental analysis can offer a holistic perspective. This chapter explores the role of fundamental analysis within the Microtrading landscape, highlighting how economic indicators, news events, and global trends can enhance your micro trading strategy.

Understanding Fundamental Analysis in Microtrading: Fundamental analysis traditionally focuses on assessing the intrinsic value of assets based on economic factors, company performance, and broader market trends. In the realm of Microtrading, fundamental analysis takes on a nuanced role, as its impact is often more immediate and pronounced within shorter timeframes. By considering economic indicators, interest rates, geopolitical developments, and news events, you expand your perspective and make informed micro trading decisions.

Economic Indicators: Unveiling Micro Opportunities: Economic indicators, such as unemployment rates, GDP growth, and consumer sentiment, hold immense sway over market sentiment. In Microtrading, understanding how these indicators influence short-term price movements is invaluable. By aligning your trades with the release of key economic data, you capitalize on micro-opportunities that arise from sudden shifts in market sentiment.

News Trading in Microtrading: News trading involves capitalizing on the immediate market impact of breaking news and events. Within the Microtrading context, news trading takes on greater significance due to the rapid execution required. By analyzing news releases, earnings reports, and geopolitical events, and gauging their potential impact on micro price movements, you position yourself to execute swift and well-timed trades.

Macro Factors and Micro Strategy: Macro trends, such as global economic shifts and geopolitical developments, can exert a substantial influence on micro price movements. By understanding the interplay between macro factors and micro strategies, you gain insights into the broader context that shapes the microcosmic landscape. This chapter will explore how to integrate macro perspectives into your micro trading decisions.

Conclusion: Chapter 9 has unveiled the integration of fundamental analysis into the Microtrading landscape, showcasing how economic indicators, news events, and macro factors can enhance your micro trading strategy. As you navigate the intricacies of Microtrading, the insights from this chapter will enable you to approach the market with a holistic view, considering both technical and fundamental aspects to make informed decisions and capture micro-opportunities with precision.

Chapter 10: The Psychology of Microtrading

In the fast-paced world of Microtrading, mastering your psychology is as essential as mastering trading strategies. This chapter delves into the psychology of Microtrading, exploring the emotions, discipline, and mental resilience required to navigate micro trades with clarity and confidence.

The Emotional Landscape of Microtrading: Microtrading's rapid pace can evoke a range of emotions, from euphoria to frustration. Emotional reactions can cloud judgment and lead to impulsive decisions. This chapter delves into the emotions commonly experienced in Microtrading and offers techniques to manage them. Cultivating emotional intelligence is pivotal in making rational decisions that align with your strategy.

Maintaining Discipline in Microtrading: Discipline is the bedrock of Microtrading success. The ability to adhere to your trading plan, execute trades with precision, and avoid impulsive deviations is integral to consistent gains. This chapter explores techniques for building and maintaining discipline, such as setting clear rules, establishing trading routines, and learning to detach emotionally from individual trades.

Staying Focused Amidst Micro Flurries: Microtrading demands intense focus and concentration. Swift execution, monitoring multiple trades simultaneously, and processing information rapidly require a heightened level of attention. Techniques like mindfulness meditation and mental rehearsal can enhance your ability to maintain focus during micro trading sessions, enabling you to capitalize on opportunities without succumbing to distractions.

Overcoming Psychological Biases in Microtrading: Psychological biases, inherent in all traders, can distort decision-making. Anchoring, overconfidence, and loss aversion are examples of biases that can impact Microtraders. By recognizing these biases and implementing cognitive strategies, you empower yourself to make more objective and informed micro trading decisions.

Conclusion: Chapter 10 has explored the psychology of Microtrading, highlighting the emotional landscape, the importance of discipline, techniques for staying focused, and strategies to overcome psychological biases. As you navigate the world of Microtrading, the insights from this chapter will serve as a guide to cultivate a resilient mindset that empowers you to navigate micro trades with clarity, confidence, and emotional equilibrium. By mastering your psychology, you enhance your ability to capitalize on micro-opportunities and nurture consistent gains

Chapter 11: The Role of Ethics and Integrity in Microtrading

Ethics and integrity are essential pillars of any trading strategy, including Microtrading. This chapter delves into the significance of ethical conduct within the Microtrading landscape, emphasizing the importance of transparency, honesty, and responsible trading practices.

The Ethical Landscape of Microtrading: Microtrading, like any form of trading, operates within a broader ethical framework. Ethical considerations include transparency in trade execution, avoiding market manipulation, and adhering to regulations. This chapter explores how ethical conduct fosters trust and credibility, not only benefiting your own trading journey but also contributing to the integrity of the trading community as a whole.

Transparency in Microtrading: Transparency is a cornerstone of ethical Microtrading. Disclosing trade execution methods, using clear and honest communication, and providing accurate information to fellow traders and clients are vital practices. This chapter will explore how transparency enhances trust and reinforces your reputation as an ethical Microtrader.

Responsible Trading Practices: Responsible trading involves recognizing the impact of your actions on the markets and other participants. Overtrading, aggressive risk-taking, and excessive leveraging can undermine ethical trading practices. This chapter will guide you in adopting responsible trading practices that prioritize the long-term sustainability of your Microtrading journey.

Adherence to Regulations and Laws: Regulations are in place to ensure fairness, transparency, and market stability. Adhering to legal and regulatory requirements is not only an ethical obligation but also a legal one. This chapter will explore the importance of staying informed about relevant regulations and how compliance contributes to maintaining the integrity of Microtrading.

Conclusion: Chapter 11 has emphasized the vital role of ethics and integrity within the Microtrading landscape. Transparency, responsible trading practices, and adherence to regulations are integral aspects of ethical conduct that contribute to your success as a Microtrader. As you continue your Microtrading journey, the insights from this chapter will guide you in upholding the highest standards of ethical behavior, fostering trust, and contributing to the positive reputation of Microtraders worldwide.

Chapter 12: Microtrading Strategies for Various Market Conditions

Effective Microtrading requires a diverse toolkit of strategies tailored to different market conditions. This chapter explores a range of strategies that Microtraders can employ to navigate various scenarios, ensuring adaptability and consistent gains.

Trending Market Strategies: In trending markets, where prices exhibit sustained upward or downward movement, trend-following strategies thrive. Microtraders can identify micro trends within the larger trend, executing trades that align with the prevailing direction. This chapter will delve into techniques such as moving average crossovers, trendline analysis, and momentum indicators for successful micro trades in trending markets.

Ranging Market Strategies: In ranging markets, characterized by price movements within a confined range, Microtraders shift their focus to range-bound strategies. Strategies such as support and resistance trading, oscillators, and Bollinger Bands are tailored to capitalize on micro-oscillations within the established range. This chapter will explore how to navigate ranging market conditions for micro gains.

Breakout Strategies: Breakout strategies excel when prices break through established support or resistance levels, signaling potential trends. Microtraders can adapt these strategies to micro timeframes, capitalizing on swift breakouts and capitalizing on micro trends that follow. This chapter will unveil the nuances of breakout strategies and their integration into the Microtrading context.

Countertrend Strategies: Countertrend strategies involve trading against the prevailing trend, aiming to capture short-term price reversals. Microtraders can deploy these strategies to capitalize on micro reversals within larger trends. This chapter will explore techniques such as RSI divergences, candlestick patterns, and Fibonacci retracements for effective countertrend micro trading.

Conclusion: Chapter 12 has explored a range of Microtrading strategies tailored to various market conditions. Whether trending, ranging, breakout, or countertrend scenarios, these strategies enable Microtraders to adapt to changing dynamics and extract value from micro movements. As you progress through your Microtrading journey, the insights from this chapter will empower you to strategically deploy the appropriate strategy for prevailing market conditions, enhancing your ability to cultivate consistent gains.

Chapter 13: Building a Microtrading Routine

A well-structured routine is the backbone of successful Microtrading. This chapter delves into the elements of building an effective Microtrading routine, including preparation, execution, review, and self-care, to optimize your trading performance and foster long-term success.

Preparation: The Foundation of a Successful Routine: Effective Microtrading begins with thorough preparation. This involves analyzing market trends, reviewing economic calendars for potential news events, and identifying micro opportunities. By dedicating time to research and analysis, you position yourself to make informed decisions during trading sessions.

Creating a Trading Plan: Guidelines for Execution: A trading plan acts as a blueprint for your Microtrading activities. It outlines your strategies, risk management techniques, and entry/exit criteria. This chapter will guide you in creating a comprehensive trading plan that provides structure and clarity to your trading activities.

Executing Trades with Precision: During trading sessions, execution is key. Swiftly placing orders, adhering to your trading plan, and managing multiple trades require focus and discipline. Techniques such as utilizing trading platforms' advanced features, setting alerts, and maintaining a trading journal contribute to effective trade execution.

Review and Analysis: Learning from Each Trade: Post-trading analysis is an integral component of your Microtrading routine. By reviewing your trades, identifying strengths and weaknesses, and assessing how well you adhered to your trading plan, you continuously refine your approach. This chapter explores techniques for constructive self-assessment and continuous improvement.

Incorporating Self-Care: Nurturing the Trader's Well-being: Microtrading demands mental and emotional resilience. Incorporating self-care practices, such as exercise, healthy nutrition, and stress management, supports your overall well-being. This chapter emphasizes the importance of nurturing your mental and physical health to enhance your trading performance.

Conclusion: Chapter 13 has unveiled the process of building a well-structured Microtrading routine, from preparation and execution to review and self-care. By following these steps, you establish a framework that optimizes your trading performance, enhances decision-making, and fosters long-term success in the world of Microtrading. As you proceed on your journey, the insights from this chapter will guide you in creating a routine that aligns with your goals and ensures consistency and discipline in your Microtrading endeavor

Chapter 14: Risk Management in Depth

Effective risk management is a cornerstone of Microtrading success. This chapter delves deeper into the intricacies of risk management, exploring advanced techniques and considerations that empower Microtraders to safeguard their capital and navigate the dynamic micro trading landscape with precision.

Advanced Position Sizing Strategies: Position sizing goes beyond basic risk calculation. This chapter explores advanced position sizing techniques, such as the Kelly Criterion and the Fixed Fractional Method, which dynamically adjust position sizes based on evolving account balances and market conditions. These techniques enhance your risk management capabilities and optimize your capital allocation.

Correlation and Portfolio Diversification: Portfolio diversification is extended to the micro level by assessing the correlation between your micro trades. By understanding how your trades interact and ensuring they are not overly correlated, you reduce the risk of simultaneous losses. This chapter will guide you in incorporating correlation analysis into your risk management strategy.

Stress Testing and Scenario Analysis: Stress testing involves simulating extreme market conditions to assess the impact on your portfolio. Scenario analysis evaluates the potential outcomes of various market scenarios. Both techniques empower you to anticipate and prepare for adverse conditions, enhancing your ability to manage risk effectively.

Adjusting Risk Management for Volatile Markets: Volatility introduces unique challenges to risk management. During periods of high volatility, adjusting position sizes, widening stop-loss orders, and reducing exposure become crucial techniques. This chapter will explore how to modify your risk management strategies to accommodate the heightened uncertainty of volatile micro trading environments.

Conclusion: Chapter 14 has delved deeper into risk management techniques tailored for the Microtrading landscape. Advanced position sizing strategies, portfolio diversification, stress testing, and adjustments for volatile markets have been explored. Armed with these insights, you're equipped to take your risk management to a higher level, ensuring that your Microtrading endeavors are grounded in prudent risk mitigation while capitalizing on micro opportunities. As you continue your Microtrading journey, these advanced risk management techniques will contribute to your overall success and sustainability.

Chapter 15: Real-Time Analysis and Decision-Making

Microtrading demands the ability to make split-second decisions based on real-time data. This chapter delves into the art of real-time analysis and decision-making, providing insights into how Microtraders can process information rapidly and execute trades with precision.

The Need for Swift Decision-Making: Microtrading operates at a rapid pace, necessitating quick analysis and decision-making. Understanding market sentiment, interpreting indicators, and identifying micro-opportunities in real time are essential skills for Microtraders. This chapter explores techniques to enhance your decision-making speed without sacrificing accuracy.

Real-Time Chart Analysis: Patterns and Trends in the Moment: Real-time chart analysis involves identifying patterns and trends as they unfold. This requires proficiency in recognizing micro trends, candlestick patterns, and key support and resistance levels in the midst of rapid price movements. By mastering real-time chart analysis, you gain a competitive edge in capturing micro-opportunities.

Utilizing Instantaneous News and Data: News and economic data can have an immediate impact on micro price movements. Incorporating news feeds and economic calendars into your trading platform enables you to react swiftly to market-moving events. This chapter will guide you in effectively integrating instantaneous news and data into your real-time analysis.

The Role of Intuition and Gut Feel: Intuition, honed through experience and market observation, plays a role in Microtrading decision-making. While data-driven analysis is paramount, trusting your intuition can provide valuable insights. This chapter explores how to balance data-driven decisions with intuitive judgments in the dynamic micro trading environment.

Conclusion: Chapter 15 has unveiled the world of real-time analysis and decision-making within the Microtrading landscape. Swift decision-making, real-time chart analysis, utilizing instantaneous news, and the role of intuition have been explored. As you proceed on your Microtrading journey, the insights from this chapter will empower you to navigate the rapid pace of micro trades with clarity, confidence, and the ability to capitalize on opportunities in the moment.

Chapter 16: Continuous Learning and Evolution

The world of Microtrading is ever-evolving, demanding a commitment to continuous learning and adaptation. This chapter explores the importance of ongoing education, the role of feedback, and strategies for evolving your Microtrading approach to remain at the forefront of this dynamic field.

The Imperative of Continuous Learning: Market trends, strategies, and technologies evolve rapidly. Continuous learning ensures that your Microtrading knowledge remains current and relevant. This chapter emphasizes the significance of staying informed about new developments and integrating new insights into your trading approach.

Feedback as a Catalyst for Improvement: Feedback, whether from your own post-trading analysis or mentorship, is invaluable in identifying areas for improvement. Constructive feedback can shed light on blind spots, refine your strategies, and enhance your overall trading performance. This chapter explores how to seek and utilize feedback to drive growth.

Adapting to Technological Advancements: Technological advancements continually reshape the trading landscape. Embracing new trading platforms, analytical tools, and automation technologies can amplify your Microtrading capabilities. This chapter will guide you in staying abreast of technological trends and incorporating them into your Microtrading toolkit.

Evolving Strategies in Changing Markets: As markets shift, your strategies should evolve accordingly. Whether due to regulatory changes, shifts in market sentiment, or the emergence of new trends, adapting your approach is essential. This chapter explores how to recognize when your strategies need adjustment and how to pivot effectively.

Conclusion: Chapter 16 has emphasized the importance of continuous learning and evolution within the Microtrading landscape. Ongoing education, feedback, adapting to technological advancements, and evolving strategies are essential components of remaining competitive and successful in the ever-changing world of Microtrading. As you progress on your journey, the insights from this chapter will guide you in cultivating a mindset of growth and adaptability, ensuring that your Microtrading approach remains effective and responsive to the evolving market dynamics.

Chapter 17: Building a Resilient Mindset

Microtrading's fast-paced nature requires a resilient mindset to navigate both wins and losses. This chapter delves into the art of building mental resilience, exploring techniques that enable Microtraders to maintain focus, discipline, and emotional equilibrium in the face of challenges.

Cultivating Emotional Control: Emotions can influence trading decisions. Developing emotional control involves acknowledging emotions without letting them drive your actions. This chapter explores techniques such as mindfulness, meditation, and emotional awareness to cultivate a balanced emotional state during Microtrading.

Staying Disciplined Amidst Uncertainty: Discipline is a cornerstone of Microtrading success. A resilient Microtrader remains disciplined even in the face of uncertainty and adverse outcomes. This chapter will guide you in building the discipline to stick to your trading plan, execute trades with precision, and avoid impulsive decisions.

Managing Stress and Pressure: Microtrading can be intense, with rapid decision-making and market fluctuations. Effective stress management techniques, such as deep breathing, visualization, and time management, enable you to maintain clarity and focus in high-pressure situations. This chapter explores strategies to manage stress and pressure effectively.

Developing a Growth Mindset: A growth mindset views challenges as opportunities for growth rather than setbacks. Adopting a growth mindset enhances your ability to learn from mistakes, adapt to changing conditions, and persist in the face of challenges. This chapter delves into techniques for fostering a growth-oriented perspective.

Conclusion: Chapter 17 has delved into the art of building a resilient mindset within the Microtrading landscape. Cultivating emotional control, maintaining discipline, managing stress, and adopting a growth mindset are integral aspects of building mental resilience. As you proceed on your Microtrading journey, the insights from this chapter will empower you to navigate the highs and lows of Microtrading with clarity, composure, and the ability to bounce back from challenges.

Chapter 18: The Path Forward: Mastery and Consistency

As you approach the culmination of your journey in Microtrading, this final chapter serves as a guide to achieving mastery and consistency in your micro trading endeavors. Drawing from the insights and techniques explored throughout this book, this chapter offers a roadmap for continued growth and success.

Synthesizing Your Microtrading Knowledge: By now, you've delved deep into the intricacies of Microtrading – from strategies and risk management to psychology and adaptability. This chapter encourages you to synthesize this knowledge into a holistic approach that aligns with your trading style, risk tolerance, and financial goals.

Committing to Continuous Improvement: Mastery is a journey, not a destination. Embracing a commitment to continuous improvement ensures that you stay ahead of market trends, refine your strategies, and adapt to changing conditions. This chapter explores how to maintain the momentum of growth through ongoing education and self-assessment.

Cultivating Consistency Through Discipline: Consistency is a hallmark of successful Microtraders. By adhering to your trading plan, executing trades with precision, and managing risk effectively, you lay the foundation for consistent gains. This chapter will guide you in building and maintaining the discipline required for sustained success.

Embracing the Long-Term Perspective: Microtrading success is not solely measured by individual trades but by your overall progress over time. Embracing a long-term perspective allows you to ride out the inevitable ups and downs, focusing on cumulative gains rather than short-term fluctuations. This chapter encourages you to cultivate patience and perseverance.

Embarking on Your Microtrading Journey: As you conclude this book, you stand at the precipice of a thrilling and rewarding journey in Microtrading. The insights, strategies, and techniques presented in each chapter equip you with the tools to navigate the dynamic micro trading landscape with skill and confidence. Your path forward involves continual learning, persistent practice, and the unwavering commitment to master the art of Microtrading and achieve consistent gains.

Final Thoughts: This book has provided you with a comprehensive exploration of Microtrading, from its strategies and risk management to its psychology and ethics. As you embark on your Microtrading journey, remember that success is a product of both knowledge and application. By integrating the principles and techniques discussed in these chapters, you position yourself for a rewarding and prosperous Microtrading career. Best of luck in your Microtrading endeavors, and may your journey be characterized by mastery, consistency, and enduring success.

Conclusion:

In this comprehensive guide, we've delved deep into the world of Microtrading, uncovering its intricacies, strategies, and nuances. From the foundational concepts to the advanced techniques, each chapter has contributed to your understanding of how to navigate the dynamic micro trading landscape with precision and skill.

Microtrading is not just about making quick trades; it's about mastering the art of capturing micro-opportunities, managing risk, maintaining discipline, and fostering a resilient mindset. Throughout this journey, you've gained insights into technical and fundamental analysis, risk management, real-time decision-making, and the psychological aspects of trading.

As you step forward into the world of Microtrading, remember that success is a continuous process. It's about the dedication to ongoing learning, the commitment to adaptability, and the persistence to cultivate a mindset of growth. By incorporating the strategies and techniques discussed in this guide, you're well-equipped to embark on a journey that has the potential to yield consistent gains and financial prosperity.

Whether you're a novice trader venturing into the world of Microtrading or an experienced trader seeking to refine your approach, the principles and knowledge shared in this guide are designed to support your growth and success. May your Microtrading journey be marked by resilience, discipline, continuous improvement, and, above all, the achievement of your trading goals.

Quantitative Trading:

Utilize mathematical models and statistical analysis to drive trading strategies

Introduction

In the intricate realm of financial markets, where precision and foresight are paramount, the practice of quantitative trading emerges as a formidable approach. At its core, quantitative trading harnesses the power of mathematical models and statistical analysis to unearth patterns, identify trends, and execute trading strategies with unparalleled accuracy. This intricate fusion of data-driven methodologies and financial acumen has revolutionized the landscape of trading, rendering traditional approaches mere relics of a bygone era.

Definition of Quantitative Trading

Quantitative trading, often referred to as algorithmic trading or quant trading, is a systematic approach to the financial markets that hinges on quantitative analysis and mathematical modeling. In stark contrast to discretionary trading, where human intuition guides decision-making, quantitative trading relies on meticulously designed algorithms to dissect and interpret vast volumes of market data. This methodological approach emphasizes objectivity, mitigating the influence of emotions that can plague human traders, and instead relies on empirical evidence and mathematical rigor.

At its core, quantitative trading revolves around formulating trading strategies based on predefined rules and parameters. These rules are informed by historical data analysis, statistical patterns, and complex mathematical models that attempt to capture the underlying dynamics of market behavior. The ultimate goal of quantitative trading is to capitalize on inefficiencies, discrepancies, and trends within the market that might be imperceptible to the human eye.

This book delves into the multifaceted world of quantitative trading, delving deep into the intricate mathematical foundations and statistical underpinnings that empower traders to navigate the complexities of financial markets with unparalleled precision. Through an exploration of algorithmic strategies, risk management techniques, and real-world case studies, we endeavor to equip traders and enthusiasts alike with the tools and insights needed to thrive in an increasingly data-driven trading landscape. As we embark on this journey, let us unravel the intricacies of quantitative trading, a symphony where mathematics orchestrates the harmonious interplay between market dynamics and strategic execution.

Importance of Quantitative Approaches in Modern Trading

In the ever-evolving tapestry of financial markets, the importance of quantitative approaches stands as an indelible testament to the dynamic shift in trading paradigms. The modern trading landscape has undergone a remarkable transformation, catalyzed by the proliferation of technology, the explosion of data availability, and the relentless pursuit of optimizing trading strategies. Within this context, quantitative approaches have emerged as a linchpin, driving trading operations to new echelons of precision, efficiency, and adaptability.

The paramount significance of quantitative approaches can be distilled into several compelling facets:

1. Data-Driven Decision Making: In an era characterized by data abundance, quantitative approaches harness the power of advanced statistical techniques to extract actionable insights from voluminous datasets. These data-driven insights serve as the cornerstone of informed decision-making, allowing traders to identify hidden patterns, correlations, and anomalies that hold the potential to shape profitable strategies. By embracing data as a strategic asset, quantitatively-oriented traders stand at the vanguard of precision trading.

2. Mitigation of Emotional Bias: Human psychology, while invaluable in various aspects of life, can be a double-edged sword in trading. Emotional biases, such as fear, greed, and overconfidence, can exert a significant influence on trading decisions, often leading to suboptimal outcomes.

Quantitative approaches circumvent this vulnerability by relying on systematic rules and algorithms that operate devoid of emotions, thereby enhancing objectivity and consistency in trading strategies.

3. Exploitation of Market Inefficiencies: Financial markets are rife with transient inefficiencies that arise from information disparities, liquidity imbalances, and behavioral biases. Quantitative approaches excel in identifying and exploiting these inefficiencies by leveraging sophisticated models that process real-time data and swiftly execute trades. This agility allows quant traders to seize fleeting opportunities that might elude traditional traders relying on manual analysis.

4. Adaptation to Dynamic Market Conditions: Modern markets are characterized by rapid shifts, driven by macroeconomic events, geopolitical factors, and technological disruptions. Quantitative approaches thrive in this dynamic environment, as they can rapidly recalibrate strategies based on evolving data and market conditions. The ability to adjust and optimize strategies in real-time positions quant traders to navigate tumultuous market landscapes with resilience.

5. Risk Management and Portfolio Diversification: Quantitative trading places a robust emphasis on risk management, a cornerstone of sustainable trading endeavors. By employing quantitative models to assess risk exposure and optimize portfolio allocation, traders can mitigate the potential impact of adverse market movements. This approach bolsters long-term sustainability by safeguarding against catastrophic losses.

In the modern trading arena, quantitative approaches are not just a toolset; they represent a paradigm shift that transcends traditional trading methodologies. As technology continues to advance and data proliferates, the role of quantitative trading will only intensify. This ebook embarks on a comprehensive exploration of how quantitative approaches harness mathematical models and statistical analysis to navigate the complexities of modern financial markets, equipping traders with the knowledge to unlock new dimensions of success.

Overview of Mathematical Models and Statistical Analysis in Trading Strategies

Within the intricate tapestry of financial markets, where uncertainty and volatility reign, the utilization of mathematical models and statistical analysis stands as a beacon of rationality and strategic acumen. At the intersection of quantitative finance and empirical science, these methodologies form the bedrock upon which modern trading strategies are built. This section provides a profound exploration into the symbiotic relationship between mathematical models and statistical analysis, unraveling their profound impact on the art and science of trading.

Mathematical Models in Trading Strategies

The deployment of mathematical models within trading strategies represents a culmination of mathematical rigor and practical application. These models encapsulate the essence of market dynamics, distilling intricate relationships into quantifiable equations that pave the way for strategic decision-making. Key facets of mathematical modeling in trading include:

1. Predictive Models: Predictive models harness historical price and market data to forecast future price movements. Time series analysis, autoregressive integrated moving average (ARIMA) models, and GARCH models are some prominent examples. These models enable traders to anticipate trends and inflection points, facilitating informed entry and exit decisions.

2. Option Pricing Models: In the realm of derivatives, options pricing models, such as the Black-Scholes model, unravel the complex interplay between underlying asset prices, volatility, and time to maturity. These models facilitate the valuation of options and guide option trading strategies.

3. Portfolio Optimization Models: Portfolio optimization is a cornerstone of risk management and asset allocation. Mathematical models, like the mean-variance optimization framework, optimize portfolio allocation based on risk and return objectives. These models aid traders in constructing diversified portfolios that balance risk and reward.

4. Market Microstructure Models: For high-frequency and algorithmic trading, market microstructure models delve into the granular mechanics of order execution, bid-ask spreads, and market impact. These models underpin strategies that capitalize on transient market inefficiencies.

Statistical Analysis in Trading Strategies

The strategic deployment of statistical analysis empowers traders to navigate the labyrinthine maze of market data with acumen and precision. Statistical techniques bring empirical validation to trading hypotheses, enabling data-driven decision-making. Notable aspects of statistical analysis in trading strategies encompass:

1. Hypothesis Testing: Statistical hypothesis testing evaluates the validity of trading strategies by subjecting them to rigorous statistical scrutiny. It allows traders to ascertain whether observed returns are statistically significant or merely the result of random chance.

2. Risk Assessment: Volatility estimation, value-at-risk (VaR) modeling, and stress testing employ statistical techniques to quantify and manage risk exposure. These tools enable traders to gauge potential losses and make informed risk mitigation decisions.

3. Correlation and Cointegration Analysis: Statistical analysis unveils relationships between financial instruments through correlation and cointegration analysis. These insights guide pairs trading and spread strategies, which capitalize on divergences and convergences between related assets.

4. Backtesting and Validation: Statistical backtesting evaluates the historical performance of trading strategies against actual market data. It provides empirical evidence of strategy effectiveness, offering insights into potential future performance.

In the realm of quantitative trading, mathematical models and statistical analysis coalesce to provide a comprehensive framework for strategy development, risk management, and performance evaluation. By melding quantitative methodologies with financial acumen, traders can navigate the capricious currents of the financial markets with enhanced precision and strategic finesse. This ebook embarks on an immersive journey through these intricate methodologies, unraveling the intricacies that drive modern trading strategies to unprecedented heights of success.

Chapter 1: Fundamentals of Quantitative Trading

The foundational cornerstone of the intricate world of quantitative trading unveils itself within the contours of this chapter. As we embark on a comprehensive exploration, the fundamental principles that underpin quantitative trading come into focus, elucidating the essence of this systematic approach and its profound implications for modern trading paradigms. Through a meticulous dissection of its evolution, benefits, challenges, and the symbiotic role of technology, we delve into the very heart of quantitative trading, setting the stage for an in-depth journey into its mathematical and statistical intricacies.

Evolution of Quantitative Trading

The origins of quantitative trading trace back to the mid-20th century, ignited by the pioneering works of economists and mathematicians. This nascent endeavor evolved in tandem with the burgeoning field of computational technology, which provided the computational power needed to process extensive datasets and implement complex algorithms. Over the decades, quantitative trading has metamorphosed from a niche pursuit into a dominant force within financial markets, driven by advancements in mathematical modeling, data analysis techniques, and algorithmic execution.

Benefits and Challenges of Quantitative Approaches

Quantitative approaches bestow an array of benefits upon traders that are deeply rooted in their systematic nature and empirical foundation. These include heightened objectivity, data-driven decision-making, enhanced risk management, and the capacity to exploit fleeting market inefficiencies. However, the pursuit of quantitative trading is not devoid of challenges. The intricate calibration of mathematical models, the ever-present threat of model overfitting, the need for continuous adaptation to changing market conditions, and the potential pitfalls of technological glitches all form a mosaic of challenges that must be deftly navigated.

Role of Technology in Quantitative Trading

Inextricably linked with the evolution of quantitative trading is the pivotal role played by technology. The relentless advancement of computational power, coupled with the proliferation of high-speed data feeds, has propelled quantitative trading into the realm of high-frequency and algorithmic trading. Technological innovation enables traders to implement intricate models in real-time, execute orders with unparalleled speed, and monitor market conditions with minute precision. However, this rapid technological evolution has also necessitated the implementation of robust risk management protocols to mitigate the potential fallout from algorithmic errors and market disruptions.

As we venture deeper into the annals of quantitative trading, the foundational insights garnered within this chapter lay the bedrock upon which the subsequent exploration of mathematical models, statistical analysis, and strategic execution will flourish. With an unwavering commitment to mathematical rigor and empirical validation, quantitative trading emerges not only as a trading strategy but as a transformative paradigm that revolutionizes the way modern financial markets are navigated and understood.

Chapter 2: Mathematical Foundations for Trading Strategies

Within the intricate fabric of quantitative trading, the edifice of mathematical foundations stands as a bedrock, imparting structural integrity to trading strategies. In this chapter, we embark on an immersive exploration of the pivotal mathematical underpinnings that empower traders to navigate the complexities of financial markets with precision and foresight. From the bedrock of probability and statistics to the multifaceted realms of time series analysis and linear algebra, we delve into the tapestry of mathematical tools that illuminate the path toward effective trading strategies.

Understanding Probability and Statistics in Trading

At the heart of quantitative trading lies the seamless fusion of probability theory and statistical analysis. Probability provides the lens through which traders interpret the inherently uncertain nature of market movements. It enables the quantification of risk and reward, forming the basis for informed decision-making. Statistical analysis, on the other hand, serves as the empirical bridge between theoretical concepts and real-world data. Through techniques such as hypothesis testing, regression analysis, and distribution modeling, traders extract actionable insights from historical data, enabling them to identify patterns, assess market conditions, and validate trading strategies.

Time Series Analysis for Market Data

The dynamic nature of financial markets necessitates the application of time series analysis—a robust methodology for analyzing sequential data points collected at discrete time intervals. Time series analysis equips traders with the tools to discern trends, seasonality, and cyclic patterns within market data. Techniques such as moving averages, autoregressive models, and exponential smoothing allow traders to filter noise, uncover underlying trends, and make informed predictions about future price movements. By deciphering the temporal dynamics of market data, traders gain a nuanced understanding of market behavior, enhancing the efficacy of their trading strategies.

Linear Algebra and Matrix Operations in Trading Models

Linear algebra emerges as an indispensable toolkit for constructing and interpreting trading models. Matrices and vectors serve as the language through which relationships between multiple variables are encoded. In the realm of trading, these relationships often manifest in the form of factors influencing asset prices, correlations between assets, and portfolio allocations. Matrix operations, including multiplication, inversion, and eigenvalue decomposition, enable traders to transform data, optimize portfolios, and extract latent factors from market data. Linear algebra empowers the formulation of quantitative models, from risk assessment to factor-based strategies, allowing traders to harness the latent power of multidimensional data.

As we delve into the depths of mathematical foundations within this chapter, the intricate interplay between probability, statistics, time series analysis, and linear algebra unfolds as the cornerstone of quantitative trading. These mathematical tools provide traders with a formidable arsenal to dissect market behavior, unravel hidden patterns, and construct models that transcend the confines of intuition. Through the prism of mathematics, trading strategies acquire a rigorous foundation, positioning traders to navigate the complex currents of financial markets with unrivaled precision and strategic acumen.

Chapter 3: Data Collection and Preprocessing

In the mosaic of quantitative trading, the integrity of data serves as the fundamental substrate upon which trading strategies are meticulously woven. This chapter peels back the layers of data collection and preprocessing, unveiling the meticulous processes that transform raw market data into a canvas of actionable insights. From the diversity of market data types to the imperative of data cleaning, transformation, and integration, and the intricate dance with missing data and outliers, this exploration sheds light on the meticulous artistry required to render data into a potent tool for informed trading decisions.

Types of Market Data and Their Significance

Market data, the lifeblood of quantitative trading, comes in an array of forms, each carrying distinct information and implications. From historical price data and order book snapshots to news sentiment scores and macroeconomic indicators, each data type contributes a unique facet to the mosaic of market understanding. These data types serve as the fuel that powers trading models, enabling traders to discern trends, assess volatility, and identify opportunities. Understanding the nuances and significance of these data types is paramount, as they collectively paint a comprehensive picture of market dynamics.

Data Cleaning, Transformation, and Integration

The journey from raw data to actionable insights is paved with the rigorous processes of data cleaning, transformation, and integration. Data cleaning involves the meticulous removal of inaccuracies, inconsistencies, and errors that can distort analysis. Data transformation entails normalization, scaling, and structuring to ensure uniformity and comparability across datasets. Data integration harmonizes diverse data sources, consolidating information from multiple streams into a coherent whole. These processes form the crucible within which raw data is refined, tempered, and molded into a reliable foundation for trading strategies.

Handling Missing Data and Outliers in Trading Datasets

Within the realm of data, imperfections manifest as missing values and outliers—challenges that demand deft handling to preserve data integrity. The presence of missing data can distort analyses and impair model performance. Techniques such as imputation and interpolation are employed to fill in missing values without compromising the validity of the dataset. Outliers, on the other hand, can skew statistical measures and lead to misguided conclusions. Outlier detection and robust statistical methods are deployed to identify and mitigate their impact, ensuring that outliers do not unduly influence trading strategies.

In the symphony of quantitative trading, data collection and preprocessing emerge as the symphonic overture, setting the tone for the intricate compositions of trading strategies. The meticulous orchestration of data types, the rigor of data cleaning, transformation, and integration, and the mastery of handling missing data and outliers culminate in a crescendo of data-driven insights. Through this chapter, traders are equipped with the knowledge and tools to navigate the intricacies of data, harnessing its potential to illuminate the path to strategic success.

Chapter 4: Building Quantitative Trading Models

In the crucible of quantitative trading, the art of model construction takes center stage. This chapter delves into the intricacies of crafting quantitative trading models, unraveling the intricate threads that weave together to form strategies that capitalize on market dynamics. From the exploration of algorithmic trading strategies to the taxonomy of trading models encompassing mean reversion, trend following, arbitrage, and more, and culminating in the rigorous processes of backtesting and optimization, this chapter immerses traders in the craftsmanship of building models that navigate the financial landscape with precision and finesse.

Exploring Algorithmic Trading Strategies

Algorithmic trading, the embodiment of systematic execution, introduces traders to a realm where the pace of decision-making is matched only by the velocity of market movements. Algorithmic strategies harness the power of predetermined rules, executing trades with mechanical precision. These strategies encompass an array of methodologies, from simple execution algorithms to complex multi-factor models. Algorithmic trading strategies offer speed, efficiency, and discipline—attributes that resonate within modern trading paradigms.

Types of Trading Models: Mean Reversion, Trend Following, Arbitrage, etc.

Trading models are the architectural blueprints that channel quantitative insights into actionable strategies. The tapestry of trading models comprises diverse genres, each with its unique approach to capturing market dynamics. Mean reversion models capitalize on the tendency of prices to revert to their historical means. Trend-following models identify and ride market trends, aiming to capture sustained price movements. Arbitrage models exploit price discrepancies between related assets, seeking to profit from inefficiencies. These models represent a mere fraction of the rich tapestry of trading models that quantitative traders wield, each tailored to seize opportunities within specific market conditions.

Backtesting and Optimization of Trading Strategies

The crafting of a trading model culminates in the meticulous processes of backtesting and optimization. Backtesting immerses the trading model in historical data, subjecting it to the trials of past market conditions. This empirical trial provides insights into the model's performance, revealing strengths and vulnerabilities. Optimization fine-tunes the model's parameters, seeking to enhance its effectiveness across a range of historical scenarios. However, the quest for optimal parameters is tempered by the risk of overfitting—a phenomenon where models excel in historical data but falter in live markets. Striking the delicate balance between optimization and robustness is the hallmark of a well-crafted trading model.

As we navigate this chapter, the essence of quantitative trading models is unveiled—an intricate fusion of data-driven decision-making, mathematical rigor, and strategic execution. These models serve as the compass that guides traders through the tumultuous waters of financial markets, translating quantitative insights into executable strategies. Through exploration, taxonomy, and empirical validation, this chapter equips traders with the knowledge and tools to embark on the journey of building trading models that leverage data, analytics, and strategy to navigate the market labyrinth.

Chapter 5: Statistical Analysis Techniques for Trading

In the realm of quantitative trading, statistical analysis unfurls as a formidable toolkit, empowering traders to distill meaning from market data, quantify risk, and validate trading strategies. This chapter delves into the intricate world of statistical techniques, illuminating the methodologies that underpin data-driven decision-making. From hypothesis testing that scrutinizes the validity of trading strategies, to the measurement of volatility and risk, and the elucidation of relationships through correlation and cointegration analysis, this exploration uncovers the methodologies that enable traders to navigate the financial labyrinth with analytical acuity.

Hypothesis Testing in Trading Strategies

At the heart of empirical validation lies hypothesis testing—a rigorous process that subjects trading strategies to statistical scrutiny. Traders formulate hypotheses about the efficacy of strategies and utilize statistical tests to assess whether observed returns are statistically significant or merely a product of chance. Hypothesis testing empowers traders to distinguish between strategies that exhibit genuine predictive power and those that are merely the outcome of randomness, ensuring that trading decisions are grounded in empirical evidence.

Volatility and Risk Measurement

In the volatile milieu of financial markets, the measurement of risk is paramount. Volatility, a measure of price fluctuations, serves as a barometer of market uncertainty. Through methodologies such as historical volatility, implied volatility, and the calculation of value-at-risk (VaR), traders quantify the potential range of price movements and assess the risk exposure of trading strategies. These risk measurement techniques provide a crucial compass, steering traders toward strategies that align with their risk tolerance and objectives.

Correlation and Cointegration Analysis

Market dynamics are often governed by intricate interrelationships between assets. Correlation analysis uncovers the strength and direction of relationships between different assets, guiding diversification strategies and risk mitigation efforts. Cointegration analysis delves deeper, identifying long-term relationships between assets that move together over time. This analysis underpins pairs trading strategies, capitalizing on divergences and convergences between cointegrated assets. By unraveling these relationships, traders gain insights that drive strategy construction and portfolio optimization.

As we journey through this chapter, the alchemy of statistical analysis techniques reveals itself as a cornerstone of quantitative trading. These techniques transform data into insights, validate trading hypotheses, and offer a systematic means of navigating market uncertainty. In the hands of skilled traders, statistical analysis serves as a beacon of empirical rigor, allowing for the crafting of strategies that are fortified by data-driven insights. Through hypothesis testing, risk quantification, and relationship elucidation, this chapter empowers traders with the methodologies to illuminate the path toward informed and effective trading decisions.

Chapter 6: Machine Learning Applications in Quantitative Trading

In the dynamic nexus of quantitative trading, the advent of machine learning heralds a new era of strategy development and analysis. This chapter unfurls the canvas of machine learning applications within trading, painting a portrait of innovation and advancement. From the rudiments of machine learning's role in trading to the dichotomy between supervised and unsupervised learning for strategy formulation, and the intricate nuances of employing neural networks, random forests, and support vector machines, this exploration delves into the marriage of data-driven algorithms and financial acumen.

Introduction to Machine Learning in Trading

Machine learning, a paradigm that empowers systems to learn from data, has forged an indelible impact on trading strategies. It endows traders with the capability to uncover complex patterns, model intricate relationships, and adapt strategies to evolving market conditions. By leveraging algorithms to detect insights hidden within vast datasets, machine learning resonates as a potent tool to bolster decision-making and foster innovation within the realm of quantitative trading.

Supervised vs. Unsupervised Learning for Trading Strategies

The terrain of machine learning unveils two prominent branches—supervised and unsupervised learning—each tailored to distinct aspects of trading strategy development. Supervised learning thrives on historical data, training algorithms to recognize patterns and relationships that can inform future trading decisions. Unsupervised learning, conversely, delves into the uncharted territories of data, identifying inherent structures and groupings without predefined labels. Both approaches harbor unique potential, empowering traders to navigate market complexities through both predictive insights and novel discoveries.

Neural Networks, Random Forests, and Support Vector Machines in Trading

Within the gamut of machine learning algorithms, neural networks, random forests, and support vector machines shine as luminaries that drive innovation in trading strategies. Neural networks, inspired by the human brain, harness intricate layers of interconnected nodes to uncover intricate patterns within data. Random forests amalgamate diverse decision trees, collectively delivering robust and adaptable predictions. Support vector machines delineate hyperplanes that optimally segregate data points, enabling classification and regression tasks. These algorithms converge as powerful tools for traders seeking to decipher market dynamics and exploit latent insights.

As we traverse this chapter, the convergence of machine learning and quantitative trading emerges as an intricate symphony that elevates strategy development to unprecedented heights. By fusing the predictive prowess of algorithms with the strategic acumen of traders, machine learning enriches the quantitative trader's toolkit. Through supervised and unsupervised learning paradigms, and the deployment of neural networks, random forests, and support vector machines, this chapter empowers traders to harness the transformative potential of machine learning, setting a course toward strategies that resonate with the cadence of data-driven precision.

Chapter 7: Risk Management and Portfolio Optimization

Amidst the intricacies of quantitative trading, the art of risk management emerges as the sentinel that safeguards trading endeavors from the tempestuous currents of financial markets. This chapter delves into the profound realm of risk management and portfolio optimization, illuminating the methodologies that mitigate exposure to potential losses and amplify the prospects of sustained success. From the paramount importance of risk management to the strategic orchestration of portfolio diversification, asset allocation, and capital allocation techniques, this exploration unveils the strategies that underpin prudent and resilient trading operations.

Importance of Risk Management in Quantitative Trading

The turbulent seas of financial markets are characterized by volatility, uncertainty, and unforeseen events. In this dynamic milieu, risk management stands as the linchpin that upholds trading sustainability. Quantitative trading, rooted in empirical rigor and data-driven insights, thrives on strategies fortified by risk management protocols. These protocols encompass the identification, quantification, and mitigation of risk exposures. By setting limits on position sizes, defining stop-loss levels, and employing robust risk assessment models, traders bolster their resilience against adverse market movements, ensuring that losses are contained and trading capital is preserved.

Portfolio Diversification and Asset Allocation

Portfolio diversification, a cornerstone of risk management, hinges on the principle that a well-constructed portfolio should encompass a spectrum of assets with varying risk-return profiles. Diversification leverages the idiosyncratic behavior of assets to offset losses in one area with gains in another. Asset allocation extends this principle, apportioning capital across different asset classes in alignment with investment objectives and risk tolerance. By diversifying across equities, bonds, commodities, and more, traders cultivate portfolios that are poised to weather diverse market conditions.

Capital Allocation Techniques to Manage Risk

Capital allocation techniques, often grounded in mathematical models, refine the art of risk management by optimizing the distribution of capital across individual trades or strategies. Techniques like the Kelly Criterion and the Capital Asset Pricing Model (CAPM) guide traders in allocating capital proportionally to the expected return and risk of each opportunity. These methods align capital allocation with risk exposure, enabling traders to capitalize on high-potential opportunities while tempering the impact of losses. Strategic capital allocation ensures that resources are judiciously deployed, promoting long-term sustainability and minimizing the impact of adverse market movements.

In this chapter, the symphony of risk management and portfolio optimization harmonizes with the precision of quantitative trading. Through the meticulous management of risk exposure, the strategic orchestration of diversified portfolios, and the nuanced application of capital allocation techniques, traders not only shield themselves from market turbulence but also cultivate an environment where prudent decision-making thrives. As we journey through this exploration, the interplay between quantitative methodologies and strategic risk management underscores the essence of trading resilience, positioning traders to navigate the multifaceted landscape of financial markets with confidence and prudence.

Chapter 8: High-Frequency and Algorithmic Trading

In the technologically-driven nexus of modern finance, the chapters of high-frequency and algorithmic trading unfold as a symphony of speed, precision, and innovation. This chapter delves into the rapid-fire world of trading strategies executed within microseconds, where algorithmic prowess merges with market microstructure insights. From the exploration of high-frequency trading (HFT) strategies, the dissecting of market microstructure and order book dynamics, to the scrutiny of challenges and regulatory considerations that accompany algorithmic trading, this exploration encapsulates the paradigm shift that has reshaped the contours of trading in the digital age.

Exploring High-Frequency Trading (HFT) Strategies

High-frequency trading emerges as a paradigm that harnesses technology's swiftness to execute a plethora of trades within fractions of a second. This chapter unravels the intricate tapestry of HFT strategies, each crafted to exploit fleeting market inefficiencies. Market making strategies provide liquidity by constantly quoting bid and ask prices, while statistical arbitrage strategies seek to capitalize on momentary price discrepancies. Execution strategies ensure swift order execution at optimal prices. As the heartbeat of modern trading, HFT epitomizes the union of speed and strategy.

Market Microstructure and Order Book Analysis

Market microstructure—the fabric that governs order flow, price discovery, and transaction mechanisms—unveils itself as the foundational bedrock of high-frequency and algorithmic trading.

Order book analysis, a key facet of market microstructure, scrutinizes the interplay between buy and sell orders, unraveling supply and demand dynamics. By discerning hidden liquidity, bid-ask spreads, and price impact, traders gain insights into optimal execution strategies. Market microstructure insights guide HFT algorithms, enabling them to navigate market depths with precision.

Challenges and Regulations in Algorithmic Trading

In the realm of algorithmic trading, technological prowess must harmonize with regulatory compliance. This chapter acknowledges the challenges that accompany algorithmic trading, including the potential for flash crashes, the risks of overreliance on models, and the emergence of market manipulation. Regulatory considerations, both nationally and internationally, have underscored the need for transparency, risk management protocols, and oversight. The delicate balance between technological innovation and market stability forms the fulcrum upon which algorithmic trading operates.

As we traverse this chapter, the convergence of algorithmic acumen and market microstructure insights unfolds as a tapestry that redefines trading paradigms. The symphony of high-frequency strategies, the nuances of order book analysis, and the vigilant awareness of challenges and regulations forge a narrative of transformation in the world of quantitative trading. Through speed, precision, and regulatory compliance, this exploration emboldens traders to navigate the fast-paced landscape of modern finance, where algorithmic strategies resonate as the pulse that animates the markets of today.

Chapter 9: Real-world Case Studies

In the crucible of quantitative trading, theory finds its resonance in practice through the crucible of real-world case studies. This chapter immerses traders in the realm of application, unraveling the intricacies of trading strategies through tangible examples that bridge the gap between theory and execution. From the statistical arbitrage strategy that capitalizes on market inefficiencies, to the marriage of mean reversion and machine learning, and the swift precision of high-frequency trading, these case studies illuminate the art of translating quantitative insights into tangible trading success.

Case Study 1: Statistical Arbitrage Strategy

The symphony of statistical arbitrage strategy unfolds as a compelling example of harnessing quantitative methodologies to exploit market anomalies. This case study delves into the art of identifying cointegrated pairs—assets that move in harmony over time but experience temporary divergences. By pinpointing these discrepancies, traders construct strategies that buy undervalued assets and short overvalued ones, capitalizing on the eventual reversion to their historical relationships. The case study unfurls the meticulous processes of data analysis, hypothesis testing, and model calibration that underpin a statistical arbitrage strategy's execution and validation.

Case Study 2: Mean Reversion Strategy using Machine Learning

This case study melds the timeless concept of mean reversion with the transformative potential of machine learning. Traders are immersed in the process of formulating and executing a mean reversion strategy through the lens of machine learning algorithms. Historical price data becomes the canvas upon which machine learning models identify optimal entry and exit points, capturing opportunities presented by temporary price deviations. The case study explores the symbiotic relationship between quantitative trading methodologies and the data-driven precision of machine learning, culminating in a strategy that navigates market turbulence with a data-driven edge.

Case Study 3: High-Frequency Trading Implementation

The chapter's final case study propels traders into the realm of high-frequency trading, where milliseconds determine success. This study unfurls the architecture of a high-frequency trading strategy, offering insights into the technological infrastructure, data feeds, and execution mechanisms that facilitate rapid decision-making and swift execution. From market data ingestion to the deployment of algorithmic strategies, this case study paints a vivid portrait of how traders leverage speed, precision, and technology to execute a high-frequency strategy that capitalizes on fleeting market opportunities.

As we delve into these case studies, theory seamlessly melds with reality, offering a panoramic view of quantitative trading in action. Each case study unveils the synthesis of data, algorithms, and strategic acumen that distinguishes effective trading strategies from mere concepts. These real-world examples illuminate the art of strategy construction, validation, and execution, serving as compasses that guide traders through the complexities of modern financial markets. Through statistical arbitrage, machine learning-driven mean reversion, and high-frequency trading, traders gain insights that transcend theory, equipping them with the tools to navigate the ever-evolving landscape of quantitative trading with acumen and efficacy.

Chapter 10: Future Trends in Quantitative Trading

In the perpetual evolution of financial markets, the visage of quantitative trading is inexorably transformed by the currents of innovation and shifting paradigms. This chapter casts a discerning gaze toward the horizon, exploring the future trends that are poised to redefine the contours of quantitative trading. From the dawn of advanced artificial intelligence and the enigmatic realm of quantum computing, to the integration of big data analytics that magnify insights, and the ethical and regulatory considerations that guide this transformation, this exploration invites traders to anticipate and prepare for the waves of change that will shape the landscape of quantitative trading.

Advancements in Artificial Intelligence and Quantum Computing

The relentless march of artificial intelligence (AI) continues to reshape the terrain of quantitative trading. Machine learning algorithms evolve into more complex and adaptive entities, capable of deciphering intricate patterns and predicting market dynamics with unprecedented accuracy. Concurrently, quantum computing emerges as a potential catalyst, promising exponential leaps in computational power that can revolutionize optimization, risk assessment, and strategy development. The fusion of AI and quantum computing heralds an era of strategic innovation, where data-driven insights and algorithmic precision ascend to new heights.

Integration of Big Data Analytics in Trading

The volume and diversity of data in modern financial markets surge with exponential force, demanding an equally formidable response. Big data analytics emerges as the elixir that extracts insights from this deluge of information. Techniques such as data mining, sentiment analysis, and real-time data processing empower traders to uncover hidden correlations, identify market sentiment, and discern patterns that might elude traditional methodologies. The integration of big data analytics transforms quantitative trading into a landscape of granular insights and actionable intelligence.

Ethical and Regulatory Considerations in Quantitative Trading

As quantitative trading evolves, the nexus of ethics and regulation ascends in significance. Ethical considerations encompass the responsible use of algorithms, guarding against manipulation and market disruption. Regulatory frameworks evolve to ensure transparency, fair access, and systemic stability in a landscape increasingly shaped by algorithms. From algorithmic trading policies to surveillance mechanisms that monitor algorithmic behavior, ethical and regulatory considerations serve as sentinels that safeguard market integrity while promoting the transformative potential of quantitative trading.

In this chapter, we peer into the future, where quantitative trading converges with the frontiers of technology and ethics. The crystalline vistas of advanced artificial intelligence, the quantum vistas of computing, the transformative power of big data analytics, and the moral compass of ethics and regulations collectively shape a trajectory that redefines trading paradigms. As the winds of change whisper through the corridors of quantitative trading, traders are beckoned to navigate these trends with prudence and foresight, poised to harness innovation while upholding the values that underpin market integrity.

Chapter 11: Machine Learning Interpretability and Explain ability in Trading

In the realm of quantitative trading, the black-box nature of advanced machine learning models has sparked a growing need for interpretability and explainability. This chapter delves into the critical discourse surrounding the transparency of machine learning algorithms within trading strategies. From the challenges posed by complex models to the methodologies employed to demystify their decision-making processes, this exploration sheds light on how traders can navigate the trade-off between model complexity and the ability to comprehend and trust the insights they generate.

Challenges in Machine Learning Interpretability

As machine learning algorithms become more intricate, the opacity of their decision-making becomes a concern. Traders often grapple with the challenge of understanding how models arrive at specific predictions or decisions. This opacity can hinder the adoption of advanced models, as traders seek to align their strategies with comprehensible insights. This chapter dissects the complexities that give rise to this challenge, from the intricacies of neural networks to the entanglement of features within ensemble models.

Methodologies for Model Explainability

To bridge the gap between model complexity and transparency, a suite of methodologies has emerged to bestow interpretability upon machine learning models. From feature importance techniques that pinpoint the variables influencing predictions, to model-specific tools like SHAP (SHapley Additive exPlanations) that quantify the impact of each feature, these approaches unlock the inner workings of algorithms. By elucidating the rationale behind model decisions, traders gain insights that enhance their confidence in employing these algorithms within trading strategies.

Trust, Validation, and Interpretability

In the high-stakes arena of quantitative trading, the ability to trust the insights derived from machine learning algorithms is paramount. This chapter examines how model interpretability not only aids in comprehending decisions but also validates the reliability of the algorithms. Transparent models empower traders to validate strategies against known market behavior, identify instances of model bias, and pinpoint potential areas of model failure. By enhancing model trustworthiness, interpretability strengthens the nexus between quantitative insights and strategic execution.

In traversing this chapter, traders are equipped to navigate the nexus of complexity and clarity within machine learning-driven trading strategies. Through an exploration of challenges, methodologies, and the pivotal role of trust and validation, this chapter invites traders to unravel the inner workings of sophisticated algorithms. In a landscape where innovation and comprehension coexist, machine learning interpretability emerges as the compass that guides traders toward strategies fortified by data-driven insights while preserving the principles of transparency and confidence.

Chapter 12: Evolution of Market Sentiment Analysis in Trading

Within the dynamic tapestry of quantitative trading, the role of market sentiment has evolved from a subtle undercurrent to a potent force that shapes market movements. This chapter delves into the realm of market sentiment analysis, tracing its trajectory from rudimentary approaches to the sophisticated methodologies that harness textual data and social media trends to gauge investor sentiment. From the foundational theories that underpin sentiment analysis to the fusion of natural language processing and machine learning, this exploration unveils how the interpretation of market sentiment becomes a cornerstone in formulating informed trading decisions.

Foundations of Market Sentiment Analysis

The inception of market sentiment analysis harkens back to the premise that investor emotions and perceptions impact market dynamics. This chapter scrutinizes the psychological theories that underpin sentiment analysis, exploring how factors such as fear, greed, and overconfidence influence the behavior of market participants. Understanding the psychological underpinnings forms the bedrock upon which sentiment analysis methodologies are erected.

Advancements in Text Analysis and Natural Language Processing

With the digital era comes an avalanche of textual data from sources such as news articles, social media posts, and financial reports. This chapter navigates the terrain of natural language processing (NLP), a field that leverages algorithms to decipher and interpret human language. Sentiment analysis blossoms as an NLP application, enabling traders to quantify the positive, negative, or neutral sentiments expressed within text. Advanced NLP techniques, such as sentiment lexicons and deep learning models, enable nuanced sentiment analysis that transcends mere keyword matching.

Machine Learning Fusion with Sentiment Analysis

The synergy between machine learning and sentiment analysis ushers in a new era of predictive insights. This chapter delves into how machine learning algorithms learn from historical sentiment data, forging predictive models that anticipate market movements. From classification models that predict price directions based on sentiment scores to time series analysis that correlates sentiment patterns with price changes, machine learning invigorates sentiment analysis with the power to inform trading strategies.

Real-world Impact and Challenges

Market sentiment analysis has transformed from a theoretical concept to a practical tool that influences trading decisions. This chapter examines the real-world impact of sentiment analysis across various asset classes, from equities to cryptocurrencies. However, challenges persist, including the noise inherent in social media data, the need for context-aware analysis, and the ever-evolving linguistic nuances that challenge sentiment interpretation.

As we traverse this chapter, the evolution of sentiment analysis unfurls as a testament to the symbiosis of psychology, technology, and quantitative trading. From foundational theories to cutting-edge machine learning fusion, sentiment analysis underscores the importance of comprehending investor emotions within trading strategies. With each advancement, sentiment analysis becomes a compass that guides traders through the tumultuous seas of market sentiment, equipping them to navigate market dynamics with acumen and foresight.

Chapter 13: Decentralized Finance (DeFi) and Quantitative Strategies

The emergence of decentralized finance (DeFi) ushers in a paradigm shift, reimagining traditional financial services through blockchain technology and smart contracts. This chapter delves into the intersection of DeFi and quantitative trading, unveiling how blockchain's transparency, accessibility, and programmability transform trading strategies. From decentralized exchanges and liquidity provision to algorithmic stablecoin trading and yield farming, this exploration navigates the novel landscape where quantitative strategies intertwine with the decentralized ethos of the blockchain era.

DeFi Infrastructure and Decentralized Exchanges

The foundational pillars of DeFi rest upon smart contracts and decentralized exchanges (DEXs), offering traders a new frontier to execute trades with unprecedented transparency and security. This chapter dissects the mechanics of DEXs, elucidating the architecture that replaces intermediaries with code. Traders navigate the intricacies of trading on decentralized platforms, where assets are swapped directly between participants, altering the trading landscape by removing barriers and introducing novel possibilities.

Liquidity Provision and Automated Market Making

Automated market makers (AMMs) emerge as the engines that power DeFi's liquidity landscape. This chapter immerses traders in the world of AMMs, where algorithms replace traditional order books. Liquidity providers deposit assets into AMM pools, earning fees for facilitating trades. The utilization of mathematical models to determine asset prices within pools creates opportunities for traders to deploy quantitative strategies that capitalize on arbitrage and market inefficiencies.

Algorithmic Stablecoin Trading and Yield Farming

Stablecoins, the bedrocks of DeFi, underpin a plethora of trading strategies. This chapter delves into algorithmic stablecoin trading, where automated algorithms maintain price stability by adjusting supply and demand. Yield farming, another facet of DeFi, leverages liquidity provision to earn rewards in the form of tokens. Traders navigate the intricacies of these strategies, unveiling how quantitative methodologies can guide decisions in the DeFi ecosystem.

Integration of Traditional and DeFi Strategies

The convergence of traditional and DeFi strategies forms an intriguing nexus. This chapter explores how traders can integrate quantitative methodologies with DeFi's decentralized architecture. Strategies that bridge these realms leverage tokenized assets and smart contract functionality to construct strategies that transcend traditional market boundaries, enabling strategies that leverage the strengths of both domains.

As we venture into this chapter, the synergy of DeFi and quantitative strategies unfolds as a symphony of innovation and decentralization. From decentralized exchanges to algorithmic stablecoin trading, the world of DeFi beckons traders to navigate a landscape where blockchain's principles resonate with the rigor of quantitative trading. Through liquidity provision, algorithmic decision-making, and the integration of traditional and DeFi strategies, traders traverse uncharted waters, poised to leverage technology's transformative potential in a realm where blockchain and quantitative acumen converge.

Chapter 14: Behavioral Finance and its Implications for Quantitative Trading

The intricate interplay between human behavior and financial markets forms the foundation of behavioral finance—a discipline that illuminates the irrationalities that shape trading decisions. This chapter navigates the realm of behavioral finance and its profound implications for quantitative trading. From cognitive biases that drive market anomalies to the fusion of behavioral insights with quantitative strategies, this exploration delves into how understanding human psychology can enhance the efficacy of trading strategies.

Cognitive Biases and Market Anomalies

The human mind is prone to a plethora of cognitive biases that influence decision-making. This chapter dissects these biases—such as overconfidence, loss aversion, and herding behavior—that steer traders toward irrational decisions. These psychological predispositions often give rise to market anomalies, creating opportunities for quantitative strategies to capitalize on mispricings and inefficiencies.

Incorporating Behavioral Insights into Quantitative Strategies

Quantitative trading thrives on data and analytics, but it cannot exist in isolation from human psychology. This chapter explores how behavioral insights can be seamlessly woven into quantitative strategies. By identifying instances where cognitive biases drive market behaviors, traders can devise strategies that anticipate and exploit these patterns. The fusion of data-driven quantitative methodologies with behavioral insights augments the precision of trading strategies.

Algorithmic Trading and Behavioral Signals

The algorithmic heartbeat of quantitative trading resonates with the nuances of behavioral signals. This chapter delves into how traders leverage behavioral data, sentiment analysis, and social media trends to quantify investor sentiment and glean insights into market movements. By integrating behavioral signals into algorithmic strategies, traders create a synergy that amplifies the predictive power of their models.

Risk Management and Behavioral Considerations

Behavioral finance extends its influence into the realm of risk management. This chapter examines how understanding the psychology of risk can shape risk management protocols. Behavioral insights illuminate the factors that drive traders to deviate from risk management strategies, enabling the formulation of protocols that align with the realities of human behavior.

As we journey through this chapter, the marriage of behavioral finance and quantitative trading unfolds as a captivating voyage into the depths of market psychology. By unraveling cognitive biases, incorporating behavioral insights, and infusing algorithmic trading with behavioral signals, traders not only decode the mysteries of irrational decision-making but also embrace these insights to fortify trading strategies. In a world where data meets human nature, behavioral finance serves as the compass that steers quantitative trading toward strategies that resonate with both the empirical and emotional dimensions of financial markets.

Chapter 15: Cybersecurity and Resilience in Quantitative Trading

As technology fortifies the foundations of quantitative trading, the specter of cybersecurity and resilience looms ever larger. This chapter delves into the critical realm of safeguarding trading operations from cyber threats and ensuring continuity in the face of disruptions. From the vulnerabilities posed by interconnected systems to the strategies that mitigate risks, this exploration navigates the intricate landscape where technology and security intersect, shaping the contours of secure and robust quantitative trading practices.

Cybersecurity Threat Landscape

The digital era opens doors to opportunities, but it also ushers in an era of heightened cyber threats. This chapter dissects the evolving cybersecurity landscape, from malware and phishing attacks to sophisticated hacking endeavors. Traders are exposed to the myriad vulnerabilities that can compromise trading operations, necessitating proactive strategies to protect valuable data, systems, and strategies.

Risk Mitigation and Resilience Strategies

Traders navigate the realm of risk mitigation, where proactive measures bolster defenses against cyber threats. This chapter unveils strategies to safeguard trading systems, including firewalls, encryption, multi-factor authentication, and intrusion detection systems. Moreover, the importance of contingency planning and disaster recovery protocols takes center stage, ensuring that trading operations can recover swiftly from disruptions and maintain continuity.

Regulatory Compliance and Data Privacy

The nexus of technology and trading is intertwined with regulatory frameworks that demand cybersecurity compliance and data privacy adherence. This chapter scrutinizes the regulatory considerations that guide cybersecurity practices, from the protection of sensitive trading data to compliance with standards that safeguard client information. The importance of alignment with global regulations underscores the imperative of maintaining robust cybersecurity measures.

Human Element in Cybersecurity

While technology is at the forefront of cybersecurity, the human element remains pivotal. This chapter underscores the significance of cybersecurity education and awareness training for traders and personnel. Human error can expose vulnerabilities, making training an essential component of a comprehensive cybersecurity strategy.

As we embark on this chapter, the fusion of technology and security takes center stage, reshaping the paradigm of quantitative trading. From cyber threats and risk mitigation strategies to regulatory compliance and the human element, the realm of cybersecurity and resilience emerges as a sentinel that guards against disruptions. By navigating the intricate landscape of cybersecurity, traders not only safeguard their operations but also cultivate an environment of trust and reliability in a digital era where technology's potential converges with the imperative of security.

Chapter 16: Evolution of Market Structure and its Impact on Quantitative Trading

The evolution of financial markets is an inexorable force that shapes the contours of quantitative trading. This chapter delves into the ever-changing landscape of market structure, unveiling how shifts in trading venues, order types, and regulatory frameworks reverberate through quantitative strategies. From the rise of electronic trading platforms to the influence of algorithmic execution, this exploration navigates the dynamic interplay between market structure and quantitative trading.

Electronic Trading and Algorithmic Execution

The proliferation of electronic trading platforms revolutionized the speed and accessibility of market participation. This chapter dissects the transformation from manual to electronic trading and explores the emergence of algorithmic execution, where trading decisions are executed by pre-programmed algorithms. Traders delve into the nuances of algorithmic strategies, unveiling how these algorithms navigate market microstructure and optimize trade execution.

Dark Pools and Fragmentation

Market fragmentation, spurred by the emergence of diverse trading venues, is a hallmark of modern market structure. Dark pools—private trading venues that conceal order information—add complexity to the landscape. This chapter delves into how dark pools and fragmentation shape trading strategies, from optimizing execution through multiple venues to grappling with the challenges posed by the opacity of dark pool trading.

High-Frequency Trading and Market Liquidity

The rise of high-frequency trading (HFT) plays a pivotal role in shaping market liquidity and dynamics. This chapter immerses traders in the world of HFT, where speed and precision coalesce to capture fleeting opportunities. The impact of HFT on market microstructure, liquidity provision, and price discovery unfolds as a key consideration that traders must navigate.

Regulatory Frameworks and Market Structure

Regulatory bodies play a fundamental role in shaping market structure. This chapter examines how regulatory frameworks influence trading practices, from MiFID II in Europe to Reg NMS in the United States. Traders traverse the terrain where regulations intersect with quantitative strategies, adapting strategies to adhere to market integrity and investor protection mandates.

As we delve into this chapter, the evolution of market structure emerges as an intricate tapestry that shapes quantitative trading's landscape. From electronic trading's transformation to the nuances of algorithmic execution, dark pools, and regulatory frameworks, traders navigate a dynamic landscape where strategy formulation harmonizes with market realities. The symphony of market structure and quantitative trading resounds as a narrative where innovation meets adaptation, poised to navigate the ever-evolving terrain of modern financial markets with precision and acumen.

Chapter 17: Social Impact and Responsible Quantitative Trading

Beyond the numbers and algorithms, the realm of quantitative trading reverberates with social impact and ethical considerations. This chapter delves into the intersection of responsible trading practices and quantitative strategies, unveiling how traders can embrace ethical considerations and contribute positively to society. From sustainable investing and environmental, social, and governance (ESG) factors to the role of algorithmic trading in market stability, this exploration navigates the dimensions where quantitative strategies intersect with responsible decision-making.

Sustainable and Responsible Investing

The emergence of sustainable investing ushers in an era where trading decisions transcend financial metrics alone. This chapter dissects the principles of responsible investing, where environmental, social, and governance (ESG) factors guide investment choices. Traders navigate how quantitative strategies can be aligned with ESG principles, forging a path that not only seeks returns but also fosters positive societal impact.

Ethical Considerations in Algorithmic Trading

The ethical underpinnings of algorithmic trading extend beyond profitability. This chapter examines how algorithmic strategies should be imbued with principles that safeguard market integrity, prevent manipulation, and ensure fair access. Traders contemplate the ethical challenges posed by high-frequency trading, flash crashes, and the potential for unintended consequences driven by algorithms.

Market Stability and Algorithmic Impact

Algorithmic trading, while propelling innovation, has also raised concerns about market stability. This chapter delves into how quantitative strategies influence market dynamics, exploring instances where algorithmic behaviors may amplify market fluctuations. The role of circuit breakers, market surveillance, and stress testing emerges as pivotal to maintaining market resilience in the age of algorithmic dominance.

Transparency and Reporting in Quantitative Trading

The principles of transparency and reporting uphold accountability within quantitative trading. This chapter navigates how traders can provide transparency to investors and regulators, disclosing trading strategies, risk management practices, and performance metrics. Transparency fosters trust and cultivates an environment where quantitative strategies are guided by the principles of openness and integrity.

As we navigate this chapter, the symphony of quantitative trading resounds with echoes of responsible decision-making. The fusion of sustainable investing, ethical considerations, market stability, and transparency underscores the potential for quantitative strategies to be a force for positive societal impact. Traders transcend the confines of profit-centric thinking, embracing a landscape where quantitative prowess aligns with principles that uphold social responsibility, ethical conduct, and market stability.

Chapter 18: Cognitive Biases in Trading and Decision-Making

In the heart of quantitative trading lies the human mind—a complex canvas colored by cognitive biases that influence decision-making. This chapter delves into the intricate interplay between cognitive biases and trading strategies, unraveling how awareness of these biases can enhance the efficacy of quantitative decision-making. From anchoring and confirmation bias to the endowment effect, this exploration navigates the psychological terrain that shapes trading choices.

Anchoring and Confirmation Bias

Anchoring bias—where individuals anchor their decisions to initial information—profoundly influences trading behavior. This chapter dissects how traders' perceptions of asset values are often skewed by the first piece of information encountered. Confirmation bias compounds the challenge by causing traders to seek information that reinforces existing beliefs. Unveiling the strategies that mitigate these biases empowers traders to foster a more impartial and data-driven approach.

Overconfidence and Loss Aversion

Overconfidence bias fuels a sense of invulnerability, prompting traders to overestimate their expertise and make risky decisions. Conversely, loss aversion drives traders to avoid losses at the cost of missing out on gains. This chapter navigates the ramifications of these biases on trading strategies, from overtrading fueled by overconfidence to the reluctance to cut losses driven by loss aversion.

Disposition Effect and Hindsight Bias

The disposition effect—the propensity to hold onto losing investments and prematurely sell winners—emerges as another cognitive pitfall. Hindsight bias compounds this challenge, distorting traders' perceptions of the predictability of past events. This chapter explores how these biases can hinder quantitative strategies, prompting suboptimal trade exits and impairing strategy refinement.

Applying Behavioral Insights to Strategy Design

Understanding and mitigating cognitive biases equips traders to devise more effective quantitative strategies. This chapter illuminates the role of data-driven decision-making in overcoming biases, as well as the integration of stop-loss mechanisms and position sizing protocols that counteract emotional-driven trading choices.

As we delve into this chapter, the psychology of decision-making unfolds as a profound undercurrent in quantitative trading. Traders traverse the intricate maze of cognitive biases, uncovering how these psychological predispositions influence trading behavior. Armed with strategies to mitigate these biases, traders chart a course that harmonizes quantitative methodologies with the rigor of data-driven, bias-aware decision-making. In a landscape where data and psychology intertwine, this exploration empowers traders to navigate the complexities of financial markets with acumen and self-awareness.

Conclusion

As we draw the curtain on this comprehensive exploration of quantitative trading, the synthesis of theory, practice, and innovation resonates as a symphony that shapes the contours of modern finance. The journey through these chapters has illuminated the multifaceted dimensions of quantitative trading, unveiling a landscape where mathematical models, data analytics, and technology converge to inform trading strategies that transcend traditional paradigms.

Summarizing the Key Takeaways from the book

In our voyage through these pages, we've traversed a panorama of quantitative trading's intricacies. We've delved into the foundational concepts, from mathematical models and statistical analysis, to data preprocessing and machine learning applications. We've navigated through real-world case studies that bridge theory and execution, and explored the future trends, behavioral considerations, and cybersecurity safeguards that underscore the dynamic nature of quantitative trading.

We've witnessed the emergence of decentralized finance, the fusion of behavioral insights with quantitative strategies, and the confluence of market structure and algorithmic acumen. The interplay of ethical considerations, responsible trading practices, and cognitive biases has illuminated a landscape where quantitative prowess intersects with human values.

Encouraging Further Exploration of Quantitative Trading Concepts

As the final page of this ebook beckons, we encourage you to delve deeper into the world of quantitative trading. The journey has only begun, and the horizon is rich with unexplored territories. Continue to refine your understanding of mathematical models, experiment with algorithmic strategies, and stay attuned to the evolving market landscape.

Quantitative trading is an ever-evolving discipline, where innovation is a constant companion. Harness the power of data, technology, and quantitative methodologies to craft strategies that navigate the complexities of modern financial markets. Whether you are an aspiring quant or a seasoned trader, the voyage into quantitative trading promises continuous learning, innovation, and a front-row seat to the transformation of finance.

The realm of quantitative trading awaits your exploration. Embrace the challenges, seize the opportunities, and continue your journey toward becoming a proficient navigator of the quantitative landscape.

Fundamental Analysis

Concentrate on analyzing economic indicators, company financials, and market news

Introduction

Fundamental Analysis is a cornerstone of investment decision-making, rooted in the comprehensive assessment of various factors that impact the value and potential of an asset. It serves as a guiding light for investors seeking to make informed choices in the dynamic and complex world of financial markets. This section delves into the very essence of Fundamental Analysis, shedding light on its core definition and elucidating the crucial role it plays in the realm of investments.

Defining Fundamental Analysis

At its essence, Fundamental Analysis is a meticulous examination of intrinsic factors that influence the intrinsic value of an asset. These factors encompass a wide range of elements, including economic indicators, company financials, industry trends, and market news. This analysis strives to unveil the true worth of an asset, discerning whether its market price is overvalued, undervalued, or fairly valued. By delving into the fundamentals of an asset, investors aim to identify opportunities for growth, income, and capital preservation.

The process of Fundamental Analysis involves a systematic evaluation of both quantitative and qualitative aspects. Quantitative aspects encompass tangible elements like financial statements, ratios, and metrics, while qualitative factors consider management quality, competitive positioning, and broader economic trends. The amalgamation of these aspects furnishes a holistic understanding of an asset's potential trajectory.

Importance of Fundamental Analysis in Investment

In the world of finance, where market dynamics are shaped by a multitude of factors, Fundamental Analysis stands as a bedrock of rational decision-making. It provides investors with a compass to navigate the treacherous waters of uncertainty by offering insights that extend beyond fleeting market sentiment.

Fundamental Analysis serves as a counterbalance to the volatility and speculation that often govern markets. It empowers investors to make well-founded decisions based on concrete data and tangible evidence, fostering a long-term perspective that is crucial for sustainable wealth creation. By examining economic indicators, company financials, and market news, investors can unearth opportunities, mitigate risks, and align their portfolios with their financial goals.

Moreover, the significance of Fundamental Analysis is amplified in periods of market turbulence and economic upheaval. When markets are in flux, relying solely on short-term trends can be perilous. Fundamental Analysis acts as a stabilizing force, enabling investors to decipher the underlying factors that drive asset values, thus aiding in crafting strategies that withstand market storms.

In essence, Fundamental Analysis is not merely an investment tool; it's a mindset that cultivates a deep understanding of the underlying forces that shape financial markets. By grounding investment decisions in solid fundamentals, investors can navigate the ever-changing landscape with confidence and prudence.

As we delve deeper into the realms of Economic Indicators, Company Financials Evaluation, and Analysis of Market News and Events, the multifaceted significance of Fundamental Analysis will become increasingly apparent, underscoring its role as an indispensable compass for investors seeking to traverse the complexities of the investment landscape.

Chapter 1: Economic Indicators and Their Analysis
Section 1.1 Understanding Economic Indicators

Economic indicators serve as the pulse of a nation's economic health, providing invaluable insights into its overall performance and trajectory. These indicators are vital components of Fundamental Analysis, as they aid investors in comprehending the prevailing economic conditions and anticipating future trends. Within this context, economic indicators can be categorized into three distinct types: leading, lagging, and coincident indicators, each offering unique perspectives on the state of an economy.

Leading Indicators

Leading indicators are instruments that provide preliminary indications of shifts in economic activity before they are reflected in broader economic data. These indicators are considered precursors to changes and offer insights into potential economic shifts in the near future. Examples of leading indicators include:

Stock Market Indices: The performance of stock market indices, such as the S&P 500, can provide early signals about investor sentiment and economic expectations.

Consumer Confidence Index: This index measures consumer optimism about the economy's future prospects, indicating potential changes in consumer spending patterns.

Building Permits: The number of building permits issued can indicate future construction activity, providing a glimpse into housing and real estate trends.

Lagging Indicators

Lagging indicators, as the name implies, follow changes in the economy after they have occurred. These indicators confirm or validate trends that have already taken shape and offer retrospective insights. Lagging indicators are crucial for confirming the accuracy of predictions made based on leading indicators. Examples of lagging indicators include:

Unemployment Rate: Changes in the unemployment rate are typically observed after shifts in economic activity, providing insights into labor market conditions.

Corporate Profits: Profits generated by businesses serve as a lagging indicator, reflecting the overall performance of companies during a specific period.

Interest Rates: Central banks often adjust interest rates in response to economic trends. Changes in interest rates are observed after economic shifts have transpired.

Coincident Indicators

Coincident indicators are those that reflect the current state of economic activity. These indicators provide real-time snapshots of the economy's health, offering immediate insights into its performance. Examples of coincident indicators include:

Gross Domestic Product (GDP): GDP is a comprehensive measure of an economy's output. It reflects the value of goods and services produced within a country's borders and serves as a primary indicator of overall economic health.

Industrial Production Index: This index measures the output of the industrial sector, including manufacturing, mining, and utilities, providing a gauge of production activity.

Retail Sales: Retail sales data offer insights into consumer spending patterns and the demand for goods and services.

Understanding the distinctions between leading, lagging, and coincident indicators is paramount for investors engaged in Fundamental Analysis. These indicators collectively contribute to a holistic understanding of an economy's trajectory, allowing investors to anticipate shifts, validate trends, and gauge the current state of economic affairs. By interpreting and analyzing these indicators in conjunction with company financials and market news, investors can forge strategies that are both well-informed and adaptable to changing economic landscapes.

Section 1.2 Importance of Economic Data in Market Analysis

The bedrock of informed investment decisions lies in the comprehensive analysis of economic data. Economic indicators, often released on scheduled intervals, offer invaluable insights into the health and direction of an economy. These data points play a pivotal role in the practice of Fundamental Analysis, serving as guiding lights for investors navigating the complexities of financial markets.

Importance of Economic Data in Market Analysis:

Economic data is akin to a financial compass, guiding investors through the turbulent waters of market dynamics. It provides a factual foundation upon which investment strategies can be built, enabling investors to base their decisions on concrete evidence rather than conjecture. This is particularly crucial in a market climate often characterized by short-lived trends and volatile sentiment.

Economic data functions as a diagnostic tool for the broader economy. It empowers investors with the ability to gauge the effectiveness of economic policies, assess the impact of regulatory changes, and identify potential risks and opportunities. This information is indispensable for devising strategies that are adaptive and resilient, capable of withstanding both favorable and adverse market conditions.

The timeliness and accuracy of economic data are of paramount importance. Timely access to economic indicators allows investors to react swiftly to unfolding events and changing conditions. Accurate data provides a reliable foundation for making well-informed decisions, reducing the risk of acting on misleading or outdated information.

Key Economic Indicators for Fundamental Analysis:

Within the realm of Fundamental Analysis, certain economic indicators hold particular significance due to their ability to provide comprehensive insights into an economy's health and trajectory. These indicators are like signposts, offering clues about the future direction of financial markets. Some of the key economic indicators that investors closely monitor include:

- **Gross Domestic Product (GDP):** GDP is the most comprehensive measure of an economy's output. It quantifies the value of all goods and services produced within a country's borders and serves as a benchmark for overall economic health.

- **Consumer Price Index (CPI) and Inflation:** CPI measures changes in the prices of a basket of consumer goods and services. Inflation, as indicated by CPI, is a key economic metric that influences purchasing power, interest rates, and investment decisions.

- **Unemployment Rate:** The unemployment rate offers insights into the labor market's health and is a reflection of economic vitality. It has a direct impact on consumer spending, production levels, and overall economic growth.

- **Purchasing Managers' Index (PMI):** PMI measures the manufacturing and services sectors' activity. It provides insights into business sentiment, demand, and supply dynamics, making it an indicator of economic expansion or contraction.

- **Interest Rates and Central Bank Policies:** Central banks' decisions on interest rates influence borrowing costs, investment decisions, and monetary policy. Monitoring interest rate movements offers insights into economic stability and monetary policy direction.

- **Trade Balance and Current Account:** These indicators provide insights into a country's international trade performance and its fiscal position in the global economy. They shed light on export-import dynamics and currency strength.

As investors traverse the landscape of Fundamental Analysis, the importance of economic data becomes evident. By meticulously examining these key indicators, investors can decode the intricate interplay between economic conditions and market trends. Armed with this knowledge, they are better equipped to make well-informed investment choices that align with their financial goals and risk tolerance.

Gross Domestic Product (GDP): Unveiling Economic Landscape
Understanding Gross Domestic Product (GDP)

Gross Domestic Product (GDP) stands as one of the fundamental pillars of economic measurement, casting a wide-reaching and comprehensive net over a nation's economic activity. It serves as a cornerstone in economic analysis, providing a quantitative measure of the total value of all goods and services produced within a country's borders over a specific period. GDP encapsulates the intricate web of economic transactions, reflecting the collective efforts of industries, businesses, and individuals.

Components of GDP: Unraveling Economic Complexity

GDP is constructed through the aggregation of four primary components, each shedding light on a distinct facet of economic activity:

1. **Consumption:** The total expenditure by households on goods and services forms the bedrock of consumption. This includes spending on necessities, such as food and housing, as well as discretionary purchases.

2. **Investment:** Investment embodies the capital outlays by businesses and individuals aimed at enhancing productive capacity. It encompasses expenditures on machinery, equipment, infrastructure, and research and development.

3. **Government Spending:** Government spending represents expenditures on public services, defense, infrastructure, and other government-led initiatives that contribute to economic growth.

4. **Net Exports:** Net exports account for the difference between a country's exports and imports. If exports exceed imports, a positive net export value contributes to GDP; conversely, a negative value detracts from GDP.

GDP Calculation: A Technical Framework

GDP can be calculated through three distinct approaches, all of which yield the same result when accurately executed:

1. **Production Approach:** This method calculates GDP by summing the value added by all industries in the economy. It accounts for the value created at each stage of production, eliminating double-counting.

2. **Income Approach:** The income approach calculates GDP by aggregating all the income generated within an economy. This encompasses wages, profits, rents, and taxes less subsidies on production and imports.

3. **Expenditure Approach:** The expenditure approach computes GDP by summing all expenditures on final goods and services. It encompasses consumption, investment, government spending, and net exports.

GDP's Significance: A Window into Economic Health

GDP's significance transcends mere numerical representation. It serves as a barometer of an economy's size, growth rate, and overall health. Changes in GDP can signal shifts in economic activity, indicating periods of expansion, contraction, or stagnation. Moreover, GDP comparisons across different periods and countries offer insights into relative economic performance, enabling governments, policymakers, and investors to gauge economic progress and make informed decisions.

Limitations of GDP: A Nuanced Perspective

While GDP is a powerful tool, it does have limitations. It does not account for factors such as income distribution, quality of life, environmental impact, or underground economy activities. Additionally, GDP growth does not necessarily equate to equitable prosperity. Hence, experts often advise complementing GDP analysis with other indicators to obtain a more comprehensive view of an economy.

In conclusion, Gross Domestic Product is more than just a numerical value; it is a reflection of an economy's vibrancy, a quantifiable portrayal of its activity and vitality. Its calculation, analysis, and interpretation form the cornerstone of economic evaluation, offering stakeholders a window into a nation's economic landscape and the foundation upon which strategic decisions are crafted.

Consumer Price Index (CPI) and Inflation: Deciphering Price Dynamics
Understanding Consumer Price Index (CPI)

The Consumer Price Index (CPI) stands as a pivotal economic metric, meticulously crafted to illuminate the complex interplay between consumer spending patterns and price fluctuations. As a principal component of economic analysis, the CPI provides critical insights into the cost of living and inflationary pressures, making it an indispensable tool for economists, policymakers, and investors alike.

Measuring Price Changes: CPI's Essence

At its core, the CPI quantifies the average change in prices of a predetermined basket of goods and services consumed by households over time. This basket reflects the typical consumption patterns of households, encompassing items ranging from food and housing to clothing, healthcare, and transportation. By meticulously tracking these prices and calculating their average change, the CPI unveils the trajectory of inflation and deflation, offering a tangible gauge of how purchasing power evolves over time.

CPI Components: Unveiling Price Movements

The CPI is meticulously divided into a set of core components, each representing a distinct segment of consumer spending:

1. **Housing:** This component encompasses the costs associated with shelter, including rents, homeownership costs, and utility bills.
2. **Transportation:** Transportation costs, including vehicle purchases, fuel, and public transportation, constitute this segment.
3. **Food and Beverages:** Food items purchased for at-home consumption, as well as those consumed away from home, contribute to this category.
4. **Apparel:** The cost of clothing and footwear is encapsulated within this component.

5. **Healthcare:** Healthcare-related expenses, including medical services and prescription drugs, constitute a significant portion of the CPI.
6. **Recreation:** Costs associated with entertainment, leisure, and recreational activities are included in this segment.
7. **Education and Communication:** Educational expenses, along with communication services, are considered within this category.

CPI and Inflation: A Vital Nexus

The CPI's primary role lies in unveiling the extent of inflation or deflation within an economy. Inflation refers to the general increase in prices, eroding purchasing power over time, while deflation signifies a decrease in prices. A rising CPI implies inflation, indicating that the cost of living is increasing. Conversely, a declining CPI could signal deflation, which, although seemingly advantageous, can hinder economic growth.

CPI Calculation: A Technical Endeavor

The calculation of the CPI involves a meticulous process that encompasses the following steps:

1. **Selection of the Basket:** Economists choose a representative basket of goods and services based on consumer expenditure patterns.
2. **Price Collection:** Prices for these items are collected at regular intervals from diverse locations, reflecting a broad cross-section of the population.
3. **Weighting:** Each item's importance in the average consumer's budget is considered to assign appropriate weights.
4. **Calculation:** The CPI is calculated by comparing the current cost of the basket to its cost in a base year, then adjusting for changes in prices.

CPI's Significance: Economic Navigation

The CPI stands as a compass guiding economic navigation. Policymakers utilize CPI data to adjust fiscal and monetary policies, while investors factor in inflation trends when crafting investment strategies. Moreover, the CPI's impact extends to wage negotiations, social security adjustments, and cost-of-living indexation.

In conclusion, the Consumer Price Index embodies the intricate dynamics between consumer spending and price movements. Its role as a harbinger of inflationary pressures and economic health cannot be overstated. By quantifying changes in the cost of living, the CPI empowers stakeholders to make informed decisions that navigate the complexities of an ever-evolving economic landscape.

Unemployment Rate: Deciphering Labor Market Dynamics
Understanding Unemployment Rate

The Unemployment Rate, a linchpin of economic analysis, unveils the intricate dance between labor supply and demand within an economy. It serves as a poignant indicator of economic health, reflecting the vitality of the labor market and its capacity to absorb and sustain the workforce. As a critical component of Fundamental Analysis, the Unemployment Rate provides invaluable insights into the broader economic landscape.

Defining Unemployment: A Nuanced Perspective

Unemployment, in economic terms, signifies the state of individuals who are actively seeking employment yet are unable to secure jobs. The Unemployment Rate quantifies this phenomenon, representing the percentage of the labor force that is unemployed within a specific period. It encapsulates the complex interplay between workforce dynamics, business cycles, and economic policies.

Unemployment Rate Categories: A Multi-Faceted View

Within the Unemployment Rate, distinct categories emerge, each portraying a distinct facet of the labor market:

1. **Frictional Unemployment:** This category encompasses individuals transitioning between jobs or entering the workforce for the first time. It is often considered temporary, arising due to factors such as skill mismatch or location changes.

2. **Structural Unemployment:** Structural unemployment arises from a mismatch between available jobs and the skills possessed by job seekers. It often occurs when technological advancements render certain skills obsolete.

3. **Cyclical Unemployment:** This form of unemployment is closely linked to economic cycles. During recessions, businesses may lay off workers due to reduced demand, leading to an increase in cyclical unemployment.

4. **Seasonal Unemployment:** Seasonal unemployment occurs due to fluctuations in demand tied to specific seasons. Industries like agriculture and tourism often experience fluctuations in labor demand.

Unemployment Rate Calculation: A Precise Endeavor

The Unemployment Rate is calculated using a formula that divides the number of unemployed individuals by the total labor force and then multiplies by 100 to express it as a percentage. The labor force comprises individuals who are either employed or actively seeking employment.

Unemployment Rate's Role: A Reflection of Economic Health

The Unemployment Rate's significance extends far beyond numerical representation. It mirrors the broader economic landscape, providing insights into labor market dynamics, consumer spending patterns, and overall economic health. A low Unemployment Rate typically signifies a robust economy with opportunities for job seekers, whereas a high rate can indicate economic distress and underutilized human capital.

Unemployment Rate and Monetary Policy: An Intertwined Connection

Central banks often take the Unemployment Rate into account when formulating monetary policies. A lower Unemployment Rate can lead to increased wage pressures, potentially spurring inflation. Conversely, a higher rate may prompt accommodative measures to stimulate economic growth and reduce unemployment.

Conclusion: A Glimpse into Labor Realities

The Unemployment Rate is more than a statistic; it's a window into the lives of individuals seeking livelihoods. Its fluctuations encapsulate the triumphs and challenges of the labor force, reflecting economic prosperity and struggles alike. As investors and policymakers delve into this metric, they gain a deeper understanding of the forces shaping labor market dynamics, enabling them to make informed decisions that resonate with economic realities.

Purchasing Managers' Index (PMI): Decrypting Business Sentiment

Understanding Purchasing Managers' Index (PMI)

The Purchasing Managers' Index (PMI) stands as a lighthouse guiding economic navigation, offering critical insights into the pulse of business activity. An integral component of Fundamental Analysis, the PMI serves as a harbinger of economic expansion or contraction, providing stakeholders with a real-time gauge of manufacturing and service sector sentiment.

Interpreting Business Sentiment: PMI's Essence

The PMI is a composite indicator that encapsulates the purchasing intentions, production levels, and overall business conditions within an economy. It acts as a thermometer, measuring the temperature of the manufacturing and service sectors. With a scale that ranges from 0 to 100, the PMI holds significance in the 50-50 range. A reading above 50 signals expansion, while a reading below 50 points to contraction.

Components of PMI: A Holistic View

The PMI's construction involves surveying purchasing managers across various industries. These professionals provide insights into different facets of business operations, which are categorized into five primary components:

1. **New Orders:** This component gauges the influx of new orders, reflecting changes in demand for goods and services. A rise in new orders often indicates increased business activity.
2. **Production:** The production component assesses output levels. An increase in production typically corresponds to higher demand and economic expansion.
3. **Employment:** Employment levels are a reflection of hiring intentions. Higher employment suggests economic growth and increased business confidence.
4. **Supplier Deliveries:** Slower supplier deliveries can signify increased demand, as suppliers may struggle to keep up with orders during periods of economic expansion.
5. **Inventory Levels:** Inventory levels provide insights into supply chain dynamics. Declining inventories may indicate robust demand and the need for increased production.

PMI and Economic Cycles: A Dynamic Relationship

The PMI's dynamic nature lies in its ability to reflect economic cycles with remarkable accuracy. During periods of economic growth, businesses often experience heightened demand, leading to increased production, new orders, and employment. Conversely, economic contraction is mirrored by decreased demand and subsequently lower readings on the PMI.

PMI and Investment Decisions: Informed Strategies

Investors glean invaluable insights from the PMI when crafting investment strategies. A rising PMI suggests economic expansion, potentially driving equity markets higher and boosting investor confidence. Conversely, a declining PMI can foretell economic challenges, prompting a more cautious approach to investments.

PMI Calculation: A Rigorous Process

The PMI is calculated through a meticulous process that involves aggregating data collected from purchasing managers' surveys. A weighted average of the five components produces the final PMI value.

Conclusion: A Barometer of Business Vibrancy

The Purchasing Managers' Index offers more than just a numerical snapshot; it encapsulates the dynamic interplay between economic sentiment and business activity. It empowers stakeholders with real-time insights, enabling them to anticipate economic shifts, make strategic decisions, and navigate the intricacies of the market landscape. By deciphering the language of business sentiment through the PMI, investors and policymakers alike obtain a nuanced understanding of economic vitality.

Interest Rates and Central Bank Policies: Navigating Economic Currents
Understanding Interest Rates

Interest rates, an integral facet of monetary policy, serve as the financial heartbeat of an economy. They influence borrowing costs, savings incentives, investment decisions, and overall economic activity. As a cornerstone of Fundamental Analysis, comprehending the nuances of interest rates and central bank policies is crucial for investors seeking to navigate the intricate currents of the financial landscape.

The Role of Central Banks: Monetary Stewards

Central banks, entrusted with the responsibility of maintaining economic stability, wield interest rates as a potent tool in their monetary policy arsenal. The management of interest rates allows central banks to influence economic conditions, either stimulating growth or curbing inflation.

Interest Rate Types: Unveiling Complexity

Interest rates manifest in several forms, each carrying its own significance:

1. **Nominal Interest Rate:** The nominal interest rate represents the raw interest charged or earned without accounting for inflation.

2. **Real Interest Rate:** The real interest rate adjusts the nominal rate for inflation, reflecting the actual purchasing power gained or lost through lending or borrowing.

3. **Policy Rate:** Also known as the target rate, the policy rate is the interest rate at which central banks lend money to commercial banks. Changes in the policy rate influence overall borrowing costs.

Central Bank Policies: The Catalyst for Change

Central banks wield a toolkit of policies to achieve economic objectives:

1. **Expansionary Policy:** During economic slowdowns, central banks may implement an expansionary policy by lowering interest rates. This stimulates borrowing and spending, fostering economic growth.

2. **Contractionary Policy:** In times of high inflation, central banks may adopt a contractionary policy by raising interest rates. This curtails borrowing, spending, and lending, moderating inflationary pressures.

3. **Forward Guidance:** Central banks communicate future policy intentions to guide market expectations. This influences long-term interest rates and investment decisions.

Interest Rates' Impact on Investments: Multi-Faceted Effects

Interest rate changes ripple through financial markets, impacting various asset classes:

1. **Bonds:** Rising interest rates often lead to falling bond prices, as higher yields on new bonds diminish the appeal of existing bonds.

2. **Equities:** The impact of interest rates on equities is complex. Lower rates can boost corporate borrowing and investment, potentially driving stock prices higher. However,

higher rates can make fixed-income investments more attractive, potentially affecting stock valuations.

3. **Real Estate:** Real estate is sensitive to interest rate shifts. Lower rates can stimulate demand for mortgages and potentially drive real estate prices higher.

Interest Rates and Global Interplay: A Complex Dance

Interest rates do not operate in isolation; they are influenced by global economic dynamics, exchange rates, and geopolitical events. Central banks also engage in coordinated efforts to manage global financial stability.

Conclusion: Navigating the Interest Rate Terrain

Interest rates and central bank policies form a critical cornerstone of economic stability and investment decision-making. Understanding their intricate interplay empowers investors to anticipate shifts in economic conditions, assess risk, and align portfolios with market trends. As we navigate the terrain of interest rates and monetary policies, it becomes evident that their impact extends beyond the financial realm, shaping the broader economic landscape.

Section 1.3: Interpreting Economic Data
Trade Balance and Current Account: Decoding Economic Flows

Understanding Trade Balance and Current Account

In the realm of economic analysis, the Trade Balance and Current Account stand as vital gauges, offering insights into a nation's international economic interactions. These metrics play a pivotal role in the practice of Fundamental Analysis, unraveling the dynamics of trade, investment, and financial flows on the global stage.

The Trade Balance: Measuring Exports and Imports

The Trade Balance, often referred to as the balance of trade, reflects the difference between a country's exports and imports of goods. It's a reflection of trade performance on a global scale. A positive trade balance occurs when exports exceed imports, signifying a trade surplus. Conversely, a negative trade balance, or trade deficit, arises when imports surpass exports.

Interpreting the Trade Balance: Economic Implications

A positive trade balance can be indicative of competitive industries, strong global demand for exports, and a potential inflow of foreign capital. However, a prolonged trade surplus might also suggest an undervalued currency or limited domestic consumption. A trade deficit might signify robust domestic demand for imported goods, possibly due to higher income levels or preferences for certain products not domestically produced.

Current Account: A Comprehensive Snapshot

The Current Account extends beyond the Trade Balance, encompassing a broader array of economic transactions. It includes not only trade in goods but also services, income flows, and transfers between a country and the rest of the world.

Components of the Current Account: Diving Deeper

The Current Account is typically divided into four primary components:

1. **Trade in Goods:** Similar to the Trade Balance, this segment captures the export and import of physical goods.

2. **Trade in Services:** This includes transactions related to services like tourism, transportation, financial services, and intellectual property.

3. **Primary Income:** Primary income reflects earnings from investments, such as interest, dividends, and profits generated by foreign assets.
4. **Secondary Income:** Secondary income accounts for transfers between countries, such as foreign aid, remittances, and grants.

Interpreting the Current Account: Economic Impacts

A Current Account surplus can signal a country's competitive edge in exporting goods and services, along with earning more from foreign investments than paying abroad. Conversely, a Current Account deficit might suggest heavy reliance on imported goods, outflows of income generated by foreign investments, or significant capital outflows.

Balancing Act: Implications for Economic Health

The Trade Balance and Current Account collectively depict a nation's economic health in the global context. A consistent surplus might point toward economic vitality, but it's crucial to assess its sustainability. Similarly, a deficit should be evaluated in terms of its underlying causes and potential consequences.

Conclusion: Economic Connectivity on the Global Stage

The Trade Balance and Current Account serve as windows into a country's economic interactions with the world. These metrics go beyond numerical values, unveiling the intricacies of trade relationships, investment patterns, and financial flows. By meticulously interpreting the Trade Balance and Current Account, investors, policymakers, and analysts gain insights into the broader economic landscape and make well-informed decisions that resonate across international borders.

Impact of Economic Indicators on Markets: Unraveling Market Dynamics
Understanding the Significance

Economic indicators, the pulse of economic health, reverberate through financial markets with profound implications. The release of these indicators triggers a cascade of reactions, reshaping market sentiments, guiding investment strategies, and influencing trading decisions. An integral facet of Fundamental Analysis, understanding the impact of economic indicators on markets is essential for investors navigating the tumultuous waters of financial landscapes.

Immediate Market Response

As economic indicators are released, markets respond instantaneously. This swift reaction is especially evident in the realm of high-frequency trading, where algorithms capitalize on nanoseconds to adjust positions. Traders monitor deviations from consensus estimates, seeking opportunities to capitalize on market overreactions or corrections.

Interest Rates and Monetary Policy Connection

Indicators such as inflation and employment data bear direct relevance to central banks' monetary policy decisions. These data points can influence interest rate expectations, which, in turn, shape bond yields, equity valuations, and foreign exchange rates. Anticipating shifts in monetary policy is a cornerstone for many investment strategies.

Equities and Earnings Outlook

Economic indicators illuminate broader economic conditions, influencing companies' earnings outlook. A robust GDP growth or healthy consumer spending can drive increased corporate revenues and higher stock prices. Conversely, indicators suggesting economic downturns can cast shadows over earnings forecasts, leading to market pullbacks.

Currency Market Volatility

Economic indicators are key drivers of foreign exchange markets. Strong economic data often leads to currency appreciation, as investors anticipate higher interest rates and a favorable economic environment. On the contrary, weak data can lead to currency depreciation.

Commodity Price Movement

Commodity markets are highly sensitive to economic indicators. Indicators like manufacturing activity influence demand for raw materials, affecting commodity prices. For instance, a decline in manufacturing can lead to decreased demand for industrial metals.

Market Sentiment and Risk Appetite

Economic indicators contribute to overall market sentiment and risk appetite. Positive data can foster confidence and encourage risk-taking, driving investors toward equities and other high-yield assets. Conversely, negative data can trigger risk aversion, leading to shifts into safe-haven assets like bonds and gold.

Long-Term Strategic Planning

Investors also use economic indicators to inform long-term investment strategies. A comprehensive understanding of economic cycles, unemployment trends, and GDP growth rates guides asset allocation decisions, enabling investors to position themselves favorably over extended periods.

Conclusion: The Indicators' Symphony

The interplay between economic indicators and markets is akin to a symphony, with each data release contributing its unique note to the overall composition. These indicators act as the heartbeat of market sentiment, influencing short-term trading decisions and long-term investment strategies alike. By deciphering the intricate relationship between economic indicators and market dynamics, investors gain the ability to anticipate trends, navigate volatility, and make informed decisions that resonate across financial landscapes.

Historical Data Analysis and Trends: Deciphering the Past for Future Insights
Understanding Historical Data Analysis

The practice of analyzing historical data stands as a cornerstone in the realm of Fundamental Analysis, offering a panoramic view of economic, financial, and market trends. By meticulously examining patterns, fluctuations, and correlations that have unfolded over time, analysts and investors gain valuable insights that guide decision-making and forecast potential future scenarios.

The Power of Patterns

Patterns inherent in historical data offer a window into the cyclicality and predictability of economic and market behavior. These patterns can span economic cycles, business cycles, and market cycles, revealing recurring phenomena that help shape strategies and allocate resources effectively.

Unveiling Long-Term Trends

Long-term trends emerge from the annals of historical data, shedding light on the gradual shifts that underpin economic growth, technological advancements, and social changes. These trends enable investors to identify industries with staying power, anticipate demographic shifts, and align portfolios with emerging opportunities.

Analyzing Economic Indicators Across Time

By juxtaposing economic indicators with historical context, analysts gain a profound understanding of cause-and-effect relationships. This practice allows for the assessment of the impact of various events, policies, and market dynamics on economic performance over time.

Market Behavior and Sentiment

Historical data analysis offers insights into market sentiment and behavior during different economic conditions. By examining how markets responded to similar scenarios in the past, investors can gauge potential reactions to current or future events.

Cyclical Fluctuations

Economic and market cycles are etched into historical data, presenting periods of expansion, contraction, and stabilization. These cyclical patterns aid in identifying entry and exit points for investments and optimizing strategies for various market conditions.

Risks and Opportunities

Historical data analysis provides a holistic view of risks and opportunities that have manifested over time. By identifying instances of market turbulence, financial crises, and sudden shifts, investors can better prepare for unforeseen challenges and capitalize on trends that lead to growth.

Predictive Modeling

Historical data serves as the bedrock for predictive modeling, enabling analysts to build models that forecast future trends based on historical patterns and relationships. These models assist in scenario planning and risk assessment.

Conclusion: Insights from the Past to Shape the Future

Historical data analysis is a portal to the past, unlocking insights that guide decisions in the present and future. By delving into trends, patterns, and cycles etched within data, investors and analysts can navigate uncertainties with greater confidence, recognize evolving market dynamics, and capitalize on emerging opportunities. With historical data as their compass, stakeholders in the financial world can chart a course that aligns with both the lessons of the past and the aspirations of the future.

Relationship Between Economic Indicators and Investment Choices: Informed Decision-Making

Understanding the Interplay

The intricate relationship between economic indicators and investment choices forms a cornerstone of informed decision-making in the financial realm. Investors, analysts, and financial institutions meticulously analyze a diverse array of economic indicators to gauge the health of economies, industries, and markets. This practice guides investment strategies, enabling stakeholders to allocate resources effectively and capitalize on emerging opportunities while mitigating risks.

Economic Indicators as Signposts

Economic indicators serve as signposts, offering insights into the prevailing economic conditions and trends. Investors closely monitor indicators such as GDP growth, unemployment rates, and consumer sentiment to gauge the overall health of an economy. This understanding is pivotal in shaping investment choices across asset classes.

Investment Allocation Strategies

Economic indicators influence investment allocation strategies. For instance, during periods of robust economic growth, investors might allocate more funds to equities, anticipating higher corporate earnings and potential stock price appreciation. Conversely, during economic downturns, diversification into defensive assets like bonds or precious metals might be favored to preserve capital.

Sectoral and Industry Analysis

The relationship between economic indicators and investment extends to sectoral and industry analysis. Certain economic indicators, such as housing starts and consumer spending, can have a direct impact on industries like real estate, retail, and construction. Investors leverage this knowledge to position themselves in industries poised for growth based on prevailing economic conditions.

Fixed Income Investments

Economic indicators play a crucial role in fixed income investments, particularly in the bond market. Investors assess indicators such as inflation rates and interest rate trends to gauge the potential purchasing power erosion and yield on fixed income investments. Anticipating interest rate changes guides decisions regarding the duration and type of bonds in a portfolio.

Currency and Foreign Exchange Markets

Economic indicators have a direct impact on currency markets. Indicators like trade balances, interest rate differentials, and economic growth influence currency exchange rates. Investors engaged in foreign exchange trading incorporate these indicators into their strategies to capitalize on currency appreciation or depreciation.

Risk Assessment and Management

Economic indicators aid in risk assessment and management. By analyzing indicators like unemployment rates, inflation rates, and consumer confidence, investors can assess the overall economic stability and potential market volatility. This information guides decisions on risk exposure, hedging strategies, and portfolio diversification.

Informed Investment Timing

Economic indicators provide insights into investment timing. Investors often wait for specific indicators to signal optimal entry points. For instance, a decline in interest rates might prompt investors to enter the real estate market, anticipating increased demand due to lower borrowing costs.

Conclusion: A Strategic Nexus

The relationship between economic indicators and investment choices weaves a strategic nexus, connecting macroeconomic dynamics with individual investment decisions. By deciphering the language of economic data, stakeholders gain the ability to navigate uncertainty, adapt to changing market conditions, and make informed choices that align with their financial objectives. This symbiotic relationship empowers investors to harness the insights gleaned from economic indicators to chart a course that balances risk and reward, ultimately driving financial success.

Chapter 2: Company Financials Evaluation
Section 2.1: Basics of Company Financial Statements
Understanding the Foundation: Company Financial Statements

Delving into the evaluation of company financials unveils a comprehensive framework for assessing the financial health and performance of businesses. Company financial statements, comprising the Income Statement, Balance Sheet, and Cash Flow Statement, serve as the bedrock of this analysis. In this section, we dissect the fundamental components of these statements and explore how they collectively provide a panoramic view of a company's financial standing.

The Income Statement: Profits and Losses Unveiled

The Income Statement, often referred to as the Profit and Loss Statement, captures a company's revenues, expenses, and ultimately its profitability over a specific period. It illuminates the revenue streams generated from operations, the costs associated with production and operation, and the resulting net income or loss. This statement provides a snapshot of a company's ability to generate profits from its core operations and reveals its cost structure and margins.

The Balance Sheet: Assets, Liabilities, and Equity

The Balance Sheet portrays a snapshot of a company's financial position at a specific point in time. It balances the company's assets, liabilities, and shareholders' equity. Assets encompass resources owned by the company, such as cash, inventory, and property. Liabilities comprise the company's obligations, including loans, debts, and other payables. Shareholders' equity represents the residual interest of owners in the company's assets after deducting liabilities. The Balance Sheet offers insights into a company's solvency, liquidity, and capital structure.

The Cash Flow Statement: Tracking Cash Movements

The Cash Flow Statement unravels the intricate web of a company's cash inflows and outflows over a given period. It categorizes cash flows into operating activities, investing activities, and financing activities. Operating activities encompass cash flows from the core business operations, reflecting the company's ability to generate cash from its day-to-day activities. Investing activities encompass cash flows from the acquisition and disposal of assets. Financing activities capture cash flows related to the company's capital structure, such as equity issuances, debt repayments, and dividend payments. The Cash Flow Statement provides insights into a company's ability to manage its cash resources effectively.

Holistic Insights Through Integration

These three financial statements collectively offer holistic insights into a company's financial landscape. The Income Statement portrays its operational profitability, the Balance Sheet showcases its financial position, and the Cash Flow Statement tracks the movement of cash. Together, these statements enable investors and analysts to assess a company's financial performance, its liquidity position, its ability to generate cash, and its overall financial stability.

The Investor's Lens: Strategic Decision-Making

For investors, these financial statements become a toolkit for strategic decision-making. They allow for comparisons across different companies and industries, providing a basis for identifying industry leaders, assessing growth prospects, and estimating intrinsic values. Evaluating the trends and ratios derived from these statements enables investors to identify red flags, gauge the effectiveness of management, and make informed investment choices.

Conclusion: A Financial Mosaic

The evaluation of company financials, facilitated through the interpretation of Income Statements, Balance Sheets, and Cash Flow Statements, is akin to assembling a financial mosaic. Each statement contributes a unique piece, unveiling different dimensions of a company's financial health and performance. Investors, analysts, and stakeholders adept in deciphering these statements acquire a lens that pierces through complexities, enabling them to navigate the investment landscape with precision and confidence.

Section 2.2: Analyzing Company Financial Statements Ratios and Metrics for Analysis: Decrypting Financial Health

In the intricate landscape of analyzing company financial statements, the spotlight turns to an array of ratios and metrics that act as powerful tools for assessing a company's financial health, performance, and efficiency. These ratios serve as magnifying glasses, enabling investors, analysts, and stakeholders to delve deeper into the nuances of financial data, identify trends, and make informed decisions. This section unveils the significance of these ratios and metrics in painting a comprehensive picture of a company's financial standing.

Liquidity Ratios: Assessing Short-Term Solvency

Liquidity ratios offer insights into a company's ability to meet its short-term financial obligations. The Current Ratio, calculated by dividing current assets by current liabilities, quantifies a company's ability to cover short-term obligations with its readily available resources. Similarly, the Quick Ratio considers only the most liquid assets in relation to current liabilities, offering a more stringent measure of liquidity.

Profitability Ratios: Gauging Earnings Efficiency

Profitability ratios gauge a company's ability to generate profits relative to its various metrics. The Gross Profit Margin assesses the percentage of revenue that remains after deducting the cost of goods sold. The Net Profit Margin, on the other hand, indicates the portion of revenue that translates into net profit after all expenses. Return on Equity (ROE) measures the return generated for shareholders relative to their equity investment.

Efficiency Ratios: Unveiling Operational Efficiency

Efficiency ratios shed light on a company's ability to manage its assets, liabilities, and operations efficiently. The Inventory Turnover Ratio gauges how quickly inventory is sold and replaced within a period. The Receivables Turnover Ratio measures the efficiency of credit management and collection. Additionally, the Payables Turnover Ratio evaluates how effectively a company manages its accounts payable.

Solvency Ratios: Evaluating Long-Term Viability

Solvency ratios assess a company's long-term viability by analyzing its capital structure and debt management. The Debt-to-Equity Ratio reveals the proportion of debt used to finance the company's assets relative to shareholders' equity. The Interest Coverage Ratio measures the company's ability to cover interest expenses with its earnings before interest and taxes (EBIT).

Investor Ratios: Market Perception and Valuation

Investor ratios delve into the market's perception of a company's valuation. The Price-to-Earnings (P/E) Ratio compares a company's stock price to its earnings per share, reflecting how much investors are willing to pay for each dollar of earnings. The Price-to-Book (P/B) Ratio compares the stock's market price to its book value per share, indicating whether the stock is overvalued or undervalued.

Conclusion: The Financial Symphony

The ratios and metrics used to analyze company financial statements orchestrate a symphony of insights, revealing the financial performance, health, and viability of a company from various angles. These tools allow stakeholders to assess liquidity, profitability, efficiency, solvency, and market perception with precision. The harmonious interplay between these ratios offers a dynamic canvas that empowers investors, analysts, and decision-makers to unravel financial intricacies and navigate the investment landscape with acumen and confidence.

Revenue and Profitability Analysis: Unveiling Financial Performance
Understanding Revenue and Profitability Analysis

The scrutiny of a company's financial performance delves deeply into revenue and profitability analysis, essential components of evaluating its operational efficiency and success. Revenue serves as the lifeblood of any business, while profitability determines its sustainability and growth prospects. By dissecting these aspects with precision, investors and analysts gain insights into a company's ability to generate income, control costs, and ultimately yield profits that drive its long-term viability.

Revenue Analysis: The Top Line

Revenue, often referred to as the top line of the income statement, showcases the total income generated from a company's primary operations. Revenue analysis unveils the sources of income, be it from product sales, services rendered, or other operating activities. Through revenue breakdown, analysts discern trends, seasonal variations, and shifts in customer preferences, empowering them to gauge the company's competitive position within its industry.

Segment Revenue Analysis: Deeper Insights

Segment revenue analysis takes a granular approach by dissecting revenue sources across different product lines, geographical regions, or customer segments. This practice provides a nuanced understanding of revenue contributions, enabling strategic decisions that optimize resource allocation, marketing efforts, and product development to maximize profitability.

Profitability Analysis: The Bottom Line

Profitability analysis peers into the bottom line, focusing on how effectively a company translates its revenue into profit. Gross Profit Margin evaluates the profitability of each unit of product sold, factoring in production costs. Operating Profit Margin measures the efficiency of core operations, excluding interest and taxes. Net Profit Margin reveals the portion of revenue that transforms into net profit after all expenses.

Return on Investment (ROI) and Return on Assets (ROA)

Return on Investment (ROI) and Return on Assets (ROA) delve into profitability from an investment perspective. ROI quantifies the return generated from an investment relative to its cost. ROA assesses the profitability of assets employed by the company in generating earnings. These ratios enable comparisons across different investments and industries, guiding capital allocation strategies.

Profitability Ratios in Context

Evaluating profitability ratios in context offers insights into a company's competitive positioning and financial health. High profitability ratios signify efficient operations, pricing power, and effective cost management. However, excessively high ratios might raise questions about sustainable growth and reinvestment in the business.

Conclusion: A Financial Compass

Revenue and profitability analysis act as a financial compass, guiding stakeholders through the intricate landscape of a company's financial performance. The exploration of revenue sources and the efficiency with which revenue translates into profit provide invaluable insights for investment decisions and strategic planning. By interpreting these aspects with rigor and precision, investors and analysts harness the power to discern opportunities, identify challenges, and navigate the ever-evolving realm of business with informed confidence.

Liquidity and Solvency Assessment: Navigating Financial Stability
Understanding Liquidity and Solvency Assessment

The evaluation of a company's financial health extends to the realms of liquidity and solvency assessment, integral components that gauge its ability to meet short-term obligations and ensure long-term viability. The delicate balance between liquidity, ensuring the availability of cash for immediate needs, and solvency, assuring the ability to cover debts over time, holds the key to a company's financial stability. In this section, we delve into the significance of these assessments in deciphering a company's financial robustness.

Liquidity Assessment: The Short-Term Horizon

Liquidity assessment revolves around a company's capacity to cover its short-term financial obligations using its readily available assets. The Current Ratio and Quick Ratio are pivotal metrics in this domain. The Current Ratio compares current assets to current liabilities, reflecting whether a company can meet its obligations with assets expected to turn into cash within a year. The Quick Ratio offers a stricter measure, considering only the most liquid assets like cash and marketable securities.

Operating Cash Flow and Liquidity

Liquidity assessment extends to a company's ability to generate operating cash flows. Positive operating cash flows signify that a company is generating more cash from its core operations than it's spending. This cash can be allocated to debt repayment, expansion, or distribution to shareholders.

Solvency Assessment: The Long-Term Horizon

Solvency assessment delves into a company's long-term financial health by analyzing its ability to meet its debt obligations. The Debt-to-Equity Ratio serves as a crucial metric, showcasing the proportion of debt relative to shareholders' equity. A lower ratio suggests a healthier capital structure with less reliance on debt financing.

Interest Coverage Ratio and Solvency

The Interest Coverage Ratio gauges a company's ability to meet interest payments on its outstanding debt. A higher ratio indicates greater financial capacity to cover interest expenses. This metric not only reflects solvency but also offers insights into the company's profitability and cash flow generation.

Striking the Balance: Liquidity vs. Solvency

Balancing liquidity and solvency is essential. Overemphasizing liquidity might lead to underutilized assets and missed growth opportunities. Conversely, focusing solely on solvency might lead to inadequate cash reserves to cover immediate needs. Striking the right balance ensures that a company can manage both short-term demands and long-term obligations effectively.

Liquidity and Solvency in Decision-Making

Liquidity and solvency assessments significantly influence decision-making. Lenders and creditors rely on these metrics to assess creditworthiness. Investors use them to evaluate risk and potential returns. Management uses them to make strategic financial decisions, such as debt issuance or dividend distribution.

Conclusion: The Financial Foundation

Liquidity and solvency assessments form the bedrock of a company's financial foundation. By evaluating its ability to manage immediate obligations and long-term debts, stakeholders gain insights into its resilience, stability, and capacity to weather economic fluctuations. The delicate balance between liquidity and solvency determines not only a company's survival but also its potential for growth and prosperity in an ever-evolving financial landscape.

Efficiency and Operating Performance Metrics: Unveiling Operational Excellence
Understanding Efficiency and Operating Performance Metrics

In the realm of company financial analysis, delving into efficiency and operating performance metrics illuminates the inner workings of a business, revealing its ability to optimize resources, manage costs, and maximize operational output. These metrics serve as powerful tools for investors, analysts, and stakeholders to gauge a company's effectiveness in converting inputs into outputs, ultimately shaping its competitive edge and long-term success. In this section, we delve into the significance of these metrics in deciphering a company's operational excellence.

Operating Efficiency Analysis: Optimizing Resources

Operating efficiency metrics assess a company's capacity to optimize its resources and manage costs. The Inventory Turnover Ratio measures how effectively a company manages its inventory by evaluating how quickly it sells and replaces its inventory within a given period. A high turnover ratio indicates efficient inventory management, reducing carrying costs and capital tied up in inventory.

Days Sales Outstanding (DSO) and Days Payables Outstanding (DPO)

Days Sales Outstanding (DSO) evaluates how efficiently a company collects its accounts receivable. A lower DSO indicates a faster collection process, translating into improved cash flow. Days Payables Outstanding (DPO) assesses how efficiently a company manages its accounts payable. A higher DPO suggests the company is taking longer to pay its suppliers, potentially improving cash flow.

Asset Turnover Ratio: Asset Utilization

The Asset Turnover Ratio measures a company's efficiency in utilizing its assets to generate sales. A higher ratio signifies effective asset utilization, indicating that the company generates more revenue per unit of assets. This ratio is particularly relevant for capital-intensive industries.

Operating Performance Metrics: Enhancing Productivity

Operating performance metrics delve into a company's productivity and effectiveness in generating profits from its core operations. The Operating Profit Margin reveals the efficiency of generating operating profit from revenue after considering all operating expenses. The Return on Assets (ROA) assesses how efficiently a company employs its assets to generate earnings.

Operating Performance in Decision-Making

Operating performance metrics play a pivotal role in decision-making. Investors use them to assess the efficiency and profitability of a company's operations. Management relies on these metrics to identify areas for improvement, streamline processes, and enhance overall productivity. Additionally, analysts leverage these metrics to benchmark a company's performance against its peers.

Conclusion: The Operational Compass

Efficiency and operating performance metrics act as a compass guiding stakeholder through the intricate terrain of a company's operational landscape. By assessing resource optimization, cost management, asset utilization, and profitability, these metrics provide a lens into a company's ability to excel in its core activities. The insights derived from these metrics empower investors, analysts, and decision-makers to align strategies with operational excellence, enhance productivity, and chart a course for sustained growth and success.

Section 2.3: Financial Ratios and Their Significance Debt Management and Leverage Ratios: Balancing Financial Structure

In the intricate tapestry of financial analysis, the spotlight turns to debt management and leverage ratios, critical tools that evaluate a company's ability to manage debt obligations while optimizing its capital structure. These ratios illuminate a company's risk appetite, its reliance on external financing, and its ability to safeguard long-term solvency. As integral components of financial ratios, debt management and leverage ratios provide stakeholders with insights crucial for strategic decision-making. This section explores the significance of these ratios in deciphering a company's financial structure and stability.

Debt Management Ratios: Ensuring Financial Discipline

Debt management ratios delve into a company's debt-related obligations, shedding light on its capacity to service its debts. The Debt-to-Equity Ratio quantifies the proportion of debt to equity in a company's capital structure. This ratio underscores the risk associated with debt financing and the extent to which a company relies on creditors to fund its operations and expansion.

Interest Coverage Ratio: Assessing Debt Servicing Capability

The Interest Coverage Ratio assesses a company's ability to meet its interest payments using its operating profits. A higher ratio indicates a healthier capacity to cover interest expenses, reflecting a lower risk of defaulting on interest payments. This ratio is particularly crucial for investors and creditors evaluating a company's creditworthiness.

Leverage Ratios: Balancing Risk and Returns

Leverage ratios analyze the financial risk associated with a company's capital structure. The Equity Ratio, also known as the Equity Multiplier, gauges the extent to which a company uses debt to finance its assets. A high equity multiplier suggests higher financial leverage and amplified risk exposure. Conversely, a lower multiplier indicates a more conservative capital structure.

Debt-to-Assets Ratio: Capital Structure Assessment

The Debt-to-Assets Ratio evaluates the proportion of a company's assets financed by debt. A higher ratio indicates greater financial leverage and a higher risk profile. This ratio plays a pivotal role in assessing a company's financial risk and its ability to absorb financial shocks.

Significance in Decision-Making

Debt management and leverage ratios play a vital role in decision-making across various spheres. Investors use these ratios to evaluate the risk-return trade-off associated with a company's financial structure. Creditors rely on them to assess the creditworthiness of borrowers. Management uses these ratios to make informed financing decisions, including the optimal mix of equity and debt to achieve growth and stability.

Balancing Act: Optimizing Debt and Equity

The interpretation of debt management and leverage ratios involves a delicate balancing act. While debt can enhance returns, excessive leverage heightens financial risk. Striking the optimal balance between equity and debt financing ensures that a company can capitalize on growth opportunities without compromising its financial stability.

Conclusion: The Financial Symphony's Tempo

Debt management and leverage ratios resonate as essential notes in the financial symphony, harmonizing the interplay between debt, equity, and risk. These ratios encapsulate a company's financial structure, guiding stakeholders in assessing its ability to meet obligations and sustain growth. By deciphering these ratios with precision, investors, analysts, and decision-makers gain the ability to navigate the intricate landscape of financial decisions, orchestrating a harmonious balance between leverage and stability.

Price-to-Earnings (P/E) Ratio: Decoding Market Valuation Understanding the Price-to-Earnings (P/E) Ratio

The Price-to-Earnings (P/E) ratio stands as a fundamental metric in the world of financial analysis, illuminating the intricate relationship between a company's stock price and its earnings. This ratio serves as a crucial tool for investors, analysts, and stakeholders seeking to assess a company's valuation, understand market sentiment, and make informed decisions in the dynamic landscape of the stock market. Delving into the nuances of the P/E ratio unveils its significance in decoding market valuation.

Calculating the P/E Ratio

The P/E ratio is computed by dividing a company's current stock price by its earnings per share (EPS). This ratio essentially quantifies the price investors are willing to pay for each dollar of earnings generated by the company. A high P/E ratio suggests that investors have high expectations for future growth and are willing to pay a premium for a company's shares. Conversely, a low P/E ratio may indicate undervaluation or lower growth prospects.

Interpreting the P/E Ratio

Interpreting the P/E ratio requires context and comparison. A company's P/E ratio should ideally be assessed relative to its peers in the same industry or sector. A high P/E ratio might indicate that the market anticipates robust future growth, but it could also imply overvaluation. A low P/E ratio could signify an undervalued stock, but it might also reflect market skepticism about the company's prospects.

Growth Stocks vs. Value Stocks

The P/E ratio plays a pivotal role in distinguishing growth stocks from value stocks. Growth stocks tend to have higher P/E ratios due to the anticipation of future earnings growth. These companies often reinvest their earnings to fuel expansion. On the other hand, value stocks, which are perceived as undervalued, typically have lower P/E ratios.

Market Sentiment and Investor Behavior

The P/E ratio also mirrors market sentiment and investor behavior. During periods of market exuberance, stocks may trade at elevated P/E ratios as investors chase growth opportunities. Conversely, during economic uncertainty or market corrections, P/E ratios may contract as investors seek safety and stability.

Limitations and Considerations

While the P/E ratio offers valuable insights, it has limitations. It does not consider other factors like debt, industry dynamics, or macroeconomic conditions. A company with a high P/E ratio may carry higher risk, and a low P/E ratio might indicate structural challenges. Moreover, cyclical industries might experience fluctuations in P/E ratios due to changes in economic conditions.

Conclusion: Unveiling Valuation Dynamics

The Price-to-Earnings (P/E) ratio functions as a window into the intricate dynamics of market valuation. By quantifying the relationship between stock price and earnings, this ratio provides stakeholders with insights into investor sentiment, growth prospects, and the perceived value of a company's shares. As a versatile tool for decision-making, the P/E ratio empowers investors and analysts to navigate the complexities of stock valuation, ultimately guiding them in making informed choices in the ever-evolving financial landscape.

Price-to-Book (P/B) Ratio: Evaluating Market Value and Book Value Understanding the Price-to-Book (P/B) Ratio

In the intricate landscape of financial analysis, the Price-to-Book (P/B) ratio emerges as a significant metric that unveils the interplay between a company's market value and its underlying book value. This ratio holds a pivotal role for investors, analysts, and stakeholders seeking to understand a company's valuation relative to its tangible assets. The exploration of the nuances of the P/B ratio reveals its essence in evaluating market perception and financial health.

Cracking the P/B Ratio Calculation

The P/B ratio is a straightforward calculation achieved by dividing a company's current market price per share by its book value per share. The book value encompasses the net value of a company's assets after deducting its liabilities. This ratio provides insights into whether a company is trading at a premium or discount to its intrinsic value as reflected in its book value.

Interpreting the P/B Ratio

Interpreting the P/B ratio necessitates a contextual understanding. A P/B ratio greater than 1 implies the market values the company's net assets more highly than its book value, signifying optimism about future growth prospects, intellectual property, brand value, or other intangible assets. A P/B ratio less than 1 might indicate the market perceives the company's book value as higher than its market value, potentially hinting at undervaluation.

Comparing P/B Ratios

A robust analysis of the P/B ratio requires comparison against industry peers, historical data, and broader market trends. A company with a lower P/B ratio compared to its peers might signal an attractive investment opportunity, provided the reasons for the undervaluation are assessed. Conversely, a higher P/B ratio may warrant scrutiny to ensure it aligns with the company's growth potential and market dynamics.

Market Perception and Financial Health

The P/B ratio is a lens through which market perception and financial health become discernible. A high P/B ratio might indicate the market's recognition of a company's intangible assets, innovation, or strong brand presence. A low P/B ratio may indicate market skepticism or potentially point to challenges in generating substantial returns on equity.

Limitations and Considerations

While the P/B ratio offers insights, it has limitations. It doesn't account for factors like earnings growth, profitability, or market sentiment. Additionally, certain industries with high intellectual property or research and development investments might have intangible assets that aren't adequately captured by book value.

Conclusion: The Valuation Compass

The Price-to-Book (P/B) ratio operates as a valuation compass, guiding stakeholders through the intricate web of market perception and financial fundamentals. By evaluating the equilibrium between market value and book value, this ratio offers a glimpse into investor sentiment, tangible assets, and potential undervaluation or overvaluation. As an indispensable tool for decision-making, the P/B ratio empowers investors and analysts to navigate the intricacies of stock valuation, enabling them to make informed choices amidst the ebb and flow of financial dynamics.

Debt-to-Equity Ratio: Navigating Financial Structure and Risk Understanding the Debt-to-Equity Ratio

In the realm of financial analysis, the Debt-to-Equity (D/E) ratio emerges as a pivotal metric that provides insights into a company's financial structure, risk profile, and the manner in which it finances its operations. This ratio holds significant implications for investors, analysts, and stakeholders aiming to evaluate a company's capitalization strategy and its potential exposure to financial risks. Delving into the intricacies of the D/E ratio unveils its essence in deciphering financial leverage and stability.

Comprehending the D/E Ratio Calculation

The D/E ratio is derived by dividing a company's total liabilities by its total shareholders' equity. This ratio unveils the extent to which a company relies on debt financing to support its operations and growth endeavors. A higher D/E ratio signifies a higher proportion of debt relative to equity, highlighting a greater reliance on external financing.

Interpreting the D/E Ratio

Interpreting the D/E ratio necessitates careful consideration of the company's industry, stage of development, and financial goals. A high D/E ratio might indicate that the company has aggressively used debt to finance expansion or acquisitions. While this could amplify returns during favorable economic conditions, it also exposes the company to higher financial risk during economic downturns.

Comparative Analysis and Industry Norms

Understanding the D/E ratio is enhanced through comparative analysis within the industry. Companies within capital-intensive sectors might naturally have higher D/E ratios due to the nature of their operations. Comparing a company's D/E ratio to industry norms and its historical performance allows for a more comprehensive assessment of its financial leverage.

Risk and Reward Trade-Off

The D/E ratio epitomizes the risk and reward trade-off. Higher leverage through debt can magnify returns during prosperous times, but it also heightens the risk of default during economic downturns. A lower D/E ratio might signify a more conservative financial strategy, aiming to safeguard against financial distress.

Investor Perception and Creditworthiness

The D/E ratio significantly influences investor perception and creditworthiness. Investors seeking higher returns might be attracted to companies with higher leverage, anticipating amplified growth. On the other hand, creditors might scrutinize companies with high D/E ratios as they represent a higher likelihood of defaulting on debt payments.

Limitations and Considerations

While the D/E ratio provides valuable insights, it's important to consider its limitations. It doesn't capture the nuances of the types of debt or the interest rates attached to them. Additionally, cyclical industries might experience fluctuations in D/E ratios due to changes in economic conditions.

Conclusion: The Financial Balance Beam

The Debt-to-Equity (D/E) ratio acts as a financial balance beam, assessing the equilibrium between debt financing and equity capital. By quantifying the proportion of debt relative to equity, this ratio unveils a company's approach to capitalization, its risk appetite, and its capacity to navigate financial uncertainties. As a decisive tool for decision-making, the D/E ratio empowers investors and analysts to navigate the complexities of financial leverage, aiding them in making informed choices in the ever-evolving landscape of business and finance.

Section 2.4: Identifying Strengths and Weaknesses
Return on Equity (ROE) and Return on Assets (ROA): Unveiling Performance Metrics

In the realm of financial analysis, the metrics of Return on Equity (ROE) and Return on Assets (ROA) emerge as beacons, illuminating a company's efficiency in generating returns from its resources. These performance indicators stand as critical tools for investors, analysts, and stakeholders seeking to evaluate a company's operational effectiveness, profitability, and capacity to create value for shareholders. This section delves into the significance of ROE and ROA in identifying strengths and weaknesses within a company.

Return on Equity (ROE): Unlocking Shareholder Value

Return on Equity (ROE) serves as a key performance metric, unveiling how efficiently a company utilizes shareholders' equity to generate profits. The formula divides net income by shareholders' equity, reflecting the return earned on the investment made by shareholders. A higher ROE signifies effective capital utilization and value creation, while a lower ROE might point to inefficiencies in generating returns.

Interpreting ROE: Efficiency and Profitability

Interpreting ROE requires context and comparison. A higher ROE can result from effective management of assets, prudent cost control, and favorable industry conditions. However, a high ROE might also be due to excessive financial leverage, which amplifies risk. Comparing a company's ROE to its industry peers and its historical performance aids in assessing its competitive positioning.

Return on Assets (ROA): Maximizing Asset Efficiency

Return on Assets (ROA) evaluates a company's ability to generate profits from its assets. The formula divides net income by average total assets, revealing the proportion of earnings generated relative to the assets employed. A higher ROA signifies efficient asset utilization, while a lower ROA might indicate suboptimal operational efficiency or overcapitalization.

ROE vs. ROA: Balancing Investment and Financing

ROE and ROA offer distinct perspectives. ROE emphasizes the returns generated for shareholders relative to their investment, highlighting the equity financing aspect. ROA focuses on operational efficiency in generating returns from all assets, regardless of their financing source. Balancing both metrics provides a comprehensive view of a company's performance.

Strengths and Weaknesses: Strategic Insights

ROE and ROA help identify strengths and weaknesses in a company's financial performance. A consistently high ROE suggests a company effectively leverages equity to generate returns, indicating shareholder value creation. A high ROA signifies operational efficiency, while a declining ROA might indicate deteriorating asset productivity or eroding profitability.

Comparative Analysis and Industry Norms

Understanding strengths and weaknesses through ROE and ROA is augmented by comparative analysis. Benchmarking against industry norms and peer companies provides insights into a company's relative performance. Deviations from industry averages can signal unique strengths or challenges within the company's operations.

Conclusion: The Performance Compass

Return on Equity (ROE) and Return on Assets (ROA) function as a performance compass, guiding stakeholders through the labyrinth of financial efficiency and profitability. By evaluating a company's ability to generate returns from equity and assets, these metrics provide valuable insights into operational excellence, shareholder value creation, and growth potential. As indispensable tools for decision-making, ROE and ROA empower investors and analysts to assess a company's strengths and weaknesses, enabling them to make informed choices in navigating the intricate landscape of financial analysis.

Benchmarking Against Industry Peers: Measuring Performance in Context
Understanding Benchmarking Against Industry Peers

In the realm of financial analysis, the practice of benchmarking against industry peers emerges as a fundamental strategy to evaluate a company's performance within the broader competitive landscape. This approach allows investors, analysts, and stakeholders to gain insights into a company's relative strengths and weaknesses, enabling them to assess its standing, identify areas for improvement, and make informed decisions. This section delves into the significance of benchmarking against industry peers in measuring performance within a contextual framework.

The Concept of Benchmarking

Benchmarking involves comparing a company's financial metrics, ratios, and performance indicators to those of its industry peers or competitors. This process sheds light on how the company fares in terms of efficiency, profitability, and other key aspects. Benchmarking offers a comparative yardstick against which a company's performance can be measured, providing valuable insights for strategic planning.

Identifying Performance Gaps and Opportunities

By benchmarking against industry peers, stakeholders can identify performance gaps and opportunities for enhancement. If a company's financial metrics consistently fall below industry averages, it may signify potential weaknesses that require attention. Conversely, outperforming industry peers might indicate areas of competitive advantage that can be leveraged for growth.

Determining Industry Norms and Best Practices

Benchmarking also aids in determining industry norms and best practices. Understanding what constitutes typical performance within an industry helps stakeholders set realistic expectations and align their strategies accordingly. Additionally, observing best practices of high-performing peers provides actionable insights to improve operational efficiency and financial health.

Comparative Analysis: A Comprehensive View

Comparative analysis through benchmarking offers a comprehensive view of a company's performance. It enables a deeper understanding of the dynamics driving financial success or challenges. Furthermore, this analysis extends beyond financial ratios, encompassing operational efficiency, market share, innovation, and other qualitative factors.

Strategic Decision-Making

Benchmarking informs strategic decision-making. A company falling short of industry norms might reevaluate its operational strategies, cost structures, and resource allocation to close the performance gap. Companies outperforming their peers can capitalize on their strengths to differentiate themselves and pursue growth opportunities.

Industry-Specific Considerations

Benchmarking should consider industry-specific dynamics. Industries vary in terms of capital intensity, growth cycles, regulatory environment, and competitive landscape. Therefore, benchmarks should be tailored to reflect these nuances, ensuring accurate and relevant comparisons.

Conclusion: The Performance Compass

Benchmarking against industry peers acts as a performance compass, guiding stakeholders through the intricacies of financial analysis within a contextual frame. By juxtaposing a company's performance against its peers, this practice provides a panoramic view of its standing, strengths, and areas for improvement. As an indispensable tool for strategic decision-making, benchmarking empowers investors and analysts to make informed choices, fostering growth, competitiveness, and success within the dynamic currents of the business landscape.

Historical Performance Analysis: Unveiling Insights through Time Understanding Historical Performance Analysis

In the realm of financial analysis, the practice of historical performance analysis emerges as a cornerstone for evaluating a company's trajectory and deciphering its past financial performance. This analytical approach allows investors, analysts, and stakeholders to gain valuable insights into a company's growth patterns, volatility, and resilience across various economic landscapes. This section delves into the significance of historical performance analysis in unveiling insights that span the dimensions of time.

The Essence of Historical Performance

Historical performance analysis entails examining a company's financial data, ratios, and key indicators over a defined period. This practice provides a retrospective view of how the company navigated through different market conditions, economic cycles, and internal changes. By studying historical trends, stakeholders can extrapolate potential future scenarios and make more informed decisions.

Insights through Time: Identifying Patterns

One of the primary goals of historical performance analysis is to identify patterns and trends. By examining historical financial data, stakeholders can recognize recurring cycles, growth spurts, and potential factors influencing fluctuations in performance. These insights contribute to a deeper understanding of a company's operational dynamics.

Volatility and Stability Assessment

Analyzing historical performance unveils a company's volatility and stability. A company with consistently stable financial performance might attract risk-averse investors seeking reliability. On the other hand, companies with fluctuating results may appeal to risk-tolerant investors who anticipate higher potential returns during periods of growth.

Adaptability and Resilience

Historical performance analysis also illuminates a company's adaptability and resilience. By studying how a company responded to challenges and capitalized on opportunities in the past, stakeholders can gauge its ability to weather uncertainties and innovate in the face of change.

Comparative Analysis: Tracking Progress

Comparing historical performance with industry peers, benchmarks, or the company's own historical data enhances the analysis. Such comparisons provide insights into whether the company is improving or lagging behind in terms of growth, profitability, efficiency, and other key performance indicators.

Strategic Decision-Making

Historical performance analysis informs strategic decision-making. Insights gained from past successes and failures aid in setting realistic goals, formulating strategies, and aligning resources. Companies can learn from past mistakes and leverage past achievements to chart a path for future growth.

Industry-Specific Considerations

It's crucial to consider industry-specific nuances in historical performance analysis. Industries have their own cycles, seasonality, and market dynamics. Understanding these unique characteristics allows for a more accurate interpretation of historical data.

Conclusion: The Insights Time Capsule

Historical performance analysis acts as a time capsule, encapsulating a company's journey through the tides of time. By delving into past financial performance, stakeholders glean insights that transcend timeframes, offering lessons from successes and challenges alike. As an invaluable tool for strategic foresight, historical performance analysis empowers investors and analysts to make informed decisions, fostering resilience, adaptability, and growth across the ever-evolving landscapes of business and finance.

Assessing Long-Term Sustainability: Navigating the Path to Resilience
Understanding the Assessment of Long-Term Sustainability

In the intricate landscape of financial analysis, the practice of assessing long-term sustainability emerges as a vital strategy for evaluating a company's ability to endure, thrive, and create value over extended periods. This analytical approach allows investors, analysts, and stakeholders to gauge a company's resilience against market fluctuations, changing industry dynamics, and evolving consumer preferences. This section delves into the significance of assessing long-term sustainability in navigating the path to lasting success.

The Essence of Long-Term Sustainability

Assessing long-term sustainability involves evaluating a company's strategies, operations, and financial health in light of future challenges and opportunities. This approach extends beyond short-term profitability to encompass factors that influence a company's ability to maintain relevance and value in the years ahead.

Key Indicators of Long-Term Sustainability

Several key indicators shed light on a company's long-term sustainability. Strong corporate governance practices, ethical business conduct, innovation, and a commitment to environmental and social responsibility contribute to a company's durability. Furthermore, financial health, investment in research and development, and adaptability to market changes play pivotal roles in long-term viability.

Resilience in the Face of Change

Assessing long-term sustainability unveils a company's resilience in the face of change. By scrutinizing its capacity to weather economic downturns, industry disruptions, and shifting consumer preferences, stakeholders gain insights into whether the company is poised for enduring success or vulnerable to challenges.

Environmental, Social, and Governance (ESG) Considerations

ESG considerations are integral to evaluating long-term sustainability. Companies that prioritize environmental conservation, social impact, and strong governance practices tend to exhibit higher resilience and value creation over time. ESG performance reflects a company's commitment to operating responsibly and creating positive societal and environmental outcomes.

Strategic Vision and Adaptation

Companies that embrace long-term sustainability prioritize strategic vision and adaptation. They continuously innovate to meet evolving customer needs, embrace new technologies, and align their operations with global trends. This adaptability fosters long-term competitiveness and relevance.

Investor Confidence and Stakeholder Trust

Assessing long-term sustainability enhances investor confidence and stakeholder trust. Companies that prioritize sustainability and demonstrate a commitment to long-term value creation are more likely to attract investors aligned with their values. Stakeholders, including employees, customers, and communities, also gravitate toward companies that exhibit responsible and sustainable practices.

Conclusion: The Resilience Blueprint

Assessing long-term sustainability acts as a resilience blueprint, guiding stakeholders through the ever-evolving terrain of business dynamics. By evaluating a company's adaptability, ethical compass, and commitment to enduring value creation, this practice provides insights that transcend short-term gains. As an instrumental tool for strategic decision-making, assessing long-term sustainability empowers investors and analysts to make informed choices, fostering resilience, stability, and growth across the sweeping horizons of business and finance.

Chapter 3: Analysis of Market News and Events
Section 3.1 Role of Market News in Fundamental Analysis

In the dynamic world of fundamental analysis, Chapter 3 embarks on a journey to explore the profound impact of market news and events on the evaluation of financial assets. This chapter delves into the intricate relationship between real-time information dissemination and the decision-making processes of investors, analysts, and stakeholders. Through a comprehensive understanding of the role of market news, stakeholders gain insights into how external events shape market sentiment and influence investment strategies.

Understanding the Role of Market News

Market news holds a pivotal role in fundamental analysis by providing a continuous stream of information that drives market sentiment, investment decisions, and asset valuation. News encompasses a wide spectrum of events, ranging from economic data releases and corporate announcements to geopolitical developments and global economic trends. The influence of market news is undeniable, as it molds perceptions, prompts actions, and shapes the trajectory of financial markets.

Impact on Investor Sentiment

Market news exerts a profound influence on investor sentiment. Positive news can fuel optimism, leading to buying activity and price appreciation. Conversely, negative news triggers caution, potentially resulting in selling pressure and price declines. The ebb and flow of market sentiment, often influenced by news cycles, plays a significant role in determining short-term market movements.

Incorporating News into Analysis

Fundamental analysts integrate market news into their analysis to gauge its potential implications on asset values. News related to economic indicators, interest rate changes, corporate earnings reports, and regulatory developments can alter market dynamics and investment outlooks. Analysts assess the relevance, credibility, and potential impact of news to align their strategies with evolving market conditions.

Event-Driven Analysis

Event-driven analysis focuses on understanding the potential market reaction to specific events. It involves anticipating how news, such as central bank decisions, trade agreements, or geopolitical tensions, could shape investor behavior and asset prices. By factoring in event-driven scenarios, investors and analysts aim to position themselves advantageously.

Risk Management and Volatility

Market news introduces an element of unpredictability and volatility. Unexpected news, such as natural disasters, political crises, or technological breakthroughs, can lead to sharp price fluctuations. Investors must implement robust risk management strategies to navigate such uncertainties and protect their portfolios.

Integration with Other Analysis Techniques

The role of market news intersects with other fundamental analysis techniques, such as economic indicators and financial statement analysis. By synthesizing news with macroeconomic trends and company-specific data, stakeholders gain a holistic perspective that informs comprehensive investment decisions.

Conclusion: News as a Catalyst

Chapter 3 underscores the indispensable role of market news as a catalyst in the world of fundamental analysis. The continuous flow of information shapes market sentiment, influences investor behavior, and serves as a compass for strategic decisions. By comprehending the multifaceted impact of market news, stakeholders are empowered to navigate the intricate currents of financial markets with a discerning eye, fostering informed choices and resilient strategies.

Chapter 4: Market Sentiment and Information Flow
Navigating the Tides of Perception Understanding Market Sentiment and Information Flow

In the intricate landscape of financial analysis, the exploration of market sentiment and information flow stands as a critical endeavor for comprehending the dynamics that shape investor behavior and asset valuation. This exploration unveils the intricate interplay between real-time information dissemination, collective investor psychology, and the resultant impact on financial markets. Through a comprehensive understanding of market sentiment and the flow of information, stakeholders gain insights into how perception drives decision-making and influences market trends.

Market Sentiment: The Pulse of Perception

Market sentiment embodies the collective emotions, attitudes, and beliefs of investors and participants within financial markets. It serves as a barometer that gauges whether investors are optimistic, cautious, or pessimistic about future market prospects. Sentiment can influence the timing and direction of investment decisions, thereby impacting asset prices and market volatility.

Influences on Market Sentiment

Market sentiment is influenced by a multitude of factors, including economic data releases, corporate earnings reports, geopolitical events, central bank pronouncements, and media coverage. Positive news may drive bullish sentiment, while negative developments can foster bearish sentiment. Social media platforms and online forums also contribute to the amplification of sentiment, magnifying its impact.

Psychology of Investor Behavior

Understanding the psychology of investor behavior is central to comprehending market sentiment. Herd behavior, where investors tend to follow the actions of the majority, can amplify sentiment-driven movements. Fear, greed, and the fear of missing out (FOMO) can prompt irrational decision-making, contributing to market bubbles and crashes.

Information Flow: Catalyst for Sentiment Shifts

Information flow serves as the catalyst that triggers shifts in market sentiment. Timely dissemination of news, data, and events prompts investors to recalibrate their views and reassess their investment strategies. Rapid information dissemination, facilitated by digital platforms, has intensified the speed at which sentiment can change.

Media Influence and Noise

Media plays a crucial role in information flow and sentiment formation. Media coverage can either amplify or distort news, influencing investor perception. Noise, characterized by excessive and irrelevant information, can cloud judgment and exacerbate sentiment-driven swings.

Risk and Opportunity Perception

Market sentiment and information flow create a spectrum of perceived risks and opportunities. Bullish sentiment might lead to perceived opportunities for growth, while bearish sentiment could prompt a heightened awareness of risks and potential losses. Understanding this interplay aids investors in managing risk and capitalizing on opportunities.

Impact on Investment Decisions

Market sentiment significantly influences investment decisions. Fundamental analysts and traders alike factor in sentiment trends to gauge potential market movements. Long-term investors may utilize contrarian strategies, taking advantage of sentiment-driven market mispricings.

Conclusion: The Perception Prism

The exploration of market sentiment and information flow unveils the intricate prism through which investors perceive and react to financial markets. By delving into the psychology of investor behavior, the influences on sentiment, and the catalytic role of information, stakeholders gain a deeper understanding of the forces shaping market dynamics. Armed with insights into sentiment-driven movements, stakeholders can navigate the nuanced currents of financial markets, fostering informed choices, strategic decision-making, and resilient portfolios.

Chapter 5: Impact of News on Asset Prices
Unveiling the Market Reaction Understanding the Impact of News on Asset Prices

In the realm of financial analysis, Chapter 3 ventures into the exploration of the profound influence that news exerts on asset prices. This section illuminates the intricate relationship between news dissemination, investor sentiment, and the resultant market reactions. By delving into the dynamics that dictate how news shapes the valuation of financial assets, stakeholders gain insights into the mechanisms driving short-term and long-term price movements.

News as a Market Catalyst

News acts as a catalyst that can trigger significant fluctuations in asset prices. Be it economic data releases, corporate earnings announcements, geopolitical events, or policy changes, news disseminates information that prompts investors to recalibrate their expectations, reassess risks, and realign their investment strategies. This recalibration often results in rapid market responses that influence price direction.

Market Efficiency and Reaction Speed

Financial markets are characterized by varying degrees of efficiency. In highly efficient markets, news is swiftly incorporated into asset prices, leaving little room for arbitrage opportunities. In less efficient markets, news might lead to significant price adjustments as participants react to new information.

Immediate vs. Delayed Reactions

The impact of news on asset prices can manifest as both immediate and delayed reactions. Some news, particularly unexpected developments, can trigger rapid and pronounced price movements in the short term. Other news might have a more gradual influence, taking time to unfold and reflect in asset valuations.

Volatility and Risk Management

News-driven price fluctuations often introduce heightened volatility to markets. Investors must adopt effective risk management strategies to navigate this volatility, safeguarding their portfolios against unexpected adverse events and capitalizing on opportunities that emerge from positive news.

Chapter 6: Evaluating News Sources
Ensuring Credibility Understanding the Significance of Source Evaluation

The analysis of market news requires a discerning approach to evaluating the credibility and reliability of news sources. As the accuracy and objectivity of news directly influence market sentiment and investment decisions, stakeholders must navigate a sea of information sources to extract accurate insights from the noise.

Established News Outlets

Established and reputable news outlets often adhere to journalistic standards, ensuring accurate and unbiased reporting. Investors and analysts frequently rely on sources such as financial newspapers, business news channels, and official government releases for credible information.

Digital and Social Media Platforms

The rise of digital and social media platforms has democratized news dissemination but has also led to information proliferation and misinformation. While these platforms provide real-time updates, stakeholders must exercise caution and verify information from reliable sources.

Expert Analysis and Commentary

Expert analysis and commentary can provide valuable insights into the implications of news events. Investors often turn to reputable financial analysts, economists, and industry experts for contextual understanding and interpretation of news developments.

Bias and Objectivity Assessment

Evaluating news sources requires an assessment of potential bias and objectivity. Sources with an overt bias or vested interests may present information selectively, influencing the perception of events. Seeking multiple perspectives and cross-referencing information aids in forming a comprehensive view.

Chapter 7: Reliable Financial News Outlets
Navigating the Sea of Information Understanding the Significance of Reliable Financial News Outlets

In the realm of financial analysis, the selection of reliable financial news outlets holds paramount importance as a strategic compass for investors, analysts, and stakeholders seeking accurate and unbiased information. This section delves into the critical role that credible news sources play in shaping investment decisions, guiding market perceptions, and fostering informed choices within the ever-evolving landscape of finance.

Credibility and Accuracy as Pillars

Reliable financial news outlets serve as pillars of credibility and accuracy. These outlets adhere to rigorous journalistic standards, prioritizing objectivity, fact-checking, and comprehensive reporting. The commitment to these principles ensures that the information disseminated is factual, unbiased, and relevant to the financial markets.

Established Financial Newspapers and Magazines

Established financial newspapers and magazines often lead the way in delivering reliable news content. Renowned publications have dedicated teams of journalists, analysts, and experts who provide in-depth coverage of market trends, economic indicators, corporate earnings, and global events. Investors frequently turn to these sources for insightful analysis and objective reporting.

Business News Television Channels

Business news television channels provide real-time coverage of market events, economic data releases, and corporate developments. Reputable channels offer insights from financial experts, industry leaders, and economists, contributing to a holistic understanding of market dynamics. These platforms facilitate immediate access to breaking news and expert commentary.

Official Government Releases and Regulatory Authorities

Official government releases and statements from regulatory authorities are invaluable sources of information. These releases provide accurate data on economic indicators, policy changes, and regulatory updates. Investors and analysts consider government sources as reliable references for making informed decisions.

Financial News Websites and Online Platforms

Financial news websites and online platforms offer a wealth of information accessible at users' fingertips. Reputable websites curate news from diverse sources, providing comprehensive coverage of global markets, economic trends, and financial developments. However, users must exercise caution and verify information from reliable sources to avoid misinformation.

Reputation and Recognition

Reputation and recognition are key indicators of reliable financial news outlets. Trusted sources have a history of accurate reporting and are recognized within the industry for their commitment to excellence. Investors and analysts rely on these outlets for trustworthy insights and dependable analysis.

Cross-Referencing and Verification

Cross-referencing and verification of information from multiple reliable sources enhance confidence in the accuracy of news reports. This practice reduces the risk of relying on potentially biased or erroneous information. Comparing information from different reputable outlets aids in forming a well-rounded perspective.

Conclusion: Anchoring Knowledge with Credibility

The selection of reliable financial news outlets is a fundamental step in anchoring knowledge and guiding decisions in the domain of financial analysis. By tapping into credible sources that prioritize accuracy, objectivity, and comprehensive reporting, stakeholders equip themselves with the tools needed to navigate the intricate currents of market information. In a world inundated with data, choosing reputable news outlets ensures that investors, analysts, and stakeholders can make well-informed choices, charting a course towards informed decisions and strategic success.

Chapter 8: Differentiating Between News and Opinion
Navigating the Spectrum of Analysis Understanding the Distinction Between News and Opinion

In the intricate landscape of financial analysis, Chapter 3 delves into the art of distinguishing between news and opinion, an essential skill for investors, analysts, and stakeholders seeking clarity amidst the sea of information. This section underscores the significance of recognizing the boundaries that separate factual reporting from subjective interpretation. By mastering the art of differentiating between news and opinion, stakeholders can glean accurate insights, refine their analysis, and make informed decisions within the ever-evolving dynamics of financial markets.

News: A Foundation of Facts

News represents the foundation of factual reporting. It consists of objective information that has been verified, researched, and presented without personal bias or interpretation. News provides data on events, developments, and occurrences that shape the financial landscape, offering stakeholders a basis for understanding market dynamics.

Opinion: A Spectrum of Interpretation

Opinion, on the other hand, resides within the realm of interpretation and analysis. It reflects the subjective viewpoints, insights, and perspectives of individuals, experts, and commentators. Opinions may be influenced by personal beliefs, experiences, and analytical frameworks, which can introduce bias and subjectivity.

Identifying Opinion in Analysis

Analyzing news and events involves identifying the presence of opinion within analysis. Opinion-driven content often contains subjective language, personal judgments, and qualitative assessments. Financial experts and commentators may offer interpretations of market trends, economic data, and corporate performance, which can guide investors but should be weighed against other sources.

Verifying Sources and Credentials

Verifying the sources and credentials of analysts and commentators is crucial when evaluating opinion-driven content. Reputable experts often have a track record of accurate insights and possess a deep understanding of financial markets. Relying on opinions from recognized and experienced professionals enhances the reliability of analysis.

Balanced Perspectives: News and Opinion Synergy

Effectively navigating the distinction between news and opinion involves seeking a balanced synthesis of both. Combining factual news reporting with expert opinions enriches the analytical process, offering stakeholders a comprehensive perspective that accounts for both objective realities and interpretive insights.

Cautious Interpretation: Forming Informed Views

Stakeholders must approach opinion-driven content with caution and discernment. While opinions can offer valuable insights and alternate viewpoints, it's essential to critically evaluate the reasoning, evidence, and context presented. Informed views are built on a foundation of well-researched information and a diversity of perspectives.

Chapter 9: Earnings Reports and Conference Calls
Deciphering Corporate Performance Insights Understanding Earnings Reports and Conference Calls

In the realm of financial analysis, the exploration of earnings reports and conference calls unveils a critical avenue for deciphering the intricacies of corporate performance. This section delves into the significance of earnings reports as windows into a company's financial health and the role of conference calls in providing context, insights, and management perspectives. By comprehending the nuances of earnings-related communications, stakeholders gain valuable insights to inform investment decisions within the dynamic landscape of finance.

Earnings Reports: Financial Health Disclosed

Earnings reports are comprehensive documents released by publicly-traded companies that detail their financial performance for a specific period. These reports provide a breakdown of revenues, expenses, profits, losses, and other key financial metrics. Stakeholders rely on earnings reports to assess a company's revenue growth, profitability, efficiency, and overall financial health.

Key Components of Earnings Reports

Earnings reports comprise several essential components, including the income statement, balance sheet, cash flow statement, and notes to financial statements. These components provide a holistic view of a company's operations, liquidity, and ability to generate value for shareholders.

Conference Calls: Contextual Insights Unveiled

Conference calls are an integral part of the earnings reporting process. Following the release of earnings reports, companies hold conference calls to provide investors, analysts, and stakeholders with additional insights, context, and management perspectives. These calls facilitate a direct dialogue between company management and the investment community.

Management Discussions and Q&A Sessions

During conference calls, company executives often deliver prepared remarks, highlighting key financial results, business strategies, and performance highlights. Additionally, conference calls feature a question-and-answer session where analysts and investors can directly engage with management to seek clarifications, gain deeper insights, and explore strategic decisions.

Interpreting Management Guidance

Management guidance, a crucial aspect of conference calls, offers insights into the company's future expectations, outlook, and potential challenges. Analysts assess this guidance to gauge the company's growth prospects, alignment with market trends, and strategic focus.

The Intersection of Analysis and Communication

The analysis of earnings reports and conference calls involves a convergence of quantitative analysis and qualitative interpretation. Analysts scrutinize financial metrics and ratios within earnings reports, seeking patterns and trends. Simultaneously, they critically assess management's narrative during conference calls to understand the rationale behind financial results and strategic decisions.

Investor Reaction and Market Impact

Earnings reports and conference calls often prompt market reactions. Positive results and optimistic guidance can lead to price appreciation, while disappointing figures or cautious outlooks can result in price declines. The market's interpretation of earnings-related communications contributes to short-term price movements.

Chapter 10: Mergers and Acquisitions:
Navigating the Complex Terrain of Corporate Consolidation Understanding
Mergers and Acquisitions

In the intricate landscape of financial analysis, the exploration of mergers and acquisitions (M&A) unveils a complex and transformative facet of corporate activities. This section delves into the significance of M&A as a strategic avenue for companies seeking growth, diversification, and enhanced competitive positioning. By comprehending the intricacies of M&A transactions, stakeholders gain insights into the motivations, processes, and implications of corporate consolidation within the ever-evolving dynamics of the business world.

Mergers and Acquisitions: Types and Definitions

Mergers and acquisitions encompass a spectrum of transactions that involve the combination of two or more companies. Mergers occur when two companies integrate to form a single entity, while acquisitions involve one company purchasing the assets, stocks, or equity of another. These transactions vary in complexity, scope, and strategic objectives.

Motivations for M&A

Companies engage in M&A for a myriad of motivations. Strategic objectives may include achieving economies of scale, expanding market share, diversifying product portfolios, accessing new technologies, entering new markets, or enhancing competitive advantages. Financial considerations, such as cost savings, revenue synergies, and increased shareholder value, also drive M&A decisions.

Due Diligence: Unveiling the Details

Due diligence is a pivotal phase in the M&A process. It involves comprehensive research and analysis to assess the financial, operational, legal, and strategic aspects of the target company. Due diligence aims to uncover potential risks, liabilities, and opportunities, guiding the decision-making process.

Valuation and Negotiation

Valuation is a crucial component of M&A transactions. Companies must accurately assess the value of the target company to determine an appropriate purchase price or exchange ratio. Valuation methods may include discounted cash flow analysis, market comparables, and asset-based approaches. Negotiations involve finding common ground on terms, pricing, and transaction structure.

Integration and Post-Merger Management

Successful M&A transactions extend beyond the deal closing. Integration of processes, systems, cultures, and personnel is critical to realizing the expected benefits of consolidation. Effective post-merger management involves aligning strategies, streamlining operations, and ensuring a smooth transition for all stakeholders.

Implications for Stakeholders

M&A transactions have implications for various stakeholders, including shareholders, employees, customers, and regulatory bodies. Shareholders assess the impact on share prices, ownership structures, and potential for value creation. Employees consider job security, roles, and cultural changes. Customers assess potential service quality and product offerings.

Market Reaction and Investor Perception

M&A transactions often prompt market reactions. Positive reactions may signal approval of strategic alignment, while negative reactions might reflect skepticism about integration challenges or the alignment of strategic goals. Investor perception of M&A can influence asset valuations and market trends.

Chapter 11: Regulatory Changes and Policy Announcements
Navigating the Landscape of Legal and Economic Impact Understanding

Regulatory Changes and Policy Announcements

In the intricate realm of financial analysis, the exploration of regulatory changes and policy announcements unveils a critical dimension that significantly influences market dynamics and investment strategies. This section delves into the significance of regulatory changes and policy announcements as catalysts for economic shifts, market reactions, and investor sentiment. By comprehending the nuances of these announcements, stakeholders gain insights into the intersection of legal frameworks and economic landscapes within the dynamic domain of finance.

Regulatory Changes: A Framework for Governance

Regulatory changes encompass alterations in legal and operational guidelines that govern industries, sectors, and financial markets. These changes may stem from government agencies, regulatory bodies, or international agreements. Regulatory shifts impact the operational landscape of businesses, financial institutions, and market participants, leading to adjustments in practices, compliance, and strategic decision-making.

Policy Announcements: Economic and Monetary Impact

Policy announcements involve decisions made by government bodies or central banks that influence economic conditions and monetary policies. These announcements encompass changes in interest rates, fiscal policies, trade agreements, and macroeconomic strategies. Policy decisions have a direct impact on market sentiment, investor behavior, and asset valuations.

Market Reaction and Sentiment

Regulatory changes and policy announcements trigger market reactions that reflect investor sentiment and anticipation of economic shifts. Positive policy changes can lead to increased investor optimism, driving market rallies. Conversely, unfavorable changes may result in market declines as investors adjust their strategies to align with altered economic conditions.

Industry-Specific Implications

Regulatory changes and policy announcements often have sector-specific implications. Industries subject to increased regulations may experience compliance costs, operational adjustments, and shifts in competitive dynamics. Conversely, policy announcements that stimulate economic growth may benefit industries that rely on consumer spending and investment.

International Impact and Global Markets

Regulatory changes and policy announcements have a global impact, particularly in interconnected economies. Trade policies, tariffs, and international agreements can influence cross-border trade and investments. Investors must consider the broader international context when assessing the implications of regulatory changes.

Investment Strategy Adjustments

Regulatory changes and policy announcements prompt investors to reassess their investment strategies. Long-term investors may adjust portfolios to align with anticipated economic trends, while short-term traders may capitalize on immediate market reactions following policy announcements.

Predictability and Volatility

The degree of predictability and volatility associated with regulatory changes and policy announcements varies. Well-telegraphed policy shifts may have a more muted market impact, as investors have time to adjust. Unanticipated changes can lead to heightened market volatility and sudden price movements.

Chapter 12: Geopolitical Events and Macro Trends
Merging Global Dynamics with Investment Strategy Understanding Geopolitical Events and Macro Trends

Within the landscape of financial analysis, the exploration of geopolitical events and macro trends reveals a profound intersection between global dynamics and investment strategies. This section delves into the significance of geopolitical events and macroeconomic trends as catalysts that shape market sentiment, asset valuation, and investor decision-making. By comprehending the intricate interplay between geopolitical forces and investment strategies, stakeholders gain insights to navigate the complexities of financial markets within the evolving realm of global affairs.

Geopolitical Events: Global Catalysts

Geopolitical events encompass international developments that impact political, economic, and social landscapes. These events range from geopolitical conflicts and diplomatic negotiations to trade agreements and international policy shifts. Geopolitical events can trigger market volatility, reflecting investor responses to shifting geopolitical dynamics.

Macro Trends: Broad Economic Forces

Macro trends represent overarching economic forces that influence markets over extended periods. These trends encompass factors such as economic growth, inflation, interest rates, and demographic shifts. Understanding macro trends enables investors to align their strategies with broader economic trajectories.

Influence on Market Sentiment

Geopolitical events and macro trends have a direct influence on market sentiment. Positive developments, such as peace agreements or favorable economic indicators, can drive optimism among investors. Conversely, geopolitical uncertainties or economic downturns can foster cautious sentiment and risk aversion.

Market Volatility and Risk Management

Geopolitical events and macro trends introduce market volatility, potentially leading to abrupt price fluctuations. Investors must employ effective risk management strategies to navigate this volatility, preserving capital and mitigating potential losses during periods of uncertainty.

Incorporating News into Investment Strategies

Aligning News with Investment Goals

Incorporating news into investment strategies involves aligning current events, news releases, and macroeconomic trends with investment goals and risk tolerance. News serves as a valuable source of information that can aid in formulating tactical and strategic investment decisions.

Short-Term vs. Long-Term Strategies

Investors adopt different strategies to capitalize on news-driven opportunities. Short-term traders may engage in event-driven trading, capitalizing on immediate market reactions to news releases. Long-term investors consider how geopolitical events and macro trends align with their portfolio's objectives and risk profile.

Analyzing Historical Patterns

Analyzing historical market reactions to similar geopolitical events and macro trends can provide insights into potential outcomes. Historical patterns help investors anticipate potential price movements and manage expectations based on past reactions.

Global vs. Regional Impact

Geopolitical events and macro trends can have varying levels of impact on different markets. Global events may have a broader influence, affecting multiple asset classes and regions. Regional events may exert a more localized impact on specific industries or sectors.

Chapter 13: Short-Term vs. Long-Term Impact
Navigating Time Horizons in Financial Analysis Understanding Short-Term vs. Long-Term Impact

Within the realm of financial analysis, the exploration of short-term vs. long-term impact unveils a critical dimension that shapes investment decisions and strategies. This section delves into the significance of differentiating between short-term and long-term effects of various factors on financial markets. By comprehending the nuanced interplay between immediate reactions and prolonged consequences, stakeholders gain insights to navigate the complexities of investment within the evolving landscape of finance.

Short-Term Impact: Immediate Responses

Short-term impact refers to the immediate and often pronounced responses that financial markets exhibit in response to events, news releases, or economic indicators. These reactions are driven by market sentiment, investor emotions, and the swift adjustment of positions in response to new information.

Volatility and Sentiment

Short-term impact is often associated with increased market volatility. Rapid and dramatic price movements can occur as investors quickly recalibrate their positions based on the perceived implications of recent developments. Short-term impact is influenced by sentiment, perceptions, and news-driven market psychology.

Trading Strategies

Short-term traders, such as day traders and scalpers, capitalize on short-term impact by seeking opportunities in volatile markets. These traders engage in event-driven trading, aiming to profit from swift price movements that occur immediately after news releases or events.

Long-Term Impact: Prolonged Effects

Long-term impact encompasses the lasting and fundamental changes that unfold over extended periods. These effects are driven by underlying economic, structural, and strategic shifts that shape market trajectories beyond immediate reactions. Long-term impact often aligns with broader trends and economic fundamentals.

Structural Changes and Trends

Long-term impact is characterized by structural changes and trends that reshape industries, economies, and investment landscapes. Examples include demographic shifts, technological advancements, regulatory reforms, and shifts in consumer behavior. Long-term impact aligns with the evolution of economic and business fundamentals.

Investment Strategies

Long-term investors, such as buy-and-hold investors and institutional funds, focus on long-term impact by considering economic fundamentals, industry trends, and sustainable growth prospects. These investors make decisions based on the potential for enduring value creation over time.

Balancing Short-Term and Long-Term Considerations

Effectively navigating short-term vs. long-term impact involves striking a balance between immediate reactions and enduring trends. While short-term impact may drive market fluctuations, long-term impact influences the strategic positioning of portfolios and investment decisions aligned with broader economic forces.

Investor Behavior and Decision-Making

Investor behavior is influenced by both short-term and long-term impact. Short-term reactions can lead to emotional decisions driven by fear or greed, while long-term considerations guide rational decisions that align with investment objectives and time horizons.

Chapter 14: Using News to Identify Opportunities and Risks
Navigating the Information Landscape for Informed Decision-Making

Understanding the Power of News in Identifying Opportunities and Risks

In the intricate world of financial analysis, the exploration of using news to identify opportunities and risks unveils a critical skill that empowers investors, analysts, and stakeholders to make informed decisions amidst the sea of information. This section delves into the significance of leveraging news as a strategic tool to identify potential investment opportunities and assess inherent risks. By comprehending how news shapes market dynamics, stakeholders gain insights to navigate the complexities of financial markets and capitalize on strategic prospects within the ever-evolving landscape of finance.

News as a Catalyst for Market Movement

News serves as a catalyst that propels financial markets into action. Events, developments, economic releases, and policy announcements trigger responses that influence asset prices, investor sentiment, and market trends. News creates a dynamic environment where opportunities emerge and risks materialize.

Identifying Opportunities: Strategic Insights

News-driven events often create investment opportunities. Positive news, such as strong earnings reports, favorable economic indicators, or technological breakthroughs, can lead to price appreciation and capital growth. Investors use news insights to align their strategies with emerging trends and growth prospects.

Assessing Risks: Early Warning Signals

News is equally instrumental in identifying and assessing risks. Negative news, such as economic downturns, geopolitical tensions, or regulatory changes, can lead to market declines and heightened uncertainty. Investors utilize news to recognize potential risks that might impact portfolios and to develop risk management strategies.

Impact of News on Market Sentiment

News plays a pivotal role in shaping market sentiment. Positive news can generate optimism and bullish sentiment, encouraging investors to take positions. Negative news can lead to fear and risk aversion, prompting investors to adopt defensive stances. The interpretation of news drives shifts in sentiment that impact asset prices.

Informed Decision-Making

Using news to identify opportunities and risks involves careful analysis and critical thinking. Investors must evaluate news sources for credibility, assess the potential impact of news events, and consider the broader economic and industry context. Informed decision-making entails assessing the reliability of news information and its alignment with strategic goals.

Event-Driven vs. Long-Term Analysis

Investors adopt different approaches when using news for decision-making. Event-driven analysis focuses on immediate reactions to news releases, aiming to capitalize on short term market movements. Long-term analysis involves considering how news events align with long-term investment strategies and industry trends.

Holistic Perspective: Synthesizing News Insights

Synthesizing news insights requires a holistic perspective. Investors must consider a range of news sources, assess the consensus view, and analyze potential scenarios and their implications. Integrating news insights with fundamental analysis and technical indicators enriches decision-making.

Conclusion: Integrating Analysis for Informed Decision-Making

The culmination of this comprehensive exploration underscores the vital role of fundamental analysis in shaping informed decision-making within the dynamic landscape of financial markets. As we recap the essential components, emphasize the integration of economic indicators, company financials, and market news, and stress the importance of holistic analysis, we recognize the intricate tapestry that underlies successful investment strategies.

Recap of Fundamental Analysis Components

Fundamental analysis, the cornerstone of effective investment strategies, comprises a spectrum of critical components. From dissecting economic indicators that reflect the health of economies to evaluating company financials that mirror organizational prowess, and from deciphering market news that fuels sentiment to navigating geopolitical dynamics and macro trends, each component offers unique insights that guide investment choices.

Integration for Informed Decision-Making

The integration of economic indicators, company financials, and market news is at the heart of effective fundamental analysis. This integration fosters a comprehensive understanding of the multifaceted influences that shape market behavior. Economic indicators offer macroeconomic context, company financials provide microeconomic insights, and market news catalyze immediate reactions. Integrating these components empowers stakeholders to navigate the complexities of financial markets with a broader perspective.

Holistic Analysis: The Path to Informed Decisions

Holistic analysis emerges as a paramount principle that underpins success in financial analysis. The interplay of economic indicators, company financials, market news, geopolitical factors, and macro trends necessitates a well-rounded approach. Holistic analysis empowers investors to recognize opportunities, assess risks, and make informed decisions that account for both short-term reactions and long-term trends. By weaving these threads of information into a cohesive narrative, stakeholders can make decisions with enhanced clarity and strategic acumen.

Navigating the Path Forward

As the financial landscape evolves, so too does the art and science of fundamental analysis. The ability to decipher economic data, dissect company financials, interpret news, and anticipate market reactions is a dynamic skill that requires continuous refinement. Equipped with the knowledge, tools, and insights gained from this exploration, investors, analysts, and stakeholders are prepared to navigate the path forward with adaptability, resilience, and a commitment to informed decision-making.

In closing, the journey through the components of fundamental analysis, the integration of economic indicators, company financials, and market news, and the emphasis on holistic analysis is a testament to the intricate dance between information and strategy. As financial markets continue to evolve, the wisdom gained from this exploration serves as a compass guiding stakeholders toward success in their pursuit of well-informed investment choices.

Appendix: Tools and Resources for Fundamental Analysis

In the pursuit of comprehensive and effective fundamental analysis, access to reliable tools and resources is paramount. This appendix compiles a selection of essential tools and resources that empower investors, analysts, and stakeholders to navigate the intricate landscape of financial analysis with precision and insight. From online data sources for economic indicators to specialized financial statement analysis software and recommended news outlets, these resources serve as indispensable aids in the journey toward informed decision-making.

Online Data Sources for Economic Indicators

1. **Bureau of Economic Analysis (BEA)** - A U.S. government agency providing comprehensive economic data, including GDP, inflation, and trade balance.
2. **Federal Reserve Economic Data (FRED)** - Offers a vast collection of economic data, indicators, and financial market information for the United States.
3. **World Bank Data** - A repository of global economic and financial data, including income, poverty, and population statistics.
4. **Eurostat** - The statistical office of the European Union, providing economic and demographic data for member countries.
5. **Trading Economics** - Offers a wide range of global economic indicators, historical data, and forecasts.

Financial Statement Analysis Software

1. **Bloomberg Terminal** - A professional platform that provides real-time financial data, news, and analytics for global financial markets.
2. **Thomson Reuters Eikon** - Offers financial data, news, and analytics to aid in decision-making for investment professionals.
3. **FactSet** - Provides financial data, analytics, and research for investment professionals and corporations.
4. **Morningstar Direct** - Offers investment research and analysis tools, including data on mutual funds, stocks, and other assets.

Recommended News Outlets and Aggregators

1. **Bloomberg** - A premier source of global financial news, data, and analysis, covering a wide range of markets and industries.
2. **Reuters** - Offers real-time news, analysis, and financial information across various sectors and markets.
3. **The Wall Street Journal** - A respected publication providing in-depth coverage of business, finance, and global events.
4. **Financial Times** - Offers comprehensive news, analysis, and commentary on global business and financial matters.
5. **CNBC** - A multimedia platform providing real-time financial news, market analysis, and insights.

Conclusion: Empowering Informed Analysis

As the financial landscape evolves, the tools and resources available for fundamental analysis continue to expand and refine. This appendix serves as a guide to some of the key tools and resources that facilitate comprehensive research, informed decision-making, and strategic acumen. By harnessing these tools and resources, stakeholders can navigate the complexities of financial analysis with precision, confidence, and the ability to extract valuable insights from economic indicators, financial statements, and market news.

Stress and Decision-making in Trading

Quantitative Analysis and Qualitative Analysis

Introduction

The realm of trading, with its myriad complexities and fast-paced environment, is not for the faint-hearted. For individuals and institutions, the opportunities to generate substantial profits are significant. However, so are the risks. In this era of globalization and technological advancement, traders are equipped with a vast array of tools and resources. Yet, ironically, many still fall prey to the snares of inadequate risk management. The introduction to this comprehensive guide aims to elucidate the vital importance of risk management in trading, providing a precursor to the in-depth strategies and methodologies elaborated upon in subsequent chapters.

The Imperative of Risk Management in Trading

At its core, trading involves making educated guesses about the future, based on data from the past and present. Every trade, regardless of how well-informed, carries an inherent risk. The volatility inherent in the markets, impacted by geopolitical, economic, and even environmental factors, makes predictability a challenge. This uncertainty is the reason risk management becomes an indispensable facet of trading. Without risk management, traders expose themselves to potential catastrophic losses. Proper risk management does not merely protect assets; it ensures sustainability, promotes longevity in the trading profession, and paves the way for consistent profitability.

Consider the landscape of historical market events — from the 1929 Great Depression to the 2008 financial crisis, and beyond. These episodes serve as grim reminders of what can transpire when risks spiral out of control. Financial markets, by their nature, are rife with uncertainty. But these uncertainties should not deter potential investors and traders. Instead, they highlight the necessity of developing and implementing robust risk management protocols.

Preview of the Comprehensive Strategies Discussed in the Book

In this guide, readers will embark on a detailed exploration of various strategies to manage and mitigate trading risks effectively. The range of topics covered is both broad and deep, ensuring a holistic understanding of the subject matter.

1. **Foundational Understanding**: Before delving into strategies, it's crucial to understand the very nature and types of trading risks. By categorizing and defining these risks, traders can create a foundation upon which effective strategies can be built.

2. **Quantitative and Qualitative Analysis**: The marriage of numbers and intuition is at the heart of trading. This guide underscores the importance of quantitative techniques like statistical analysis while also emphasizing the psychological factors that influence trading decisions.

3. **Tools and Techniques**: From the judicious use of stop-loss orders to the intricate realms of hedging and correlation analysis, a plethora of tools are available to traders. Knowing when, why, and how to use these tools is vital, and this guide seeks to impart that knowledge effectively.

4. **The Human Element**: Machines, algorithms, and statistical models play significant roles in modern trading. However, the human element — understanding psychological biases, staying updated with continual education, and recognizing the importance of risk tolerance — remains paramount.

5. **Real-world Applications**: Theory, while invaluable, needs practical application. Through a series of case studies, this guide will delve into real-world scenarios, drawing lessons from traders and institutions that have navigated the treacherous waters of the financial markets, both successfully and otherwise.

In concluding this introduction, it is vital to reiterate a foundational belief that permeates this guide: risk management is not about eliminating risks. Such a goal is not only unfeasible but also counterproductive. Trading, at its essence, is about taking risks. Effective risk management, therefore, is about understanding these risks, controlling them, and harnessing them to one's advantage. It's about making informed decisions that balance potential rewards against potential dangers.

As readers progress through this guide, they will gain insights, strategies, and tools to achieve precisely this balance. By internalizing the principles and methodologies presented, traders can position themselves to not just survive in the volatile world of trading, but to thrive.

In the ensuing chapters, we embark on a journey, one that charts a course through the intricate maze of trading risks, providing clarity, insight, and actionable strategies every step of the way. Whether a novice trader or a seasoned professional, this guide seeks to provide invaluable tools and knowledge to navigate the financial markets with confidence and proficiency.

Chapter 1: The Fundamentals of Trading Risks

The world of trading is akin to a vast ocean, its depths teeming with hidden perils and opportunities. Like seasoned sailors navigating these waters, traders must be aware of the dangers that lurk beneath the surface. Recognizing and understanding these risks is the first step toward successfully mitigating them.

Delineation of the Various Forms of Trading Risks

Trading risks can be broadly classified into several categories, each with its unique characteristics and challenges:

1. **Market Risk (Systematic Risk)**: This is the risk that the entire market will decline, affecting almost all assets. Factors like economic downturns, interest rate changes, geopolitical crises, and global pandemics can trigger market-wide shocks. No asset or strategy is immune to market risk; however, its impact can vary depending on the asset class and geographical exposure.

2. **Liquidity Risk**: Liquidity refers to the ease with which an asset can be quickly bought or sold without causing a significant price change. An asset that cannot be easily sold due to market stagnation or lack of buyers poses a liquidity risk. This can result in traders holding onto a devaluing asset or selling at a reduced price.

3. **Credit Risk (Counterparty Risk)**: This arises when one party in a trading contract default or fails to meet their obligations. For example, if a broker becomes insolvent or a counterparty in a derivatives contract default, traders might face financial losses.

4. **Operational Risk**: These are risks arising from operational failures, be it technical glitches, human errors, or problems arising from external factors like natural disasters. Even with the most advanced systems, occasional malfunctions can occur, disrupting trading activities.

5. **Model Risk**: Many trading strategies rely on financial models to predict future price movements. If these models are based on flawed assumptions or inadequate data, they can lead to erroneous predictions and subsequent losses.

6. **Regulatory and Legal Risks**: Changes in governmental or regulatory policies can affect trading dynamics. For instance, sudden changes in tax laws, trade regulations, or policies can impact specific sectors or the entire market.

7. **Leverage Risk**: While leverage can amplify profits, it can also magnify losses. A trader who borrows heavily to invest might face significant losses if the market moves against their position.

Understanding these risks is the first layer of defense for any trader. By recognizing the potential pitfalls inherent in the market, one can devise strategies to counteract or mitigate them. However, it is crucial to remember that risks often intersect, intertwine, and influence each other. For instance, an operational glitch might lead to a liquidity problem, which can then exacerbate market risks during volatile periods.

Risk as an Inherent Part of Trading

Every trader, whether they realize it or not, makes risk decisions with every trade. The decision to buy or sell, the choice of asset, the amount invested, the use of leverage – each of these is a risk decision. And every trade, regardless of outcome, provides feedback on those decisions. Over time, repeated feedback allows traders to refine their understanding and approach to risk.

It's also essential to recognize that not all risks are negative. In many cases, risks represent opportunities. Market downturns, for instance, might present chances to buy assets at discounted prices. Similarly, a high-volatility environment, while risky, might offer significant profit opportunities for short-term traders. The key lies in understanding, managing, and optimizing these risks.

Conclusion

Risk, in its myriad forms, is the constant companion of every trader. It is a multifaceted entity, sometimes lurking in the shadows, at other times starkly evident. But in every guise, risk presents both a challenge and an opportunity. By delving deep into its nature and nuances, traders can transform risk from an adversary into an ally, using it as a tool to hone strategies, refine decisions, and drive profitability. The subsequent chapters of this guide delve deeper into each form of risk, providing insights, strategies, and tools to navigate the complex landscape of trading risks effectively.

Chapter 2: Importance of a Risk Management Plan

In the intricate and often unpredictable world of trading, entering the market without a risk management plan is akin to sailing stormy seas without a compass. A risk management plan serves as a trader's guiding star, offering direction in times of uncertainty and acting as a safeguard against potential pitfalls. This chapter delves into the significance of such a plan and the foundational elements that constitute it.

Establishing the Foundation: Why No Trader Should Operate Without a Plan

1. Clarity in Decision Making: Uncertainty is an inherent aspect of trading. However, a well-structured risk management plan offers clarity, ensuring that decisions are not impulsive but are based on predefined criteria. This proactive approach minimizes reactive, emotion-driven decisions that often lead to losses.

2. Consistency in Trading Approach: Trading can be influenced by a multitude of external factors, from global events to market sentiment. A risk management plan ensures consistency in approach, regardless of external pressures or market volatility. It acts as a framework, guiding traders in maintaining a uniform approach irrespective of market conditions.

3. Preservation of Capital: At its core, a risk management plan is designed to protect a trader's capital. By setting predefined loss limits and employing protective strategies like stop-loss orders, traders can ensure that they live to trade another day, even after facing adverse market movements.

4. Enhancing Profitability: Risk management isn't just about preventing losses; it's also about optimizing profits. By defining risk-reward ratios and profit targets, traders can ensure they capitalize on favorable market movements, taking profits at optimal points rather than getting swayed by greed or fear.

5. Building Confidence: Knowing that there's a robust plan in place offers traders confidence. This psychological benefit cannot be overstated. A confident trader, buoyed by a sense of preparedness, is less likely to make impulsive decisions and more likely to stick to their strategy.

6. Continuous Evaluation and Improvement: A good risk management plan is not static. It includes provisions for periodic review, allowing traders to evaluate its effectiveness and make necessary adjustments. This iterative process ensures that the plan remains relevant and effective, adapting to changing market conditions and evolving trading goals.

Creating a Robust Risk Management Plan

Crafting a risk management plan involves a series of deliberate steps:

1. **Risk Assessment**: Before formulating a plan, traders must first assess the potential risks they might encounter. This involves understanding market dynamics, the specific risks associated with the assets they're trading, and their personal risk tolerance.

2. **Defining Risk Limits**: Based on the assessment, traders should define clear risk limits. This could be in the form of a maximum percentage of capital at risk per trade or a total dollar amount they're willing to lose in a specific timeframe.

3. **Selecting Risk Management Tools**: With clear limits in place, traders can then select the tools and strategies that best fit their trading style and risk profile. This could range from basic tools like stop-loss orders to more advanced strategies like hedging.

4. **Monitoring and Review**: Implementing the plan is just the beginning. Constant monitoring is essential to ensure its effectiveness. Regular reviews, ideally after a set number of trades, will provide insights into potential improvements.

Conclusion

In the vast and dynamic world of trading, a risk management plan stands out as a trader's most trusted ally. It provides clarity in chaos, consistency in volatility, and protection against unforeseen adversities. The subsequent chapters of this guide will delve into specific strategies and tools that traders can incorporate into their risk management plans, providing a holistic roadmap to trading success.

Chapter 3: Quantitative Analysis in Risk Management

In the domain of risk management, quantitative analysis acts as a beacon, offering precise metrics, statistical interpretations, and mathematical models that guide traders in their decision-making processes. This chapter explores the realm of quantitative analysis, elucidating its pivotal role in managing and mitigating trading risks effectively.

Decoding Quantitative Analysis

At its core, quantitative analysis uses mathematical and statistical techniques to understand and predict market behaviors. This rigorous, data-driven approach helps traders identify patterns, analyze market trends, and make informed decisions based on objective information.

Key Components of Quantitative Analysis in Trading

1. **Historical Data Analysis**: By examining past market data, traders can identify recurring patterns, anomalies, and potential trends. This retrospective analysis provides a foundation upon which future predictions can be built.
2. **Probability and Statistics**: These tools assist traders in assessing the likelihood of specific market events. For instance, standard deviation can be used to gauge the volatility of an asset, while regression analysis can help ascertain relationships between variables.
3. **Time Series Analysis**: This involves studying sequenced data points (usually ordered in time) to forecast future price movements. Techniques such as moving averages and autoregressions fall under this category.
4. **Risk Metrics**: Tools such as Value at Risk (VaR) and Conditional Value at Risk (CVaR) provide traders with quantitative measures of the potential losses they might face within a given confidence interval.
5. **Optimization Models**: These mathematical algorithms assist traders in determining the best asset allocation in a portfolio, maximizing returns for a given level of risk.

Advantages of Implementing Quantitative Analysis

1. **Objectivity**: Quantitative analysis minimizes emotional and subjective biases, grounding decisions in solid, objective data.
2. **Scalability**: Quantitative models, especially when automated, can analyze vast datasets quickly, providing insights on a scale that's difficult to achieve through manual methods.
3. **Predictive Insights**: The algorithms and models used in quantitative analysis can identify subtle patterns and relationships that might be overlooked in a qualitative review, aiding in predictive forecasting.
4. **Risk Measurement**: By offering concrete metrics and numerical assessments of risk, quantitative analysis gives traders a clear understanding of their exposure.
5. **Portfolio Diversification**: Quantitative models can assist traders in crafting well-diversified portfolios that are designed to optimize returns while mitigating risks.

Challenges and Considerations

While quantitative analysis is an invaluable tool, traders should be wary of its limitations:

1. **Model Risk**: Relying heavily on models can be perilous if the models are based on flawed assumptions or outdated data. It's essential to continually validate and update models to ensure their relevance.
2. **Over-reliance**: Quantitative analysis should be part of a broader risk management strategy. Solely depending on it, while disregarding qualitative factors, can lead to oversight.
3. **Data Quality**: The effectiveness of quantitative analysis hinges on the quality of the underlying data. Inaccurate or incomplete data can lead to erroneous conclusions.

Conclusion

Quantitative analysis, with its arsenal of statistical tools and mathematical models, plays a pivotal role in the landscape of risk management. By offering traders objective metrics, predictive insights, and concrete risk measurements, it empowers them to navigate the complexities of the market with confidence and precision. Future chapters will further delve into specific quantitative tools and techniques, illuminating their applications and nuances in the context of trading risk management.

Chapter 4: Qualitative Analysis in Risk Management

While quantitative analysis provides an empirical and data-driven approach to understanding trading risks, it's equally essential to recognize the critical role of qualitative analysis. Qualitative analysis delves into the more intangible aspects of trading, focusing on factors that cannot be easily quantified but play a significant role in shaping market dynamics.

The Essence of Qualitative Analysis

Qualitative analysis centers on understanding the non-numeric factors that influence the trading environment. These could be socio-political events, market sentiments, trader psychology, or regulatory changes, among others. It employs descriptive methods to gain insights into these subjective elements.

Core Elements of Qualitative Analysis in Trading

1. **Fundamental Analysis**: This method involves evaluating an asset's intrinsic value by considering related economic, financial, and other qualitative and quantitative factors. For stocks, this could involve examining a company's management quality, industry position, and competitive advantages.

2. **Market Sentiment Analysis**: Here, traders gauge the overall mood or feeling of market participants. Sentiment analysis can provide insights into potential market movements based on collective perceptions.

3. **Behavioral Finance**: These studies the effects of psychological factors on market behaviors. It seeks to understand why traders might act irrationally at times, leading to bubbles or crashes.

4. **Geopolitical and Economic News Analysis**: World events, from elections to wars, can have profound impacts on markets. Qualitative analysis in this domain assesses the potential ramifications of such events on trading landscapes.

Advantages of Using Qualitative Analysis

1. **Comprehensive Understanding**: While numbers and statistical models can provide a clear picture of past and current market conditions, qualitative analysis offers a deeper understanding of the reasons behind those numbers.

2. **Predicting Black Swan Events**: Unforeseen and rare events, which might not be evident in historical data, can be anticipated with the aid of qualitative analysis.

3. **Balancing the Quantitative**: Qualitative insights can validate or challenge quantitative models, ensuring a more holistic trading strategy.

Pitfalls and Precautions

However, there are challenges to be navigated:

1. **Subjectivity**: Unlike quantitative analysis, qualitative methods are open to interpretation. This subjectivity can sometimes lead to biased or inconsistent conclusions.

2. **Time-Consuming**: Given the depth of analysis and the multitude of factors to consider, qualitative analysis can be more time-intensive than its quantitative counterpart.

3. **Over-reliance on Expert Opinions**: While expert insights are valuable, they are still opinions. Blindly following them without personal assessment can be risky.

Conclusion

Qualitative analysis enriches a trader's understanding of the market, adding depth and dimension to the cold hard facts presented by quantitative methods. It paints a vivid picture of the myriad influences at play, from the rational to the emotional, from the tangible to the abstract. When combined effectively with quantitative tools, qualitative analysis provides traders with a comprehensive toolkit to navigate the intricate terrains of risk management. The forthcoming chapters will delve into specific qualitative techniques, highlighting their relevance and application in the intricate world of trading.

Chapter 5: The Role of Portfolio Diversification in Risk Management

Diversification, a cornerstone concept in the investment arena, is rooted in the age-old adage, "Don't put all your eggs in one basket." Portfolio diversification is the practice of spreading investments across various assets or asset classes to mitigate risks. This chapter sheds light on the mechanics of diversification, its significance in trading risk management, and best practices to achieve an optimally diversified portfolio.

Understanding Portfolio Diversification

At a fundamental level, diversification aims to reduce the unpredictability of an investment's return by investing in different areas that would each react differently to the same event. It is based on the premise that individual assets are not entirely correlated in their price movements.

Mechanisms Driving Diversification Benefits

1. **Uncorrelated Assets**: When two assets are uncorrelated, the price movement in one doesn't necessarily mirror the other. Having a mix of such assets can dampen the volatility of a portfolio.
2. **Law of Averages**: By spreading capital across a variety of investments, the poor performance of a few can be offset by the strong performance of others.

Benefits of Diversification

1. **Risk Reduction**: Diversification can significantly reduce the volatility and potential loss in a portfolio. While it doesn't guarantee against loss, diversification is an essential component of reaching long-range financial goals while minimizing risk.
2. **Return Potential**: By diversifying across various sectors and asset classes, investors can capitalize on robust performers, thereby potentially enhancing returns.
3. **Flexibility**: A diversified portfolio allows traders to adjust their portfolio based on the evolving market conditions, rebalancing assets as needed.

Achieving Effective Diversification

1. **Across Asset Classes**: This includes diversifying investments across stocks, bonds, commodities, real estate, and more.
2. **Geographic Diversification**: Spreading investments across different countries or regions can protect against regional downturns or geopolitical events.
3. **Sectoral Diversification**: Within an asset class like equities, diversification can be achieved by investing in different sectors like technology, healthcare, finance, etc.
4. **Time Horizon Diversification**: This involves staggering your investments across various time horizons, mitigating risks associated with a particular period.

5. **Diversifying Strategies**: Implementing a range of trading strategies can also be a form of diversification, ensuring that a downturn in one approach doesn't decimate your portfolio.

Limitations and Misunderstandings

1. **Over-Diversification**: It's possible to spread investments too thin. This can dilute potential gains and lead to mediocre performance, negating the benefits of standout assets.
2. **False Security**: Diversification mitigates but doesn't eliminate risks. Traders must still be vigilant and responsive to changing market conditions.
3. **Cost Implications**: Building and maintaining a diversified portfolio might entail higher costs in terms of transaction fees, management fees, and others.

Conclusion

Portfolio diversification is a powerful tool in a trader's risk management arsenal. While it's not a foolproof strategy against losses, it effectively reduces the severity of potential downturns, smoothing out the investment journey. By understanding the intricacies of diversification and integrating them effectively, traders can create a resilient and adaptive portfolio, well-equipped to navigate the complexities of the trading landscape. The subsequent chapters will delve deeper into portfolio construction, emphasizing the interplay of various assets and the intricacies of effective asset allocation.

Chapter 6: Leverage and Margin: Tools and Risks

Leverage, often entwined with margin trading, amplifies both potential gains and potential losses in the trading arena. This chapter dissects the concepts of leverage and margin, explicating their advantages, inherent risks, and best practices for their judicious utilization.

Demystifying Leverage and Margin

Leverage involves using borrowed capital as a funding source when investing to expand the potential return on investment. In the context of trading, brokers typically offer leverage, allowing traders to open positions larger than their initial capital.

Margin, on the other hand, represents the initial deposit required to open and maintain a leveraged position. In essence, it's a good faith deposit that ensures a trader can cover potential losses from that position.

How Leverage Works in Trading

1. **Multiplying Exposure**: With leverage, a trader can significantly increase their market exposure. For example, with a 10:1 leverage, a trader can control a position worth $10,000 with just $1,000 of their own capital.
2. **Enhanced Returns**: The primary allure of leverage is the potential for higher returns. If a trade moves in a favorable direction, the ROI is significantly amplified.

Inherent Risks of Leverage

1. **Magnified Losses**: Just as gains are amplified, so are losses. If the market moves against a leveraged position, the losses incurred can quickly deplete the trader's capital.
2. **Margin Calls**: If a leveraged position goes against a trader and their account equity drops below the margin requirement, the broker might issue a margin call. This requires the trader to deposit additional funds to maintain the position or face its liquidation.
3. **Interest Charges**: Leverage often comes with interest charges on the borrowed amount, which can eat into profits or exacerbate losses.

Best Practices for Using Leverage and Margin

1. **Understand the Terms**: Before employing leverage, understand the broker's terms, including the margin requirements and interest charges.
2. **Start Conservatively**: Especially for those new to leveraged trading, it's wise to start with lower leverage levels, gradually increasing exposure as one gains experience.
3. **Risk Management Tools**: Employ tools such as stop-loss orders to limit potential losses. These tools automatically close positions when losses reach a predetermined level.
4. **Continuous Monitoring**: Leveraged positions require constant monitoring. Rapid market movements can result in swift capital depletion, so it's essential to be vigilant.
5. **Avoid Emotional Decisions**: Given the heightened stakes with leveraged trading, traders might be tempted to make hasty decisions driven by fear or greed. It's crucial to remain analytical and avoid emotional trading.

Conclusion

Leverage and margin, while offering the allure of magnified returns, come with equally magnified risks. Their judicious use demands a deep understanding of their mechanics, a disciplined approach, and robust risk management strategies. When employed cautiously and wisely, they can be powerful tools in a trader's repertoire, allowing for greater market exposure and potential profit maximization. Subsequent chapters will delve into other advanced trading tools, elaborating on their uses, benefits, and associated risks in the realm of risk management.

Chapter 7: Technological Tools in Risk Management

In today's digital age, technology plays a pivotal role in the trading realm. From sophisticated algorithms to real-time data analytics, technology equips traders with tools to enhance decision-making processes and manage risks adeptly. This chapter elucidates the spectrum of technological tools available, their functionalities, and their integral role in modern risk management.

The Digital Transformation in Trading

The evolution of trading from floor-based exchanges to electronic platforms has been monumental. This digital transformation has brought forth a plethora of tools designed to streamline, optimize, and enhance trading processes.

Prominent Technological Tools in Risk Management

1. **Trading Platforms**: These are software applications that allow traders to place trades, monitor accounts, and analyze market data. Platforms like MetaTrader, NinjaTrader, and Thinkorswim offer a suite of tools, from charting to back-testing, aiding traders in risk management.
2. **Algorithmic Trading**: Algorithms, based on a predefined set of criteria, can execute trades automatically. They minimize human error, execute trades at unmatched speeds, and can be tailored to specific risk management strategies.
3. **Risk Analytics Software**: These tools provide quantitative insights into potential risks. They can simulate various market scenarios, assess portfolio vulnerabilities, and predict potential losses.
4. **Real-Time Data Feeds**: Access to real-time market data ensures traders can make informed decisions promptly, adapting to rapid market shifts.

5. **Artificial Intelligence (AI) and Machine Learning (ML)**: These technologies analyze vast datasets, identifying patterns and trends that might be imperceptible to the human eye. They can forecast market movements, enhancing predictive risk management.

Advantages of Leveraging Technology in Risk Management

1. **Speed and Efficiency**: Automated tools can process information and execute trades far quicker than human traders, ensuring timely responses to market changes.

2. **Objective Decision-Making**: Algorithms and software tools minimize emotional and subjective biases, leading to more rational trading decisions.

3. **Advanced Analysis**: Technological tools can perform complex calculations, simulations, and analyses that would be cumbersome or impossible manually.

4. **Continuous Monitoring**: Automated systems can surveil markets round the clock, ensuring no crucial market movement goes unnoticed.

Caveats and Considerations

1. **Over-reliance**: While technology is invaluable, blind reliance can be perilous. It's essential to use these tools as aids rather than replacements for human judgment.

2. **Technical Glitches**: Software and systems are prone to bugs and glitches. Traders should have contingency plans for technical failures.

3. **Security Concerns**: Digital platforms are susceptible to cyberattacks. It's imperative to ensure robust cybersecurity measures are in place.

Conclusion

Technology, with its array of sophisticated tools, has revolutionized risk management in trading. It augments a trader's capabilities, offering enhanced insights, rapid response mechanisms, and advanced analytical prowess. However, while these tools are transformative, they should complement, not replace, a trader's expertise and judgment. The following chapters will delve deeper into specific technological advancements, elucidating their intricacies and best practices for their integration into a trader's risk management arsenal.

Chapter 8: Behavioral Biases in Trading and Risk Management

Human psychology plays an often-underestimated role in trading decisions. Despite the technicalities and quantitative aspects of trading, human behavior and its inherent biases can significantly impact risk perception and subsequent actions. This chapter delves into the realm of behavioral finance, identifying common biases in trading and strategies to counteract them for effective risk management.

The Intersection of Psychology and Trading

The trading world isn't governed solely by numbers and algorithms; human emotions, perceptions, and behaviors significantly influence market dynamics and individual trading decisions. Recognizing and understanding these behavioral biases is pivotal to instituting effective risk management.

Common Behavioral Biases in Trading

1. **Overconfidence Bias**: Traders, buoyed by a string of successes, might overestimate their abilities or the accuracy of their information. This can lead to taking on excessive risks.

2. **Loss Aversion**: Traders might hold onto losing positions longer than advisable, hoping the market will rebound, driven by the psychological pain of realizing a loss.

3. **Confirmation Bias**: Traders might seek out information that aligns with their existing beliefs or predictions, ignoring contradicting data.
4. **Anchoring**: This involves relying heavily on the first piece of information encountered (the "anchor") when making decisions, even if newer data suggests a different course of action.
5. **Herd Behavior**: Traders might follow the actions of the majority, believing there's safety in numbers, even if it contradicts their analysis.
6. **Recency Bias**: Giving more weight to recent events, neglecting historical data, and potentially misjudging risks.

Mitigating the Impact of Behavioral Biases

1. **Self-awareness**: Regularly reflecting on trading decisions and outcomes can help identify personal biases and tendencies.
2. **Diversified Information Sources**: Ensure information is sourced from a variety of outlets to counteract confirmation bias.
3. **Set Defined Rules**: Establish clear trading rules and criteria, making decisions more systematic and less impulsive.
4. **Feedback Mechanisms**: Peer reviews or mentorship can provide an external perspective, highlighting potential biases in decision-making.
5. **Regular Training**: Engage in continuous learning, attending workshops, or seminars on behavioral finance to remain aware of biases and develop strategies to counteract them.
6. **Technological Aids**: Use automated tools, like stop-loss orders, to counteract emotional decision-making.

Conclusion

Behavioral biases, deeply rooted in human psychology, can often be the Achilles' heel for traders. By understanding these biases and their impact on trading decisions, traders can develop strategies to counteract their influence, ensuring more objective and effective risk management. Subsequent chapters will delve into other cognitive and emotional factors in trading, emphasizing the interplay between human psychology, market dynamics, and risk management strategies.

Chapter 9: Stress and Decision-making in Trading

While behavioral biases concern intrinsic human tendencies, external pressures such as stress can also significantly sway trading decisions. Stress, a natural human response to challenging situations, can distort rational thinking and amplify risks in trading. This chapter delves into the nexus between stress and trading, elucidating its implications and offering strategies to manage and mitigate its effects.

Stress in the Trading Realm

Trading, by its very nature, is a high-pressure activity. Rapid market fluctuations, substantial financial stakes, and the unpredictability of global events can make trading a crucible of stress. Understanding how stress affects decision-making is imperative for effective risk management.

Impacts of Stress on Trading

1. **Impaired Judgment**: Chronic stress can cloud judgment, making it difficult to interpret market data accurately.

2. **Reduced Cognitive Function**: Stress can hinder memory recall and analytical thinking, pivotal components of the trading process.
3. **Reactivity**: Traders under stress might react impulsively to market changes, bypassing thorough analysis.
4. **Physical Effects**: Chronic stress can lead to physical ailments, affecting overall well-being and reducing trading efficiency.

Managing Stress for Effective Decision-making

1. **Structured Trading Plan**: Having a clear and structured trading plan can reduce ambiguity and uncertainty, alleviating some sources of stress.
2. **Physical Exercise**: Regular physical activity has been proven to reduce stress levels, enhancing overall cognitive function.
3. **Mindfulness and Meditation**: Techniques like mindfulness meditation can help manage stress, promoting clarity and calmness.
4. **Breaks and Downtime**: Taking regular breaks away from screens and ensuring adequate downtime can prevent burnout and reduce stress.
5. **Peer Support**: Engaging with a community of traders can offer support, perspective, and camaraderie, helping alleviate stress.
6. **Continuous Learning**: Upgrading one's skills and knowledge can boost confidence, reducing stress associated with uncertainty.

Stress-Testing in Trading

Aside from personal stress, traders can apply the principle of "stress-testing" to their portfolios. This involves simulating extreme but plausible adverse conditions to evaluate potential vulnerabilities.

1. **Scenario Analysis**: Identify specific known risks and model their potential impact on a portfolio.
2. **Sensitivity Analysis**: Determine how different changes in a single variable, like interest rates, might affect a portfolio.
3. **Simulation**: Use statistical processes to predict the likelihood of different outcomes based on historical data.

Conclusion

Stress, both as a personal experience and a modeling technique, plays a significant role in the trading world. By understanding and managing stress, traders can ensure that their decisions remain rational, clear, and aligned with their risk management strategies. The subsequent chapters will further explore the emotional and cognitive challenges faced by traders, offering insights and techniques to navigate the tumultuous waters of the financial markets.

Chapter 10: Portfolio Diversification: Spreading Risks

Diversification is one of the foundational principles in investment and trading risk management. By distributing investments across various assets or asset classes, traders can shield themselves from unsystematic risks, ensuring that potential adverse outcomes in one area don't jeopardize the entire portfolio. This chapter provides an in-depth analysis of portfolio diversification, its importance, and strategies to implement it effectively.

The Rationale Behind Diversification

Investments and trades inherently come with risks. While some risks are specific to individual assets, others affect the broader market. Diversification seeks to mitigate the former, unsystematic risks, which are unique to specific assets or sectors.

Key Benefits of Diversification

1. **Risk Reduction**: Spreading investments reduces the impact of poor performance by any single asset or asset class.
2. **Return Enhancement**: Diversified portfolios can harness growth across sectors, potentially boosting overall returns.
3. **Protection Against Volatility**: Diverse portfolios tend to be more stable, cushioning against short-term market fluctuations.

Diversification Strategies

1. **Across Asset Classes**: Diversifying across stocks, bonds, commodities, and other asset classes to exploit their uncorrelated behavior.
2. **Within Asset Classes**: Even within a particular asset class, like stocks, diversifying across sectors (e.g., technology, healthcare, finance) can be beneficial.
3. **Geographic Diversification**: Investing across various geographical regions can protect against localized economic downturns or political instabilities.
4. **Temporal Diversification**: Also known as dollar-cost averaging, it involves spreading out investments over time, thereby reducing the impact of any unfavorable market timing.

Common Misconceptions about Diversification

1. **Guaranteed Protection Against Loss**: While diversification reduces risk, it doesn't eliminate it. Market-wide downturns can still affect a diversified portfolio.
2. **Over-diversification**: There's a fine line between diversification and over-diversification. Holding too many assets can dilute potential gains and make portfolio management unwieldy.
3. **Static Strategy**: The effectiveness of diversification isn't static. As market conditions change, the diversification strategy might need adjustments.

Tools and Analysis for Effective Diversification

1. **Correlation Analysis**: Assessing how different assets move in relation to one another. Assets with low or negative correlations are ideal for diversification.
2. **Variance-Covariance Matrix**: A more advanced tool that gives a comprehensive view of how assets interact, aiding in optimizing portfolio diversification.
3. **Modern Portfolio Theory (MPT)**: A framework that seeks to maximize returns for a given level of risk through effective diversification.

Conclusion

Portfolio diversification, while a powerful tool, requires careful planning and continuous oversight. When implemented judiciously, it serves as a robust shield against unsystematic risks, ensuring that traders and investors can navigate the markets with a degree of resilience. The following chapters will delve deeper into other holistic strategies and methodologies that complement diversification in the quest for comprehensive risk management in trading.

Chapter 11: Leverage and Margin: Understanding Amplified Risks

Leverage, while an enticing tool for traders, presents its own set of risks. It allows traders to amplify their trading position using borrowed funds, thereby potentially magnifying both profits and losses. This chapter dissects the concept of leverage, its correlation with margin, and the inherent risks and rewards.

Leverage Explained

In its essence, leverage entails using borrowed capital to increase the potential return of an investment. In the trading realm, brokers often provide leverage, allowing traders to open positions larger than their actual capital would permit.

Margin: The Flip Side of Leverage

Margin is the trader's own investment, which acts as collateral for the leveraged position. Brokers set margin requirements to ensure that traders have enough capital to cover potential losses from their leveraged positions.

Advantages of Using Leverage

1. **Potential for Higher Profits**: With a larger position size, even small market movements can result in significant profit.
2. **Capital Efficiency**: Traders can maintain a diverse portfolio without tying up all their capital in a single position.
3. **Flexibility**: Allows traders to react quickly to market opportunities without liquidating other assets.

Risks Associated with Leverage

1. **Amplified Losses**: Just as potential profits are magnified, losses can also be amplified, potentially exceeding the original investment.
2. **Margin Calls**: If a leveraged position moves against a trader and their equity falls below the margin requirement, brokers may issue a margin call. This requires the trader to deposit additional funds or close positions to meet the requirement.
3. **Interest Costs**: Leveraged positions often incur interest charges on borrowed funds, which can accumulate over time.

Best Practices for Leveraged Trading

1. **Know Your Limits**: Traders should be aware of their risk tolerance and set limits on leverage accordingly.
2. **Continuous Monitoring**: Leveraged positions require close attention due to their amplified volatility.
3. **Use of Stop-Loss Orders**: This can help limit potential losses from leveraged positions.
4. **Stay Informed**: Understand the broker's margin requirements and the implications of a margin call.
5. **Risk Management**: Only a fraction of the trading capital should be allocated to leveraged trades.

Conclusion

Leverage, while offering the allure of substantial profits, is a double-edged sword. Without careful management and a deep understanding of its mechanics, it can lead to significant financial losses. This chapter has underscored the importance of prudence and informed decision-making when employing leverage in trading. Upcoming chapters will continue to explore advanced trading concepts, tools, and strategies, emphasizing their role in effective risk management.

Chapter 12: Advanced Derivative Instruments: Hedging and Speculation

Derivative instruments like options, futures, and swaps are fundamental tools in the trading world. These financial instruments derive their value from underlying assets, offering traders opportunities to hedge their portfolios or speculate on market movements. This chapter offers insights into these advanced instruments, elucidating their functionalities, risks, and strategic applications.

Understanding Derivative Instruments

At the core, derivatives are contracts between two parties that stipulate future transactions involving an underlying asset at a predefined price. These assets can range from stocks and bonds to commodities and currencies.

Types of Derivative Instruments

1. **Options**: Contracts offering the right, but not the obligation, to buy or sell an asset at a specific price within a set period.
2. **Futures**: Agreements to buy or sell an asset at a predetermined price on a specific future date.
3. **Swaps**: Contracts in which two parties exchange cash flows or other financial instruments.
4. **Forward Contracts**: Non-standardized contracts between two parties to buy or sell an asset at a specified future time at a price agreed upon today.

Hedging with Derivatives

Hedging is a strategy employed to offset potential losses in an investment. Derivatives can serve this purpose effectively.

1. **Commodity Hedging**: Companies can lock in prices for raw materials using futures, insulating themselves from volatile price movements.
2. **Interest Rate Hedging**: Financial institutions and companies can use interest rate swaps to manage exposure to fluctuating interest rates.
3. **Currency Hedging**: Multinational corporations and investors can utilize currency forwards and options to protect against adverse currency movements.

Speculation with Derivatives

Speculation involves attempting to profit from price changes in a financial instrument. Derivatives provide a leveraged means to speculate on asset price movements.

1. **Leverage**: Since derivatives often require a small upfront investment compared to the asset's actual price, potential profits (and losses) are magnified.
2. **Broad Market Access**: Derivatives allow traders to speculate on a variety of markets without owning the actual asset.

3. **Flexibility**: Various derivatives can be combined to create complex strategies based on the trader's market predictions.

Risks Associated with Derivatives

1. **Leverage Risks**: The amplified returns also mean amplified losses.
2. **Complexity**: Some derivative strategies can be intricate, leading to misunderstood risks.
3. **Liquidity Risks**: Some derivatives might not be easily tradable, posing challenges during rapid market shifts.
4. **Counterparty Risk**: The risk that the other party in the derivative contract will default.

Conclusion

Derivative instruments, while complex, offer a potent toolkit for traders. Whether seeking protection from market uncertainties or capitalizing on anticipated market movements, derivatives play a crucial role. However, their complexity and leverage necessitate a thorough understanding and prudent management. Subsequent chapters will delve deeper into the intricacies of the trading world, laying the groundwork for comprehensive and informed risk management strategies.

Chapter 13: Behavioral Finance: Navigating Cognitive Biases in Trading

In the complex world of trading, decision-making isn't solely based on cold, hard facts. Human emotions and cognitive biases significantly influence trading behaviors, often leading to irrational decisions that can amplify risks. Behavioral finance seeks to understand these psychological factors, offering insights and strategies to navigate the cognitive pitfalls that traders often encounter.

Understanding Behavioral Finance

Behavioral finance is an interdisciplinary field bridging finance and psychology. It challenges the traditional finance premise of rational and utility-maximizing investors, positing that psychological influences and biases often result in irrational financial decisions.

Key Cognitive Biases in Trading

1. **Overconfidence Bias**: The belief that one's skills or insights are superior, leading to excessive trading or underestimation of risks.
2. **Confirmation Bias**: Seeking or valuing information that aligns with one's existing beliefs while ignoring contradictory evidence.
3. **Loss Aversion**: The tendency to prefer avoiding losses over achieving equivalent gains, often resulting in holding onto losing positions for too long.
4. **Anchoring**: Relying heavily on the first piece of information (the "anchor") encountered when making decisions.
5. **Herd Behavior**: Mimicking the actions of the majority, irrespective of one's own analysis or beliefs.

Emotional Traps in Trading

1. **Fear**: Can result in panic selling or avoiding opportunities.
2. **Greed**: Pushing traders to chase after high returns without adequate risk assessment.
3. **Regret**: The emotional response to missed opportunities, which can influence future trading decisions.

4. **Over-attachment**: Holding onto assets based on emotional factors rather than rational analysis.

Strategies to Counteract Biases and Emotions

1. **Awareness**: Recognizing and understanding one's biases is the first step to mitigating their influence.
2. **Objective Analysis**: Relying on data-driven analysis, avoiding decisions based purely on emotions or gut feelings.
3. **Structured Trading Plans**: Setting clear entry, exit, and stop-loss criteria, and adhering to them.
4. **Regular Review**: Periodically assessing trading decisions to identify patterns of biases and learn from them.
5. **Seeking Diverse Opinions**: Engaging with a community or mentor to gain different perspectives, challenging one's own biases.

Conclusion

Human psychology plays a profound role in trading, often presenting as much of a challenge as market volatility itself. By understanding the intricacies of behavioral finance and actively working to recognize and counteract biases, traders can make more rational, objective decisions. The following chapters will further explore the confluence of human behavior and financial strategies, highlighting tools and methods to enhance the decision-making process in trading.

Chapter 14: Technological Tools: Harnessing Advanced Analytics in Risk Management

With the advent of technology and big data, the trading landscape has evolved dramatically. Advanced analytics, powered by artificial intelligence (AI) and machine learning (ML), provide traders with a competitive edge, enabling more precise predictions and proactive risk management. This chapter delves into the intersection of technology and trading, showcasing how modern tools can refine trading strategies and risk management approaches.

The Technological Revolution in Trading

As digital transformation sweeps across industries, the financial sector is no exception. From high-frequency trading to algorithmic strategies, technology's imprint on the trading world is undeniable and profound.

Benefits of Technological Tools in Trading

1. **Precision**: Advanced algorithms analyze vast data sets with impeccable accuracy, allowing for precise trading decisions.
2. **Speed**: Automated systems can execute trades in milliseconds, capitalizing on fleeting market opportunities.
3. **Data Analysis**: With the ability to process and interpret vast amounts of data, traders can glean insights previously inaccessible.
4. **Adaptive Learning**: Machine learning models can adapt to changing market conditions, refining their predictions over time.

Key Technological Tools in Modern Trading

1. **Algorithmic Trading Platforms**: Systems that execute trades automatically based on predefined criteria.
2. **Risk Management Software**: Tools designed specifically to assess and mitigate trading risks, often in real-time.
3. **Predictive Analytics**: Using historical data to forecast future market movements.
4. **Sentiment Analysis Tools**: Analyzing news articles, financial reports, and social media to gauge market sentiment.

Considerations and Risks of Technological Reliance

1. **Over-reliance**: Blindly trusting algorithms without human oversight can lead to unforeseen issues.
2. **Model Risk**: The potential inaccuracy of models, especially if they're based on flawed assumptions or data.
3. **Technological Failures**: Glitches, crashes, or cyberattacks can disrupt trading operations.
4. **Ethical Considerations**: The rise of algorithmic trading raises questions about market fairness and the potential for manipulation.

Staying Ahead: Continuous Learning and Adaptation

1. **Regular System Updates**: Keeping trading systems up-to-date ensures they operate efficiently and securely.
2. **Training**: As technology evolves, continuous learning becomes crucial for traders to harness new tools effectively.
3. **Diversified Strategies**: Avoid putting all eggs in one technological basket. Diversifying strategies can hedge against tech-specific risks.

Conclusion

Technology has irrevocably altered the face of trading, offering opportunities and challenges in equal measure. By integrating advanced analytics and maintaining a balanced perspective on their strengths and limitations, traders can navigate the digital age of finance with confidence. As we progress through this book, we will further discuss the confluence of traditional trading wisdom with modern technological advancements, setting the stage for a holistic approach to risk management.

Chapter 15: Global Macroeconomic Factors: Assessing Broader Influences on Trading

The world of trading isn't isolated; it's deeply intertwined with global events and macroeconomic shifts. From geopolitical tensions to central bank decisions, a myriad of external factors can influence asset prices and trading risks. This chapter offers a panoramic view of these macroeconomic influences, guiding traders in their assessment and response to larger economic narratives.

The Interconnectedness of Global Markets

No market operates in a vacuum. The symbiotic relationship between different economies means that a ripple in one part of the world can create waves elsewhere, affecting asset valuations and investor sentiment.

Key Macroeconomic Indicators and Their Impact

1. **Gross Domestic Product (GDP)**: A reflection of an economy's health, influencing currency strength and equity markets.
2. **Interest Rates**: Central bank decisions on interest rates can sway currency values, bond yields, and equity market sentiments.
3. **Inflation**: Affecting purchasing power and potentially prompting central bank interventions.
4. **Employment Data**: Indicators of economic health, impacting consumer spending and, by extension, equity markets.
5. **Trade Balances**: Affecting currency strength and reflecting the economic relationship between countries.

Global Events and Their Influence

1. **Geopolitical Tensions**: Wars, territorial disputes, or diplomatic spats can lead to market uncertainties.
2. **Natural Disasters**: Events like hurricanes or earthquakes can impact local economies and specific sectors, like insurance or commodities.
3. **Epidemics and Pandemics**: As evidenced by COVID-19, health crises can lead to global economic slowdowns and heightened market volatility.
4. **Technological Breakthroughs**: Innovations can drive sectoral growth and shift market dynamics, as seen with the rise of the tech sector in recent decades.

Strategies to Navigate Macroeconomic Factors

1. **Stay Informed**: Regularly follow reputable financial news sources to keep abreast of global events.
2. **Diversification**: Spreading investments across regions and asset classes can provide a buffer against localized economic downturns.
3. **Use of Hedging Instruments**: Derivatives can be employed to mitigate risks arising from anticipated macroeconomic shifts.
4. **Adopt a Long-term Perspective**: While short-term market fluctuations can be influenced by immediate events, long-term trends often align more closely with fundamentals.

Conclusion

Understanding the broader macroeconomic landscape is crucial for traders aiming to make informed decisions. By recognizing the interconnectedness of global markets and staying updated on significant global events, traders can better anticipate market movements and implement strategies to manage associated risks. As we delve deeper into the complexities of risk management in subsequent chapters, the significance of a well-rounded, global perspective becomes increasingly evident.

Chapter 16: Portfolio Diversification: Spreading Risk Across Assets and Geographies

The old adage, "Don't put all your eggs in one basket," resonates profoundly in the realm of trading and investments. Diversification, the practice of spreading investments across different assets or geographies, is a cornerstone of risk management. By reducing exposure to any single asset or market, traders can buffer their portfolios against unpredictable downturns. This chapter explores the nuances of diversification, highlighting its importance and outlining effective strategies for its implementation.

The Essence of Diversification

At its core, diversification is a risk management strategy, aiming to spread exposure and thereby reduce the impact of adverse movements in any single asset or market on the overall portfolio.

Benefits of Portfolio Diversification

1. **Risk Reduction**: By holding a variety of investments, the decline in one can potentially be offset by the performance of others.
2. **Potential for Higher Returns**: Diversification provides exposure to assets or markets with growth potential that might have been otherwise overlooked.
3. **Flexibility**: A diverse portfolio can be adjusted based on changing risk appetites or market conditions.
4. **Mitigation of Unsystematic Risks**: Risks specific to a particular company or sector can be diluted through diversification.

Types of Diversification

1. **Asset Diversification**: Distributing investments across asset classes like equities, bonds, commodities, and real estate.
2. **Geographical Diversification**: Investing in assets from different countries or regions.
3. **Sectoral Diversification**: Spreading investments across various industry sectors.
4. **Temporal Diversification**: Investing at different times, often done through strategies like dollar-cost averaging.

Challenges and Limitations of Diversification

1. **Over-diversification**: Holding too many assets can dilute potential gains and make portfolio management cumbersome.
2. **Correlation Misunderstanding**: Assets that usually behave differently might become correlated during market crises.
3. **Costs**: Expanding into multiple assets or geographies can lead to increased transaction and management fees.
4. **Knowledge Gaps**: Effectively diversifying requires understanding various assets and markets, which can be challenging for individual investors.

Effective Diversification Strategies

1. **Regular Portfolio Review**: Continuously assess the risk and return profile of the portfolio, making adjustments as necessary.
2. **Rebalancing**: Periodically realigning the portfolio to ensure it adheres to the desired asset allocation.
3. **Seek Expertise**: Leveraging financial advisors or robo-advisors can guide diversification decisions.
4. **Utilize Diversified Funds**: Investment vehicles like mutual funds or exchange-traded funds (ETFs) can offer instant diversification.

Conclusion

Diversification stands as a time-tested strategy in the risk management toolkit. While it doesn't guarantee against loss, it plays a pivotal role in mitigating specific risks and ensuring that traders don't bear the brunt of adverse movements in any one investment. As we journey further into the intricacies of risk management in the chapters ahead, the foundational principles of diversification will continually echo, emphasizing its enduring relevance in the trading realm.

Chapter 17: Leveraging and Margin Trading: Understanding the Double-Edged Sword

Trading on leverage, or margin trading, allows investors to open positions much larger than their initial investment or account balance. While this can amplify potential profits, it can also magnify losses, making it a potent tool that must be used judiciously. This chapter unravels the intricacies of leverage and margin trading, offering a comprehensive understanding of their benefits, risks, and best practices for effective utilization.

The Basics of Leverage and Margin

Leverage is the ability to control a large position with a relatively small amount of capital. The margin is the required deposit an investor makes to open such a leveraged position. In essence, trading on margin involves borrowing funds to amplify exposure.

Advantages of Margin Trading

1. **Increased Profit Potential**: A successful leveraged trade can result in returns that are proportionally higher than the initial margin.
2. **Flexibility**: Traders can capitalize on both rising and falling markets by going long or short, respectively.
3. **Diversification**: With the ability to take larger positions, traders can diversify across various assets without committing significant capital.
4. **Access to Higher Capital**: Particularly beneficial for traders with limited funds but a robust trading strategy.

Risks of Leveraging

1. **Magnified Losses**: Just as profits can be amplified, so can losses, potentially leading to significant financial setbacks.
2. **Margin Calls**: If a leveraged position moves against a trader, brokers may issue a margin call, demanding additional funds to maintain the position.
3. **Potential for Account Liquidation**: If the trader cannot meet a margin call, the broker might liquidate assets at potentially unfavorable prices.
4. **Interest Costs**: Borrowing funds to trade on margin often incurs interest, which can erode profits if trades aren't successful.

Best Practices for Safe Margin Trading

1. **Risk Management**: Always use stop-loss orders to limit potential losses and have a clear exit strategy for every trade.
2. **Stay Informed**: Monitor leveraged positions closely and stay updated on market news that could affect trades.

3. **Limit Leverage**: Just because high leverage is available doesn't mean it should always be used. Determine the appropriate level based on risk tolerance and strategy.
4. **Educate and Research**: Understand the terms and conditions of margin agreements and be aware of the costs involved.

Conclusion

Leverage and margin trading, while offering enticing prospects, are not suitable for all investors due to their inherent risks. The ability to navigate this double-edged sword hinges on knowledge, disciplined risk management, and continuous monitoring. As we delve deeper into trading strategies in the subsequent chapters, the role of leverage, both as an ally and an adversary, will be further illuminated, highlighting the importance of cautious and informed decision-making in the high-stakes world of trading.

Chapter 18: Behavioral Finance: Navigating the Psychological Pitfalls of Trading

Trading is as much a psychological endeavor as it is a strategic one. While market analytics, risk models, and trading strategies are critical, understanding and managing one's psychological tendencies can be the key differentiator between successful and unsuccessful trading. Behavioral finance, which explores the intersection of psychology and financial decision-making, offers invaluable insights into the common cognitive biases that traders face. This chapter provides a deep dive into these biases and equips traders with strategies to navigate them effectively.

Introduction to Behavioral Finance

Behavioral finance challenges the traditional economic theory that investors are always rational, profit-maximizing individuals. It posits that various cognitive biases can distort judgment, leading to irrational financial decisions.

Common Cognitive Biases in Trading

1. **Overconfidence Bias**: Overestimating one's abilities or information, which can lead to excessive trading and increased risks.
2. **Confirmation Bias**: Focusing on information that confirms existing beliefs while ignoring contradicting evidence.
3. **Loss Aversion**: The pain of a loss is felt more intensely than the pleasure of a similar gain, leading traders to hold onto losing positions in the hope of recovery.
4. **Anchoring Bias**: Relying heavily on an initial piece of information (the "anchor") to make subsequent judgments.
5. **Herd Mentality**: Following the actions of the majority, even if they contradict one's own analysis or judgment.

Impact of Emotional Responses

1. **Fear**: Can lead to panic selling or avoiding opportunities.
2. **Greed**: Might result in over-leveraging or holding onto a position for too long.
3. **Regret**: The pain of missing out or making a wrong decision can skew future trading choices.

Strategies to Mitigate Psychological Pitfalls

1. **Self-awareness**: Regular introspection to identify personal biases or emotional triggers.
2. **Set Clear Rules**: Predefine entry and exit strategies, and adhere to them.

3. **Diversification**: A diversified portfolio can help distribute risk and reduce the emotional impact of poor performance in any single asset.
4. **Continuous Education**: Understanding behavioral finance and its principles can arm traders against common pitfalls.
5. **Seek External Views**: Discussing strategies with peers or mentors can offer a fresh perspective and challenge ingrained biases.

Conclusion

The complexities of the human psyche play a pivotal role in the trading journey. By recognizing and addressing inherent cognitive biases and emotional responses, traders can cultivate a more balanced, disciplined, and ultimately successful approach to the markets. As this book concludes in the subsequent sections, the melding of strategic analysis with psychological understanding emerges as the bedrock of effective risk management in the ever-evolving world of trading.

Conclusion: Synthesizing Strategies for Effective Risk Management in Trading

Trading, by its very nature, is an endeavor rife with uncertainty. The confluence of global events, market dynamics, individual behaviors, and sheer randomness ensures that risk is an ever-present companion for every trader. However, as this book has illuminated, risk isn't something to be shunned; rather, it's a variable to be understood, embraced, and adeptly managed.

Recap of Key Insights

1. **Foundation of Risk Management**: Before delving into strategies, understanding the inherent risks in trading is paramount. These range from market risks to operational challenges and even psychological pitfalls.
2. **Toolkits and Techniques**: Various instruments and methods, from diversification to leverage, can be employed to shape a trader's risk profile. Yet, each tool comes with its set of nuances that must be grasped for effective utilization.
3. **Macro to Micro**: While global macroeconomic factors set the broader trading backdrop, individual behavioral biases can significantly influence trading decisions. Both these spectra, expansive and introspective, are critical to holistic risk management.

The Way Forward

1. **Continuous Learning**: The world of trading is dynamic. New strategies, tools, and risks continually emerge. As such, the successful trader is a perpetual student, always attuned to shifts and advancements in the field.
2. **Embracing Technology**: Modern technology, including AI and machine learning, offers novel ways to analyze and manage risks. Leveraging these can offer traders an edge.
3. **Staying Grounded**: While techniques and tools are vital, the human element — intuition, judgment, ethics — remains at the core of trading. Balancing analytical rigor with human insights is key.

Parting Thoughts

Risk management, as detailed throughout this book, isn't merely a set of techniques; it's a mindset. It's about acknowledging that the future is uncertain, but rather than being paralyzed by that uncertainty, one is empowered by the ability to shape responses and strategies around it. Through a blend of knowledge, discipline, intuition, and continuous adaptation, traders can transform risk from an adversary into an ally, making it a catalyst for growth, learning, and success in the exhilarating world of trading.

Alternative Investments

Explore trading strategies involving non-traditional assets like art, wine, or collectibles.

Introduction
Understanding the realm of non-traditional assets

In the vast world of investments, most financial discourse predominantly revolves around traditional assets. These typically encompass equities, bonds, cash, and, more recently, certain types of commodities. At their core, traditional investments have established marketplaces, standardized evaluation metrics, and robust regulatory frameworks. For the average investor, these assets serve as the primary building blocks of a diversified portfolio. They offer a predictable balance of risk and reward, backed by historical performance data and widespread acceptance among financial professionals.

However, as the global economy evolves and becomes more interconnected, there emerges a niche but growing segment of the market known as non-traditional or alternative assets. Unlike their traditional counterparts, these assets don't have the luxury of universally accepted valuation metrics. Instead, their value often hinges on subjective factors such as rarity, aesthetic appeal, historical significance, or sheer market demand.

These alternative assets can range from tangible items like art, collectibles, and wine, to intangible assets such as intellectual property rights or even certain digital commodities. The intrigue around these assets lies not just in their uniqueness but also in the opportunities they present for significant returns. In several instances, the appreciation in value for some alternative investments has outpaced the returns from more mainstream assets. For instance, certain works of art or vintage wines have appreciated exponentially within relatively short time frames, delivering windfall gains to their holders.

Importance of diversifying into alternative investments

Diversification has long been heralded as the cornerstone of prudent investment strategy. At its essence, diversification is the act of spreading one's investments across a range of asset classes to minimize risk. While equities might offer high returns, they come with volatility. Bonds, on the other hand, while being more stable, often deliver lower yields. By blending these assets, an investor can achieve a desired risk-return profile.

Enter alternative investments. Their inclusion in an investment portfolio serves a dual purpose. Firstly, they provide a hedge against the more cyclical behavior of traditional markets. When stock markets are in turmoil, the value of a rare piece of art or a vintage wine collection might remain unaffected or even appreciate. This counter-cyclical nature makes them valuable stabilizers in a diversified portfolio.

Secondly, alternative investments often come with unique value propositions that are not found in mainstream assets. Take art, for instance. The value of an artwork doesn't just depend on the name of the artist or the age of the piece. Factors like provenance, historical significance, condition, and even current art market trends can significantly influence its price. The same logic applies to other alternative assets, be it wine, collectibles, or luxury watches. This complexity introduces an element of research, expertise, and even passion into the investment equation.

However, it's essential to underscore that while alternative investments can offer lucrative returns, they are not devoid of risks. Their markets can be less liquid, meaning selling them at the desired price can be challenging. Additionally, their valuation can be highly subjective, leading to potential mispricing. And, given the absence of standardized regulatory oversight, the potential for fraud can be higher.

In conclusion, as investors look to diversify their portfolios and seek out assets that can deliver both financial and intrinsic value, the realm of non-traditional assets becomes increasingly pertinent. This book aims to delve deep into the intricacies of alternative investments, shedding light on their historical context, psychological appeal, potential risks, and strategies for effective trading. As we journey through the world of art, wine, collectibles, and beyond, the reader will gain comprehensive insights into this niche yet immensely fascinating segment of the investment landscape.

Chapter 1: Defining Alternative Investments
Beyond stocks and bonds: A comprehensive look at non-traditional assets

At its core, the essence of investing revolves around allocating capital with the expectation of a future financial return. While traditional investment mediums like stocks, bonds, and even commodities like gold have long dominated this space, the realm of alternative investments is expansive and intricate. So, what truly defines an alternative investment?

Alternative investments are typically characterized as any investment that falls outside the purview of traditional asset classes. This category can encompass a diverse range of assets, from tangible items like real estate and art to more intangible assets such as hedge funds or even private equity.

Several distinct features demarcate alternative investments from their traditional counterparts:

1. **Liquidity**: Unlike stocks or bonds, which can be swiftly sold on centralized exchanges, alternative investments often lack such platforms. This can make liquidating these assets more time-consuming and sometimes less predictable in terms of return.

2. **Valuation Complexities**: With stocks or bonds, valuation metrics like price-to-earnings ratios, yield curves, or credit ratings provide clear benchmarks. However, alternative assets often require specialized knowledge for accurate valuation. Factors like provenance in art, vintage year in wines, or zoning regulations in real estate can play pivotal roles in determining worth.

3. **Regulation**: Traditional investments often operate within stringent regulatory environments designed to protect investors. Alternative assets, given their diverse and niche nature, might not always have such comprehensive oversight. This can result in both opportunities and risks.

4. **Investment Horizon**: Alternative investments often necessitate longer investment horizons. For instance, a real estate project or a private equity stake in a startup requires patience and a longer-term outlook compared to equities which can be traded daily.

5. **Unique Risk Profile**: Alternative assets come with their own set of risks, often distinct from market risks affecting traditional assets. These could range from environmental risks in real estate, to authentication risks in art, to storage risks in wine.

6. **Specialized Expertise**: The successful trading of alternative assets usually mandates a deep understanding of the specific market. Whether it's recognizing the potential of a young artist or identifying the growth trajectory of a startup, specialized expertise is crucial.

Understanding the nuances of alternative investments requires a keen eye for detail, an appetite for research, and often, a passion for the asset itself. Investing in a piece of art, for instance, isn't merely a financial decision; it's an intersection of aesthetic appreciation, historical significance, and market dynamics.

This book will navigate these multifaceted terrains, providing readers with in-depth knowledge on various alternative assets, their market dynamics, and strategies to effectively trade and invest in them. Whether you're an ardent art aficionado or a wine connoisseur, or simply an investor looking to diversify and tap into new avenues of growth, this exploration will equip you with the tools and insights to make informed decisions in the world of alternative investments.

Chapter 2: Historical Context of Alternative Investments
A journey through time: The evolution and significance of alternative assets

Alternative investments, while a relatively recent classification in the contemporary financial landscape, have roots that stretch deep into the annals of history. Civilizations throughout the ages have revered, traded, and cherished assets that today fall within this category. Understanding the historical context is vital not only for the deeper appreciation of these assets but also for discerning patterns, trends, and cyclical behaviors that might repeat in contemporary times.

Ancient Civilizations and the Dawn of Collectibles In ancient Egypt, art and jewelry were considered both status symbols and investments. Pharaohs and nobility hoarded gold, jewelry, and intricate artifacts, understanding their intrinsic and lasting value. Similarly, in ancient China, porcelain and silk, due to their unique production methods and aesthetic appeal, became sought-after collectibles, often exchanged for hefty sums and considered assets of prosperity.

The Middle Ages: Land and Property as Prime Assets During the feudal era, land was the most dominant form of asset, conferring both wealth and power. Those who controlled vast tracts of land were not just economically affluent but also wielded significant political influence. Property and land, in many ways, became the first widely-accepted alternative investment forms, setting the foundation for real estate as an investment class in modern times.

The Renaissance: Art as an Investment and Status Symbol The European Renaissance period saw a surge in the production and trade of art. Patronage by wealthy families, most notably the Medici in Florence, saw artists like Leonardo da Vinci and Michelangelo rise to prominence. Artworks, commissioned by the elite, were clear symbols of status, wealth, and culture. They were also seen as tangible assets, with their value appreciating over time, setting the early precedents for art as an investment.

The Age of Exploration: Commodities and Trade Goods As European explorers set sail to discover new lands, commodities such as spices, silks, and even exotic artifacts became significant trade assets. These items, rare in Europe but abundant in Asia or the Americas, were traded for substantial sums, underscoring the principles of supply, demand, rarity, and desirability - factors that play a pivotal role in the valuation of alternative investments even today.

The Industrial Revolution and the Rise of Intellectual Property The 18th and 19th centuries saw an explosion in inventions and innovations. With this came the concept of intellectual property, where inventors could protect and monetize their creations. This era laid the groundwork for understanding and valuing intangible assets, from patents and trademarks to copyrights, which today form a significant portion of alternative investments.

The 20th Century: From Collectibles to Digital Assets The past century has seen a proliferation of collectibles as investments. From rare stamps to vintage cars, from baseball cards to first edition books, the 20th century expanded the horizons of what could be considered an "asset". Furthermore, with the advent of the digital age, the late 20th and early 21st centuries have introduced the concept of digital or virtual assets, like domain names or, more recently, non-fungible tokens (NFTs).

Conclusion The historical journey of alternative investments is not just a testament to their enduring appeal but also a guide to understanding their future trajectory. By studying the past, investors can glean insights into how societal, cultural, and economic shifts influence the desirability, and thereby the value, of non-traditional assets. The following chapters will dive deeper into individual asset classes, but this historical context provides a foundation, ensuring readers approach each asset not as an isolated entity but as a part of a grand tapestry woven through time.

Chapter 3: The Psychological Appeal of Alternative Investments
Beyond monetary value: The intrinsic appeal and emotional attachment

While the financial aspect of investments is paramount, it is essential to recognize that alternative investments often tread a path where emotions, passions, and psychological factors significantly influence decisions. This unique blend of intrinsic appeal and potential financial return sets alternative investments apart from traditional assets.

The Emotional Connection to Tangible Assets Human beings have an innate inclination towards the tactile. The ability to touch, see, and experience an asset amplifies its perceived value. A collector might derive immense satisfaction from flipping through vintage comic books, savoring a rare bottle of wine, or wearing a luxury watch. This emotional connection transcends the realm of mere financial valuation. For many, it's not just about potential returns; it's about the joy, memories, and experiences these assets provide.

The Sense of Exclusivity and Rarity Owning something rare or unique offers a sense of exclusivity, elevating the owner's status in certain social or collector circles. This psychological appeal is evident when we look at the world of art collectors or car enthusiasts. Possessing a piece that few others have can be a significant driving force, often leading to competition and driving up prices, especially in auction scenarios.

Nostalgia: A Potent Driver Many alternative assets, especially collectibles, tap into the powerful emotion of nostalgia. Vintage toys, stamps, or even certain pieces of music or art can transport individuals back to a different time, evoking powerful memories. This emotional connection can significantly influence purchasing decisions, sometimes leading investors to pay premiums for assets that resonate with their past.

Investing in Passions While traditional investments are typically driven by cold, hard data and financial metrics, alternative investments allow individuals to invest in their passions. A lover of fine wines might delve into wine investment not just for potential profits but because they love the intricacies of viticulture, the art of wine-making, and the sheer joy of tasting and collecting.

The Desire for Tangible Wealth In an age of digital currencies, online stocks, and virtual assets, there's a segment of investors who find comfort in tangible wealth – assets they can see, touch, and experience. This psychological need for physicality can be a driving force behind investments in real estate, gold, or other tangible alternative assets.

Diversification Not Just of Portfolio, but of Experience For some investors, diversifying into alternative assets isn't merely a financial strategy. It's a diversification of experience. Attending art auctions, visiting vineyards, or participating in collectors' conventions can offer experiences that standard stock or bond investments cannot provide.

Conclusion The psychological dynamics intertwined with alternative investments highlight the multifaceted nature of this domain. While potential returns remain a crucial consideration, the intangible benefits – emotional satisfaction, unique experiences, and personal connections – play an equally, if not more, significant role. As we delve deeper into individual alternative assets in the coming chapters, understanding this emotional and psychological underpinning will be vital in comprehending the complexities of the market dynamics and valuation principles.

Chapter 4: Art as an Investment Medium
Decoding the canvas: From historical significance to market dynamics

Art, with its rich tapestry of history, culture, and emotion, has long been a sought-after investment medium. Yet, the world of art investments is intricate, governed not just by monetary considerations but also by aesthetic appeal, societal trends, and historical significance.

Historical Value vs. Market Value While a piece of art might have immense historical or cultural value, it doesn't necessarily translate to a high market value. Factors such as the artist's prominence, the era during which it was created, its provenance, and its condition play pivotal roles. Conversely, a contemporary piece with no historical significance might fetch a high price due to current market demand or trends.

Understanding Authenticity and Provenance Authenticity is the cornerstone of art investment. Ensuring that a piece is genuine is paramount, given the myriad of forgeries in the market. Provenance, or the record of ownership, can not only affirm authenticity but can also add value, especially if previously owned by notable personalities or featured in esteemed exhibitions.

The Role of Art Auction Houses Institutions like Christie's, Sotheby's, and Bonhams play a significant role in the art investment world. They not only help determine market value but also set trends, with high-profile auctions often influencing the market direction for certain artists or styles.

Evaluating Emerging Artists Investing in established artists offers a sense of security, but the highest returns often come from identifying and investing in emerging talents. Understanding the art world, networking with galleries, and having an eye for potential can yield significant dividends.

Art Funds and Investment Groups Given the high entry costs for notable art pieces, art funds or investment groups allow individuals to invest in art collectively. These funds pool resources to purchase significant pieces, aiming for appreciation over time.

Insurance, Maintenance, and Storage Unlike stocks or bonds, art requires maintenance to retain its value. This includes considerations related to storage conditions, insurance against damage or theft, and periodic restoration efforts.

Digital Art and NFTs: The New Frontier The advent of digital art, especially with the rise of Non-Fungible Tokens (NFTs), has revolutionized the art investment landscape. While the principles remain similar, the digital medium introduces new considerations, especially related to authenticity, digital storage, and market dynamics in online platforms.

Conclusion Investing in art is a journey that blends the heart and the mind. While aesthetic appreciation and emotional connection form the core, understanding market dynamics, historical trends, and the nuances of authentication and maintenance are crucial. This chapter sets the foundation for a deeper exploration of strategies and considerations specific to art investment, ensuring the reader is equipped to navigate this colorful and complex world.

Chapter 5: Fine Wine Investments
From vineyards to cellars: Navigating the nuances of viticulture economics

The appreciation of fine wine goes beyond the palate. Over time, wine has solidified its position as a lucrative investment avenue, combining the intricacies of viticulture, market dynamics, and aging potential. Investing in wine is a multifaceted endeavor, necessitating understanding far beyond mere taste preferences.

Historical Context of Wine as an Asset Wine's journey as a valued commodity traces back to ancient civilizations. The Romans, for instance, recognized the economic potential of viticulture, with some vintages even used as currency or barter goods. This historical backdrop provides context for wine's enduring appeal both as a consumable and an investment.

Terroir, Vintage, and Varietal: The Trifecta of Wine Valuation Three primary factors influence a wine's potential value:

1. **Terroir**: This refers to the unique environmental factors, including soil, climate, and topography, where grapes are grown. Certain regions, like Bordeaux in France or Napa Valley in the USA, command premium valuations due to their renowned terroir.
2. **Vintage**: The year of production can significantly impact a wine's value. Factors like weather conditions during the growing season can influence the quality of grapes and, by extension, the wine.
3. **Varietal**: The grape variety used plays a role in valuation. Certain varietals, like the Cabernet Sauvignon or Pinot Noir, typically command higher prices due to their global appeal and aging potential.

The Role of Wine Critics and Ratings Prominent wine critics, like Robert Parker, can significantly sway market demand. A high rating from a reputed critic can catapult a wine's value overnight. As such, staying attuned to reviews and ratings is pivotal for wine investors.

Storage, Aging, and Provenance Unlike many other assets, wine's value can fluctuate based on its storage conditions. Proper aging can enhance a wine's flavor profile and, consequently, its market value. Conversely, improper storage can degrade its quality. Additionally, provenance, or the wine's ownership and storage history, can influence its desirability among collectors.

Investing in Wine Funds and Futures For those looking to invest in wine without maintaining a personal cellar, wine funds offer a collective investment avenue. Additionally, wine futures allow investors to purchase wine while it's still in the barrel, speculating on its future market value once bottled and aged.

Diversifying with New World Wines While European wines, especially from regions like France and Italy, have traditionally dominated the investment scene, New World wines from regions like South America, Australia, and South Africa are gaining traction. Investing in these emerging markets can offer diversification and untapped growth potential.

Conclusion Fine wine investment is a delicate blend of science, art, and market acumen. Whether you're a seasoned oenophile or a novice looking to dip your toes into viticulture economics, understanding the nuances of wine production, valuation, and storage is crucial. The subsequent chapters will delve deeper into strategies, risks, and opportunities in the ever-evolving world of wine investments

Chapter 6: Collectibles – Stamps, Coins, and More
Tangible treasures: Navigating the world of collectible investments

The realm of collectible investments is a captivating intersection of history, culture, and finance. These tangible treasures hold within them not just the allure of aesthetics, but also the stories of civilizations, the resonance of eras long gone, and the craftsmanship of artisans. From the intricate designs on coins to the delicate engravings on stamps, from the nostalgia of vintage toys to the wisdom encapsulated in rare books, the collectibles universe is a testament to human creativity and the passage of time.

The Charm of Tangible Heritage

Collectibles, by their very nature, captivate our imagination and sense of wonder. They beckon us to a past rich with memories, accomplishments, and moments frozen in time. Stamps, with their miniature canvases depicting historical events and cultural icons, provide insights into societies as they once were. Coins, bearing the mark of their era's rulers and the symbols of their age, serve as silent witnesses to the passage of civilizations. Vintage toys, icons of playfulness and creativity, echo the joys of childhood across generations. And rare books, repositories of knowledge, stories, and the human experience, connect us to authors and eras that shaped our world.

Investing in Numismatics – The Study of Coins

Numismatics, the study and collection of coins, is an intricate realm where art, history, and finance intersect. Coins are not just tokens of exchange; they embody the cultures, economies, and aspirations of the times in which they were minted. Collecting coins offers a glimpse into the evolution of societies – their symbols, leaders, and technological advancements. Rarity is a key driver in numismatic investment. Coins with limited mintages or those bearing unique errors can command significant premiums. Condition, graded on standardized scales, influences a coin's value, with uncirculated specimens often fetching higher prices.

Stamps: A Philatelist's Pursuit

Philately, the study and collection of stamps, is a voyage through the stories of nations and peoples. Stamps mirror historical events, commemorate cultural icons, and reflect technological progress. Each stamp carries a narrative – whether it's a postage stamp from a wartime era, a commemorative stamp celebrating a historical event, or a thematic stamp set depicting a nation's natural beauty. The rarity of stamps often stems from printing errors, limited editions, or historical context. As with coins, condition matters, and stamps in mint condition tend to hold greater investment value.

Vintage Toys and Comics: Playful Investments

Vintage toys and comic books evoke the innocence of childhood and the cultural zeitgeist of their eras. Collecting vintage toys is akin to preserving the joys of yesteryears. Action figures, dolls, and toy cars evoke memories of play and wonder. As investments, rarity, condition, and demand from nostalgic collectors drive their value. Similarly, comic books are not just narratives in panels; they are historical artifacts documenting popular culture, social changes, and storytelling trends. Iconic characters like Superman, Batman, and Spider-Man are embedded in global consciousness, and their first appearances in comic books hold immense value.

Books as Collectible Assets

Rare books are more than repositories of knowledge; they are time capsules of human thought, creativity, and expression. First editions, limited printings, and manuscripts carry the essence of their authors' ideas and eras. Collecting rare books involves understanding not only the literary merit but also the historical and cultural context. Condition, original bindings, and provenance contribute to a book's value. Manuscripts, letters, and autographed copies offer unique insights into authors' minds and can command premium prices.

Art of Authentication and Valuation

Authenticating collectibles is a critical process in ensuring their value. Expert appraisers, collectors' associations, and provenance documentation play essential roles in confirming the legitimacy of items. For stamps and coins, understanding mint marks, engravers' signatures, and printing techniques is crucial. Authentication of rare books involves examining bindings, watermarks, and signatures. The expertise of professional authenticators provides a layer of confidence for investors.

Investment Funds and Indices

While individual collectibles can be highly specialized, investment funds and indices offer avenues for broader exposure to the asset class. Collectible investment funds pool resources from multiple investors to acquire and manage collections. Indices track the performance of various collectibles categories, offering insight into market trends and value appreciation.

Cultural and Economic Trends

Collectibles' markets are not immune to shifts in cultural preferences and economic dynamics. Pop culture phenomena, anniversaries, and societal trends can influence demand and, consequently, value. The rise of nostalgia-driven purchasing and the increasing digitalization of content have also impacted the collectibles landscape.

In conclusion, the world of collectible investments is a harmonious blend of sentiment and strategy. Whether driven by nostalgia, historical curiosity, or financial aspirations, understanding the nuances of numismatics, philately, vintage toys, and rare books equips investors to navigate this captivating realm. As you delve further into the subsequent chapters, you'll uncover the intricacies of valuation, market trends, and investment strategies, allowing you to embark on your own journey through tangible treasures and historical narratives.

Chapter 7: Luxury Watches and Jewelry
Timeless investments: The blend of craftsmanship, rarity, and demand

Luxury watches and jewelry are more than adornments; they are embodiments of human artistry, engineering precision, and aesthetic beauty. These opulent assets have carved a niche in the investment world, where rarity, brand reputation, and timeless appeal converge to create a unique value proposition.

Craftsmanship and Design: The Heart of Luxury

Luxury watches and jewelry are the result of meticulous craftsmanship and artistic vision. Watches, with their intricate movements and complications, showcase the mastery of horology. Jewelry, often bearing rare gemstones and intricate designs, epitomizes the fusion of aesthetics and skill. The blend of form and function imbues these items with lasting value.

Brand Identity and Rarity

In the realm of luxury watches and jewelry, brand identity holds immense sway. Established names like Rolex, Patek Philippe, and Cartier carry not just reputations but legacies. Limited editions and unique designs add an element of rarity that drives demand. Collectors and enthusiasts vie for pieces that are not just beautiful but also hold the promise of exclusivity.

Market Trends and Collectibility

The luxury watch and jewelry market thrives on trends, much like the fashion industry. Iconic designs or vintage pieces can witness resurgences in popularity, leading to increased demand and higher values. Similarly, the allure of owning a piece worn by a celebrity or linked to a historical event can significantly enhance its collectibility and investment appeal.

Precious Metals and Gemstones

Precious metals and gemstones are inherent components of luxury watches and jewelry. The value of gold, silver, platinum, and precious gemstones plays a role in determining the baseline worth of these items. Understanding the market dynamics of these materials is crucial for gauging the intrinsic value of a piece.

Investment vs. Collection

While some individuals invest in luxury watches and jewelry purely for financial gain, others view these assets as forms of personal expression and heirlooms. The distinction between investing and collecting lies in the motivations behind acquisition. Investors focus on potential returns, whereas collectors often prioritize aesthetic appreciation and emotional connections.

Authentication and Certification

In a market where counterfeits can be sophisticated, authentication and certification are paramount. Expert horologists and gemologists provide authentication services, validating the authenticity and quality of luxury items. Certificates of authenticity enhance buyer confidence and protect against fraudulent transactions.

Investment Funds and Portfolios

For those seeking exposure to luxury watches and jewelry without direct ownership, investment funds offer an avenue. Such funds pool resources to acquire pieces, providing investors with fractional ownership. Building a diversified portfolio of luxury assets can mitigate risks associated with individual pieces.

Conclusion

The allure of luxury watches and jewelry extends beyond their material worth. These items are conduits of artistry, history, and human aspiration. Investing in them is an intricate dance between understanding craftsmanship, tracking market trends, and recognizing the intangible elements that contribute to value. As you delve further into this chapter and the ones to come, you'll gain insights into the world of luxury investments – a realm where timepieces and adornments become not just accessories but vehicles of timeless elegance and financial potential.

Chapter 8: Intellectual Property and Digital Assets
Unveiling the intangible: Exploring the value of ideas and digital creations

In a world increasingly driven by technology and innovation, the concept of investing in intellectual property (IP) and digital assets has gained prominence. These intangible assets, ranging from patents and copyrights to digital tokens and virtual real estate, represent a new frontier where creativity intersects with financial opportunity.

Intellectual Property as an Investment

Intellectual property encompasses patents, copyrights, trademarks, and trade secrets. Investing in IP involves recognizing the value of ideas, innovations, and creative works. Patents grant exclusive rights to inventions, copyrights protect artistic and literary works, and trademarks safeguard brands. IP investments offer both potential licensing revenue and the ability to enforce exclusivity.

Digital Tokens and Cryptocurrencies

The rise of blockchain technology has introduced digital tokens and cryptocurrencies as investable assets. Tokens represent ownership, access, or other rights within digital ecosystems. Cryptocurrencies, like Bitcoin and Ethereum, have garnered attention for their potential to store value and offer alternative investment avenues.

Non-Fungible Tokens (NFTs)

Non-fungible tokens (NFTs) have revolutionized digital ownership and collectibility. NFTs represent unique digital assets, from artwork and music to virtual real estate and in-game items. Their scarcity, verifiable ownership, and transferability have opened new vistas for artists, creators, and investors alike.

The Role of Digital Real Estate

Virtual real estate, often hosted on blockchain-based platforms, is a novel concept in digital assets. Owning digital land, spaces, or structures in virtual worlds holds potential for real-world monetization through gaming, events, or social interactions. The value of digital real estate is intertwined with the growth and popularity of virtual ecosystems.

Challenges and Opportunities

Investing in intellectual property and digital assets comes with its share of challenges. Valuing intangible assets can be complex, involving considerations beyond traditional financial metrics. Regulatory uncertainties, technological vulnerabilities, and market volatility also present risks. However, these challenges are counterbalanced by the potential for diversification, innovation, and disruptive growth.

Market Trends and Speculation

The market for intellectual property and digital assets is dynamic, driven by technological advancements and shifting cultural trends. NFT marketplaces, for instance, have witnessed skyrocketing prices for digital art and collectibles. While some investments are fueled by speculation, others are underpinned by genuine utility and innovation.

Creating Value in the Digital Economy

Investing in intellectual property and digital assets extends beyond financial gain. It involves recognizing the value of innovation, creativity, and the evolving digital economy. Creators, artists, and entrepreneurs can tokenize their work, enabling fractional ownership, wider distribution, and novel revenue streams.

Conclusion

Investing in intellectual property and digital assets delves into the realm of the intangible, where ideas manifest as value and creativity shapes opportunity. As technology continues to reshape industries, these assets provide a lens into the future of finance, innovation, and the evolving ways in which value is created and exchanged. In the upcoming chapters, you'll delve deeper into the strategies, considerations, and implications of investing in intellectual property and the digital landscape.

Chapter 9: Real Estate Investment Trusts (REITs) and Infrastructure
Building wealth through bricks and bridges: Exploring REITs and infrastructure investments

Real estate investment trusts (REITs) and infrastructure projects offer avenues for investors to tap into physical assets with the potential for steady income and long-term growth. These investment vehicles provide exposure to real property and essential infrastructure, while also offering the benefits of liquidity and diversification.

Real Estate Investment Trusts (REITs)

REITs are investment vehicles that allow individuals to invest in real estate properties without owning physical assets. They pool resources from multiple investors to acquire, develop, and manage properties, such as commercial buildings, residential complexes, and shopping centers. REITs offer dividends from rental income and the potential for capital appreciation.

Types of REITs

REITs come in various forms, including equity REITs that own and manage properties, mortgage REITs that provide financing for real estate, and hybrid REITs that combine aspects of both. Specialized REITs focus on specific sectors, such as healthcare, hospitality, or data centers, offering targeted exposure to particular segments of the real estate market.

Infrastructure Investments

Infrastructure investments involve funding and owning essential facilities and systems that underpin modern societies. These include transportation networks, energy grids, water supply systems, and communication networks. Infrastructure assets often have stable cash flows and long-term revenue potential, making them attractive for income-focused investors.

Public vs. Private Infrastructure

Investors can access infrastructure through both public and private avenues. Public infrastructure includes publicly traded companies that operate and maintain essential services. Private infrastructure investments involve direct ownership or investing in funds that finance projects like toll roads, airports, and renewable energy installations.

Income, Growth, and Risk

REITs and infrastructure investments offer a balance between income and growth potential. REIT dividends come from rental income, while infrastructure assets generate revenue through user fees or government contracts. Both asset classes can provide a hedge against inflation due to their tangible nature and long-term revenue streams.

Liquidity and Diversification

One of the benefits of investing in REITs and infrastructure is their liquidity compared to owning physical properties. REIT shares can be bought and sold on stock exchanges, providing ease of entry and exit. Additionally, these investments offer diversification by allowing exposure to real assets across different sectors and geographical regions.

Regulation and Tax Considerations

REITs are subject to specific regulations that dictate their structure, operations, and tax treatment. To qualify as a REIT, a company must distribute a significant portion of its earnings to shareholders. Infrastructure investments can have tax implications based on ownership structure, jurisdiction, and the type of income generated.

Global Infrastructure Trends

Infrastructure investments are influenced by demographic shifts, urbanization, technological advancements, and environmental concerns. Renewable energy projects, smart cities, and digital connectivity are emerging trends that shape the infrastructure landscape, offering opportunities for forward-looking investors.

Conclusion

REITs and infrastructure investments bridge the gap between physical assets and financial markets. They provide a way to access the tangible benefits of real property and essential systems while offering the flexibility and liquidity of traditional investments. As you explore these investment avenues further in the subsequent chapters, you'll gain insights into strategies, risks, and considerations that can guide your decisions in building wealth through bricks and bridges.

Chapter 10: Hedge Funds and Private Equity
The realm of sophisticated investments: Unveiling hedge funds and private equity

Hedge funds and private equity are two categories of investment vehicles that cater to sophisticated investors seeking alternative avenues for potentially higher returns. These vehicles often involve complex strategies, active management, and limited accessibility, making them a distinctive corner of the financial landscape.

Hedge Funds: Dynamic and Diverse

Hedge funds are investment pools managed by skilled professionals who aim to generate returns by implementing various strategies. These strategies can range from long-short equity positions to arbitrage and macroeconomic plays. Hedge funds offer potential returns that are uncorrelated with traditional markets, providing diversification benefits for investors.

Risk Management and Hedging

Hedge funds derive their name from their initial purpose: to hedge against market risks. While modern hedge funds go beyond traditional risk mitigation, they still incorporate elements of hedging to manage potential losses. The flexibility to short-sell assets allows hedge fund managers to profit from declining markets.

Alternative Investment Strategies

Hedge funds deploy a wide array of investment strategies. Global macro funds focus on economic trends and global events, while quantitative funds use algorithms and mathematical models for trading decisions. Distressed debt funds invest in undervalued or troubled assets, seeking to profit from turnarounds.

Private Equity: Unveiling Potential

Private equity involves investing in private companies or acquiring public companies to take them private. These investments are typically made by institutional investors, high-net-worth individuals, or private equity firms. The aim is to enhance a company's performance, streamline operations, and eventually exit for a profit.

Value Creation and Active Management

Private equity investors actively participate in the companies they invest in, aiming to create value through operational improvements, strategic direction, and efficient management practices. The goal is to enhance a company's profitability and increase its market value over time.

Venture Capital and Growth Equity

Venture capital is a subset of private equity focused on early-stage startups. These investments are characterized by higher risk and potentially higher returns. Growth equity, on the other hand, targets established companies with the potential for significant expansion.

Liquidity and Lock-Up Periods

Hedge funds and private equity investments often come with limited liquidity compared to traditional assets. Hedge fund investors may have redemption restrictions, and private equity investments often have lock-up periods during which capital cannot be withdrawn.

Access and Accreditation

Both hedge funds and private equity investments typically require higher minimum investments and are accessible to accredited investors, who meet specific wealth or income criteria. This exclusivity aims to ensure that investors have the financial capacity to understand and weather potential risks.

Conclusion

Hedge funds and private equity represent investment strategies that go beyond traditional market participation. These vehicles cater to investors seeking potentially higher returns, active management, and exposure to unique market dynamics. As you continue exploring this chapter and the ones to follow, you'll delve deeper into the strategies, risk considerations, and opportunities that characterize these sophisticated investment avenues.

Chapter 11: Risk Management and Due Diligence
Navigating uncertainty: Strategies for managing risk and conducting due diligence

In the world of alternative investments, where opportunities often come with complexities, risk management and due diligence play a pivotal role. Effective risk assessment and thorough due diligence are critical to making informed investment decisions and safeguarding capital.

Understanding Risk in Alternative Investments

Alternative investments offer potential rewards but also come with inherent risks. These risks can vary widely based on the asset class, market conditions, and macroeconomic factors. From market risk and liquidity risk to regulatory and operational risks, investors must evaluate a spectrum of potential vulnerabilities.

Diversification and Portfolio Allocation

Diversification is a cornerstone of risk management. Allocating investments across different asset classes can help mitigate the impact of poor performance in any single category. By spreading risk, investors aim to achieve a balanced portfolio that can withstand market fluctuations.

Risk-Return Trade-off

The risk-return trade-off is a fundamental principle in investing. Generally, higher returns come with higher risks. Investors must assess their risk tolerance and align their investment choices with their financial goals and comfort level with potential volatility.

Due Diligence: Uncovering the Facts

Due diligence involves thorough research and analysis before making an investment. It encompasses examining financials, assessing management teams, understanding market dynamics, and evaluating legal and regulatory aspects. Proper due diligence helps investors make informed decisions and identify potential pitfalls.

Assessing Investment Strategies

Understanding the strategies employed by alternative investment vehicles is essential. For instance, when investing in hedge funds, analyzing trading methodologies, risk management approaches, and historical performance can provide insights into how the fund may fare in different market conditions.

Evaluating Managers and Teams

In the realm of private equity and hedge funds, the expertise and track record of fund managers play a significant role. Examining their past performance, investment philosophy, and alignment with investor interests is crucial for predicting future success.

Market and Economic Analysis

Alternative investments are influenced by economic trends, geopolitical events, and regulatory changes. Conducting a comprehensive analysis of macroeconomic factors that could impact the asset class is an integral part of due diligence.

Legal and Regulatory Considerations

Understanding the legal and regulatory environment is paramount. Depending on the asset class and jurisdiction, there could be compliance requirements, tax implications, and regulatory risks that need to be carefully considered.

Conclusion

Risk management and due diligence are the cornerstones of successful alternative investment strategies. By effectively assessing and mitigating risks and conducting comprehensive due diligence, investors can position themselves to navigate the complexities of the alternative investment landscape. As you delve further into the subsequent chapters, you'll gain insights into specific risk management strategies and due diligence processes that can guide your investment decisions.

Chapter 12: Tax Considerations in Alternative Investments

Balancing returns and obligations: Navigating tax complexities in alternative investments

Investing in alternative assets brings not only potential returns but also a web of tax considerations. These investments often come with unique tax implications that require careful planning to optimize returns and manage obligations.

Understanding Tax Efficiency

Tax efficiency involves structuring investments and transactions in a way that minimizes tax liabilities while maximizing after-tax returns. For alternative investments, where tax rules can be intricate, seeking tax-efficient strategies is crucial to preserving investment gains.

Types of Taxes

Various taxes can impact alternative investments, including income tax, capital gains tax, and estate tax. The specific tax treatment depends on factors such as the asset class, holding period, and jurisdiction.

Pass-Through Entities

Many alternative investments, such as partnerships and limited liability companies (LLCs), are structured as pass-through entities. This means that income and losses flow through to the investors' individual tax returns. Understanding how pass-through taxation works is key to accurately estimating tax obligations.

Capital Gains and Holding Periods

Capital gains tax applies to profits earned from the sale of assets. Holding periods can impact tax rates, with short-term gains often taxed at higher rates than long-term gains. Investors should be aware of how the length of ownership affects tax liabilities.

Depreciation and Amortization

Certain alternative investments, like real estate, allow for depreciation and amortization deductions. These deductions can reduce taxable income and potentially provide significant tax benefits to investors.

Tax-Efficient Exit Strategies

Exit strategies in alternative investments can have significant tax implications. Whether selling a property, liquidating a fund, or transferring ownership, understanding the tax consequences of different exit paths is essential for making informed decisions.

International Tax Considerations

For investors with international exposure, cross-border investments come with additional tax complexities. Double taxation treaties, withholding taxes, and reporting obligations can impact the overall tax burden.

Tax-Efficient Structures

Investors often employ tax-efficient structures, such as self-directed retirement accounts or tax-deferred exchanges, to optimize their alternative investment strategies. These structures can offer advantages in terms of deferring taxes or achieving tax-free growth.

Seeking Professional Advice

Navigating the tax landscape of alternative investments requires expertise. Consulting with tax professionals who specialize in the specific asset class and jurisdiction can provide valuable insights and help investors make tax-smart decisions.

Conclusion

Tax considerations are a critical aspect of the alternative investment journey. By understanding the tax implications of different asset classes, investment structures, and exit strategies, investors can proactively manage their tax obligations and enhance their after-tax returns. As you continue your exploration of alternative investments in the upcoming chapters, you'll gain deeper insights into the strategies and considerations for achieving tax efficiency in your investment portfolio.

Chapter 13: Managing Liquidity and Exit Strategies

Unlocking value: Navigating liquidity challenges and exit strategies in alternative investments

One of the distinctive aspects of alternative investments is their varying degrees of liquidity. Managing liquidity effectively and planning exit strategies are crucial for optimizing returns and aligning investments with financial goals.

Understanding Liquidity Spectrum

Liquidity refers to how easily an asset can be converted into cash without significantly affecting its market price. Traditional assets like stocks and bonds are generally highly liquid, while alternative investments can span a wide liquidity spectrum – from relatively liquid real estate investment trusts (REITs) to less liquid private equity holdings.

Factors Influencing Liquidity

Several factors impact the liquidity of alternative investments. Asset class, market conditions, investor demand, and the complexity of the investment structure all play roles in determining how quickly an investment can be monetized.

Liquidity Risk

Liquidity risk is the potential for an investor to be unable to quickly sell an investment at the desired price. This risk is particularly relevant in investments with longer holding periods or less active secondary markets.

Balancing Liquidity and Return Objectives

Investors must strike a balance between liquidity and return objectives. While more liquid investments can provide faster access to cash, less liquid investments often offer the potential for higher returns. Aligning liquidity needs with investment goals is key to making informed choices.

Exit Strategies for Private Investments

Exit strategies are critical in private investments like private equity and venture capital. Investors seek to monetize their investments through strategies like initial public offerings (IPOs), mergers and acquisitions (M&A), or secondary market transactions.

Holding Periods and Illiquidity Discounts

Alternative investments with longer holding periods may require a trade-off between illiquidity and potentially higher returns. Illiquidity discounts are reductions in the value of an investment due to its limited marketability.

Secondary Markets and Liquidity Solutions

For investors seeking liquidity before an investment's natural exit, secondary markets provide a way to sell or buy stakes in private investments. These markets offer opportunities to access cash without waiting for the completion of the investment's lifecycle.

Real Estate Exit Strategies

Real estate investments come with diverse exit strategies, including selling the property, refinancing, or converting to a different use. Investors must consider market conditions, rental income, and property appreciation when planning their exit.

Conclusion

Managing liquidity and planning exit strategies are integral aspects of alternative investments. By assessing the liquidity needs, understanding the factors affecting liquidity, and aligning exit strategies with investment objectives, investors can unlock the value of their alternative investment portfolios. As you delve into the subsequent chapters, you'll gain insights into specific exit strategies for different asset classes and the nuances of managing liquidity effectively in alternative investments.

Chapter 14: Evaluating Performance and Benchmarking

Measuring success: Evaluating performance and benchmarking in alternative investments

Assessing the success of alternative investments requires specialized tools and benchmarks due to the unique characteristics of these asset classes. Evaluating performance accurately and benchmarking against relevant standards are essential for making informed investment decisions.

Challenges in Performance Evaluation

Alternative investments pose challenges in performance evaluation due to their illiquidity, complexity, and varying risk profiles. Traditional metrics like market indices and total returns might not capture the full picture of an alternative investment's performance.

Risk-Adjusted Returns

Risk-adjusted returns consider the level of risk taken to achieve a certain level of return. Metrics like the Sharpe ratio and the Sortino ratio account for volatility and downside risk, providing a more accurate measure of investment success.

Comparing Apples to Apples

Benchmarks are crucial for evaluating alternative investments in context. These benchmarks should be relevant to the specific asset class and investment strategy, allowing for accurate comparisons and performance assessment.

Private Equity Benchmarks

Benchmarking private equity investments involves comparing them against relevant industry benchmarks like the Cambridge Associates Private Equity Index. These benchmarks provide insight into the performance of private equity investments compared to public market equivalents.

Real Estate Benchmarks

Real estate benchmarks help evaluate the performance of property investments. These benchmarks might include indices that track property values, rental income, and total returns within specific geographic regions and property types.

Benchmarking Hedge Funds

Benchmarking hedge funds can be challenging due to the diverse strategies they employ. Custom benchmarks, peer groups, or indices that track specific hedge fund strategies can provide a more accurate measure of performance.

Evolving Benchmarking Standards

The alternative investment landscape is constantly evolving, leading to the development of new benchmarking standards. Institutional investors and industry associations often collaborate to establish benchmarks that reflect the changing dynamics of the market.

Due Diligence and Benchmark Selection

Selecting appropriate benchmarks requires due diligence and understanding the investment's objectives and strategies. The benchmark should align with the investment's risk profile, asset class, and geographical focus.

Conclusion

Evaluating performance and benchmarking alternative investments requires a nuanced approach that takes into account the unique characteristics of these asset classes. By using relevant benchmarks, risk-adjusted metrics, and performance evaluation tools, investors can make informed decisions and accurately measure the success of their alternative investment endeavors. As you proceed to explore the final chapters, you'll delve deeper into the practical aspects of evaluating performance and benchmarking in specific alternative investment scenarios.

Chapter 15: Building a Holistic Alternative Investment Strategy
Creating a blueprint for success: Constructing a well-rounded alternative investment strategy

Crafting a successful alternative investment strategy involves weaving together various elements, from asset allocation and risk management to due diligence and portfolio construction. Building a holistic approach that aligns with your financial goals is key to navigating the complexities of alternative investments.

Defining Investment Objectives

The first step in creating an alternative investment strategy is defining clear investment objectives. Whether seeking income, capital appreciation, or diversification, understanding your goals will guide your decision-making process.

Asset Allocation and Diversification

Asset allocation involves determining how much of your portfolio should be allocated to alternative investments. Diversification across different asset classes and strategies helps manage risk and enhances the potential for consistent returns.

Assessing Risk Tolerance

Understanding your risk tolerance is crucial in alternative investments, where risk profiles can vary widely. Assessing how much volatility and illiquidity you are comfortable with will shape your investment choices.

Identifying Investment Opportunities

Identifying suitable investment opportunities involves conducting thorough due diligence. This includes researching investment options, evaluating managers, and assessing the potential risks and returns.

Building a Balanced Portfolio

A well-rounded alternative investment strategy incorporates a mix of asset classes that complement each other. Combining assets with different risk profiles and return characteristics can lead to a more balanced and resilient portfolio.

Staying Informed and Adaptive

The alternative investment landscape evolves over time. Staying informed about market trends, regulatory changes, and emerging opportunities is essential for adapting your strategy to changing conditions.

Monitoring and Adjusting

Regularly monitoring the performance of your alternative investments and assessing their alignment with your investment objectives is critical. Making adjustments based on market dynamics and changes in your financial situation can help you stay on course.

Access and Professional Guidance

Accessing alternative investments might require specialized platforms, networks, or advisors. Engaging professionals with expertise in specific asset classes or strategies can provide valuable insights and guidance.

Conclusion

Building a holistic alternative investment strategy is a dynamic process that requires careful planning, continuous monitoring, and adaptability. By aligning your investment objectives, assessing risk tolerance, and constructing a diversified portfolio, you can navigate the complexities of alternative investments and work towards achieving your financial goals. As you conclude your journey through the chapters ahead, you'll gain further insights into practical strategies, considerations, and approaches to building a successful alternative investment portfolio.

Chapter 16: Case Studies in Alternative Investments

Learning from experience: Exploring real-world case studies in alternative investments

Examining real-world case studies provides valuable insights into the practical application of alternative investment strategies. By delving into these examples, you can gain a deeper understanding of the challenges, opportunities, and outcomes that investors have encountered in their alternative investment journeys.

Case Study 1: Real Estate Investment Trust (REIT) Success

In this case study, we explore the journey of an investor who strategically allocated a portion of their portfolio to REITs. Through careful research and diversification, they achieved a steady stream of income and capital appreciation from a mix of residential, commercial, and industrial properties.

Case Study 2: Venture Capital Triumph

This case study highlights an investor who ventured into the realm of venture capital, investing in early-stage startups with high growth potential. By partnering with experienced venture capital firms, they gained exposure to innovative technology companies and realized substantial returns from successful exits.

Case Study 3: Private Equity Turnaround

In this case study, we delve into the story of an investor who participated in a private equity fund focused on distressed companies. Through active management, operational improvements, and strategic restructuring, they transformed struggling businesses into profitable enterprises, generating impressive returns.

Case Study 4: Navigating Crypto Investments

This case study follows an investor who entered the world of cryptocurrencies and non-fungible tokens (NFTs). By conducting thorough research, staying updated on market trends, and embracing a long-term perspective, they navigated the volatile crypto landscape and capitalized on opportunities.

Case Study 5: Successful Hedge Fund Strategy

This case study examines the journey of an investor who allocated a portion of their portfolio to a hedge fund employing a global macro strategy. By leveraging the fund manager's expertise in macroeconomic trends and geopolitical events, they achieved consistent returns that were uncorrelated with traditional markets.

Case Study 6: Balancing Illiquidity and Returns

In this case study, we explore an investor's decision to invest in illiquid assets like private real estate. By considering their long-term investment horizon and accepting illiquidity, they achieved significant capital appreciation and rental income, aligning their strategy with their financial goals.

Case Study 7: Navigating Tax Efficiency

This case study highlights an investor's approach to managing tax implications in alternative investments. Through careful structuring, leveraging tax-advantaged accounts, and optimizing exit strategies, they minimized tax liabilities and enhanced after-tax returns.

Conclusion

Case studies offer a window into the practical application of alternative investment strategies. By examining real-world scenarios and outcomes, you can gain valuable insights that can inform your own investment decisions. As you conclude your exploration of alternative investments, remember that each case study provides a unique perspective on the challenges and successes that investors encounter in this dynamic and diverse landscape.

Chapter 17: The Future of Alternative Investments
Anticipating change: Exploring the evolving landscape of alternative investments

As the investment landscape continues to evolve, the world of alternative investments is no exception. This chapter delves into the potential trends, innovations, and transformations that could shape the future of alternative investments.

Technological Advancements

Technology is likely to play a significant role in the future of alternative investments. Blockchain technology could further enhance transparency, security, and liquidity in illiquid assets. Artificial intelligence and data analytics may refine investment strategies and risk assessment.

Sustainable and Impact Investing

The demand for sustainable and impact investments is on the rise. Alternative investments aligned with environmental, social, and governance (ESG) criteria could become more prevalent, catering to investors seeking both financial returns and positive societal impact.

Digital Securities and Tokenization

The emergence of digital securities and tokenization could revolutionize ownership and trading of alternative assets. Non-fungible tokens (NFTs) and security tokens might provide more efficient and accessible ways to invest in real estate, art, collectibles, and more.

Innovations in Due Diligence and Risk Management

Advancements in data analytics and machine learning could reshape due diligence and risk management in alternative investments. Predictive analytics and AI-driven risk assessments might enhance decision-making processes and identify potential pitfalls.

Regulatory Developments

Regulatory changes will continue to shape the alternative investment landscape. Governments and regulatory bodies are likely to adapt to the evolving nature of these investments, influencing how they are structured, traded, and taxed.

Globalization and Access

Advancements in technology and communication could further globalize the alternative investment market. Investors may gain easier access to international opportunities, expanding their investment horizons beyond their local markets.

Evolving Asset Classes

New asset classes could emerge as alternatives to traditional investments. As industries evolve, new investment opportunities may arise in areas such as space exploration, biotechnology, and renewable energy.

Conclusion

The future of alternative investments holds a tapestry of possibilities, driven by technological advancements, changing investor preferences, and regulatory shifts. As you conclude your exploration of this guide, remember that staying informed about these trends and innovations will be crucial for navigating the ever-evolving landscape of alternative investments. By embracing a forward-thinking mindset and adapting to new opportunities, you can position yourself to thrive in this dynamic and diverse investment arena.

Chapter 18: Taking the Next Steps
Embarking on your journey: Navigating the path forward in alternative investments

As you conclude your exploration of alternative investments, this final chapter provides guidance on taking the next steps in your investment journey. Whether you're a seasoned investor or just starting out, these insights can help you make informed decisions and embark on a successful path in the world of alternative investments.

Continuing Education and Research

The landscape of alternative investments is vast and constantly evolving. Commit to ongoing education and research to stay updated on market trends, emerging opportunities, and regulatory changes that could impact your investment decisions.

Building a Network of Experts

Surrounding yourself with a network of professionals and experts can provide valuable insights and guidance. Consider engaging financial advisors, investment managers, legal experts, and mentors who specialize in alternative investments.

Assessing Risk Tolerance and Goals

Evaluate your risk tolerance and financial goals before making any investment decisions. Align your alternative investment strategy with your broader financial objectives to ensure that it complements your overall wealth-building plan.

Diversification and Portfolio Construction

Diversification remains a key principle in alternative investments. Balance your portfolio with a mix of asset classes, strategies, and risk profiles to enhance stability and potential returns.

Starting Small and Gradually

If you're new to alternative investments, consider starting with a smaller allocation and gradually increasing it as you become more comfortable and knowledgeable. This approach allows you to learn from experiences and adjust your strategy accordingly.

Seeking Professional Advice

Complexities abound in the world of alternative investments. Engaging with experienced professionals who understand the intricacies of different asset classes and strategies can provide valuable insights and mitigate potential risks.

Staying Patient and Long-Term Focused

Alternative investments often require a longer investment horizon to realize their full potential. Embrace a patient and long-term perspective, recognizing that the value of illiquid assets may take time to materialize.

Adapting to Market Dynamics

Be prepared to adapt your investment strategy as market dynamics change. The ability to pivot and adjust to new opportunities or challenges is essential for success in the ever-evolving world of alternative investments.

Conclusion

As you navigate the world of alternative investments, remember that each step you take contributes to your growth as an investor. Embrace a spirit of continuous learning, seek expert guidance, and make decisions that align with your risk tolerance and financial objectives. By doing so, you can confidently chart your path forward and unlock the potential that alternative investments offer. Your journey in this dynamic and diverse investment landscape is just beginning, and the opportunities ahead are boundless.

Conclusion

The journey through this comprehensive guide has provided you with a profound understanding of the intricate world of alternative investments. This knowledge serves as a solid foundation for your exploration of these unique and diverse avenues within the investment landscape. By delving into the nuances of various asset classes, strategies, risk considerations, and practical approaches, you have gained the tools needed to navigate the complexities of alternative investments with confidence and clarity.

As you reflect on the insights gathered from each chapter, it becomes evident that alternative investments offer a realm of possibilities beyond traditional asset classes. From real estate and private equity to hedge funds, cryptocurrencies, and more, the spectrum of opportunities is vast and dynamic. Furthermore, the case studies showcased real-world scenarios, illustrating both the potential challenges and substantial rewards that alternative investments can offer.

As you move forward on your investment journey, keep in mind the importance of strategic planning and due diligence. Diversification remains a cornerstone principle, helping to mitigate risks and enhance the potential for long-term gains. Moreover, the critical role of assessing your risk tolerance, aligning investment objectives, and staying informed cannot be understated.

The future of alternative investments is promising, driven by technological advancements, shifting investor preferences, and evolving market dynamics. Embracing a forward-thinking approach will position you to seize emerging opportunities while navigating potential obstacles effectively.

Ultimately, your success in the world of alternative investments will be a culmination of knowledge, preparation, and adaptability. Continuously educate yourself, engage with experts, and remain open to refining your strategy as you encounter new insights and developments. Your journey into this realm is marked by potential for growth, financial prosperity, and a deeper understanding of the diverse investment landscape.

With the lessons learned and insights gained from this guide, you are well-equipped to embark on a journey filled with exploration, growth, and accomplishment in the realm of alternative investments. As you navigate the opportunities that lie ahead, remember that every decision you make is a step towards realizing your financial aspirations and securing a prosperous future.

Advanced Tools and Analytics in Social Trading

Diversification in Social Trading

Introduction
A Prelude to the Modern Trading Landscape: The Emergence of Social Trading Platforms.

In the vast realm of financial markets, trading has consistently been at the confluence of technology, strategy, and human psychology. Traditionally, individual traders and financial institutions relied on a combination of fundamental and technical analysis to make informed decisions. However, with the proliferation of the internet and rapid advancements in technology, a novel paradigm has emerged, drastically altering the landscape of trading: Social Trading.

Origins of Trading and the Evolution of Financial Markets

Historically, trading was a privilege accorded to those with direct access to financial markets, typically in centralized physical locations such as the stock exchange floors in major cities. Access was, for the most part, limited to professional traders, brokerage firms, and wealthy individuals. The vast majority of the general populace was distant, both physically and cognitively, from these nerve centers of financial activity.

But as time progressed and technology evolved, this landscape began to change. The late 20th century saw the dawn of electronic trading, which democratized market access and led to a surge in retail participation. Suddenly, trading wasn't just the purview of those in power suits on Wall Street; it was increasingly becoming a global activity, engaged in by enthusiasts from all walks of life.

The Digital Disruption: Birth of Social Trading

With the turn of the millennium, further technological disruptions, especially the rise of the internet and social media, brought forth the next phase in the evolution of trading: the conceptualization and realization of social trading. In essence, social trading merged the world of financial trading with the principles of social networking. Just as platforms like Facebook or LinkedIn allowed people to connect, share, and follow each other, social trading platforms provided a medium for traders to display their strategies, share their insights, and allow others to follow or replicate their trades.

This was revolutionary in several ways. First, it lowered the barriers to entry even further. Novices with little to no experience in trading could now leverage the expertise of seasoned professionals. By simply choosing to follow a particular trader, newcomers could replicate the trading strategies of experts in real-time, without needing to spend years acquiring the knowledge and experience themselves.

Second, it added a layer of transparency to the world of trading. Unlike traditional fund managers who might keep their strategies cloistered, social trading platforms necessitated openness. Traders, especially those who wanted a following, had to be transparent about their wins, losses, strategies, and thought processes.

The Psychological Paradigm and Group Dynamics

However, with these advantages came nuances in human psychology. Traditional trading required individual decision-making, often isolated and based on one's research and intuition. In contrast, social trading introduced group dynamics into the mix. Decisions could now be influenced by popular sentiment, the actions of a well-followed trader, or the collective behavior of a group. This dynamic introduced both opportunities and challenges. While there was the benefit of collective wisdom, there was also the risk of herd mentality, where traders might blindly follow a popular figure without adequate understanding or analysis, leading to potential market bubbles or irrational behaviors.

Conclusion

The introduction of social trading platforms heralded a new era in the world of finance. As with any revolutionary concept, it came with its set of advantages and challenges. On one hand, it democratized access to trading expertise, enabling novices to benefit from the experience of seasoned traders. On the other hand, it introduced complexities in market dynamics, influenced by collective behaviors and psychological factors. As we delve deeper into this book, we will explore the mechanics of social trading, its key players, strategies for success, and the potential pitfalls to be wary of. The world of social trading, as we will discover, is as much about understanding human behavior as it is about understanding market trends.

Chapter 1: Social Trading Defined

Unraveling the Basics: What Social Trading Means in Today's Digital Era.

Introduction to the Concept

In an age where information flows at the speed of light and digital interactions form the crux of many activities, the financial market has not remained untouched by the digital revolution. The advent of social trading epitomizes this transformation. At its core, social trading combines elements of traditional trading with modern-day social networking. It provides a platform where traders can share their strategies, insights, successes, and failures in a communal setting. But what precisely does this entail?

Defining Social Trading

Social trading can be succinctly defined as a type of financial trading that uses social networks to gather information, strategies, and trade suggestions from other traders in real-time. It essentially bridges the knowledge gap between novice and experienced traders. By leveraging these platforms, inexperienced traders can replicate the actions of their more seasoned counterparts, thereby benefiting from the latter's expertise without undergoing the steep learning curve.

This doesn't mean that it's merely a follow-the-leader approach. Most advanced social trading platforms come equipped with various tools, analytics, and filters that allow users to discern which traders align with their investment goals and risk tolerance.

Components of Social Trading

Several key components underpin social trading:

1. **Trader Profiles**: Just as one would have a profile on a social media platform, traders have profiles on social trading platforms. These profiles typically detail their trading performance, strategies employed, risk metrics, and more.

2. **News Feed**: This feature shares similarities with mainstream social media platforms. Here, traders can post updates, share insights, or discuss market trends. These feeds become a hub for real-time market analysis and discussion.

3. **Follow and Copy**: Perhaps the most distinctive feature of social trading is the ability for users to "follow" other traders. Once followed, users can opt to manually implement the trader's strategies or automatically copy their trades.

4. **Dashboard and Analytics**: Comprehensive insights are provided about followed traders, helping users understand the performance metrics, potential risks, and profitability of each trader they follow.

The Democratization of Trading Knowledge

Before the age of the internet, acquiring trading knowledge was a cumbersome process. It required dedicated efforts, resources, and often, a significant financial outlay. However, social trading has democratized this access to knowledge. Today, someone in a remote part of the world, with limited financial means but an internet connection, can learn from a trader in a global financial hub. This global sharing and accessibility of knowledge have leveled the playing field, to some extent, between the 'haves' and the 'have-nots' in the trading world.

Conclusion

Understanding the basic tenets of social trading is fundamental before delving deeper into its intricacies. As with any tool or platform, it's not just about what it offers, but also about how one uses it. While social trading brings the wisdom of crowds to an individual's fingertips, it's imperative to approach it with an analytical mind and not be swayed by mere herd mentality. In subsequent chapters, we will dissect the mechanics of how these platforms operate, their benefits, pitfalls, and the strategies that can optimize their potential.

Chapter 2: Historical Context of Social Trading
From Traditional Markets to Digital Engagement: The Evolutionary Path.

The Genesis of Trading

The history of trading stretches back millennia, with ancient civilizations engaging in barter systems and later transitioning to coinage and other standardized currency forms. As societies evolved, so did the complexity of their financial systems. This led to the establishment of more organized marketplaces where goods, services, and eventually financial instruments were traded.

Traditional Markets and Their Limitations

By the 19th and 20th centuries, major cities worldwide boasted centralized trading floors – a physical space where traders would gather to buy and sell securities. These stock exchanges, as they came to be known, represented the pinnacle of financial activity. However, they came with inherent limitations:

1. **Geographical Restrictions**: Participation was largely confined to those who could physically access these trading floors or had connections to brokers on the floor.

2. **Information Asymmetry**: Due to technological constraints, real-time market data and analytics were reserved for a privileged few, leading to significant informational advantages.

3. **Entry Barriers**: Significant capital requirements and a lack of knowledge-sharing mechanisms made it challenging for novices to break into the trading arena.

Emergence of Electronic Trading

The latter half of the 20th century heralded significant change. The combination of advanced telecommunication infrastructures and computing capabilities facilitated the transition from physical trading floors to electronic platforms. This digital shift brought about profound changes:

1. **Global Accessibility**: Traders from around the world could now access major markets without physical presence.

2. **Democratization of Information**: Real-time data, previously the domain of a select few, became widely available, leveling the informational playing field.

3. **Increased Trading Volume**: With easier access came an influx of new participants, leading to a surge in daily trading volumes.

The Inception of Social Trading

While electronic trading was revolutionary, it was the rise of Web 2.0 in the early 21st century that set the stage for social trading. As the internet transitioned from a static informational medium to a dynamic, user-generated content platform, the financial world took note.

Early social trading platforms emerged as forums where traders would discuss strategies, share insights, and provide trade suggestions. However, it was the integration of brokerage services into these platforms that truly marked the birth of modern social trading. This allowed users to not just discuss trades but to automatically replicate the trades of others in real-time.

The Modern Landscape of Social Trading

Today, social trading platforms are multifaceted entities. They combine the features of traditional brokerages with social networking tools, comprehensive analytics, and user-generated content. The collaborative nature of these platforms fosters a sense of community, where knowledge is openly shared and the wisdom of the crowd can be harnessed.

Conclusion

The trajectory of social trading mirrors the broader evolution of the financial world. From the hustle and bustle of trading floors to the silent hum of server racks powering digital platforms, the way we trade has transformed dramatically. Social trading is the latest chapter in this storied history, representing the intersection of finance, technology, and community. As we move forward, understanding this historical context will be crucial in anticipating future trends and ensuring the sustainable growth of the social trading ecosystem.

Chapter 3: The Psychological Aspects of Social Trading

Group Dynamics and Herd Mentality: Navigating the Emotional Landscape.

The Human Element in Trading

The essence of trading, despite its quantitative veneer, is deeply rooted in human psychology. Emotions such as fear, greed, hope, and regret often exert powerful influences on trading decisions, sometimes superseding logic and objective analysis. This emotional aspect becomes even more intricate and intensified within the realm of social trading, given its communal nature.

The Psychology of Following

In social trading, the act of following another trader's actions represents a psychological phenomenon. It is driven by:

1. **Trust**: The belief that the followed trader possesses superior knowledge or skill.
2. **Convenience**: The comfort of relinquishing decision-making responsibility, especially for novice traders.
3. **Validation**: Seeing others follow the same trader or strategy can instill a sense of validation and reassurance.

Herd Mentality in Financial Decisions

Herd mentality, also known as herd behavior, is a psychological phenomenon where individuals follow the majority's actions or beliefs. It is not exclusive to financial markets but can be particularly pronounced due to the high stakes and uncertainty inherent in trading. When applied to social trading:

1. **Positive Feedback Loops**: When a significant number of users follow and replicate a particular trader's actions, it can lead to amplifying effects. For example, if a well-followed trader buys a particular stock, and thousands replicate this trade, it can drive the stock's price up.

2. **Exacerbation of Bubbles and Crashes**: Herd behavior can contribute to market bubbles when many traders rush to buy a rising asset, and likewise, lead to steeper crashes when they collectively rush to sell.
3. **Dilution of Individual Responsibility**: When following the crowd, there can be a perceived dilution of personal responsibility. If a trade goes wrong, the blame can be externally attributed to the trader being followed, rather than introspectively analyzing one's decision to follow.

Contrarian Approaches and the Value of Dissent

Within the dynamics of group behavior, there exists a subset of traders who adopt a contrarian approach. These individuals intentionally go against the prevailing sentiment or the actions of the majority. Their strategies underscore the value of dissent in an ecosystem where herd mentality can dominate. Contrarians serve as a reminder that popular opinion isn't always right and that there can be value in independent thought.

Managing Emotional Dynamics

For those navigating social trading platforms, understanding and managing these psychological aspects is crucial:

1. **Self-awareness**: Recognize and check one's biases and emotional drivers. Understand why you choose to follow a particular trader or strategy.
2. **Diversification**: Just as one diversifies financial portfolios, diversifying sources of information and traders to follow can mitigate the risks of herd behavior.
3. **Continuous Learning**: While the convenience of following experienced traders is tempting, continuous self-education remains invaluable. This equips individuals to better assess the quality of traders they follow and make more informed decisions.

Conclusion

The foray into social trading is not just a journey through financial markets, but also a deep dive into the intricacies of human psychology. Emotions, biases, and group dynamics play pivotal roles in shaping trading outcomes. To thrive in this environment, one must strike a delicate balance: harnessing the collective wisdom offered by social trading platforms, while also maintaining a level of critical thinking and emotional detachment. The subsequent chapters will delve into the practical aspects of doing just that.

Chapter 4: Choosing the Right Social Trading Platform
Navigating the Digital Landscape: Key Considerations in Platform Selection.

Introduction: The Plenitude of Choices

In the expansive realm of social trading, numerous platforms have emerged, each boasting unique features, tools, and community dynamics. For traders, both novice and experienced, selecting the appropriate platform can be both an opportunity and a challenge. This chapter aims to elucidate the key criteria to consider in making an informed choice.

Platform Reputation and Credibility

At the forefront of selection criteria should be the platform's reputation:

1. **Operational History**: While newer platforms might offer innovative features, platforms with a longer operational history often have proven track records and have withstood market stresses.

2. **User Testimonials and Reviews**: Hearing from current and former users provides invaluable insights into the platform's reliability, user experience, and potential pitfalls.
3. **Regulatory Compliance**: Ensure the platform adheres to the requisite financial regulations in your jurisdiction. Compliance not only speaks to the platform's legitimacy but also to the safety of your investment.

Range of Offered Instruments

Different platforms might cater to different segments of the financial market. Consider:

1. **Asset Types**: Does the platform allow trading in equities, commodities, cryptocurrencies, forex, or other derivatives? Your investment preferences should align with the platform's offerings.
2. **Global Access**: Some platforms might grant access to global markets, while others might be restricted to specific regional exchanges.

Technological Infrastructure and User Interface

The backbone of any social trading platform is its technological prowess:

1. **Platform Stability**: Regular downtimes, glitches, or technical issues can be detrimental to trading experiences and outcomes.
2. **User Experience (UX)**: An intuitive and user-friendly interface is crucial, especially for traders who might not be tech-savvy.
3. **Mobile Access**: In today's age, having a robust mobile application or mobile-responsive platform is non-negotiable for those who wish to trade on-the-go.

Tools and Analytics

The strength of a social trading platform often lies in the quality of its tools:

1. **Analysis Tools**: From charting tools to predictive analytics, the platform should offer a suite of instruments to aid decision-making.
2. **Social Interaction Features**: Features like chat rooms, forums, and direct messaging can enhance the communal experience.
3. **Transparency in Trader Metrics**: Platforms should provide comprehensive data on the traders you can follow, encompassing their performance history, risk metrics, and trading style.

Cost Structures and Fees

While often overlooked, understanding a platform's fee structure can have long-term implications on net returns:

1. **Trade Commissions**: Are fees charged per trade? If so, how do they compare with industry standards?
2. **Subscription or Platform Fees**: Some platforms might charge monthly or annual fees for premium features.
3. **Hidden Costs**: Be wary of any undisclosed fees. Transparency in cost structures speaks volumes about a platform's integrity.

Conclusion

Choosing a social trading platform is a decision that sets the stage for one's trading journey. Given the myriad of options available, a methodical approach, grounded in research and introspection, is imperative. With the right platform, traders can seamlessly meld the advantages of digital technology, community wisdom, and personal trading goals. Future chapters will delve deeper into optimizing the use of chosen platforms and strategies to enhance trading outcomes.

Chapter 5: Identifying and Evaluating Top Traders to Follow

Harnessing Collective Wisdom: A Guide to Distilling Expertise.

Introduction: The Significance of Selection

One of the foundational pillars of social trading is the ability to follow and replicate the trades of others. However, with thousands of traders vying for attention on platforms, how does one discern true expertise from mere noise? This chapter provides a framework to identify and critically assess traders worth following.

Performance Metrics: Beyond the Obvious

While a trader's past performance is not a guarantee of future returns, it remains a crucial evaluation metric:

1. **Consistency Over Time**: Rather than mere short-term gains, look for traders who have consistently performed well over extended periods.
2. **Risk-Adjusted Returns**: High returns might come with high risks. Platforms often provide risk metrics that give insights into a trader's risk profile. A high Sharpe ratio, for instance, indicates better risk-adjusted performance.
3. **Drawdowns**: Consider the maximum drawdowns (peak-to-trough declines) the trader has experienced. Frequent or deep drawdowns can indicate high-risk strategies.

Trading Style and Strategy

Understanding a trader's approach can help ascertain if they align with your financial goals and risk appetite:

1. **Investment Horizon**: Does the trader engage in long-term, positional trades or short-term, intraday trades?
2. **Asset Preference**: Does the trader specialize in equities, forex, commodities, or other financial instruments? Ensure this aligns with your investment interests.
3. **Strategy Clarity**: Top traders often articulate their trading strategies, be it technical analysis, fundamental analysis, news-based trading, or a combination.

Volume and Frequency of Trades

The trading frequency can impact potential returns and costs:

1. **High-Frequency Traders**: Traders who trade frequently might generate more signals for you to follow. However, consider the associated transaction costs.
2. **Low-Frequency Traders**: Those who trade less often might be following a more long-term strategy, potentially leading to fewer transaction fees but also requiring patience.

Community Interaction and Feedback

Engagement with the community is a testament to a trader's commitment:

1. **Response to Queries**: Top traders often engage with their followers, answering questions and providing insights into their decisions.
2. **Peer Reviews**: Look at reviews and feedback from other users. Positive testimonials can reinforce credibility, while negative reviews can offer critical insights.
3. **Follower Count and Retention**: While a high follower count can indicate popularity, also consider the retention rate. If many users are frequently unfollowing a trader, it might be a red flag.

Transparency and Honesty

Integrity remains paramount in the world of trading:

1. **Disclosure of Losses**: Every trader incurs losses. Assess if traders openly discuss and analyze their setbacks, as it indicates transparency.
2. **Avoiding Overpromising**: Be wary of traders who guarantee specific returns or present their strategies as foolproof. Trading inherently involves risks.

Conclusion

The art of selecting traders to follow is a nuanced process that goes beyond mere performance metrics. It's an amalgamation of analytical assessment, alignment of investment philosophies, and gut instinct. As followers embark on their social trading journey, continuous evaluation and, if necessary, realignment of chosen traders is crucial. Future chapters will delve into effective strategies to diversify following, ensuring risk is spread across multiple trading philosophies and styles.

Chapter 6: Diversification in Social Trading

Strategically Spreading Risk: Leveraging Multiple Expertise.

Introduction: The Core Principle of Investment

Diversification, often termed as "not putting all your eggs in one basket," is a cardinal rule in the investment world. The premise is simple: by spreading investments across various assets or strategies, the risk of a significant loss is diminished. Social trading, with its unique nature, offers opportunities to diversify not just across assets, but also across strategies, styles, and traders.

Diversifying Across Traders

The foundation of diversification in social trading is to follow multiple traders. This has several advantages:

1. **Risk Spread**: Just as with assets, no trader is infallible. By following multiple traders, the impact of any single trader's poor performance is mitigated.
2. **Multiple Strategies**: Different traders bring varied strategies to the table, from technical analysis to fundamental research. Following multiple traders allows followers to benefit from diverse market approaches.
3. **Regional Diversification**: If traders specialize in different geographical markets, followers can gain exposure to various economies, further spreading risk.

Balancing Portfolio by Asset Classes

Traders often have preferences for specific asset classes, such as equities, commodities, or cryptocurrencies:

1. **Asset Performance Variability**: Different assets perform differently under varied market conditions. For instance, during economic downturns, certain commodities might perform better than equities.
2. **Liquidity Considerations**: Assets like blue-chip stocks or major forex pairs tend to be more liquid than certain niche commodities or altcoins. Following traders dealing in a mix of assets can ensure portfolio liquidity.

Adjusting Leverage and Exposure

While social trading platforms allow followers to replicate traders' moves proportionally, they often also provide flexibility to adjust leverage:

1. **Personal Risk Tolerance**: Followers can choose to allocate more or less capital to specific traders based on their risk tolerance and trust in the trader's strategy.
2. **Active Portfolio Rebalancing**: Continuously monitor and adjust exposure to traders based on performance metrics and changing market conditions.

Periodic Review and Realignment

Diversification is not a one-time activity:

1. **Performance Analysis**: Periodically review the performance of followed traders. Replace underperforming traders or reduce exposure to them.
2. **Market Evolution**: As markets evolve, new asset classes or trading strategies might emerge. Stay updated and consider diversifying into these new areas.
3. **Feedback Loop**: Engage with traders and the community to get insights into changing market dynamics or emerging strategies.

Conclusion

Diversification in social trading is a multi-faceted approach that goes beyond traditional asset diversification. By leveraging the collective wisdom of multiple traders, followers can effectively spread risk and potentially enhance returns. However, this approach requires active involvement, continuous learning, and periodic realignment. In the upcoming chapters, we will explore the nuances of managing and optimizing a diversified social trading portfolio for long-term success.

Chapter 7: The Ethical Dimensions of Social Trading

Responsibility, Transparency, and Integrity in a Connected Trading Ecosystem.

Introduction: The Intersection of Technology and Ethics

As with any technology-driven paradigm shift, social trading is not devoid of ethical considerations. While it offers immense advantages in democratizing access to trading expertise, it also presents unique challenges related to trust, responsibility, and the ethical use of shared information.

Responsibility of Signal Providers

Traders, often referred to as signal providers in the social trading realm, hold significant influence. With this power comes considerable responsibility:

1. **Honesty in Reporting**: Traders should provide a truthful account of their performance, including losses and not just the wins.

2. **Transparency in Strategy**: While proprietary strategies might be a trader's unique selling point, a degree of transparency in their approach helps followers understand the risks involved.
3. **Avoidance of Overpromising**: Ethical traders steer clear of guarantees in a realm as uncertain as financial markets.

Ethical Considerations for Followers

While much is discussed about the responsibilities of traders, followers too, have their ethical considerations:

1. **Due Diligence**: Blindly following any trader, especially based on hyped claims, is detrimental not just for the individual but also for the ecosystem's credibility.
2. **Constructive Feedback**: When engaging on platforms, providing constructive feedback, rather than baseless criticism, contributes to a positive community.
3. **Understanding of Leverage**: Misusing leverage, especially when replicating trades, can lead to significant losses. Ethical investing involves understanding and responsibly using the tools at one's disposal.

Platform's Role in Upholding Ethics

Social trading platforms, as facilitators, have a pivotal role in ensuring an ethical trading environment:

1. **Vetted Signal Providers**: Platforms should have rigorous processes to vet traders before allowing them to provide signals to the community.
2. **Transparent Fee Structures**: All costs, from platform fees to transaction charges, should be transparently communicated to users.
3. **Robust Grievance Redressal**: An effective system to address user grievances and concerns enhances trust in the platform's ethical stance.
4. **Educational Resources**: Platforms should invest in educating users about risks, strategies, and ethical trading practices.

Potential Pitfalls and Malpractices

As with any financial ecosystem, social trading isn't immune to malpractices:

1. **Churning**: Unethical traders might frequently trade to generate commissions rather than genuine market strategies.
2. **Fake Reviews and Testimonials**: Be wary of platforms or traders with only positive reviews, as they might be fabricated.
3. **Conflict of Interest**: Traders might have affiliations with certain assets or companies. Transparent disclosure of such affiliations is crucial.

Conclusion

The ethical dimensions of social trading extend beyond mere trading strategies. They encompass the entire ecosystem, from traders and followers to the facilitating platforms. In an environment that heavily relies on trust and communal engagement, upholding ethics isn't just a moral imperative but a crucial factor for sustainable success. As we delve deeper in the subsequent chapters, the importance of trust, credibility, and ethics will be recurrent themes, underlying the very fabric of social trading.

Chapter 8: Risk Management in Social Trading

Strategic Approaches to Safeguarding Capital in a Collaborative Environment.

Introduction: The Inevitability of Risk

No investment endeavor is devoid of risks. While social trading offers the allure of tapping into the expertise of seasoned traders, it's imperative to understand that it does not negate the inherent risks of trading. This chapter sheds light on how followers can strategically manage and mitigate risks in a social trading environment.

Understanding the Nature of Risk

Before diving into risk management strategies, one must understand the various types of risks associated with social trading:

1. **Market Risk**: The inherent risk associated with fluctuations in the financial markets.
2. **Strategy Risk**: Risks arising from the trading strategies adopted by the traders you follow.
3. **Operational Risk**: Risks related to the trading platform's stability, technical glitches, or execution delays.
4. **Leverage Risk**: The amplification of potential losses when leveraging investments.

Setting Capital Allocation Limits

One of the foremost steps in risk management is determining how much capital to allocate:

1. **Fixed Capital Allocation**: Dedicate a fixed amount of capital to follow each trader, irrespective of their past performance or strategy.
2. **Performance-Based Allocation**: Allocate capital based on a trader's past performance, with better-performing traders getting a larger capital share.
3. **Strategy-Based Allocation**: Distribute capital based on the perceived risk of a trader's strategy. For instance, allocate less to high-frequency traders or those using high leverage.

Utilizing Stop-Loss Mechanisms

Most social trading platforms offer automated tools that can be invaluable in risk management:

1. **Individual Trade Stop-Loss**: Set a threshold for each trade, and if losses exceed this threshold, the trade is automatically closed.
2. **Trader-Based Stop-Loss**: Set a cumulative loss threshold for each trader you follow. If a trader's actions lead to losses exceeding this limit, you stop following their trades.
3. **Portfolio-Wide Stop-Loss**: Set a maximum loss limit for your entire portfolio. If aggregate losses from all followed traders exceed this amount, all trades are closed.

Periodic Review and Re-evaluation

Risk management is a dynamic process, necessitating regular re-evaluation:

1. **Performance Audit**: Regularly assess the performance of the traders you follow. Replace or reduce allocation to consistently underperforming traders.
2. **Strategy Shifts**: Be aware if traders deviate significantly from their stated or typical strategies, as this might introduce new risks.

3. **Market Landscape Evaluation**: Adjust your risk parameters based on broader market conditions. For example, during highly volatile periods, consider reducing leverage or tightening stop-loss thresholds.

Education and Continuous Learning

An informed follower is better equipped to manage risks:

1. **Platform Tutorials**: Ensure you understand all the risk management tools offered by the platform.
2. **Engage with the Community**: Discuss strategies, share experiences, and learn from the collective wisdom of the community.
3. **Stay Updated**: Regularly update yourself on market news, emerging risks, and global economic indicators.

Conclusion

Risk management, while crucial in all forms of trading, takes on a nuanced dimension in social trading due to the interplay of multiple traders and strategies. An effective risk management approach combines strategic capital allocation, use of automated tools, continuous learning, and periodic re-evaluation. As we progress into subsequent chapters, we'll delve deeper into advanced strategies that can be combined with these foundational risk management principles for optimized outcomes.

Chapter 9: The Psychological Dynamics of Social Trading

Understanding Human Behavior, Emotional Triggers, and Collective Decisions.

Introduction: The Mind and the Market

While trading might seem predominantly about numbers, charts, and algorithms, the human psyche plays an indomitable role. Emotions, biases, and herd mentality can often overshadow objective decision-making. When magnified in a social trading environment, these psychological elements become even more paramount.

The Double-Edged Sword of Collective Wisdom

Pooling together the expertise of multiple traders can be beneficial, but it also introduces new psychological dynamics:

1. **Reinforcement Bias**: Seeing many traders adopt a particular strategy can reinforce one's belief in that strategy, sometimes ignoring contrary indicators.
2. **Fear of Missing Out (FOMO)**: Watching others profit from a trade can trigger a fear of missing out, leading followers to hastily jump on the bandwagon.
3. **Overconfidence Effect**: Over-relying on top traders might lead to overconfidence, making followers underestimate risks.

Emotional Resilience in Volatile Times

Markets can be unpredictable, and watching real-time fluctuations in a social trading platform can be emotionally taxing:

1. **Panic Selling**: Observing multiple traders exit a position can trigger panic, prompting followers to sell prematurely.

2. **Greed-Driven Decisions**: On the flip side, seeing a wave of traders enter a seemingly profitable trade might lead to greed-driven buying without proper analysis.
3. **Handling Losses**: Emotionally coping with losses, especially when they result from following reputed traders, can be challenging. Maintaining perspective and not making impulsive decisions is crucial.

Overcoming Cognitive Biases

Awareness of inherent cognitive biases can lead to more informed decisions:

1. **Confirmation Bias**: The tendency to seek out and give more weight to information that confirms one's pre-existing beliefs.
2. **Recency Bias**: Overemphasizing recent events or trends while making decisions, sidelining historical data.
3. **Anchoring**: Relying heavily on the first piece of information encountered (the "anchor") when making decisions.

Strategies for Sound Psychological Health

Emotionally navigating the world of social trading requires specific strategies:

1. **Set Clear Goals**: Define what you seek from social trading – whether it's learning, capital growth, or diversifying strategies.
2. **Limit Exposure**: Do not incessantly monitor trades or the platform. Set specific times for review to avoid emotional exhaustion.
3. **Seek Community Support**: Engage with the community, sharing experiences and feelings, and seeking advice when faced with emotional dilemmas.
4. **Educate and Empower**: Continual learning about markets, strategies, and psychological dynamics can instill confidence.

Conclusion

The intertwining of psychology and trading is profound, and in a community-driven environment like social trading, it's amplified. Being cognizant of the emotional rollercoasters, understanding inherent biases, and adopting strategies to maintain psychological balance are integral. As we move ahead, we'll explore how these psychological aspects impact long-term strategies and how followers can optimize their journey by combining emotional intelligence with trading acumen.

Chapter 10: Advanced Tools and Analytics in Social Trading

Harnessing Technology for Informed Decisions and Enhanced Outcomes.

Introduction: The Technological Revolution in Trading

Modern trading is deeply intertwined with technological advancements. From algorithm-driven trading to real-time analytics, technology has revolutionized how traders and investors approach the market. In the realm of social trading, these advancements provide followers with powerful tools to make informed decisions.

Real-Time Performance Dashboards

Most social trading platforms are equipped with dashboards that display real-time metrics:

1. **Trader Performance Metrics**: Track the performance of individual traders, including their wins, losses, drawdowns, and overall ROI.

2. **Portfolio Overview**: Get a holistic view of your portfolio, including asset allocation, overall performance, and risk metrics.
3. **Market Insights**: Real-time market data, news, and insights to keep followers informed about global market dynamics.

Algorithmic Filtering of Traders

With thousands of traders to choose from, selecting the right ones can be daunting. Advanced algorithms can help:

1. **Risk-Adjusted Performance**: Algorithms that filter traders based on risk-adjusted returns, ensuring followers aren't just seeing those who take excessive risks.
2. **Consistency Scoring**: Prioritize traders who have demonstrated consistent performance over time rather than sporadic high returns.
3. **Strategy Classification**: Algorithms that categorize traders based on their strategies – be it scalping, long-term investing, technical analysis, etc.

Automated Portfolio Rebalancing

Ensuring an optimized portfolio distribution is key for risk management:

1. **Asset Diversification**: Tools that automatically rebalance portfolios to maintain a desired asset allocation.
2. **Trader Exposure**: Set limits to how much exposure you want to a particular trader, and automated tools ensure this is maintained, adjusting for profits or losses.
3. **Market Condition Adjustments**: Algorithms that adjust portfolio allocations based on broader market conditions and volatility indicators.

Predictive Analytics and AI Integration

The next frontier in social trading technology:

1. **Market Prediction Models**: AI-driven models that forecast market trends based on historical data, current events, and global economic indicators.
2. **Trader Performance Forecasts**: Analytical tools that project traders' future performance based on their historical data and current market conditions.
3. **Sentiment Analysis**: AI tools that gauge market sentiment by analyzing news articles, social media posts, and financial reports.

Conclusion

The fusion of advanced technology with social trading is ushering in an era of enhanced decision-making capabilities for followers. These tools, when used judiciously, can empower individuals to not only choose the right traders to follow but also manage and optimize their portfolios with precision. In the following chapters, we will delve deeper into optimizing these tools, ensuring followers are equipped to harness technology's full potential in the realm of social trading.

Chapter 11: Social Trading vs. Traditional Fund Management
Analyzing the Paradigms, Advantages, and Disadvantages of Both Approaches.

Introduction: A Shift in Financial Management

Financial management has witnessed a significant evolution over the past few decades. Traditional fund management, which has been the bedrock of investments for many years, is now being juxtaposed against the relatively new yet rapidly evolving arena of social trading. This chapter aims to provide an analytical comparison between the two, elucidating their distinct advantages and challenges.

The Traditional Fund Management Paradigm

Understanding traditional fund management involves recognizing its key characteristics:

1. **Centralized Decision Making**: Investment decisions are made by a fund manager or a team of experts.
2. **Structured Portfolio**: Investments are made based on a predetermined strategy, often encapsulated in a prospectus.
3. **Fee Structures**: Typically involves a management fee and, in some cases, a performance fee.
4. **Regulation and Oversight**: Managed by regulated institutions with rigorous compliance requirements.

The Social Trading Model

Social trading diverges from traditional fund management in several ways:

1. **Decentralized Decision Making**: Followers choose from a multitude of traders based on personal preferences.
2. **Dynamic Portfolios**: Portfolios evolve based on the strategies of the selected traders and real-time decisions.
3. **Varied Fee Structures**: Often entails platform fees, trader commissions, and spread costs.
4. **Community Engagement**: Features a community-driven model where followers can interact, share insights, and learn.

Comparative Advantages

Both paradigms come with their unique set of advantages:

Traditional Fund Management:

- **Expertise**: Managed by professional experts with vast industry experience.
- **Stability**: Often provides a stable, albeit sometimes conservative, return.
- **Regulatory Protection**: Strong regulatory frameworks often ensure investor protection.

Social Trading:

- **Flexibility**: Allows for dynamic portfolio adjustments.
- **Diverse Strategies**: Access to a myriad of trading strategies, assets, and risk profiles.
- **Learning Opportunity**: Enables followers to learn from real-time trades and community insights.

Challenges and Considerations

Both also present certain challenges:

Traditional Fund Management:

- **Limited Transparency**: Daily trading decisions are often opaque to investors.
- **Higher Fees**: Traditional funds sometimes come with higher fees, impacting net returns.
- **Limited Customization**: Investors have minimal influence over the portfolio's constituents.

Social Trading:

- **Varying Expertise**: Not all traders on social platforms are professionals; discernment is crucial.
- **Potential for Herd Mentality**: Popular decisions might overshadow sound strategies.
- **Platform Reliability**: The operational integrity of the platform is vital for seamless execution.

Conclusion

Both social trading and traditional fund management have their unique places in the investment landscape. While traditional funds might appeal to those seeking stability and expert-managed portfolios, social trading resonates with the tech-savvy, interactive investor looking for flexibility and a hands-on approach. The subsequent chapters will delve deeper into optimizing social trading strategies, but understanding its position vis-à-vis traditional models is foundational for making informed choices.

Chapter 12: Navigating Regulation and Compliance in Social Trading

The Legal Landscape, Implications, and Ensuring Safe Investment Practices.

Introduction: The World of Financial Regulation

The world of finance, given its vast potential and inherent risks, is extensively regulated. This regulation aims to protect investors, maintain market integrity, and foster trust. As social trading emerges as a dominant force in the investment landscape, understanding its regulatory nuances becomes paramount.

The Evolution of Financial Regulation

Historical context is essential for grasping the state of today's financial regulations:

1. **Pre-digital Era**: Regulation traditionally focused on physical trading floors, broker-dealers, and investment advisors.
2. **Digital Revolution**: The onset of online trading brought with it the challenge of regulating electronic trading platforms and ensuring cybersecurity.
3. **Advent of Social Trading**: This newer modality requires the adaptation of existing regulations to ensure investor protection, transparency, and fairness.

Regulatory Considerations in Social Trading

Social trading platforms operate within a multifaceted regulatory framework:

1. **Licensing and Registration**: Depending on the jurisdiction, social trading platforms might need licenses as brokers, investment advisors, or alternative trading systems.
2. **Transparency Requirements**: Platforms must ensure transparency in trader performance metrics, fee structures, and potential conflicts of interest.

3. **Investor Education and Marketing**: Regulatory bodies often mandate platforms to provide accurate educational resources and ensure that marketing materials aren't misleading.
4. **Data Security and Privacy**: Ensuring the security of financial transactions and personal data is paramount in today's digital age.

The Role of Global Jurisdictions

Regulation is not uniform across the globe:

1. **US Regulatory Bodies**: In the US, agencies like the Securities and Exchange Commission (SEC) and the Commodity Futures Trading Commission (CFTC) play pivotal roles in overseeing different aspects of social trading.
2. **European Framework**: The European Securities and Markets Authority (ESMA) provides guidelines for member countries, which then have their specific regulatory bodies like the UK's Financial Conduct Authority (FCA).
3. **Asia-Pacific and Others**: Diverse regulatory landscapes exist in countries like Australia, Singapore, and Japan, each with its distinctive approach to social trading.

For the Investor: Ensuring Safe Practices

For participants in social trading:

1. **Platform Due Diligence**: Ensure that the chosen platform adheres to regulatory requirements and is licensed in its operational jurisdiction.
2. **Understand Your Rights**: Being informed about investor rights and grievance redressal mechanisms is crucial.
3. **Stay Updated**: Regulatory landscapes evolve; periodic checks on platform compliance are prudent.

Conclusion

While social trading offers a plethora of opportunities, it also necessitates vigilance and awareness regarding the regulatory environment. Ensuring compliance, both as a platform operator and as an investor, is integral to the long-term success and sustainability of social trading. As we venture into further chapters, the focus will shift to nuanced strategies within this regulatory framework, helping investors harness the full potential of social trading.

Chapter 13: Risk Management in Social Trading

Strategies, Tools, and Practices to Safeguard Investments.

Introduction: The Nature of Risk in Investments

All forms of investment carry inherent risks, and social trading is no exception. The interconnected nature of social trading – where the decisions of one trader can influence the portfolios of many followers – presents unique risk scenarios. It's imperative for investors to recognize, evaluate, and manage these risks to ensure sustainable returns.

The Multi-Dimensional Nature of Risk

Several types of risk are especially pertinent to social trading:

1. **Market Risk**: The possibility of an investor experiencing losses due to factors affecting the overall performance of financial markets.

2. **Trader Risk**: The potential for a chosen trader to underperform or make unsound decisions.
3. **Platform Risk**: Concerns regarding the operational integrity, security, and reliability of the social trading platform.
4. **Liquidity Risk**: The risk that an asset or security cannot be traded quickly enough in the market without affecting its price.

Tools for Risk Assessment

Modern social trading platforms provide tools to help investors gauge and manage risk:

1. **Risk Scorecards**: Many platforms rate traders based on their risk-adjusted performance, enabling followers to make informed decisions.
2. **Portfolio Diversification Tools**: Instruments that help distribute investments across various traders and assets to reduce exposure to any single entity.
3. **Real-time Alerts**: Notifications about market volatility, significant losses, or drastic strategy changes by followed traders.

Strategies for Managing Risk

A proactive approach can substantially mitigate risks:

1. **Diversify Trader Followings**: Just as one diversifies assets, diversifying the traders one follows can spread risk.
2. **Set Loss Thresholds**: Decide on a maximum loss percentage and commit to reevaluating if that threshold is reached.
3. **Stay Informed**: Continuously monitor market news, trader communications, and platform updates. Knowledge is the first line of defense against unforeseen risks.
4. **Avoid Over-leverage**: Leveraging amplifies both gains and losses. It's essential to understand the implications and use leverage judiciously.

Emphasizing Continuous Learning

Given the dynamic nature of social trading:

1. **Educational Resources**: Use platform-provided tutorials, webinars, and articles to understand risk management better.
2. **Community Interaction**: Engage with other users to learn from their experiences, strategies, and risk management techniques.
3. **Periodic Portfolio Review**: Regularly review and adjust your portfolio based on performance, market conditions, and personal financial goals.

Conclusion

Risk management is a foundational element of successful investing in any domain, and in the realm of social trading, it takes on distinct characteristics. By understanding the sources of risk, utilizing platform tools, and maintaining a proactive approach, investors can navigate the exciting world of social trading with confidence and prudence. The ensuing chapters will delve deeper into the strategies and nuances of social trading, always with an eye on risk-adjusted returns.

Chapter 14: The Psychological Dynamics of Social Trading
Understanding Behavioral Influences and Ensuring Rational Decision Making.

Introduction: The Human Factor in Trading

While trading is often viewed through the lens of numbers, charts, and algorithms, the human psychological element remains profoundly influential. Emotions, cognitive biases, and herd mentality can impact decision-making. In social trading, where community interactions are heightened, understanding these psychological dynamics is pivotal.

Cognitive Biases in Decision Making

Cognitive biases can inadvertently skew perceptions and decisions:

1. **Confirmation Bias**: The tendency to search for, interpret, and recall information in a way that confirms one's pre-existing beliefs.
2. **Overconfidence Bias**: Overestimating one's knowledge or the accuracy of one's predictions.
3. **Loss Aversion**: The disposition to strongly prefer avoiding losses over acquiring gains.
4. **Herd Mentality**: Following the actions of larger groups, irrespective of one's own research or beliefs.

Emotional Drivers in Social Trading

Being a communal platform, emotions can run high:

1. **Fear of Missing Out (FOMO)**: Seeing many on the platform succeeding with a particular trader or strategy might drive an irrational urge to follow suit.
2. **Regret Aversion**: Avoiding making a decision for fear of it turning out to be wrong.
3. **Elation and Despair**: Experiencing extreme emotions with wins and losses, which can cloud judgment.

Strategies for Objective Decision Making

Staying rational amidst the noise is crucial:

1. **Educate and Self-Reflect**: Understand cognitive biases and frequently reflect on decisions to recognize if they were unduly influenced.
2. **Diversify Sources of Information**: Do not rely solely on the platform's community. Seek information from external trusted sources to form a holistic view.
3. **Set Clear Goals and Stick to Them**: Define your investment objectives, risk tolerance, and time horizon. Make decisions aligned with these, rather than fleeting emotions or popular sentiment.
4. **Periodic Detachment**: Take breaks from continuous monitoring. Over-engagement can lead to emotional exhaustion and impulsive decisions.

The Value of Community

While there are challenges:

1. **Collective Wisdom**: A large group's aggregated decisions and insights can sometimes outperform individual experts.

2. **Support During Volatility**: Sharing concerns, experiences, and strategies with peers can be comforting during market downturns.
3. **Diverse Perspectives**: Engaging with a diverse set of traders and investors can provide different angles on the same issue, leading to more informed decisions.

Conclusion

The world of social trading is vibrant and dynamic, enriched by its community's collective experiences and insights. However, the very strength of this community can also present psychological challenges. By understanding these dynamics, investors can harness the community's power while maintaining objective, rational decision-making. Future chapters will delve further into optimizing social trading strategies with an understanding of these psychological underpinnings.

Chapter 15: Technological Innovations in Social Trading

Exploring the Advancements Powering the Future of Community-driven Investments.

Introduction: The Confluence of Technology and Finance

The realm of finance has been significantly influenced by technological advancements. This synergy has been particularly pronounced in the evolution of social trading platforms. From data analytics to Artificial Intelligence (AI), technology is revolutionizing how traders connect, share, and prosper.

The Data Revolution

A vast amount of data flows through social trading platforms. Harnessing this effectively is pivotal:

1. **Big Data Analytics**: Platforms can process vast amounts of trade data, user interactions, and market metrics to derive insights that can guide traders and investors.
2. **Personalized Recommendations**: Using data patterns, platforms can suggest traders, assets, or strategies that align with a user's profile and preferences.
3. **Forecasting Tools**: By analyzing historical data, platforms can offer predictive insights about market trends or trader performance.

Artificial Intelligence (AI) and Machine Learning (ML)

The incorporation of AI and ML has transformative implications:

1. **Automated Risk Analysis**: Algorithms can assess a trader's past performance and strategies to generate a risk profile, aiding followers in their decisions.
2. **Sentiment Analysis**: AI can gauge community sentiment by analyzing discussions, comments, and feedback, providing a pulse of the prevailing market sentiment.
3. **Enhanced Security**: AI-driven tools can detect fraudulent activities or security breaches by recognizing patterns that deviate from the norm.

Blockchain and Decentralization

While traditionally associated with cryptocurrencies, blockchain technology is finding its niche in social trading:

1. **Transparent Track Records**: Blockchain can maintain immutable records of traders' performances, ensuring transparency and trust.
2. **Decentralized Platforms**: Some platforms are exploring decentralization, reducing the control of any single entity and increasing community governance.

3. **Secure Transactions**: Blockchain provides enhanced security for financial transactions, ensuring data integrity and reducing fraud risks.

The Future: Virtual Reality (VR) and Augmented Reality (AR)

Emerging technologies are further enhancing user experience:

   1. **Virtual Trading Floors**: VR can simulate traditional trading floors, allowing users to "meet" and discuss in a virtual space.
   2. **AR-enhanced Data Visualization**: Augmented reality can overlay data and insights on real-world views, offering interactive and immersive analytics.

Conclusion

As technology continues to evolve, so will the face of social trading. These innovations not only enhance user experience but also drive efficiency, security, and transparency. With a firm grasp of the technological underpinnings, traders and investors can optimize their engagement in social trading. Upcoming chapters will delve deeper into leveraging these technological advancements for better trading outcomes.

Chapter 16: Crafting a Personalized Social Trading Strategy

Blending Personal Goals, Market Insights, and Community Wisdom.

Introduction: The Need for Personalization

In the vast ocean of social trading, where a multitude of strategies, assets, and trader personas exist, finding a path that aligns with one's unique goals and risk tolerance is paramount. Crafting a tailored strategy ensures that one's investment journey remains aligned with personal aspirations and financial realities.

Understanding Personal Financial Goals

Before diving deep into social trading, clarity on one's financial objectives is crucial:

   1. **Short-Term vs. Long-Term**: Whether one aims for quick returns or sees social trading as a long-term investment avenue will significantly influence strategy.
   2. **Income Generation vs. Wealth Accumulation**: Determining if the goal is regular income or growing a nest egg will guide asset and trader choices.
   3. **Risk Appetite**: Recognizing one's comfort level with market volatility and potential losses is foundational to crafting a strategy.

Research and Due Diligence

A personalized strategy begins with informed choices:

   1. **Trader Analysis**: Beyond just performance metrics, understanding a trader's strategies, preferred assets, and risk management techniques is essential.
   2. **Market Trends**: Keeping an eye on macroeconomic indicators, industry news, and global events can offer insights into potential market shifts.
   3. **Platform Features**: Fully leveraging platform tools, from analytics to risk management, can enhance strategy effectiveness.

Balancing Community Insights with Independent Research

While the community is a valuable asset, independent thought is essential:

1. **Avoiding Echo Chambers**: Diversify the sources of information and ensure that one isn't just hearing reinforced biases.
2. **Engage, But Evaluate**: Engage with the community, participate in discussions, but always evaluate advice against personal research and understanding.
3. **Benefit from Diverse Opinions**: Social trading platforms often have a global user base. Engage with users from different regions to gain varied market perspectives.

Continuous Review and Adaptation

The financial landscape is dynamic, and so should be one's strategy:

1. **Quarterly Strategy Reviews**: Set aside time periodically to review and adjust your strategy based on performance and changing financial goals.
2. **Stay Updated**: With technology and regulatory shifts impacting the trading ecosystem, staying informed ensures that one's strategy remains relevant.
3. **Learning and Upgradation**: The world of finance is ever-evolving. Continuous learning, be it through courses, webinars, or books, can significantly enhance strategy effectiveness.

Conclusion

A well-crafted personalized social trading strategy is the compass that guides traders and investors through the exciting yet complex world of social trading. By balancing personal goals, market research, and community wisdom, one can navigate the intricacies of the platform with confidence. Subsequent chapters will dive deeper into advanced strategies and tools to further refine and enhance one's investment approach.

Chapter 17: The Ethical Dimensions of Social Trading

Exploring Responsibility, Transparency, and Integrity in Community-driven Finance.

Introduction: The Ethical Pillars in Trading

The financial sector, historically, has been under scrutiny for its ethical considerations. Social trading, as a fusion of finance and community, brings forth unique ethical challenges. Addressing these concerns ensures not only the trustworthiness of the platform but also enhances the quality of community interactions and decisions.

Transparency in Performance and Intent

For a system built on trust, transparency is vital:

1. **Honest Reporting**: Traders must ensure that their performance metrics, strategies, and trade histories are reported accurately, without any manipulations.
2. **Clear Intentions**: Traders who share insights or tips must clarify their intentions, revealing any potential conflicts of interest.
3. **Platform's Role**: Social trading platforms must be clear about their revenue models, potential conflicts, and algorithms governing trader rankings.

Responsible Trading and Advice

Given the influence experienced traders have, responsibility is paramount:

1. **Avoiding Over-promotion**: Traders must avoid over-hyping certain strategies or assets, especially if they stand to benefit disproportionately.

2. **Understanding Audience**: Offering a high-risk strategy to novice traders or those with limited risk appetite can be ethically questionable.
3. **Guarding Against Misinformation**: Ensuring that any information shared, whether about market trends or specific assets, is factually accurate.

Community Respect and Integrity

As a community-driven platform, certain behavioral norms enhance the ecosystem:

1. **Avoiding Toxic Behavior**: Discouraging behaviors such as trolling, insults, or spreading unnecessary panic.
2. **Promoting Healthy Debate**: Encouraging discussions based on facts and logic rather than emotions or biases.
3. **Protecting Privacy**: Respecting the privacy of other users, not sharing their personal or financial details without explicit consent.

Regulatory Oversight and Compliance

The legal and regulatory angle:

1. **Staying Updated**: Both traders and platforms need to be aware of the ever-evolving regulatory landscape surrounding social trading.
2. **Ensuring Compliance**: Platforms must ensure mechanisms to comply with financial regulations, especially around transparency, data protection, and fraud prevention.
3. **Addressing Grievances**: A robust mechanism for users to report ethical violations and seek redressal enhances trust in the platform.

Conclusion

Ethical considerations in social trading are not just moral imperatives but are crucial for the sustainable growth and credibility of the platform. Ensuring transparency, promoting responsible behavior, and adhering to regulatory standards elevates the quality of interactions and decisions on the platform. As we explore further into the nuances of social trading in the following chapters, the underlying theme of ethics will remain a consistent touchpoint.

Chapter 18: Advanced Tools and Analytics for Optimal Decision Making
Harnessing the Power of Sophisticated Instruments in Social Trading.

Introduction: Beyond Basic Tools

In the contemporary era of social trading, users have access to an arsenal of advanced tools and analytics. Leveraging these sophisticated instruments can significantly enhance decision-making capabilities, allowing traders to delve deeper into data, trends, and patterns.

Deep Dive into Data Analytics

Advanced data analytics offer deeper insights:

1. **Trend Analysis**: Identifying patterns over extended periods can provide insights into potential future movements and trader consistency.
2. **Comparative Analytics**: Comparing multiple traders or assets side by side allows for a holistic evaluation.

3. **Behavioral Analytics**: Understanding how certain news or global events affect trading patterns and asset values.

Machine Learning for Predictive Insights

Machine learning brings predictive capabilities:

1. **Future Performance Predictions**: Algorithms that assess the likelihood of traders maintaining or improving their performance based on historical data.
2. **Market Movement Forecasts**: Using past trends, global events, and other data points to predict potential market shifts.
3. **Personalized Suggestions**: Algorithms that suggest traders, assets, or strategies based on user behavior, preferences, and past decisions.

Simulation and Backtesting Tools

Before committing resources, these tools offer a test environment:

1. **Trade Simulators**: Allows users to simulate trades without actual investments to understand potential outcomes.
2. **Strategy Backtesting**: Testing a particular trading strategy against historical data to gauge its effectiveness.
3. **Scenario Analysis**: Creating hypothetical market conditions to see how certain strategies or decisions would fare.

Integration with External Data Sources

Merging platform data with external sources:

1. **News Feed Integration**: Real-time news updates integrated into the platform can significantly influence decision-making.
2. **Economic Calendar**: Integrating global economic events that might affect market conditions.
3. **Third-party Analytics**: Allowing users to integrate tools or data analytics platforms they are familiar with.

Advanced Risk Management Tools

Ensuring that risks are always in check:

1. **Automated Stop Loss**: Setting predefined conditions where trades are automatically stopped to limit losses.
2. **Portfolio Rebalancing Tools**: Algorithms suggesting rebalancing strategies to ensure optimal asset distribution.
3. **Risk-Reward Calculators**: Tools that help assess the potential reward of a decision against its associated risk.

Conclusion

The world of social trading has grown beyond just following and replicating trades. With the integration of advanced tools and analytics, traders are empowered to make informed, data-backed decisions. This sophisticated environment, while offering increased capabilities, also demands a thorough understanding to be harnessed effectively. As this book wraps up in the next section, it reiterates the importance of continuous learning and adaptation in the dynamic domain of social trading.

Conclusion: The Future Landscape of Social Trading

Synthesizing the Learnings and Gazing into What Lies Ahead.

Introduction: Reflecting on the Journey

This odyssey through the intricacies of social trading has spanned from foundational concepts to advanced tools and strategies. It's evident that social trading has solidified its place in the financial world, offering both novices and experts a unique confluence of community and commerce.

The Power of Community

The essence of social trading lies in harnessing collective intelligence:

1. **Shared Wisdom**: The platform is not just about individual successes but the collaborative growth of its community.
2. **Global Interconnectedness**: The social trading realm underlines the importance of global perspectives, reflecting the interconnected nature of today's world.
3. **Continuous Learning**: The diverse experiences and backgrounds of community members ensure a constant flow of new knowledge and insights.

Technology as the Catalyst

Technological advancements will continue to drive evolution:

1. **Data-driven Insights**: As data analytics become more sophisticated, traders will be equipped with even deeper insights into market trends and behaviors.
2. **Blockchain and Beyond**: Innovations like blockchain could further enhance transparency and trust within the platform.
3. **AR and VR**: With Augmented and Virtual Reality technologies maturing, they might offer immersive and interactive trading experiences.

Ethics and Responsibility

As the platform grows, so does its responsibility:

1. **Regulatory Oversight**: As social trading becomes mainstream, regulatory frameworks might become more stringent, ensuring user protection.
2. **Enhancing Transparency**: Ensuring ethical conduct and transparency will be paramount for sustaining user trust.
3. **Educating the Masses**: Platforms might invest more in educating users, ensuring they make informed and responsible decisions.

The Road Ahead

1. **Diversification**: We might see a diversification in assets and strategies available for social trading, reflecting the broader financial market.
2. **Integration with Traditional Finance**: There could be a stronger integration between social trading platforms and traditional financial institutions, bringing the best of both worlds.

3. **Focus on Sustainability**: With global shifts towards sustainable finance, social trading platforms might prioritize assets and strategies that align with sustainable and responsible investing.

Final Thoughts

Social trading, at its core, represents the future of finance – a domain where technology, community, and commerce seamlessly merge. For traders and investors, the journey does not end here. The ever-evolving nature of this field means continuous adaptation, learning, and growth are imperative. As platforms evolve, and as global finance shifts, the principles and strategies discussed in this book will remain invaluable guiding posts for all aspirants in the world of social trading.

Risk Management Strategies

Utilize historical patterns to take trading decisions.

Introduction

The realm of financial markets is an intricate tapestry woven by myriad factors that influence price movements, trends, and ultimately, trading decisions. One often overlooked yet potent force in this intricate dance is the concept of trading. In this comprehensive guide, we delve into the depths of trading, unearthing the historical patterns and ity that hold the potential to revolutionize trading strategies.

Section A: The Significance of Trading

At the core of financial markets lies the eternal pursuit of understanding market behavior. Traders, analysts, and investors endeavor to decipher the enigma of price fluctuations, seeking reliable tools to navigate the complex waters of profit and loss. Amidst this quest, trading emerges as a compelling avenue, providing a distinct lens through which market dynamics can be viewed.

trading, at its essence, revolves around the recognition and exploitation of recurring patterns in market behavior. These patterns, tied to specific periods of time, are driven by a variety of factors including natural cycles, economic events, and human behavior. The beauty of trading lies in its ability to offer foresight based on historical precedent. By observing how markets have historically responded to certain conditions during specific times of the year, traders can potentially enhance their decision-making prowess.

Section B: Objectives of the Book

The objectives of this book are two-fold: to establish a solid foundation for comprehending the nuances of trading and to equip traders with actionable insights that empower them to make informed decisions.

In pursuit of the former, we will embark on a journey through the annals of market history, exploring the evolution of trading from its nascent stages to its modern-day applications. By delving into the historical perspective, we will trace the origins of patterns and examine how they have shaped market dynamics over time. Through this exploration, readers will gain a deep appreciation for the historical underpinnings that have paved the way for contemporary analysis.

Furthermore, this guide is committed to providing practical tools and insights that transcend theoretical knowledge. We understand that information without actionable application holds limited value. Therefore, our aim is to furnish traders with the tools and techniques necessary to identify, analyze, and leverage patterns effectively. From data collection methods to advanced technical indicators, we will equip traders with a comprehensive toolkit designed to amplify their trading prowess.

In essence, this book aspires to bridge the gap between theoretical understanding and real-world application. It endeavors to empower traders with the ability to decipher the underlying rhythms of the market, harnessing the power of historical patterns and ity to make calculated and well-informed trading decisions.

In the chapters that follow, we will unravel the intricacies of trading, guiding you through the fundamental principles, analytical techniques, and strategic considerations that underpin this approach. We will explore the diverse sectors where trends manifest, dissect case studies of successful (and not-so-successful) trades, and unveil the potential of incorporating analysis into broader trading strategies.

As we embark on this journey, I invite you to open your mind to the possibilities that trading offers. With diligence and the insights garnered from these pages, you hold in your hands the key to unlocking a deeper understanding of market behavior—one that has the potential to transform your trading trajectory. Let us delve into the heart of trading and embark on a voyage that intertwines historical insight with contemporary application, illuminating the path to informed and astute trading decisions

Chapter 1: Fundamentals of Trading

Section A: Defining Trading

trading, as a methodology, rests upon the recognition that markets exhibit consistent patterns that repeat at specific intervals of time. These patterns, often influenced by external factors such as weather, holidays, and economic cycles, provide traders with a unique perspective to anticipate potential price movements. At its core, trading is a form of technical analysis that goes beyond conventional price charts and indicators, focusing instead on the temporal dimension of market behavior.

The heart of trading lies in identifying these recurring patterns and exploiting them to gain a competitive edge. A pattern could manifest as increased consumer spending during the holiday season, resulting in an upsurge in retail stocks, or as the cyclic demand for heating oil during colder months, driving the energy market. By understanding the driving forces behind these patterns and their historical consistency, traders can align their strategies to capitalize on predictable price movements.

Section B: Historical Perspective on Patterns

To comprehend the roots of trading, one must delve into the annals of market history. The practice of recognizing patterns is as old as markets themselves, with ancient traders observing the ebb and flow of supply and demand during specific times of the year. These early practitioners recognized that certain agricultural products exhibited recurring price patterns tied to planting and harvesting seasons. Over time, this simple observation evolved into a nuanced trading strategy, as traders sought to exploit these patterns to their advantage.

In more recent history, the advent of technology and data analysis has refined the practice of trading. The availability of vast amounts of historical market data has enabled traders to quantify and validate patterns across various asset classes and markets. Modern trading platforms equipped with advanced charting tools and data analytics capabilities have democratized access to this wealth of information, allowing traders of all sizes to engage in analysis.

Moreover, the integration of machine learning and algorithmic trading techniques has elevated trading to a new level of sophistication. By utilizing complex algorithms, traders can sift through immense datasets, identifying subtle patterns and anomalies that might evade manual analysis. This amalgamation of historical wisdom and cutting-edge technology forms the foundation of the contemporary approach to trading.

In the chapters that lie ahead, we will dissect the intricate mechanics of trading, guiding you through the various dimensions that comprise this methodology. From data collection methods to advanced analytical techniques, our objective is to equip you with the knowledge and tools necessary to harness the power of patterns. By immersing ourselves in the historical journey and modern advancements of trading, we will prepare you to navigate the complexities of the market with a seasoned perspective, unearthing opportunities where others might perceive randomness.

As we embark on this exploration, I encourage you to approach each concept with an open mind and a willingness to challenge preconceived notions. trading is not a crystal ball that guarantees success, but rather a disciplined approach that can significantly enhance your trading acumen. With historical insights as our compass and technical analysis as our map, let us embark on this enlightening voyage into the world of trading.

Chapter 2: Analyzing Historical Data

Section A: Data Sources and Collection Methods

The cornerstone of effective trading lies in the meticulous analysis of historical data. Robust and accurate data serves as the canvas upon which patterns are painted and insights are gleaned. In this section, we delve into the essential aspects of data collection and the various sources that fuel the analytical engine of trading.

Historical market data is a treasure trove of information, encapsulating the ebbs and flows of price movements over time. The process of collecting this data is two-fold: sourcing reliable data and organizing it for meaningful analysis. A plethora of financial data providers, both free and subscription-based, offer historical price data for a wide range of asset classes including stocks, commodities, and currencies.

When selecting data sources, it is imperative to consider the accuracy, completeness, and consistency of the data. Inaccurate or incomplete data can lead to erroneous conclusions and skewed analysis. Additionally, the choice of data frequency (daily, hourly, minute-by-minute) depends on the trading horizon and the granularity of patterns under investigation.

Once data is procured, the organization and preprocessing stage begins. This involves cleaning the data to remove outliers, handling missing values, and adjusting for corporate actions such as stock splits and dividends. Furthermore, the data needs to be transformed into a format suitable for analysis. This might involve calculating rolling averages, identifying trends, and creating custom indices that reflect relevant market dynamics.

Section B: Identifying Key Data Points for Analysis

Amidst the deluge of historical data, pinpointing the key data points for analysis is paramount. Not all data is equally relevant; specific data points hold the potential to unveil the intricate patterns that define trading. The identification of these key data points forms the bedrock of successful analysis.

For instance, in the realm of agricultural commodities, data points such as planting and harvest dates, weather conditions, and government reports play a pivotal role in capturing the dynamics of crop prices. In the equities market, corporate earnings announcements, economic indicators, and geopolitical events become critical data points that shape patterns.

In addition to the quantitative data, qualitative factors also hold significance. News events, regulatory changes, and shifts in investor sentiment can catalyze shifts in market behavior. By integrating qualitative factors with quantitative data, traders can achieve a more holistic understanding of the forces driving patterns.

As we traverse the chapters ahead, we will delve deeper into the intricacies of data analysis. From constructing custom indicators to visualizing patterns using advanced charting tools, we will equip you with the technical skills necessary to unravel the hidden narratives within historical data. By cultivating an acute sense of data discernment, you will be primed to uncover the gems of insight that lie beneath the surface, ultimately honing your ability to capitalize on the predictable rhythms of the market.

In the quest for trading mastery, the mastery of data analysis is a formidable milestone. Armed with the knowledge and techniques encapsulated within this chapter, you are poised to embark on a data-driven expedition into the realm of patterns. Remember, within the labyrinth of historical data, lies the map to profitable insights. It is now up to you to follow its trails and decode the cryptic language of the markets.

Chapter 3: Understanding ity in Different Markets

Section A: Equities and Stock Markets

ity is a force that transcends geographical boundaries and permeates various asset classes. In this chapter, we turn our attention to the world of equities and delve into the nuances of trends within stock markets.

Equities, often regarded as the cornerstone of financial markets, are subject to a multitude of factors that shape their performance. Beyond fundamental analysis, understanding the ebb and flow of patterns can provide traders with a distinctive edge. While stock prices are influenced by a plethora of factors including company performance, economic indicators, and geopolitical events, patterns offer an additional layer of insight.

Certain sectors, such as retail and technology, experience distinct cycles. Retail stocks often surge during the holiday shopping season, while technology companies might exhibit patterns tied to product release cycles. By identifying these patterns, traders can position themselves strategically to capitalize on anticipated price movements.

Section B: Commodities and Futures Markets

Commodities and futures markets constitute another arena where ity wields significant influence. These markets, rooted in tangible assets such as agricultural products, energy resources, and precious metals, exhibit distinct patterns driven by natural cycles and supply-demand dynamics.

A classic example of commodity ity is seen in agricultural products. Planting, growing, and harvesting seasons directly impact supply levels, consequently affecting prices. Similarly, energy markets experience fluctuations as demand for heating and cooling resources shifts with changing weather conditions. By understanding these cycles, traders can proactively adjust their positions to align with impending price trends.

Section C: Forex and Currency Markets

The dynamic world of forex and currency markets is not exempt from the grip of ity. While currency pairs do not follow planting and harvesting cycles like commodities, they are influenced by economic cycles, interest rate differentials, and geopolitical events.

Certain currencies exhibit patterns tied to economic data releases. For instance, a currency might strengthen during a nation's positive economic data releases and weaken during times of uncertainty. By keeping a keen eye on the economic calendar and understanding historical trends, forex traders can enhance their ability to predict price movements and make informed decisions.

As we delve into the subsequent chapters, each dedicated to different sectors, we will dissect the intricacies of trends unique to each domain. By immersing ourselves in the specifics of equities, commodities, and currencies, we aim to equip you with the specialized knowledge necessary to discern and leverage patterns within diverse markets.

The world of trading is vast and multifaceted, with each market presenting its own set of challenges and opportunities. By embracing the power of ity across these markets, you are embarking on a journey that transcends traditional analysis, delving into the realm where historical wisdom meets contemporary application. Armed with sector-specific insights, you will be primed to navigate the nuanced world of trading with a seasoned understanding of the temporal forces that shape market behavior.

Chapter 4: Tools and Techniques for Analysis
Section A: Moving Averages and Averages

In the realm of analysis, tools and techniques serve as the compass guiding traders through the intricate web of historical data. Moving averages and averages are among the foundational tools that offer insights into the underlying patterns of market behavior.

Moving averages, a staple in technical analysis, are particularly useful in identifying trends and smoothing out price fluctuations. When applied to analysis, moving averages can help discern long-term patterns from short-term noise. By calculating moving averages over specific time frames, traders can visualize the broader trends and make informed decisions based on the prevailing direction.

averages take this concept a step further by aggregating data points specific to the same time periods across multiple years. This process effectively filters out random fluctuations and reveals the consistent patterns that emerge over time. averages provide a clearer representation of historical trends, enabling traders to spot recurring price movements and align their strategies accordingly.

Section B: Oscillators and Indicators for Trends

Oscillators and indicators are vital tools for identifying momentum shifts and potential reversal points in trading. When applied to analysis, these tools can provide nuanced insights into the strength of trends and potential turning points.

One commonly used indicator in analysis is the Relative Strength Index (RSI). RSI measures the speed and change of price movements, indicating whether a security is overbought or oversold. By applying RSI to patterns, traders can identify periods of excessive bullishness or bearishness, potentially indicating reversals or continuation of trends.

Additionally, traders often employ the Moving Average Convergence Divergence (MACD) indicator. MACD compares two moving averages and generates signals based on crossovers and divergence. In the context of analysis, MACD can offer insights into the convergence or divergence of trends, aiding in decision-making.

By integrating these oscillators and indicators into your analysis toolkit, you gain a more comprehensive understanding of the underlying dynamics of market behavior. With these tools at your disposal, you are poised to navigate the complex interplay between historical patterns and technical signals, harnessing the power of data-driven insights to refine your trading strategy.

As we delve deeper into the realm of tools and techniques, you will be introduced to a plethora of analytical instruments designed to illuminate the hidden patterns within historical data. By mastering the application of moving averages, averages, and oscillators, you will possess the arsenal necessary to unlock the potential of analysis in a manner that transcends theoretical knowledge, translating into actionable insights within the dynamic landscape of trading.

Chapter 5: Identifying Patterns
Section A: Regular vs. Irregular Patterns

Within the realm of analysis, understanding the distinction between regular and irregular patterns is crucial. Regular patterns refer to predictable and consistent price movements that recur at specific times of the year. These patterns are often influenced by recurring events such as holidays, seasons, or economic cycles.

Irregular patterns, on the other hand, encompass price movements that deviate from historical norms due to unexpected events or shifts in market sentiment. These deviations can stem from factors such as geopolitical events, regulatory changes, or unexpected economic data releases. While irregular patterns may disrupt the predictability of regular patterns, they also present unique trading opportunities for those who can anticipate and adapt to sudden shifts.

Section B: Interpreting Charts and Graphs

Charts and graphs serve as visual representations of historical data, allowing traders to discern patterns and trends at a glance. When it comes to analysis, specific charting techniques are employed to uncover the temporal ebbs and flows within the data.

One commonly used chart for analysis is the bar chart. This chart displays the average price movement for a specific asset during different periods of the year. By plotting these averages across multiple years, traders can identify recurring patterns and trends.

Another valuable tool is the heatmap, which presents data in a color-coded grid format. Each cell in the grid corresponds to a specific period of time, and the color intensity represents price movements or other relevant metrics. Heatmaps provide a concise visual representation of how specific time periods behave in relation to others.

As we journey deeper into the world of analysis, we will explore various charting techniques that cater to the unique demands of deciphering patterns. By mastering the interpretation of these charts and graphs, you will be empowered to uncover the temporal rhythm that underpins market behavior, enabling you to make informed trading decisions that harmonize with the cadence of the seasons.

In the chapters that lie ahead, we will continue to explore the intricacies of identifying and understanding patterns within specific markets. Armed with the knowledge of regular and irregular patterns and the ability to interpret visual representations, you will develop a heightened sense of awareness for the cyclical forces that shape market dynamics.

Chapter 6: Incorporating ity into Technical Analysis
Section A: Combining Analysis with Traditional Technical Indicators

The fusion of analysis with traditional technical indicators creates a dynamic synergy that enhances trading insights. Technical indicators, such as moving averages, oscillators, and trendlines, provide a framework for assessing price trends and momentum. When integrated with analysis, these indicators offer a multidimensional perspective that can lead to more informed trading decisions.

For example, when analyzing patterns in equities, you might identify a consistent upward trend during a particular quarter. By overlaying a moving average on the chart, you can discern whether the pattern aligns with the broader trend. The convergence of trends and technical indicators can provide stronger validation for potential trades.

Section B: Visualizing Patterns on Price Charts

Price charts serve as a canvas upon which traders paint their analysis. Incorporating patterns into these charts can yield a comprehensive view that encapsulates both historical rhythms and technical signals.

One approach is to superimpose averages on price charts. This allows you to visualize how the trends interact with actual price movements. By observing the alignment or divergence between the two, you can ascertain whether patterns are translating into actionable trading opportunities.

Additionally, trendlines drawn on charts can provide insights into the sustainability of trends. By connecting highs or lows of successive cycles, you can identify the trajectory of price movements and assess whether patterns are evolving or deviating over time.

As you venture further into this chapter, you will gain an understanding of how to seamlessly integrate analysis with traditional technical tools. By merging historical patterns with contemporary indicators, you will cultivate a holistic perspective that transcends individual data points, paving the way for more robust and strategic trading decisions.

The marriage of analysis and technical indicators is not merely a juxtaposition of methodologies—it is a synergistic alliance that harmonizes historical wisdom with real-time insights. As we traverse the intricacies of this integration, you will embark on a journey that deepens your understanding of market behavior, equipping you with the tools necessary to navigate the complex interplay of trends and patterns.

Chapter 7: Risk Management Strategies for Trading
Section A: Setting Stop-Loss and Take-Profit Levels

Effective risk management is a cornerstone of successful trading, and this principle holds true in the realm of trading. patterns provide insights into potential price movements, but market dynamics can be influenced by unexpected events. Thus, setting appropriate stop-loss and take-profit levels is essential to safeguarding your capital.

When setting stop-loss levels, consider the historical volatility of the asset and the potential impact of irregular events. By placing stop-loss orders beyond the scope of expected price fluctuations, you can mitigate the risk of sudden reversals that defy trends.

Take-profit levels, on the other hand, should be aligned with the historical potential of the trend. While it's tempting to aim for aggressive targets, basing take-profit levels on the average historical price movement during similar periods can offer a more realistic perspective.

Section B: Position Sizing Based on Volatility

Position sizing is a critical aspect of risk management that takes into account the volatility inherent in trading. Volatility can amplify gains, but it also heightens the risk of losses. By adjusting your position size in accordance with the historical volatility of the asset, you can strike a balance between capitalizing on opportunities and safeguarding against adverse price movements.

Utilizing techniques such as the Average True Range (ATR) indicator can aid in determining the appropriate position size. ATR quantifies market volatility, helping you tailor your position size to match the inherent risk of the trade. During periods of higher volatility, reducing position size can limit potential losses, while during periods of lower volatility, increasing position size can maximize potential gains.

As we navigate the intricacies of risk management within trading, you will acquire a comprehensive understanding of how to preserve capital and optimize returns. By aligning stop-loss, take-profit, and position sizing strategies with the dynamics of patterns, you will be better equipped to navigate the inherent uncertainties of the market while capitalizing on the predictability that analysis offers.

In the subsequent chapters, we will explore real-world case studies that exemplify the application of risk management principles within trading. Through these illustrative examples, you will witness firsthand the interplay between strategy and safeguarding, honing your ability to navigate the trading landscape with prudence and confidence.

Chapter 8: Case Studies in Trading
Section A: Real-life Examples of Successful Trades

The true measure of any trading strategy lies in its real-world application and its ability to yield consistent results. In this chapter, we delve into a series of case studies that showcase successful trades across various markets. These case studies provide insights into the practical implementation of analysis, highlighting how historical patterns can be transformed into profitable trading decisions.

Consider a case where a trader identifies a consistent pattern in the energy sector. Historical data reveals that energy prices tend to surge during the winter months due to increased demand for heating resources. Armed with this knowledge, the trader positions themselves ahead of the uptrend, leveraging the historical precedent to their advantage.

Section B: Learning from Trading Mistakes

While successful trades offer valuable insights, learning from mistakes is equally crucial in refining trading strategies. In this section, we dissect trades that did not align with expected patterns, uncovering the lessons embedded within these missteps.

Imagine a scenario where a trader anticipated a rally in a specific commodity based on historical data. However, unforeseen geopolitical tensions triggered a price decline that defied the expected pattern. Through this case study, we explore the importance of accounting for irregular events and adapting strategies when market dynamics deviate from historical norms.

By immersing ourselves in both the triumphs and tribulations of real-world trading scenarios, we gain a profound understanding of the practical challenges and rewards of trading. Through these case studies, you will not only witness the power of historical patterns in shaping trading decisions but also learn to navigate the complexities of the market with resilience and adaptability.

As we progress through the following chapters, you will continue to encounter a collection of case studies that span diverse sectors and market conditions. Each case study serves as a window into the intricacies of trading, providing you with a comprehensive perspective on how historical analysis translates into actionable strategies within the ever-evolving landscape of trading.

Chapter 9: Developing a Trading Plan
Section A: Steps to Create a Comprehensive Trading Strategy

A well-crafted trading plan is the compass that guides traders through the labyrinth of market dynamics. In the context of trading, a comprehensive trading plan is essential to harness the power of historical patterns effectively. This section outlines the key steps involved in developing a trading plan that aligns with your goals and risk tolerance.

1. **Identify Your Objectives:** Define your trading goals, whether they involve capital growth, risk mitigation, or portfolio diversification. Determine the timeframes you plan to trade within and the markets you wish to focus on.

2. **Data Collection and Analysis:** Gather historical data relevant to your chosen markets and identify recurring patterns. Use analytical tools to extract insights and validate trends.

3. **Strategy Formulation:** Based on your analysis, formulate trading strategies that align with the identified patterns. Decide on entry and exit points, stop-loss and take-profit levels, and position sizing guidelines.

4. **Risk Management:** Establish risk management parameters, including stop-loss levels, position sizing, and overall risk exposure. Consider the historical volatility of the markets you're trading to make informed decisions.

Section B: Backtesting and Refining Strategies

Backtesting is a pivotal phase in the development of any trading strategy. In the realm of trading, backtesting involves applying your strategies to historical data to assess their performance. By analyzing how your strategies would have performed in past market conditions, you can identify strengths and weaknesses, refine your approach, and gain confidence in your strategy's potential.

Effective backtesting requires attention to detail, including accurate data, realistic transaction costs, and adherence to historical market conditions. By incorporating these elements, you can gain a realistic perspective on the viability of your trading strategies.

As you proceed through this chapter, you will gain a comprehensive understanding of how to craft a trading plan that integrates analysis with effective risk management. By following these steps and honing your strategies through rigorous backtesting, you will be poised to embark on your trading journey with precision and purpose.

In the subsequent chapters, we will explore the realm of automated trading systems, unveiling the potential of algorithmic strategies that leverage the power of historical patterns in real-time trading environments.

Chapter 10: Implementing Automated Trading Systems

Section A: Pros and Cons of Algorithmic Trading

In an era driven by technology, the integration of automation into trading strategies has become a compelling avenue for traders seeking efficiency and precision. Algorithmic trading systems, often referred to as trading bots, leverage pre-defined rules and historical data to execute trades automatically. In the context of trading, these systems offer both advantages and challenges.

Pros:

- **Precision and Consistency:** Algorithmic systems execute trades with precision and consistency, eliminating the potential for emotional biases.
- **Real-time Analysis:** Algorithms can analyze vast amounts of data in real-time, identifying patterns and potential trading opportunities swiftly.
- **Mitigation of Human Error:** Automated systems minimize the risk of human error that can occur during manual trading.

Cons:

- **Data Reliance:** Algorithmic systems heavily rely on historical data, and their performance can be affected by changes in market dynamics.
- **Complexity:** Designing, testing, and maintaining an algorithmic trading system requires a solid understanding of programming and trading principles.
- **Risk Management:** Algorithms can lead to rapid execution of trades, potentially amplifying losses if risk management protocols are not well-implemented.

Section B: Building and Testing Trading Algorithms

Developing an algorithmic trading system requires a structured approach encompassing strategy formulation, coding, and thorough testing. When creating a trading algorithm, you must encode the specific rules and conditions that correspond to the identified patterns.

Testing the algorithm is a critical phase that involves simulating its performance across historical data. Backtesting provides insights into how the algorithm would have performed under past market conditions. While backtesting can offer valuable insights, it's important to acknowledge that past performance doesn't guarantee future results. Therefore, rigorous testing and ongoing refinement are essential to ensure the algorithm's adaptability to evolving market dynamics.

As we navigate the realm of automated trading systems, you will acquire a comprehensive understanding of the advantages and challenges associated with algorithmic trading. By exploring the intricacies of building, testing, and refining trading algorithms, you will be equipped to leverage the power of automation while navigating the complexities of patterns in real-time trading environments.

In the chapters that lie ahead, we will continue our exploration of trading, examining its application across diverse sectors and markets. Armed with the insights garnered from this chapter, you will be primed to embark on the cutting-edge path of algorithmic trading with a refined understanding of its potential and limitations.

Chapter 11: Exploring Trends in Different Sectors

Section A: Agriculture and Soft Commodities

Agricultural and soft commodity markets form a fascinating tapestry where the forces of nature intricately intertwine with economic dynamics. Within this chapter, we embark on a comprehensive journey into the realm of patterns within the agricultural sector. We will uncover the profound impact of planting cycles, weather fluctuations, and supply-demand intricacies on the ebb and flow of prices across a diverse array of commodities.

From the golden fields of wheat to the verdant expanses of coffee plantations, each agricultural commodity boasts its own unique set of patterns. The cyclical rhythm of planting, growth, and harvesting intertwines with market behavior to create patterns that astute traders can decipher and capitalize upon. By understanding the influence of nature's cycles on prices, you can navigate the complexities of agricultural and soft commodity trading with greater precision.

In the world of agriculture, planting and harvesting seasons wield tremendous influence. The timing of planting, influenced by climate conditions, has a direct bearing on the eventual supply of a commodity. As the growing season unfolds, weather events such as droughts or heavy rainfall can introduce volatility into the market, impacting crop yields and subsequently affecting prices.

Section B: Analyzing Supply-Demand Dynamics

Beyond the realm of nature's capriciousness, supply and demand dynamics play a pivotal role in shaping trends within agriculture. This interplay is most evident in the realm of perishable goods. Consider the citrus industry, where the emergence of diseases can suddenly disrupt supply, leading to price spikes. By understanding the delicate balance between supply and demand, traders can anticipate potential price movements and position themselves accordingly.

Understanding the nuances of storage and stockpiling in the agricultural sector is equally crucial. Certain commodities, such as grains, are often stored for extended periods, affecting their availability in the market. As a result, harvest time isn't the sole determinant of price fluctuations. Instead, traders must also account for the inventory levels and the cyclical release of stored goods.

In the pursuit of profitable trading, having a profound comprehension of the agricultural sector's unique rhythms is paramount. By aligning your strategies with planting cycles, supply-demand dynamics, and the influence of weather, you can harness the power of historical patterns and nature's whims to navigate the intricate landscape of agricultural and soft commodity trading. As we delve deeper into other sectors, each with its own distinct trends, you'll uncover a world rich with trading opportunities influenced by both historical wisdom and real-time dynamics.

Chapter 12: Energy Markets and Natural Resources
Section A: Oil and Gas

Within the expansive realm of energy markets, a symphony of factors orchestrates price movements, from geopolitical tensions to technological advancements. In this chapter, we embark on an illuminating journey into the heart of trends within the energy sector. We will unravel the intricate dance between supply disruptions, geopolitical dynamics, and historical patterns that define the ebbs and flows of oil and natural gas prices.

Oil and gas, the lifeblood of modern economies, exhibit a complex web of patterns influenced by a myriad of factors. The cyclical nature of seasons itself plays a role, as shifts in weather patterns influence energy demand for heating and cooling. Furthermore, geopolitical tensions, production quotas, and technological advancements can introduce volatility and unpredictability into the sector.

Understanding the impact of geopolitical dynamics on energy prices is paramount. Geopolitical events, such as conflicts in oil-producing regions or shifts in global alliances, can trigger supply disruptions, sending shockwaves through energy markets. By keeping a watchful eye on these events and their historical correlations, traders can position themselves to capitalize on anticipated price movements.

Section B: Renewable Energy and Clean Technologies

In an era of growing environmental consciousness and technological innovation, the realm of renewable energy and clean technologies presents a dynamic backdrop for trading. This section sheds light on how shifts in government policies, technological breakthroughs, and changing consumer preferences intermingle with trends within the renewable energy sector.

The rise of solar and wind energy, driven by advancements in technology and an increasing focus on sustainability, introduces its own set of patterns. Solar energy production, for instance, peaks during sunny seasons, while wind energy's viability fluctuates with the strength of prevailing winds. By understanding these dynamics, traders can navigate the evolving landscape of renewable energy and position themselves for potentially lucrative opportunities.

As we journey through the energy sector, you'll gain insights into the impact of demand variations, technological advancements, and geopolitical events on energy prices. By harnessing the power of historical patterns and combining them with contemporary insights, you'll be equipped to navigate the multifaceted world of energy trading with acumen and adaptability. With each new sector explored, you'll uncover a treasure trove of insights that transcends conventional market analysis, guiding you toward informed trading decisions.

Chapter 13: Technology and Innovation Stocks
Section A: Product Release Cycles

In the realm of technology and innovation, where change is the only constant, patterns reveal a fascinating interplay between consumer sentiment and market behavior. Within this chapter, we embark on a captivating exploration of how product release cycles drive the rhythms of price movements within the technology sector. We will dissect the impact of product launches, software upgrades, and industry events on the trajectory of technology and innovation stocks.

The technology sector thrives on innovation, with companies continually unveiling new products and updates. The timing of these releases plays a pivotal role in influencing market sentiment and stock prices. Consider the anticipation and buzz leading up to a smartphone launch – such events can trigger significant price fluctuations as investors speculate on the product's potential impact on the company's revenues and market share.

Understanding the rhythm of product release cycles empowers traders to capitalize on anticipated price movements. By aligning your strategies with the historical trends of market response to past launches, you can position yourself to make informed trading decisions.

Section B: Earnings Seasons and Tech Trends

In the tech sector, the release of earnings reports becomes a focal point, shedding light on the financial health and growth prospects of companies. This section delves into the significance of earnings seasons and how broader tech trends can guide trading decisions throughout the year.

During earnings seasons, investors scrutinize financial results and guidance, impacting stock prices. By understanding how historical earnings trends align with patterns, traders can anticipate potential price movements and adjust their strategies accordingly.

Moreover, tracking broader tech trends is essential for staying ahead of market shifts. From shifts in consumer preferences to technological advancements like artificial intelligence and cybersecurity, understanding these trends allows traders to pivot their strategies in response to evolving market dynamics.

As we journey through the tech sector, you'll uncover the art of aligning your strategies with product releases, earnings seasons, and industry trends. By harmonizing historical wisdom with contemporary insights, you'll gain a competitive edge in navigating the ever-evolving world of technology and innovation stocks. Each sector we explore enriches your trading toolkit, equipping you with a multifaceted perspective that transcends traditional analysis and empowers you to make well-informed trading decisions.

Chapter 14: Holiday-Related Trading Opportunities
Section A: Retail and Consumer Goods

In the realm of trading, holidays and special occasions aren't just about celebration – they also offer unique windows of opportunity driven by shifts in consumer behavior. Within this chapter, we embark on an insightful journey into the influence of patterns tied to holidays on the retail and consumer goods sectors. We will delve into how these patterns intermingle with market dynamics, shaping price movements and creating trading opportunities.

Holidays like Black Friday, Christmas, and back-to-school periods create pronounced surges in consumer spending. These events have the power to significantly impact stock prices within the retail sector. As consumers flock to stores and online platforms during festive seasons, the anticipation of increased sales can drive up stock prices in retail companies. Conversely, a lackluster holiday season can lead to price declines.

Understanding the patterns of consumer behavior during holidays enables traders to anticipate and capitalize on potential price movements. By analyzing historical data and the effects of previous holiday seasons, traders can position themselves strategically to take advantage of short-term trends driven by collective celebrations.

Section B: Travel and Hospitality

The travel and hospitality industry experiences its own set of trends tied to holiday periods and vacation seasons. In this section, we explore how these patterns interact with broader economic indicators and market dynamics to create trading opportunities within this sector.

As holiday periods approach, travel and hospitality stocks may experience fluctuations in prices due to changing demand for travel services, accommodations, and leisure activities. By understanding historical trends in these sectors during holiday periods, traders can make informed decisions about potential trading opportunities.

By delving into the interplay between holidays, consumer behavior, and market dynamics, you'll uncover a world of short-term trading opportunities within the retail and travel sectors. Each holiday brings with it a unique set of dynamics, allowing traders to align their strategies with the sentiments of the season. As we continue our exploration through different sectors, you'll gain a broader understanding of the multifaceted influence of historical patterns on trading decisions.

Chapter 15: Applying Patterns in Financial Markets
Section A: Forex and Currency Markets

The world of forex and currency trading is a complex interplay of global economies, geopolitical events, and historical trends. In this chapter, we embark on a comprehensive exploration of how patterns intersect with the currency markets. We will unravel how economic cycles, political developments, and global economic trends interact with historical patterns to shape price movements in the forex arena.

Currency pairs are influenced by a myriad of factors, including interest rates, inflation, trade balances, and geopolitical tensions. Yet, beneath these complexities lies the potential for discernible patterns. For example, central bank decisions to adjust interest rates can create predictable trends in currency pairs over specific periods.

Understanding the correlations between economic events, political shifts, and patterns can empower traders to anticipate potential price movements and make informed decisions in the forex market.

Section B: Bonds and Interest Rate Cycles

Within the realm of fixed income markets, trends are influenced by interest rate cycles, economic data releases, and broader market dynamics. This section delves into the interplay between these factors, revealing how historical patterns intersect with bond market behavior.

Interest rate cycles play a pivotal role in shaping bond prices. By understanding how economic conditions and central bank policies correlate with trends, traders can position themselves to capitalize on potential opportunities. For instance, during periods of economic uncertainty, bonds may experience increased demand as investors seek safe-haven assets, leading to predictable patterns in prices.

As we journey through the financial markets, you'll gain insights into the intricate dance between economic data releases, interest rate fluctuations, and trends. By merging historical wisdom with real-time insights, you'll be equipped to navigate the complex landscape of financial markets, using patterns as a guiding light in your trading decisions. With each sector explored, you'll unveil a new layer of trading opportunities that transcend conventional analysis, allowing you to make well-informed and strategic choices.

Chapter 16: Navigating Patterns in Global Markets
Section A: Emerging Markets

Emerging markets, characterized by diverse economic conditions and geopolitical dynamics, offer a unique tapestry of trends. In this chapter, we embark on a comprehensive exploration of how historical patterns intersect with the intricacies of emerging markets. We will unravel how economic cycles, political developments, and regional trends influence price movements, presenting traders with a mosaic of opportunities and challenges.

Emerging markets are a diverse landscape, each with its own set of economic conditions and growth prospects. The ebb and flow of commodities, changes in trade relationships, and shifts in geopolitical alliances can create distinct trends within these markets.

Understanding the impact of economic indicators, political shifts, and cultural factors on emerging markets can guide traders in identifying potential opportunities and managing risks. By combining historical patterns with real-time insights, traders can navigate the dynamic landscape of emerging markets with a nuanced understanding of their rhythms.

Section B: Global Indices and International Equities

Global stock indices and international equities present yet another facet of trends driven by regional economic trends and geopolitical events. This section delves into how these factors intersect with historical patterns to shape price movements across global markets.

From European stock exchanges to Asian markets, each region's economic conditions and market dynamics create their own set of trends. Understanding the interplay between economic cycles, regional developments, and historical patterns equips traders with a comprehensive perspective to navigate international markets.

As we traverse global markets, you'll uncover the complexity of emerging markets and the diversity of international equities. By melding historical wisdom with real-time observations, you'll be prepared to navigate the global landscape with an acute awareness of its patterns. Each sector explored enhances your trading knowledge, allowing you to make well-informed decisions that transcend traditional analysis and harness the power of historical patterns.

Chapter 17: Strategies in Options and Derivatives Markets
Section A: Leveraging Options for Trading

Within the realm of options and derivatives markets lies a realm of sophisticated strategies that can harness the power of patterns. In this chapter, we embark on a journey into the intersection of options trading and historical trends. We'll delve into how traders can use options to capitalize on the predictive potential of historical patterns and enhance their trading strategies.

Options offer a versatile toolkit for traders to manage risk and capitalize on market movements. patterns can enhance these strategies by providing insights into potential price movements during specific periods. By combining options contracts with historical patterns, traders can create tailored strategies to navigate the ebbs and flows of the market.

From covered calls to spreads and straddles, options strategies can be adapted to align with anticipated movements. For instance, a trader might use a bull call spread to capture anticipated upward price movements during a season of historically positive performance.

Section B: Commodity Futures and Trading

Commodity futures markets provide a fertile ground for traders seeking to capitalize on supply-demand dynamics and patterns. This section delves into how traders can leverage commodity futures contracts to navigate the complexities of the commodity sector.

patterns often align with supply and demand cycles within the commodities sector. By aligning futures contracts with historical trends and supply fluctuations, traders can potentially benefit from both price movements and the inherent leverage of the futures market.

Understanding the interplay between options and futures markets, along with historical patterns, equips traders with the ability to design sophisticated strategies that reflect insights. By mastering the nuances of these derivative markets and merging them with historical wisdom, traders can position themselves to navigate the complexities of market movements with precision.

As we explore the realm of options and derivatives, you'll gain insights into the art of blending historical patterns with intricate trading strategies. Each sector we've traversed adds to your trading toolkit, allowing you to synthesize diverse insights into a well-rounded approach that transcends conventional market analysis, ultimately guiding you toward strategic and informed trading decisions.

Chapter 18: Adapting to Evolving Market Conditions
Section A: Recognizing Changes in Trends

The world of trading is dynamic, and market conditions evolve over time. In this chapter, we explore the art of recognizing shifts in trends and adapting trading strategies accordingly. By staying attuned to macroeconomic shifts, industry developments, and emerging technologies, traders can proactively adjust their approaches to remain aligned with changing market dynamics.

As economies evolve and industries transform, patterns may shift or change in response. For instance, changes in consumer behavior due to technological innovations or shifts in preferences can disrupt traditional trends. Recognizing these shifts early on can help traders adjust their strategies to capture new opportunities or mitigate potential risks.

Section B: Integrating Fundamental Analysis with Patterns

Fundamental analysis, which examines economic indicators and company-specific data, can complement the insights gained from analysis. This section delves into the synergy between fundamental and analysis, showcasing how these approaches can be integrated to refine trading decisions.

By marrying the macroeconomic context provided by fundamental analysis with the historical context of patterns, traders can gain a more comprehensive understanding of market behavior. This integration empowers traders to make well-rounded trading decisions that consider both the bigger picture and the nuances of movements.

Adaptability is a hallmark of successful traders. By combining the insights from recognizing shifts in trends and integrating fundamental analysis, traders can navigate the dynamic world of finance with agility and acumen. The culmination of this comprehensive guide equips traders with a versatile toolkit that transcends conventional analysis, enabling strategic and informed trading decisions across various market conditions.

Conclusion

The journey through the intricacies of trading has led us on a voyage of discovery, unveiling a world where historical patterns intersect with market dynamics to create a tapestry of opportunities. As we draw the final curtain on this comprehensive guide, let us reflect on the insights gained and the path ahead for traders who seek to leverage the power of ity in their pursuits.

Throughout the chapters, we've traversed sectors and markets, delving into the influence of trends on prices and trading decisions. From agriculture to technology, energy to international equities, each sector presented its own unique set of patterns and intricacies. We've explored how planting cycles, weather conditions, geopolitical tensions, and consumer sentiment all play a role in shaping the ebbs and flows of prices.

One of the key takeaways from this journey is the importance of understanding history's role in guiding the future. Historical patterns serve as invaluable guideposts, allowing traders to anticipate potential price movements and make informed decisions. However, the path to success in trading is not one of complacency, but rather of adaptability and continuous learning.

Trading is a dynamic endeavor, with markets evolving and shifting over time. As we've discussed in the final chapters, recognizing changes in trends and integrating fundamental analysis can be powerful tools in adapting to evolving market conditions. The ability to pivot strategies in response to shifts in economic dynamics, technological innovations, or geopolitical developments is a hallmark of successful traders.

As you close the final chapter of this guide, remember that while historical patterns offer insights, they are not infallible predictors of the future. Trading requires discipline, risk management, and a commitment to ongoing education. The pursuit of consistent profitability demands an unwavering dedication to refining strategies, adapting to changing market dynamics, and embracing the inherent uncertainties of trading.

Armed with the knowledge gleaned from this guide, you are poised to approach the markets with a fusion of historical wisdom and contemporary insights. As you navigate the complexities of trading, may your decisions be guided by a holistic perspective that marries the power of trends with an adaptable approach. Embrace each trading day as a new opportunity, and may your journey be one of growth, fulfillment, and success.

Manufactured by Amazon.ca
Bolton, ON

42823133R00269